MUSIC AND THE MAKING OF MODERN JAPAN

Music and the Making of Modern Japan

Joining the Global Concert

Margaret Mehl

https://www.openbookpublishers.com
©2024 Margaret Mehl

This work is licensed under a Creative Commons Attribution-NonCommercial-NoDerivatives 4.0 International license (CC BY-NC-ND 4.0). This license allows you to share, copy, distribute and transmit the work for non-commercial purposes, providing attribution is made to the author (but not in any way that suggests that she endorses you or your use of the work). Attribution should include the following information:

Margaret Mehl, *Music and the Making of Modern Japan: Joining the Global Concert*. Cambridge, UK: Open Book Publishers, 2024, https://doi.org/10.11647/OBP.0374

Copyright for the reuse of the image included in this publication differ from the above; this information is provided in the caption.

Further details about CC BY-NC-ND licenses are available at
http://creativecommons.org/licenses/by-nc-nd/4.0/

All external links were active at the time of publication unless otherwise stated and have been archived via the Internet Archive Wayback Machine at https://archive.org/web

Any digital material and resources associated with this volume will be available at https://doi.org/10.11647/OBP.0374#resources

ISBN Paperback: 978-1-80064-252-2
ISBN Hardback: 978-1-80064-839-5
ISBN Digital (PDF): 978-1-80064-384-0
ISBN Digital eBook (EPUB): 978-1-80064-705-3
ISBN HTML: 978-1-80064-927-9

DOI: 10.11647/OBP.0374

Cover illustration: 'Picture of the Tokyo Youth Band', *Fūzoku Gahō* (8 October 1895), p. 4. Public domain
Cover design by Jeevanjot Kaur Nagpal

'Picture of the Tokyo Youth Band', *Fūzoku Gahō* (8 October 1895). Public domain.

In memory of my father
Dieter Mehl
A lover of music

Contents

Acknowledgements	xiii
Introduction: Music and Japan	1
Overview and Chapters of the Book	17
A Note on Terminology	26
Japanese Names	27
Part One: Global History, Modernity, and Western Music	29
1. Global History, Musical Modernity, and the Globalization of Western Music	31
Global Modernity	33
Musical Modernity	38
The Globalization of Western Music	48
Transnational Circulation in Northeast Asia	55
'Western' versus 'Modern'	59
2. Under Reconstruction: Japan, the United States, and the European Model	63
The Beginnings of Music Education in America	66
Concerts and the Veneration of European Art Music	70
The Quest for a National Music	76
3. The Case of Japan	87
Western Music and Musical Reform	89
Traditional Musical Genres and the Meiji Reforms	93
The Meiji Reforms and the Introduction of Western Music	100
The Expansion of the Musical Infrastructure	108
Globalization, Sound Technology, and the Quest for a Japanese Sound	113
The Postwar 'Musical Miracle' and Its Critics	121

Part Two: Music for the Nation	125
4. From Rites and Music to National Music	127
5. Isawa Shūji: Music, Movement, Science, and Language	139
Keeping Them Together in Time: Froebel's Movement Games	141
Music, Language, and Science	147
Music Education	152
6. Civilizing Citizens: Music Reform	157
Isawa Shūji and the Tokyo Academy of Music	162
The Debate about the Existence of the Tokyo Academy of Music	167
Shikama Totsuji's Contribution	172
7. Shikama Totsuji: Music Reform and a Nationwide Network	181
Global Ambitions and a Nationwide Network: The Musical Magazine (*Ongaku zasshi*)	185
Shikama Totsuji's Other Publications	190
Shikama Totsuji as a Performer, Collector and Inventor of Musical Instruments, and Band Instructor	192
8. Playing Modern: Blending Japanese and Western Music	203
Music Reform in Practice: Graduates of the Tokyo Academy of Music and Blended Music	205
Blended Music as a Commercial Enterprise	222
Part Three: The World, Japan, and Sendai	237
9. Local Pioneers and the Beginnings of Western Music in Sendai	243
The Shikama Brothers in Sendai	246
Music in the Second High School	263
Sendai's Concert Culture around 1907	282
10. Foreign Actors: Kate I. Hansen	293
A Transnational Life and a Musical Mission	295
Kate Hansen and the Music of Others: Sendai's Concert Culture Through Foreign Ears	300
Teaching Japanese Girls to Sing	328

11. The World in Sendai	345
Tōhoku Ongakuin	351
The Second High School	357
Miyagi Normal School	366
Miyagi College	374
Other Institutions	378
Representing the Nation and the World in Sendai	381
Conclusion	387
Appendix: Chronological List of Concerts in Sendai Reported in *Ongakukai*	405
Bibliography	409
Index	439
About the Author	451

Acknowledgements

Throughout the many years it took me to complete this book I benefited from the help and support of more people and institutions that I can attempt to enumerate, so the following list is limited and selective.

A large part of my research was conducted during a sabbatical in 2013, thanks to generous support from the Japan Foundation. Then, as on several previous and subsequent occasions, Waseda University (with Gay Rowley as my host) provided generous support. Waseda University even enabled me to purchase a few major reference volumes that proved invaluable during the coronavirus-induced lockdown.

While travel was still an option, I spent an inspiring sabbatical in summer 2019 at the Friedrich-Meinecke-Institut of the Free University of Berlin, thanks to Sebastian Conrad. He and his group of PhD candidates and postdoctoral researchers, as well as the invited speakers of the global history seminar series, provided invaluable intellectual stimulation.

Back in 2015, I was invited by Jürgen Osterhammel to participate in an authors' workshop entitled 'Global Encounters in Musical Life since the 19th Century' at the University of Konstanz, together with Thomas Irvine (University of Southampton) and Harry Liebersohn (University of Illinois at Urbana-Champaign). I still think with gratitude of that opportunity to present my work and to receive thoughtful questions and feedback from the other presenters and the audience at a time when I was still unsure about where I was going with my work.

My long-time colleagues and friends in Tokyo, including Furukawa Eriko, Furukawa Takahisa, Suzuki Akiko, and Suzuki Jun have continuously provided hospitality and valuable hints for my research. Tsukahara Yasuko has patiently answered my various queries over the years, both in person and by e-mail.

In Sendai, my thanks go to Ōuchi Fumi at Miyagi Gakuin Women's University for her help in examining the university's materials relating to Kate Ingeborg Hansen. I also thank the staff at the archives at Miyagi Gakuin, Tohoku Gakuin, and Tohoku University, as well as from the Miyagi Prefectural Library and the Sendai City Library. Staff at the latter introduced me to Watanabe Shin'ya, editor for several years of the local history magazine *Sendai bunka*, who let me have copies of his materials relating to the history of Western music in Sendai.

My thanks also go to Dōrinji temple and the Russian Orthodox Church in Sendai for providing information about Maedako Shinkin and his family.

Research on Kate Hansen's activities in Sendai also took me to the University of Kansas at Lawrence, where I was grateful for the help of the staff at the Kenneth Spencer Research Library.

A particularly heartfelt thanks goes to Shikama Tatsuo, grandson of Shikama Totsuji, for meeting me in Sendai and Tokyo and for sharing information about Shikama Totsuji and his family.

Finally, I thank the reviewers for Open Book Publishers for their suggestions for improvement, and David Hughes for valuable editorial suggestions, as well as Lucy Barnes at Open Book Publishers for perceptive copyediting, and Tessa Carroll for expert proofreading and insightful suggestions for additional edits.

Margaret Mehl, Copenhagen, February 2024

Introduction: Music and Japan

The word 'Music' has a special ring to it [...] When I teach a class at university with 'music' in the title, [...] this gap [between music-lovers and those who feel less strongly about music] seems to widen. From my perspective, I do not intend to delve deeply into a discussion of 'music' itself, using specialist terminology. Rather, I am simply treating music as a theme for thinking about questions like the cultural circumstances of an age; the processes through which culture is formed and transformed, and the mechanisms behind them. But my aim is not understood.[1]

Although Western intellectuals love music, they claim that it's difficult to understand and draw a sharp line between 'musicians' and others.[2]

Japan's enforced opening to the West by the American naval officer Commodore Matthew Perry and his fleet was accompanied by music. Not only did his show of military strength in 1853 and 1854 include a military band: his men also entertained their reluctant hosts with an 'Ethiopian concert' of popular American plantation songs that were by no means militant in content. Some of these later found their way into the Japanese song repertoire.[3] Whether the Japanese audience enjoyed the sounds they heard is doubtful. As a German observer wrote two decades later, 'If I had to describe the effect of European music on the Japanese, I think I should be right in saying that they find our music still more horrible than we find theirs.'[4] Illustrations preserved in Japanese

---

1   Hiroshi Watanabe, *Saundo to media no bunka shigengaku: kyōkai senjō no ongaku* (Tokyo: Shunjūsha, 2013), 5.
2   Bruno Nettl, *Encounters in Ethnomusicology: A Memoir* (Warren, MI: Harmonie Park Press, 2002), 64.
3   On plantation songs, see Chapter 2. For details about the musical encounter, including programmes, see Kiyoshi Kasahara, *Kurobune raikō to ongaku* (Tokyo: Yoshikawa Kōbunkan, 2001).
4   Quoted in Alexander J. Ellis, 'Appendix to Mr. Alexander J. Ellis's Paper on "The Musical Scales of Various Nations" Read 25th March 1885', *Journal of the Society of the*

archives, however, show that the musical performances were at least regarded with interest.

Music, in other words, was introduced as part of the modernization package from the beginning of Japan's enforced opening in the mid-nineteenth century. Even today, visitors from Western countries arriving in Tokyo for the first time often express surprise at how 'Western' music seems to dominate the musical landscape. Japan is widely perceived as a country that has managed to preserve its cultural traditions even while becoming one of the most modern nations in the world. Music, however, does not seem to conform to this perception. European art music, popularly referred to as classical music, is now more widely enjoyed in Japan than even in the part of the world where it originated. For decades, Japanese and other East Asian musicians have won prestigious international competitions, performed on the world's most famous stages, and populated leading symphony orchestras.[5]

Back in Japan, even indigenous genres such as J-pop sound familiarly 'Western'. Traditional genres survive, but have been relegated to a niche existence. In the realm of popular music (in the widest sense), the boundaries between 'Western' and 'Japanese' are not clear-cut. This is especially the case in vocal music, where 'folk songs' (*min'yō*) might be older or more recent, and the sentimental *enka* ballad, perceived as expressing the Japanese soul, mixes traditional Japanese and Western musical elements. Among the instrumental genres, there are *tsugarujamisen*, a modern style of *shamisen* music that can have an almost jazz-like flavour, and *taiko* drumming. None of these modern Japanese genres is free from the influence of Western music.

Arts 33, no. 1719 (30 October 1885): 1109, http://www.jstor.org/stable/41335239 For the original German, see Leopold Benjamin Karl Müller, "Einige Notizen ueber die Japanische Musik', *Mitteilungen der Gesellschaft für Natur- und Völkerkunde Ostasiens* (*MOAG*) 1, no. 6, 8, 9 (1873–76): 13.

5   See Nicholas Cook, 'Western Music as World Music', in *The Cambridge History of World Music*, ed. Philip Vilas Bohlman (Cambridge: Cambridge University Press, 2013), https://doi.org/10.1017/CHO9781139029476.005 While Cook does not discuss Japan explicitly, his main argument certainly applies to that country. On the music scene in contemporary Japan, see Bonnie C. Wade, *Music in Japan* (Oxford: Oxford University Press, 2005). For a recent comment on Western art music in Japan, see Lasse Lehtonen. 'Western Art Music Taken to Heart by the Japanese', *Finnish Music Quarterly* [*online*], 2 April 2020. https://fmq.fi/articles/western-art-music-japan

In this, Japan is merely an extreme example of a general trend: European expansion and the accompanying dissemination of European music left no part of the world unaffected. Japan was the first non-Western country to transform into a modern nation that could compete with the Western powers on their terms. After its complete defeat in 1945, Japan again astonished the world with its rapid recovery and so-called economic miracle. This was paralleled by the country's equally spectacular rise to become a major player on the stage of Western classical music. The worldwide reach of Western music, including European art music, cannot be denied, but neither can its dominance in modern Japan. 'Modernity' as a concept will be discussed in the following chapter, but as one scholar has observed, the modernization process involved the absorption and, indeed, the indigenization of Western music.[6] One of the most remarkable aspects of this process is the complete change in musical sensibilities that the Japanese people experienced within a few decades. A liking for alien-sounding music does not usually develop quickly or easily. As Bruno Nettl, one of the pioneers of ethnomusicology, noted:

> In my experience of them, American and Western European university professors in all fields oscillate between cultural relativism and ethnocentrism. But among those domains of culture that are importantly aesthetic [...] they tend to be particularly ethnocentric about music and food. They will gladly have African sculptures in their living rooms, but they shy away from trying the recipes in Jessica Kuper's *Anthropologist's Cookbook*. They read *The Tale of Genji* but don't want to hear *gagaku*.[7]

Nettl's assertion about alien music, including *gagaku* (Japanese court music), still stands and does not apply exclusively to university professors (indeed, these days Western intellectuals may well be more inclined to eat sushi than to read *The Tale of Genji*). We can, moreover, assume that Nettl deliberately selected the most rarefied of Japan's music genres to make his point. In fact, most Japanese do not want to hear *gagaku* either, nor most of the other traditional genres. The musicologist Watanabe Hiroshi, discussing the nature of Japanese culture, points out the contradiction between what many Japanese perceive as Japanese music

---

6 Bonnie C. Wade, *Composing Japanese Musical Modernity* (Chicago: University of Chicago Press, 2014), 4, https://doi.org/10.7208/chicago/9780226085494.001.0001
7 Nettl, *Encounters*, 64.

(*Nihon ongaku*) writ large and the music they actually listen to. Many foreigners, including myself, have experienced the kind of Japanese host described by Watanabe: one who takes their guest to a performance of 'Japanese culture' they themselves are barely familiar with.[8]

In *Music and the Making of Modern Japan*, I argue that musical modernization, including the importation and adoption of European music, played an essential role in Japan's modernization following Western models. Music was part of the action on centre stage, an important vehicle for empowering the people of Japan to join in the shaping of the modern world. In order to understand the process in which Western music came to play a dominant role in the making of modern Japan, five points must be kept in mind. First, music became a focus of both official and non-official attention not because of its intrinsic merits but because of its functions within the modern state. Second, while strengthening the nation and moulding its citizens was at the heart of their efforts, most of the actors introduced in the following pages were acutely conscious of being part of a global community of nations in which they wanted Japan to be accepted as equal by the leading powers. Third, while traditional music was ultimately relegated to a niche existence, it was simultaneously accorded a vital role in the re-imagining of Japanese culture: this development was a result of the first two points. Fourth, 'Western music' is a blanket term, and European art music as we know it today was, arguably, the least important genre to be introduced, at least initially. And fifth, while neither the effects of the music itself nor of active music-making are easy to assess—much of the literature on the subject appears to be based on personal experience, anecdotes, and speculation—there is good reason to accept that many of the effects described in the research literature are real. These effects support the argument that engaging with Western music (as well as approaching indigenous music in a new way) was a means for Japanese people to engage with global modernity itself and to play an active part in shaping it.

Music and the Making of Modern Japan covers the period from the 1870s to the early 1920s. During this period the foundations for Japan's contributions to the global music scene were laid. This is all the more

---

[8]   Hiroshi Watanabe, *Nihon bunka modan rapusodi* (Tokyo: Shunjūsha, 2002), 5–6.

remarkable since, for most of this period, recordings were unavailable and the only way Japanese people could hear Western music was through live performance or by attempting to play it themselves. Nevertheless, by the end of this period, Western music was widely heard and played in the country. The standard of musical performance 'was approaching that of some of the musically less-developed countries in Europe'.[9] Meanwhile, modern popular song, whose development is closely linked to the growth of the global record industry, successfully blended inspiration from the West with musical characteristics perceived as Japanese.[10] In music, as in other areas, the ambitions of the political reformers who strove to modernize Japan following the Meiji Restoration of 1868 had largely been fulfilled, albeit not quite in the way they had envisaged.[11]

The period under examination here coincides roughly with the period highlighted by Osterhammel in his outline of the global contexts of European art music, 1860 to 1930. In terms of musical globalization, the period is marked by European musicians extending their activities overseas thanks to the increase in passenger ships, culminating in the massive overseas migration of musicians fleeing from Nazism. As a result, Europe lost any claim to a monopoly in determining musical standards.[12] Even before the Nazis came to power, in the wake of the Russian Revolution, refugees were leaving Europe and, although only a few of them ended up in Japan, they contributed significantly to the rapid rise in musical standards in the period between the world wars. Arguably, it was in the decades treated in this book that the foundations

---

9 Luciana Galliano, *Yōgaku: Japanese Music in the Twentieth Century*, trans. Martin Mayes (Lanham, Maryland, and London: The Scarecrow Press, 2002), 94.

10 See, for example, Toru Mitsui, *Popular Music in Japan: Transformation Inspired by the West* (New York: Bloomsbury Academic & Professional, 2020), https://doi.org/10.5040/9781501363894.

11 For a comprehensive introduction to the history of modern Japan, see Andrew Gordon, *A Modern History of Japan: From Tokugawa Times to the Present (4th International Edition)* (Oxford: Oxford University Press, 2020).

12 See Jürgen Osterhammel, 'Globale Horizonte europäischer Kunstmusik, 1860–1930', *Geschichte und Gesellschaft* 38, no. 1 (2012): 89. https://doi.org/10.13109/gege.2012.38.1.86 The first travelling violin virtuoso to arrive in Japan, in 1863, was Augusto Robbio, who claimed to be a student of Paganini. See Margaret Mehl, *Not by Love Alone: The Violin in Japan, 1850–2010* (Copenhagen: The Sound Book Press, 2014), 40.

were laid for Japan's significant contribution to what might be dubbed the 'musical provincialization' of Europe.[13]

Japan, as should be clear from this brief outline, must be examined in the context of global modernity, which is one of the aims of *Music and the Making of Modern Japan*. This wider context is discussed in more detail in the following chapter. First, however, a brief justification for choosing music as the central subject of an exploration of Japan's modern history seems in order. As Michael P. Steinberg, whose scholarship spans both the discipline of history and that of music, has observed that 'the case for music as a dimension of history, and therefore as a concern of professional historians, seems still to require special pleading'.[14] Certainly, music has not received the attention from historians that it deserves. In historical works not explicitly dealing with music, it tends to be treated as a side show, if at all. When I first contemplated writing a book about the history of music in Japan, my limited musical expertise made the idea seem presumptuous. Then I began to question the prevailing assumption about music as a field of inquiry being particularly 'difficult' and best left to the experts. Nettl, quoted above (in the second epigraph), is not the only one to have drawn attention to the notion. The musician and neuroscientist Daniel Levitin has observed that '[t]he chasm between musical experts and everyday musicians that has grown so wide in our culture makes people feel discouraged, and for some reason this is uniquely so with music.' He adds that this phenomenon seems to be 'cultural, specific to contemporary Western society'.[15] Susan McClary, writing thirty years earlier, expressed the paradox even more sharply: 'Now it is quite clear to most listeners that music moves them, that they respond deeply to

---

13 For East Asia as the new centre for European art music, see Nicholas Cook, 'Western Music as World Music', in *The Cambridge History of World Music*, ed. Philip Vilas Bohlman (Cambridge: Cambridge University Press, 2013). For a similar periodization, with the focus on musical globalization in the United States and Europe, see Harry Liebersohn, *Music and the New Global Culture: From the Great Exhibitions to the Jazz Age* (Chicago: University of Chicago Press, 2019), 3, 18–19, https://doi.org/10.7208/9780226649306

14 Quoted in Julian Johnson, *Out of Time: Music and the Making of Modernity* (Oxford: Oxford University Press, 2015), 6, https://doi.org/10.1093/acprof:oso/9780190233273.001.0001

15 Daniel Levitin, *This Is Your Brain On Music: Understanding a Human Obsession* (London: Atlantic, 2008 (2006)), 194.

music in a variety of ways, even though in our society they are told that they cannot know anything about music without having absorbed the whole theoretical apparatus necessary for music specialization.' Music, she observed, has long been treated as self-contained, and 'Musicology remains innocent of its own ideology'.[16]

Others, too, have commented on the peculiar position of music as a field of inquiry. The ethnomusicologist Bell Yung has remarked on the relative isolation of musicology as a discipline, although with the possible exception of ethnomusicology: 'Music research continues to be relatively isolated from cognate disciplines.'[17] While ethnomusicologists have borrowed ideas and methods from the social sciences, social scientists, according to Bell, are not aware of advances in ethnomusicology. The same applies to other disciplines: scholars who are neither professional musicians nor musicologists seem hesitant to make music part of their investigations. Even historians, while generally eclectic both in their choice of methods and subjects, have long been reluctant to include music in their examination of the past. Celia Applegate, a historian of Germany who has pioneered the inclusion of music as a central theme of its history, writes, 'I came to musical investigations as a historian of modern Germany who had some limited musical training. I wondered why so few of my fellow German historians, many of whom I knew to be passionate about music, "classical" and otherwise, wrote about it in their scholarship.'[18]

Recent years have seen what Applegate describes as 'a kind of Schengen zone of scholarship'[19]: musicologists have branched out considerably, into a variety of disciplines, while historians are venturing into musical investigations. Even so, music is noticeably absent in most historical writing. What is true of history in general is also true of the relatively new field of global history, which, as two scholars remarked

---

16 Susan McClary, 'Afterword: The Politics of Silence and Sound', in *Noise: The Political Economy of Music*, ed. Brian Massumi (Minneapolis: University of Minnesota Press, 1985), 150, 153.

17 Bell Yung, 'The Nature of Chinese Ritual Sound', in *Harmony and Counterpoint: Ritual Music in Chinese Context*, ed. Bell Yung, Evelyn S. Rawski, and Rubie S. Watson (Stanford, CA: Stanford University Press, 1996), 14.

18 Celia Applegate, *The Necessity of Music: Variations on a German Theme* (Toronto: University of Toronto Press, 2017), 4.

19 Applegate, *Necessity*, 4.

recently, has so far largely been a 'silent undertaking'.[20] Ironically, the same scholars use the visual metaphor of the lens, which seems symptomatic.[21]

The tendency among researchers to privilege the visual is pointed out and called into question by the proponents of another relatively new field: that of sound studies, which represents an attempt to remedy the perceived neglect of the auditory. The editors of *The Auditory Culture Reader* note that '[i]n the hierarchy of the senses, the epistemological status of hearing has come a poor second to that of vision'.[22] Attributing this relegation to the nature of modern scientific approaches, they write, 'Both the impetus to objectify and to universalize appear to be rooted in the historical ascendancy of visual epistemologies in Western culture.' They even claim that 'Western narratives of sound are associated with dominance, exoticism and Orientalism.'[23] In a similar vein, the editors of *The Oxford Handbook of Sound Studies* state that science tends to be associated with seeing rather than hearing and pose the question whether listening can produce new knowledge. They do not answer it directly, but suggest several potential lines of inquiry.[24] Sound studies, for them, is by definition an interdisciplinary undertaking that aims to study 'the material production and consumption of music, sound, noise, and silence, and how these have changed through history and within different societies'.[25]

It may be that scholars who shy away from music because they feel they lack relevant expertise are less inhibited when it comes to sound in general. Some musicologists, meanwhile, have embraced sound studies in reaction to the perceived shortcomings of musicology, which has too often concentrated on the pantheon of European art music, or else, in the case of ethnomusicology, on the exotic other. Music is, of course,

---

20 Martin Rempe and Claudius Torp, 'Cultural Brokers and the Making of Glocal Soundscapes, 1880s to 1930s', *Itinerario* 41, no. 2 (2017): 223, https://doi.org/doi:10.1017/S0165115317000420
21 Rempe and Torp, 'Making of Glocal Soundscapes', 223.
22 Bull, Michael, and Les Back. 'Introduction: Into Sound', in *The Auditory Culture Reader*, ed. Michael Bull and Les Back (Oxford: Berg, 2003), 1.
23 Bull and Back, *Auditory Culture Reader*, 4, 8.
24 Trevor Pinch and Karin Bijsterveld, 'New Keys to the World of Sound', in *The Oxford Handbook of Sound Studies*, ed. Trevor Pinch and Karin Bijsterveld (Oxford University Press, 2012), 3–36, https://doi.org/10.1093/oxfordhb/9780195388947.001.0001
25 Pinch and Bijsterveld, *Oxford Handbook Sound Studies*, 6–7.

sound—'humanly organized sound', to be more precise[26]— although not all organized sound is recognized as music. A wholly satisfactory definition of music is elusive, although most people tend to recognize music when they hear it, even when they profoundly dislike what they are hearing. This is the case with the sonic events discussed in this book. Definitions, then, need not detain us, as long as we keep in mind that music is, among other things, a social construct. The Italian composer Luca Lombardi (b. 1945) has expressed this succinctly: 'Music is that which a sufficiently large number of listeners regard as music.'[27] Similarly, Watanabe Hiroshi, musicologist scholar of cultural resources studies (*bunka shigen gaku*), has summed up his premise that music is a social construct by observing that music (*ongaku*) is not so much *aru mono*, something that is, but *naru mono*, something that comes into being, that is constructed.[28]

Watanabe might have added that music is *yaru mono*, that is, something we do. The abstract term 'music' tends to obscure this. The music-related activities humans engage in are, however, arguably more accessible to historians and other scholars concerned about their perceived lack of musical expertise. The musicologist Christopher Small emphasized activity by resurrecting the verb 'musicking' from its forgotten existence in dictionaries.[29] His proposal does not appear to have caught on; perhaps his definition, taking part in a musical performance in any capacity, seemed too unspecific. A more manageable concept was introduced by the musicologist Tsukahara Yasuko, in her groundbreaking account of how Western music was introduced into Japan in the nineteenth century. She uses 'music-related activities' (*ongaku katsudō*) to describe the support system that enables the creation, performance, and reception of a given type of music, including the places and occasions, actors, and systems of preservation and transmission.[30]

---

26 John Blacking, *How Musical is Man?* (Seattle: University of Washington Press, 1973), 10.
27 Luca Lombardi, 'On the Meaning of Music', online essay, [n.d.], http://lucalombardi.net/pdf/Text%20Lombardi%20Meaning.pdf
28 Watanabe, *Saundo to media*, 39.
29 Christopher Small, *Musicking: The Meanings of Performing and Listening* (Middletown, CT: Wesleyan University Press, 1998).
30 Yasuko Tsukahara, *Jūkyū seiki no Nihon ni okeru Seiyō ongaku no juyō* (Tokyo: Taka Shuppan, 1993), 9–10.

Musicking or music-related activities, then, are just particular forms of human activity; and human activity of any kind is the object of history as a field of inquiry. There are good reasons why historians would do well to pay more attention to such activities. As Applegate so rightly argues in summing up her reasons for venturing into music in the 1990s:

> The enormous range of ways in which people have made and made use of music over the centuries represented a rich source of knowledge about how people lived, the beliefs they held, and the means they devised to express themselves, both in public and in private. Historians could look to musical life as a way to understand more fully the other aspects of the past we had long studied—social classes and gender roles, parliaments and protest movements, wars and revolutions, religions and ideas, and identities of all kinds.[31]

Another historian, Jessica Gienow-Hecht, describes music as 'part of the fabric of history' and mentions historians who have treated music as 'an instrument to analyse questions of power, political hegemony and cultural change', in other words, as 'a tool to reconstruct the past by shedding light on groups, individuals, organizations, events, objects, actions and phenomena'. She adds, however, that 'historians are called upon to investigate music not simply as a tool, but as a forum of values, customs, and ideas'.[32] In a similar vein, Jane Fulcher, in her introduction to *The Oxford Handbook of the New Cultural History of Music*, describes music as 'a privileged point of entry' for, among other things, 'questions of cultural identity and its expression, or its constructions, representations, and exchanges'.[33]

The Oxford Handbook deals almost exclusively with Europe, but the non-verbal nature of music and the vagueness and mutability of musical meaning mean that these questions are particularly interesting when asked about cultural interactions across the globe. Jürgen Osterhammel describes music as the globalized cultural resource *par*

---

31 Applegate, *Necessity*, 4.
32 Jessica C. E. Gienow-Hecht, 'Introduction', in *Music and International History in the Twentieth Century*, ed. Jessica C. E. Gienow-Hecht (New York/Oxford: Berghahn, 2015), 4, 12.
33 Jane F. Fulcher, 'Introduction: Defining the New Cultural History of Music, Its Origins, Methodologies and Lines of Inquiry', in *The Oxford Handbook of the New Cultural History of Music*, ed. Jane F. Fulcher (Oxford: Oxford University Press, 2011), 9, 10.

excellence and highly suited to globalization because of its mobility.[34] Likewise, the editors of a special issue entitled 'Cultural Brokers and Glocal Soundscapes, 1880s to 1930s' for the journal *Itinerario* highlight the significance of music in global history when they argue 'that a musical lens provides fresh insights into the history of global cultural exchange.'[35] A related argument is made by the editors of *The Auditory Culture Reader:* 'Listening to music offers new opportunities to address issues of globalization, place, identity, belonging, history and memory.'[36] Increasingly, there is a perception that music is far too important to be left to the musical experts alone and deserves—even demands—the attention of scholars of several disciplines.

Of course, it would be foolish to ignore the work done by musical specialists. Nor is it possible or desirable to separate the activity entirely from the music itself. As Nettl states, 'It seems that, for whatever reason, a special relationship exists between a society and the special musical language of its culture.'[37] This begs the question: What happens when society changes and, in particular, when change includes encounters with the musical language of another culture? More broadly, what is it that makes music and musicking special and more than worthy of attention from non-specialists? The links between social and musical change will be examined with Japan as a case in the course of this book. As for the broader question, three possible answers are attempted here.

First, music or 'musicking' is a human activity—or, rather, a cluster of activities—found in all known human societies and throughout recorded history. Music-making, like dancing (which is inseparable from music in many cultures), can thus be regarded as a 'microcosm of holistic culture' and as reflecting 'powerful social forces that demand explanation'.[38] Both music and dance are expressions of human

---

34 See Jürgen Osterhammel, 'Globale Horizonte', 86-87 . I am not sure I agree that music does not require translation, but this might be a question of how 'translation' is defined. At the very least, European art music demands a degree of literacy.
35 Rempe and Torp, 'Making of Glocal Soundscapes', 223.
36 Bull and Back, *Auditory Culture Reader*, 14.
37 Nettl, *Encounters*, 70.
38 Joann Kealiinohomoku, 'Dance Culture as a Microcosm of Holistic Culture', in *New Dimensions in Dance Research: Anthropology and Dance - The American Indian. Proceedings of the Third Conference on Research in Dance*, ed. Tamara Comstock (New York: Committee on Research in Dance, 1972), 99; Paul Spencer, *Society and the Dance* (Cambridge: Cambridge University Press, 1985), 2–3.

behaviour, and their various forms are unique to the culture they are part of.[39] Studying the music and dance of other cultures 'can help us achieve a balance between understanding cultural difference and recognizing our common humanity'.[40]

Second, music as an activity (musicking) expresses the whole of our nature as humans—spiritual, intellectual, emotional, and physical.[41] Music, or more broadly, 'ritual sound', is associated with religion and with the spiritual more generally in many, if not most, cultures.[42] The history of European art music is closely linked to that of the church. Even when the authority of the church was increasingly challenged, composers still wrote sacred music, and, in the increasingly secularized society of the nineteenth century, art music took on the role of a substitute religion.[43] In Japan, Buddhism and Shinto each have their own musical genres.

Music also engages the intellect. Indeed, it has at times served primarily as an intellectual preoccupation. In ancient Greece it was the subject of mathematical investigation. According to one historian, 'The oldest law of "science" is the law of music.'[44] Greek theories were received and transformed both in Western Europe and in the Arab world. In China, too, music was the subject of mathematical investigation. Common to ancient Greece and China was the idea of music as the manifestation of an ordered world that could be understood in terms of mathematics. In Europe, this concept is known as the Harmony of the Spheres. Although European music came to be thought of primarily as an art in modern times, it continued to be the subject of scientific investigation, and the fact that European music was perceived to be

---

39 Judith Lynne Hanna, *To Dance Is Human* (Austin: University of Texas Press, 1980).
40 Thomas Turino, *Music as Social Life: The Politics of Participation* (Chicago and London: The University of Chicago Press, 2008), 3.
41 Several parts of the human brain have been shown to be involved in the processing of music. See Levitin, *This Is Your Brain On Music*.
42 On ritual sound, and distinguishing musical elements, see Yung, 'The Nature of Chinese Ritual Sound', 17. In order to distinguish music from sound in a complex ritual Yung suggests eight possible musical elements in a sonic event, each of which are typically subject to prescription (p.18).
43 Nicholas Cook, *Music: A Very Short Introduction* (Oxford: Oxford University Press, 2000), 31–38; Tim Blanning, *The Triumph of Music: Composers, Musicians and Their Audiences, 1700 to the Present* (London: Allan Lane (Penguin), 2008), 135–39.
44 Rens Bod, *A New History of the Humanities: The Search for Principles and Patterns from Antiquity to the Present* (Oxford: Oxford University Press, 2015 (2013)), 37.

rooted in scientific laws of harmony was a major reason for its appeal to reformers in Japan and elsewhere.

The emotional power of music is universally recognized. For Gienow-Hecht, this is a major reason why historians should include music in their examination of the past.[45] The effects of different kinds of music on those who listen are, however, far from universal. Music is not a universal language in the sense that any kind of music can be understood by a listener who is not familiar with it; nor will it arouse the same emotions as it would in a listener who is.[46] One only has to listen to music from different cultures to realize that, like a foreign language, foreign music requires some degree of learning or at least habituation. Moreover, even listeners familiar with a given piece of music and its characteristic idiom might experience a variety of emotions.

There are several reasons for this. Musical meaning, in the succinct wording of Alex Ross, is 'vague, mutable, and, in the end, deeply personal'.[47] It is also strongly dependent on the context in which it is performed and heard. This is true even of a work by a known composer, written down and including detailed instructions for the performer. The circumstances under which a certain piece of music was heard for the first time may have a profound influence on the way the listener experiences the same music on a subsequent occasion. Music has the power to evoke other times and places in the mind of the listener; 'musical experience incites us to respond as if to a whole perceptual world.'[48] Ultimately, the listeners themselves find their own meaning.[49] This does not preclude a piece of music from acquiring a particular emotional significance for a group or even a whole society's collective experience.

---

45 Jessica C. E. Gienow-Hecht, *Sound Diplomacy: Music and Emotions in Transatlantic Relations, 1850–1920* (Chicago: University of Chicago Press, 2009), 10.7208/chicago/9780226292175.001.0001

46 For a discussion of the question, see Kathleen Marie Higgins, *The Music between Us: Is Music a Universal Language?* (Chicago: University of Chicago Press, 2012), 10.7208/chicago/9780226333274.001.0001

47 Alex Ross, *The Rest is Noise: Listening to the Twentieth Century* (New York: Picador, 2007), xvii.

48 Higgins, *Music between Us*, 106. Higgins describes the phenomenon as 'musical synesthesia'; Higgins, 106–118.

49 See also Andrew Gant, *Music*, Ideas in Profile: Small Introductions to Big Topics, (London: Profile Books, 2017), 91.

Emotions are associated with physical actions and reactions in complex ways that are only partially understood. Music, as well as engaging the emotions, stimulates physical responses in listeners. The bodily practices demanded from those who perform it are often so complex that they require years of training, starting in early childhood. In other words, like dance, or sports, learning to sing in a certain way or to play a musical instrument depends on the transmission of particular techniques of the body, and the same kind of questions may be explored in relation to music-making as to the more obviously physical activities, including the concept of 'embodied identities'.[50] The notion of learning with and through the body forms an integral part of training in the traditional arts in Japan, perhaps more explicitly so than when, for example, learning a musical instrument in Europe.[51] And if we accept that the human body is both an object of social construction and that bodily practices can reshape social lives, we need to treat music-making as a bodily practice.[52]

Of particular interest in the context of music's role in shaping (and re-shaping) a society is the significance of synchronized physical movement in groups, whether marching to the sounds of a military band, playing in a musical ensemble, dancing, or singing. In *Keeping Together in Time*, William H. McNeill argues that such rhythmical movement as part of a group gives most people pleasure and results in what he calls 'muscular bonding', and that communities and societies that have learnt to make use of this have reached a high level of cohesion and power.[53]

This certainly applies to modern Japan. Given that military drill is one of McNeill's prime examples, and that military bands were one of the first paths for Western music to be introduced to non-Western countries,

---

50 Noel Dyck and Eduardo P. Archetti, *Sport, Dance and Embodied Identities* (Oxford: Berg, 2003).
51 On learning and remembering with the body (*karada de oboeru*), see, for example: Yasuo Yuasa, *The Body: Toward an Eastern Mind-Body Theory*, trans. Thomas P. Kasulis and Shigenori Nagatomo (Albany: State University of New York Press, 1987); Tomie Hahn, *Sensational Knowledge: Embodying Culture through Japanese Dance* (Middletown, Connecticut: Wesleyan University Press, 2007).
52 Dyck and Archetti, *Sport, Dance and Embodied Identities*.
53 William McNeill, *Keeping Together in Time: Dance and Drill in Human History* (Cambridge, MA: Harvard University Press, 1997).

including Japan, [54] the bodily practices involved in the adoption of Western music surely merit more attention than they have received so far. We might even ask whether the Japanese were so enthusiastic to form bands and later orchestras because it enabled them to bodily enact Western civilization and Western-style modernity, even to create a piece of it: music, after all, exists in the performance. Another question might be whether the Japanese group mentality, insofar as the stereotype has any basis at all in fact, might be a result of the time devoted to singing together and to movement games with music in the country's modern education system.

A third reason why music merits the attention of historians, besides its ubiquity and ability to express all aspects of our human nature, is that music can be related to all areas of human existence and activity. Music-related activities always take place in a political, economic, and social context, and developments in music are related to developments in other areas. Musical performance has even been described as a microcosm for social interaction.[55]

The potential for studying and gaining a better understanding of society by examining connections between music and activities in other fields has yet to be fully explored, but the following examples suggest that such efforts are likely to be fruitful. Pioneering work in the fields of social and economic history was done by an economic historian, Cyril Ehrlich, who published books on the social and economic history of the piano and on the history of the music profession in Britain.[56] Music has, in fact, been claimed to have a particularly strong affinity with economics, 'with which it shares a peculiar ultimate object which

---

54 Not only Japan of course: see Martin Rempe, 'Cultural Brokers in Uniform: The Global Rise of Military Musicians and Their Music', *Itinerario* 41, no. 2 (2017), https://doi.org/10.1017/S0165115317000390 Besides, the first Japanese efforts to learn drum rhythms to accompany Western-style drill were not perceived as music: see Yasuto Okunaka, *Kokka to ongaku: Isawa Shūji ga mezashita Nihon kindaika* (Tokyo: Shunjūsha, 2008).

55 Giacomo Novembre Alessandro D'Ausilio, Luciano Fadiga, Peter E. Keller, 'What can music tell us about social interaction?', *Trends in Cognitive Sciences* 19, no. 3 (2015): 111, https://doi.org/10.1016/j.tics.2015.01.005

56 Cyril Ehrlich, *The Piano: A History. Revised edition* (Oxford: Oxford University Press, 1990 (1976)); Cyril Ehrlich, *The Music Profession in Britain Since the Eighteenth Century: a Social History* (Oxford: Clarendon Press, 1985).

is *number*.⁵⁷ More obviously, the attention given to music might reflect a society's economic prosperity (or lack thereof). Purchasing a piano, for example, represents (among other things) a significant economic investment. The economic boom Japan experienced as a result of the First World War was cited by Kate Ingeborg Hansen, a music teacher and long-time observer of the progress of Western music in Japan, as a major reason for the rapidly rising standards of musical performance after 1918.⁵⁸

A recent exploration of the of the relationship between music and changes in several areas of society in modern times was presented by the historian Tim Blanning, who argued that music benefited more than any art from several of the major changes that characterize the period from around the 1700s to the present and especially the nineteenth century: status, purpose, places and spaces, technology, and liberation.⁵⁹ Blanning's theme of 'liberation' includes 'nation, people, sex'. Of these, the nation will receive particular attention in the following chapters. Music played and plays an important role in the process of shaping the imagined community that forms the basis of any nation.⁶⁰

The examples named here justify Rens Bod's claim that musicology 'can be called the most interdisciplinary humanistic discipline'.⁶¹

The question remains: what exactly can historians gain from examining musicking and music (for the one can hardly be separated completely from the other) that might not be gained from studying other areas of human activity? Musical activities are accessible enough, but their product is elusive compared to those of other activities: Applegate refers to the dilemma as the 'problem of music's fleeting existence', which poses a challenge to historians quite apart from their perceived

---

57 Frederic Jameson, 'Foreword', in *Noise: The Political Economy of Music*, ed. Brian Massumi (Minneapolis: University of Minnesota Press, 1985), vii. (The emphasis is Jameson's.)
58 See Chapter 10.
59 Blanning, *Triumph*. See Chapter 1.
60 See, for example, Turino, *Music as Social Life*, 142-47, 210. That Benedict Anderson's much-cited work on imagined communities barely mentions music (except for a brief reference to singing national anthems) is symptomatic of the reluctance of non-specialists to address music, even when it is highly relevant. See *Imagined Communities* (London: Verso, 1991), 145.
61 Bod, *New History*, 310.

lack of specialist competences.⁶² Can we 'hear' the past through its music, as Alex Ross implies with his subtitle to *The Rest is Noise*: *Listening to the Twentieth Century*?⁶³ Even if the answer is yes, what exactly is it that we hear? And what do we do about most of the nineteenth century, for which we have no recorded music and therefore no way of hearing how contemporary performers played it? Equally significantly, we have no way of hearing a piece of music in the way contemporaries would have heard it at its first performance, so our experience will always be different from theirs.

Perhaps the only way to find out what we might learn from including music in our investigations is to actually do it and see, or, whenever possible, hear, where it leads us. Perhaps it is only when we have multiple investigations relating to music that we will know why they were worth the effort. While writing *Music and the Making of Modern Japan* I have given considerable thought to these questions, and I believe that I have at least demonstrated that the activities that involved singing and playing music had a vital role transforming the Japanese people into modern citizens of the nation and the world. I have also—tentatively—concluded that the act of making music was more significant than the standard of any resulting performance. But that does not mean that the music itself was of no significance at all. Government officials and intellectuals who advocated the introduction of Western music, for example, while interested chiefly in music's functions, comment on the character of Western and Japanese music respectively in their discourse. I include only limited discussion of music itself; nevertheless, I hope to have demonstrated that the topic is worth exploring further.

Overview and Chapters of the Book

As mentioned previously, a major aim of this book is to situate the history of music in Japan in the context of Western expansion and globalization, which was accompanied by the worldwide reach of Western music. Japan absorbed and even indigenized Western music as part of the nation-building process. There is, therefore, some justification for a

---

62 Celia Applegate, 'Introduction: Music Among the Historians', *German History* 30, no. 3 (2012): 330–31, https://doi.org/10.1093/gerhis/ghs039
63 Ross, *The Rest is Noise*.

strong focus on the introduction of Western music in any narrative about music and modern Japan. But what about indigenous Japanese music? Existing literature has tended to focus almost exclusively on either Japanese music (*hōgaku*) or Western music (*yōgaku*). This poses practical challenges for researchers attempting to give equal weight to both, as they are faced with a situation similar to that of moving between different disciplines. More significantly, it reflects the separation of Western and traditional indigenous music that characterizes contemporary Japan. Practitioners of traditional musical genres tend to move in a world of their own, one dominated by a system of transmission which severely limits influence from other musical styles and genres. There appears to be a tacit assumption that the separation was in effect from the time when Western music was first introduced in the nineteenth century.[64] This, however, was not the case: the separation was only cemented after 1945.[65] Nevertheless, as will be shown, the tendency to distinguish sharply between Western and Japanese music was already discernible by the end of the period examined here. In practice, even advocates of music reform, who had in mind some sort of fusion between both musical worlds, tended to privilege Western music.

I have made every effort to pay attention to the changes that affected traditional Japanese music, including the relationship between Western and indigenous musics. I believe that I have at least succeeded in demonstrating the importance of this line of inquiry. Other previously neglected topics I discuss are the global context of developments in Japan; the influence of Confucianist ideas about the role of music in government (*reigaku* or the 'Rites and Music' concept of music) on Japan's intellectual and political leaders; and the role of non-state actors, including local actors, on the Japanese musical landscape. The Tokyo-centeredness of much research means that we still do not know enough

---

64 This may be changing. See Watanabe, *Nihon bunka modan rapusodi*; Yūko Chiba, *Doremi o eranda Nihonjin* (Ongaku no Tomosha, 2007); Yasuto Okunaka, *Wayō setchū ongakushi* (Tokyo: Shunjūsha, 2014). For a short treatment of traditional music after 1868, see Eta Harich-Schneider, *A History of Japanese Music* (London: Oxford University Press, 1973).
65 See Watanabe, *Nihon bunka modan rapusodi*.

about the way musical life was transformed in other parts of Japan; what we do know suggests that there were wide variations.⁶⁶

The main section of the book is divided into three interconnected parts, relating to the global, the national, and the local level. Globalization and nation-building were two major trends in the nineteenth and twentieth centuries, and music played a major role in global as well as national integration. A nation state has to unite the entire people within its borders. In Japan, as in many other emerging nations, this meant transcending considerable regional and local differences.⁶⁷ Indeed, it is at the local level that we see most clearly the vital role played by music in drawing together the Japanese people in order to actively participate in the nation, as well as experiencing themselves as part of a world of nations. It is also at the local level that the importance of individuals demonstrating personal initiative is most evident.

Part One: Global History, Modernity, and the Spread of Western Music situates the theme of the book both conceptually and historically.

Chapter 1, 'Global History, Musical Modernity, and the Globalization of Western Music' discusses the concepts of global history, globalization, modernity, and musical modernity, and relates these to the themes explored in this book. The global historical context is then described in more detail. The introduction of Western music to Japan has usually been treated in isolation, or from a bilateral perspective, rather than as a part of a global process. While Western music was disseminated to varying degrees in most parts of the world in the nineteenth century, Japan was unique in that its government took the adoption of Western music to the extreme of privileging it over indigenous music, which was increasingly marginalized.

---

66   See Chapter 3 for references to previous research. Research on regions outside Tokyo has often focused on the Kansai region. See, for example, Watanabe, *Nihon bunka modan rapusodi*; Hugh De Ferranti and Alison Tokita, eds., *Music, Modernity and Locality in Prewar Japan: Osaka and Beyond* (Farnham, Surrey: Ashgate, 2013). A number of (usually narrowly focused) articles on local musical culture have been published in the in-house journals of universities in that region. A recent book with a focus on Northern Japan (particularly Akita) is Kanako Kitahara and Kenji Namikawa, eds., *Kindai ikōki ni okeru chiiki keisei to ongaku: tsukurareta dentō to ibunka sesshoku* (Kyoto: Mineruba Shobō, 2020).

67   This is true even without considering the Ryukyu Islands and Hokkaido (formerly Ezo), which were only incorporated into the Japanese state in the Meiji period. The music of the Ryukyuan people and the Ainu are beyond the scope of this book.

Chapter 2, 'Under Reconstruction: Japan, the United States, and the European Model' examines similarities between two nations whose relationship is usually regarded as asymmetrical. The United States played a dominant role in forcing Japan to give up its isolation policy in the mid-nineteenth century. Culturally, however, there were remarkable parallels as well as synchronicity in the two countries' efforts to develop a national music. Post-Civil-War America and Meiji Japan both engaged in an intense process of nation-building, and the creation of their own musical identity was part of the process. Although both countries treated European music as a model, they endeavoured to develop a distinctive national music by merging local and imported musical elements. While a full-scale comparison of these countries' musical developments is beyond the scope of this book, the chapter shows one of the most powerful Western nations in a position of perceived cultural inferiority compared to European nations and thus challenges facile assumptions about 'the West'.

The main intention with Chapter 3, 'The Case of Japan', is to position Japan in the wider field of musical encounters and to provide readers unfamiliar with Japan with the necessary context for what follows in the other parts of the book. No comprehensive survey is attempted, as this would fill a book in its own right, but a brief outline of developments after the period treated in this book is included. Particular attention is given to the effects of post-1868 social transformations on indigenous musics and on the relationship between Japanese and Western music.

Part Two: Music for a Modern Nation zooms in on Japan in order to shed light on specific aspects of the country's musical modernization that illustrate its global dimension and the role of music in nation-building.

Chapter 4, 'From Rites and Music to National Music', illustrates how 'music' is about much more than music. In both Europe and the Sinosphere (that is, the East Asian cultural sphere), of which Japan is a part, concepts of music were intimately linked to concepts of civilization. When Japan embarked on re-inventing itself as a modern nation—one modelled on the most powerful Western nations—Eastern and Western conceptions of civilization became intertwined. The first book-length history of music in Japan, *Kabu ongaku ryakushi* (A concise history of singing, dancing and music in Japan, 1888), represents a landmark in the epistemic transformation that resulted from these geopolitical changes.[68] In effect, this work both legitimized musical borrowing, whether from China in the past or the West in the present, and elevated the music of the common people of Japan to a national asset.

Against this backdrop, the introduction of Western music into the education system is discussed in Chapter 5, 'Isawa Shūji: Music, Movement, Science, and Language'. His pivotal role in this process is well known, but it can only be fully understood in the context of his other concerns, particularly language reform and moral and physical education, as well as his preoccupation with the scientific basis for musical harmony. For Isawa, music was part of what in modern parlance might be called holistic education. Combined with language and physical movement, music became a powerful tool for educating the citizens of the new nation state.

Isawa was, moreover, one of the advocates of music reform, which is treated in Chapter 6, 'Civilizing Citizens: Music Reform'. Influenced by their education in the Chinese classics (*kangaku*), reformers argued that improving music (*ongaku kairyō*) was an essential means of refining the manners and customs of the people. Japanese music was perceived to be unsuited to this purpose, while Western music was perceived to have desirable—civilizing—characteristics that Japanese music lacked. Reform was to be achieved by blending elements of Western and Japanese music, but the official reform efforts were short-lived, and the dominance of Western music in the education system continued into the twenty-first century.

Compared to Isawa, the role of non-state actors in the dissemination of Western music has received relatively little attention. Chapter 7, 'Shikama Totsuji: Music Reform and a Nationwide Network' introduces one of them, Shikama Totsuji, whose importance is equal to Isawa's. In 1890 Shikama founded Japan's first magazine devoted to music: *Ongaku zasshi*, which had the additional English title *The Musical Magazine*. His stated purpose for the publication was to promote music reform. In addition, Shikama engaged in several other music-related activities to further this agenda. These underline the scope of his ambitions and

---

68 Kiyonori Konakamura, *Kabu ongaku ryakushi* (Tokyo: Konakamura Kiyonori, 1888).

illustrate the way individual actors, despite minimal training in Western music, contributed to transforming Japan's musical culture.

Unofficial efforts to reform music, by Shikama and other individuals, continued after official efforts had ceased. Chapter 8, 'Playing Modern: Blending Japanese and Western Music', examines the widespread, albeit short-lived, fashion for performing Japanese music (chiefly *koto* and *shamisen* genres) on Western instruments; a practice known as *wayō chōwa gaku* (music harmonizing Japanese and Western elements, which I will refer to as 'blended music').[69] The propagators of the practice can be categorized loosely as 'reformers' and as 'entrepreneurs'. The second group, people who promoted the practice of playing blended music, was particularly significant for transforming musical practices. It included enterprising musicians, often performers of indigenous music. Their activities included the publication of sheet music for traditional and modern Japanese-style composition in Western staff notation. As a result, traditional repertoire that previously would have been confined to particular regions and only available for study by direct transmission through personal contact with a teacher, became widely available. The popularity of performing blended music, moreover, suggests that the strict separation between Western and Japanese music (which, from around 1900, began to be called *hōgaku*) was not a foregone conclusion, despite the privileging of Western music by the Meiji government.

Part Three: The World, Japan, and Sendai focuses on the northern provincial city of Sendai, placing the transformation of local musical culture in the context of globalization and national unification. Detailed local studies are almost non-existent, although the region around Osaka and Kobe has received a fair amount of attention. Like Tokyo, however, it is exceptional: Osaka is another metropolis, and Kobe is a major port town.[70] The choice of Sendai may seem somewhat arbitrary. My main reason for selecting it was the surprising number of reports on musical activities in the city that appear in *Ongaku zasshi*. The magazine's special attention paid to the place was soon explained when I learnt that its editor, Shikama Totsuji, was himself from Sendai and that his brother

---

69   Also known as *wayō setchū* (mixing Japanese and Western elements) or *wayō gassō* (Japanese-Western ensemble playing).

70   Watanabe, *Nihon bunka modan rapusodi*. De Ferranti and Tokita, *Music, Modernity and Locality*.

Jinji was one of the principal actors in the local music scene. Shikama Totsuji thus represents a link between the national and the local level. As will be explained in the introduction to Part Three, there are a number of reasons that make Sendai a good case study, offering the opportunity to examine what kind of conditions were necessary to enable the musical transformations that occurred in the capital to reach a provincial town.

Chapter 9, 'Local Pioneers', highlights the decisive role of determined individuals, including Shikama Totsuji and his brother Jinji, in promoting music in general and disseminating Western music in particular. Having received the bare minimum of musical training in the capital, these local pioneers taught music, wrote songs, helped establish local associations for the promotion of music, and organized concerts.

Although the decisive reforming initiatives came from locals, foreign actors were indispensable in the years around the turn of the century, when levels of knowledge and skill among the Japanese were low. The most notable foreign actor in Sendai is discussed in Chapter 10, 'Foreign Actors: Kate I. Hansen'. Hansen, a missionary, was both typical and unique. Missionaries played an important role in introducing basic Western musical education, and in Sendai Hansen stands out as the most significant of them. Not only did she have professional training as a musician: she spent most of her working life in Sendai, where she was instrumental in building a music department at Miyagi School for Girls. It offered training at conservatoire level at a time when few schools outside Tokyo did so. Hansen was, moreover, an astute observer of musical life, and her detailed descriptions of local concerts as well as of the methods she developed in order to teach her students Western-style singing give unique insights into the changing musical landscape.

But what kind of 'Western music' was actually performed in concerts in Sendai? This is the main theme of Chapter 11, 'The World in Sendai'. Based on the programmes of local concerts between 1907 and 1921 published in the magazine *Ongakukai* (Music world), this chapter shows how local concerts, in which different groups came together to perform an eclectic repertoire to a mixed audience, helped transform the people of Sendai into members of a nation within a wider world of nations. The modern institution of the public concert represented a space where Japanese and foreigners met and played and listened to music that was being performed and heard worldwide. The repertoire included a wide range of genres and countries of origin. Together, this variety, and the locations, scenes, and stories evoked by the pieces reveal much that is obscured by the blanket term 'Western music'. Works from the narrow canon of the 'great masters' of European art music, in fact, represented only a small fraction of what was performed.

The Conclusion, after briefly outlining how the changes in musical culture in the 1920s made themselves felt in Sendai, returns to the larger framework. It places the emergence of a new musical culture in Sendai in the context of national consolidation, as well as of Japan's growing importance on the international stage after the First World War. This discussion leads back to the question posed in this introduction: what can music contribute to our understanding of history?

Examining musical practices can greatly enhance our understanding of historical developments, provided that these practices are examined in their wider historical context. The case of Japan demonstrates that music and musical modernization were an integral part of its transformation into a modern nation. This transformation was motivated in large part by the need to respond to Western dominance and was inspired by Western models. Traditional genres of Japanese music flourished in the period examined, but, ultimately, they were relegated to a niche existence. Arguably, official neglect at the time when Western music was systematically adopted ensured their preservation as (supposedly) unadulterated elements of traditional culture. In this way, Western and indigenous music each played (and still play) their part in defining modern Japan.

Japan successfully negotiated two significant global transformations in the late nineteenth and into the twentieth century: nation-building and globalization. Its ability to do so was in part due to the ability of officials and non-state actors to harness the power of music in support of their aims. The commonalities between European and East Asian, including Confucian, ideas about music as a civilizing force made it possible to accept European claims to universality without fully appreciating the epistemological gap between those concepts. Western music was perceived by Isawa and other political and intellectual leaders to be based on universal scientific laws and to represent an assumed universal modernity. Combined with two other powerful tools for building community—synchronized movement and language – and promoted in modern institutions, namely the school and the army, the performance and reception of Western music promoted national bonding. At the same time, learning to listen to and perform Western music linked the Japanese people, even those who lived in provincial towns and cities such as Sendai, to the global circulation of music and enabled then to join in the global performance of modernity.

Finally, I hope that my detailed treatment of this decisive phase in Japan's musical modernization will help to deepen our understanding of the process and thereby dispel the stereotypes about Japanese (and, by extension, Asian) musicians that prevail to this day. There is still widespread ignorance of just how deeply rooted in Japanese history and culture is the music that we tend to describe as 'Western'. As my draft for this book was nearing completion, this ignorance was demonstrated at a masterclass at the Juilliard School of Music. The world-famous violinist Pinchas Zukerman employed cultural stereotypes while addressing two American students with Japanese ancestry. He reportedly told them that their playing was too perfect and lacked expression, advising them to add 'a little more vinegar—or soy sauce!' to their performance and topping these remarks with 'I know in Korea they don't sing.'[71]

The example of Sendai suggests that such stereotypes could pass for accurate characterizations of performances in Japan in the nineteenth and early twentieth centuries. There is good reason to believe that Kate Hansen's assertions about her students were based on accurate observations. Western music was still unfamiliar and, before commercial recordings became available, opportunities to hear it performed well were extremely limited. By the end of the few decades examined here, however, the situation had changed completely; by the latter half of the twentieth century, earlier assumptions about the ability of the Japanese to understand and master foreign music had been proven wrong.

---

71 The class took place on 25 June 2021. For a report by a violinist who witnessed the class, see Laurie Niles, 'Juilliard acts after Pinchas Zukerman uses "offensive cultural stereotypes"', *Violinist.com* (blog), 27 June 2021, https://www.violinist.com/blog/laurie/20216/28825/ The case was widely reported. See, for example, Javier C. Hernández, 'Violinist Apologizes for "Culturally Insensitive" Remarks About Asians', *The New York Times,* 28 June 2021 (updated 11 November 2021), https://www.nytimes.com/2021/06/28/arts/music/pinchas-zukerman-violinist-asians.html

A Note on Terminology

I have aimed to use English translations for some central Japanese terms to avoid confusing readers without knowledge of Japanese. Many terms, however, including musical instruments and genres, defy easy translation. The following terms have for the most part been rendered in English, but require explanation.

The term 'music', although common to many European languages, did not have an obvious equivalent in Japanese in the nineteenth century. The term *ongaku*, in general use today, was used from the Tokugawa period (1603–1868) to translate 'music', but it did not attain common currency until well into the Meiji period (1868–1912). Music imported from the West was referred to as *yōgaku* (Western music) regardless of genre. Today, (Western) classical music is referred to as *kurashikku*. I have used 'European art music' for classical music, since the music originated in Europe.[72] 'Western music' includes all genres that are perceived as 'Western' (which usually means European and North American) in origin.

Japanese musical genres were known by their individual names: a blanket term only became necessary in order to distinguish all indigenous music collectively from that imported from the West. From the early twentieth century, *hōgaku* (indigenous Japanese music) came into use. Then, the term referred to the traditional genres (unlike today, when *hōgaku* can also refer to modern genres such as J-pop). In this book, 'Japanese music' refers to traditional musical genres unless otherwise stated.

The music of the common people, primarily for entertainment, was known as *zokugaku*, translated here as 'common music'. Eta Harich-Schneider, pioneering author of Japanese musical history, states that Western music was initially ranked with *zokugaku*.[73] Given the circumstances of its introduction, this would not be surprising. But in the debates of Meiji reformers, *zokugaku* often implied a moral judgement. 'Common', which in some contexts can imply contempt, therefore seems a fitting translation.

---

72 See Osterhammel, 'Globale Horizonte', 96.
73 Eta Harich-Schneider, *A History of Japanese Music* (London: Oxford University Press, 1973), 546.

A musical genre popular in late-nineteenth and early-twentieth century Japan was *minshingaku* (literally 'Ming and Qing music'; Ming and Qing dynasty music) or *shingaku* (Qing music), a regional style of popular music from China that was first transmitted to Japan by Chinese merchants in the Tokugawa period.

The custom of playing pieces from the *hōgaku* repertoire on Western instruments was referred to as *wayō setchū gaku* (music mixing Japanese and Western elements), *wayō chōwa gaku* (music harmonizing Japanese and Western elements), or *wayō gassō* (Japanese-Western ensemble playing). I have translated this as 'blended music' or 'blended performance'.

A term I have left untranslated is *shōka*. It has sometimes been translated as 'school songs', but this invites confusion with the songs celebrating a particular school (*kōka*). The basic meaning of *shōka* is 'song', but its use is more specific. The term was initially used mainly for Western-style songs imported, or composed by Japanese, for use in education. Many of these songs achieved popularity outside the school system. Several of the early *shōka* feature in the Collection of 100 Japanese songs (*Nihon no uta hyakusen*) published by the Agency of Cultural Affairs in 2007.[74]

Japanese Names

Japanese names in the main body of the book are given in the conventional Japanese order, that is with the surname first. In the footnotes, bibliography, and index they are given in the same order as the Western names in order to avoid confusion.

---

74 Bunkachō (Agency of Cultural Affairs), 'Nihon no uta hyakusen', *Bunkachō geppō* 2007, no. 2 (2007), https://www.bunka.go.jp/tokei_hakusho_shuppan/hakusho_nenjihokokusho/archive/pdf/93732401_03.pdf

Part One: Global History, Modernity, and Western Music

While this book centres on Japan, it is essential to keep in mind that Japan was not an isolated case, even if it was in some ways exceptional. So, before turning to developments within Japan, an examination of the global context is in order. The nineteenth century was an age of accelerating globalization, and dissemination of the ideas, institutions, and practices that we generally associate with modernity, including nationalism and a world of nation states, capitalism, constitutional government, and universal military service and schooling. It was also an age of Western imperialism and colonialism, but, as Harry Liebersohn has rightly observed: 'Overall, it is a fundamental misconception to imagine the late nineteenth century as a time when Western colonizers imposed and the colonized reacted by simply deferring or rebelling. Rather, in an age of globalization a *circulation* of ideas and sensibilities took place.'[1] The cases of educator Isawa Shūji (1851–1917) and physicist and music theorist Tanaka Shōhei (1862–1945) provide early examples of exchanges: both played a role as informants for Alexander J. Ellis (1814–90), a pioneer of comparative musicology.[2]

In any case, Japan was never colonized, although the threat of colonization was real and represented a strong incentive for the Meiji government to respond by abolishing the feudal domains and unifying the country, and by introducing reforms based on Western models. The Meiji reforms and Japan's emergence as a powerful modern nation

---

1 Harry Liebersohn, *Music and the New Global Culture: From the Great Exhibitions to the Jazz Age* (Chicago: University of Chicago Press, 2019), 118. https://doi.org/10.7208/9780226649306 The emphasis is Liebersohn's.
2 See Chapter 5.

have received much attention from researchers, but there has long been a tendency to neglect the wider context of these processes.[3] There is a certain irony in this, given that the Japanese reformers were always aware of acting, as it were, on a global stage. Historically, nation-building and globalization are closely connected to each other. Together, they are among the most important characteristics of modernity, and music played a crucial role in both national and global integration. A third characteristic of modernity that is particularly relevant in our context is its self-consciousness, the acute perception among the people experiencing it that they were living in a world that was 'transforming away from itself with terrifying speed'.[4] It is these three characteristics of modernity that are central to the subject of this book.

Japan's (relative) isolation from European power politics was a characteristic it shared with the United States.[5] The structures within the two countries were different, but processes of national integration occurred at the same time following the Meiji Restoration and the end of the American Civil War. And while America was one of the Western countries Japan looked towards as a model in music edication and in many areas, both countries looked to Europe as the source of musical culture. It is therefore meaningful to compare and contrast the reception of European music in the two countries that were not European colonies but nevertheless revered and strove to adopt European music, before moving on to focus on Japan. Japan is treated here as a case of the global dissemination of Western music and its effects on traditional Japanese music.

---

[3] Kenneth Pyle, 'Profound Forces in the Making of Modern Japan', *Journal of Japanese Studies* 32, no. 2 (2006).

[4] Stefan Zweig, 'Lafcadio Hearn', in *Das Japanbuch: Eine Auswahl aus den Werken von Lafcadio Hearn* (Frankfurt a. M.: Rütten & Loening, 1923 (1911)), 1.

[5] Osterhammel treats the two countries as special cases in the process of national integration: Jürgen Osterhammel, *Die Verwandlung der Welt: Eine Geschichte des 19. Jahrhunderts* (Munich: C. H. Beck, 2009), 599.

1. Global History, Musical Modernity, and the Globalization of Western Music

The world-wide facility of communication has allowed the wind of Western civilization to blow into the East [...] still, to anyone who has seen with his eyes the present state of world affairs and knows its [i.e. resistance's] actual impossibility there can be no other policy than to move on with the rest of the world and join them in dipping into the sea of civilization, joining them in creating the waves of civilization, and joining them in the pains and joys of civilization.[1]

The people of India, Africa, and China all love Mozart – is this not remarkable? How has Classical music spread so widely throughout the world? How was classical music able to become the global standard? [...] The music we listen to, whether rock, pop, or *kayōkyoku*, are in fact hybrid genres, born from the principles of harmony (chord progression) brought forth by Western classical music, as well as from rhythms that developed from their African origins. If Japanese emotions (*jōcho*) are added to this harmony and rhythm, they become *enka* and J-pop; if Korean emotions are added, they become K-pop. And on the American continent, travelling up North, they became jazz, while travelling down South they became tango.[2]

Fukuzawa's words illustrate that, whatever criticisms scholars today level at concepts of modernity and progress, for an intellectual writing in Japan in the late nineteenth century the case was clear: Western

---

1 Yukichi Fukuzawa, 'On De-Asianization by Fukuzawa Yukichi, March 16, 1885', in *Meiji Japan through Contemporary Sources*, ed. Tokyo The Centre for East Asian Cultural Studies (Tokyo: The Centre for East Asian Cultural Studies, 1972), 179.

2 Shigeaki Saegusa, *Kyōten dōchi kurashikku* (Tokyo: Kino Bukkusu, 2014), 2. Saegusa's questions are also part of the text on the book's sleeve (*obi*).

civilization was the way to go; resistance was not an option. Western music was part of what we might call the 'civilization package', and the spread of music can thus be linked to Western imperialism and dominance. On the other hand, no one forced the Japanese (or other non-Western peoples) to adopt Western music, much less European art music, to the extent they did. So it is legitimate to ask whether something in the music itself encouraged its worldwide adoption.

Saegusa (b. 1942), a composer whose works include operas with Japanese themes, introduced his book (it has the English subtitle *Astonishing Classical Music*) by noting the omnipresence and prestige of music that originated in Europe and outlined what he called the 'three great achievements' of (European) classical music: staff notation, harmony, and 'an attitude of "progress" that continuously demands renewal'.[3] Harmony relates to the music itself, while notation is a practice that is fundamental to European art music. To what extent the 'attitude of progress' can be heard in the music itself must remain open to question. However one chooses to answer, classical music came to be closely associated with modern times and was perceived as desirable for that reason.

Geopolitics, musical practices, and musical characteristics contributed to the global reach of Western music, and if we treat global history as the history of increasing global integration, we might describe music as a major integrating force.[4] The concept of integration implies that the different parts of the world are interconnected and that events in one part of the world are likely to have an effect on other parts of the world. Whether or not connections and transnational movements of people, objects, ideas, and institutions, even on a global scale, have significant effects on the societies involved, depends on the overall geopolitical environment in which they happen.[5] The case of music in Japan illustrates this point very well. Western music was first brought to Japan in the sixteenth century, when it was taught to Japanese by Jesuit

---

3   Saegusa, *Kyōten dōchi kurashikku*, 26–27, 32–33, 38–39. Saegusa uses the word *hatsumei*, a term that implies both 'invention, contrivance' and 'cleverness'.
4   Sebastian Conrad, *What is Global History?* (Princeton: Princeton University Press, 2016), 6–11. Conrad distinguishes three types of global history; the one based on the notion of global integration is narrower than the other two.
5   Conrad, *What is Global History?*, 68–69. Conrad uses the introduction of Western clocks to Japan as an example.

missionaries. But the early encounter ultimately left no lasting traces. The well-known story of the hidden Christians and their sung liturgy, also mentioned by Saegusa, does not fundamentally alter this fact.[6] The main reason for this is that, by around 1600, political and military leaders who were aiming to unify the country had good reasons to keep the Western intruders at bay, which was largely achieved with the suppression of Christianity and the shogunate's seclusion policy. By the mid-nineteenth century, however, the geopolitical situation in East Asia had changed completely. The power of China was in decline: although it escaped colonization, it was unable to resist heavy foreign encroachment. Foreign ships increasingly appeared on Japan's shores, and in 1853 Commodore Perry forced Japan to conclude the first of the 'unequal treaties', precipitating the fall of the Tokugawa shogunate. The Meiji government then embarked on a course of reform, and their first priority was to resist Western imperialism and, crucially, to be accepted as an equal to the great powers. Thus, three hundred years after the first encounter with Western culture, the government had good reasons not only to tolerate but to embrace much of it, including music.

Global Modernity

Japan's course of pursuing Western-style modernization, including the adoption of Western music, took place in the context of global developments from the mid-nineteenth century: Western expansion, global integration, and state-building.[7] The reforms enacted by the Meiji government and the resulting political, economic, social, and cultural transformations have often been described as 'modernization', a concept originally developed with reference to Europe. Although problematic when applied to other parts of the world and much criticized, it has proved hard to avoid (resorting to 'modern' or 'modernity' hardly solves the problem of Eurocentric bias) and has found its defenders,

---

6 Saegusa, *Kyōten dōchi kurashikku*, 80–81. For a detailed treatment of the period, see Harich-Schneider, *A History of Japanese Music*.

7 For the broader history of the period, see Jürgen Osterhammel, *The Transformation of the World: A Global History of the Nineteenth Century*, trans. Patrick Camiller (Princeton: Princeton University Press, 2014); John Darwin, *After Tamerlane: The Rise & Fall of Global Empires, 1400–2000* (London: Penguin Books, 2007).

albeit with more modest claims.[8] Modernity can be usefully defined as 'a condition, historically produced over three centuries around the globe in processes of change that have not ended yet'. The modern 'possesses commonalities across time and space'.[9] Commonalities include the nation state, the call for national political participation, major social shifts, major changes in values, and 'global forces of capitalism and industrialization', as well as 'incorporation into the reigning geopolitical world order' and experience of tensions between global and the local.[10] The different types of interplay between these global commonalities and local specifics, including differences in timing, mean that modernity is experienced in significantly diverse ways across the globe. In order to recognize the modern in its many different forms, we need to examine individual cultures closely, so that we do not end up regarding cultural differences as 'evidence of stunted modernity'.[11] In other words, although many elements that are regarded as characteristic of modernity historically originated in the West, we must not fall into the trap of assuming modernity is intrinsically Western or that modernization is the same as Westernization.[12] Instead, we must train ourselves to recognize innovation that is not immediately derived from Western influences.[13] In Japan, for example, culture and society had begun to transform and

---

8   See, for example, Hans-Ulrich Wehler, *Modernisierungstheorie und Geschichte* (Göttingen: Vandenhoeck & Ruprecht, 1975). For Japan, see Sheldon Garon, 'Rethinking Modernization and Modernity in Japanese History: A Focus on State-Society Relations', *Journal of Asian Studies* 53, no. 2 (1994), https://doi.org/10.2307/2059838; Sebastian Conrad, Hans Martin Krämer, and Tino Schölz, eds., *Geschichtswissenschaft in Japan: Themen, Ansätze und Theorien* (Göttingen: Vandenhoeck & Ruprecht, 2006).

9   Carol Gluck, 'The End of Elsewhere: Writing Modernity Now (AHR Roundtable)', *American Historical Review* 116, no. 3 (2011): 676, https://doi.org/10.1086/ahr.116.3.676 Part of the following is also based on Margaret Mehl, *History and the State in Nineteenth-Century Japan: The World, the Nation and the Search for a Modern Past* (*Second edition with new preface*) (Copenhagen: The Sound Book Press, 2017 (1998)).

10 Gluck, 'End of Elsewhere', 676–77.

11 Christopher Goto-Jones, *Modern Japan: A Very Short Introduction* (Oxford: Oxford University Press, 2009), 10.

12 Volker H. Schmidt, 'How Unique is East Asian Modernity?', *Asian Journal of Social Science*, no. 39 (2011), https://doi.org/10.1163/156853111X577596; Osterhammel, *Verwandlung der Welt*, 1281–83; Christopher Alan Bayly, *The Birth of the Modern World 1780–1914: Global Connections and Comparisons* (Malden, MA: Blackwell, 2004); De Ferranti and Tokita, *Music, Modernity and Locality*, 10–12; Goto-Jones, *Modern Japan: A Very Short Introduction*, 7–10; Garon, "Rethinking Modernization'.

13 See George Akita, *Evaluating Evidence: A Positivist Approach to Reading Sources on Modern Japan* (Honolulu: University of Hawai'i Press, 2008), 118–24.

develop characteristics associated with modern times before its enforced opening to the West. In Tokyo (then still named Edo) and other cities a consumer culture emerged. As a result, when, for example, the Meiji government abolished the monopolies protecting certain groups of musicians and their genres, the more enterprising found a receptive audience for their art among the townspeople. Increased mobility, both social and geographical, provided the possibility of disseminating regional genres, such as the Satsuma-style of *biwa*[14] performance, nationwide. The adoption by the government of Western music did ultimately affect the traditional musics of Japan, but innovation in these genres and their successful adaptation to the changing conditions was not a direct result of Westernization.[15]

The different forms modernity takes in different times and places result from the 'plurality of pasts' and the 'plurality of futures'[16] or, in other words, the variations in 'preexisting conditions' and 'available modernities'.[17] For Japan, at the time of the Meiji Restoration in 1868, Western expansion in East Asia, as well as the political, economic, and social conditions of the Tokugawa system of rule represented these 'preexisting conditions'.[18] While some of these can, with hindsight, be regarded as having been conducive to modernization, it is important to note that the leaders of Meiji Japan did not deliberately seek to build on Japan's legacy, at least not its most recent legacy.[19] The 'preexisting conditions' determine what choices are available at the conjunction of a society's history when 'modernization' is on the agenda. The same applies to 'available modernities'. The version of modernity aspired to

---

14   The *biwa* is a type of plucked lute; *satsumabiwa* is a modern style of the instrument in its own right.
15   Kazushi Ishida, *Modanizumu hensōkyoku: Higashi Ajia no kindai ongakushi* (Tokyo: Sakuhokusha, 2005), 24–37.
16   Sudipta Kaviraj, 'An Outline of a Revisionist Theory of Modernity', *European Journal of Sociology* 46, no. 3 (2005): 498, 500, https://doi.org/10.1017/S0003975605000196
17   Gluck, 'End of Elsewhere', 679, 681.
18   Ibid., 679.
19   See Mark Lincicome, *Imperial Subjects as Global Citizens: Nationalism, Internationalism, and Education in Japan* (Lanham, MD: Lexington Books, 2009), 1–29; Mark Ravina, *To Stand with the Nations of the World: Japan's Meiji Restoration in World History* (New York: Oxford University Press, 2017), 9-10. Ravina introduces the term 'radical nostalgia' to describe the 'invocation of the distant past to promote radical change in the present', although he adds that this kind of discourse had precedents in the Tokugawa era.

by Meiji Japanese was known to them as 'civilization and enlightenment' (*bunmei kaika*) modelled by Western countries (*Ō-Bei shokoku* or 'the countries of Europe and America'), which they understood to be to a greater or lesser degree ahead of them on a universal ladder towards progress.[20]

In other words, leading intellectuals such as Fukuzawa Yukichi did in fact perceive a single, universal modernity. For him, as for other intellectual and political leaders, 'an aspiration to be "up with the times"'[21] was certainly an essential ingredient of being modern, and modernization was thus also the 'adaptation to the contemporary situation.'[22] Likewise, the global dimension of modernity was obvious to Fukuzawa and others. It was the outside world encroaching on Japan that forced the Tokugawa shogunate to abandon its isolation policy, precipitating the collapse of the regime and the establishment of the Meiji government. The new leaders, at both national and local levels, saw from the start the need to act within a global context. The pledge in the Imperial Oath of 1868 that 'knowledge shall be sought from all the countries of the world' found its remarkable expression in 1871, when half of the new government, which had only just managed to secure control over the entire country, embarked on the Iwakura Embassy which took the Ambassador Extraordinary and Plenipotentiary, four vice-ambassadors and an entourage of nearly one hundred men, over a period of twenty-one months, to twelve countries as well as to every major sea port between Marseilles and Nagasaki.[23]

Meanwhile, in the remote prefecture of Kashiwazaki (soon to be absorbed into Niigata Prefecture), in the spring of 1873, the Deputy Councillor, in a public notification to all village headmen

---

20 Gluck, 'End of Elsewhere', 681.
21 Bayly, *Birth of the Modern World*, 10. Gluck refers to an 'aspirational modernity': Gluck, 'End of Elsewhere', 677.
22 Margaret J. Kartomi, 'The Processes and Results of Musical Culture Contact: A Discussion of Terminology and Concepts', *Ethnomusicology* 25, no. 2 (1981): 246 n.10, https://doi.org/10.2307/851273
23 In addition, the embassy included students who stayed abroad, among them six girls. See introduction in Kunitake Kume, *The Iwakura Embassy 1871–73: A True Account of the Ambassador Extraordinary and Plenipotentiary's Journey of Observation through the United States of America and Europe*, ed. Graham Healey and Chushichi Tsuzuki, trans. Graham Healey, Martin Colcutt, Andrew Cobbing, P. F. Kornicky, Eugene Soviak, Chushichi Tsuzuki, 5 vols., vol. 1: The United States of America (Kamiyakiri, Matsudo, Chiba: The Japan Documents, 2002).

concerning the 'Control of Customs during the Spring and Autumn Festivities', condemned young people's dancing together, pointed out the government's efforts 'for our country to hold its own among the countries of the world (*bankoku to gotaiji*)'[24] and that Japan must not be put to shame by those countries (*bankoku no chijoku o ukuru*).[25] And when Shikama Totsuji (1859-1928) founded the first journal dedicated to music, *Ongaku zasshi*, in 1890, the additional English title, 'The Musical Magazine', on the cover signalled clearly that he too had his eyes on the world beyond Japan. These examples show that local actors in Japan (as elsewhere) were conscious of being caught up in global trends.[26] The speed of global interaction increased dramatically in the course of the nineteenth century with the development of the railway, steamships, and the telegraph. Likewise, 'ideas of modernity–progress, science, and rationality–meant a great deal to the Japanese themselves from the Meiji Restoration of 1868 to the recent past.'[27]

'Modernity' is nevertheless likely to remain a contested term, and never more so than when it is applied to music. Efforts to 'provincialize' Europe have been combined with attempts at 'decentring musical modernity'.[28] While it is certainly important to recognize and study developments that challenge Eurocentrism in music history and the sharp distinctions between 'the West and the rest', no amount of decentring can deny the global impact of music that originated in Europe, including European art music, in modern times. Increasing and accelerating global integration is one of the defining characteristics of modernity and can also be observed in relation to music.

---

24 The expression *bankoku to gotaiji* appears twice in the *haihan chiken* order of Meiji 4 (1871). 7.14 about the abolition of the domains and the establishment of prefectures. See *Dajō ruiten 1* (Available on the website of the National Archives: http://www.archives.go.jp/ayumi/kobetsu/m04_1871_04.html).
25 Niigata-ken, ed., *Shin Niigata-kenshi: Shiryō hen 14* (*Kindai 2: Meiji ishin hen II*) (Niigata: Niigata-ken, 1983), 931–32. See Margaret Mehl, ,'Verbote der Bon-Tänze in den Präfekturen Kashiwazaki und Niigata (1872/73)', in *Wege zur Japanischen Geschichte: Quellen aus dem 10. bis 21. Jahrhundert in deutscher Übersetzung*, ed. Anke Scherer and Katja Schmidtpott (Hamburg: Gesellschaft für Natur-und Völkerkunde Ostasiens, 2020).
26 Osterhammel, *Verwandlung der Welt*, 13. Bayly, *Birth of the Modern World*, 10–11.
27 Garon, 'Rethinking Modernization', 350.
28 Tobias Janz and Chien-Chang Yang, 'Introduction', in *Decentering Musical Modernity: Perspectives on East Asian and European Music History*, ed. Tobias Janz and Chien-Chang Yang (Bielefeld: Transcript, 2019). The authors discuss Dipesh Chakrabarty, *Provincializing Europe: Postcolonial Thought and Historical Difference*, on pp. 26–30.

Musical Modernity

Musical modernity is, however, about more than the global spread of Western music. The term can be applied to describe both the music itself and the changing characteristics and conditions of music-making. The first is more difficult to define than the second, and to do so requires considerable expertise in musicology as well as history. Max Weber (1864–1920) was the first to attempt a definition of the entity we call (European) art music from a comparative perspective. He developed a theory of musical rationalization, based on his understanding of rationalization as a defining characteristic of modernity.[29] According to Weber, music as a cultural complex comprises four major elements: the material logic of tone production and its systematization in the form of a tonal musical language; the application of this language in the creative process of composing individual musical works; the meanings ascribed to these works by musicians and their audiences; finally, the institutional organization of musical life. He then attempted to identify what made the West and its music unique, while avoiding the kind of Eurocentrism that would elevate art music of Europe above all other music. His work was based on the latest research in acoustics, musicology, and ethnomusicology.[30] Although he attempted to identify cross-cultural commonalities, he concluded that European art music represented an outstanding case of rationalization, evinced in the development of the tonal system and its standardization through equal temperament embodied in the mechanics of the piano, the notation system, and the rules of composing polyphonic works. The tonal language, as Weber knew from the works of acousticians and musicologists of his time, is based on scientific observation, even if the reverence for masterpieces

---

29 Most of the following is based on Jürgen Osterhammel, 'Globale Horizonte europäischer Kunstmusik, 1860–1930',' *Geschichte und Gesellschaft* 38, no. 1 (2012): 97–99, https://doi.org/10.13109/gege.2012.38.1.86 See also Michael Fend, 'Witnessing a 'Process of Rationalisation'? A Review-Essay of Max Weber's Study on Music', *Max Weber Studies* 10, no. 1 (2010), https://doi.org/10.15543/MWS/2010/1/9; Max Weber, '[Zur Musiksoziologie] ', in *Max Weber: Zur Musiksoziologie (Nachlaß 1921)*, ed. Christoph Braun and Ludwig Finscher, Max Weber Gesamtausgabe (Tübingen: J. C. B. Mohr (Paul Siebeck), 2004 (1921)).

30 Weber did not cite his sources in detail, but most have been identified. See Christoph Braun and Ludwig Finscher, eds., *Max Weber: Zur Musiksoziologie (Nachlaß 1921)*, Max Weber Gesamtausgabe (Tübingen: J. C. B. Mohr (Paul Siebeck), 2004 (1921)).

by genius composers is, as Weber knew equally well, a result of social construction. Its basis in scientific facts (facts that cannot be explained away with postmodern or postcolonial theory) was one of the characteristics that contributed to its image of being modern, and was certainly a major reason for Japanese reformers such as Isawa Shūji to privilege Western music.

A different approach to the question of musical modernity in European art music is presented by the musicologist Julian Johnson in *Out of Time*. Johnson argues that it extends over the 400-year period that is marked by Monteverdi's *Orfeo* at the beginning of the seventeenth century and Birtwistle's *The Mask of Orpheus* towards the end of the twentieth. The recurrence of motifs from the Orpheus myth throughout this period is just one example of the continuities Johnson identifies in the music of the last 400 years: continuities that conventional periodization into epochs and styles tends to obscure. Johnson argues that rather than a linear development, comparable to a train line, the history of music might be likened to a map of the London underground; in this way one might account for the several seemingly contradicting currents in the nineteenth century.[31] Johnson's overall argument is that music does not merely reflect the fundamental differentiations and tensions of the modern experience, but that in exploring them it has also reshaped them and by doing so helped shape modernity itself: 'music is entwined with the making of modernity'.[32] He demonstrates his point by examining a wealth of European art music from the early seventeenth to the late twentieth centuries and discussing music's exploration of time and space and music's relationship with language: music is both like a language and quite different, characterized by sound that is both produced and listened to by the physical actions and through the bodies of performers and their instruments and listeners.

A long-term perspective on modernity emphasizing continuities across the conventional style periods does not mean that they are irrelevant. It merely means that musical modernity 'led to a constant transformation and destabilization of the foundations of music' well

---

31 Johnson, *Out of Time: Music and the Making of Modernity* (Oxford: Oxford University Press, 2015), 11, https://doi.org/10.1093/acprof:oso/9780190233273.001.0001
32 Ibid., 312.

before the mid-nineteenth century,[33] even while significant commonalities across time remained. Indeed, in *Out of Time*, transformation in musical styles is not ignored, but related to developments in literature, scientific advances, social changes, and cultural trends. For example, the completion of Beethoven's *Eroica* Symphony in 1804, described by Richard Wagner as the beginning of musical modernity, coincided with the first steam locomotive train, built by Richard Trevithick in Wales; the coincidence has been noted by several observers. While the two events are not directly connected, Johnson argues that the dynamism of train travel experienced by the public a few decades into the nineteenth century 'had already been prefigured in music by about half a century. Music thus articulated a new sensibility of time which the railway later realized'.[34] The railway was a major symbol of modernity worldwide. In Japan, from 1900, it was celebrated by so-called railway songs. Beethoven, meanwhile, was revered as 'the sage of music' even before his symphonic music could be heard. The first railway line was already in operation by the end of 1871, while the first performance of the *Eroica* by a Japanese full symphony orchestra did not take place until 1924.[35]

Johnson does not discuss European art music in relation to other musics, but he outlined his view of what makes it unique in an earlier work intended for a wider audience, *Who Needs Classical Music?* As he himself noted, several other authors published books in defence of 'Classical music' at the beginning of the new millennium.[36] They

---

[33] Tobias Janz and Chien-Chang Yang, 'Introduction', in *Decentering Musical Modernity: Perspectives on East Asian and European Music History*, ed. Tobias Janz and Chien-Chang Yang (Bielefeld: Transcript, 2019), 22.

[34] Johnson, *Out of Time*, 47–49. (Quote on p. 49.)

[35] The *Eroica* was premiered by the orchestra of the Tokyo Academy of Music, under Gustav Kron. Previously, the first movement had been performed under August Junker: Tōkyō Geijutsu Daigaku Hyakunenshi Hensan Iinkai, ed., *Tōkyō Geijutsu Daigaku hyakunenshi: Ensōkai hen 1* (Tokyo: Ongaku no Tomosha, 1990), 281, 351,517. For a treatment of Beethoven's reception in Japan, see Minoru Nishihara, *'Gakusei' Bētōven no tanjō* (Tokyo: Heibonsha, 2000).

[36] Julian Johnson, *Who Needs Classical Music? Cultural Choice and Musical Value* (New York: Oxford University Press, 2002), xiv. (Introduction to the paperback edition, 2011). Johnson refers to Lawrence Kramer, *Why Classical Music Still Matters* (Berkeley and Los Angeles: University of California Press, 2007); Joshua Fineberg, *Classical Music, Why Bother? Hearing the World of Contemporary Culture through a Composer's Ears* (New York: Routledge, 2006); Carolyn Beckingham, *Moribund Music: Can Classical Music be Saved?* (Brighton: Sussex Academic Press, 2009). Another is Ian Hewett, *Music: Healing the Rift* (New York: Continuum, 2003).

1. *Global History, Musical Modernity, and the Globalization of Western Music* 41

seemed to be driven by a sense of crisis that, while not new, appeared to have become even more acute, and argued, albeit in different ways, that classical music can offer an experience not gained from popular music to those who make the required effort to listen.[37]

In Japan too, the place of (Western) classical music was a subject of debate, although from a different angle: its dominant position in Japan's cultural life and in particular in the education system at the expense of Japan's traditional music had begun to be challenged. In 2002, the Ministry of Education (MEXT) published new guidelines, which for the first time stipulated that playing a Japanese musical instrument would become a compulsory component of music education in public schools.[38] Likewise in 2002, two books by musicologists presented a critical evaluation of the history of Western music in modern Japan. Aikawa Yumi, a singer and musicologist, in her book *'Enka' no susume* (An encouragement of 'enka'—a type of popular song that originated in the late 1920s and is regarded as quintessentially Japanese), diagnosed a 'Western music complex' as a result of Japan's music education.[39] Watanabe Hiroshi challenged contemporary misconceptions about both Western and traditional Japanese music. He drew attention to the interaction between them and highlighted the different forms musical modernity took in the Kansai region, in contrast to Tokyo.[40] And in *Doremi o eranda Nihonjin* (When the Japanese chose 'do re mi'), published in 2007, Chiba Yūko, a musicologist specializing in Japanese music, presented a history of what she called the 'dual structure' of music in Japan. Highlighting the impact of Western music on indigenous music and on the musical perceptions of the Japanese, Chiba too identified a Japanese 'complex' in the face of Western music.[41] Although different on the face of it, the two trends—the perceived crisis of classical music noted by writers in Europe and North America, and the unease expressed by Japanese about the overwhelming dominance of that same music and the resulting neglect

---

37 Johnson, *Out of Time*, 245; Hewett, *Music: Healing the Rift*, 23, 120; Fineberg, *Classical Music, Why Bother? Hearing the World of Contemporary Culture through a Composer's Ears*; Beckingham, *Moribund Music: Can Classical Music be Saved?*, 71. Fineberg is himself a noted composer.
38 Rinko Fujita, 'Music education in modern Japanese society', in *Studies on a Global History of Music*, ed. Reinhard Strohm (London: Routledge, 2018).
39 Yumi Aikawa, *"Enka" no susume* (Tokyo: Bungei Shunjū, 2002), 16162.
40 Hiroshi Watanabe, *Nihon bunka modan rapusodi*, (Tokyo: Shunjūsha, 2002).
41 Yūko Chiba, *Doremi o eranda Nihonjin* (Ongaku no Tomosha, 2007), 173.

of Japanese traditional music—may well be regarded as reactions to global trends in music, including the blurring of boundaries between Western and non-Western, or classical and popular music.

While it seems reasonable to assume that European art music has characteristics that marked it as 'modern' and therefore made it attractive to non-Western societies aspiring to modernity, there remain two problems with this assumption. First, few of these characteristics are likely to register with an audience to whom it is completely unfamiliar. Second, European art music was not the only Western music that was globalized; its impact, at least initially, was comparatively limited. In fact, the very category of 'classical music' is a modern invention.[42] The creation of this category involved establishing and cultivating a canon, or repertoire of works, often by dead composers, that were considered timeless, although this involved a value judgment that was very much of its time. The expressive aesthetic and the importance of individuality and originality were treated as axiomatic and were accepted as such by musicians working in the tradition of 'great' classical composers.[43]

We are on much firmer ground when we attempt to define the modern in relation to the context of music-related activities, including performance. Western music was modern, because it was performed in modern settings and for modern purposes. 'Places and spaces', as well as 'purpose', are two of five areas where, according to Tim Blanning, a historian of early modern and modern Europe, music benefited more than any other art from major transformations between 1700 and the present day. The other three are status, technology, and liberation.[44] Blanning's account centres on Europe and the Western world, but the areas that he highlights can usefully serve as a basis for examining non-Western cases.

Modernity brought new purposes for music, while old functions, including religious worship, affirmation and representation of power, and recreation and entertainment, remained significant. The power that was represented could and did change: new institutions and modern

---

42 Tim Blanning, *The Triumph of Music: Composers, Musicians and Their Audiences, 1700 to the Present* (London: Allan Lane (Penguin), 2008), 111–14.
43 Blanning argues that these values even inform leading jazz and rock artists of the late twentieth century: Blanning, *Triumph*, 114–21.
44 Ibid..

ceremonies required appropriate music, such as military bands playing at political and diplomatic ceremonies.⁴⁵ Military bands also played for public entertainment. Indeed, military music was often the first Western music that people in other cultures encountered, and anyway, the boundaries between European art music and military music are at best fluid: military bands played arrangements from operas, and musical elements of marches are common in symphonic music.⁴⁶

A new development in (early) modern Europe that spread to other parts of the world was the institution of the public concert, open to anyone who could afford a ticket. Music performed at concerts was enjoyed for its own sake and involved a new kind of listening, in which performers and audience were clearly distinguished from each other.⁴⁷ The public concert, particularly the symphonic concert, required a new kind of space in the form of the purpose-built concert hall. Like other modern 'places and spaces', the concert hall was an urban space, catering to the demands of the increasing populations of cities. The symphony, a central genre of musical modernity, is an urban phenomenon by definition and depends on an orchestra, a substantial paying audience, and a large hall, all of which are only available in cities.⁴⁸ In smaller towns, concerts had to be held in venues intended for other purposes, and performers were most often amateurs.⁴⁹

Even in the major cities, however, not all performance spaces were temples of high art. The majority of the urban middle classes craved lighter fare, and represented a growing market for commercial entrepreneurs, who staged big concerts in large halls offering programmes that mixed demanding works with more accessible pieces of various orchestral genres. Dance venues, another musical space, also

---

45 For the global reach of military music, see Martin Rempe, 'Cultural Brokers in Uniform: The Global Rise of Military Musicians and Their Music', *Itinerario* 41, no. 2 (2017), https://doi.org/10.1017/S0165115317000390
46 See, for example, Maiko Kawabata, 'Virtuoso Codes of Violin Performance: Power, Military Heroism and Gender (1789–1830)', *19th-Century Music* 28 (2004), https://doi.org/10.1525/ncm.2004.28.2.089
47 Blanning, *Triumph*, 85–6; Cook, *Music*, 19–21.
48 Johnson, *Out of Time*, 132.
49 Amateurs have received less attention than professional musicians. For a brief commentary on amateur concerts in England, see George Bernard Shaw, 'A ladylike tremolando in Richmond', in *Music for Love*, ed. Christopher Driver (London: Weidenfeld & Nicolson, 1994 (1890–94)).

reflected social hierarchies with the more exclusive venues only open to the upper classes. Dances were increasingly standardized, and in the early twentieth century large dance halls attracted huge and diverse audiences. For the working classes unable to afford opera and concert tickets, the music hall became a major space for enjoying music. An extension of traditional performance spaces in pubs, inns, and coffee houses, music hall performances featured opera extracts, burlesque, and songs of various types ranging from patriotic to sentimental to comic, with catchy tunes.[50]

The public concert provided new opportunities for composers and performers.[51] While this did not necessarily result in a higher status for musicians—dependence on an aristocratic patron came to be replaced by other kinds of dependency—it did allow more freedom and independence, especially for musicians with entrepreneurial flair. A significant transformation of the musician's status was the development of musical professions in line with other middle-class professions, with the establishment of conservatoires providing training and accreditation in composition and performance, as well as in teaching.[52] In Germany, the first conservatoire was established in Leipzig in 1843 and offered a broad curriculum of theoretical and practical subjects, with members of the Gewandhaus Orchestra teaching orchestral instruments.[53] The number of conservatoires increased over the next decades.

The new professions were open to men only. Women, although admitted to conservatoires, were systematically excluded from the professions, apart from teaching. Those who did perform for a living tended to come from the 'artist-musician class' and from families where women's employment was taken for granted.[54] Women from the

---

50   Blanning, *Triumph*, 163–65.
51   Ibid., 84, 85–89.
52   Blanning does not treat professionalization; nor does he take into account the enormous variations in status between a rock star (such as Brian May) and, for example, a freelance classical musician. For the latter, see Stephen Cottrell, *Professional Music-Making in London: Ethnography and Experience*, SOAS Musicology Series, (Aldershot: Ashgate, 2004). Or, for a more graphic account: Blair Tindall, *Mozart in the Jungle: Sex, Drugs and Classical Music* (London: Atlantic Books, 2005).
53   Wilfried Gruhn, *Geschichte der Musikerziehung: Eine Kultur- und Sozialgeschichte vom Gesangsunterricht der Aufklärungspädagogik zu ästhetisch-kultureller Bildung*, second ed. (Hofheim: Wolke, 2003), 98–99.
54   Nancy Reich, 'Women as Musicians: A Question of Class', in *Musicology and Difference: Gender and Sexuality in Musical Scholarship*, ed. Ruth A. Solie (Berkeley:

aristocracy or the educated middle classes (*Bildungsbürgertum*) might be trained to professional level, but their music-making was limited to the home or, possibly, charity concerts. A woman's supposedly natural role was that of a housewife, mother, and, on occasion, the inspiring muse to her artist husband. The new romantic ethos, moreover, not only defined the artist creator and genius as male, but even the music itself was defined as masculine.[55] In Japan, the situation was different, at least initially, because the male elite regarded music-making as an inappropriate occupation for men.

Technology revolutionized the performance and reception of music in direct and indirect ways. Railways and, later, steamships enabled musicians, traditionally an itinerant group in many societies, to travel further and with more ease and enabled the phenomenon of the travelling virtuoso. Means of mass-production (whether a result of technology, organization, or economy of scale) brought the prices of musical instruments down, making them affordable for more people. Technical improvements to instruments, such as adding valves to brass instruments, increased the scope of what could be played on them, and also made them easier to learn. The technical changes to brass instruments, together with lower prices, made possible the proliferation of amateur brass bands.[56] Two instrumental technologies in particular were 'central to the development of musical modernity': the orchestra and the piano. The orchestra, in the form of the 'specifically *symphonic* orchestra', displayed the latest instrument technology (woodwind with keys, an expanded section of brass instruments with valves), as well as the working together of individual parts as in an industrial machine, or the division of labour in a modern factory. The resulting sound fit the Romantic category of the sublime.[57]

The development of the piano into a robust and loud instrument that could fill the new, large venues and hold its own against a full symphony orchestra, promoted its entry into the new concert halls, while its versatility, its pleasing sound even when played by the unskilled, and

---

University of California Press, 1995). See also Martin Rempe, *Kunst, Spiel, Arbeit: Musikerleben in Deutschland, 1850 bis 1960* (Göttingen: Vandenhoeck & Ruprecht, 2020).

55 Reich, 'Women as Musicians', 133; Kawabata, 'Virtuoso Codes'.
56 Blanning, *Triumph*, 191-97; Rempe, *Kunst, Spiel, Arbeit*, 94–112.
57 Johnson, *Out of Time*, 142, 145–48. Johnson's italics.

its affordable price made it the instrument of choice for middle-class homes. Meanwhile, another keyboard instrument, the reed organ or harmonium, besides rivalling the piano in the home, was widely played in small churches, village halls, and schools.[58] More affordable and easier to tune and maintain than a piano, it was, moreover, widely disseminated overseas, chiefly by missionaries. In Japan, reed organs were produced domestically and sold nationwide from the 1880s.

Technical improvements to the piano and lower prices transformed music-making in many ways.[59] But Liszt certainly put his finger on one vital capability of the piano when he remarked that, '[t]hrough its mediation, works can be broadcast that otherwise would remain unknown, due to the difficulties of assembling a full orchestra.'[60] Before the advent of recording technology, piano arrangements (together with arrangements for small ensembles) were the only way of hearing operas and symphonic works in remoter parts of the country, or overseas. When the first performance of a European opera in Japan—Gluck's *Orpheus*[61]—was staged in 1903, the piano replaced the orchestra.

Audio technology, although first invented in the nineteenth century, did not have a major impact until the twentieth century, when gramophone recordings could be made and sold in large quantities. Then, however, it fundamentally changed the practice of music. Recorded performances made it possible to separate the music from the performer and bring it to places where it would otherwise not be heard, thus making a wider range of music accessible to more people. Radio broadcasting, whether live or with pre-recorded music, increased accessibility even further. Recordings widened the audience for classical music in both Western and non-Western countries and thus contributed significantly to its globalization, but also to the 'ossification' of the classical canon.[62] Recordings also introduced new music. Jazz, for example, which came into being at around the same time as large-scale

---

58 Blanning, *Triumph*, 196–97.
59 For discussion of the piano, see, for example, James Parakilas and E. Douglas Bomberger, *Piano Roles: Three Hundred Years of Life with the Piano* (New Haven: Yale University Press, 1999).
60 Quoted in Blanning, *Triumph*, 181.
61 For the Orpheus motive, see Johnson, *Out of Time*; for Japanese performance, see Tōkyō Geijutsu Daigaku Hyakunenshi Hensan Iinkai, ed., *Tōkyō Geijutsu Daigaku hyakunenshi: Tōkyō Ongaku Gakkō hen 1* (Tokyo: Ongaku no Tomosha, 1987), 541–52.
62 Blanning, *Triumph*, 201.

commercial recording, owed much of its worldwide dissemination and popularity to the new medium. Recording companies moreover played a role in popularizing music that was produced to suit the medium, namely the popular song.[63]

Recording technology also made it possible to collect and archive performance-based musics that did not rely on a written score, including music of the 'folk' at home, and that of other cultures, and thus revolutionized both folk music research and ethnomusicology.[64] In Japan, Tanabe Hisao (1883–1984), one of the founders of Japanese ethnomusicology, collected recordings both within Japan and in the territories of the expanding Japanese colonial empire, and played a major part in defining *hōgaku* (Japanese indigenous music) but also *tōa ongaku* and *tōyō ongaku* (East Asian music and Oriental music).[65] Meanwhile, collecting the music of the 'folk' with the aid of sound recordings lent impetus to musical nationalism; perhaps most famously demonstrated by Béla Bartòk (1881–1945) and Zoltán Kodály (1882–1967) whose collections of folk music provided material for their nationalist and modernist compositions and made them 'national cultural heroes' in their home country.[66]

Nationalism, including musical nationalism, predated the modern nation state. In Europe, nationalism emerged as a liberating, revolutionary, and democratic force during the wars following the French Revolution and fuelled the movements for unification in Italy and Germany. Blanning treats it in the context of 'liberation'. He argues that music played a decisive part in forming the imagined communities

---

63 Blanning, *Triumph*, 197–204; Christiana Lubinski and Andreas Steen, 'Travelling Entrepreneurs, Travelling Sounds: The Early Gramophone Business in India and China', *Itinerario* 41, no. 2 (2017), https://doi.org/10.1017/S0165115317000377 For Japan, see Kerim Yasar, *Electrified Voices: How the Telephone, Phonograph, and Radio Shaped Modern Japan, 1868–1945* (New York: Columbia University Press, 2018), 83–113, https://www.degruyter.com/document/doi/10.7312/yasa18712/html

64 Philip V. Bohlman, *World Music: A Very Short Introduction* (Oxford: Oxford University Press, 2002), 23–34, 64–69, 140–43.

65 See Shuhei Hosokawa, 'In Search of the Sound of Empire: Tanabe Hisao and the Foundation of Japanese Ethnomusicology', *Japanese Studies* 18, no. 1 (1998), https://doi.org/10.1080/10371399808727638; Seiko Suzuki, '"Kagaku" to shite no Nihon ongaku kenkyū: Tanabe Hisao no gagaku kenkyū to Nihon ongakushi no kōchiku' (Ph.D. Doctoral thesis, University of Tokyo, 2014). For more on the term *hōgaku*, see Chapter 3.

66 Bohlman, *World Music*, 64–69.

that, according to Benedict Anderson, represented the indispensable foundation of nation states.[67] One example is national and transnational travel to amateur music festivals, including large choral meetings. Enabled by modern transport, travelling helped participants to develop both a sense of nation and an awareness of being part of a world of nations.[68]

Once authoritarian rulers aligned themselves with the idea of the nation, however, nationalism's liberating potential gave way to more repressive forms—for example, in the unified German Empire after 1871, or in Japan at around the same time. But whether state-led or not, music represented an important vehicle to promote a sense of community and national destiny, and the belief that a nation had to have its own national music persisted. National anthems and songs, and military music, featured prominently in the ceremonies and in mass traditions of nation states.

The Globalization of Western Music

Nations exist in a world of nations, that is, in relation to each other. The concept of the nation state originated in Europe, and began to gain worldwide currency as an ideal in the late nineteenth century, although the nation state did not become the dominant state form until well into the twentieth century. The growth of nationalism was accompanied by the dissemination of European art music. While not the only form of Western music with a global reach, it played a major role in the construction of national music traditions worldwide. This is particularly true of the theoretical concepts and practices associated with it. The trend towards standardization identified by Max Weber helped pave the way for the globalization of equal temperament tuning and modern functional harmony along with Western music.[69]

---

67 Blanning, *Triumph*, 231–300, 284–85. Blanning also treats 'people' and 'sex' under this heading.
68 Celia Applegate, *The Necessity of Music: Variations on a German Theme* (Toronto: University of Toronto Press, 2017), 70–99; Blanning, *Triumph*, 284.
69 Bob van der Linden, 'Non-Western National Music and Empire in Global History: Interactions, Uniformities, and Comparisons', *Journal of Global History* 10 (2015): 433, https://doi.org/10.1017/S1740022815000212

Elite music reformers in Japan and around the globe established modern institutions for music education, rationalized music theory, collected local music and transcribed it in staff notation or indigenous notation systems modified with reference to Western ones, defined canonical repertoire, published music manuals and books for self-instruction, and organized concerts and conferences.[70] The fact that European art music was globalized in the context of European expansion does not, however, mean that it was necessarily linked to colonial rule.[71] Comparing the influence of Western music on the development of music to represent the nation in non-Western countries, Bob van der Linden speaks of a continuum 'between the two extremist poles of the adoption of Western music and simultaneous neglect of indigenous music (Japan), and the rejection of Western music but modernization of high-cultural traditional music (India)'.[72] Given that India was a British colony and Japan was never colonized but, on the contrary, became a colonial power itself, it should be clear that colonial expansion cannot be more than part of any explanation for the globalization of European art music and Western musical idiom.

On the other hand, even in India, musical reformers referred to Western ideas about music to 'systematize their own music traditions scientifically' and adopted a Western-style distinction between 'classical' and 'non-classical' music'.[73] They studied Western Orientalist and musicological writings on Indian music, as well as works on European music and musicology. The creation of modern institutions was likewise inspired by Western models. Some Indian musical traditions even adopted Western instruments: the violin into Carnatic music, and the harmonium.[74] This is in marked contrast to Japan, where, ultimately, no Western musical instrument found a place in any of the traditional genres before the explorations of new, blended, musical forms from the late twentieth century.

---

70   van der Linden, 'National Music', 438. The dissemination of Western music in the context of European expansion and its influence on the negotiation of local identities is also covered by Nicholas Cook, 'Western Music as World Music', in *The Cambridge History of World Music*, ed. Philip Vilas Bohlman (Cambridge: Cambridge University Press, 2013), https://doi.org/10.1017/CHO9781139029476
71   Osterhammel, 'Globale Horizonte', 111.
72   van der Linden, 'National Music', 440. See also Osterhammel, 'Globale Horizonte'.
73   van der Linden, 'National Music', 438.
74   Ibid., 450–53.

In Muslim countries from Central Asia to Morocco, there existed a shared elite music culture, which, during the period of the Ottoman Empire, was influenced by the performance of musicians who travelled between the different courts.[75] Initiatives to reform and modernize music with reference to Western models took off in the early twentieth century, with the first Congress on Arab Music in Cairo in 1932 representing a major landmark for Arab music. Ultimately, however, Western art music did not come to play a dominant role in the musical life of the participating countries. In the Ottoman Empire, musical reform following Western models began as early as the end of the eighteenth century, under Sultan Selim III (r. 1789–1807) and continued under his successor Mahmut II (r. 1808–39). Borrowing from Europe continued into the twentieth century, by which time Japan as well as Europe served as a model.[76] After the end of the Ottoman Empire, the radical reforms under Mustafa Kemal Atatürk included music, and efforts were made to establish European art music. But ultimately it did not gain ground among the masses. As of the early 1970s it was 'governmentally sanctioned and supported as the price for being accepted in the international community of nations'. A few European-trained musicians and composers had gained international recognition. But the masses 'detested' it, and even the educated, urban elite merely 'tolerated' it.[77]

In the Americas, the situation of Western music was different in that the musics of the indigenous peoples were marginalized in the face of massive immigration from Europe. In North America (which will be treated in more detail in the following chapter), music from Europe dominated, reflecting the dominance of European immigrants. These immigrants, however, brought with them a variety of musics, and it is wrong to take the high prestige of European art music and its dominance as given.

In Mexico and South America, European art music remained the focus of the European elites, who 'invented European military music, Italian-opera-inspired anthems, and classical music with vernacular

---

75 van der Linden, 'National Music', 446–49.
76 Karl Signell, 'The Modernization Process in Two Oriental Music Cultures: Turkish and Japanese', *Asian Music* 7, no. 2 (Symposium on the Ethnomusicology of Culture Change in Asia (1976), https://doi.org/10.2307/833790
77 Signell, 'Modernization Process', 81

references as national music'.⁷⁸ Meanwhile, the musics that came to represent Brazil, Cuba, Argentina, and Mexico were popular genres that developed in the context of slavery and the intermingling of races, and were strongly influenced by African rhythms.⁷⁹

In the countries of Northeast Asia, China, Japan, Taiwan, and Korea, Western music represented a significant element of the modernization that advocates of reform envisaged when they propagated modernization and national strengthening from the second half of the nineteenth century onwards. While the threat from the Western powers motivated the reforms, none of these countries was colonized by a Western power. From the late nineteenth century onwards, the foundations were laid for the much-noted presence of Western art music in these countries and of their musicians on the global stage during the second half of the twentieth century and subsequently. Japan, as the first Asian country to be transformed into a modern nation, went furthest in the adoption of Western music, including European art music. Already by the end of the nineteenth century, moreover, following the acquisition of Taiwan in 1895, Japan began to act as a disseminator of 'colonial modernity'.⁸⁰

China, like Japan, first encountered Western music through Christian missionaries in the early modern period, without the encounter having much significance for the dissemination of Western music in modern times.⁸¹ Until the encroachment into the region by the Western powers, the Chinese empire and its culture held a dominant place in the region. But by the late nineteenth century, Japan was well on its way to becoming

---

78   van der Linden, 'National Music', 455. For Latin America, especially Mexico, see also Helmut Brenner, 'Absorption und Adaption als Faktoren traditioneller Music in Lateinamerika', *Archiv für Musikwissenschaft* 62, no. 1 (2005), https://doi.org/ https://www.jstor.org/stable/25162318

79   van der Linden, 'National Music', 453–55. Van der Linden's focus is on Brazil and Samba; see also Hermano Vianna, *The Mystery of Samba: Popular Music and National Identity in Brazil*, trans. John Charles Chasteen (Chapel Hill and London: The University of North Carolina Press, 1999). For Tango, both in and outside Argentina, including Japan, see Marta E. Savigliano, *Tango and the Political Economy of Passion* (Boulder: Westview Press, 1995).

80   Faye Yuan Kleeman, *In Transit: The Formation of the Colonial East Asian Cultural Sphere* (Honolulu: University of Hawai'i Press, 2014), 4–5, 7, https://doi.org/10.1515/9780824838614

81   The following is based on Heinrich Geiger, *Erblühende Zweige: Westliche klassische Musik in China* (Mainz: Schott, 2009), 17–41.

a modern nation and, after defeating China in war in 1895, a model for successful modernization. The defeat, together with the collapsing domestic order during the last years of the Qing dynasty, increased the pressure for China to modernize. Reformers looked to Meiji Japan as well as to the West as their model. Educational reformers strove to create modern institutions following Western examples. Music was seen as a means to inspire the heart, cultivate character, and awaken and strengthen national sentiment. Thousands of Chinese students travelled to Japan. Among the reformers who studied music in Japan was Xiao Youmei, born in 1884 and known as 'the father of music education in modern China'.[82] In 1901, at the age of just sixteen, he went to Tokyo, where he studied at the Tokyo Academy of Music (Tōkyō Ongaku Gakkō) and later at Tokyo Imperial University. He returned to China in 1909. Three years later, he travelled to Germany where he studied music in Leipzig and Berlin, just as many Japanese students did, but foundations of his musical training were laid in Japan.

While Xiao Youmei studied at the state-sponsored Tokyo Academy of Music, many more studied at private colleges, particularly the Music College of the East (Tōyō Ongaku Gakkō), founded in 1907 by Suzuki Yonejirō (1868–1940). Just before founding the college, Suzuki had travelled to China to study the state of education there. Even before opening his college, Suzuki taught music to Chinese students at the hall of residence for Chinese students opened in Kanda in 1902. The students had their own music society, established in 1904. Suzuki opened his new college in the same neighbourhood.[83] While the number of Chinese students who specialized in music may have been small, many more studied music as part of a teacher training course. Waseda University, for example, opened a teacher training department for Chinese students in 1905, and *shōka* (singing of Western-style songs for use in schools) was one of the subjects taught; the same was true of the (accelerated) teacher training department of the private girls' school Jissen Jogakkō.[84]

---

82 Geiger, *Erblühende Zweige*, 36–38. See also Sheila Melvin and Jindong Cai, *Rhapsody in Red: How Western Classical Music Became Chinese* (New York: Algora, 2004).
83 Midori Takeishi, *Ongaku kyōiku no ishizue: Suzuki Yonejirō to Tōyō Ongaku Gakkō* (Tokyo: Shunjusha, 2007), 77–89; Mehl, *Not by Love Alone*, 87–90.
84 Hiroshi Abe, *Chūgoku no kindai kyōiku to Meiji Nihon* (Tokyo: Fukumura Shuppan, 1990), 86, 100.

In the second and third decades of the twentieth century, the foundations for a new musical culture were established, and the period from 1919 to 1949 marked the creative breakthrough in the field of European art music in China.[85] Chinese intellectuals, starting with Cai Yuanpei, who in 1917 published an essay entitled 'About replacing religion with aesthetic education', saw music as a replacement for religion.[86] European art music, particularly that of Beethoven, came to represent the highest ideals. The early promoters of European art music were scholars educated first in the Confucian tradition and then abroad, where they personally experienced Western-style musical culture. They perceived music as a means for education and social reform. From the late 1920s they were joined by musicians, either Western foreigners in China, or Chinese who had learnt musical instruments from them or had studied at mission schools.[87] In 1927 the first public music college was established in Shanghai. The majority of its teachers in the first decades were foreigners. The choice to adopt Western music, however, owed much to the ideas and actions of strong Chinese individuals who believed that they could save the essence of Chinese culture by strengthening it with the help of Western techniques. Those who were trained musicians actively created a place for Western music in the midst of Chinese society.[88]

In Taiwan, too, missionaries were the first to introduce Western music. British Presbyterian missionaries came first to northern, then to southern Taiwan in the 1860s to spread their faith among the aborigines and they distributed hymn books. They were joined by Canadian Presbyterians from the 1870s. The missionaries also trained girls for Christian service and set up a school in 1884.[89] When Taiwan became Japan's first colony in 1895, the Japanese established a public education system with Western music as a school subject. Isawa Shūji (1851–1917), who had acted as the driving force behind the establishment of music education in Japanese schools, was appointed acting chief of

---

85 Geiger, *Erblühende Zweige*, 26–27, 32, 33.
86 *Yi meiyu dai zongjiau shuo*, Geiger, *Erblühende Zweige*, 35.
87 Geiger, *Erblühende Zweige*, 40.
88 Ibid., 40–41.
89 Angela Hao-Chun Lee, 'The Influence of Governmental Control and early Christian Missionaries on Music Education of Aborigines in Taiwan', *British Journal of Music Education* 23, no. 2 (2006).

the education bureau (*gakumu bu*), established in the civil department (*minsei kyoku*) of the government-general in May 1895. His tenure only lasted until July 1897, and his ambitious plans for education in Taiwan were only partly realized. Nevertheless, Isawa 'had mapped out the direction for education in Taiwan',[90] including music education.

In Korea, efforts to modernize the country were made in the years following the enforced opening of the country in 1876 by Japan.[91] They continued under Japanese dominance. The colonial government introduced a programme of reforms similar to that conducted in Japan, including a school curriculum with singing lessons, often taught by Japanese school teachers. Like the Japanese, Koreans embraced Western music, although initially they did not much like it, because they regarded it as part of the general reform package. The state school system was introduced in 1906, but, as in Japan, schools founded by missionaries played a major role in providing education. In Korea too, hymns and songs taught in school represented the first introduction to Western music for many people.

The capital, Seoul, offered more opportunities to hear Western music. In 1901, the German Franz Eckert was appointed to teach military music at the Korean court. Eckert, who had previously taught in Japan for twenty years (from 1879 to 1899), worked in Korea for fifteen years until his death in 1916.[92] Under his baton, the military band gave weekly concerts in Pagoda Park, performing a repertoire that included arrangements of Classical and Romantic works as well as military music. A concert culture evolved in Seoul and the other larger cities. In the early twentieth century, gramophone recordings and radio broadcasting also did much to disseminate European art music. The Japanese composer Miyagi Michio (1894–1956) lived in Seoul during some of his formative years, where he enjoyed and benefited from new opportunities to attend concerts and listen to imported records. Although his works are in the

---

90   Patricia E. Tsurumi, *Japanese Colonial Education in Taiwan, 1895–1945* (Cambridge, Mass.: Harvard University Press, 1977), 17.
91   Much of the following is based on Jin-Ah Kim, 'Transfer und Aneignung. Europäische Kunstmusik in Korea', *Asien* 143 (April 2017), https://asien.asienforschung.de/wp-content/uploads/sites/6/2018/01/143_abs_Kim.pdf
92   Hermann Gottschewski and Kyungboon Lee, 'Franz Eckert und "seine" Nationalhymnen. Eine Einführung', *OAG Notizen*, no. 12 (2013), http://www.oag.jp/images/publications/oag_notizen/Feature_II_-_Kimigayo.pdf

traditional Japanese genre, it was while being exposed to Western music in Korea that he began to compose.[93]

As he had done in Japan, Eckert composed musical arrangements of local songs, including a folk song that became the basis for the pre-war Korean national anthem.[94] Korean composers likewise re-arranged melodies as well as composing their own. Missionaries adapted the melodies of their hymns to the local tonal system and published new versions with Korean lyrics that took on the character of folk songs. In this way new hybrid genres of song emerged.

Traditional Korean music was discouraged and marginalized in the colonial period. This did not immediately change after liberation. Even Korean nationalists did not reject Western music. On the other hand, a nation state's ideological legitimation lies in invoking tradition. Thus, as in Japan, European art music was promoted as part of modern culture, while selected genres of traditional music were promoted and protected as national heritage.[95]

Transnational Circulation in Northeast Asia

Although Japan became a dominant power in Northeast Asia and a model of successful modernization, the dissemination of Western music in the region happened in the midst of cultural flows in several directions. In the early twentieth century, Japan owed much of its success in assimilating Western music to impulses from the Asian continent. The growth of the symphony orchestra and the general rise in standards of music-making after the First World War can hardly be imagined without the cities of Harbin and Shanghai and their significant foreign populations as sites of encounter and cultural interaction, both between East Asia and Europe and within East Asia.

Harbin, sometimes known as the 'St. Petersburg of the East', had a distinctly Russian flavour as a result of the Russian treaty with China in 1896, which secured Russia a concession to build and operate a

---

93 Kim, 'Transfer und Aneignung', 51; Henry Johnson, 'A Modernist Traditionalist: Miyagi Michio, Transculturalism, and the Making of a Music Tradition', in *Rethinking Japanese Modernism*, ed. Roy Starrs (Leiden: Brill, 2012), 256–57.
94 Gottschewski and Lee, 'Franz Eckert'.
95 Kim, 'Transfer und Aneignung', 53–55.

railway in northeast China. Russians in search of work and a living had settled there. After 1917 they were joined by Russian Jews and White Russians fleeing from the revolution, and by 1922 about a quarter of the population were Russians. Harbin had its own music academy and symphony orchestra, the China Eastern Railway Symphony Orchestra, founded in 1909.[96]

Even more significant as a city of musical encounters was Shanghai. After the Opium War, the International Settlement and the French Concession were established. Shanghai had a public band as early as 1879, which in the early twentieth century evolved into a full professional symphony orchestra under the Italian conductor Mario Paci. Like Harbin, Shanghai experienced an increase in its Russian population, even more so after Japan's seizure of Manchuria in 1931, when many Russians fled Harbin. The Russian refugees gave a considerable boost to the city's musical life, both as musicians and as audience members. Japanese immigrants moved into the International Settlement from the 1920s. The Chinese population of Shanghai likewise increased as many fled from other parts of the country into the foreign concessions during the Taiping Rebellion (1850–64), the Boxer Rebellion (1901), the fall of the Qing, the rule of the warlords, and during the Sino-Japanese War from 1937 to 1945.[97]

Russian musicians, particularly from Harbin, played a major role in the formation of professional symphony orchestras in Japan, including the present-day NHK Orchestra.[98] The Kansai region in particular benefited from Russian musicians who settled around Kobe and Osaka. Orchestral performance received a major boost when Emmanuel Metter (1878–1941), the conductor of the symphony orchestra in Harbin, was invited as a conductor of the Osaka Philharmonic Orchestra and then the Kyoto University Orchestra in 1926.[99] Under his baton, the latter became a major orchestra of the region. Among his students were

---

96 Yūichi Iwano, *Ōdō rakudo no kōkyōgaku: Manshū – shirazaru ongakushi* (Tokyo: Ongaku no Tomosha, 1999); Melvin and Cai, *Rhapsody in Red*, 100–02; Yasuko Enomoto, *Shanhai ōkesutora monogatari: Seiyōjin ongakukatachi no yume* (Tokyo: Shunjūsha, 2006).
97 Geiger, *Erblühende Zweige*, 43.
98 Margaret Mehl, *Not by Love Alone: The Violin in Japan, 1850–2010* (Copenhagen: The Sound Book Press, 2014), 140–59.
99 Ben Okano, *Metteru Sensei: Asahina Takashi, Hattori Ryōichi no Gakufu, Bōmeisha Ukurainejin shikisha no shōgai* (Tokyo: Rittōmyūjikku, 1995).

the future conductor of the Osaka Philharmonic Orchestra, Asahina Takashi (1908–2001) and the highly successful composer and arranger of popular music, Hattori Ryōichi (1907–1993). Both worked for a time on the Asian continent.

Osaka by the 1920s was an industrial metropolis with a growing, multi-ethnic population that included immigrants from Okinawa and Korea, and Shanghai significantly contributed to the distinctive musical developments in the Kansai region.[100] Jazz in Japan received significant influences from Shanghai, which had become a veritable Asian jazz mecca. Many Japanese performed in the Shanghai International Settlement's dance halls, restaurants, and jazz clubs: they were known as 'Shanghai returnees' (*Shanhai-gaeri*).[101] A similar pattern can be discerned for tango.[102]

The dissemination and circulation of Western music in East Asia was facilitated by the technological innovations already mentioned: modern forms of transport, which enabled the increase in migration over long distances, and recording technology, which made music transportable independently of the travelling performer. The gramophone business was highly international from its beginnings, with major manufacturers dividing up the world market between them.[103] South and East Asia, particularly the large populations of India and China, were then perceived as having huge potential. Once they recognized the local populations' preference for their own music, the manufacturers sent recording engineers, who with the help of local intermediaries, recorded local performers. In September 1902 the Anglo-American Gramophone Co. sent the recording engineer Frederick Gaisberg (1873–1951) to Asia, accompanied by an assistant and a businessman. Over the next months they travelled to Colombo, Calcutta, Singapore, Hong Kong, Shanghai, Tokyo, Bangkok, and Rangoon and made hundreds of recordings (the

---

100 Junko Iguchi, 'Osaka and Shanghai: Revisiting the Reception of Western Music in Metropolitan Japan', in *Music, Modernity and Locality in Prewar Japan: Osaka and Beyond*, ed. Hugh De Ferranti and Alison Tokita (Farnham, Surrey: Ashgate, 2013). The role of the Russian musical community in the Kansai area, however, has yet to be examined in detail.

101 Iguchi, 'Music, Modernity and Locality', 286–87.

102 Yuiko Asaba, In between the 'Continents': Japanese Tango Musicians in China,1920s-1940s. Talk given at Oxford International History of East Asia Seminar (online), 25 May 2020.

103 The following is based on Lubinski and Steen, 'Travelling Entrepreneurs'.

finished records were manufactured in Germany). In 1904, Gramophone, together with Victor, published its first Chinese record catalogue. These early recordings (like those made in India) included popular artists who were regarded as disreputable. Their music, separated from its performers, moved into the houses of respectable society.[104]

Soon Western record companies were competing with each other, which resulted in lower prices. Japan also joined the competition, with a gramophone type named 'Nipponophone' that sold at prices well under those for similar European devices.[105] During the First World War, Japanese manufacturers managed to take over market shares from European producers, just as they did for other products. Record companies, besides producing recordings in a wide range of musical genres, created musical styles specifically for mass consumption. After the First World War, Japanese record companies began to produce hits: popular songs in various, blended styles, which came to be known as *ryūkōka*.[106] Recordings of popular music were exported to Japan's colonies, including Taiwan from the late 1920s. In 1933 the Columbia Record Company of Japan set up an operation in Taiwan in order to record popular songs composed and performed by local artists to suit local tastes. As a result, local people had the chance 'to link themselves to the global music/dance scene (albeit through the mediation of the Japanese colonial culture)'.[107] Columbia also had operations in Korea, where Japanese popular songs were often covered in Korean.

In a rare reverse case, a Japanese-language cover of the Korean folk song *Arirang* became a hit throughout the region. In 1932 a musical arrangement by the famous singer Koga Masao was recorded by Columbia Japan in Seoul and sung as a duet by the Korean singer Hasegawa Ichirō (Ch'ae Kyuhwa) and the well-known Japanese singer Awaya Noriko. Victor Japan had already released its own Japanese-language cover version the previous year, and in 1933 Dynaphone

---

104 Lubinski and Steen, 'Travelling Entrepreneurs', 284.
105 Ibid., 287.
106 Toru Mitsui, *Popular Music in Japan: Transformation Inspired by the West* (New York: Bloomsbury Academic & Professional, 2020), 159–62, https://doi.org/10.5040/9781501363894. See also Hiromu Nagahara, *Tokyo Boogie-Woogie: Japan's Pop Era and its Discontents* (Cambridge, MA 2017), https://doi.org/10.4159/9780674978409
107 Kleeman, *In Transit: The Formation of the Colonial East Asian Cultural Sphere*, 187.

Recording released a version of *Arirang* under its Kirin label.[108] *Arirang* in fact enjoyed what Atkins has called a 'dual career': as a 'Korean resistance anthem' and a 'Japanese pop hit'; as a national song, and as a 'transnational pop song' and an expression of colonial modernity.[109] One might even add a third: during the Korean War, *Arirang* became a marching tune for the U.S. Army Seventh Infantry Division and is still performed at commemorative ceremonies.[110] Today *Arirang* is regarded as a Korean national song, both in North and South Korea.

'Western' versus 'Modern'

The transformations of the allegedly traditional folk song *Arirang* illustrate salient characteristics of musical modernity: the impact of Western music and the importance of music for fostering national sentiment, as well as a sense of living in a modern world of nations and different cultures. The lyrics of Japanese pop versions of the 1930s expressed emotions such as longing for lost love and home, just as many other Japanese pop songs did. But they also represented 'a means for critique of modernity itself' and its alienation of the Japanese from their own cultural heritage, as well as an 'ethnographic lens' through which to observe the perceived essence of the Korean psyche.[111] The postcolonial history of *Arirang* in both Koreas illustrates the kind of streamlining and standardization that transform a folk song, the transmission of which is characterized by inconsistencies and variants, into a national song. The most familiar lyrics of *Arirang* sung in Korea today refer to lost love and to Baekdu (or Paektu) mountain, a location of national cultural significance. Musically, most versions of the song heard today have more in common with modern sentimental popular songs in many other countries than with specifically Korean folk music: the use of Western instruments and harmonization demonstrate the influence of a Western

---

108 *Sōgyō 1910 nen koronbia rekōdo no otakara ongaku*, CC-R 2, Columbia Music Entertainment 2007, liner notes for *Arirang*; see also 'Senzen no Chōsen ryūkōka rekōdo' http://busan.chu.jp/toko/fal/10.html
109 E. Taylor Atkins, 'The Dual Career of "Arirang": The Korean Resistance Anthem that Became a Japanese Pop Hit', *The Journal of Asian Studies* 66, no. 3 (2007): 646, https://doi.org/http://www.jstor.org/stable/20203201 As Atkins notes, *Arirang* is not really one song; there are thousands of versions.
110 The Seventh Infantry Division Association, *History*, https://www.7ida.us/history.asp
111 Atkins, '"Arirang",' 666–67.

musical aesthetic. Both the music and the discursive characteristics represent what might be described as a common 'grammar' of musical modernity, as does the prevalence of a de facto standard version (even if it exists side by side with other versions).[112]

The example of *Arirang* also reminds us that the term 'Western music' broadly covers two types of music that can no longer be regarded as 'Western' at all.[113] One is the 'global hybrid' (Cook), including popular songs such as *Arirang* and the genres named by Saegusa (quoted earlier): rock, pop, *kayōkyoku* (a genre of Japanese popular song), K-pop, jazz, and tango. The other is the art music that originated in Europe, popularly known as 'classical', that served as a kind of gold standard for musical modernization worldwide.

Paradoxically, at the time when European dominance was at its height, opportunities to hear its most iconic products, operas and large symphonic works, performed as the composer wrote them (as opposed to various arrangements) were limited even within Europe, because until the wide availability of recorded music, these genres depended on the physical presence of a large group of competent performers. European art music's enormous prestige was in part based on influential literary works, such as the writings of Romain Rolland.[114] This prestige endures. Even in the twenty-first century—so far—the historian David Schoenbaum only slightly overstates his case when he observes, 'When people join the modern world, their kids get piano and violin lessons'.[115]

Whatever the 'modern' elements of the music itself, Western music's modern image was chiefly based on non-musical features. Arguably, it was the first music to benefit from modern innovations that originated in the West. The musical features themselves were less significant than the fact that they were presented to the world as a rational system, including staff notation, equal temperament, and other elements of standardization. Its tonal system, moreover, was claimed to be based on science. Above all, it was modern, because it was played in modern

---

112 The designation as an Important Intangible Cultural Asset by the South Korean Cultural Heritage Administration reportedly 'applies to all folk tunes called *Arirang* that have been handed down in local provinces across the country'. See https://world.kbs.co.kr/service/news_view.htm?lang=e&Seq_Code=113609
113 Cook, 'Western Music as World Music', 89.
114 Ibid., 79. This certainly applies to Japan, particularly to the image of Beethoven.
115 David Schoenbaum, 'Countries and Western: The Geopolitics of Music', *The Wilson Quarterly*, Winter (2015), http://wilsonquarterly.com/quarterly/fall-2014-the-great-wars/what-spread-classical-music-tells-us-about-globalization/

spaces and for modern purposes, as the case of Japan illustrates. The military served to defend the nation and to expand its borders, while at the same time uniting men from all social classes in one institution and imbuing them with a sense of national purpose. Universal schooling, too, served as a powerful unifying force and to transform the nation's young into citizens. School auditoriums could also serve as concert venues. The concert, another modern institution imported from Europe, was potentially a shared space, where performers and composers of Western music, and performers and (performer-) composers of traditional musics could meet and their musical worlds could connect.[116]

The encounter with Western music, while certainly not the only impulse, transformed indigenous musical cultures in several ways.[117] Modernizing indigenous music could take the form of standardizing intonation on the basis of equal temperament; publishing scores in staff notations or in indigenous notation modified with reference to it; rationalizing music theory, or subjecting it to Western performance practices. Modernizing could involve 'classicizing' indigenous music by defining a canonized repertoire, formalizing teaching, creating a sharp distinction between recognized specialists and amateurs, and treating it as absolute by separating it from its social context. Finally, where different musical traditions existed, indigenous music could be invented as a new category, bringing together previously separate musical worlds, as was the case with 'Japanese music' (*hōgaku*) in Japan. Thus, standards that originated in the West are no longer exclusively Western. Nor is European art music: it is particularly firmly established in East Asia.[118]

In one of the most powerful Western countries, on the other hand, the assimilation of European art music and the high prestige it was accorded were not a given: the United States of America's musical history in the nineteenth and early twentieth centuries is in several respects remarkably similar to that of Japan.

---

116 Wade, *Composing Japanese Musical Modernity*, 10.
117 See Cook, 'Western Music as World Music'; van der Linden, 'National Music'. My understanding of the 'classical model' is in part based on Ruth Finnegan, *The Hidden Musicians: Music-Making in an English Town* (Cambridge: Cambridge University Press, 1989), 133–36, likewise my use of the term 'musical worlds'.
118 Cook, 'Western Music as World Music', 89. Whether Cook is right in describing it as 'most strongly rooted in Asia' depends on how 'rooted' is understood. Saegusa describes Asia as the new centre of classical music, but only in terms of consumption, in what he characterizes as a region where classical music is still underdeveloped (*mikai*). See Saegusa, *Kyōten dōchi kurashikku*, 170–71.

2. Under Reconstruction: Japan, the United States, and the European Model

> Having journeyed through a realm of civilization and enlightenment, we were now crossing a very ancient, uncivilized wilderness.[1]

> Compared to classical music in its European homeland, classical music in the United States is a mutant transplant. Deep roots were not importable, nor in the main were they newly cultivated. The resulting foliage, oftentimes resplendent, was often "peculiar".[2]

Kume Kunitake (1839–1931), in his record of the Iwakura Embassy to the United States and Europe, was recalling the Embassy's train journey from San Francisco through the states of Nevada and Utah in February 1872. His remarks suggest that he was thinking in terms of the spatial conception of civilization versus barbarism (*ka'i*) that characterized the world view of the Sinosphere.[3] At the same time, he and the other members of the embassy may well have been aware of the North American frontier mythology that was so central to the country's national narrative, and which posited civilization against barbarism in a similar way. The American 'Wild West' is arguably the

---

1 Kunitake Kume, *The Iwakura Embassy 1871–73: A True Account of the Ambassador Extraordinary and Plenipotentiary's Journey of Observation through the United States of America and Europe*, ed. Graham Healey and Chushichi Tsuzuki, trans. Graham Healey, Martin Colcutt, Andrew Cobbing, P. F. Kornicky, Eugene Soviak, Chushichi Tsuzuki, 5 vols., vol. 1: The United States of America (Kamiyakiri, Matsudo, Chiba: The Japan Documents, 2002), 126–31, 127.
2 Joseph Horowitz, *Classical Music in America: A History of Its Rise and Fall* (New York: Norton, 2005), xiii. See also Wolfgang Rathert and Bernd Ostendorf, *Musik der USA: Kultur- und Musikgeschichtliche Streifzüge* (Hofheim: Wolke, 2018), 16, 311.
3 See Chapter 4.

most mythologized among the frontiers of the nineteenth century, and the conquest of the West became a central element in the construction of the history of the nation.[4]

Kume's report only hints at the amazement he and his Japanese fellow travellers must have felt when, after visiting schools, factories, a shipyard, and locomotive works, they began to traverse territories that were not yet fully incorporated into the nation. While travelling through the Humboldt wilderness, the members of the embassy first caught sight of the continent's native population, and Kume discussed their similarities with the unruly populations that resisted the Yamato court in ancient Japan. The train that Kume and the other members of the Iwakura Embassy boarded in San Francisco was the first transcontinental railway, completed less than three years earlier in May 1869 and running via Salt Lake City to Chicago, and from there to New York. Westward expansion into the territories between Kansas and California was still ongoing, as were the American Frontier Wars. Not until 1890 was the frontier officially declared closed.

Traversing the frontier in the middle of the United States by train may well have provided the most spectacular evidence of a nation under construction. By the time Commodore Perry arrived in Japan in 1853, sparking off the turmoil that led to the fall of the Tokugawa shogunate, the United States' borders with Canada in the north and Mexico in the south had largely been determined (1842 with British Canada; 1848 with Mexico).[5] But territorial expansion was still under way, and internal tensions were rising and culminated in the Civil War. Bayly, who describes the war as a 'global event', may well be right when he observes that it 'may also have aborted the emergence of a more aggressive American expansionist policy in the Pacific and the Far East, where Japan was afforded a short, but critical respite from Western pressure.'[6] Once the war ended, the United States had to virtually found itself all over again, and with the period of reconstruction entered a

---

4 See Jürgen Osterhammel, *Die Verwandlung der Welt: Eine Geschichte des 19. Jahrhunderts* (Munich: C. H. Beck, 2009), 465–500.
5 Osterhammel, *Verwandlung der Welt*, 685, 687.
6 Christopher Alan Bayly, *The Birth of the Modern World 1780–1914: Global Connections and Comparisons* (Malden, MA: Blackwell, 2004), 161.

new phase of nation-building at the same time as Japan.⁷ Thus, both the United States and Japan were under reconstruction in the last third of the nineteenth century, and they knew it.⁸

Besides this synchronicity of the processes of nation-building in the two countries, there were other parallels, albeit superficial. At the same time that the colonization of the West was in its final stage in the United States, the Meiji government had its own wilderness to tame. Japan's early territorial consolidation, by incorporating the northern island of Ezo as Hokkaido in September 1869 and the Ryukyu Islands as Okinawa in 1879, tends to be taken for granted, but it required significant effort. In Hokkaido, the government engaged in a project of internal colonization, administered through the Hokkaido Colonization Office.⁹ Unsurprisingly, the Japanese government hired American teachers to support their efforts: General Capron, the U.S. Commissioner of Agriculture, resigned from his post to take up a position in the Japanese government's Frontier Development Bureau (Kaitakushi) from 1871 to 1875; William Clark, president of Massachusetts Agricultural College, was appointed president of the newly founded Sapporo Agricultural College, where he taught from 1876 to 1877, assisted by two young colleagues from Massachusetts, William Wheeler and David Penhallow, who continued their work after Clark's departure. Some of the advisors explicitly cited the colonization of the American West as a model.¹⁰

The closing of the frontier and the United States' subsequent rise to an imperial power (it acquired the Philippines as a colony in 1898), moreover, roughly coincided with the emergence of 'Imperial Japan', which is generally associated with the proclamation of the constitution

---

7   Osterhammel, *Verwandlung der Welt*, 600–01. Osterhammel even treats Japan and the United States together in one section, although not because of similarities, but rather as two special cases ('Sonderwege', pp. 596–601) of nation-building.
8   'Reconstruction' is not a term usually employed to describe Japan after 1868. 'Under Reconstruction' is, however, the English title of Mori Ōgai's famous short story *Fushinchū*.
9   Hokkaidō Kaitakushi (1869–82). See Mark Ravina, *To Stand with the Nations of the World: Japan's Meiji Restoration in World History* (New York: Oxford University Press, 2017), 173–75.
10 Mark Ravina, *To Stand with the Nations of the World*, 175. On Capron, see also Edward Boyle, 'Imperial Practice and the making of Modern Japan's Territory: Towards a Reconsideration of Empire's Boundaries', *Geographical Review of Japan Series B* 88, no. 2 (2016): 72, https://doi.org/10.4157/geogrevjapanb.88.66

in 1889, the first elections in 1890 and the revision of the unequal treaties and colonial expansion from the 1890s onwards.[11]

Obviously, in some respects the situation of the United States could not have been more different from that of Japan. The frontier the Iwakura Embassy witnessed was geographically in the middle of the emerging nation rather than at the periphery like Hokkaido. The original inhabitants of North America were excluded and forced onto reservations. The differences between the two nations are even more obvious with regard to the populations within their borders. The United States was dominated by a population that had only arrived recently, as a result of migration on an unsurpassed scale that was still ongoing.

The Beginnings of Music Education in America

The diversity of the immigrant population and the successive waves of immigration decisively influenced the history of music in the United States. After the Civil War, massive industrial growth, led by the Northern states, and the resulting economic prosperity provided the basis for science, scholarship, and the arts to flourish, including music. European music was already well-established, brought by the immigrants. Many of the early, chiefly German and British, immigrants had left Europe seeking freedom to live according to their religious convictions, and thus church music initially dominated in New England. The early Puritans strongly believed in music as an instrument of symbolic politics and theological guidance. This emphasis on music for moral and religious edification was significantly stronger than in Europe, and continued well into the nineteenth century.[12] It was not lost on the members of the Iwakura Embassy, who also noted the importance accorded to singing education. The Puritans, while restrictive in the range of music they considered acceptable, accorded high importance to singing as part of worship, and efforts to improve the quality of singing in church lay at the roots of music education in America.[13] In the course of the eighteenth

---

11   It should be noted that 'Imperial Japan' is a term used in English-language scholarship, and that the Japanese term *teikoku* ('empire') has significantly different connotations and is often used differently.
12   Rathert and Ostendorf, *Musik der USA*, 135.
13   Following based on Michael L. Mark, *A Concise History of American Music Education* (Lanham, MD: Rowman & Littlefield Education, 2008), 9–77.

century, ministers began to propagate formal instruction in music in the belief that an ability to read music would help improve the quality of singing. Singing schools were established, and continued until well into the nineteenth century, and this tradition of teaching music to the public provided the basis for the introduction of music into public schools.

As later in Japan, pragmatic considerations dominated the efforts to establish systematic instruction in music from the start. Among the pioneers of music education in schools were William Channing Woodbridge (1794–1845) and Lowell Mason (1792–1872), who has been described as the 'father of singing among the children'.[14] Woodbridge had travelled to Europe and observed Pestalozzi's colleague and disciple Georg Nägeli teach music to children. He adopted Pestalozzi's idea that music served to develop a child's intellectual, moral, and physical capacities. Mason moved to Boston in 1827, having spent fifteen years promoting music education in Savannah, Georgia. He fully embraced the nineteenth-century belief in progress through science. In musical terms this meant shunning the older practices of psalmody in favour of music by European composers and teaching music in a way similar to other school subjects. Mason was one of the founders of the Boston Academy of Music, established in 1833 to train teachers, offer music classes to children and adults, and operate music programmes in private schools. Music was also taught at music conventions, where singing masters, directors of church choirs, and others could further their musical training. Mason, together with George Webb, held his first convention in 1834, and they continued for about thirty years. For teacher training, summer courses ('normal institutes') were introduced in the 1850s. They offered several weeks of practical and theoretical instruction. The first one was held in New York City from 23 April to 15 July 1853 under the direction of Lowell Mason, George F. Root and William B. Bradbury.[15] Music as a curricular subject in public schools was first introduced in Boston in 1838. Lowell Mason was appointed Superintendent of Music, the first in the United States. Other communities followed, and on the eve of the Civil War several large cities had introduced music education in their schools. The numbers rose after the war, particularly in the Northern states.

---

14   Quoted in Mark, *A Concise History of American Music Education*, 34.
15   Bonlyn G. Hall, 'The American Education of Luther Whiting Mason', *American Music* 6, no. 1 (1988): 68, https://doi.org/10.2307/3448346

After the Civil War this tendency increased, as did the trend towards what was regarded as a scientific approach to teaching music, with graded courses of drills and prescribed songs, and examinations.[16] Here again, Lowell Mason was a pioneer: he was the first to use the phrase 'graded music series', to describe his *Song Garden*, published in three volumes from 1864.

The most influential graded series in the following decades was the *National Music Course*, first published in Boston in 1870. Although it met increasing competition from the 1880s, it continued to be in use into the twentieth century. Its author was Luther Whiting Mason (1818–96), the future pioneer of music education in Japan. A distant relative of Lowell Mason,[17] he had received informal musical training in his native Maine before enrolling in the teachers' classes at the Boston Academy of Music in 1838. In October 1845 he attended the three-day American Music Convention in New York City. In 1853 he studied for three months at the New York Normal Music Institute. He continued to attend training courses even after beginning his career in public school music in Louisville in autumn 1853. In January 1856 he started teaching in Cincinnati public schools. That summer he attended the Normal Musical Institute in North Reading, Massachusetts. This ended his formal musical education.[18] Mason was one of 'hundreds of American school music teachers of that era' who received their training through 'a rigorous course of continuing education'.[19]

Having thus received the best training available in his day, Luther Whiting Mason became a pioneer of music education in his own right. In Cincinnati, where music was already being taught in the public school system (established in 1830), he was introduced to the textbooks of Christian Heinrich Hohmann (1811–61), namely his *Praktischer Lehrgang*

---

16 Mark, *A Concise History of American Music Education*, 40, 54–55.
17 Bonlyn G. Hall, 'Luther Whiting Mason's European Song books', *Notex, Second series* 41, no. 3 (1985): 483, https://doi.org/10.2307/941157 Hall cites genealogical research to the effect that Luther Whiting Mason's father and Lowell Mason were eighth cousins. On his musical education, see Hall, 'The American Education of Luther Whiting Mason'. See also Sondra Wieland Howe, *Luther Whiting Mason: International Music Educator* (Warren, MI: Harmonie Park Press, 1997).
18 Hall, 'The American Education of Luther Whiting Mason', 69. Hall calculated that his total hours of formal training compared well with present-day requirements, apart from the absence of courses in music history (pp. 70–71).
19 Ibid., 71.

für den Gesang-*Unterricht in Volksschulen*, translated into English as *Practical Course of Instruction in Singing* (1856–58). Hohmann, whose works were introduced by German immigrants, was also known for his tutors for piano (1847) and violin (1849).[20] Mason began to develop his own musical charts for teaching, based on those of Hohmann, making use of German folk songs.

In 1864 Mason was appointed Superintendent of Music in the Primary Schools in Boston, where, after serving in the Civil War, he taught until 1878. Here he continued to develop his method, published as the *National Music Course*. In the course of his work he travelled to Europe twice, in 1872 and 1874, to observe musical education and collect song books. During his time in Boston, Mason firmly established his reputation as a music educator; his *National Music Course* earned him honours at the world exhibitions in Vienna (1873) and Paris (1878) as well as the Philadelphia Centennial Exposition in 1876. Mason hoped to develop an international music course, which is one of the reasons he readily took up an appointment in Japan (1879–82), where he could build on his experience at home. He subsequently travelled to Europe twice more: in 1882, and in September 1890, when he did not return to America until spring 1893. In the 1890s, as well as continuing to train teachers at summer schools in Boston, Detroit, and Maine, Mason headed an editorial committee that published a German work, *Neue Gesangsschule*, based on his methods.

Luther Whiting Mason's pioneering work in America attracted the attention of Japanese officials, and led to his appointment by the Japanese government in 1879. As his biographer sums up: 'Luther Whiting Mason was a significant international music educator, because he transported nineteenth-century European methodology and song materials to America, synthesized these materials in the popular National Music Course, and brought Western music education to Japan.'[21] That he could fulfil this double role is another illustration of how Japan and the United States were in a comparable position when it came to introducing what they perceived as the most advanced musical education of the time: that of Europe, specifically Germany.

---

20 Howe, *Luther Whiting Mason*, 13–17.
21 Ibid., 144.

Concerts and the Veneration of European Art Music

America's (and Japan's) dependence on European models was not limited to education. By the time of Mason's pioneering work in Boston, the city had a thriving music scene. Standards of artistic performance, however, were mixed. European art music was highly venerated, but the musical infrastructures to support professional performance developed only after the Civil War. The Boston critic John Sullivan Dwight, who began publishing *Dwight's Journal of Music* in 1852 and who 'more than any other individual first defines what Americans meant by "classical music"',[22] was instrumental in fostering the reverence for European art music, including the cult of Beethoven, whose music he described as the 'presentation of coming social harmony'.[23]

Dwight was also among the founders of the New England Conservatory of Music, established in 1867 as a private institution. The founders included both Americans and recent immigrants, and the first head was Carl Stasny, a pupil of Franz Liszt.[24] Two years later, Boston became the scene of the 'Great National Peace Jubilee', intended to celebrate the restoration of peace after the Civil War. The official programme of 1869 boasted, 'this glorious event in our national history will be celebrated by the grandest musical festival ever known in the history of the world.'[25] The festival was the brainchild of the Irish-born bandmaster Patrick S. Gilmore (1829–92) who, together with Philip Sousa (1865–1932), did more than any other to popularize music in America.[26] He and his band had taken part in the Civil War. About a thousand instrumentalists and ten thousand choristers took part in five concerts; art and showmanship combined, and the result represented a triumph for Boston.

---

22 Horowitz, *Classical Music in America*, xiv.
23 Boyles, quoted in Rathert and Ostendorf, *Musik der USA*, 291.
24 Rathert and Ostendorf, *Musik der USA*, 165. The other American founders were the pedagogue Eben Tourjée and the music publisher Oliver Ditson; the German-born immigrants were the pianist Robert Goldbeck and the flautist Carl Zerrahn.
25 Horowitz, *Classical Music in America*, 16. The following outline is taken from ibid., 15–25.
26 Rathert and Ostendorf, *Musik der USA*, 143.

Gilmore attempted to surpass his previous success with the 1872 World Peace Jubilee, which was on an even grander scale, billed as 'the greatest series of concerts ever given in the world', with three weeks of concerts in a newly built Coliseum seating twenty-one thousand.[27] The French, British, and Prussian governments sent bands, and Johann Straus Jr, Vienna's waltz king, performed for the first time in America.

The Jubilee was attended by the members of the Iwakura Embassy. Already on the day after their arrival in San Francisco on 15 January 1872 they had been treated to an evening 'serenade' by a band from the San Francisco artillery regiment. Their sightseeing trip of San Francisco Bay and to the Navy Yard on Mare Island on 19 January was likewise accompanied by a band.[28] The Embassy's next encounter with Western music was during a visit to the Denman School for Girls on 23 January, where they were greeted by singing, as they were to be at all the elementary schools they visited, and Kume concludes his short description by stating that he would not mention the fact each time.[29] Kume does not appear to have had a particular interest in music, but his few descriptions of the delegates' musical experiences are revealing in that they concern those functions of Western music deemed the most relevant to the Japanese (and indeed to other nations who adopted Western music).

Kume's description of the Jubilee in the Embassy's official report is the longest description of a musical performance, reflecting the fact that it was almost certainly the most overwhelming musical event the delegates attended. They were invited as guests of honour for the second and third days (18 and 19 June). The concerts they attended featured a massive choir and orchestra with thousands of participants. The programme featured patriotic items:

> the British National Anthem *God Save the Queen*, English version, sung by a full chorus of twenty thousand voices, with solo by the eminent artiste Madame Eiminia Rudersdorff, accompanied by the band of the Grenadier Guards, the grand orchestra of one thousand performers, the military band of one thousand, full corps of drums, all the bells of Boston in chime and several batteries of artillery fired by electricity.

---

27 Horowitz, *Classical Music in America*, 27.
28 Kume, *Iwakura Embassy, Vol. 1*, 1: The United States of America, 65, 70.
29 Ibid., 75.

The British band then followed this up with *The Star-Spangled Banner*.[30] The audience went wild.

What the Japanese delegates made of it is another matter. Presumably, they hardly knew what had hit them; Kume's description is far from conclusive: 'they gracefully performed the falling snow' must be regarded as a rhetorical flourish rather than an accurate description of what he actually heard, with 'falling snow' (*hakusetsu*; literally 'white snow') being the metaphor for a particularly intricate (and incomprehensible) piece of music.[31] Significantly, Kume followed up his description of the concert with observations about patriotism in Western countries.[32]

All three encounters described by Kume are examples of music's uses in the context of the modern nation: as part of ceremonies and hospitality in diplomatic relations, in the education of its citizens, and in commemoration as a display of power and an expression of patriotism. Western music was already beginning to fulfil the same functions in Japan. Ironically in the face of Kume's remarks, American patriotism did not provide as obvious a premise for the 1872 Peace Jubilee as it had for the 1869 one, since there was no specifically American peace to celebrate. The new hall was not filled, the festival failed to make money, Dwight condemned it and concluded: 'The great, usurping, tyrannizing, noisy and pretentious thing is over ...'.[33] Kume and the other Japanese

---

30 Official Programme for the Second Day, 'English Day', *Boston Daily Evening Transcript*, 19 June 1872, quoted in Kunitake Kume, *The Iwakura Embassy 1871–73: A True Account of the Ambassador Extraordinary and Plenipotentiary's Journey of Observation through the United States of America and Europe* ed. Graham Healey and Chushichi Tsuzuki, trans. Graham Healey Martin Colcutt, Andrew Cobbing, P. F. Kornicky, Eugene Soviak, Chushichi Tsuzuki, 5 vols. (Kamiyakiri, Matsudo, Chiba: The Japan Documents, 2002), 318.

31 The English translation reads 'The sound was so serene that it could have been the music of falling snow.' Kume, *Iwakura Embassy, Vol. 1*, 1: The United States of America, 310. This, presumably is based on the interpretation given by a Japanese scholar of Western music in Japan (Nakamura Kōsuke), but given the sheer noise of the spectacle, this seems implausible. Dictionary definitions *hakusetsu* (the character combination can also be read *shirayuki* but the Sinitic *hakusetsu* is more likely) include the proper name of a (lost) piece of music of ancient China, and a metaphor for a difficult and intricate piece of music. This seems a plausible literary expression for Kume to use for what to him and the other delegates must have been an inaccessible piece of music.

32 Kume, *Iwakura Embassy, Vol. 1*, 1: The United States of America, 311–12.

33 On 13 July 1872; quoted in Horowitz, *Classical Music in America*, 28.

2. Under Reconstruction: Japan, the United States, and the European Model 73

delegates would probably have agreed. Anyway, no event on this scale was repeated either in Boston or elsewhere.

Performances of symphonic and large-scale music, however, continued to be popular. They played a central part in the consolidation of European art music as one central element in modern American musical culture. With the increasing segmentation of American society and culture after the Civil War, European art music was firmly adopted by the economic and social elites as 'high culture', together with the other classical traditions of Europe, whether art, theatre, or architecture. 'Eurocentric ideals of cultural superiority' were enshrined in the institutions of this culture, including the concert hall and the opera house.[34] In the years following the Boston jubilees, professional symphony orchestras were founded in several major cities. The Boston Symphony Orchestra was founded in 1881; it became the model for the Chicago Symphony Orchestra in 1891, which in turn became the model for orchestras in other cities: Cincinnati in 1895, Pittsburgh in 1898, Philadelphia in 1900 and Minneapolis in 1907.[35]

The founder and musical director of the Chicago Orchestra was Theodore Thomas (1835–1905), one of many German immigrants with a cultural mission.[36] The son of a town musician who emigrated with his family to New York in 1845, he joined the Philharmonic Society of New York. By 1862 he was arranging his own orchestral concerts. His mission was to improve the musical tastes of his audiences, and besides performing he also founded several new institutions, including the Cincinnati Festival and the Cincinnati College of Music. In Chicago, Thomas's tasks included preparing for the World Exhibition in 1893, for which he was appointed musical director. The Orchestra was expanded to 130 players. One of them was August Junker (1868–1944), who after a short period as a violinist in the Berlin Philharmonic Orchestra and, possibly, a stint in Boston, joined the Chicago Orchestra in early 1892 as principal of the viola section. He even helped to find more German players.[37] Junker also performed as a soloist and a member of a string

---

34 Eric Avila, *American Cultural History: A Very Short Introduction* (Oxford: Oxford University Press, 2018), 58, https://doi.org/10.1093/actrade/9780190200589.001.0001
35 Horowitz, *Classical Music in America*, 175–76.
36 Rathert and Ostendorf, *Musik der USA*, 82–83.
37 Norman Schweikert, *Interview with Iwakura Tomokazu* (1995), Cassette tape, Rosenthal Archives of the Chicago Symphony Orchestra. For details on Junker's

quartet, and taught violin at the Columbian College of Music. In 1897 he became naturalized as August Yunker.[38] Nevertheless, he decided to leave America for Japan: by 18 February 1898 he was performing with local amateurs at a meeting of the Yokohama Literary Society.[39] A year later, he was appointed professor at the Tokyo Academy of Music, a post he held until 1913. He premiered several symphonic works in Japan and is remembered as the 'father of the Japanese symphony orchestra'.[40]

By the time Junker left the United States for Japan, Germany rather than America had become the direct source of musical imports, as far as education and European art music was concerned—although, in the twentieth century, American popular music would become a new import, with jazz introduced almost as soon as it came into being. Having laid the foundations with American support, the Japanese turned directly to the European heartland. From the 1880s, the government primarily hired German musicians as teachers, and Europe (particularly Germany) became the primary destination for music students. Although Kōda Nobu, a pupil of Mason and the first music student sent abroad by the Meiji government in 1889, initially studied at the New England Conservatory in Boston, she stayed there only for a year before continuing her studies in Vienna.[41]

The reliance on and reverence for Europe's musical tradition in both America and Japan may well have resulted in the similar attitudes in both countries towards the source of their modern musical culture. While the sacralization of art music was characteristic of nineteenth-century Europe, it manifested itself even more strongly in these two new nations. As Horowitz remarked in *Classical Music in America*, 'More than Europeans, Americans have worshipped musical masterpieces and deified their exponents.'[42] Similarly, it has been observed that 'Japan has

---

work in Japan, see Margaret Mehl, *Not by Love Alone: The Violin in Japan, 1850–2010* (Copenhagen: The Sound Book Press, 2014).

38 According to his grandson, he renounced his American nationality when he returned to Germany in 1913: Schweikert, *Interview with Iwakura Tomokazu*.

39 'A Violin Virtuoso', *The Japan Times*, 21 February 1898.

40 Tōkyō Geijutsu Daigaku Hyakunenshi Hensan Iinkai, ed., *Tōkyō Geijutsu Daigaku hyakunenshi: Tōkyō Ongaku Gakkō hen 1* (Tokyo: Ongaku no Tomosha, 1987), 535.

41 Margaret Mehl, 'A Man's Job? The Kōda Sisters, Violin Playing and Gender Stereotypes in the Introduction of Western Music in Japan', *Women's History Review* 21, no. 1 (2012), https://doi.org/10.1080/09612025.2012.645675

42 Horowitz, *Classical Music in America*, 26.

also led the rest of Asia in the iconization (fetishization) of Western classical music. The very high status ascribed to learning piano or violin has elevated *kurashikku* to the pinnacle of cultural admiration.'[43]

In both countries, the reverence for European art music, particularly German music, contributed to a strong emotional affinity. In America, 'nonverbal cultural and artistic contacts [...] proved much more intense and enduring than political ties, surviving broken treaties, mutual alienation and even several wars.'[44] American actors promoting German Kultur, and particularly orchestral music, believed that it was 'both unique and universalistic', and that classical music was a 'means for providing evidence of culture' and 'an essential element of Western civilization'.[45] American students flocked to Europe, above all Germany, clinging persistently to the 'almost mythical belief in a "musical atmosphere" that Germany had' and their own country lacked, and went in search of 'the magic'.[46]

Similarly, in Japan, the affinity Japanese felt for Germany as a result of their strong cultural links survived Germany's participation in the Triple Intervention of 1895 and Japan's joining the Allies in the First World War. The alliance between Japan and Nazi Germany owed much to this pre-existing affinity, and the cultural links forged in the 1930s and 1940s endured even after the Anti-Comintern Pact of 1936 and the Tripartite Pact of 1940 had proved unsuccessful in political and military terms.[47] Indeed, post-war cultural exchanges between the two countries show significant continuities on closer examination.[48] The links were only in part a result of government policies. They were promoted by people who had their own agenda and acted if not independently then at least

---

43 David W. Hughes and Alison McQueen Tokita, eds., *The Ashgate Research Companion to Japanese Music* (Aldershot, Hampshire: Ashgate, 2008), 7–8.

44 Jessica C. E. Gienow-Hecht, *Sound Diplomacy: Music and Emotions in Transatlantic Relations, 1850–1920* (Chicago: University of Chicago Press, 2009), 5, 10.7208/chicago/9780226292175.001.0001

45 Gienow-Hecht, *Sound Diplomacy*, 7–8.

46 Ibid., 57, 61.

47 Political, military, and cultural relations are treated in Gerhard Krebs and Bernd Martin, eds., *Formierung und Fall der Achse Berlin-Tōkyō* (Munich: iudicium, 1994).

48 The cultural relations between Japan and Germany from 1933 to 1945 have received detailed treatment in Hans-Joachim Bieber, *SS und Samurai: Deutsch-Japanische Kulturbeziehungen 1933–1945* (Munich: iudicium, 2014).

in a semi-official capacity, displaying initiative and resourcefulness that went beyond government expectations.

Both American and Japanese elites were conscious of their dependence on European models, and a perception of cultural inferiority resulted.[49] In both cases, the sense of inferiority had its counterpart in European stereotypes. The question of whether America had any distinctive culture at all was debated by intellectuals on both sides of the Atlantic.[50]

The Quest for a National Music

The heavy dependence on an imported culture represented the backdrop for the quest for a national sound in both Japan and the United States. To some extent this corresponded to musical nationalism in Europe, but the timing is not the same, as the efforts to create a specific national music did not reach their peak in the United States (and, to a lesser extent, in Japan) until the twentieth century.[51] The search for an American cultural identity and, in musical terms, an American sound is a major theme in the history of music in the United States.[52] Arguably, the debates about a specifically American music were even more intense than their equivalent in Japan. Unlike Japan, where the divide between traditional Japanese and Western music was obvious, American culture was dominated by immigrants from Europe, who brought their music with them. European styles and aesthetics dominated American musical culture, well into the nineteenth century.[53] Other major differences were that America was multi-ethnic in a way that Japan was not, and that popular music came to play a major role in defining America musically. Nevertheless, the parallels are significant enough to warrant a brief discussion, because, besides showing that the challenges Japan faced in its search for a way to express and celebrate the nation musically were not unique, they highlight the questions associated with the very concept of a national music. In theory, a national music is one that is

---

49   Rathert and Ostendorf, *Musik der USA*, 16, 311.
50   Barbara A. Zuck, *A History of Musical Americanism* (Ann Arbor, MI: UMI, 1980 (1978)), 17.
51   For America: Zuck, *Musical Americanism*, 7. For Japan, see following chapters.
52   Rathert and Ostendorf, *Musik der USA*, 1.
53   Ibid., 282.

shared by all the nation's citizens, as opposed to musical genres that are attributed to a particular class or group within a society. But what exactly should that music express? Who decides? Whom is the music for? And whose music is it anyway?

The quest for a specifically American art music (or 'cultivated' music, which is 'usually created by trained composers to be interpreted by professional performers'[54]) was an internal contest between 'cultivated music in America' and 'American cultivated music' that had a 'conceptual' and a 'compositional' dimension.[55] Conceptual Americanism refers to advocating music composed by Americans, as well as writings and activities to promote American music. Compositional Americanism refers to using native elements in the composition of music. There was some attempt to develop new styles independently of European models by composers of the so-called First New England School in the eighteenth century, but contrary to the name they did not establish a lasting tradition.[56] While conceptual Americanism became a noticeable trend from the mid-nineteenth century, compositional Americanism did not become a significant trend until the end of the century.[57] By then, the question of how to define American music preoccupied all musical actors.[58]

The debate about a specifically American music reached its height when Antonín Dvořák was appointed to the National Conservatory of Music in New York in 1892, where his symphony 'From the New World' was premiered in the 1893–94 concert season.[59] Dvořák, who in his Bohemian homeland had drawn inspiration from peasant songs and dances, advocated the use of melodies of African and Native Americans in composition, although he had limited knowledge of either. Not everyone agreed with him. One of the most original American composers, Edward MacDowell, felt strongly that quality, not nationality, should set the standard and was scathing of Dvořák's suggestion:

---

54   Zuck, *Musical Americanism*, 7.
55   The following is based on Zuck, *Musical Americanism*, 8–9.
56   Rathert and Ostendorf, *Musik der USA*, 276.
57   Zuck, *Musical Americanism*, 9, 10.
58   Rathert and Ostendorf, *Musik der USA*, 299.
59   Horowitz, *Classical Music in America*, 5–11, 211–41; Gienow-Hecht, *Sound Diplomacy*, 151–75.

Moszkowski the Pole writes Spanish Dances. Cowen in England writes a Scandinavian Symphony. Grieg the Norwegian writes Arabian music; and to cap the climax, we have here in America been offered a pattern for an 'American' national musical costume by the Bohemian Dvořák– though what the Negro melodies have to do with Americanism in art still remains a mystery. Music that can be made by 'recipe' is not music, but 'tailoring'.[60]

The music critic Henry Krehbiel, on the other hand, in an article in the *New York Daily Tribune* on 15 December 1893, justified his description of Dvorak's Symphony no. 9 as 'American' by pointing out various musical features.[61] What precisely is quintessentially American about them is, however, open to question: the 'Scottish snap' is (as the name suggests and he himself points out) not limited to the music of 'the negroes of our South'. Of a melodic element he stated that 'the phrase is built on the pentatonic, or five-note, scale, which omits the fourth and seventh tones of our ordinary diatonic series, and admits that the same scale feature in Scottish, Irish, or Chinese music, as well as songs by the Omaha Indians.' And, we might add, in Japanese music, where it is known as *yonanuki* (the fourth and seventh degrees omitted) scale and commonly regarded as reflecting Japanese musical sensibilities and preferences, particularly in its minor version (*yonanuki tan'onkai*).[62] A subsidiary phrase is described as having a 'distinctly negro characteristic', giving the (first) movement a 'somewhat Oriental tinge'. Another phrase (in the last movement) is described as 'a paraphrase of "Yankee Doodle"'. The musicologist Michael Beckerman in his analysis of Krehbiel's article calls these musical devices 'multicultural puns', meaning that they are common to at least two cultures.[63] In fact, if *Yankee Doodle* were

---

60 Quoted in Zuck, *Musical Americanism*, 56. For more examples of critics' reactions, see Horowitz, *Classical Music in America*, 59, 66–69.
61 The article is quoted in full in Michael Beckerman, 'Henry Krehbiel, Antonín Dvořák, and the Symphony "From the New World"', *Notes* 49, no. 2 (1992), https://doi.org/10.2307/897884 Krehbiel, who was in close contact with the composer, wrote it after hearing the symphony in rehearsal. On Krehbiel's characterizing the symphony as 'American', see also Gienow-Hecht, *Sound Diplomacy*, 168.
62 The *yonanuki* modes, whether major (*yonanuki chōonkai*) or minor, which dominated Japanese-style popular songs (*kayōkyoku, enka*), are hybrids of the pentatonic mode of traditional music with a Western harmonic orientation. They are not a typical feature of traditional Japanese music.
63 Beckerman, 'Henry Krehbiel, Antonín Dvořák, and the Symphony "From the New World"', 462.

replaced with the title of a Japanese folk song, these 'American' musical devices might equally well be described as characteristic of Japanese national music of the early twentieth century. Krehbiel himself seemed to be aware of the 'multicultural' dimensions, as is suggested by his observations written immediately after the premiere and published two days later in the same newspaper:

> If the melodies which he has composed and moulded into a symphony contain elements which belong also to the music of other peoples, so does the American people contain elements of the races to which those elements are congenial. Let them be Scotch, let them be Irish, let them be German, let them be African or Indian, in them there is that which makes the appeal to the whole people, and therefore, like the people, they are American.[64]

Subsequent discussions of the symphony often centred on whether 'negro' and 'Indian' tunes could be regarded as representative of America. More broadly, the question was what in fact constituted American sound. Charles Ives, perhaps the most emblematic of American composers in that period, explicitly rejected the appropriation of slave plantation and native Indian melodies in his music.[65] Nevertheless, although there was no agreement on the question of which folk tunes might be considered truly 'American', ultimately this was a minor issue. As Dvořák himself stated, 'Undoubtedly the gems for the best of music lie hidden among all the races that are commingled in this great country.'[66] Dvořák's major contribution was that he inspired Americanist composers' interest in vernacular music, that is American folk or popular music. As a result, American composers took up a variety of sources. Compositional Americanism received a major boost, and continued as a significant trend until 1945.[67]

A significant group among the composers embracing folk music were the Indianists. Musical Indianism is the trend that can most usefully be compared to efforts in Japan to compose art music in the European idiom while including traditional Japanese elements. Unlike

---

64 *New York Daily Tribune* 17 December 1893, p. 7. Quoted in Beckerman, 'Henry Krehbiel, Antonín Dvořák, and the Symphony "From the New World"', 471.
65 Horowitz, *Classical Music in America*.
66 Quoted in Zuck, *Musical Americanism*, 59.
67 Zuck, *Musical Americanism*, 59.

other American folk music, but like traditional Japanese music, the music of Native Americans was so different from European art music as to render the two incompatible.[68] During Dvořák's tenure in New York, Alice Fletcher published her pioneering ethnographical *Study of Omaha Indian Music* in 1893, the result of extensive collaboration with her Omaha informant Francis La Flesche. Fletcher envisaged the creation of a national music, and saw to it that Dvořák received a copy of her *Study*, including ninety-two transcriptions. Although the study was not the only collection of its kind, the timing and Fletcher's lobbying meant that it had significant influence on Indianist composers and in the construction of 'Indian Sound' in the decades between 1890 and 1930 out of a mixture of indigenous music mediated (and often distorted) by ethnographers, and composers using Western musical devices with a long history of association with the exotic and the primitive, as well as their individual imaginative creations. Native performers both played on and challenged expectations, resulting in 'a peculiar pastiche in which racist stereotypes might be simultaneously reinforced and questioned through Indian musical performances'.[69]

But the Indianist movement sought to do more than importing a few Indian tunes into European art music to create a 'national' music.[70] Arthur Farwell, one of its leading representatives, explicitly challenged the 'great definite machinery for the performance of European music':[71] the Old World institutions as well as the music itself. Musically, he and others envisioned a new language, created by bringing together two musical spheres. Romantic notions of Indian culture combined with ideas of progress: at the time, the Frontier Wars were in their final phase and there was a general assumption that Indians would vanish in the face of unstoppable modern progress. Ethnographers saw their efforts to collect and record Indian culture, including Indian music, as salvage work. The native peoples, while viewed as primitive, were simultaneously accorded a certain dignity, based on the patina of an

---

68 The following discussion of Indianism is based chiefly on Philip J. Deloria, *Indians in Unexpected Places* (Lawrence, KS: University Press of Kansas, 2004), 183–223, https://doi.org/10.1353/book111312 See also Rathert and Ostendorf, *Musik der USA*, 317–26.
69 Deloria, *Indians in Unexpected Places*, 210.
70 Rathert and Ostendorf, *Musik der USA*, 317.
71 Quoted in Horowitz, *Classical Music in America*, 260.

ancient culture. Indianist composers saw their work in part as an act of translation.

But what does translation mean in a musical context? The key for Alice Fletcher and her associate John Filmore was harmony (as with many would-be reformers of Japan's traditional music). In the Western musical system, melodies fit within a clear harmonic structure. The music of the Omaha and of Indians in general did not use harmony, and melodies were not structured in the same way as Western ones.[72] Nevertheless, Filmore operated with the idea of 'implied harmony': he harmonized Omaha melodies and came to believe that by doing so he was highlighting their natural structure. In reality, he was imposing Western conceptions of music in the belief that they were universal. The fact that his and Fletcher's Omaha informants reportedly approved of the result is no evidence for this supposed universal harmonic sense. By this time most Indians had long been exposed to Western music and especially the harmonized hymns taught by Christian missionaries playing them on the harmonium or piano.[73]

The 'Indian Sound' of twentieth-century popular culture resulted to a large extent from the addition of harmony by the Indianist composers to the melodies collected by ethnographers. Arguably the most successful example was Charles Wakefield Cadman (1881–1945), whose well-known *Four American Indian Songs Founded upon Tribal Melodies* (Op. 45, first published in 1909) even found their way to Japan.[74] Cadman's 'Indian' opera—tellingly, he himself preferred to call it 'American'—*The Robin Woman* (*Shanewis*) was the first successful opera by an American composer, premiered in March 1918 at the New York Metropolitan Opera and running for two seasons as well as being performed in other American cities. A major reason for the opera's success was the singer in the title role: Tsianina Redfeather Blackstone (1882 or 1892–1985).[75] A Creek Indian trained by Denver's leading voice instructor and well-known singer John C. Wilcox, she had been touring the United States with Cadman since 1913, performing in his highly successful *Indian Music Talks*.

---

72 Deloria, *Indians in Unexpected Places*, 200.
73 Ibid., 202, 279. The quote comes from Fletcher, *Omaha Music*.
74 See Chapter 10.
75 According to Deloria, the 1892 date is more likely.

Redfeather, who also had a successful singing career independently of Cadman, performed in pieces which encapsulated Indianness. She was perceived as authentic and she herself actively used white people's fascination with Indians. In that way her career is not unlike that of her Japanese contemporary Miura Tamaki (1884–1946) and her performances as the eponymous *Madame Butterfly*.[76] Both were talented, conservatoire-trained singers who, in performing their ethnicity, consciously played to Western stereotypes, even while their mastery of Western-style singing and European art music confounded white people's expectations.

By the time of Cadman's success with *Shanewis*, the Indianist movement had, however, already passed its zenith. Indianist composers such as Cadman and Indian performers such as Redfeather Blackstone faded into oblivion. There are several reasons why Native American music failed to become part of an American national music. The distance between the musical systems made it almost impossible for the former to be integrated convincingly into European art music.[77] Arguably, the most significant reason, however, was that Native Americans themselves in the twentieth century pursued a version of 'inclusion' in American society that included recognition as sovereign nations, based on their memories of independence, their claims to the land, their legal rights, and their distinct national status. This version of inclusion rested on 'distinct cultural and social status', that is, on 'distinctiveness and difference'.[78]

Meanwhile, African Americans, who sought 'inclusion' during the same period, sought it in the form of legal and social equality and equal opportunities for full participation in the ideal of American freedom. Their history of close contact and interdependence with the white population was reflected in Afro-American music, which had a history of exchange and acculturation that had started early, particularly in the Southern states.[79] The Civil War sped up the process, which after the

---

76 Mari Yoshihara, 'The Flight of the Japanese Butterfly: Orientalism, Nationalism, and Performances of Japanese Womanhood', *American Quarterly* 56, no. 4 (2004), https://doi.org/10.1353/aq.2004.0067
77 Rathert and Ostendorf, *Musik der USA*, 317.
78 Deloria, *Indians in Unexpected Places*, 235–37.
79 Deloria, *Indians in Unexpected Places*, 237; Rathert and Ostendorf, *Musik der USA*, 219, 276.

war was accompanied by serious research into Afro-American music, represented in the landmark collection, *Slave Songs of the United States*, published in 1867, and discussions of the music's positive qualities, with *Dwight's Journal* even referring to an 'American School of Music' in the making.[80] The period from 1890 to 1920 was one of 'crucial development' in Afro-American music, which morphed from 'folk' music (understood as the music associated with a particular group) to 'popular' music (music played and heard throughout the nation). Unlike Indian music, ragtime and jazz were the result of 'cross-pollination', and their appeal was broad enough to allow their integration into the musical mainstream.[81] While the Indianist movement waned after 1920, the new hybrid genres, together with European modernist music, became the main inspiration for compositional Americanism.[82]

Even the integration of music that included Afro-American roots into European art music, however, was limited. The music of the United States was virtually colonized by the aesthetic characteristics and values of European art music, and the dream of a uniquely American music that integrated all the heterogenic musics prevalent in America was not realized.[83] It may well have been an impossible dream, at least within the genre of European art music and beyond the 'cautious integration' of elements from foreign musical systems.[84] Besides, any effort to create the authentically American through complete adoption and mastery of European models, without reference to the diverse local traditions, meant that the composers who attempted it isolated themselves from the 'popular' in the sense of being owned by the people.[85]

Ultimately, popular music, not art music, came to be recognized as quintessentially American. As early as 1864, after the death of Stephen Foster, his songs were described by *Harper's Magazine* as 'our national music'.[86] Foster's formative musical experiences were minstrel shows and music-making at home, and he aimed to write music 'for the people', and

---

80   Rathert and Ostendorf, *Musik der USA*, 305.
81   Zuck, *Musical Americanism*, 74. For her definition of 'folk' and 'popular', see pp. 14–15.
82   Zuck, *Musical Americanism*, 74–86.
83   Rathert and Ostendorf, *Musik der USA*, 207.
84   Ibid., 303–14.
85   Ibid., 303.
86   Quoted in Rathert and Ostendorf, *Musik der USA*, 44.

succeeded in transforming 'certain sentimental and nostalgic everyday myths' into music.[87] Songs such as *Oh! Susannah* and *Old Folks at Home* became immensely popular. His early minstrel or plantation songs contained lyrics in pseudo-African American dialect, but songs such as *Nelly was a Lady* (1849) and *Massa's in de Cold Ground* portrayed slaves as having dignity and human feelings, beyond the prevailing stereotypes.[88] Some of his songs became popular worldwide. In Japan they were heard for the first time when Commodore Perry's men treated their reluctant hosts to a number of minstrel shows, held on the steamship *Powhatan* in Yokohama, Hakodate, Shimoda, and Naha in the Ryukyu Islands. The programme included several songs by Foster.[89] While only very few Japanese witnessed these performances, Foster's songs found their way into school textbooks and hymnbooks in Japan, often with Japanese lyrics that had nothing to do with the English ones. The tune of *Old Folks at Home* first appeared in a singing textbook for schools in 1888, and again in subsequent editions in 1891, 1892, 1895, 1902, 1905, and 1908, and in a hymnbook in 1901. *Massa's in de Cold Ground*, with Japanese lyrics, can be found in school books published in 1903, 1908, and 1911 and in hymn books published in 1909 and 1915. Both songs appeared in volumes of songs in English.[90] The recurring themes of Foster's songs: yearning for one's native place, loss of loved ones through death, and nostalgia in general, are similar to those of several other songs published in Japan at the time, as well as sentimental popular songs played in both countries throughout the twentieth century.[91]

Given the pains American elites went to in order to distinguish cultivated music from vernacular, 'popular' music, a fundamental conflict that characterized debates from around the end of the eighteenth century and into the twentieth century,[92] it is ironic that 'American'

---

[87] Ibid., 45.
[88] Ibid., 46–48. Only 23 of 287 were written in dialect (p. 23).
[89] Kiyoshi Kasahara, *Kurobune raikō to ongaku* (Tokyo: Yoshikawa Kōbunkan, 2001), 102–70.
[90] Details of the Japanese versions in Kazuko Miyashita, 'Foster's Songs in Japan', *American Music* 30, no. 3 (2012): 313, https://doi.org/10.5406/americanmusic.30.3.0308 For the original lyrics, see Sakai, Katsuisa. *Eigo shōka shū*. Tokyo: Uedaya Shoten, 1903 vol. 1, pp. 6–9; vol. 2, pp. 16–19.
[91] For America, see Rathert and Ostendorf, *Musik der USA*, 50. For Japan: Miyashita, 'Foster's Songs in Japan', 313–14.
[92] Rathert and Ostendorf, *Musik der USA*, 136, 303.

music came to be defined by popular genres, starting with Foster's songs, and eventually including jazz, blues, gospel, music theatre, and others. A similar irony in Japan is that it was popular music that came closest to embodying the elite reformers' ideal of a harmonization of Western and Japanese music. Japanese genres, meanwhile, could be and were elevated and preserved as 'traditional', thus serving to represent specifically Japanese music and thus what Deloria, with reference to Native Americans, described as 'distinctiveness and difference'.[93]

The United States, in the person of Luther Whiting Mason, played a major role in the introduction of Western music in Japan in the crucial early phase of establishing the teaching of singing, reading staff notation, and basic music theory in schools and setting up teacher training. Americans, whether Mason on a national level, or Kate I. Hansen in the provincial city of Sendai, also acted as mediators of European musical traditions. For both countries, the art music of Europe was an object of veneration, and when Horowitz, describing the efforts of Dwight and others to sacralize European art music in its purest form, remarks, 'This zeal reflected insecurities inherent to a borrowed high culture [...]',[94] he might just as well be referring to Japan. The process of adopting and establishing a musical high culture based on European models went hand in hand with nation-building in both countries and almost contemporaneously, as did the quest for a national music integrating indigenous elements (however defined) into the European idiom. In both countries, this trend waned after 1945.[95]

---

93 Deloria, *Indians in Unexpected Places*, 237.
94 Horowitz, *Classical Music in America*, 27.
95 For America: Zuck, *Musical Americanism*, 273–78.

3. The Case of Japan

> After all, never has there been a country more unskilled in [cultivated] music than ours.[1]

> Few things were more astonishing than the growth during the past forty years of a taste for 'foreign' music. In no other respect did the civilization of Japan differ from that of Europe so much as in its music which, through centuries of assiduous cultivation, has become a highly developed and complete system, oriental in its general character, yet distinctly national. [...] Their own still holds first place in the hearts of all the music loving people and some of them who are capable of thoroughly understanding and enjoying both systems, sturdily maintain that it possesses certain qualities and characteristics of such excellence that it will have a large contributory influence in the evolution of the 'music of the future' and must be reckoned with accordingly.[2]

That European music should play a leading role in the United States' quest for an American music is not surprising, given that the dominant class of immigrants came from European countries. Japan, however, had a highly developed musical culture and, although threatened by the European powers, was never colonized. Relatively few Europeans settled in Japan and fewer still as immigrants. Japan nevertheless represents an

---

[1] Kōhei Kanda, 'Kokugaku o shinkō subeki no setsu,' *Meiroku zasshi* 18 (1874); Kōhei Kanda, 'On Promoting Our National Music,' in *Meiroku Zasshi: Journal of the Japanese Enlightenment*, ed. and trans. William R. Braisted (Cambridge, Massachusetts: Harvard University Press, 1976). Braisted translates *onritsu* as harmony, but that seems incorrect. Kanda apparently means 'music' in the meaning of 'the art or science of composing or performing music' (OED), or what Zuck describes as 'cultivated' music. See Yasuko Tsukahara, *Meiji kokka to gagaku: dentō no kindaika/kokugaku no sōsei* (Tokyo: Yūshisha, 2009), 109; e-mail to author, 29 December 2021.

[2] Thomas C. Mendenhall, 'Japan Revisited after Thirty Years', *The Journal of Race Development* 2, no. 3 (January 1912), 229.

'extreme case' of musical Westernization.³ Nowhere was Western music adopted and assimilated as rapidly and thoroughly as in Japan; and in no other nation was a highly developed, diverse, and flourishing native musical culture marginalized to quite the same extent.⁴ Less than fifty years after the Meiji Restoration, foreign observers were beginning to express astonishment at the rising standards of musical performance. In 1940, moreover, Japan celebrated the 2,600th anniversary of the founding of its empire by commissioning large symphonic works from acclaimed Western composers.⁵ More than anything else, the use at the height of military nationalism of European-style symphonic music to celebrate the ascension of the (legendary) first emperor demonstrates that the formerly alien music had become an integral part of the culture of modern Japan.

What processes resulted in the dominance of Western music to the extent that traditional Japanese music was marginalized? We can rule out an inherent superiority of European art music (even if contemporaries did not), or direct pressure from the Western powers. No-one forced the Japanese to found a Western-style conservatoire, or symphony orchestras.

---

3   Bob van der Linden, 'Non-Western National Music and Empire in Global History: Interactions, Uniformities, and Comparisons', *Journal of Global History* 10 (2015): 440, https://doi.org/10.1017/S1740022815000212

4   The most comprehensive overview of the process is still Luciana Galliano, *Yōgaku: Japanese Music in the Twentieth Century*, trans. Martin Mayes (Lanham, Maryland, and London: The Scarecrow Press, 2002). See also Bonnie C. Wade, *Music in Japan* (Oxford: Oxford University Press, 2005); Judith Ann Herd, 'Western-influenced "classical" music in Japan,' in *The Ashgate Research Companion to Japanese Music*, ed. David W. Hughes and Alison McQueen Tokita (Aldershot, UK: Ashgate, 2008); Margaret Mehl, 'Introduction: Western Music in Japan: A Success Story?', *Nineteenth-Century Music Review* 10, no. 2 (2013), https://doi.org/10.1017/S1479409813000232; Margaret Mehl, *Not by Love Alone: The Violin in Japan, 1850–2010* (Copenhagen: The Sound Book Press, 2014).

The most useful comprehensive works by Japanese scholars are Yasuko Tsukahara, *Jūkyū seiki no Nihon ni okeru Seiyō ongaku no juyō* (Tokyo: Taka Shuppan, 1993); Kōsuke Nakamura, *Kindai Nihon yōgaku josetsu* (Tokyo: Tōkyō Shoseki, 2003). Yūko Chiba, *Doremi o eranda Nihonjin* (Ongaku no Tomosha, 2007).

5   Takahisa Furukawa, *Kōki, Banpaku, Orinpikku: Kōshitsu burando to keizai hatten* (Tokyo: Chūō Kōronsha, 1998), 61–127. For a broader treatment of the anniversary celebrations in English, see Kenneth J. Ruoff, *Imperial Japan at its Zenith: The Wartime Celebrations of the Empire's 2,600th Anniversary* (Ithaca, NY: Cornell University Press, 2010). It is symptomatic of historians' neglect of music that Ruoff hardly mentions the subject at all and does not mention the musical activities referred to here.

There were several reasons why Meiji leaders nevertheless saw the introduction of Western music as a necessity, although sidelining Japanese music was not what they had in mind. Their ultimate goal was the creation of a new national music, and Western models were to provide the means and inspiration for reform, as with so many other areas of politics, society, and culture. This ideal of a national music created by blending Western and Japanese elements never became a reality. Cross-fertilization and hybridization did occur, but not in the way political and intellectual leaders intended. These developments were the result of several circumstances.

One is the incompatibility of the two musical worlds at the time. Thomas Mendenhall (1841–1924), who taught physics at the University of Tokyo from 1878 to 1881, remarked on a 'chasm that yawned between Japanese and European music, the difference being everywhere so great as to make them mutually exclusive'.[6] Decades later, Eta Harich-Schneider, the author of the first comprehensive history of music in Japan in English, observed that Japan's encounter with Western art music in the nineteenth century 'took place at a moment when the contrast [with its own music] was at its strongest'.[7] The nineteenth-century Western idea of 'absolute music', she asserted, had no equivalent in Japan.[8] Meanwhile, Western music, including European art music, was changing: fundamental ideas that had shaped its traditions were being challenged.[9]

Western Music and Musical Reform

The decision-makers in government, however, were not in a position to appreciate the difficulties. They had minimal musical training or expertise and were motivated by pragmatic rather than aesthetic considerations. For them, Western music was not superior *per se*, but

---

6   Mendenhall, 'Japan Revisited', 229.
7   Eta Harich-Schneider, *A History of Japanese Music* (London: Oxford University Press, 1973), 546.
8   She may have overstated her case; see Alison Tokita, 'Takarazuka and the Musical *Modan* in the Hanshin Region 1914–1942', in *Rethinking Japanese Modernism*, ed. Roy Starrs (Leiden: Brill, 2012), 413.
9   Gerald Groemer, 'The Rise of "Japanese Music"', *The World of Music* 46, no. 2 (2004): 21, https://www.jstor.org/stable/41699564

possessed qualities Japanese music lacked and that were perceived as indispensable for their overall reform agenda. One, frequently mentioned, was harmony. Others had less to do with the music itself than with the way it was discussed and practised: Western music came to Japan with a universal (as opposed to instrument-specific) system of notation and teaching methods suitable for large groups in the classroom; a theoretical framework and vocabulary that facilitated intellectual discussions about music (in the abstract), and—thanks to modern instrument technology and suitable compositions—a potential for large-scale and high-volume displays of power and unity in public performances. In short, it appeared highly suitable to the needs of the modern state they were in the process of building.

Western music was, moreover, perceived as being based on scientific principles and as representing an essential element of modern civilization. In the ideology of universal progress that the Meiji leaders adopted from the West, the state of a nation's music corresponded to its state of civilization. The music of Japan, with the possible exception of court music (*gagaku*), which lacked popular appeal, was perceived as backward by the elites, who were brought up to regard the common people with contempt. For most men of the samurai class, the Confucian ideal of 'rites and music' (*reigaku*) as two essential means of government contrasted with the reality of their lives, where music-making was not regarded as an appropriate occupation. On the other hand, common music (*zokugaku*), enjoyed by the lower classes was far too prevalent and popular to be suppressed, and 'reform' proved easier to discuss than to accomplish.

In order to understand the process better, it is instructive to compare and contrast the advance of Western music in Japan with the fate of another musical import, known as Ming-Qing music (Ming and Qing dynasty music, *minshingaku*).[10] Transmitted in the 1820s and 1830s by Chinese merchants in Nagasaki, Ming-Qing music was a genre of popular music that until mid-Meiji was far more widely enjoyed among the people than Western music.[11] Fashionable among men of letters since

---

10 The following is based on Tsukahara, *Seiyō ongaku no juyō*, 315–28.
11 On the characteristics of *minshingaku*, see William P. Malm, 'Chinese Music in the Edo and Meiji Periods in Japan', *Asian Music* 6 no. 1/2 (1975), https://doi.org/10.2307/833846 On its provenance and transmission, see Kuei-Hsiang Yang, 'Minshingaku: Nagasaki ni tsutaerareta Chūgoku ongaku', *Ochanomizu Joshi Daigaku Daigakuin Ningen Bunka Kenkyūka (Journal of the Musicological Society of*

the Tokugawa era (1603–1868), it reached the height of its popularity in the period from the 1860s. The instruments of Ming-Qing music included several types of Chinese fiddles and the Chinese version of the *biwa*, but the most popular instrument was the *gekkin*, a plucked lute with a round, flattish body and frets. From the 1880s, a veritable craze for the *gekkin* swept Japan; easier to learn than the fretless *shamisen*, it became popular among geisha in Kyoto and in ordinary families. During the Sino-Japanese war of 1894–95, Ming-Qing music lost its popularity and never really recovered, although it continued to enjoy a limited measure of popularity and was taught (privately) as a separate genre in Osaka until 1940.[12] Changing geopolitics, however, were not the only or even the main reason for its decline.

An examination of the general circumstances of their introduction and of performance spaces, actors, and social structures reveals essential differences between Ming-Qing music and Western music. Introduced through informal channels during the last decades of the Tokugawa shogunate, Ming-Qing music was not supported through regular contact with China after the initial transmission. Western music, on the other hand, was systematically adopted by the new government after 1868 and maintained and developed with continuous input from Western countries (foreign teachers, imported instruments, tutors, sheet music, and Japanese studying abroad). Official promotion by the Meiji government meant that spaces, both physical and in terms of occasions for performance, were created, starting with performance at state ceremonies. Western music was thus accorded special status from the outset and performed in entirely new, modern spaces. The early actors, moreover, included musical professionals, and systematic training was established within government structures. Ming-Qing music, on the other hand, was largely the domain of amateurs, with only a small number of specialized musicians to teach them. Unlike the government structures that supported Western music, Ming-Qing music was entirely dependent on private enterprise, and popular demand.

Ochanomizu University) 2 (2000), https://teapot.lib.ocha.ac.jp/record/33890/files/KJ00004857924.pdf; Chunli Piao, 'Nagasaki no minshingaku to Chūgoku no minshin jichō shōkyoku kenkyū,' *Chūkyō Daigaku Bunka Kagaku Kenkyūsho/Fukuoka Daigaku Jinbun Gakubu (Cultural Science)* 17, no. 2 (2006).

12 Tsukahara, *Seiyō ongaku no juyō*; Kōichi Yumoto, *Bakumatsu Meiji ryūkō jiten* (Tokyo: Kashiwa Shobō, 1998), 186–89.

The decisive difference was that the adoption of Western music was part of the overall Westernization package; that is, it was tightly bound up with political relations and diplomatic protocol, activities and considerations outside the realm of music. Ming-Qing music, meanwhile, was not an inseparable part of any significant non-musical context. Finally, although this might at first glance seem counter-intuitive, the relative similarities in musical practice of Ming-Qing music and traditional Japanese music since the Edo period, especially the similar ways in which they were transmitted and performed, ultimately worked against Ming-Qing music, allowing it to melt into the latter and thus lose its independent status.[13]

Japanese music, meanwhile, although it suffered official neglect and was increasingly marginalized, nevertheless had a significant role to play in the making of modern Japan. Arguably, its very neglect and marginalization meant that the music itself and some of the associated practices changed less than they would have done with systematic government interference. As it was, the major genres flourished in the hands of private practitioners and sponsors, ready to be recast, when the time came, as representative of unadulterated Japanese cultural traditions in order to balance the universalizing forces of Western-style modernity by emphasizing the distinctiveness of the Japanese nation and its culture.

At the beginning of the Meiji period, however, the very concept of 'Japanese music' had yet to become fully formed; this came gradually in the course of the Meiji period, as a result of the encounter with Western music.[14] A short characterization of Japanese music will be sufficient in the present context.[15] The different musical genres were highly context-bound, played by different social groups in different settings. With the possible exceptions of the theatre, the *gagaku* orchestra, and music played at festivals, most settings were small and intimate. Large-scale public performances comparable to the symphony concert or the military parade, modern

---

13 Tsukahara, *Seiyō ongaku no juyō*, 327–28.
14 See Chapter 1; Groemer, 'Rise of "Japanese Music"'.
15 Based on David W. Hughes and Alison McQueen Tokita, 'Context and Change in Japanese Music', in *The Ashgate Research Companion to Japanese Music*, ed. Alison McQueen Tokita and David W. Hughes (Aldershot, UK: Ashgate, 2008), 18–27. For more comprehensive treatments of indigenous music, see Harich-Schneider, *A History of Japanese Music*; William P. Malm, *Traditional Japanese Music and Musical Instruments* (Tokyo: Kodansha International, 2000).

phenomena even in the West, were almost unknown. The only exceptions were some of the larger festivals, which were, however, restricted to certain days of the year and clearly separated from everyday life.

Scales and modes vary among the different genres. Vertical harmony is rarely used; instruments playing together tend to play in a kind of loose unison, or with a melody and counter-melody. Apart from dance music the rhythm is often quite free, while the timing or the space between sounds (*ma*) holds particular significance. Significant differences lie in what is considered a beautiful sound: unlike the Western *bel canto* tradition with its ideal of pure notes, the unstable pitch of a twanging string, or the sound of blowing mixed with the note of a *shakuhachi* are essential ingredients of the music; the skilled musician creates variety by subtly changing timbres. Moreover, in contrast to the passionate expression of the Classical and particularly Romantic music of Europe, most Japanese music lacks overt emotional expression; sober refinement or decorum characterized the performance of the most highly regarded music.

Transmission was by ear, from teacher to pupil. It was commonly organized in the so-called *iemoto* system of fictive family ties, with a hereditary master as the 'head of house' (*iemoto*) ensuring the continuation of the lineage or school (Japanese *ryūha*). Licensed members of the school assumed a professional name (*natori*), part of which was the name of the school. The *iemoto* system was particularly marked in the elite genres that today are described as 'Japanese classical music' (*Nihon koten ongaku*), including several of the recital and instrumental genres as well as noh and kabuki theatre. It is characteristic of other traditional arts as well as the martial arts and continues to this day.

Traditional Musical Genres and the Meiji Reforms

Western observers in the nineteenth century were quick to point out that Japan's music owed much to outside influence from the continent, particularly China. By the nineteenth century, however, these imports had long been assimilated and were not perceived as foreign.[16] One of the

---

16 Leopold Benjamin Karl) Mueller (Müller, 'Einige Notizen ueber die Japanische Musik', *Mitteilungen der Gesellschaft für Natur- und Völkerkunde Ostasiens* 1, no. 6

oldest imports is *gagaku*, the orchestral music of the imperial court and certain shrines. It came to Japan between the seventh and ninth centuries, and while it has changed over time it can still claim to be one of the world's oldest continuous orchestral traditions.[17] Other genres likewise have roots on the Asian continent, even if they originated in Japan.

In the course of the early modern period, the different kinds of music crystallized into the separate genres identified today.[18] They included *shōmyō* (Buddhist chant), *kagura* (music performed at Shintō shrines), the accompanying music of the noh, kabuki, and bunraku theatres, as well as various styles of recitation and song to the accompaniment of the *biwa* (plucked lute), *shamisen* (three-stringed plucked lute) and *koto* (plucked zither), and as purely instrumental genres. Like Tokugawa society itself, music was highly stratified and its practice affected by class, gender, and geographical divides.[19] The *biwa, koto, kokyū* (bowed lute) and *shamisen* were often (though not exclusively) played by blind musicians organized in special guilds with official support. Playing the *shakuhachi* was, at least in theory, restricted to members of the Zen Buddhist Fuke sect. Several genres were associated with the pleasure quarters. The common people enjoyed folk songs (*min'yō*) and various genres now described as folk performing arts (*minzoku geinō*). The Ainu in the north of Japan and the Okinawans in the south also each had their own musical traditions.

The Meiji Restoration and the resulting political, social, and economic transformations brought changes to the world of Japanese music even before the privileging of Western music made itself felt. Some of these changes had already begun in the Tokugawa period, such as the general blurring of social boundaries, which was reflected in musical practice. Government policies merely sanctioned them; for example, the *shakuhachi* was already being played by amateurs as a leisure pursuit when the Meiji government abolished the Fuke sect in 1871 and with it the right of the *komusō* (mendicant monks) to solicit donations as

---

(1874), https://oag.jp/books/band-i-1873-1876-heft-6/; Rudolf Dittrich, 'Beiträge zur Kenntnis der japanischen Musik', *MOAG* 6, no. 85 (1897).
17   William P. Malm, 'The Special Characteristics of Gagaku', in *Gagaku: Court Music and Dance*, ed. Masataro Togi (Tokyo: Weatherhill, 1971), 5.
18   Galliano, *Yōgaku*: 16.
19   Groemer, 'Rise of "Japanese Music"', 13–18.

itinerant players. Guilds were abolished, while genres previously sponsored by the shogunate lost their support.[20]

Gagaku, closely associated with the imperial court, was the one music that had a place in the government's reforms. As a result, it was transformed by the typical government measures of the time: centralization, standardization, regulation. As early as 1870 the government began to reorganize the *gagaku* musicians in the imperial household's *gagaku* department.[21] The different orchestras and their traditions were brought together in Tokyo; the musicians were ordered to submit information about the music and the training, including pieces and methods of playing that had always been transmitted secretly from teacher to disciple. They had to copy and edit their repertoire according to general principles and their status was newly defined. The system of secret transmission was abolished; in 1873 the government permitted the study of *gagaku* by anyone who wished to do so, provided they applied for permission. *Gagaku* musicians, just like the samurai, were no longer privileged by virtue of their birth, and they had to share the function of performing music at important ceremonies with the new army and navy bands. Their salaries decreased, causing some to leave and make a living elsewhere.[22] At the same time, the government took measures to preserve *gagaku*.[23] The heads of the traditional *gagaku* families received government stipends to ensure that they continued to practise and teach their art. *Gagaku* was thus not completely displaced by Western music. It continues to play a limited but significant role to this day. *Gagaku* musicians played at modern ceremonies, sharing this function with the military bands. One such occasion was the official opening of the first railway line.[24]

---

20 Kiku Day, 'The Effect of the Meiji Government's Policy on Traditional Japanese Music During the Nineteenth Century: The Case of the *Shakuhachi*', *Nineteenth-Century Music Review* 10, no. 2 (2013): 370, https://doi.org/doi:10.1017/S1479409813000268
21 The following is based on Nakamura, *Kindai Nihon yōgaku josetsu*, 403–510. Masataro Togi, *Gagaku: Court Music and Dance*, trans. Don Kenny (New York: Weatherhill, 1971), 133–37. On the *gagaku* musicians and the Meiji state in general: Tsukahara, *Meiji kokka to gagaku*.
22 Harich-Schneider, *A History of Japanese Music*, 550–78; Tsukahara, *Seiyō ongaku no juyō*; Yasuko Tsukahara, 'Meiji 30 nen no kunaishō shikibushoku gagakubu', *Tōkyō Geijutsu Daigaku Ongakubu kiyō*, no. 31 (2006), https://geidai.repo.nii.ac.jp/records/505; Tsukahara, *Meiji kokka to gagaku*.
23 Nakamura, *Kindai Nihon yōgaku josetsu*, 500.
24 On that occasion a bugle corps from the army played the French military march *Aux Champs* outside the station building. Inside, on the other hand, a *gagaku* orchestra

The officials in the Department of Court Ceremonies, which included the *gagaku* department, nevertheless read the signs of the times: soon several of the musicians began to study Western music in addition to *gagaku*, and thus in effect attained bi-musicality.[25] A rehearsal schedule published in English by the *gagaku* department in December 1878—the rehearsals were open to the public, which in itself was an innovation— stated that Western music was rehearsed on Wednesdays and Saturdays, the other days being devoted to 'Kagura or music belonging to the oldest Japanese song' and 'Gaku or several kind [sic] of classical music'.[26]

Other types of music were affected by national and local government policies to various degrees. Music associated with Shintō and Buddhism was affected by the government's policies relating to religion. Buddhism suffered suppression and persecution in the early years of Meiji. In response, Buddhist reformers reconfigured Buddhism to ensure its place in the modern world.[27] Some even looked to Protestant hymns in their efforts to reform religious music. In 1907, one of the Buddhist denominations published a collection of Buddhist hymns, half of which used melodies of Protestant hymns.[28]

The fate of genres associated with the theatre was in part linked to that of the theatre itself, but some of them flourished independently. The noh theatre lost the support of the shogunate, but from the late 1870s, members of the government and the nobility initiated measures to protect and revive noh. A new theatre, the Nōgakudō was opened in 1881 in Shiba Park in Tokyo, and from the late Meiji period noh, like court music, enjoyed protection as a cultural asset.[29] *Yōkyoku* (noh singing) was (and is) practised by amateurs.

---

played *Manzairaku* (Dance of Longevity). Nihon Fūzokushi Gakkai, ed. *Shiryō de kataru Meiji no Tōkyō hyakuwa* (Tokyo: Tsukubanesha, 1996), 118–119. *Manzairaku* is traditionally played on auspicious ceremonial occasions.
25 See Alison M. Tokita, 'Bi-Musicality in Modern Japanese Culture', *International Journal of Bilingualism* 18, no. 2 (2014 (2012)): 159–74, https://doi.org/10.1177/1367006912458394
26 Nakamura, *Kindai Nihon yōgaku josetsu*, 430.
27 See James Edward Ketelaar, *Of Heretics and Martyrs in Meiji Japan: Buddhism and Its Persecution* (Princeton: Princeton University Press, 1990).
28 *Sanbutsuka*, published by the True Pure Land Honganji sect; see Chiba, *Doremi*, 19–20.
29 Yasuko Tsukahara, 'Nihon ongaku no kindai kara gendai', in *Nihon no dentō geinō kōza: ongaku*, ed. Nihon Geinō Bunka Shinkōkai and Kokuritsu Gekijō (Kyoto: Tankōsha, 2008), 463.

Kabuki, *jōruri* and related genres, including the vocal genres with *shamisen* accompaniment (*nagauta, tokiwabushi, kiyomotobushi, gidayūbushi*), were less influenced by the reforms. Widely enjoyed in the Tokugawa period, they continued to be popular, and some artists and performers became highly successful.[30] The kabuki theatre itself became a focus for efforts to reform the theatre (*engeki kairyō*) in the 1880s. The aims were similar to those of music reform: to cleanse it of its supposed decadence, its erotic innuendos, and its vulgarity and turn it into an art that could be shown to Western dignitaries to convince them that Japan was a civilized country. The politicians involved were motivated by a sense of urgency following the opening of a 'Japanese village' in London in January 1885, and the premiere on 14 March 1885 of Gilbert and Sullivan's opera *The Mikado* at the Savoy theatre. With an opening run of 672 performances, it became the most successful Savoy Opera ever and went on to thrill audiences in the United States, Germany, Austria, and Denmark. In the eyes of the Japanese, however, both events perpetuated exactly the quaint and exotic image they were making every effort to discard.[31] The reform efforts had little permanent effect on kabuki; instead, a new theatre movement that aimed to break with tradition gained ground after the Sino-Japanese war.

For practitioners of the instrumental genres, the abolition of the specially protected guilds, while depriving them of a monopoly, offered opportunities to profit from the increasing commercialization. The *shakuhachi* became widely popular as a solo as well as a chamber music instrument in the three-part ensemble (*sankyoku*) together with the *koto* and the *shamisen*. New schools emerged and the repertoires were standardized. The enterprising *shakuhachi* player and teacher Nakao Tozan (1876–1956) introduced a new school with its own teacher-licensing system.

The *koto* survived as a popular instrument of domestic music-making, albeit with increasing competition from the piano in the twentieth century. Performance came to be dominated by women. In this role it persisted well into the post-war period, until it was displaced by the

---

30 Ibid., 464.
31 Yoshihiro Kurata, *Geinō no bunmei kaika: Meiji kokka to geinō kindaika* (Tokyo: Heibonsha, 1999), 260–88.

piano in the 1970s.³² The repertoire of *koto* music (*sōkyoku*) was developed and extended further through new compositions (*shinkyoku*).³³ From the late 1880s, the Ikuta style of playing spread from the Kansai region, where it originated, to other parts of the country.³⁴ One characteristic of the school was the performance of *jiuta* (originally a term describing *shamisen* music in the Kyoto style), usually in an ensemble with *koto*, *sangen* (as the *shamisen* was referred to in such an ensemble), and *kokyū* or *shakuhachi*.

The *shamisen*, played in a variety of vocal genres as well as in instrumental music such as *jiuta*, continued to be popular, although its strong association with the pleasure quarters gave it a dubious reputation. Several vocal genres experienced something of a heyday in the Meiji period, both spoken storytelling (such as *rakugo*) and singing or chanting accompanied by a musical instrument. *Naniwabushi*, sung ballads accompanied by the *shamisen* and performed by street performers in Tokugawa Japan, became one of the most popular genres of the Meiji period. It moved from the streets into the variety theatre (*yose*), where it was performed along with other narrative genres. In the twentieth century, recordings and radio broadcasts helped maintain and increase the popularity of these vocal genres.³⁵

Music performed on the *biwa* consisted of several styles, each with its own tradition and played on a slightly different instrument. *Heikebiwa* performance, formerly a monopoly of the blind, suffered a temporary decline after the abolition of that monopoly in 1871. Meanwhile *satsumabiwa* and *chikuzenbiwa*, both originating in Kyushu, represent good examples of a style of musical performance that was originally a local speciality developing into genres enjoyed nationwide.³⁶ *Chikuzenbiwa* was a newly developed, eclectic style, while *satsumabiwa*

---

32 Thomas R. H. Havens, *Artist and Patron in Postwar Japan: Dance, Music, Theater and the Visual Arts, 1955-1980* (Princeton, NJ: Princeton University Press, 1982), 188, 190.
33 Philip Flavin, 'Meiji shinkyoku: The Beginnings of Modern Music for the Koto,' *Japan Review: Journal of the International Research Center for Japanese Studies*, no. 22 (2010), https://nichibun.repo.nii.ac.jp/record/211/files/JN2204.pdf .
34 Tsukahara, 'Nihon ongaku no kindai', 464.
35 Tsukahara, 'Nihon ongaku no kindai', 466. See also Malm, *Traditional Japanese Music*, 218–19.
36 Tsukahara, 'Nihon ongaku no kindai', 465. Hugh de Ferranti, 'Taming the Reciting Voice: *Satsumabiwa* Text-scores and their Roles in Transmission and Performance', *Context: Journal of Music Research* 31 (2006): 138–39.

had a history of several centuries. After the Meiji Restoration, *biwa* players from Satsuma domain (present-day Kagoshima prefecture) moved to the capital at the same time as the new political leaders from the region. Yoshimizu Tsunekazu (Kin'ō, 1844–1910), who moved from Kagoshima to Tokyo in the late 1870s, was particularly successful; he toured regional cities, including Sendai, and founded his own school, attracting many students.[37] Associated with the samurai class in Satsuma domain (Yoshimizu was sent to Tokyo as a student from the domain school[38]), in the capital *satsumabiwa* initially became popular with the social elite, but from around the turn of the century it was taken up by commoners and enjoyed as an amateur pursuit. Numerous collections of *biwa* songs were published, many of them new compositions, narrating events from the recent wars.[39] From the beginning of the twentieth century Yoshimizu began to call the style of playing he taught *teikoku biwa* ('imperial' *biwa*), an indication that he saw his art as a national one rather than a local speciality;[40] the *satsumabiwa* had first attracted attention in Tokyo after Yoshimizu had performed for the emperor in May 1882.

New practices helped bring the different musical worlds together and thus contributed to the formation of 'Japanese music' as a concept. Public concerts, a modern institution, often featured performances of both Western and different genres of Japanese music. In April 1893 the Association for Native Japanese Music (Kokufū Ongaku Kai), whose goal was to 'promote the characteristic music of this country (*honpō tokuyū no ongaku*)', held a concert. Organized by Takano Shigeru (1847-1929), a *koto* teacher of the Ikuta school, it reportedly brought together musicians of different genres and from different parts of the country.[41] Takano, moreover, intended to open a school for the study of all music (*ongyoku*), whether refined or common, and regardless of school (*ryūha*), as well as create a truly Japanese music (*kokufū ongaku*) that could be performed abroad without shame. People with disabilities

---

37 Kakushō Kitagawa, *Biwa Seisuiki: Shirazaru biwa no konjaku monogatari* (Osaka: Fūeisha, 2016).
38 Shōzō Koshiyama, *Satsumabiwa* (Tokyo: Perikansha, 1983), 266.
39 See Tadashi Shimazu, *Meiji Satsumabiwa uta* (Tokyo: Perikansha, 2001).
40 Koshiyama, *Satsumabiwa*, 269. *Teikoku* here, presumably, in the sense of related to the emperor.
41 *Ongaku zasshi* 32 (1893), 20. A concert by a group of the same name was reported in *Ongaku zasshi* 13 (1891), stating that the rival Yamada and Ikuta schools were organizing it together.

would be taught for free.⁴² The following month, two more concerts were held on consecutive days, each ending with an outline of the new school's aims.⁴³ By September 1893 an auditorium for the school was being constructed opposite the Peers' School for Girls, thanks to the initiative of individuals who cared for the preservation of the country's music (*kokugaku hozon*).⁴⁴ Whether 'preservation' was the association's main aim is not entirely clear, given that performances at the meeting in June 1894 featured both new works in the traditional idiom (*kokufū shinka*) and 'reformed' works (*kairyō shinka*), as well as including the well-known piece *Rokudan* played by an ensemble of *koto*, violin, and clarinet.⁴⁵

Indigenous musical culture was thus affected at least as much by economic and social changes as by the introduction of Western music, and innovation and modernization within traditional genres were not always a direct effect of Westernization.⁴⁶ Ultimately, however, the Meiji government's wholesale embrace of Western music undeniably had a far-reaching and lasting impact on musical culture. It changed the soundscape, the way music was thought about, and even the people's musical sensibilities, within a few decades. No indigenous genre could remain unaffected by the introduction of Western music, even if direct influence was limited.

The Meiji Reforms and the Introduction of Western Music

Music was an essential part of the Meiji reform package. The main channels for the official introduction of Western music by the Meiji government were the military and the public education system.

---

42 *Ongaku zasshi* 32 (1893), 21.
43 *Ongaku zasshi* 33 (1893), 23–24.
44 *Ongaku zasshi* 36 (1893), 36; a note on the same page states that eleven members of the Kokufū Ongaku Kai had been invited to perform at a concert in Sendai.
45 'Kokufū ongaku reikai', *Ongaku zasshi* 45 (25 June 1894). This is the last report on the Kokufū Ongaku Kai's activities. Whether it ceased to be active, or whether the journal's editor, Shikama Totsuji, who played the clarinet in the concert, ceased to be involved is not clear.
46 Information about how the different genres of Japanese music fared can also be gleaned by examining existing registers of active musicians: see Tsukahara, 'Nihon ongaku no kindai', 466–67.

Christian missionaries played an important role in private education.[47] Military bands formed an integral part of a modern army and navy and represented the nation state in both to the outside world, in diplomatic ceremonies, and to its citizens. The introduction of military music began already in the 1850s, following Commodore Perry's arrival in Japan in 1853, when the shoguns and several lords created what are usually described as drum and fife bands. Initially, these bands may not have been perceived as musical ensembles at all, but merely as a tool for military drill.[48]

In 1871 the national army and navy were established by dissolving the armies of the domains and forming a core out of the troops from the domains loyal to the new government (conscription was introduced in 1873). From April 1872, the army and the navy were under the jurisdiction of two separate ministries, each with their own military bands. The army employed French instructors: from 1871 to 1883 Gustave Charles Dagron (1845–88?), and from 1884 to 1889 Charles Leroux (1851–1926). The navy employed the British bandmaster John William Fenton (1828–90), previously employed by the Ministry for Military Affairs.[49] When he left Japan in 1877, he was succeeded in 1879 by the German military musician Franz Eckert (1852–1916). Eckert probably contributed more to the development of Western music in the early years than any other foreign musician. During his twenty years in Japan he taught not only the musicians of the navy (from 1879 to 1889 and 1895 to 1899), but also of the army (from 1890 to 1894) and the musicians in the *gagaku* department, where he held official appointments from 1887 to 1899, having first taught some of the musicians privately. Between 1883 and 1886 he also taught for the Music Investigation Committee (Ongaku Torishirabe Gakari; predecessor of the Tokyo Academy of Music) established in 1879. Besides teaching, he harmonized and arranged

---

47   For comprehensive treatments of the introduction of Western music, see Nakamura, *Kindai Nihon yōgaku josetsu*; Tsukahara, *Seiyō ongaku no juyō*. No treatment in English is similarly comprehensive. See Galliano, *Yōgaku*; Wade, *Music in Japan*, 7–19; Herd, 'Western-influenced "classical" music in Japan'. On the beginnings of singing education: Ury Eppstein, *The Beginnings of Western Music in Meiji Era Japan* (New York: Edwin Mellen, 1994). On the violin and its role in the process, Mehl, *Not by Love Alone*.

48   Yasuto Okunaka, *Kokka to ongaku: Isawa Shūji ga mezashita Nihon kindaika* (Tokyo: Shunjūsha, 2008), 11, 32.

49   Details about Fenton in Nakamura, *Kindai Nihon yōgaku josetsu*, 293–312.

numerous pieces of music, most famously the national anthem *Kimi ga yo*. Eckert left Japan in 1899. He briefly returned to Germany before moving to Korea in 1901.[50]

By the time Eckert began to teach the court musicians, they had already begun to study Western music, having secured official permission as well as practical support from the Navy Ministry. In 1875, about half of the court musicians, thirty-five men, were receiving instruction, and the following year Fenton was employed by both the navy and the Department of Court Ceremonies, while two court musicians were appointed conductors. The court musicians gave their first performance of Western music on 3 November 1876, at the celebrations for the emperor's birthday. In 1879, four of them applied for permission to learn the piano from Clara Matsuno (née Zitelmann, 1853–1941), who taught at the kindergarten department of the government-run Tokyo Normal School for Women (Tōkyō Joshi Shihan Gakkō Fuzoku Yōchien). She was an accomplished pianist. Members of the *gagaku* department were thus among the first civilians to be trained in Western music, and some soon began to teach it themselves.

Both *gagaku* and military musicians actively disseminated Western music among the wider population. The *gagaku* department established the Society for Western Music (Yōgaku Kyōkai) in November 1879, renamed the Society for Music (Ongaku Kyōkai) in 1882: it gave regular performances of Western music. The court musicians played on an increasing variety of occasions and did much to bring Western music to an audience beyond the confines of the imperial court. Military musicians who left the army and navy in the late 1880s likewise contributed to the dissemination of Western music among the wider population by teaching or establishing their own bands.[51] By that time the number of functions that called for Western music, including balls, had risen sufficiently to provide opportunities for civilian bands. In 1883 the Rokumeikan (Deer Cry Pavilion) was opened, an impressive

---

50   Hio-Jin Kim, *Koreanische und westliche Musikerausbildung: Historische Rekonstruktion - Vergleich - Perspektiven -* (Marburg: Tectum, 2000), 118–20; Hermann Gottschewski and Kyungboon Lee, 'Franz Eckert und ‚seine' Nationalhymnen. Eine Einführung', *OAG Notizen*, no. 12 (2013), http://www.oag.jp/images/publications/oag_notizen/Feature_II_-_Kimigayo.pdf

51   Seitarō Ōmori, *Nihon no yōgaku*, 2 vols., vol. 1 (Tokyo: Shinmon Shuppansha, 1986), 56–64.

building designed by the Englishman Josiah Conder. Its purpose was to provide a space where Japanese political leaders and their wives could mingle with foreign dignitaries and demonstrate that Japan was well on the way to measuring up to Western standards of civilization. Social events included concerts of Western music and grand balls with bands providing the music.[52]

Most important of all for disseminating Western music was the education system, but music education in schools was slow to develop. Nominally it started with the Education Law (*Gakusei*) of 1872, which stipulated universal compulsory schooling and laid the foundations for a centralized modern education system and named music among the subjects to be taught.[53] Until the 1880s, however, lessons in singing and sometimes playing the organ or violin were largely limited to missionary schools, since the government lacked the necessary resources. Mission schools played a particularly significant role in education for girls, which the Meiji government neglected in the early years. Even when music was not an independent subject in the curriculum, pupils were taught to sing hymns. At the first of these schools, the private academy of James Hepburn in Yokohama, and the Ferris Seminary established as part of Hepburn's school in 1870, hymns were taught from its establishment, while music was formally introduced into the curriculum only in 1887.[54] The influence of Protestant hymns was particularly significant, because many of them were translated and published in song collections from 1874 onwards. Some, such as *Joy to the World*, became regular hits.[55]

The systematic introduction of Western music into the public education system began with the establishment of the Music Investigation Committee[56] in 1879. The Committee, headed by Isawa

---

52 On the balls at the Rokumeikan: Margaret Mehl, 'Dancing at the Rokumeikan - A New Role for Women?', in *Japanese Women: Emerging from Subservience, 1886–1945*, ed. Gordon Daniels and Hiroko Tomida (Folkestone, Kent: Global Oriental, 2005).

53 More precisely, the law named *shōka* (Western-style songs taught in schools) for primary schools and *sōgaku* (performing instrumental music) for lower secondary schools. See Nakamura, *Kindai Nihon yōgaku josetsu*, 523. The following summary is based on Nakamura, *Kindai Nihon yōgaku josetsu*.

54 Ibid., 725.

55 Japanese: Morobito kozorite mukaematsure; Nakamura, *Kindai Nihon yōgaku josetsu*, 732.

56 Renamed Ongaku Torishirabe Sho (Institute of Music Investigation) from February to December 1885.

Shūji (1851–1917), had two main tasks: research into Japanese and Western music with the aim of creating a national music (*kokugaku*), and the implementation of music teaching in schools by producing suitable teaching materials and training teachers. From March 1880, Luther Whiting Mason was appointed as advisor and teacher.[57] Teacher training at the Music Institute began in 1880 and the first song book for use in schools was published in 1881. Of the first twenty-two students, which included several court musicians and thirteen women, only three completed the entire course and graduated in 1885. The court musicians, with their previous experience in Western music, were soon promoted to assistant teachers. In order to disseminate singing in schools as rapidly as possible, students from teacher training schools in several prefectures were enrolled for short courses in 1883 and 1884. When they graduated, they returned to the prefectures that had sent them and several became local pioneers in the dissemination of Western music.

Mason was dismissed in 1882 and was succeeded by Franz Eckert and Guillaume Sauvlet (1843–after 1898; in Japan 1885–89), both of whom had other commitments and taught part-time. Sauvlet earned his living as a travelling performer, conductor, and teacher, and first came to Japan in 1885 as a conductor and pianist for the British Mascotte Opera Company.[58] The appointment of Rudolf Dittrich (1861–1919) as artistic director and the upgrading of the Music Investigation Committee to the Tokyo Academy of Music (Tōkyō Ongaku Gakkō) represent the first indication that the government's ambitions extended beyond teacher training and towards a conservatoire, rivalling those that were founded in Europe and the United States in the course of the nineteenth century for training composers and performers—that is, artists as well as pedagogues.[59] Unlike his predecessors, Dittrich was an outstanding, conservatoire-trained professional, having trained at the Vienna Conservatoire. During his time at the Tokyo Academy of Music, from 1888 to 1894, he not only taught, but performed in fifty

---

57 For the following see especially Nakamura, *Kindai Nihon yōgaku josetsu*, 511–630; Eppstein, *Beginnings*.

58 Rihei Nakamura, *Yōgaku dōnyūsha no kiseki: Nihon kindai Yōgakushi josetsu* (Tokyo: Tōsui Shobō, 1993), 643–88.

59 'Academy' is used here rather than 'School' because this was the English translation used in the Meiji period. Between 1893 and 1899 it lost its independence again and became a department of the Higher Normal School (Kōtō Shihan Gakkō).

concerts, including solo performances and chamber music with pupils, colleagues, and foreign amateurs, and conducted choral concerts.

A few months after Dittrich's arrival, the school was reorganized into a preparatory department and a core department; the latter included a two-year teacher training course and a three-year specialist course. That same year, 1889, Kōda Nobu (1870–1946), one of only three students to graduate in 1885, became the first music student to be sent abroad by the Meiji government. This pioneering role fell to a woman, because music was still regarded by the former samurai families as a frivolous pastime, inappropriate for men. Consequently, women represented a substantial proportion of the student body and were even among the staff. Kōda Nobu returned to teach in 1895, having studied violin and piano in Boston and Vienna. Gradually, foreign teachers and the school's graduates, often after studying abroad, raised the standards at the Tokyo Academy of Music.

Although the Tokyo Academy of Music came to teach almost exclusively Western music, in the early years the reform of Japanese music and the creation of a national music were still on the agenda. Early concerts at the Music Research Institute and the Academy included both Japanese and Western music, although, in the course of the 1890s, concerts increasingly featured only Western music.[60]

Like Eckert, Dittrich harmonized Japanese songs, presumably in response to the expectations of their employers.[61] Dittrich published harmonizations of *shōka* (Western-style songs taught in schools) as well as Japanese songs from the collection of *koto* pieces compiled by the Music Research Committee and published by the Ministry of Education in 1888.[62] In a lecture about Japanese music given in German he expressed

---

60 Programmes of concerts under the auspices of the Music Research Committee in Tōkyō Geijutsu Daigaku Hyakunenshi Hensan Iinkai, *Tōkyō Ongaku Gakkō hen 1*, 198–228. For the presence of Japanese music (or lack thereof) at the Music Research Committee and the Academy, see Chiba, *Doremi*, 93–101.

61 Irene Suchy, 'Deutschsprachige Musiker in Japan vor 1945. Eine Fallstudie eines Kulturtransfers am Beispiel der Rezeption abendländischer Musik' (Ph.D. doctoral thesis, University of Vienna, 1992), 79–80.

62 Dittrich's compositions based on Japanese songs include Rudolf Dittrich, *Nippon Gakufu. Sechs japanische Volkslieder gesammelt und für das klavier bearbeitet* (Leipzig: Breitkopf und Härtel, 1894); Rudolf Dittrich, *Nippon Gakufu 2: Zehn japanische Volkslieder gesammelt und für das klavier bearbeitet* (Leipzig: Breitkopf und Härtel, 1894); Rudolf Dittrich, *Rakubai: Fallende Pflaumenblüten: Japanische Lieder mit Koto für*

doubts about attempting to harmonize according to Western principles the songs from another age and culture.[63] But apart from pleasing his employers, Dittrich (presumably) realized that music with an exotic flavour appealed to audiences in Europe. The title pages of German editions carried lavish illustrations in full colour and with an English as well as a German title.[64]

By the mid-Meiji period, Western music was thus well established in government institutions.[65] The army, the navy, the imperial court and the public education system each had a group of active specialists who were recruited and trained through formal channels. Equally importantly, occasions for the performance of Western music had been created as part of the process of reform: imperial tours, diplomatic events such as welcoming foreign representatives and state visitors, court ceremonies, and various new ceremonies in schools and businesses. This systematic importation by the government is one of the main reasons why Western music could take such a strong hold in Japan within a short time. Nevertheless, it took some further time for these developments to reach beyond the capital and the larger cities; the dissemination throughout the country's schools had only begun. Most people still had few opportunities to hear Western music. For example, Kate Hansen, the American missionary who began to teach music in Sendai in 1907, observed that the provincial town had a less developed Western music scene than Tokyo, and that the smaller towns and villages she toured were even more backward in this respect (see Chapter 10).

Dedicated concert halls, like that of the Academy, were rare, even in the larger cities. Concerts took place in school auditoriums and other multi-purpose halls, theatres, and restaurants. They tended to offer mixed fare, sometimes including other kinds of entertainment. Bands parading in the streets or performing in public parks were a common feature in the cities. Their repertoire included arrangements of popular Japanese tunes (including *nagauta* and other vocal genres with *shamisen*, or well-known songs).

Klavier bearbeitet (Leipzig: Breitkopf und Härtel, 1894). For an analysis of Dittrich's compositions, see Suchy, 'Deutschsprachige Musiker', 107–23.
63   Dittrich, 'Beiträge zur Kenntnis der japanischen Musik', 390.
64   See, for example, *Rakubai*, in the collection of the International Research Center for Japanese Studies https://kutsukake.nichibun.ac.jp/obunsiryo/book/005696489/
65   The process is particularly well outlined in Tsukahara, *Seiyō ongaku no juyō*.

Informal channels played a significant role in the dissemination of Western music, although evidence of amateur music-making in private homes is limited and often anecdotal. The German engineer Gottfried Wagener, a keen violinist, reportedly gave private lessons in Tokyo.[66] Christian missionaries and other foreign teachers, many of them amateur musicians, associated informally with the Japanese around them, offering opportunities for music-making at social gatherings. An example is the family of Clara Whitney, who came to Japan in 1875. Clara mentions several musical events in her diary.[67] The participation of missionaries and other foreign amateurs in public concerts in Sendai is well attested (see Chapters 9 and 11). In the Kobe area, the German merchant Hans Ramsegger (1867–1933) conducted, performed, composed, and taught for several years.[68]

Associations, semi-official or private, both in and outside Tokyo, promoted Western music by staging concerts. In 1887, high-ranking aristocrats, government officials, and leading industrialists, together with members of the Imperial University and the Tokyo Academy of Music, founded the Japan Music Society (Nihon Ongaku Kai).[69] Its president was Marquis Nabeshima Naohiro (1846–1921); Isawa Shūji acted as vice-president. Their aim was to disseminate Western music by sponsoring regular concerts. The foreign music teachers, including Eckert and Sauvlet, participated as a matter of course and took part in the concerts organized by the society. Sixteen concerts were held between the society's establishment and 1894; the society disbanded in 1897 and was replaced in 1898 by the Meiji Music Society (Meiji Ongaku Kai), which had similar aims and organized fifty-four concerts in Tokyo and in the Kansai area between 1898 and 1910. The Tokyo Municipal Music Society (Tōkyō Shichū Ongaku Kai) was founded in 1886 by a former navy band member as a joint stock company with financial support from Shibusawa Eiichi (1840–1931), a prominent businessman. Its band recruited twenty young men, bought musical instruments, and hired an Italian director. As the first commercial ensemble for Western

---

66 Kurt Meissner, *Deutsche in Japan* (Tokyo: OAG, 1961), 47, 57.
67 Clara Whitney, *Clara's Diary: An American Girl in Meiji Japan* (Tokyo: Kodansha International, 1981), 173–74, 223–24.
68 Suchy, 'Deutschsprachige Musiker', 149–63, 229.
69 Hiroko Fujimoto, 'Meiji 20 nendai no Tōkyō Ongaku Gakkō to Nihon Ongaku Kai', *Ochamomizu ongaku ronshū*, no. 8 (2006).

music, the band played at private functions and public ceremonies; it even managed to secure a regular engagement at the weekly ball at Yokohama Grand Hotel. The band did much to introduce Western light music to the public.[70]

Youth bands began to proliferate and contributed to musical training, as well as increasing opportunities to hear music. One of the first was founded in Tokyo in 1895 by Shikama Totsuji (see Chapter 7). A few years later, the major department stores began to establish and employ their own youth bands. Led by former members of the navy, the bands recruited and trained young people, who had to commit themselves for a fixed number of years. The Mitsukoshi store recruited twelve youths between the ages of eleven and fifteen in 1909. They were not expected to have previous experience with instruments or written music. Rehearsing after school, they gave their first performance after two months. Membership lasted four years, after which several members turned professional. The Osaka Mitsukoshi Band followed in 1914. In 1911, the Itō clothing store in Nagoya (predecessor of the Matsuzakaya department store) recruited twenty young musicians for a band. In 1914 it performed together with the Mitsukoshi band in Ueno Park; at this time string players were added, several of whom later became professionals.[71] The Mitsukoshi Band ceased performing in May 1925, but new youth bands formed in the 1920s. Many of the young men trained in these bands became members of the first professional symphony orchestras founded in the 1920s.

The Expansion of the Musical Infrastructure

In the early twentieth century, opportunities for professional training increased with the opening of several new schools. The Tokyo Academy of Music remained the most important institution of professional music education, but from the turn of the century, private music colleges were founded. One of the first was the Music College of the East (Tōyō Ongaku Gakkō), founded in 1907 by Suzuki Yonejirō, an early graduate of the

---

70 Ōmori, *Nihon no yōgaku*, 1, 56–57; Nihon Fūzokushi Gakkai, ed., *Shiryō de kataru Meiji no Tōkyō hyakuwa* (Tokyo: Tsukubanesha, 1996), 256–59.
71 Zenzō Matsumoto, *Teikin yūjō: Nihon no vaiorin ongaku shi* (Tokyo: Ressun no Tomosha, 1995), 100, 120, 202.

Tokyo Academy of Music. Suzuki's connections with the business world enabled him to help his graduates find employment as performers. The expansion of higher education in general in the 1920s included several music colleges.[72]

Magazines did much to spread knowledge of music beyond the major cities.[73] The earliest articles about music appeared in general scholarly and literary journals. The first magazine devoted to music, *Ongaku zasshi* (The musical magazine), began publication in September 1890. It ceased publication in 1897 and a series of short-lived publications followed until the appearance of *Ongakukai* (Music world). Published from 1908 to 1923, it attained the largest readership of all the music magazines. The Tokyo Academy of Music's alumni association began publishing a magazine named *Ongaku*, perhaps the most scholarly of the magazines, in 1910. From 1907 to 1916 the musical instruments division of the Jūjiya store in Kyoto published *Ongaku sekai* (The world of music; Latin subtitle *Mundus Musicae*). Yamano Gakki, a company based in Tokyo, published *Gekkan gakufu* (Monthly scores) from 1912 to 1941. As the title suggests, the magazine included music scores, as did some of the other magazines.

From the 1890s, sheet music of Japanese music began to be published, much of it for the increasing number of people attempting to play the accordion, violin, or (if they could afford it) the reed organ. While earlier sheet music collections of Japanese genres were motivated by the idea of reforming Japanese music, the newer publications catered to the fashion for playing Japanese tunes on Western instruments. This fashion persisted well into the twentieth century, and led to increased familiarity with the sounds of Western music as well as with the repertoire of Japanese music (see Chapter 8). Domestic publication of foreign music began in 1915, when Koyo Senow (1891–1961) founded his music publishing company Senow Gakufu.[74]

Western musical instruments, like sheet music, initially had to be imported until they could be produced in Japan. Of particular

---

72 On Suzuki, see Midori Takeishi, *Ongaku kyōiku no ishizue: Suzuki Yonejirō to Tōyō Ongaku Gakkō* (Tokyo: Shunjusha, 2007).

73 For the following see Setsuko Mori, 'A Historical Survey of Music Periodicals in Japan: 1881–1920', *Fontis Artis Musicae* 36, no. 1 (1989).

74 Mai Koshikakezawa, 'Senoo gakufu kara miru Taishō jidai no yōgaku juyō', *Tōkyō Geijutsu Daigaku Ongaku Gakubu kiyō* 41 (2015).

importance were the production and sale of instruments used in music education. Already in the 1880s, Suzuki Masakichi and Yamaha Torakusu, the founders of companies that still exist today, began by producing violins and reed organs (and, later, pianos) respectively for the new domestic market created by music education in schools. Just before the First World War, Yamaha's company, Nihon Gakki, began to produce harmonicas, until then almost exclusively the domain of German manufacturers such as Hohner. When Germany went to war in 1914, Yamaha and Suzuki took over German markets in Europe and America. While this first success was short-lived, it anticipated the post-1945 export boom in mass-produced Japanese instruments, particularly keyboards. A single instrument newly invented by a Japanese also gained a measure of popularity outside Japan: the *taishōgoto*, a type of *koto* with keys resembling those of a typewriter, invented in Nagoya by Morita Gorō in 1912, is still played in a few parts of Indonesia and India, where it has been adapted to local musical culture.[75]

By the early twentieth century, opportunities for listening to and practising Western music were increasing throughout the country. Japanese children growing up from the late 1880s onwards received some measure of singing education in schools. *Shōka* were increasingly composed by Japanese. The Meiji wars against China in 1894–95 and Russia in 1904–05 created a surge in patriotic feelings, which found their expression in military songs with rousing rhythms (*gunka*). Numerous collections of different types of *shōka* were published by private individuals, including themed songs such as the popular 'railway songs' (*tetsudō shōka*). They celebrated the railway, that powerful symbol of modern times, and, by describing landmarks along the main lines, they presented geography and history lessons as well as entertainment. Besides military bands, civic bands could be heard in public spaces. Particularly in cities, public concerts offered a greater range of music. For those who progressed beyond elementary education, girls' schools often provided instrumental teaching (violin and organ or piano),

---

75 Takako Tanaka, Akiko Odaka, and Hideharu Umeda, 'Taishōgoto no denpan to hen'yō: Taiwan, Indoneshia oyobi Indo no jirei', *Kyōto Kyōiku Daigaku kiyō* 120 (2012); Hideharu Umeda, 'Bari shima nishi bu Pupuan mura ni denshō sareru taishōgoto o kigen to suru gakki mandorin', *Shizuoka Bunka Geijutsu Daigaku kenkyū kiyō* 19 (2018), https://suac.repo.nii.ac.jp/records/1551

while at boys' schools extracurricular activities included Western music. Meanwhile, traditional Japanese music still represented a major element in the musical soundscape and was preferred at least by the older generations.[76]

Several trends are discernible around this time that continued well into the twentieth century: the accelerating dissemination of different genres of Western music, including European art music; the continued quest for a national music; and the construction of traditional Japanese music as a cultural asset to be preserved. One indication of the latter was the establishment in 1907 of the Committee for Research into Traditional Japanese Music (Hōgaku Kenkyū Kakari) at the Tokyo Academy of Music. The term *hōgaku* for (traditional) Japanese music came into common use from around this time. At the leading national institution, almost exclusively devoted to the cultivation of European art music, Japanese music now became an object of research and preservation. The measure was in part a response to a petition submitted by the *heikebiwa* player Tateyama Zennōshin (1845–1916), calling for the preservation of Japan's traditional music. Tateyama subsequently became a member of the committee. Preservation took the form of creating scores in staff notation and recordings. Regular concerts of traditional music were held, which from 1913 onwards were open to the public. The work continued until the early 1940s.[77]

Nor was the Committee the only project related to traditional Japanese music. In 1903 Tanaka Shōhei (1862–1945) established a private research institute for Japanese music in his home. Four years earlier, he had returned from fifteen years of research in Germany, where he studied with Helmut Helmholtz and made a name for himself as the inventor of the enharmonium, a harmonium-like instrument that divided the octave into twenty-two pitches and had a transposing mechanism, making it possible to play with just intonation. Tanaka had learnt the violin while studying physics at Tokyo University, but although he perceived European music to be superior, he asserted

---

76 For the successive generations' exposure to Western music, see Yūko Tamagawa, 'Kindai Nihon ni okeru katei ongaku ron: "ikka danraku" no mikan no yume', *Tōhō Gakuen Daigaku kenkyū kiyō* 43 (2017): 69–70.

77 Details about the committee and its work in Tōkyō Geijutsu Daigaku Hyakunenshi Hensan Iinkai, ed., *Tōkyō Geijutsu Daigaku hyakunenshi: Tōkyō Ongaku Gakkō hen 2* (Tokyo: Ongaku no Tomosha, 2003), 553–748.

that he did not feel moved by it as he did by Japanese music.[78] He also founded the Bion Kai (Association for Beautiful Sound), in order to promote traditional Japanese music. The association organized public concerts with leading artists of different genres. Like the committee at the Tokyo Academy of Music, where Tanaka was at times engaged as an advisor, work at his institute included creating scores of Japanese pieces in staff notation.[79] Tanaka's object was not just preservation: he advocated reforming Japanese music with reference to Western music, as had Isawa Shūji, only in 'a more nuanced and sophisticated' version.[80] Among those who regularly worked with Tanaka was a young physics graduate, Tanabe Hisao (1883–1984), the future founder of Japanese ethnomusicology, who in 1910 and 1911 also worked for the Academy's research committee.[81]

New forms of Western-style musical entertainment emerged in the cities. One of them was musical theatre. Japan's first attempt to establish a permanent repertoire company for opera, at the Imperial Theatre (which, despite its name, was a private venture), failed. The director employed for the purpose in 1912, G.V. Rossi, was dismissed in 1916 and left Japan in 1918 after a failed attempt to establish his own company. But the singers trained by Rossi enjoyed successful careers, most famously Fujiwara Yoshie (1898–76), who even enjoyed success abroad. Having studied in Italy, he performed in several European countries as well as America between 1920 and 1934. In Japan, he became a star of the 'Asakusa Opera'. Named after Tokyo's major entertainment district, Asakusa Opera mixed all kinds of musical performance, from opera proper to light musical theatre and chorus line revues. It flourished from the late 1910s and reached a wide audience. The Great Kantō Earthquake in 1923 completely destroyed the Asakusa district, however, and Asakusa Opera never really recovered. Musicians and other performers

---

78 Jonathan Service, 'Harmony outside the Iron Cage: Tanaka Shōhei's Strategic Deconstruction of the Music-Theoretical Edifice', *History of Humanities* 2, no. 2 (2017): 378, 382, https://doi.org/10.1086/693320

79 Memo by Tateyama recommending Tanaka, 15 April 1910, Tōkyō Geijutsu Daigaku Hyakunenshi Hensan Iinkai, *Tōkyō Ongaku Gakkō hen 2*, 564–66. See Hisao Tanabe, *Meiji ongaku monogatari* (Tokyo: Seiabō, 1965), 279–85. See also Service, 'Harmony outside the Iron Cage'.

80 Service, 'Harmony outside the Iron Cage', 385.

81 See Chapter 1; Hosokawa, 'In Search of the Sound of Empire'; Suzuki, '"Kagaku" to shite no Nihon ongaku kenkyū'.

in general had to seek work outside Tokyo at least temporarily, which benefited musical culture in other parts of the country.[82]

Meanwhile, another operatic venture, in the Kansai area, had lasting success, although not as the 'opera' envisaged by its founder. In 1914 the Takarazuka Girls' Opera (*Shōjo Kageki*), known in English as the Takarazuka Revue, gave its first performance. Established in a popular tourist spot at the Hankyū Railway's terminus by the railway company's president Kobayashi Ichizō (1873–1957), it was intended to offer high-quality musical theatre for the masses. True to the spirit of the times, it aimed to combine the best of Japanese and Western performance art, including kabuki and opera (Kobayashi regarded both as too elitist in their pure forms). Kobayashi favoured Western music for its sophisticated image, and for the first performance Japanese women played the violin in kimono. A few years later the Takarazuka Symphony Orchestra was formed. The theatre's programme included musicals based on Western and Japanese stage works. In 1938, Takarazuka toured Europe, North America, and China.[83]

Globalization, Sound Technology, and the Quest for a Japanese Sound

The 1920s and 1930s saw rapidly rising standards in the performance of European art music. They resulted from several developments. Increasing wealth brought a growing demand for both entertainment and cultural pursuits, among them learning to play Western instruments, buying gramophone records, and attending concerts and other events where Western music was played. International stars included Japan on their tour circuit, thanks to the enterprising spirit of Avray Strok, a Russian-Jewish businessman and musical impresario based in Shanghai, and his Japanese co-organizer Yamamoto Kyūzaburō, the manager of the Imperial Theatre in Tokyo.[84] Japanese who had developed a taste

---

82   The standard work on the history of opera in Japan is Keiji Masui, *Nihon opera shi – 1952* (Tokyo: Suiyōsha, 2003). See also Keiji Masui, *Asakusa opera monogatari: rekishi, sutā, jōen kiroku no subete* (Tokyo: Geijutsu Gendai Sha, 1990).

83   Makiko Yamanashi, *A History of the Takarazuka Revue Since 1914: Modernity, Girls' Culture, Japan Pop* (Leiden: Global Oriental, 2012).

84   Sheila Melvin and Jindong Cai, *Rhapsody in Red: How Western Classical Music Became Chinese* (New York: Algora, 2004), 18, 97; Kōichi Nomura, Kenzō Nakajima, and

for European art music thus had the chance to hear the world's leading performers. Several top-class musicians, moreover, stayed longer: European refugees, including Jews fleeing from persecution, first from Russia, then from Nazi Germany.[85]

Compared to the influx of foreign performers, Japanese musicians performing European art music abroad were a rarity, but a few nevertheless enjoyed success in Europe and America. They included the singers Fujiwara Yoshie, mentioned earlier, and Miura Tamaki, who gained fame performing in the title role of Puccini's opera *Madame Butterfly* (see Chapter 2). Others were Yamada Kōsaku (1886–1965), commonly regarded as the first Japanese composer of note, as well as one of the pioneers of the symphony orchestra, together with Konoe Hidemaro (1898–1973). Yamada gave two concerts at Carnegie Hall in New York to considerable acclaim. The first, in October 1918, consisted entirely of his own compositions, the second, in January 1919, in part. His experience abroad caused him to reflect on his ideas about a Japanese national music in a Western idiom, and in his works from 1919 he self-consciously employed Japanese elements.[86] Konoe conducted in Germany in the 1930s and, during the Second World War, in the countries occupied by Germany. He impressed his audiences not only with his own achievements, but also with his reports about Western music's triumph in Japan.[87] In 1934, the violinist, composer and conductor Kishi Kōichi (1909–37) had his works performed at a widely reviewed 'Japanese Evening' in Berlin and conducted the Berlin Philharmonic Orchestra, only the second Japanese after Konoe (in 1924 and 1933) to do so.[88] Other Japanese composers in the 1930s were taking part in festivals of the International Society for Contemporary Music (ISCM), and a number of them won prizes at international competitions.

Kiyomichi Miyoshi, *Nihon yōgaku gaishi: Nihon gakudan chōrō ni yoru taikenteki yōgaku no rekishi* (Tokyo: Rajio Gijutsusha, 1978), 148.

85   Mehl, *Not by Love Alone*, 135–59.
86   Galliano, *Yōgaku*, 36, 48.
87   Friedrich-Heinz Beyer, 'Deutsche Musik in Japan: Völkisch-nationale Musikpflege im Fernen Osten', *Zeitschrift für Musik*, no. 6 (June) (1941). For a recent account of Konoe's activities in Germany, which included forming an orchestra of displaced musicians, see Fuyuki Sugano, *Konoe Hidemaro: Bōmei ōkesutora no shinjitsu* (Tokyo: Tōkyōdō Shuppan, 2017).
88   Mehl, *Not by Love Alone*, 207–12.

Foreign artists contributed significantly to the rise of symphonic music, which until then could hardly be heard in Japan at all. When Yamada and Konoe founded the New Symphony Orchestra (Shin Kōkyō Gakudan), the predecessor of the present-day NHK Symphony Orchestra, in 1926, they relied heavily on the support of foreign musicians as conductors and concert masters. Although commonly described as Japan's first professional symphony orchestra, the New Symphony Orchestra was in fact predated by the Takarazuka Symphony Orchestra, which gave its first Concert in 1924 under the Austrian musician Josef Laska (1886–1964). Laska conducted the orchestra in 150 subscription concerts from 1926 until he left Japan in 1935.[89] The New Symphony Orchestra's affiliation with national broadcasting, introduced in 1925, nevertheless assured it a pioneering role, and the radio represented a decisive impulse for the rise of professional orchestras.

Amateur orchestras also began to form in the 1910s and 1920s. The Suwa Symphony Orchestra in Nagano Prefecture, founded in 1925, prides itself upon being Japan's oldest amateur orchestra.[90] Others formed at universities, where music societies began to flourish around the turn of the century. Among the earliest were those of Tokyo Imperial University, whose members often took part in concerts at the Tokyo Academy of Music; the private Keiō and Waseda Universities; Kyoto Imperial University, and the private Dōshisha University.[91] The orchestra at Kyushu Imperial University played its first symphonic concert in 1919.

New settings for music included Western-style hotels, cafés, dance halls, and cinemas. The large international hotels employed both Japanese and foreign ensembles to play for concerts and balls or in their cafes and restaurants. The repertoire required in these settings was not limited to art music. Globalization was bringing new kinds of music to Japan, including Latin American, Tango and Hawaiian, and, most notably, jazz.[92] Jazz became popular in Asian port towns, starting with

---

89 For a brief overview of the early symphony orchestras, see Mehl, *Not by Love Alone*, 149–59. For the Takarazuka Symphony Orchestra, see Suchy, 'Deutschsprachige Musiker', 167–84.
90 'Rōhō no amachua ōkesutora Suwa kōkyōgakudan sōritsu 80 shūnen', *Sarasate*, no. 11 (2006).
91 Ōmori, *Nihon no yōgaku*, 1, 125–28.
92 Taylor E. Atkins, *Blue Nippon: Authenticating Jazz in Japan* (Durham, N.C.: Duke University Press, 2001).

Manila, from where several Philippine jazz bands and musicians came to Japan, and to Shanghai, which became an Asian jazz mecca, attracting many Japanese musicians. Other Japanese musicians played on the ocean liners and, while on leave in San Francisco, they had the chance to hear American jazz musicians and to buy instruments, scores, and other equipment. Jazz was also played in the dance halls, which enjoyed great popularity until government or local authorities increasingly suppressed them as morally dubious. The first public ballroom, the Kagetsuen in Yokohama, opened in March 1920. In Osaka, restaurants and cafés began adding dance halls to their businesses until police laws forbade the practice. From 1925 an increasing number of commercial dance halls opened. At the peak of the 'golden era of dance halls' in 1936 there were eight major halls in Tokyo and a total of thirty-nine halls in the rest of the country, the majority of them in the areas around Kyoto, Osaka, and Kobe. Others opened in the colonies and on the Chinese mainland.[93]

Cinemas too offered musical entertainment. As in the West, the silent films were accompanied with live music; the Japanese ones with kabuki style music, often played by small ensembles of Japanese and Western instruments that played Western-style music for the Western films. Gradually, permanent cinemas were established, and with the advent of long films from around 1914, the bigger ones employed their own orchestras, who also played during intervals. Similar ensembles played in Kobe and Ōsaka. The new 'talkies' (the first was shown in Tokyo in 1929) put the live ensembles out of business, but provided new opportunities through the creation of soundtracks. Film music, especially the theme songs of films, was also sold on records.

Sound technology was, in fact, one of the most important developments in Japan's music history from around the 1920s, when gramophone records became widely available, and radio broadcasting was introduced (in 1925). Recordings enabled listeners to experience a wide variety of musical styles, as well as European art music performed to the highest standard. Japan soon became the biggest market for recordings of Western music. In 1924 a set by Deutsche Grammophon of Beethoven's Ninth Symphony (the first complete recording of a major

---

93   Yoshikazu Nagai, *Shakō dansu to Nihonjin* (Tokyo: Shōbunsha, 1991), 39–117.

work) sold 300 subscriptions in Japan. In 1933 the set of Beethoven's piano sonatas from Victor attracted 2,000 subscriptions from Japan, the same number as the sum of all European subscriptions. The set of Toscanini's recording of Beethoven's Fifth with the NBC Orchestra released by Victor in 1939 sold 50,000 copies in Japan.[94]

Thanks to gramophone recordings, major symphonic works and difficult chamber music and solo repertoire could be heard in Japan for the first time. In the nineteenth century, intellectuals had often discussed composers such as Beethoven and Wagner without having heard their works performed in the way the composers intended.[95] Unless they had travelled abroad, they knew Beethoven from the literary work of Romain Rolland (1866–1944) rather than from his own music. His 'Kreutzer Sonata' was familiar from Tolstoy's story rather than from hearing Beethoven's composition performed. Gramophone records enabled music enthusiasts not only to hear famous works, but also, by imitating the recordings of stars such as Elman, Kreisler, and Heifetz, to play them (or at least attempt to). One violinist who did so was Suzuki Shin'ichi, whose 'Suzuki Method' to this day makes good use of model recordings.[96]

The impact of sound recording on traditional Japanese music and contemporary popular music was equally significant. Local recording companies produced gramophone records of traditional music, as well as blended styles, often played with Western instruments. Before the large international record companies (Victor, Columbia, Polydor) took over the market, many domestic companies were founded, several of them located in the Kansai region. Nittō, for example, established in Osaka in 1920, boasted an impressive list of locally recorded Western music. But the company mainly produced gramophone records of genres such as *gidayū* (a popular narrative *shamisen* genre), *kouta* (a short *shamisen* song), and *riyō* (a rustic popular song), as well as styles characteristic

---

94 Chiba, *Doremi*, 167.
95 See Toru Takenaka, 'Wagner-Boom in Meiji-Japan', *Archiv für Musikwissenschaft* 62, no. 1 (2005); Minoru Nishihara, *'Gakusei' Bêtōven no tanjō* (Tokyo: Heibonsha, 2000).
96 Toshiya Etō, *Vaiorin to tomo ni: Nani o uttatte iru ka shiritai* (Tokyo: Ongaku no Tomosha, 1999), 224–25; Shin'ichi Suzuki, *Nurtured by Love: The Classic Approach to Talent Education*, trans. Waltraud Suzuki (Miami: Suzuki Method International, Summy-Birchard Inc., 1983), 51, 97. See also Eta Harich-Schneider, 'European Musician in Japan', *XXth Century (Shanghai)* 3, no. 6 (1942): 420.

of Osaka musical culture, which were disseminated nationwide as a result. Performers were often geisha.[97] The catalogues of Nittō and other companies reflected the listening preferences of most Japanese: Western music, although increasingly popular, was far from dominant: most Japanese preferred traditional genres. Radio broadcasting likewise prioritized traditional genres, and a poll of radio listening preferences in 1925 revealed that most listeners preferred these.[98]

From the late 1920s, companies such as Nittō began to lose ground to the big international companies, and Tokyo displaced Osaka as a centre of the recording industry. Rather than disseminating existing musical culture, these companies produced and promoted hits. The new category of popular song, which came to be known as *ryūkōka* or *kayōkyoku*, was eclectic, encompassing a broad range of styles, broadly 'Western', but most often with musical characteristics that strongly appealed to Japanese sentiments.[99] Popular songs, sharply criticized by the elites, were far from the 'national music' envisaged by Isawa and others, but they did combine Western and Japanese elements in a way that appealed to the wider population.

Popular song as a product of the recording industry is a global phenomenon and so it should not surprise us that one pioneer of popular song in Japan even enjoyed a measure of success abroad: the composer

---

97   Hiroshi Watanabe, *Nihon bunka modan rapusodi* (Tokyo: Shunjūsha, 2002), 192–218. On sound recordings and narrative genres, see also Kerim Yasar, *Electrified Voices: How the Telephone, Phonograph, and Radio Shaped Modern Japan, 1868–1945* (New York: Columbia University Press, 2018), 83–113, https://www.degruyter.com/document/doi/10.7312/yasa18712/html For a brief historical overview of genres recorded in Japan, see Toru Mitsui, 'Interaction of Imported and Indigenous Music in Japan: A Historical Overview of the Music Industry', in *Whose Master's Voice: The Development of Popular Music in Thirteen Cultures*, ed. Alison J. Ewbank and Fouli T. Papageorgiu (Westport, Connecticut: Greenwood Press, 1997).

98   Chiba, *Doremi*, 37–38..

99   The terms *ryūkōka* and *kayōkyoku* are not used consistently in the literature; *ryūkōka* is the broader term. See Watanabe, *Nihon bunka modan rapusodi*, 213–14. Hiromu Nagahara, *Tokyo Boogie-Woogie: Japan's Pop Era and its Discontents* (Cambridge, MA 2017), https://doi.org/10.4159/9780674978409 For a brief discussion of terminology for contemporary Japan, see Jennifer Milioto Matsue, *Music in Contemporary Japan*, Focus on World Music Series, (New York: Routledge, 2016), 24–25; Toru Mitsui, *Popular Music in Japan: Transformation Inspired by the West* (New York: Bloomsbury Academic & Professional, 2020), https://doi.org/10.5040/9781501363894 According to Mitsui (p. 76) *kayōkyoku* was coined as an alternative to *ryūkōka*, which had connotations of vulgarity. Characteristics perceived as Japanese include the *yonanuki* scale that omits the fourth and seventh degrees, especially in its minor version.

and performer Koga Masao (1904–78). His songs mixed elements from the Meiji *shōka* songs and American dance rhythms (as well as, possibly, Korean folk songs). He toured North and South America in 1938 and 1939, and a selection of his compositions, sung in English by the Mullen sisters, was broadcast worldwide by NBC on 31 August 1939; Koga would have continued to Europe had not the outbreak of the Second World War prevented it.[100]

Japanese composers of art music such as Yamada and Kishi, who performed their own compositions in America or Europe, mainly attracted interest on the strength of their 'Japaneseness'. They were, however, expressing Japanese sentiment in a musical style perceived as Western by their audiences and which they had fully mastered. The supposedly 'Japanese elements' in their works conformed to a common musical idiom perceived as 'Oriental'.[101] Once back in Japan, Kishi joined in the ongoing debate among composers and musicians about how to achieve a specifically Japanese music that was not just an imitation of European models. Many performers and composers of traditional music likewise sought musical renewal. By the twentieth century, they could not avoid being exposed to and influenced by Western music, and many did not even wish to. They experimented with new forms and with new versions of Japanese instruments, typically larger ones with a wider range of pitch. The most famous representative of 'New Japanese Music' composed in the traditional idiom but influenced by Western music is Miyagi Michio (1894–1956). Today, his music is widely perceived as traditional, but it is a tradition transformed by the composer's encounter with Debussy and other European composers.[102]

So deeply rooted was Western music by the 1930s that increasing jingoism and government suppression could not reverse the process.

---

100 Koga Masao Ongaku Bunka Shinkō Zaidan (The Masao Koga Music and Culture Promotion Foundation), *Yume jinsei o kanadete* (Tokyo: Koga Masao Ongaku Bunka Shinkō Zaidan, 2004).

101 For an outline of Orientalism in Western music that emphasizes the creative aspects, see John M. MacKenzie, *Orientalism: History, Theory and the Arts* (Manchester: Manchester University Press, 1995), 139–75. See also Nicholas Cook, 'Western Music as World Music', in *The Cambridge History of World Music*, ed. Philip Vilas Bohlman (Cambridge: Cambridge University Press, 2013), 83–84, https://doi.org/10.1017/CHO9781139029476

102 For a treatment of the debates around 'new Japanese music' in the early twentieth century, see Watanabe, *Nihon bunka modan rapusodi*, 37–84.

The debates about a national music intensified, with several composers' associations being formed, as composers sought to free themselves from the dominance of inherited Western (especially German) traditions of composition. This was the musical version of the efforts by intellectuals to 'overcome' (Western-style) modernity in the same period, but it was simultaneously a continuation of the quest for a national music that began with the introduction of Western music by the Meiji government.[103]

Such official opposition to Western music as there was in the late 1930s and the 1940s was mainly directed against the newer forms of popular music. Some traditional genres, such as *naniwabushi*, *gidayū*, and *biwa*, benefited from government support, and musicians were mobilized for the war effort. But hostility towards Western music, as the music critic Nomura Kōichi recalled, came from members of the public rather than government officials.[104] Western classical music sometimes took the form of bombastic performances with large symphony orchestras, part of the official efforts to use music for propaganda purposes. The biggest musical spectacle during the war were the celebrations to commemorate in 1940 the 2,600th anniversary of the ascension of the first (legendary) Emperor Jimmu. In an effort to make this an international event, the government commissioned large symphonic works from several acclaimed European composers.[105] Suppression of Western music, then, was selective, and resulted from government-enforced war austerities

---

103 For an analysis of one group of composers in this period, see Lasse Lehtonen, '"March from the Age of Imitation to the Age of Creation": Musical Representations of Japan in the Work and Thought of Shinkō sakkyokuka renmei, 1930–1940' (Doctoral Dissertation University of Helsinki, 2018), https://helda.helsinki.fi/handle/10138/233760 For a brief discussion of the Japanese intellectual current described as 'overcoming modernity' in a global context, see Alain-Marc Rieu, 'The syndrome of "overcoming modernity": Learning from Japan about ultra-nationalism', *Transtext(e)s Transcultures. Journal of Global Cultural Studies* 9 (2014), https://doi.org/10.4000/transtexts.552

104 Nomura, Nakajima, and Miyoshi, *Nihon yōgaku gaishi*, 264–72.

105 Jacques Ibert from France, Ildebrando Pizzetti from Italy, Richard Strauss from Germany, Benjamin Britten from England, and Sándor Veress from Hungary. See Furukawa, Takahisa, *Kōki, Banpaku, Orinpikku: Kōshitsu burando to keizai hatten* (Tokyo: Chūō Kōronsha, 1998), 61–127; Kazushi Ishida, *Modanizumu hensōkyoku: Higashi Ajia no kindai ongakushi* (Tokyo: Sakuhokusha, 2005), 99–103. Britten's Requiem Symphony was deemed inappropriate and was not performed. For a broader treatment of the anniversary celebrations in English, see Ruoff, *Imperial Japan at its Zenith: The Wartime Celebrations of the Empire's 2,600th Anniversary*. It is symptomatic of historians' neglect of music that Ruoff hardly mentions the subject at all and does not treat the musical activities referred to here.

and the economic and social effects of the worsening military situation rather than ideology.

In sum, by the 1920s, Western music was firmly established; so were the seeds of what one author has described as the dual structure (*nijū kōzō*) of music in Japan.[106] Western and Japanese music, the latter having begun to be known as *hōgaku* in order to distinguish it from Western music (*yōgaku*), were not yet entirely separate, as they would become, but the recasting of *hōgaku* as part of Japanese culture writ large had begun.

The Postwar 'Musical Miracle' and Its Critics

After 1945, the Japanese could build on the pre-war foundations, and the narrative of music being resurrected from the ruins is similar to that perpetuated in Germany.[107] Efforts to revive culture and entertainment, including Western classical music, did indeed start almost as soon as the war was over: conservatoires reopened, orchestras performed again, new orchestras were formed, and the production of musical instruments resumed. From the 1950s, foreign artists began to tour Japan again. They performed for increasingly large audiences as prosperity increased and audience associations provided affordable tickets for their members and made it worthwhile for artists and ensembles to tour the provinces.

The post-war 'economic miracle' was accompanied by a rising presence of Japanese musicians on the global stage: from the late 1950s, Japanese musicians began to attract attention abroad. One of the first was Ozawa Seiji, who won the International Competition of Orchestra Conductors in Besançon in 1959 and the Koussevitsky Prize at the Tanglewood Music centre in Massachusetts in 1960. Embarking on an international career, he became a household name on the global stage. In what has been called the 'reverse flow',[108] Japan became an exporter of classical music in other ways. Yamaha and Suzuki had already exported musical instruments earlier in the century and especially during the

---

106 Chiba, *Doremi*, 37.
107 See Celia Applegate, *The Necessity of Music: Variations on a German Theme* (Toronto: University of Toronto Press, 2017), 301–02.
108 Mari Yoshihara, *Musicians from a Different Shore: Asians and Asian Americans in Classical Music* (Philadelphia: Temple University Press, 2007).

First World War. Once the Suzuki Method became popular abroad in the 1960s, Suzuki Violins led the supply of fractional violins. Mass-produced pianos from Japan took over foreign markets in what has been described as 'the most significant development in modern piano history'.[109] Aided by the availability of cheap instruments, the number of people in Japan learning to play Western instruments themselves also increased: the piano, previously reserved for the elites, became affordable for middle-class families and represented the chief object of middle-class aspirations.[110]

Although traditional musical genres were popular immediately after the war, as early as 1952, a Western observer remarked: 'Thus, when one speaks about music in Japan, this means only Western music; indeed, the process of assimilation has reached the extent where the younger generation virtually denies the cultivation of its country's indigenous music.'[111] This may well have been an overstatement, but the audience for traditional indigenous music did indeed shrink. Music education in schools still excluded indigenous music, and this did not change until this side of the millennium.

For most of the twentieth century, the growth of Western classical music looked like an unqualified success story. At the time of the 'Bubble' economy of the 1980s, however, Japanese observers began to express unease with the state of musical culture. Increased spending power coupled with the very high prestige accorded to Western classical music resulted in excessive commercialization, to the point where a foreign observer described Japan as 'the world's most profitable and least critical market for classical music'.[112] In fact, many Japanese felt that Japan still somehow lagged behind the West. The weaknesses of classical music in Japan, real or imagined, were the subject of many comments and discussions in the wake of the so-called Geidai or Kanda

---

109 Cyril Ehrlich, *The Piano: A History. Revised edition* (Oxford: Oxford University Press, 1990 (1976), 195.
110 Havens, *Artist and Patron*, 188, 190.
111 Margareta Wöss, quoted in Irene Suchy, 'A Nation of Mozart-Lovers: Das Phänomen abendländischer Kunstmusik in Japan', *Minikomi (Informationen des akademischen Arbeitskreises Japan)* 1994, no. 1 (1994): 4.
112 Norman Lebrecht, *The Maestro Myth: Great Conductors in Pursuit of Power* (New York: Citadel Press, 1993), 230.

Affair in 1981.[113] Together with the privileging of Western classical music over all other forms, including Japan's traditional music, this sense of inferiority and under-achievement has led critical observers to speak of a 'classical music complex'.[114] Some commentators have even claimed that this ambivalence towards a music imposed from outside and above combined with a sense of inferiority have resulted in a secret dislike of classical music.[115]

As mentioned, the increasing dominance of Western music, and indeed Western-style modernity, gave rise to criticism even before 1945. Such criticism, however, never implied an outright rejection of Western music. On the contrary, wartime debaters highlighted the ability to absorb cultural influences from abroad as a strength of Japanese culture and advocated renewing national music with inspiration from the West.[116] It was not until the post-war era that the sharp distinction between 'Japanese' and 'Western' culture, including music, was firmly established. Western music and Japanese music (*yōgaku* and *hōgaku*), at least in their classical forms, were each placed on their separate pedestal. While the trend began earlier in the twentieth century, the hardening of the boundaries between the two musical worlds is a post-war phenomenon and resulted partly from the complete rejection of anything that was perceived as part of the wartime ideology. This meant that any discussions about renewing Japanese music was associated with the ultranationalism of the war years, although (as the following chapters will show) it had in fact been on the agenda of political and intellectual leaders as well as musicians since the 1870s.

Another reason for the separation was the internalization of Western notions of authenticity that required the music of the Other to remain pure and unsullied by outside influences, a reflection of the fact that notions of cultural and national identity are inseparable from relations

---

113 The affair, also known as the 'Kanda scandal', a case of fraudulent practices in the violin trade that attracted worldwide attention, was masterminded by a Japanese instrument dealer. Tokyo University of the Arts (Geidai) was among his customers, and one of the conservatoire's professors was arrested on charges of taking bribes. See Mehl, *Not by Love Alone*, 317–29.

114 Yumi Aikawa, '*Enka' no susume* (Tokyo: Bungei Shunjū, 2002). See Chapter 1.

115 Akeo Okada, 'Europäische Klassik in Japan - eine düstere Diagnose', in *Musik in Japan*, ed. Guignard Silvain (Munich: iudicium, 1994), 188–90. The article was originally written in 1989.

116 For this and the following, see Watanabe, *Nihon bunka modan rapusodi*, 69–84.

with other cultures and nations. Many nations in the twentieth century strove to construct a non-Western musical identity based on Western musical style.[117] Japan was, arguably, a pioneer in what became a global trend. From the start, Japanese who sought to introduce Western music and to reform Japan's music were aware that they were actors on a global stage.

---

117 Cook, 'Western Music as World Music', 84.

Part Two: Music for the Nation

As shown in Part 1, the adoption of Western music and the transformation of Japanese music must be seen in the context of the globalization of Western music and the diverse local responses to this development. For the political leaders of Meiji Japan, Western music was part of the package labelled 'Western civilization' that needed to be adopted and assimilated in order to build a strong nation that could resist Western encroachment. They were hardly in a position to analyse the music's intrinsic qualities, but they observed and appreciated the functions it performed in modern nations. The idea of music as a tool of statecraft was not new to them: it features prominently in the Confucian concept of 'Rites and Music' (*reigaku* in Japanese). In music, as in other areas, traditional concepts influenced the way new ideas and practices from the West were adopted.

That music was just one part of a wider concern with unifying the nation and creating national citizens is demonstrated by the career and initiatives of Isawa Shūji (1851–1917), for whom music was only one area in need of reform. He envisaged the creation of a national music from Western and Japanese musical characteristics, but this was not an easy task. The very concept of a national music was new, as was the emerging global geopolitical order of nation states. In order to represent the nation in the world of nations, a national music has to both reflect unique national characteristics and have common currency. One might say, it must enable both the aspects of inclusion described by Deloria: 'distinctiveness and difference' as well as equality.[1] Simultaneously, it must be inclusive enough to be shared by all the citizens of the nation, who, at least in theory, are equal.

---

1   See Chapter 2. Philip J. Deloria, *Indians in Unexpected Places* (Lawrence, KS: University Press of Kansas, 2004), 235–37, https://doi.org/10.1353/book111312

Traditional Japanese music was deficient on both counts. Most Westerners found it inaccessible and abhorrent and inferior to Western music. Music in Japan, moreover, was divided into separate musical worlds and reflected divisions within pre-Meiji society. The country's elite despised the music enjoyed by the common people and saw no place for it in their vision of a modern nation, at least not in its existing form.

Government policies produced the infrastructure for the introduction of Western music and the social order that changed the conditions for the practice of traditional musical genres. The close connection between Western music and the modern institutions shaped by the Meiji government ultimately led to the dominance of Western music and to the division of functions, in which Western music represented global integration and Japanese music national distinctiveness.

Transforming the various musics of pre-Meiji Japan into 'national' music in the sense that it had the potential to include all Japanese was largely the work of non-state actors, including self-appointed reformers such as Shikama Totsuji, Kitamura Sueharu, Takaori Shūichi and others (see Chapter 7), as well as enterprising performers and teachers of traditional Japanese music such as Kōga Musen and Nakao Tozan (see Chapter 8).[1] The publication of traditional Japanese pieces from different repertoires in staff or cipher notation by Kōga, Nakao, and others made the music accessible to Japanese throughout the nation without having to depend on direct transmission through a teacher. This nationwide dissemination and increased accessibility played a decisive role in shaping the concept of 'Japanese music' (*hōgaku*). Japanese music was modernized in that its genres were freed from their previous boundaries and could (in theory) be practised by anyone, regardless of social class, gender, and geographical location, and it became the object of systematic research and standardization. Moreover, it took on a new significance by having its own part to play in the representation of the modern nation.

---

1   See Chapters 7 and 8.

4. From Rites and Music to National Music

移風易俗，莫善於樂。

For changing their [i.e., the people's] manners and altering their customs, there is nothing better than music.[1]

Let me make the songs of a nation, and I care not who shall make the laws.[2]

Japan's success as the first non-Western country to succeed in building a modern nation as a response to Western dominance and the threat of colonization has meant that its nationhood has often been taken for granted. Tokugawa Japan, however, was not a nation state, even if it had some of the attributes associated with modern nations. Within, it was a federation of domains, or 'countries'.[3] Without, it was part of the Sinosphere, or China-centred world order, in which the Chinese empire, as well as being the most powerful entity in East Asia, represented a normative reference.[4] Western encroachment not only

---

1   *Classic of Filial Piety*, quoted from Chinese Text Project: https://ctext.org/xiao-jing?searchu=%E6%A8%82
2   Matilda H. Kriege, *The Child, Its Nature and Relations: An Elucidation of Froebel's Principles of Education. A Free Rendering of the German of the Baroness Marenholtz-Bülow*. (New York: E. Steiger & Co., 1872), 92–93. The quote (the exact wording varies) is most commonly attributed to the Scottish Politician and writer Andrew Fletcher of Saltoun (1653–1716). See Gant, *Music*, 66.
3   See Luke S. Roberts, *Performing the Great Peace: Political Space and Open Secrets in Tokugawa Japan* (Honolulu: University of Hawaii Press, 2012), 8–15. The word *kuni* (country) in Tokugawa Japan could refer both to a region and to Japan as a whole.
4   Joshua A. Fogel, *Articulating the Sinosphere: Sino-Japanese Relations in Space and Time* (Cambridge MA: Harvard University Press, 2009). For China as a normative reference, see David Mervart, 'Meiji Japan's China Solution to Tokugawa Japan's China Problem', *Japan Forum* 27, no. 4 (2015), https://doi.org/10.1080/09555803.2015.1077881

resulted in geopolitical upheaval, but in a major epistemic change, in which Sinocentric universality gave way to the assumed universality of Western standards and norms.

The universality of Western civilization was generally accepted in Meiji Japan. It was understood both as a universal stage in world history and as a description of contemporary Europe and America.[5] Characterizing Western practices worthy of introduction to Japan as markers of 'civilization' and 'enlightenment' enabled Meiji leaders to 'transcend the potential opposition of 'Japanese' and 'foreign'.[6] The new concept of *bunmei* (with its opposite, 'barbarian' or *yaban*) adopted in Meiji Japan was based on a Western concept that took Western standards as given, but claimed their universality. But this did not mean that civilization was equated with Westernization. In fact, the language of civilization and enlightenment (*bunmei kaika*—with *kaika* commonly used to describe the process of civilizing) 'was used to promote ideas at every point along the ideological spectrum'.[7]

This was possible because the Sinosphere too had a concept of a civilized world and its opposite: *ka'i*. '*Ka*' stood for the civilized realm: China. In Tokugawa Japan, *ka'i* distinguished civilized subjects of the shogun from barbarians.[8] After the Meiji Restoration, the government in the name of the emperor took the place of the shogunate, while the concept itself remained. A good example is the Imperial Rescript on Historiography, which was issued on 4 April 1869 and decreed the compilation of an official history in the tradition of Chinese and ancient Japanese ruler-centred histories as a means of legitimation. The Rescript ends with the exhortation, 'Let us set right the relations between monarch and subject, distinguish clearly between the alien and the proper (*ka'i naigai*) and implant virtue throughout our land.'[9] *Naigai* literally means

---

5 Carol Gluck, 'The End of Elsewhere: Writing Modernity Now (AHR Roundtable),' *American Historical Review* 116, no. 3 (2011): 681, https://doi.org/10.1086/ahr.116.3.676
6 Mark Ravina, *To Stand with the Nations of the World: Japan's Meiji Restoration in World History* (New York: Oxford University Press, 2017), 8, 11. Ravina refers to this strategy as 'cosmopolitan chauvinism'.
7 David L. Howell, *Geographies of Identity in Nineteenth-Century Japan* (Berkeley and Los Angeles: University of California Press, 2005), 156.
8 Howell, *Geographies*, 131, 156.
9 Author's translation from the text quoted in Toshiaki Ōkubo, *Nihon kindai shigaku no seiritsu*, Ōkubo Toshiaki rekishi chosakushū 7, (Tokyo: Yoshikawa Kōbunkan,

'inside' and 'outside', thus emphasizing the spatial element of the concept, which contrasts with the linear concept of civilization as the apex of a universal ladder of progress.

The *ka'i* concept of civilization and barbarianism, with its spatial connotations, can be discerned in the expression *bunmei no iki* or *bunmei no eiiki*;[10] Shikama Totsuji, for example, uses the latter in his editorial in the inaugural issue of *Ongaku zasshi* (The musical magazine).[11] The emphasis on reforming customs in the early Meiji period, moreover, reflected the Japanese actors' understanding of the 'relationship between correct customs and an orderly realm' as a universal truth. The fact that Westerners did view some Japanese customs as uncivilized reinforced the assumption 'that outward customs lay at the very heart of the Western conception of civilization'.[12]

Music represented a marker of civilization, whether conceived as *bunmei* versus *yaban*, or as *ka'i*. In Confucian thought, music played a central role in maintaining a well-ordered and well-governed realm where civilized customs prevailed. In the *Book of Rites*, music, together with rites, laws, and punishment, is treated as an indispensable part of good government; it is associated with heaven, with harmony, joy, similarity, and unity (in contrast to rites, which are associated with distinction and separation), with the spiritual and human affections, and with order, including the regulation of physical movement.[13] Confucius is said to have loved music, played music himself and regarded it as an important part of education and, together with ceremonies or 'rites', of government. The right music could influence people for the good, while bad music had the opposite effect. The *Five Classics*, of which the *Book of Rites* is one, formed the core of the *kangaku* (Chinese learning) canon,

---

1988), 42. See Margaret Mehl, *History and the State in Nineteenth-Century Japan: The World, the Nation and the Search for a Modern Past* (Second edition with new preface) (Copenhagen: The Sound Book Press, 2017 (1998)), 1.

10 Douglas R. Howland, *Translating the West* (Honolulu: University of Hawai'i Press, 2002).
11 Totsuji Shikama, 'Hakkan no shushi', *Ongaku zasshi* 1 (1890).
12 Howell, *Geographies*, 158.
13 Ch'u Chai and Winberg Chai, eds., *Li Chi* (*Book of Rites*): *An Encyclopedia of Ancient Ceremonial Usages, Religious Creeds, and Social Institutions*, translated by James Legge, 2 vols., vol. 2 (New Hyde Park, New York: University Books, 1967). See also Walter Kaufmann, *Musical References in the Chinese Classics*, Detroit Monographs in Musicology (Detroit: Information Coordinators Inc., 1976).

and most of the actors in the Restoration and the reforms that followed were educated in the tradition of *kangaku*.

At the same time, music and its role in society was not a major preoccupation for most Confucian scholars in the Tokugawa period.[14] Among the exceptions were Ogyū Sorai (1666–1728) and his disciple Dazai Shundai (1680–1747), who advocated a renewed focus on the ancient Confucian texts, rather than the Neo-Confucian canon. Sorai developed his own interpretation of the Confucian classics. He stressed music even more than 'rites'; performing music meant learning with the body, which in turn influenced the heart. Music could transform people in a way that words and laws could not. It was Sorai's contention that the good and right music of old (*kogaku*) approved by the ancient sages was lost in China, but preserved in Japan. One of his aims, therefore, was to recover this music. Sorai regarded the popular music of his time, including *koto* and *shamisen* music, as unacceptable and a potentially pernicious influence. Shundai further elaborated on his teacher's thinking.[15]

The legacy of Confucian thought continued to be influential even after 1868. Private academies teaching Chinese learning continued to play a significant role until the 1890s or longer, and the *Five Classics* were (at least nominally) part of the curriculum.[16] Chinese learning, in particular the Sinitic written language, was, moreover, an important vehicle for mediating the adoption of Western concepts, while Confucianism continued to provide the foundations of moral education.[17] Confucian ideas about the role of music likewise continued, as is evident in the

---

14 See, for example, Demin Tao, 'Tominaga Nakamoto no Ongakukan: "Gakuritsukō" no kenkyū', in *Nihon kangaku shisōshi ronkō: Sorai, Nakamoto oyobi kindai* (Suita: Kansai Daigaku Shuppanbu, 1999).

15 Mostly based on Yasunori Kojima, 'Ogyū Sorai ichimon no ongaku shikō to sono reigaku kan', in *Reigaku bunka: Higashi Ajia no kyōyō*, ed. Yasunori Kojima (Tokyo: Perikansha, 2013). See also Tao, 'Tominaga Nakamoto no Ongakukan'.

16 Margaret Mehl, 'Chinese Learning (*kangaku*) in Meiji Japan', *History* 85 (2000), https://doi.org/10.1111/1468-229X.00137; Margaret Mehl, *Private Academies of Chinese Learning in Meiji Japan: The Decline and Transformation of the Kangaku Juku* (Copenhagen: NIAS Press, 2003). See also Margaret Mehl, 'Transmutations of the Confucian Academy in Japan: Private Academies of Chinese Learning (kangaku juku 漢学塾) in Late Tokugawa and Meiji Japan as a Reflection and Motor of Epistemic Change,', in *Confucian Academies in East Asia*, ed. Vladimír Glomb, Eun-Jeung Lee, and Martin Gehlmann (Leiden: Brill, 2020).

17 Howland likewise emphasizes the role of *kangaku* in mediating between Japan and the West: see Howland, *Translating the West*, 60.

debates about music reform. The epistemological shift occurred gradually, and it is not certain how aware Meiji intellectuals were aware of its extent. The use of Sinitic terms to translate Western concepts made it possible to obscure the epistemological distance between them, as the examples of *ongaku* and *bunmei* illustrate.

Similarly, the link perceived between music and civilization in both the Sinitic and the European world view offered sufficient common ground for Western ideas to be assimilated. While educated Japanese derived their notions from Confucian thought, Europeans saw themselves as the heirs of ancient Greek culture. In ancient Greece, [18] the natural order of the universe was conceived of in terms of musical harmony, and with Pythagoras (c. 582–497 B.C.E.) the harmony was expressed in numbers. By Plato's time (429?–347 B.C.E.), this 'scientific' view of harmony was well-established, and, in Plato's writings, conceptions of harmony influence all spheres of philosophy. In his writings about music education, he held on to the original meaning of the Greek word *mousikē* (art of the Muses) as a unity of music, language (especially poetry), and movement (dance), with rhythm as the unifying element. Plato, Aristotle (384–322 B.C.E.), and the other Greek writers on music, although they differed with respect to details, shared a belief in music's ability to influence human behaviour and in the ethical power of music. They perceived music as essential for developing character and educating good citizens who would maintain and promote the state. The musical thinking of ancient Greece (unlike the music itself, which was not transmitted) remained influential throughout European history. Christianity baptized it, as it were: the harmony of the spheres was re-imagined as the music of angels,[19] and the power of music was enlisted to reinforce the Christian message. As in ancient Greece, musical performance and virtuosity for their own sake were regarded with suspicion.

In sum, both ancient cultures shared the belief in an ordered universe and in the important role of music within it. Both developed a theoretical

---

18 Edward A. Lippman, *Musical Thought in Ancient Greece* (New York and London: Columbia University Press, 1964); Eckhard Nolte and Reinhold Weyer, eds., *Musikalische Unterweisung im Altertum: Mesopotamien - China - Griechenland*, Beiträge zur Geschichte der Musikpädagogik (Frankfurt a. M. et al.: Peter Lang, 2011).

19 Reinhold Hammerstein, *Die Musik der Engel: Untersuchungen zur Musikanschauung des Mittelalters* (Bern: Francke, 1962).

framework of music that included a concept of harmony and the idea of music having an essential role in promoting good morals and therefore having significance for good government.

The perceived universality of Western music, moreover, did not rest solely on its link with civilization but also on the belief that it was rooted in the universal principles of the natural sciences. Here too, 'universal' essentially meant 'Western'. With the scientific revolution in Europe, principles from the natural sciences came to be applied to music theory,[20] while scientific instruments originally used for research in physics were used in efforts to standardize musical practice: the metronome (rhythm), and the tuning fork (pitch).[21] In early modern Europe, the study of music was characterized as a 'desire for unity between theory and empiricism'.[22] Theory, especially theory of harmony, was perceived as universal. Musical practice, on the other hand, was acknowledged to be dependent on time and place. The historiography of music came under the influence of Darwinian ideas, and the history of music (like history in general) came to be seen as a series of stages in human development towards maturity, with Europe having reached the most advanced stage. Herbert Spencer, one of the first to apply Darwin's ideas to culture, described musical development as 'progressive integration' from the 'simple cadence [...], which in the changes of savages is monotonously repeated', and, 'among the civilized races' becomes 'a long series of different musical phrases combined into one whole'.[23] ('Changes' here, presumably refers to a sequence of pitches as in bell-ringing.)

---

20 On the history of musicology in the context of the humanities, see Rens Bod, *A New History of the Humanities: The Search for Principles and Patterns from Antiquity to the Present* (Oxford: Oxford University Press, 2015 (2013)). On science and musical modernity, see Johnson, *Out of Time: Music and the Making of Modernity*, (Oxford: Oxford University Press, 2015), 286–89, https://doi.org/10.1093/acprof:oso/9780190233273.001.0001

21 Myles W. Jackson, 'From Scientific Instruments to Musical Instruments: Tuning Fork, Metronome, and Siren', in *The Oxford Handbook of Sound Studies*, ed. Trevor Pinch and Karin Bijsterveld (Oxford University Press, 2012).

22 Bod, *New History*, 200.

23 Quoted in Bennett Zon, 'Science and Religion', in *The Oxford Handbook of Music and Intellectual Culture in the Nineteenth Century*, ed. Paul Watt, Sarah Collins, and Michael Allis (Oxford University Press, 2020), 389–90. Spencer's thinking became known in Japan even before his works were translated. For a recent assessment of his influence, see G. Clinton Godart, 'Spencerism in Japan: Boom and Bust of a Theory', in *Global Spencerism: The Communication and Appropriation of a British Evolutionist* ed. Bernard Lightman (Leiden: Brill, 2016).

4. From Rites and Music to National Music   133

Western ideas about music as a marker of civilization and of human progress meant that music was perceived as an essential ingredient of modernization and nation-building. At the same time the notion harmonized with the 'rites-and-music' perception of music as a means for civilizing the people. Kume Kunitake's report of the Embassy's first visit to a school, where they were greeted by singing, spelt out the connection:

> Through singing students praise the divine, and it brings harmony to the heart. The piano accompaniment instils rhythm and timing into their dance steps. Both boys and girls study singing, which attunes the emotions. This corresponds in meaning to the appointment of the official K'uei Tzŭ as director of music by the legendary Emperor Shun so that spirits and men would be brought into harmony.[24]

This straddling of epistemes is even more clearly evident in the first book-length history of music in Japan, published in 1888 by Konakamura Kiyonori, a leading scholar of *kokugaku* (National learning). Entitled *Kabu ongaku ryakushi* (A brief history of music and dance), the book treats the various musical genres of Japan (including performing arts, of which music is a part) under the heading *ongaku*, which in itself is remarkable, since *ongaku*, or music, as an overarching concept for the separate genres was not yet well established. Konakamura himself, when he wrote the first version of the book in 1880, used the term *ongyoku* (musical performance) rather than *ongaku*. He changed *ongyoku* to *ongaku* sometime between 1880 and 1883, while in conference with Shigeno Yasutsugu, a prominent scholar of Chinese learning.[25] Shigeno himself is credited with having written the first, albeit short, chronological history of music in Japan, treating music comprehensively, across the genres, although the word *ongaku* does not appear in the title,

---

24 Embassy's visit to the Denman School for girls in San Francisco on 23 January 1872: Kunitake Kume, *The Iwakura Embassy 1871–73: A True Account of the Ambassador Extraordinary and Plenipotentiary's Journey of Observation through the United States of America and Europe*, ed. Graham Healey and Chushichi Tsuzuki, trans. Graham Healey, Martin Colcutt, Andrew Cobbing, P. F. Kornicky, Eugene Soviak, Chushichi Tsuzuki, 5 vols., vol. 1: The United States of America (Kamiyakiri, Matsudo, Chiba: The Japan Documents, 2002), 75.

25 For details of the correspondence between Shigeno and Konakamura, see Kei Saitō, *<Ura> Nihon ongakushi: ikei no kindai* (Tokyo: Shunjūsha, 2015), 32–34. Saitō cites Konakamura's diary and his correspondence with Shigeno.

Fūzoku kabu genryū kō (Considerations about the origin of popular music and dance).[26]

Rarely used before Meiji, *ongaku* had connotations of serious, official, predominantly instrumental music. In other words, the sort of music that could be part of 'rites and music' (*reigaku*). Another connotation of *ongaku* is 'foreign', which in ancient Japan meant Chinese, and in the Tokugawa and Meiji periods increasingly meant 'Western'.[27]

That *'ongaku'* had not yet gained general currency around 1880 is also suggested by a series of articles written by Ono Shōgorō (1841–?), an early advocate of music reform (see Chapter 7). His first article was entitled 'Ongaku okusu beshi' (Music should be promoted).[28] In the article itself, he referred to music as *'gaku'* and only uses the word *'ongaku'* one more time, in the final paragraph. The three instalments of the following article are entitled 'Ongyoku no fusei wa jinmin no hinkō o midaru' (Improper musical performance corrupts the moral conduct of the people). We can assume that Ono was aware of the different connotations of *ongaku* and *ongyoku*, and that the choice was conscious.

Ongaku was the obvious word to translate the Western term 'music', despite the fact that there was a huge 'epistemological gap between the foreignness implied in the vernacular conceptualization and the humanism and abstraction in the Western one'; a gap that Meiji intellectuals were not fully aware of.[29]

Konakamura not only consulted with Shigeno, whose name appears as the first of four scholars in Konakamura's acknowledgements at the end of the book.[30] He asked him to contribute a preface, which Shigeno

---

26   The article was published in two parts in 1881 and 1883: Yasutsugu Shigeno, 'Fūzoku kabu genryū kō', in *Zōtei Shigeno hakushi shigaku ronbunshū*, ed. Toshiaki Ōkubo (Tokyo: Meicho Fukyūkai, 1989).

27   Saitō, *<Ura> Nihon ongakushi*, 31–32; Shuhei Hosokawa, 'Ongaku, Onkyō/Music, Sound', in *Working Words: New Approaches to Japanese Studies* (20 April: Center for Japanese Studies, UC Berkeley, 2012). http://escholarship.org/uc/item/9451p047

28   Shōgorō Ono, 'Ongaku okosu beshi', *Kōshū joshi* 14 (1877); Shōgorō Ono, 'Ongyoku no fusei wa jinmin no hinkō o midaru' *Kōshū joshi* 15–17 (1877). See Kanako Kitahara and Sumire Yamashita, 'Kyū Sendai hanshi Ono Shōgorō no ongakuron, "Ongyoku no fusei wa jinmin no hinkō o midaru"', *Hirosaki Daigaku kokushi kenkyū* 143 (October 2017).

29   Hosokawa, 'Ongaku, Onkyō/Music, Sound', 3.

30   Kiyonori Konakamura, *Kabu ongaku ryakushi* (Tokyo: Konakamura Kiyonori, 1888), 56. The other three named are Kurita Hiroshi (the scholar credited with completing the *Dai Nihonshi*, begun by the lord of Mito in the Tokugawa period and faithfully modelled on Chinese dynastic histories), Kosugi Sugimura (a scholar of National

duly did. The body of the book is written in Japanese, the obvious choice for a scholar of National learning. Shigeno's preface, however, is composed in Sinitic (*kanbun*), an equally obvious choice for Shigeno, a renowned *kanbun* stylist in his time, *kanbun* having for centuries served as the language of official documents and of scholarship. National learning as a school developed in the Tokugawa period in opposition to Chinese learning, and in scholarship it emphasized the study of Japanese texts as opposed to the Chinese classics. In the early Meiji period, representatives of both schools were often in conflict as they competed for influence in shaping the institutions, scholarship, and ideology of the emerging nation state.[31] Both schools, however, were part of the Sinosphere, soon to be replaced by the modern academic disciplines introduced from the West. Indeed, this transformation is represented in Konakamura's book by a second preface, in English, contributed by Basil Hall Chamberlain (1850–1935). Chamberlain had recently (in 1886) become the first professor of Japanese and philology at the Imperial University.

Both Konakamura's choice of the term *ongaku* and his request for a preface from Shigeno served to elevate the music of Japan as a whole, including popular genres, to the status of serious and refined music that was worthy of being considered the music of the nation. This interpretation is suggested by Shigeno's words in the preface. It is remarkable for the way it combines four different frames of reference: the Sinosphere, the Japanese nation, the world of nations, and, by adding the name of his home domain, Satsuma, to his signature, Shigeno invokes a sub-national entity, suggesting that he regarded it as a defining part of his identity, even as the ideology of the unified, homogenous nation was emerging. Significantly, Shigeno's own work on music emphasizes its alleged Satsuma roots.

The contents can be divided into three sections. Shigeno begins by paraphrasing the summary presented by Konakamura himself in the conclusion of his book. He then praises Konakamura, whom he refers

---

learning), and Kashiwagi Kaichirō (an antiquarian). See Margaret Mehl, 'From Classical to National Scholarship: Konakamura Kiyonori's History of Music in Japan (1888) and Its Foreign-Language Prefaces', *History of Humanities* 8, no. 1 (2023), https://doi.org/10.1086/723948

31 See Mehl, *History and the State*.

to as 'Ryōsō', a Sinitic-style pen-name,[32] for his meticulous scholarship and for including genres of music and performance that previous generations of scholars regarded with contempt. Finally, he sums up the place of music in Japan in his own time and concludes:

> The ancient music of China and Korea has long been lost over there, but exists over here. This being so, may we not reasonably call it our own music? Nowadays, we have friendly relations with many foreign countries, and the music of many countries is being disseminated widely in our country at a rate increasing day by day. We take up and practise good and beautiful music, just as we did with the ancient music of China and Korea, which was lost in its country of origin but has been preserved in Japan. In other words, in Japan alone, all the most beautiful music of the world is brought together. Japan can be described as the world's largest *gakubu*.[33] Without doubt, no one is better placed than Ryōsō to compile a work such as the present one.[34]

Shigeno's intellectual rootedness in the Sinocentric world order is evident from his reference to the music of the Tang and Han periods as representing a gold standard and his positioning of Japan as the legitimate heir of China, cultivating this music even while it has declined in its land of origin. At the same time, he praised Konakamura for including the different genres of common music (*zokugaku*) in his work. Later, researchers would adopt the German concept of the 'Volk' to describe the music of the common people, but here already that music is ennobled by being treated as a valid expression of Japanese sentiment. The significance of this view becomes clear when contrasted with the statements of leading intellectuals in defence of the Tokyo Academy of Music in 1890 (see Chapter 6). One of the most important arguments in defence of the Academy was the perceived need to reform common music, for which several commentators expressed the deepest contempt. In their calls for music reform as a vital part, and even a decisive measure of reforming customs, several of the defenders quoted from the Confucian classics. In other words, they were expressing a world view

---

32 Literary names with their Sinitic readings and references to the Chinese classics were more common among *kangaku* scholars.
33 'Music Office'; Shigeno seems to be using the term in the sense of a repository.
34 Shigeno Yasutsugu, preface to Konakamura, *Kabu ongaku ryakushi*.

that was characterized by the *reigaku* approach to music that regarded the music of the common people as an embarrassment.

Nations exist in a world of nations, and in his conclusion, Shigeno refers to the global stage of competing nations (here, as so often in Meiji Japan, referred to as *shokoku*) as a new source of knowledge and inspiration. For Shigeno, Japan's cultural borrowing from China served as a precedent for borrowing from the West. The international angle is reinforced by Chamberlain's preface. The endorsement by a foreign professor, written in the language of the most powerful Western nations, served to further elevate the music of Japan as well as reinforce the universality implicit in the abstract term as *ongaku*. Chamberlain described music as a 'universal language', although he conceded that this supposedly single language has branched out into dialects.[35] Chamberlain, unlike Shigeno, did not receive the manuscript of the book and his preface appears somewhat perfunctory,[36] but that is hardly the point.

Konakamura's book with its two foreign prefaces legitimized indigenous music, by giving it a pedigree, and cultural borrowing from the West by treating Japan's adoption of music from China as a precedent and characterizing Japan as a cultural repository where all the different musics were assimilated and preserved. The way was thus prepared for the creation of a national music that blended imported and indigenous elements.

The creation of a national music was the goal of Isawa Shūji, whose name, more than any other, is associated with the introduction of Western music in Meiji Japan.

---

35 Konakamura, *Kabu ongaku ryakushi*. Chamberlain's preface (handwritten in the 1888 edition), is followed by a Japanese translation (anonymous), where his surname is preceded by his Sinitic penname Ōdō.

36 According to Konakamura's diary, he received Chamberlain's preface a week after having asked him to write it. See Yoshiki Ōnuma, ed., *Konakamura Kiyonori nikki* (Tokyo: Kyūko Shoin, 2010), 219, 220.

5. Isawa Shūji: Music, Movement, Science, and Language

> It has even been averred that music is an [*sic*] universal language, inasmuch as it speaks straight to the heart of all men at all times and in all countries. Nevertheless, it must be admitted that the universal language has branched off into many separate dialects. Japanese music is not the least attractive of them.[1]

> The music of western nations originated in Greece. The eight sounds are elements from which all sounds spring. As the relation and value of these eight sounds are all founded on nature, the scale, pitch and all properties are precise and they are unchangeable. [...] Our country respects 'Rites and Music' [...] Yet I am afraid that they are not founded on nature [...].)[2]

Both the idea of music as a tool for moral education and of Western music being the most progressive because it was rooted in science motivated Isawa Shūji (1851–1917) to promote the introduction of music education in the nation's schools. Isawa is rightly regarded as the man who played the most important role in the introduction of Western music into the education system. His importance as an educator and shaper of educational policy, however, went far beyond music: he contributed as a politician and practitioner to state-supported national education in general, both at home and in Japan's first colony, Taiwan. Based on expertise acquired through Western books (some of which he translated himself) and through study abroad, he pioneered specialist

---

1 Chamberlain, preface to Kiyonori Konakamura, *Kabu ongaku ryakushi* (Tokyo: Konakamura Kiyonori, 1888).
2 From the memorandum and plan submitted by Megata Tanetarō and Isawa Shūji to the vice-minister of Education, Tanaka Fujimaro, 8 April 1878 (English version 20 April 1878): quoted in Ury Eppstein, *The Beginnings of Western Music in Meiji Era Japan* (New York: Edwin Mellen, 1994), 34–35.

education in several fields besides music: teacher training, physical education, education for the deaf, and speech education, namely to correct stammering.[3]

Isawa's own education resembled that of many samurai from the lower ranks in his time: early training in Chinese learning at the domain school Shintokukan in Takatō domain, military training, and studies in Western learning. While his Western learning tends to be highlighted, his traditional education was equally significant. His study of the *Four Books* and *Five Classics* of the Confucian canon, which he claimed to have mastered by the time he was twelve or thirteen,[4] may well have predisposed him to take for granted the idea that music was indispensable for creating a harmonious society and therefore played a part in good government.

Isawa became a member of the domain's drum and fife band and learnt the basics of Western-style military drumming. He must have done well, for in 1866 he was dispatched to Kiso Fukushima as an instructor. Still as a drummer, he was part of a military detachment sent to Edo in 1867. In 1868 he followed his lord to Kyoto, where he engaged in Dutch studies (*rangaku*). Returning to Tokyo in 1869, he continued to study Western learning, including the English language, and in the 1870s he entered the new government's highest institution of Western studies.[5] For Isawa, as for other samurai of his generation, early military training followed by Western studies opened the doors to social advancement in Meiji Japan. Training in music was not normally part of samurai education, and whether Isawa's experience of drumming can be counted as experience of Western music is open to question. His recent biographer, Okunaka, argues that these bands, set up by domain lords in the 1860s, constitute not so much a Westernization of musical culture as part of the modernization process, in which music served as a tool for turning the Japanese into modern citizens and creating

---

[3] Hachirō Kaminuma, *Isawa Shūji*, Jinbutsu sōsho (Tokyo: Yoshikawa Kōbunkan, 1962). For a newer biography with a focus on music, see Yasuto Okunaka, *Kokka to ongaku: Isawa Shūji ga mezashita Nihon kindaika* (Tokyo: Shunjūsha, 2008).

[4] Kaminuma, *Isawa Shūji*, 17. See also Okunaka, *Kokka to ongaku*, 89–90, 195. The information is based on Isawa's autobiography.

[5] Daigaku Nankō: Okunaka, *Kokka to ongaku*. About the *kōshinsei* system, see Benjamin Duke, *The History of Modern Japanese Education: Constructing the National School System, 1872–1890* (New Brunswick, NJ: Rutgers University Press, 2009), 52–53.

modern physical bodies (*kindaiteki na shintai*). Military drill trained the ability to move in a group while following orders. The drumbeats, accompanied by Japanese flutes, served to provide the rhythm for exercises in military drill, and were not perceived as music. The rhythms were not even recorded with staff notation, but with special symbols, another indication that the auditory signals produced for military drill were not in the same category as the military music introduced later.[6] Nevertheless, Isawa's experience of marching to the sounds produced by the drum and fife band, musical or otherwise, certainly constituted 'keeping together in time'[7] and may well have contributed to his interest in promoting 'movement games' (*Bewegungsspiele*) as part of physical education for young children, based on the kindergarten pedagogy of Friedrich Froebel.

Keeping Them Together in Time: Froebel's Movement Games

One of Isawa's foreign teachers in Tokyo was Guido Verbeck (1830–98) who played (and sometimes taught) the organ. In 1873, Verbeck lent Isawa *The Child: Its Nature and Relations* by Matilda H. Kriege.[8] *The Child* was a modified translation of a German work, published with the intention to make the kindergarten pedagogy of Friedrich Froebel accessible to the public. Isawa became one of the first Japanese to learn about Froebel's pedagogy as it was adopted and interpreted by American educators.[9]

Kriege's book would presumably have spoken directly to Isawa right from the opening paragraphs: now that society was being completely remodelled, asserted the author, education too had to change. She described Froebel as the 'new genius' who had discovered just the right way to educate children in accordance with their nature.[10] After introducing Froebel's principles of education, Kriege devoted

---

6 Details about the bands can be found in Okunaka, *Kokka to ongaku*, 3–40.
7 William McNeill, *Keeping Together in Time: Dance and Drill in Human History* (Cambridge, MA: Harvard University Press, 1997).
8 Okunaka, *Kokka to ongaku*, 96–99. Kriege, *The Child*.
9 Okunaka, *Kokka to ongaku*, 102–06.
10 Kriege, *The Child*, 15–16.

considerable space to what she called Froebel's 'mother-cosseting songs', designed to help mothers to further their child's development through 'physical play exercises'. In this context Kriege quoted (without naming a source) the statement quoted earlier (Chapter 4), attributed to 'a great man'.[11] Citing Froebel, she described songs as 'invaluable aids in moral training'.[12] Both may well have impressed Isawa. About the role of music in education more generally, Kriege wrote:

> One powerful means of awakening the ideal side of the human being, is the early cultivation of art; and the blending of art with industry in our time makes it almost a necessity for all grades and classes of society. There is hardly any branch of industry in which drawing is not required. Music is more and more cultivated by all. "The Finger Piano" is an exercise for the fingers, and accompanied by song cultivates the ear, teaches time, rhythm and lawfulness of motion. Rattles, bunches of keys, all discordant noises, ought to be given up; songs, some pleasant instrument, the sounds of nature, are best for the young child.[13]

The 'physical play exercises' presented by Krieger impressed Isawa as much as the case she made for music. In fact, even before the systematic introduction of Western music in the form of *shōka* into the education system, educators experimented with kindergarten education, including songs combined with playful movements as taught by Froebel. Froebel's intention with his *Bewegungsspiele* was to encourage and develop children's natural inclination to engage with nature and with the everyday activities they observed around them. The playful movements performed to songs might represent simple activities or imitate animals, while games involving running or walking strengthened children's bodies and furthered their physical development, and circle games trained their ability to act as part of a group and identify themselves as members of a community and, ultimately, of society.[14] While Froebel's ideas were slow to spread in nineteenth-century Germany, they were

---

11 Kriege, *The Child*, 92–93.
12 Ibid., 122.
13 Ibid., 124.
14 See Yoshiaki Katsuyama, 'Furêberu no undō yūgi ron ni kansuru ikkōsatsu: shūdan yūgi ni yoru ningen keisei ron o chūshin ni', *Nagoya Daigaku Kyōiku Gakubu kiyō* 33 (1986); Ulf Sauerbrey, 'Froebelian Pedagogy: Historical Perspectives on an Approach of Early Childhood Education in Germany', in *Guójì jiàoyù réncái péiyù zhī cèlüè yánjiū* (*Talent Development for International Education*), ed. Sophia Ming-Lee Wen (Taiwan: Tian Ming Sheu/National Academy for Educational Research, 2016).

highly influential in the United States, the first country visited by the Iwakura Embassy. Among its members was the future minister of education, Tanaka Fujimaro (1845–1909), who thoroughly researched education in the countries the embassy visited. His detailed reports after his return include descriptions of different kinds of institutions for pre-school education.[15] During his tenure as head of the Ministry of Education (1873 to 1880), the first public kindergarten in Japan was established in the Tokyo Normal School for Women (Tōkyō Joshi Shihan Gakkō), which opened in 1876. In April 1876 Tanaka travelled to the Philadelphia Centennial, where he spent several months, returning in early 1877.[16] Although pre-school education was only one of many areas of interest, Tanaka visited the model kindergarten based on Froebel's pedagogy at the exhibition and reported his observations, not least of songs (shōka) combined with gymnastics (taisō). His report included a description of a song with an accompanying game entitled 'Cuckoo'.[17]

Variously described in the English-language sources as 'musical gymnastic exercises'[18] and 'running and walking games connected with song',[19] the playful movements to the accompaniment of songs came to be known in Japan as yūgi or shōka yūgi. Yūgi was a term rarely used before Meiji. In the Edo period, it could refer to adults' amusements or to children's play, but not in the context of education. In the early 1870s, Tanaka Fujimaro used it to describe unstructured play in pre-school institutions in Europe and America. Isawa, in his report quoted below, refers to kigi. From the late 1870s yūgi was regularly used by translators

---

15 Masae Fukuhara, 'Yōchien sōsetsuki ni okeru yūgi' no dōnyū ni kansuru kenkyū: Tanaka Fujimaro no hōkoku monjo o tegakari ni', Taiikugaku kenkyū 51 (2006). For a brief summary of Tanaka's early life and his activities as a delegate, see Duke, Modern Japanese Education, 81–83.

16 For details of the visit, see Duke, Modern Japanese Education, 219–29; specifically on the kindergarten, see Fukuhara, 'Tanaka Fujimaro', 640–43.

17 Fukuhara, 'Tanaka Fujimaro', 641. The song and movements appear in Bertha Ronge and Johann Ronge, A practical guide to the English kinder-garten (children's garden): for the use of mothers, nursery governesses, and infant teachers: being an exposition of Froebel's system of infant training: accompanied by a great variety of instructive and amusing games, and industrial and gymnastic exercises, also numerous songs, set to music and arranged to the exercises (London: J. S. Hodson, 1855). The work went through several editions and was translated into Japanese.

18 Ronge and Ronge, English Kindergarten, 43. 3

19 Adolf Douai, The Kindergarten: A Manual for the Introduction of Froebel's System of Primary Education into Public Schools, and for the Use of Mothers and Private Teachers (New York: E. Steiger, 1872 (4th ed.)), 18.

for Froebel's concept of structured games as part of his educational programme.[20]

Putting the ideas into practice, however, was another matter. At the newly established kindergarten, the lack of experts trained in Western kindergarten pedagogy meant that using Japanese material was the only way forward. Teachers there included Clara Matsuno (née Zitelmann, 1853–1941), a trained kindergarten teacher, who had married a Japanese ministry official. She was the only one at the school who could play the piano. The systematic introduction of Western music had not yet begun, and the songs taught to future kindergarten teachers (from 1877) were composed by court musicians, with lyrics in a highly Sinicized style. These *gagaku* songs are an early example of indigenous musical creativity inspired by the encounter with Western music.[21]

Kindergarten education was not a government priority; the one opened in 1876 remained the only state kindergarten until 1912. By then there were 221 other public kindergartens and 309 private ones, and a mere two percent of the nation's children attended kindergarten; the percentage rose to only 6.8 by 1945.[22] *Yūgi* nevertheless played a significant role in education, forming the basis for physical education in the infant years of elementary schools and in physical education for girls. According to a survey conducted in 1894, *yūgi* based on the principles advocated by Isawa and on the praxis at the government kindergarten were widely taught in schools nationwide.[23] Collections of *yūgi shōka* were published for use in schools as well as kindergartens.[24]

---

20   For a discussion of the terminology, including Tanaka's use of *yūki* and *yūgi*, see Fukuhara, 'Tanaka Fujimaro.' 639–40. The basic meaning of amusing and enjoying oneself is similar; before Meiji they usually referred to adults. Tanaka's use changes over time. Meanings of *kigi* include frisking, frolicking. On Isawa's terminology, see Haruko Takahashi, Sachiko Kishimoto, and Kichiji Kimura, 'Isawa Shūji no "yūki" ni kansuru ikkōsatsu', *Chūkyō taiikugaku kenkyū* (*Chūkyō Daigaku Gakujutsu Kenkyūkai*) 16, no. 1 (1975): 79.

21   Shigeo Murayama, *Meijiki dansu no shiteki kenkyū* (Tokyo: Fumaidō, 2000), 32–35; Hermann Gottschewski, 'Nineteenth-Century *Gagaku* Songs as a Subject of Musical Analysis: An Early Example of Musical Creativity in Modern Japan', *Nineteenth-Century Music Review* 10, no. 2 (2013), https://doi.org/10.1017/S1479409813000256

22   Tōru Umihara, *Nihonshi shōhyakka: Gakkō* (Tokyo: Kondō Shuppansha, 1979), 46 (appendix).

23   Murayama, *Meijiki dansu no shiteki kenkyū*, 35.

24   The catalogue of the National Diet Library (NDL) records nine titles including the expression '*yūgi shōka*', published between 1887 and 1910. There are likely to have been more. Shikama's collection, for example, is not included. See Chapter 8.

Even before the founding of the first state kindergarten, Isawa, having become acquainted with Froebel's ideas through Kriege's book, began to experiment with some of Froebel's ideas when he was appointed head of the newly established Aichi Normal School (Aichi Shihan Gakkō) in 1874. He saw music, particularly singing, and physical education as belonging together. In February 1875, he submitted a report to Tanaka Fujimaro, which was published in the Ministry of Education's yearly report. His reasoning was as follows:

On Promoting *shōka kigi*

The benefits of [singing] *shōka* are great: First of all, it heightens perception (*chikaku*) and sensitivity (*shinkei*), and gives pleasure to the mind (*seishin*). Second, it enhances the ability of people's hearts to be moved. Third, it corrects pronunciation and regulates breathing. This is just a short summary of the arguments for why *shōka* are an absolutely indispensable part of small children's education. I will not be long-winded and go into details here. Our Ministry of Education realized this early on and decreed that *shōka* would be among the subjects taught in primary school, but even so this subject has not yet been established. Now, I have followed the ideas set forth in the writings by the prominent educator Froebel as well as several other notable pedagogues, and have adapted traditional children's songs of our own country and arranged two or three short songs. I expect that with time they can be performed to good effect and I can report success.

Here, I present a couple of examples. *Shōka* are pleasing to the mind, while movement refreshes the entire body. Both should in equal measure form part of education, and neither should be neglected. Currently, many kinds of physical exercise have been made compulsory for all as gymnastics (*taisō*). But making children of tender years, with weak muscles and soft bones, do vigorous exercise can be quite harmful. This the famous [pedagogues] state with certainty. Therefore, we now establish *kigi* in the infant years of elementary school.[25]

Three examples follow: *Tsubaki shōka* (Camellia song), *Kochō* (Butterfly) and *Nezumi* (Mouse). They illustrate Isawa's aim to adapt *shōka yūgi* by using Japanese songs, thus conforming to Froebel's recommendation

---

25 Shūji Isawa, 'Aichi Shihan Gakkō nenpō', *Monbushō nenpō* 2 (1875). See also Yasuto Okunaka, 'Shōka ni yoru shintai no kokuminka: Isawa Shūji no kyōiku shisō no ichi sokumen', *Kaitoku* 68 (2000); Okunaka, *Kokka to ongaku*, 106–17.

that melodies familiar to the children be used.[26] Isawa described the movements, but did not include the music.[27] Indeed, as with military drill to the accompaniment of drum and fife bands, it can be plausibly argued that *shōka yūgi* had little to do with music. Both in the United States and subsequently in Japan, education in singing, whether or not in the form of *yūgi*, was perceived as health education and as moral training rather than art education. The continuity from Isawa's early experience of military drill to his interest in promoting *shōka yūgi* might thus be said to lie in creating modern bodies and mobilizing them in the service of the nation.[28]

Isawa's pragmatic approach to *yūgi*, as well as his emphasis on adapting Japanese songs for use in *yūgi*, reflected his aim, explicitly stated in his subsequent writings, to reform music by combining the best of Western and Japanese music. Aesthetic considerations or the idea of music as an art were not part of Isawa's educational agenda. For him, music was a tool for quite literally moving bodies, and, at the same time, disciplining them.[29] From a musical point of view the songs that accompanied *yūgi* may well seem forgettable. But their significance must be rated highly. Making infant bodies move together in time was an important part of forming modern citizens; not only in Japan. Together with other elements in Froebel's pedagogy, such as having children make things with their hands, these movement games served to prepare children for their place not only in a modern state, but also in a modern industrial society. It is, moreover, significant that the early reception of Froebel's pedagogy in Japan happened entirely through English-language sources, most of them American, whose pragmatic treatment of music Isawa followed.

Isawa's study of American pedagogy resulted in the publication of *Kyōju shinpō* (True method of teaching) during his time at Aichi Normal School. The work was based on *Theory and Practice of Teaching* by David Page, first published in 1847 and still highly regarded in the 1870s. Isawa

---

26 Okunaka, *Kokka to ongaku*, 106-16. Okunaka characterizes Isawa's ideas as Froebel 'sono mama' (i.e. as essentially a replication of Froebel's ideas.

27 Murayama, *Meijiki dansu no shiteki kenkyū*, 25. *Nezumi* is an adaptation of Douai's 'Cat and Mouse', while the movements described for *Kochō* are the same as those for *Solar System*, described by Ronge and Ronge.

28 Okunaka, *Kokka to ongaku*, 106–17; Okunaka, 'Shōka ni yoru shintai no kokuminka'.

29 Okunaka, 'Shōka ni yoru shintai no kokuminka', 31, 40.

translated selected parts of the book and added material from other publications, including sample material from *The Teacher's Assistant* by Charles Northend, published in 1873.[30] Isawa's adaptation of Page's work shows his role as one of the pioneers of developmental education and of 'object lessons' as a separate branch of study in Japan.[31]

By the time Isawa was sent by the government to study at Bridgewater Normal School in Massachusetts in July 1875, he had acquired a sound knowledge of educational theory and practice in the United States.

Music, Language, and Science

Isawa's training at Bridgewater included music, which reportedly was his worst subject; he was even advised to drop it by the school's principal, A. G. Boyden, who otherwise spoke highly of Isawa, describing him as 'well-trained in the schools of Japan'.[32] His difficulties with the Western tonal system led him to Luther Whiting Mason, with whom he took private lessons. Mason's credentials as a music pedagogue were excellent: his *National Music Course* was the most influential series of music textbook in America in the 1870s and early 1880s, and earned him honours at the world exhibitions in Vienna (1873) and Paris (1878) as well as the Philadelphia Centennial Exposition in 1876.[33] It is not surprising that Mason's work attracted the attention of Japanese studying education and teacher training in America. Megata consulted him about music education, and Isawa's lessons with Mason prepared him for supervising the introduction of music education in Japan's schools.

Similarly, his problems with English pronunciation brought him in contact with Alexander Graham Bell (1847–1922), and he began studying speech with him in 1876, around the same time as he studied with Mason.[34] Bell is, of course, known best as the inventor of the telephone.

---

30 For an analysis of Isawa's work see Mark E. Lincicome, *Principle, Praxis, and the Politics of Educational Reform in Meiji Japan* (Honolulu: University of Hawai'i Press, 1995), 38–49.
31 Ibid., 45.
32 Quoted in Sondra Wieland Howe, *Luther Whiting Mason: International Music Educator* (Warren, Michigan: Harmonie Park Press, 1997), 58.
33 For details of Mason's biography and work see Ibid.
34 Kaminuma, *Isawa Shūji*, 330.

He demonstrated an early telephone prototype at the 1876 Centennial Exposition in Philadelphia, where the international audience included the Japanese, among them Education Minister Tanaka Fujimaro and the Japanese students, including Isawa.[35] Early the following year, Isawa cooperated with Bell in two demonstrations of his invention, and thus Japanese became what Bell later called 'the first foreign language' spoken over his telephone.[36]

As with Mason, Isawa's contact with Bell (having been introduced by Megata) was about more than remedial teaching. Besides working as a speech instructor, Bell was a propagator of 'visible speech'.[37] Alexander Graham Bell's father Alexander Melville Bell (1819–1905), his grandfather Alexander Bell and his brother Melville James Bell (1845–1870) were prominent teachers of oratory and elocution. His father published several works on speech, including *The Standard Elocutionist* (1860) and *Visible Speech* (1867).[38] According to Alexander Melville Bell,

> The fundamental principle of Visible Speech is, that all Relations of Sound are symbolized by Relations of Form. Each organ and each mode of organic action concerned in the production or modification of sound, has its appropriate Symbol; and in all Sounds of the same nature produced at different parts of the mouth, are represented by a Single Symbol turned in a direction corresponding to the organic position.[39]

In other words, Bell devised a kind of phonetic alphabet, which he believed to be so logical and clear that it offered numerous advantages over conventional alphabets. He believed its simplicity would greatly facilitate teaching literacy to 'the illiterate in all countries' as well as help prevent and cure speech defects. By visualizing every imaginable

---

35 Okunaka, *Kokka to ongaku*, 134, 152.
36 Robert V. Bruce, *Bell: Alexander Graham Bell and the Conquest of Solitude* (Boston: Little, Brown and Company, 1973), 215, 18.
37 For the following, see Okunaka, *Kokka to ongaku*, 127–86; Seth Jacobowitz, *Writing Technologies in Meiji Japan: A Media History of Modern Japanese Literature and Visual Culture* (Cambridge, MA: Harvard University Press, 2015), https://doi.org/10.1163/9781684175628
38 Alexander Melville Bell, *Visible Speech: The Science of Universal Alphabetics on Self-Interpreting Physiological Letters for the Writing of All Languages in One Alphabet, Illustrated by Tables, Diagrams and Examples*, Inaugural Edition ed. (London/London and New York: Simpkin, Marshall & Co./N. Trübner & Co., 1867).
39 Ibid., 35.

speech sound and the way it was produced by the human speech organs, moreover, it provided the means to teach the deaf as well as to communicate 'the exact sounds of foreign languages to learners in all countries'. Indeed, Bell went even further and outlined the political possibilities he envisaged: 'The establishment of a Standard of the Native Pronunciation of any language', and the 'speedy diffusion of the language of a mother country throughout the most widely separated colonies'.[40]

His son Alexander Graham Bell had learned 'visible speech' as a child. At the time of his encounter with Isawa, he was using the system to teach the deaf. Having settled in Boston in autumn 1872, he gave private tuition, and had been appointed professor at Boston University's newly opened School of Oratory in 1873.[41]

Isawa soon realized the potential of visible speech. Reforming and standardizing the national spoken language was a pressing issue in Japan, where local dialects could be mutually incomprehensible. In fact, both Bell and Isawa wanted to use the system to draw 'marginal subjects into the national, or imperial, mainstream'.[42] Foreign language education was another highly relevant application, not just for the Japanese studying English and other languages but, once Japan became a colonial power, for teaching Japanese to their colonial subjects. Isawa later published several works about pronunciation and about visible speech.[43]

Both these potential applications were relevant for his practical work as a government official. *Shōka* education, after all, combined both music and language, while foreign language education became a major concern when Japan acquired Taiwan as its first colony in 1895, at the end of its war with China. That year Isawa was appointed acting chief of the education bureau (*gakumubu*) that was established in the civil department (*minseikyoku*) of the government general, which gave him the opportunity to put his ideas about state education, including

---

40 Bell, *Visible Speech*, 20–21. The other advantages Bell envisaged were the effective telegraphic communication in any language, the study and preservation of languages threatened by extinction, as well as making it easier to trace the etymology of words, and, finally the possibility of creating a universal language aided by 'the world-wide communication of any specific sounds with absolute uniformity'.
41 Biographical details in Bruce, *Bell*.
42 Jacobowitz, *Writing Technologies*, 154.
43 See Kaminuma, *Isawa Shūji*, 345–47.

language education, into practice.⁴⁴ Although his term as the head of the educational bureau ended in 1897, his plans for a system of public schools were implemented over the following years. Singing education was on the curriculum of the new schools from the start, and the song books compiled for Japanese elementary schools under Isawa's auspices were used until the Taiwan Government-General published its own collections, starting in 1915. Among the Japanese teachers whom Isawa recruited personally, Takahashi Fumiyo, a graduate of Tokyo Normal School, became the most influential music teacher in Taiwan, where he taught from 1896 to 1906.⁴⁵ He composed songs that were included in the Taiwan Government-General's song collections from 1915. The foundations for Taiwan's rise as a musical as well as an economic 'Asian Tiger' after 1945 were thus laid by Isawa in the early twentieth century.

After resigning from his post in Taiwan, Isawa was appointed president of the Tokyo Higher Normal School (Tōkyō Kōtō Shihan Gakkō), the former Tokyo Normal School, whose president he had been twenty years previously, on 30 August 1899, but illness forced him to resign the following year. This marked the end of his career in state employment (apart from his membership of the Upper House), but not of his public activities.

His most significant achievement after 1900 may well have been his work with people suffering from speech impairments, namely stammering. In 1901 he published *Shiwahō* (Visible speech; he sent a copy of the book to Bell).⁴⁶ This was followed by several works on pronunciation in which he applied the method of visible speech. In 1903 Isawa founded the association Rakusekisha. Its aim was to promote research and teaching in visible speech, and to promote good pronunciation of Japanese, English, Chinese, and Taiwanese, to correct non-standard pronunciation as a result of speaking dialects and stammering and to teach speech to deaf-mute people.⁴⁷ From January

---

44 For this and the following see Tsurumi, *Japanese Colonial Education in Taiwan, 1895–1945*, 14–21; Kaminuma, *Isawa Shūji*, 213–53.

45 *Shōgaku shōkashū* (1881–84), *Yōchien shōka* (1887), and *Shōgaku shōka* (1892–93). See Sondra Wieland Howe and Mei-Ling Lai, 'Isawa Shūji, Nineteenth-Century Administrator and Music Educator in Japan and Taiwan', *Australian Journal of Music Education* 2 (2014 (2011)): 102–04, https://files.eric.ed.gov/fulltext/EJ1061986.pdf

46 Bruce, *Bell*, 81.

47 On the founding and development of the Rakusekisha see Kaminuma, *Isawa Shūji*, 291–311.

1909 the association published the journal *Rakuseki sōshi*. It turned out that there was a huge demand for the correction of stammering, especially from young people and their families. Within a few years the number of people treated reached thousands and training courses for teachers were organized at local centres. Tuition was also offered to the hearing-impaired and for the correction of pronunciation in singing, particularly for speakers of Tohoku dialects. The first initiative for the latter came from the governor of Akita prefecture, who had noticed the flawed pronunciation of children singing the national anthem during his official visits to schools.[48] During his final years Isawa also continued his work on teaching Chinese pronunciation, begun when he was appointed to the colonial government in Taiwan. He even extended his efforts to native Chinese speakers and in 1916 travelled to the Chinese continent and to Korea. At the time of his sudden death he was planning to extend his activities to North America.

Arguably, therefore, Isawa's interest in language education exceeded his interest in music: it remained a major preoccupation for the rest of his life. His studies both with Bell and Mason were highly significant: for Isawa, the use of the voice and vocal culture were also a subject of scientific enquiry and related to his interest in theories of evolution.[49] Having graduated from Bridgewater he enrolled in the Lawrence Scientific School at Harvard University, a significant institution for the reception and teaching of evolutionist thought in America. Isawa's studies included the works of Charles Darwin, Thomas Henry Huxley, and Herbert Spencer.[50] By the time Isawa returned to Japan, he was well acquainted with both biological evolutionism and the cultural evolutionism of Herbert Spencer, including his writings on the origins and function of music. In 1879, the year he was charged with music investigation, Isawa published *Seishu genshiron* (On the origin of species), a partial translation of Thomas Henry Huxley's *On the origin*

---

48 Ibid. The Meiji government targeted certain dialects, including the Tohoku dialect, as part of the efforts to standardize the spoken language, resulting in their stigmatization. See Mie Hiramoto, 'Slaves Speak Pseudo-Toohoku-ben: The Representation of Minorities in the Japanese Translation of Gone with the Wind', *Journal of Sociolinguistics* 13, no. 2 (2009), https://doi.org/10.1111/j.1467-9841.2009.00406.x

49 Okunaka, *Kokka to ongaku*, 175–79.

50 Kaminuma, *Isawa Shūji*, 79.

of species, or, The causes of the phenomena of organic nature: a course of six lectures to working men (1863). He is credited with having translated the first work introducing Darwin's theory. He published a full translation in 1889 under the title *Shinka genron* (The principles of evolution).

Isawa's belief in science as a fundamental part of civilization lay at the root of his approach to education, whether in language or music. While Chamberlain, in the passage quoted at the beginning of this chapter, used 'dialects' to describe the different kinds of music in the world, Isawa's dialects included the varieties of indigenous music as well as variations of the Japanese language. Both had to be subjected to a national standard.[51]

Music Education

Immediately after his return to Japan in May 1878, Isawa held several appointments in quick succession, some of them simultaneously. He was appointed to the Tokyo Normal School (Tōkyō Shihan Gakkō) in June 1878, and became its president the following year. Together with Takamine Hideo, who had likewise studied education in the United States (at Oswego), he set out to reform the institution based on what they had learnt about Pestalozzi's principles. It is significant that they did this without direct input from foreign advisors. Their reforms provoked opposition, especially from the imperial court.[52] At the same time Isawa was an official in the Ministry of Education, where he was employed in various capacities until 1891. In November 1878 he became head of the National Institute of Gymnastics (Taisō Denshū Sho) established in the Ministry of Education, where, together with the American physician George A. Leland (1850–1924), he worked to establish a programme for physical education in schools and to train teachers. As his efforts to introduce *yūgi* show, Isawa attached great importance to physical education. At Bridgewater he had learnt the system of gymnastics developed by the physician Diocletian Lewis (1823–86), to improve the

---

51 Okunaka, *Kokka to ongaku*, 178–79. On Isawa's scienticism as a basis for his approach to music, see also Toru Takenaka, 'Isawa Shūji's "National Music": National Sentiment and Cultural Westernization in Meiji Japan', *Itinerario* 34, no. 3 (2010), https://doi.org/10.1017/S0165115310000719

52 Duke, *Modern Japanese Education*, 196.

physical condition of children and adults who were not fit enough for the more demanding forms of exercise. Isawa set out his thoughts in a memorandum entitled, 'Shin taisōhō jisshi' (On the implementation of new gymnastics), and in 1879, a month before his resignation, he submitted a report on the results of his work and outlined the merits of Lewis's New Gymnastics.[53]

Isawa left the National Institute of Gymnastics to become head of the Music Investigation Committee (Ongaku Torishirabe Gakari), a post he held concurrently with the presidency of the Tokyo Normal School. The Committee was established a result of Isawa's own efforts. Even before his return from America, in April 1878, Isawa and Megata Tanetarō submitted a report to Tanaka Fujimaro, then vice-minister of Education, about the need to firmly establish music in the education system. Music, the joint report stated, 'refreshes the mind of schoolchildren, provides relaxation from the efforts of hard study, strengthens the lungs, promotes the health, clears the voice, corrects the pronunciation, improves the hearing, sharpens the thinking, pleases the heart well also and forms a good character'.[54] In addition, music also benefits society by its 'capacity for providing recreation profitable for society, for turning it naturally toward the good and removing it from evil, for the advancement of society in civil manners, for elating the people, for praising royal virtue and for the enjoyment of peace'.[55] No suitable musical style existed in Japan, however, so Western music should be adapted to suit the Japanese. An additional document signed by Megata detailed the practical implementation.[56] He proposed setting up a 'singing course' in the Tokyo Normal School and Tokyo Normal School for Women, and employing Luther Whiting Mason as a teacher with Isawa Shūji as his assistant.

In spring 1879, Isawa persuaded a high-ranking official in the Ministry of Education to express his—Isawa's—ideas in a 'Plan for the Establishment of a Music Instruction Centre'. The plan referred to

---

53 Kaminuma, *Isawa Shūji*, 89–94. For details on gymnastics at Bridgewater and Isawa's work, see Shūichi Nose, 'Kei taisō no kindai Nihon taiikuka kyōiku katei e no dōnyū ni kansuru shiteki kōsatsu (A historical review on the curricular adoption of light gymnastics into modern Japanese physical education)', *Taiiku kenkyū: Japan journal of physical education, health and sport sciences* 28, no. 3 (1983).
54 Quoted in Eppstein, *Beginnings*, 30.
55 Ibid., 31.
56 Both documents (the second one in Megata's own English version) are quoted in full in Eppstein, *Beginnings*, 31–37.

combining Eastern and Western music to create a national music, and the Music Investigation Committee functioned both as a research and experimental committee and a teacher training institute. Its tasks were to investigate music at home and abroad in order to develop suitable educational materials and to implement musical education, starting with singing, at the kindergarten and primary school affiliated to the teacher training school. In June Mason was formally appointed 'Instructor of Musics in the School of Musics' for a period of two years, although no institution of that name existed. Mason arrived in Japan in March 1880.[57]

In preparation for his work in Japan, Mason had bought musical instruments and tools to tune and repair them, and collected pentatonic folk songs from Scotland, Ireland, and Wales. His work with Japanese students in America had led him to believe that these were most suited to Japanese ears. His responsibilities in Tokyo were similar to those he had had at home: teaching children, training teachers, organizing and directing performances, and creating educational materials. He taught at the Tokyo Normal School, the Tokyo Normal School for Women and the affiliated schools and the kindergarten, at the Peers' School, and the Music Institute of the Music Investigation Committee.

The most immediate task was the selection of songs deemed suitable for teaching in schools. A committee was set up in order to compile a series of graded music textbooks, chaired by Isawa and including Mason, an interpreter, three poets, five court musicians, and two general scholars.[58] The inclusion of poets demonstrates the importance attached to the lyrics, which were intended to provide suitable content. After all, singing education (*shōka*) in Isawa's view was a means for moral education.[59] The first song book was published in 1881. Most of the melodies came from Western sources, while the lyrics were composed by Japanese. Many of the songs are still popular in Japan today.[60]

Mason left Japan for Europe in July 1882, intending to learn more about music education there, particularly for the blind. He expected

---

57 For Mason's work in Japan, see Howe, *Luther Whiting Mason*; Eppstein, *Beginnings*.
58 According to Mason; see Howe, *Luther Whiting Mason*, 95.
59 Okunaka, *Kokka to ongaku*, 190.
60 For a discussion of the contents of the early song books, see Eppstein, *Beginnings*; Masato Sakurai, Heruman Gochefuski [Hermann Gottschewski], and Hiroshi Yasuda, *Aogeba tōtoshi: maboroshi no genkyoku hakken to 'Shōgaku shōkashū' zenchikuseki* (Tokyo: Tōkyōdō Shuppan, 2015).

to return to Japan, but his contract (he had been granted a one-year extension of his original contract) was cancelled that November. The reasons for this are not entirely clear, but by the 1880s, the Japanese government was aiming to reduce the number of foreign teachers. The government and Isawa may well have felt that they could now continue implementing Western vocal music in the education system without Mason. Besides, disagreements between Mason and Isawa may have influenced the decision. Mason, who regarded Japanese music as having 'a wrong scale' and was convinced of the necessity of converting his pupils to 'civilized music',[61] presumably had little time for Isawa's vision of a national music.

Isawa, meanwhile, began to lobby for transforming the Music Research Committee into a fully-fledged conservatoire. The Tokyo Academy of Music was established in 1887 and Isawa was appointed president. He had submitted a proposal to the Ministry of Education, signed by seven like-minded intellectuals as well as himself, in November 1886.[62] They stated that, while educational reform had improved physical and intellectual education, educating the emotions was equally important and, to this end, training in the arts needed to be more firmly established. The proposal referred to the theatre reform movement and asserted the necessity of training performing artists (*geijutsuka*). Besides teacher training, the new Academy included a specialist department for particularly talented students. This, together with the appointment of Rudolph Dittrich, marked the beginning of a change of course. The wording of the proposal, however, as well as most of Isawa's subsequent pronouncements suggest that Isawa's utilitarian approach to music education never really changed. Even as president of the academy (he resigned in 1891, having been suspended from his duties the year before), he held other appointments, acting as president of the Tokyo School for the Blind and Dumb (Tōkyō Mōa Gakkō) from 1890 to 1891. After 1891 he held no official appointment related to music, although he did continue to be deeply involved with education, both as

---

61 Quoted in Howe, *Luther Whiting Mason*, 90.
62 They were Sakurai Jōji, Yatabe Ryōkichi, Toyama Masakazu, Hotsumi Nobushige, Muraoka Ken'ichi, Mitsukuri Kakichi, and Kikuchi Dairoku. See Tōkyō Geijutsu Daigaku Hyakunenshi Hensan Iinkai, *Tōkyō Ongaku Gakkō hen 1*, 285.

a government official and privately.[63] Indeed, in 1907, he criticized the Tokyo Academy of Music for over-emphasizing music as art for its own sake even in the teacher training department.[64]

In sum, while music for Isawa was an essential part of national education, he had little time for music as an art. Moving together in time and singing together in tune, with correct, standardized pronunciation of suitably edifying lyrics, all served the same purpose: to unify the nation and advance its level of civilization, so that Japan could compare itself favourably with the dominant Western powers. As for the music itself, Isawa's belief in science and in theories of evolution led him to conclude that Western music provided a useful model. Ultimately, of course, Japan should create its own national music, by using that model to reform existing music. This, however, proved to be far from straightforward, as the discussions about music reform and the activities of would-be reformers illustrate.

---

63 For details about Isawa's career, see Okunaka, *Kokka to ongaku*.
64 Quoted in Okunaka, *Kokka to ongaku*, 226.

6. Civilizing Citizens: Music Reform

[...] our aim is not entire adoption of European Musics but the making or refining of Japanese Music by assimilating the elements of both Native and European Musics [sic].¹

At such a time, what is more fitting than to publish a music magazine in order to present that which will correct such abuse and prevent such harm; support what is right and guard against wrong; to help promote ever more correct and refined music, and thus ensure that we reach the realm of civilization (*bunmei no eiiki*)? I therefore believe that the time has indeed come to establish this magazine.²

Isawa Shūji, who wrote the lines quoted above in a letter to Luther Whiting Mason dated 1 July 1880, four months after Mason's arrival in Tokyo, was not the first to advocate the reform of Japanese music. Reform or improvement (*kairyō*) was one of the watchwords of the 1870s and 1880s, applied to many areas, including the noh and kabuki theatre.³ The topic had already been discussed by Kanda Kōhei (1830–96), a founding member of the Meiji Six Society (Meirokusha), in his article 'On Promoting Our National Music' published in the society's journal in October 1874.⁴ Kanda asserted that the reform of music and the performing arts needed to be addressed immediately, as this would

---

1   Ury Eppstein, *The Beginnings of Western Music in Meiji Era Japan* (New York: Edwin Mellen, 1994), 77.
2   Totsuji Shikama, 'Hakkan no shushi', *Ongaku zasshi* 1 (1890), 2.
3   See Yoshihiro Kurata, *Geinō no bunmei kaika: Meiji kokka to geinō kindaika* (Tokyo: Heibonsha, 1999), 260–88.
4   Kōhei Kanda, 'Kokugaku o shinkō subeki no setsu', *Meiroku zasshi* 18 (1874). For a full translation, see Kōhei Kanda, 'On Promoting Our National Music', in *Meiroku Zasshi: Journal of the Japanese Enlightenment*, ed. and trans. William R. Braisted (Cambridge, Massachusetts: Harvard University Press, 1976).

take time. When he claimed that Japan was unskilled in music (*onritsu*), he was presumably referring to cultivated music.⁵ He expressed the criticism that had already been expressed by Ogyū Sorai in the previous era and would be repeated many times in the following years: the music enjoyed by the common people (*zokugaku*) was vulgar and its influence on public morals pernicious. Kanda called it coarse and obscene (*hiri waisetsu*). With both the music of Tang China, brought to Japan in ancient times, and *sarugaku* (a predecessor of noh) having lost their appeal, there no longer existed any music suitable for the enjoyment of refined people and they had lost all interest in music. In order to remedy the situation, the science of music had to be studied as a branch of knowledge in its own right. The study of music was fairly advanced in China, but even more so in Europe and America. For promoting music in Japan, the most appropriate instruments were to be selected, whether Japanese, Chinese, European, or American. The lyrics, on the other hand, had to be Japanese. The ones currently sung were unsuitable, but the words of noh plays, *gidayū* ballad drama, or the Utazawa school of vocal music might be adapted for the purpose.

Kanda then went on to discuss theatre reform and concluded with a note on *sumō* wrestling, which he described as barbaric (*yaban*) and wished to see discontinued. Kanda's article shows that he regarded public entertainment as highly important: the aim of reforms should be to create performances that the entire population, from emperor to common people, could enjoy together.⁶ Kanda did not mention education, although he was writing two years after the introduction of the Education Law. Clearly, he was more concerned with public entertainment.

Education, on the other hand, was a central concern for Ono Shōgorō, another early advocate of music reform. A samurai from Sendai and educated at the domain's school, Yōkendō, Ono's activities were largely limited to his home town and his views are unlikely to have been circulated widely, but they suggest that the need for music reform was not only felt by the elite in Tokyo. Ono fled to Hakodate during the war in 1869, where he converted to the Russian Orthodox faith. Back in Sendai, he opened a private academy in 1872. Although

---

5   See Chapter 3, opening quote, and note.
6   *dōyū kairaku*: the entire phrase is apparently an allusion to Mencius. See Kotobank https://kotobank.jp/word/%E5%81%95%E6%A5%BD-458657

he was active in the Orthodox church in Sendai, education was his main concern. In 1877 he published a series of lectures in his magazine *Kōshū yoshi* (Training course magazine), in which he advocated training in Western-style choral singing.[7] Unlike other commentators introduced in this chapter, Ono laid stress on the pleasures of music. He began his first article, entitled 'Ongaku okosu beshi' (Music should be promoted), by stating, 'It is a fact that human beings must have their enjoyment.'[8] All humans, he continued, regardless of era, state of civilization, intelligence, or location, seek enjoyment. For 'pleasures', Ono used the word *'tanoshimi'*, written with the same character as the *'gaku'* in *ongaku*. In the body of the article Ono used *gaku* rather than *ongaku* for 'music'; surely a conscious choice, emphasizing the close relationship between music and enjoyment expressed by the Chinese character.[9]

Having asserted the universality of a need for enjoyment, Ono argued that the nature of what people enjoyed varied widely, not only from place to place (he mentioned the capitals of England and France, Formosa, and Hainan Island), but also between gentlemen of high standing and villains. The level of civilization (*kaika*), as well as intelligence and virtue, and nobility, was reflected in what people enjoyed. The sages recognized the universal craving for pleasure, and so music (*gaku*), vocal and instrumental (*kaei kangen*), became a tool for leading people to virtue. Music and rites served to rectify customs and support government. Music, Ono continued, was thus a necessity, but getting the people to enjoy the right kind of music and preventing regression into barbarian pleasures was difficult. In the realm of Japan (Dai Nihon Teikoku), there existed various kinds of music, but none that might be named together with rites. Instead, barbarian instrumental pieces and obscene songs prevailed. Nevertheless, it would be impossible to abolish them outright. Because civilization (*bunmei*) was characterized

---

7   Shōgorō Ono, 'Ongaku okosu beshi', *Kōshū joshi* 14 (1877); Shōgorō Ono, 'Ongyoku no fusei wa jinmin no hinkō o midaru', *Kōshū joshi* 15–17 (1877): Documents relating to the Ono family in the Sendai City Museum. The articles are reprinted in: Kanako Kitahara and Sumire Yamashita, 'Kyū Sendai hanshi Ono Shōgorō no ongakuron, Ongyoku no fusei wa jinmin no hinkō o midaru', *Hirosaki Daigaku kokushi kenkyū* 143 (October 2017), https://cir.nii.ac.jp/crid/1010282256804517896
8   Kitahara and Yamashita, 'Kyū Sendai hanshi Ono Shōgorō', 39.
9   On the significance of the character's dual meaning in ancient China, see Wolfgang Bauer, *China und die Hoffnung auf Glück: Paradiese, Utopien, Idealvorstellungen in der Geistesgeschichte Chinas* (Munich: dtv, 1974), 32–33.

by the flourishing of rites and music, Ono concluded, and because Japan aspired to be civilized but had no appropriate music, it was essential to promote refined music (*ongaku*) in order to transform manners and customs.

Why the different kinds of music in Japan were not suitable and what kind of music he proposed instead was the subject of 'Ongyoku no fusei wa jinmin no hinkō o midaru' (Improper musical performance corrupts the moral conduct of the people), published in the following issues, in three instalments.[10] Ono began by naming native genres: instrumental music (*ongaku*) with *shō* (a reed organ-like wind instrument), *hichiriki* (double reed wind instrument), and *taiko* (drum); *nōyō* (noh chanting), and *jōruri shibai* (narrative *shamisen* music and drama). In his discussion, *hichiriki*, typically used in court music and music performed at Shinto shrines (*kagura*), stood for highly refined music, whose entertainment value Ono judged deficient. Noh, he regarded as too bound up with the elite of the previous era and with Buddhism. *Jōruri*, other theatre performances, and all other vocal and instrumental music (*kakyoku kangen*) he condemned as irredeemably obscene (*inji*) and coarse (*hiya*), and their effect as harmful as poison. Even gentlemen enjoyed lowly songs such as *Kappore* and *Jinku* at banquets, making them no better than their grooms and coachmen.[11]

Next, Ono discussed the effects of bad music on children and young people and the need for education in the arts.[12] Ono argued that even if they received moral instruction at school, they would still be exposed to harmful music. Many took lessons in *gidayū* and *tokiwazu* (genres of narrative songs with *shamisen* accompaniment), and those who did not would go to the theatre or variety shows behind their parents' backs and hum songs such as *Kappore* and *Jinku* when out of earshot.

After elaborating on the harmful influence of bad music, Ono finally revealed what kind of music he proposed: 'organ', here in the meaning

---

10 Ono, 'Ongyoku no fusei'. See Kitahara and Yamashita, 'Kyū Sendai hanshi Ono Shōgorō', 40–42.

11 *Kappore* is the name of a folk song that accompanies a comic dance. *Jinku* is likewise a folksong with the lyrics varying from place to place. The lyrics of present-day versions have presumably been sanitized.

12 Kitahara and Yamashita, 'Kyū Sendai hanshi Ono Shōgorō', 41–42.

of *organum*, that is polyphonic *a cappella* singing.[13] According to Ono it was suitable for men and women of all ages; the sounds expressed joy and sorrow, bravery and gentleness, love and yearning, and the ancient lyrics all promoted righteousness and virtue. This type of music, moreover, was performed in Europe and America. Elaborating on his proposition in the final part of his article,[14] Ono stressed the importance of fostering a sense of beauty in children and the role of beauty, rites, and music as an essential part of moral education.

Finally, Ono discussed the relationship between a people's music and disposition. He recounted an anecdote about French troops invading Russia and being moved to dance when they overheard Russians singing. Ono concluded that Russia's efforts to enrich their country and strengthen their army were reflected in their invigorating music. Meanwhile, Europeans judged the melodies of Japanese songs depressing and the instrumental pieces unrefined. Now that Japan was emerging from the shackles of the past and the people could be free, it was time to rejoice and, instead of deriving enjoyment from sad and coarse music, to abandon the voice of barbarianism and promote refined music (*gagaku*). 'For this reason', Ono concluded,

> I desire that organum music be speedily promoted; that singing lyrics by saints and sages be introduced; that we develop in the young the wisdom that will make them love beauty; that we have them sing with exhilaration in order to stimulate a lively and enterprising disposition, and that by suppressing obscene songs and coarse music wash off the laughter and scorn of the people of foreign countries.[15]

Ono's view of music as a means of transforming the people's conduct and (together with rites) as a tool of government is characteristic of the 'Rites and Music' (*reigaku*) view of music that informed most of the debates on music reform. While it is unlikely that Ono knew much about the ideas that informed Russian Orthodox Church music, his encounter with its practice would have made it seem entirely compatible with the aims of 'Rites and Music'. At the same time, his desire for music that expressed the exhilaration and joy of a new departure suggest that he regarded

---

13 Ibid., 45; Rihei Nakamura, *Kirisuto-kyō to Nihon no yōgaku* (Tokyo: Ōzorasha, 1996), 62.
14 Kitahara and Yamashita, 'Kyū Sendai hanshi Ono Shōgorō', 42.
15 Ibid., 42.

organum as modern compared to Japanese music, even while he praised its ancient lyrics. His claim that it was widely practised in the West and his reference to Western opinions of Japanese music, meanwhile, show that transforming musical practices was not just a domestic affair, but also aimed to improve Japan's standing in the eyes of the world. Ono did not mention reforming Japanese music. His discussion gives the impression that he was resigned to its continued existence as a source of pleasure, but that it would gradually be marginalized once people, especially the young, learned to prefer more refined music. Ono's thoughts were not widely disseminated, but they demonstrate both the prevalence of the 'Rites and Music' view of music and the variety of ways in which musical practice could be imagined.

Isawa Shūji and the Tokyo Academy of Music

Isawa Shūji, then, was not the first to stress the importance of music education. Like Ono, he was convinced that music was a significant tool for reforming manners and customs, and that the music enjoyed by the common person was not fit for purpose and therefore needed to be reformed. Unlike Ono, however, Isawa's appointment to the Ministry of Education placed him in a position to put his ideas into practice on a national scale. As he stated in the letter to Luther Whiting Mason quoted at the beginning of this chapter, music reform meant, 'the making or refining of Japanese Music by assimilating the elements of both Native and European Musics [sic]'.[16] He outlined his argument in more detail in a memorandum entitled, 'Zokugaku kairyō no koto' (On the improvement of popular music), circulated in the Ministry of Education in 1883.[17] The music enjoyed by the common people was morally corrupt and obscene (*inja waisetsu*), and its melodies lewd in manner (*inpū*). It corrupted morals and obstructed progress, and damaged Japan's prestige in relations with foreign countries. Clearly, music reform was not just a domestic matter.

---

16 Eppstein, *Beginnings*, 77.
17 Shūji Isawa, 'Ongaku kairyō no koto', in *Isawa Shūji: Yōgaku kotohajime - Ongaku torishirabe seiseki shinpōsho*, ed. Masami Yamazumi (Tokyo: Heibonsha, 1971 (1884)). Partial translation and discussion in Eppstein, *Beginnings*, 69–70.

In the English translation the criticism of common music is not quite so harshly expressed, however. Presumably this is a reflection of 'Isawa's dilemma':[18] he despised common music, but at the same time he wished to convince Mason and other foreigners that Japan had a highly refined culture, and a wholesale condemnation of common music was hard to reconcile with this claim. Of course, there was *gagaku*, the music of the imperial court and of Shinto ritual, which could be sharply distinguished from the music of the common people. It had to be anyway, since it represented the institutions and ideology that formed the basis of the modern state. Indeed, Isawa went even further: he argued that that the Japanese music of his time was similar in tonality to ancient Greek music.[19]

The English version of Isawa's discussion was included in the collections of exhibits provided by the Music Investigation Committee for the International Health Exhibition in London in April 1884,[20] the World's Industrial and Cotton Centennial Exposition in New Orleans, held from December 1884, and for the International Inventions Exhibition in London in 1885.[21] Alexander J. Ellis (1814–90), one of the pioneers of music research based on scientific experimentation, and of comparative musicology, made good use of the information in his paper, 'On the Musical Scales of Various Nations', read in London at the Society of Arts on 25 March 1885.[22] Ellis, who was entrusted with

---

18 See Eppstein, *Beginnings*, 68–69.
19 'Extracts from the Report of S. Isawa, Director of the Institute of Music on the result of the Investigations Concerning Music Undertaken by Order of the Department of Education Tokyo Japan. Translated by the Institute of Music.' In Tōkyō Geijutsu Daigaku Hyakunenshi Hensan Iinkai, ed., *Tōkyō Geijutsu Daigaku hyakunenshi: Ensōkai hen 1* (Tokyo: Ongaku no Tomosha, 1990), 167–77. Japanese versions in Masami Yamazumi, ed., *Isawa Shūji: Yōgaku kotohajime - Ongaku torishirabe seiseki shinpōsho* (Tokyo: Heibonsha, 1971). See also Eppstein, *Beginnings*, 70–74.
20 It was entitled, 'Extracts from the Report of S. Isawa, Director of the Institute of Music on the result of the Investigations Concerning Music Undertaken by Order of the Department of Education Tokyo Japan. Translated by the Institute of Music', and dated February 1884.
21 Tōkyō Geijutsu Daigaku Hyakunenshi Hensan Iinkai, *Tōkyō Ongaku Gakkō hen 1*, 189–97. See also Liebersohn, *Music and the New Global Culture: From the Great Exhibitions to the Jazz Age* (Chicago: University of Chicago Press, 2019), 98–104.
22 Alexander J. Ellis, 'On the Musical Scales of Various Nations', *Journal of the Society of the Arts* 33, no. 1688 (27 March 1885), http://www.jstor.org/stable/41327637 In addition to Isawa, Ellis cited a 'Japanese gentleman who is studying physics in Europe', who wished to remain anonymous. This was presumably Tanaka Shōhei, inventor of the enharmonium and another advocate of music reform.

the exhibits after the 1885 exhibition (most of which were given to the South Kensington Museum), subsequently received from Isawa three sets of tuning forks and two sets of pitch pipes representing the tuning of the *koto* and *biwa* and of basic Japanese scales (*ritsu*) for his personal use. He discussed these in a lengthy addition to his previous paper. In return Ellis sent Isawa a set of French tuning forks, which, he wrote 'may prove serviceable for tuning your pianos by'.[23]

Besides giving Japanese music, or at least court music, added prestige both at home and abroad, downplaying the differences between Japanese and Western music made Isawa's aim of creating a modern 'national music' (*kokugaku*) by combining elements of the two seem achievable. In order to qualify for this synthesis, Japanese music was to be reformed by referring to what were deemed desirable qualities of Western music. As in other areas, the idea was to modernize Japanese culture by selectively imitating Western models. Meanwhile, since prohibiting the music of the common people was hardly realistic, it was to be reformed by selecting the least offensive pieces, and improving them; particularly the lyrics. Adding harmonies was intended to make them equal to Western art songs, while publishing them in staff notation would make them available for teaching and study.[24]

In practice, the early efforts made by Isawa's Committee and subsequently by the Tokyo Academy of Music seldom produced more than transcribed traditional melodies in staff notation (with all the limitations the notation entailed) and, in the case of songs, sanitized lyrics. One of the few tangible results was a collection of *koto* pieces, published under the auspices of Isawa in 1888. The publication was bilingual: the English title page and the addition of romanized lyrics (except for *Rokudan*, all the works had a vocal part) suggest that the collection was published at least in part with a foreign audience in mind. Japanese studying the *koto* in the traditional way with a teacher would not have needed sheet music, since transmission was largely by

---

23 Letter to Isawa, 11 and 24 October 1885, published in Tōkyō Geijutsu Daigaku Hyakunenshi Hensan Iinkai, *Tōkyō Ongaku Gakkō hen 1*, 196–97. For Ellis's discussion of the Japanese tuning forks, see Ellis, 'Appendix to Mr. Alexander J. Ellis's Paper on "The Musical Scales of Various Nations" Read 25th March 1885', *Journal of the Society of the Arts* 33, no. 1719 (30 October 1885), http://www.jstor.org/stable/41335239

24 Isawa, 'Ongaku kairyō'.

ear. The preface included the following information about the selection and editing process:

> Though most of the pieces contained in this collection are selected from the better portion of the old Koto music, yet for those words and tunes occurring therein, which are liable to offend the public feelings on account of their vulgarity and meanness, pure and elegant ones have been substituted, thus preventing their baneful effects upon the social character. [25]

New tunes had also been added, but great care had been taken 'not to injure that virtue which is inherent in our old Koto music'. The collection included a revised version of the traditional song *Sakura* (no.2), which gained international currency when Puccini used the tune in *Madame Butterfly* and generally acquired iconic status as a 'traditional' Japanese song.

Although musically 'Western', European songs with Japanese-themed lyrics arguably represented an attempt at blending Japanese and Western elements (*wayō setchū*) as part of the effort to create a national music; particularly when the songs were art songs rather than children's songs. In the 1880s and 1890s, several such songs were published and performed at the Tokyo Academy of Music. Most of the original Japanese lyrics are now forgotten: today these songs are either sung in the original language or in direct translation. An early example is *Yasumasa*, first published in 1889 in the collection *Chūtō shōka shū* (Intermediate level song collection). Fujiwara no Yasumasa, a courtier from the Heian period, was known for his ability to play the flute, and the lyrics tell the story of how he stopped a robber in his tracks with his music. The music of the three-part chorus was *Das klinget so herrlich* from Mozart's opera, *The Magic Flute*. The lyricist thus took his inspiration from the title of the opera (although in the actual chorus it is Papageno's glockenspiel, rather than his flute, that 'enchants' Monostatos and his men). The tune, however, does not lend itself easily to the sounds of the Japanese language, which may well be why the song never became popular.[26]

---

25 From the preface: Tokyo Academy of Music, ed., *Collection of Japanese Koto Music* (Tokyo: Department of Education, 1888); Monbushō Ongaku Torishirabe Gakari, ed., *Sōkyokushū* (Tokyo: Monbushō Henshūkyoku, 1888).)

26 Yasuto Okunaka, *Wayō setchū ongakushi* (Tokyo: Shunjūsha, 2014), 11–14. Okunaka names Kōzu Senzaburō as the composer, but the publication does not give the

A more successful example was *Satsuma-gata* (Satsuma Bay) with lyrics by Torii Makoto (1855–1917), a poet who had studied French and then Western music and was appointed Professor at the Academy of Music in 1891. The lyrics tell the famous story of Saigō Takamori and his companion, the monk Gesshō, and their attempt to drown themselves in Kinko Bay in Kagoshima in 1859. Gesshō died, but Saigō was rescued and went on to become one of the most celebrated heroes of the Meiji Restoration.[27] The words are set to the music of Robert Schumann's *Zigeunerleben* (Op. 29 No. 3), and the first recorded performance was at a concert by the Alumni Association (Gakuyūkai) of the Academy on 27 November 1892.[28] The programme in English described the work as *Zigeunerleben* without any reference to the Japanese lyrics. Several more performances followed, and by 1902 when it was performed at the graduate concert of the teacher training department on 29 March 1902, a newspaper described the work as a signature piece (*meibutsu*) of the Academy. The programme names Torii Makoto as if he were the composer.[29] This, however, may have been the last Academy concert featuring Torii's lyrics. In subsequent concerts, Schumann's work has the Japanese title *Rurō no tami* (The vagrant people/gypsies), and was sung with a translation of the original lyrics by Ishikuro Kosaburō.[30] Ishikuro (1881–1965), having graduated in German literature from Tokyo Imperial University, taught at several institutions, including (in 1906–07) the Tokyo Academy of Music. He wrote several books about German literature and music as well as translating from German.

The change may well reflect the changing priorities of the Tokyo Academy of Music, resulting in the privileging of Western music at the

---

    names of either composers or lyricists. Kōzu is also named in an exhibition catalogue compiled by the library of Kunitachi College of Music; they cite a different edition of the collection (Dai Nihon Tosho, 1889).

27 Ivan Morris, *The Nobility of Failure: Tragic Heroes in the History of Japan* (Tokyo: Tuttle, 1982 (1975)).

28 Tōkyō Geijutsu Daigaku Hyakunenshi Hensan Iinkai, *Ensōkai hen 1*, 13–14. For Torii's text see p. 631.

29 Subsequent performances are recorded on 30 May 1896, a charity concert for victims of the Meiji Sanriku tsunami, and on 2 May 1899. Tōkyō Geijutsu Daigaku Hyakunenshi Hensan Iinkai, *Ensōkai hen 1*, 35, 81–82, 115–16. The review in *Yomiuri shinbun* is quoted on p. 117.

30 First record, concert on 9 October 1908. Ishikuro Kosaburō is not mentioned in connection with the work until a concert on 8 (repeated on 9 June) 1912. See Tōkyō Geijutsu Daigaku Hyakunenshi Hensan Iinkai, *Ensōkai hen 1*, 279, 343–44.

expense of traditional music. The change of policy happened gradually: its founding in 1887 did not mean that the reform agenda of the Music Investigation Committee was abandoned. Indeed, when in 1890 the Academy became a subject of debate in the newly opened parliament and its closure was proposed, the need for music reform was cited by its defenders as a justification for its continued existence.

The Debate about the Existence of the Tokyo Academy of Music

The National Diet convened for the first time on 23 October 1890, an event that was celebrated even at the Tokyo Academy of Music.[31] The celebration turned out to be premature. Less than a month later, when the government's budget was debated, some members of the Diet suggested closing three of the government's schools in order to reduce government expenditure, including Tokyo Academy of Music. In January 1891, the question was discussed in the Diet, and a committee was set up to investigate. The chairman published a report on 20 February recommending the closures, but the vice-minister of education, a member of the committee, disagreed. The controversy over the continued existence of the Tokyo Academy of Music (*Tōkyō Ongaku Gakkō zonhai ronsō*) had begun.[32]

Ultimately, the Tokyo Academy of Music survived the crisis, although government support was reduced and it was temporarily demoted to a department within the Tokyo Higher Normal School. But the threatened existence of all three schools sparked off a heated debate in the press that reveals how their proponents thought about the role of music in relation to education, the state, and the people.

An early contributor to the debate was Yatabe Ryōkichi (1851–99), better known for his contributions to the science of botany. In 1885 he had been one of the signatories of a memorandum to the Ministry of Education calling for the establishment of the Tokyo Academy of

---

31 Tōkyō Geijutsu Daigaku Hyakunenshi Hensan Iinkai, *Tōkyō Ongaku Gakkō hen 1*, 294–96.
32 Ibid., 297–337.

Music.³³ He published an editorial entitled, 'Ongaku Gakkō ron' (On the Academy of Music), which received considerable attention from the press.³⁴ His arguments were not new. In his first section, 'Ongaku wa fūkyōjō kyōikujō kaku bekarazu' (Music is indispensable for public morals and education), Yatabe asserted that the importance of music for public morals was agreed upon in East and West, and cited titles of *shōka* designed to promote patriotism and virtue. He went on to discuss what appears to be his main concern: the state of popular music and the need to reform it. In 'Wagakuni zokkyoku no hiwai naru koto' (The popular songs of our country are obscene), he cited a collection of *hauta* (short *shamisen* songs) licenced for publication in 1883 as one example of many that he believed should not be allowed and that constituted infringements of Paragraph 259 of the criminal law.³⁵ He quoted short phrases from several songs, each followed by the remark, 'I cannot bear to write more'. Such songs, with their numerous allusions to the brothel and to illicit love, Yatabe asserted, were destructive to public morals. In his next section, 'Zokkyoku wa katō shakai no kyōkasho nari' (Popular songs are the textbooks of the lower classes), he even claimed that such songs with lewd content were the ethics textbooks and the bible (*baiburu*) of the lower classes. It was meaningless, he continued, to strive for equality with Western countries (*Seiyō shokoku to taiji suru koto*) and to call for the abolition of prostitution while neglecting to reform the education of the lower classes.

Yatabe nevertheless realized that simply prohibiting the objectionable songs would not be effective. In his last section, 'Zokkyoku kairyō no hōhō' (How to reform popular songs), he proposes three methods: 1. Promoting *shōka* in schools; 2. Correcting and improving popular songs,

---

33 Tōkyō Geijutsu Daigaku Hyakunenshi Hensan Iinkai, *Tōkyō Ongaku Gakkō hen 1*, 285.

34 Ryōkichi Yatabe, 'Ongaku Gakkō ron', in *Tōkyō Geijutsu Daigaku hyakunenshi: Tōkyō Ongaku Gakkō hen 1*, ed. Tōkyō Geijutsu Daigaku Hyakunenshi Hensan Iinkai (Tokyo: Ongaku no Tomosha, 1987 (1891)). It was first published in *Nihon* on 13 January, and then in *Kokka kyōiku* (No. 5) on 12 February. See Kimiko Hirata, 'Meiji 20 nendai no Nihon ongaku kan: Tōkyō Ongaku Gakkō zonhai ronsō o tōshite', *Ningen hattatsu bunka gakurui ronshū*, no. 8 (2008), https://www.lib.fukushima-u.ac.jp/repo/repository/fukuro/R000002158/16-51.pdf

35 This was one of several collections of *hauta* published in the 1880s. Paragraph 259 of the 1880 Penal Law stipulated that the display or sale of books and other material harmful to established customs or of obscene character was punishable with a fine.

and 3. Encouraging people to develop a liking for refined and elegant (*kōshō yūbi*) music. In order to succeed with the last two objectives, new versions of popular songs should be disseminated with the help of sheet music in Western notation, and concerts should present appropriate music. The Tokyo Academy of Music, he pointed out, was already working along these lines. The task, Yatabe concluded, was far too important to leave to private individuals or to religious bodies (presumably he was referring to missionary schools).

Inoue Tetsujirō (1856–1944), professor of philosophy at the University of Tokyo and recently returned from study in Germany, was another prominent contributor to the debate.[36] In an open letter to the journalist Asahina Chisen, published in the newspaper *Tōkyō shinpō* in February 1891, he gave his own answer to the question asked by the Diet member Yasuda Yuitsu, who had demanded to know how the Ministry of Education would categorize music in its classification of education as intellectual (*chiiku*), moral (*tokuiku*), or physical (*taiiku*). For Inoue, the Ministry's classification was itself questionable. He stated that it was based on Herbert Spencer and that English philosophers like him, unlike ancient Greek and German philosophers, hardly discussed the role of aesthetics in education. After introducing alternative classifications by the ancient Greeks and several German philosophers respectively, Inoue concluded that it was best to include aesthetic education (*biiku*) as a separate category, although he also argued that music had a positive effect on intellectual, moral, and physical education.

Inoue then enumerated the benefits of music: it could enhance pleasure, make work go more smoothly, and dispel worries and depression. He even suggested that the members of the Diet took time off from their heated debates and visited the Academy of Music in order to listen to sonorous music (*ryūryō naru ongaku*) to calm their hearts and cool their passions. The benefits of music for the state, he continued, had often been pointed out by the ancients. As well as the *Book of Rites*, he cited Plato, Aristotle, Strabo, Theophrastus, and Plutarch.[37] Given such

---

36 Tōkyō Geijutsu Daigaku Hyakunenshi Hensan Iinkai, *Tōkyō Ongaku Gakkō hen 1*, 356–57.
37 Plato, Aristotle, and Pseudo-Plutarch are the most important sources for ancient Greek thought on music. Strabo (64 or 63 BCE–c.24 CE) is known for *Geography*, his only extant work; Theophrastus (c. 371–287 BCE), a Peripatetic philosopher who

widespread agreement since ancient times, the government should invest in music education. Inoue concluded by expressing concerns about the democratic process itself as represented by the new parliament: while making decisions by majority vote could be positive, it could also cause harm if the majority vote resulted from short-sightedness and ignorance.

Kōzu Senzaburō (1852–97), who had studied teacher training in the United States at the same time as Isawa and taught at the Academy, likewise emphasized the importance of reforming music as part of reforming customs and public morals, for it was these that determined whether a country was civilized and progressive (*bunmei kaika*) or barbarian and backward (*yaban mikai*). For this reason, reforming public morals and continuing to support the Tokyo Academy of Music in its work was clearly the responsibility of the state.[38]

Other contributors to the debate argued largely along the same lines as Yatabe and Inoue. They referred to the ancient Greeks or the Confucian classics as evidence for the benefits of music in general and for the relationship between music and public morals and the prosperity and decay of states. The music enjoyed by the common people in Japan was coarse, even obscene, variously described in the debate as *hizoku* (vulgar, coarse); *hiwai* (obscene); *inwai* (obscene); *inja* (morally corrupt and evil) and generally associated with the pleasure quarters and prostitution. Such music needed to be replaced with more appropriate music, described with terms such as, *kōshō yūbi* (noble and graceful; refined), *kōshō tenga* (noble and refined), or *junsei* (pure; perfect) and *zenryō* (good, virtuous).

Creating the right kind of music and training teachers who would disseminate it was, of course, the task of the Tokyo Academy of Music, a task too important to be left to private individuals.

Several writers alluded to the competitive global climate and to Japan's efforts to join the ranks of civilized countries. In order to be recognized as civilized, the customs and morals of the people needed to be reformed, and music had an indispensable part to play in this

---

was Aristotle's close colleague as well as his successor, wrote about all areas of philosophy. His significant treatises on music are largely lost.

38 Senzaburō Kōzu, 'Mondai tōgi', in *Tōkyō Geijutsu Daigaku hyakunenshi: Tōkyō Ongaku Gakkō hen 1*, ed. Tōkyō Geijutsu Daigaku Hyakunenshi Hensan Iinkai (Tokyo: Ongaku no Tomosha, 1987 (1891)).

process. 'Ah, given today's world winners and losers where the strong defeat the weak (*yūshō reppai jakuniku kyōshoku*), who would say that the Tokyo Academy of Music is an unnecessary institution, if we want to raise the rank of our country and have our civilization progress?'[39] declared a Niitaku Ichiin (pseudonym), who also pointed out that music was a regular part of both private and public ceremonial occasions. Niitaku was one of two writers who drew a connection between the alleged decline of music in the Tokugawa period and the decline of the Tokugawa regime. He conceded, however, that while the Tokugawa rulers did not establish their own formal music, the imperial court had their *gagaku* and the warrior class cultivated noh, while in the better families, the *shamisen* was forbidden and their daughters learnt the *koto*.[40]

There were dissenting voices. The author of an article in *Tōkyō shinpō* asserted that the defenders of the Academy were overstating their case. Children, he claimed, did not understand the lyrics of either the new patriotic songs or of the obscene popular songs, so they were not significantly influenced by them.[41]

His assertion was rejected by Suzuki Yonejirō, a graduate from the Academy in 1888 and the future founder of the private Music College of the East.[42] Quoting several *shōka* with suitably uplifting lyrics, he asserted that children could well be taught to understand their content, as he knew from his own experience as a teacher. Unfortunately, he added, they also understood the less edifying content of popular songs all too well.[43]

---

39 Nitaku Ichiin Koji, 'Aete yo no shokusha ni shissu', in *Tōkyō Geijutsu Daigaku hyakunenshi: Tōkyō Ongaku Gakkō hen 1*, ed. Tōkyō Geijutsu Daigaku Hyakunenshi Hensan Iinkai (Tokyo: Ongaku no Tomosha, 1987 (1891)), 361. For another writer who referred to global competition, see Shōken Koji, 'Ongaku Gakkō no hitsuyō ni tsuite', in *Tōkyō Geijutsu Daigaku hyakunenshi: Tōkyō Ongaku Gakkō hen 1*, ed. Tōkyō Geijutsu Daigaku Hyakunenshi Hensan Iinkai (Tokyo: Ongaku no Tomosha, 1987 (1891)). Both names are pseudonyms; 'koji' means a layperson.
40 Nitaku Ichiin Koji, 'Aete yo no shokusha ni shissu', 362. The other writer was Iwasaki Kōji from Gumma prefecture: Tōkyō Geijutsu Daigaku Hyakunenshi Hensan Iinkai, *Tōkyō Ongaku Gakkō hen 1*, 364.
41 Kitarō Nakai, 'Ongaku Gakkō haisezaru bekarazu', in *Tōkyō Geijutsu Daigaku hyakunenshi: Tōkyō Ongaku Gakkō hen 1*, ed. Tōkyō Geijutsu Daigaku Hyakunenshi Hensan Iinkai (Tokyo: Ongaku no Tomosha, 1987 (1891)), 358–59.
42 See Chapter 3.
43 Yonejirō Suzuki, 'Ongaku Gakkō zonhai ni tsuite', in *Tōkyō Geijutsu Daigaku hyakunenshi: Tōkyō Ongaku Gakkō hen 1*, ed. Tōkyō Geijutsu Daigaku Hyakunenshi Hensan Iinkai (Tokyo: Ongaku no Tomosha, 1987 (1891)).

Shikama Totsuji's Contribution

The most significant commentator not affiliated with the government or its educational institutions was Shikama Totsuji (1859–1928). A native of Sendai, Shikama had graduated in 1885 from the Music Investigation Committee's nine-month course for prospective music teachers seconded by the prefectural governments, and stayed on in Tokyo (see Chapter 8). On 25 September 1890, just a couple of months before the debate about the existence of the Tokyo Academy of Music took off, he published the first issue of *Ongaku zasshi* (The musical magazine), Japan's first magazine devoted to music. An avid supporter of the Tokyo Academy of Music, Shikama published several articles of his own in its defence in *Ongaku zasshi*, as well as reporting on the controversy and printing or reprinting speeches by Isawa and others.[44] His stated intention was to promote music reform, and his first editorial began as follows:

> These days our country follows a course of reform in many areas, day by day, and we are reaching the realm of civilization (*bunmei no iki*) month by month. The old appearance of the education system is being reformed on a large scale, social interactions are being completely freed from evil customs, and in every way a new Japan is being created. Accordingly, people's knowledge is being developed with immense speed and their sensibilities are being directed towards refinement and elegance (*kōshō yūbi*). However, in order to foster this taste for refinement and elegance, the power of art and music is of utmost importance. Therefore, the government early on issued a law for all schools in the country, and as a result music courses were established far and wide.[45]

Shikama went on to detail government measures and musical activities, starting with the Music Investigation Committee, now the Tokyo Academy of Music, which had recently completed a new school building (the Sōgakudō, which housed Japan's first purpose-built concert hall) in May 1890. His other examples were the performance of Western music by the army and navy military bands; the Department of Ceremonies at the imperial court, where both *gagaku* and Western music were performed; performances at the Peeresses' School (Kazoku Jogakkō), where 'the

---

44 The chapter in *Tōkyō Geijitsu Daigaku hyakunenshi* cites *Ongaku zasshi* as its source for several of the texts.
45 Shikama, 'Hakkan no shushi'.

beautiful sound of the piano and the violin harmonize warmly with the nightingale song of the graceful young ladies', as well as several other schools. He also mentioned churches and ladies' and gentlemen's clubs, and added that even in the suburbs, there was a lively music scene, not to mention other parts of the country. However, Shikama continued, 'where there is thriving activity, abuses result and harm emerges. There is no escaping the general rule under heaven that every advantage has its drawbacks.'[46] Shikama's new magazine was intended as a timely contribution to the renewal of music. He assured his readers that he was well aware of the difficulties associated with his venture, but that despite these and his own inadequacies, he was determined to dedicate himself to the task. He concluded,

> For this journal, from now on, and for as long as it continues, I will from the bottom of my soul, with all my strength, and with sincere effort research and collect all that has to do with music, whether great or small, rough or refined (*gazoku*) and will strive to publish it in this magazine and will report everything without neglect. Thus, I will not cease to work hard in order to bring music of our country to the highest level of refinement. I beg you all, if you are making any effort at all to reform and aggrandize (*kyōsei kōchō*) the music of our country, to support our intentions and humbly hope that you will do us the honour of regularly reading our magazine.[47]

While Shikama's launch statement gives the impression that reform meant the dissemination of Western music, this is not what he had in mind. *Ongaku zasshi* in fact covered the entire musical spectrum of the time, including the various traditional genres of Japan, and Ming-Qing music (*minshingaku*). Shikama emphasized his inclusive stance in a short note in the seventeenth issue of *Ongaku zasshi*:

> Reviewers of our journal *Ongaku zasshi* have described it as a journal of Western music and I hear that it is disliked by some for this reason. The intention of this journal, however, is certainly not to proclaim Westernism or to advocate contempt for all things Japanese. It is to cover the whole world of music, whether Western or Eastern, to adopt what is right and reform what is wrong, to gather what is superior and reject what is

---

46 Shikama, 'Hakkan no shushi', 2. The quoted lines are followed by the statement quoted at the beginning of this chapter.
47 Ibid.

inferior, to adopt the strengths and to compensate for the weaknesses, and to act as a guide towards musical reform (*ongaku kairyō*). In this way, as we plan musical reform and progress, what else would we do but follow the course of fairness and integrity (*kōmei keppaku*).[48]

Shikama Totsuji elaborated on his views in further articles in *Ongaku zasshi*. In June 1892 he published an article entitled, 'Nihon ongaku' (The music of Japan).[49] Beginning with the assertion that every human society had its own music, corresponding to its level of progress and knowledge, he sketched a brief outline of music in Japan, described as part of the East (*tōyō*) with a 4,000-year history, since the age of the gods. Describing the Tokugawa period, he distinguished three kinds of music: *honpōgaku* (literally, 'the music of our country'); *hiwai naru zokugaku* (the obscene music of the common people), and *Shinagaku* (music from China). The first was music performed at the court and the shrines; he appears to mean *gagaku*, which Isawa too had singled out as a genre worth of consideration. The Meiji revolution (*kakumei*) brought a huge change with the introduction of Western or Western-derived music (*Seiyō chokuyaku-teki ongaku*) which was in the process of sweeping up (*sōtō*) the music of Japan. Japanese music, Shikama asserted, was not so much based on scientific principles (*gakuriteki*) as on the practice of technique (*shujutsu no shūren*). Moreover, seen from the rationale (*riron*) of Western music, it sounded sad by nature. Since Japan's music was born from Japan's national essence (*kokutai*), from the people's likes and dislikes, it did not suit the people from other nations and races. Making radical changes by force might be damaging. The music of Japan, whether refined or otherwise, had been part of the Japanese's sentiments for thousands of years and could not simply be classified as inferior to Western music. 'However', he continued,

> now that the tide of civilization does not permit us to continue with a half-baked situation, our best course is to compare and contrast East and West, and subject the music of our country to revision. Even so, our feelings and tastes do not allow us to merely add lyrics to Western scores. So, today's musicians must thoroughly comply with the character of our country's music: they must strive to achieve progress without acting against our national polity and tastes. Those who are first and foremost

---

48 'Waga Ongaku zasshi', *Ongaku zasshi*, no. 17 (February 1892).
49 Totsuji (Shōsen Itsudo) Shikama, 'Nihon ongaku', *Ongaku zasshi* 21 (1892).

responsible are institutions such as the Tokyo Academy of Music and the music department at the imperial court (Gagakusho). But we cannot help doubting whether the Tokyo Academy of Music and the imperial music department are following this principle. This is not the time when each can raise their own independent flag. Let all of us do our best to unite at this important time when our country's music is to be amended (*shūsei*) and bring forth something that is appropriate for advancing human intellect, as well as sentiment and tastes. We must not dishonour the wisdom of our ancestors![50]

Shikama's opinions largely reflected Isawa's, but his remark about the Tokyo Academy of Music and the Gagaku Office suggests that he had reservations about their efforts. He clearly saw a role for private individuals like himself in bringing about reform. The implication seems to be, and in this he may well have been right, that the representatives of the Academy and the court were too far removed from the common people to understand or care about their musical preferences.

That Shikama did not equate music reform with the introduction of Western music is even more evident from his longest statement on music reform (*ongaku kairyō*), a two-part article entitled, 'An outline of music reform', published in *Ongaku zasshi* in late 1893.[51] He began by stating that the introduction of Western music had brought about an impasse in the musical world of the country. Western music was welcomed by educated people, because of its scientific principles (*seiritsu naru gakuri*), but it also excited people's taste for all things new.[52] The problem, according to Totsuji, was that many members of the musical world of Japan treated the new musical current as irrelevant and remained ignorant of it. The practitioners of indigenous music held on to what was transmitted exclusively from teacher to disciple from ancient times (Shikama Totsuji is here referring to the practice of *hiden*, that is, secret transmission, in the traditional arts of Japan), and valued only their own repertoire of musical pieces. Consequently, any plan to renew music would come to nothing. The music of the common people was obscene

---

50   Shikama, 'Nihon ongaku' 11.
51   (Totsuji) Senka Shikama, 'Ongaku kairyō ippan', *Ongaku zasshi*, no. 38 (November 1893); (Totsuji) Senka Shikama, 'Ongaku kairyō ippan (ctd.)', *Ongaku zasshi*, no. 39 (1893). Although, 'to be continued' is printed at the end of the second part, Shikama does not seem to have published another instalment.
52   Shikama, 'Ongaku kairyō ippan', 1.

(*hiwai*), but as it was widely popular, it hindered the progress of the right kind of music (*seigaku*). As a result, the world of sentiments and emotions was contaminated.

The present musical genres of Japan, Shikama continued, had all come from abroad.[53] But the conditions of the country and people's tastes caused them to transform. For the renewal of Japan's music, anything from Western music that could be usefully applied to improve Japanese music should be adopted in order to remedy its shortcomings. For this purpose, its principles (*gakuritsu*) should be studied thoroughly and then transferred to Japanese music as needed. Shikama specifically mentioned scales and harmony, which he declared were underdeveloped in Japanese music, making it inferior to Western music. A full-scale transfer of Western music he rejected, because any music is the product of its environment and could not simply be imported from abroad. The ultimate aim must be to create a new music (*shin ongaku*) by combining the strengths of both Japanese and Western music. For this purpose, suitable instruments had to be selected and unsuitable lyrics improved. Shikama stressed the importance of producing sheet music in staff notation, which as he explained, made it possible to understand the composer's intention to the last detail. In particular, the transcription and publication of pieces that had always been transmitted secretly from teacher to disciple would make it possible for individuals to learn new pieces without needing a teacher, as well as making the music widely accessible to the public and for researchers. Musicians must therefore make available to the public the pieces they learnt by direct transmission from their teachers. 'The present times', Shikama asserted,

> no longer allow secretiveness, so the secret pieces should be made public, our country's music should be carefully selected, the lyrics of songs that are wrong should be discarded and instead right lyrics created from traditional or new texts; and by copiously taking Western works as a model, new instrumental works and songs should be composed. In this way we will achieve for the first time that which most of our compatriots hope for, the creation of a new music that suits the people of this country, and even the primitive and vulgar common music, which

---

53 He lists *gagaku*, *wagaku*, *shingaku* (Qing music), *zokugaku*, and *Seiyōgaku* (Western music).

cannot be expected to disappear quickly, will fade as a result and world of sentiment (*kanjōkai*) can for the first time be purified.⁵⁴

Music reform, Shikama continued in the second part of his article,⁵⁵ was advocated particularly by those who prioritized education. It was, however, an immense task that had to be combined with the transformation of learning (*gakujutsu*) and with influencing sentiment for the better (*jōsho no kanka*) in order to create new customs. Many of the people who advocated music reform did not have the expertise needed to effect this, while performers of Japanese music were set in their ways, had dubious morals, and were less concerned with education than with making a living by providing popular entertainment. Meanwhile, the attitude of those studying Western music did not help matters: they concentrated their efforts exclusively on Western music and treated Japanese music with contempt, failing even to distinguish between refined and vulgar (*seiga hizoku*) music or to consider common people's economic needs or their preferences. Conditions could change however, Shikama argued:

> Behold, we need only to look back to the people who threw themselves into Western music a few years ago: they knitted their brows and covered their ears when they heard the music of our country, and hated it greatly; like the cholera or snakes and scorpions. But is it not so that, gradually, influenced by the conditions of the times (*jisei*) and public opinion, our country's *Miyasan*-song was composed, and sheet music was produced for *sōkyoku* (*koto* music), as well as other instrumental music? This then was how the development of a new music for our country began and progressed without ceasing, and so we saw the first examples of music that reconciled Japanese and Western music by combining elements of both (*yūwa naru setchū no ongaku*).⁵⁶

Shikama envisaged a single, right music (*seigaku*) for the entire nation. But he realized that this was not likely to happen overnight, and one of the reasons was the existence of different social classes, upper, middle, and lower, and their musical preferences. The musical tastes of the lower classes were quite different from those of the middle and upper classes:

---

54 Shikama, 'Ongaku kairyō ippan', 2.
55 Shikama, 'Ongaku kairyō ippan (ctd.)'.
56 Shikama, 'Ongaku kairyō ippan (ctd.)', 2.

> Currently elite society performs on the piano elegant and refined songs and compositions with great pleasure, but even so the lower classes cannot be made to do the same. Not only would it not work, but it would not be possible to supply the musical instruments. For this reason, it will be extremely difficult to unite the country and unify its music. Moreover, the existence of the refined and vulgar (*seizoku*) music has been a natural truth in all places at all times. So rather than try to abolish or disregard common music, it is better to include it and to infuse it with refined music and thus cause the obscene and the vulgar to disappear naturally: this, I believe, will be an expedient means for the reform of music.[57]

As a practical contribution to the perceived need for suitable musical instruments that would appeal to people accustomed to common music, Shikama developed a hybrid instrument of his own, the *senkakin* (see the following chapter). In an article in which he introduced it to his readers, he continued his discussion of music reform and again stressed the need to incorporate the music of the people into the reform efforts rather than abolishing it outright. He began,

> Not only music, but all things begin by being quite uncomplicated (*kantan*); merely taking the form that is in step with the simple tastes, knowledge, and feeling of people's lives. But when it comes to music, its natural, unaffected sounds harmonize with the human body and because of this its development precedes those in other areas, and it is an obvious fact that it imperceptibly changes into something more complex.[58]

Music, Shikama continued, originated in India and continued to the East and the West. In the West, the Caucasians developed it continuously, while the Mongolian race in the East, including the Japanese, was more conservative. But although lagging behind in the development of music compared to the West, the Japanese were artistically inclined, and this extended to music, as the widespread performance of music among the common people testified. Intellectuals wanted this kind of music abolished, and to see only the most refined music widely disseminated, and even to replace Japanese music with Western music, but Shikama did not believe this was realistic or even desirable. Western music, he asserted,

---

57 Shikama, 'Ongaku kairyō ippan (ctd.)', 2.
58 Totsuji Shikama, 'Senkakin ni tsuite', *Ongaku zasshi*, no. 27 (December 1892): 10.

is composed according to scientific principles and by using harmony it gives a feeling of truly wondrous elegance, while its well-ordered melodies unite the hearts of the people (*jinshin o tōitsu narashimu*). But one cannot say that this music just as it is, is constructed in a way that allows it to be adopted by all countries. It is suited to national conditions, tastes, and sentiments of the people of the white race and expresses their attainments.[59]

Like Isawa and Kanda, Shikama identified the scientific basis and the use of harmony and systematic composition as the chief merits of Western music, and like Isawa and other government officials and teachers of the elite government schools who advocated music reform, he believed that Japan's indigenous music, with the possible exception of *gagaku*, was unsuitable for the needs of the modern nation they were striving to create, and that Western music should serve as a model for reform and become the basis for the creation of a new national music. The vulgar and obscene music of the common people needed to be discouraged and, ultimately, replaced.

For Isawa and those like him, however, music *per se* did not ultimately feature highly on their overall agenda of modernizing the country and creating a body of loyal citizens. Having limited (if any) musical expertise, they were hardly in a position to articulate how exactly their advocated synthesis of indigenous music with European art music might be successfully achieved in practice. Nothing, moreover, suggests that they were aware of the different kinds of music in Western countries, or of contemporary debates about music, such as, for example, the ongoing tensions in America between those who revered European art music as the gold standard and those who regarded modern popular genres as true American music. Ultimately, lack of musical expertise, and the absence of any genuine interest in music for its own sake, together with contempt for what they regarded as base music—and scorn for the lower classes in general—played a major part in determining the course of the development of the Tokyo Academy of Music into a Western-style conservatoire almost exclusively devoted to Western art music. When, in the early twentieth century, efforts to research indigenous music were initiated, it was with the aim of preserving it rather than developing it further.

---

59   Ibid., 10–11.

Shikama, on the other hand, while similarly dismissive of the music of the common people, was more sensitive to their needs and preferences. He had a genuine interest in music and engaged in a wide range of musical activities. He also had a better understanding of Japan's musical culture. He realized that traditional practices were closely bound up with social divisions, and that the ways in which traditional music was transmitted and practised were as much in need of reform as the music itself. Direct transmission from teacher to disciple hindered free access to the repertoire. Many players of traditional music, moreover, made a living by performing for popular entertainment, often in establishments of ill repute. On the other hand, Shikama appreciated the skills that went into performing traditional music and realized that the supposedly vulgar traditional genres appealed to the people and could not simply be abolished. He understood that music reform was a major modernization project that involved transforming not only the practice of music but also deeply rooted social and cultural practices, as well as the musical preferences of the people. He appreciated the immensity of the task that music reform represented. Above all, he was determined to take it on himself.

7. Shikama Totsuji: Music Reform and a Nationwide Network

> I intended, by importing music from the civilized countries (*bunmei koku*) to reform the music of our country and with this intent, from about Meiji 7 or 8 [1874 or 1875] I researched the various musics of our country. All the same, I achieved nothing. But finally, fortunately, I entered the Ministry of Education's Music Research Institute and for the first time I was able to study Western music thoroughly in accordance with my wishes […]. [1]

> Totsudō is not a musician: carrying a brush in one hand and a *koto* in the other, he writes and draws as he continues his pilgrimage through all the provinces.[2]

Shikama Totsuji's activities were, arguably, just as significant as Isawa's for the transformation of musical culture in the late nineteenth century. His many initiatives highlight the importance of individual actors, as does the content of *Ongaku zasshi*, which includes reports of the activities of other individuals who did not hold an official appointment, or, if they did—such as teachers in public schools—worked well beyond the scope of their employment. [3]

How exactly Shikama (1859–1928) came to play the role he did, remains somewhat of a mystery: little is known about his early education, and even less about his early experience of music, whether Japanese or Western. At the time of his birth as the first son of Shikama Nobunao, his

---

1 Totsuji Shikama, 'Yamato miyage no jo', *Ongaku zasshi* 46 (1894).
2 'Jinbutsu dōsei', *Ongakukai*, no. 160 (1915). Totsudō was Shikama's Sinitic literary name. Two years later he was living in Tsuchiura (Ibaraki prefecture): *Ongakukai*, no. 189 (1917): 50.
3 Part of the content in this chapter was previously published as Margaret Mehl, 'Between the Global, the National and the Local in Japan: Two Musical Pioneers from Sendai', *Itinerario* 41, no. 2 (2017), https://doi.org/10.1017/S0165115317000389

father, a vassal of the house of the Date (the rulers of Sendai domain), was responsible for the Date's horses (*baseika*). After 1868, Nobunao selected and bred riding horses for the emperor.[4] He was a prominent figure in the local stock-raising business. His second son Shikama Jinji (1863–1941) became a pioneer of music education in Sendai (see Chapter 9).[5] Better known than either Totsuji or Jinji is Nobunao's fourth son Kōsuke (1876–1937), a vice admiral who fought in the Russo-Japanese War in 1904–05 and in the First World War.[6]

Shikama Totsuji received his early training in the Confucian classics at the domain school Yōkendō. The school admitted boys from the age of eight, so Totsuji is likely to have been enrolled in 1866 or 1867. There was no fixed graduation age. The curriculum, as was usual for domain schools, included military training and book learning, mostly in the form of the Chinese classics, and Yōkendō printed its own copies of them.[7] A distinguishing feature of Yōkendo was that noh chanting (*yōkyoku*) had been introduced as a subject of 'rites and music' in 1817 and thus became part of education for the domain's vassals.[8] If, as his biographer states, Totsuji studied there for eight years, he would have been among a minority of students who remained there through the Restoration wars, when the school suffered severe disruption. From 1869 the school

---

4   Biographical details on Shikama Totsuji in Keiji Masui, '*Ongaku zasshi* (*Omukaku*) kaidai', in *Ongaku zasshi* (*hōkan*) (Tokyo: Shuppan Kagaku Sōgō Kenkyūsho, 1984). Besides information culled from *Ongaku zasshi*, Masui relied on documents and reports from family members, namely Shikama Tsuneo, the son of Totsuji's youngest brother Kōsuke, and the widow of Totsuji's fourth and only surviving son by a concubine.

5   He is generally described as the first music teacher of note in Sendai: see biographical details in Shin'ya Watanabe, 'Sendai sho no shōka kyōshi Shikama Jinji', *Sendai bunka*, no. 11 (2009); Miyagiken Kyōiku Iinkai, ed., *Miyagiken kyōiku hyakunenshi Vol 4* (Sendai: Gyōsei, 1977), 429; Sakae Ōmura, *Yōkendō kara no shuppatsu: kyōiku hyakunenshi yowa*, vol. 1 (Tokyo: Gyōsei, 1986), 175.

6   Shikama Nobunao's third son (Kōji?) died as a student, according to Masui; the inscription on Shikama Totsuji's family grave records the year of his death as 1891: his age is not recorded.

7   Osamu Ōtō, *Sendai-han no gakumon to kyōiku: Edo jidai ni okeru Sendai no gakuto-ka*, Kokuhō Osaki Hachimangū Sendai Edogaku Sōsho 13 (Sendai: Ōsaki Hachimangū (Sendai Edogaku Jikkō Iinkai), 2009), 38–41.

8   Sumire Yamashita, 'Tōhō seikyō no ongakaku to shizoku', in *Kindai ikōki ni okeru chiiki keisei to ongaku: tsukurareta dentō to ibunka sesshoku*, ed. Kanako Kitahara and Kenji Namikawa (Kyoto: Mineruba Shobō, 2020), 190.

underwent several transformations.⁹ Whether Shikama stayed on or whether he changed to one of the new schools specializing in Western subjects is not known. He may well have continued his studies in Tokyo. He reportedly spent two years studying both English and *kangaku* at Dōjinsha, the private academy opened in 1873 by Nakamura Masanao (1832–91), a founding member of the Meiji Six Society.¹⁰ Whatever the details of his education, Totsuji was subsequently employed by Miyagi prefecture and married Tatsu, a geisha (also known as Kotatsu; c.1862–1940).¹¹ The couple had four sons and six daughters, of whom three daughters survived them.¹² All three became musicians.

Totsuji himself claimed that he had already begun to study music in the 1870s.¹³ Even if we take his claim with a pinch of salt, he does appear to have developed an interest in music early in life and learnt various musical instruments. In 1881 he reportedly published sheet music for the *gekkin*, the popular fretted lute with a round body, used in Ming-Qing music.¹⁴ The space given to Ming-Qing music in *Ongaku zasshi* suggests that he had a special interest in that music. On 3 December 1884, Totsuji was admitted onto the short training course for prospective music teachers at the institute of the Music Investigation Committee in Tokyo. Earlier that year all the prefectures had been invited to send suitable candidates. Only twelve of them did (Fukuoka sent four).¹⁵ Miyagi prefecture sent Totsuji's younger brother Jinji, who at only eighteen years of age had become the principal of a local primary school. Whether the

---

9   The Yōkendō was established as the Gakumonjo in 1736 and renamed in 1772. The following summary is based on Kazusuke Uno, *Meiji shōnen no Miyagi kyōiku* (Sendai: Hōbundō, 1973). For the Tokugawa period, see also Ōtō, *Sendai-han no gakumon*.
10 Masui, 'Kaidai', 7–8. The chronology is uncertain.
11 According to the inscription on the family grave at Kōmyōji in Sendai, she died in 1940 at the age of seventy-eight.
12 The second daughter, Ranko (c. 1886–1968), the third Kunie (c. 1891–1969), and the sixth, Kiyoko (c. 1900–65). The eldest son Kaoru went to the United States to study and was not heard of again.
13 See the quote at the beginning of this chapter.
14 Masui, 'Kaidai', 8. I have not been able to verify this.
15 Masami Yamazumi, *Shōka kyōiku seiritsu katei no kenkyū* (Tokyo: Tōkyō Daigaku Shuppankai, 1967), 158–70; Mamiko Sakamoto, *Meiji chūtō ongaku kyōin no kenkyū: 'Inaka kyōshi' to sono jidai* (Tokyo: Kazama Shobō, 2006), 119–22. There were forty-seven prefectures at the time (the numbers fluctuated before 1888). Sakamoto's work is the most detailed about the training of secondary level music teachers in the Meiji period (although only from lower secondary level onwards).

prefecture also sent Totsuji, who was not employed as an educator, or whether his strong interest in music made him persuade the authorities to let him attend too we cannot be sure.[16] The Institute was, presumably, happy to have him, as the number of applicants fell below the Institute's quota.[17] The nine-month course consisted of *shōka*, reed organ, *koto* and *kokyū* (Japanese bowed lute). The Japanese instruments were used, sometimes in modified forms, as a substitute for the keyboard and the violin, although most schools made every effort to purchase at least one reed organ.

After graduating in July 1885,[18] Shikama Jinji returned to Sendai, while Shikama Totsuji remained in Tokyo. For the next few years he taught at Tokyo Normal School (until 1888). He is also listed as a teacher (of what exactly is not recorded) at the Tokyo Academy of Music from 1892 to 1894.[19] Most of his wide-ranging musical activities, however, he conducted privately. He taught at the Tōkyō Shōkakai in the Yūrakuchō district of Tokyo. Established in 1885, this was the first of several private music schools offering short courses in music for primary school teachers. He also engaged in publishing, collecting instruments and even inventing a new one himself, as well as performing and organizing concerts.

In May or June 1896 Totsuji returned to Sendai, ostensibly because of his father's illness (Nobunao died in December 1897).[20] Possibly, he also saw more scope for his pioneering activities in the provincial town, where there were far fewer men with even his low level of musical training. For the next ten years or so, he continued his pioneering activities in Sendai. He may have moved back to Tokyo with his family in around 1906, but left his family to travel around the Tohoku region, a lifestyle that

---

16   Masui, 'Kaidai', 8. Totsuji (unlike Jinji) is not on the list of students sent by their prefectures in 1885 compiled by Sakamoto: Sakamoto, *Meiji chūtō ongaku kyōin*, 120. Possibly he studied at his family's expense, as did his contemporary Tsunekawa Ryōnosuke, who likewise is missing from the list. See Satsuki Inoue, 'Tsunekawa Ryōnosuke to Meijiki Nihon no Ongaku', *Aichi Kenritsu Geijutsu Daigaku kiyō*, no. 41 (2011): 24, https://doi.org/10.34476/00000014

17   Masui, 'Kaidai', 9.

18   The university's later yearbooks say 1886, but 1885 is correct.

19   Tōkyō Geijutsu Daigaku Hyakunenshi Hensan Iinkai, *Tōkyō Ongaku Gakkō hen 2*, 1560, 1588.

20   A short report in *Ongaku zasshi* 58 (May 1895) stated that he was returning because his father was ill. The next volume was not published until September, by which time Kyōiku Shōsha had taken over.

a newspaper article in 1909 unflatteringly described as *hōrō* (roaming, wandering about like a vagabond).[21] For a while he stayed in Maebashi in Gunma prefecture, where he reportedly lived by his writing.[22] He acquired a concubine, Saitō Sumi from Gunma prefecture, with whom he fathered two children, a son (born in 1916 in Tochigi prefecture) and a daughter (born in 1918 in Chiba prefecture).[23] Judging from the places of birth of his youngest children, Totsuji's itinerant life continued into his final years. He died in Tokyo on 7 September 1928.

Global Ambitions and a Nationwide Network: The Musical Magazine (*Ongaku zasshi*)

The publication of *Ongaku zasshi* may well have been Shikama Totsuji's greatest achievement. As Shikama himself suggested, the time was indeed ripe for a magazine dedicated to music. Government efforts to disseminate music education nationwide had just begun, and Western music had no mass appeal. Meanwhile, traditional Japanese music and the immensely popular Ming-Qing music flourished. The world of traditional Japanese music, while still fairly closed, with its strict division into genres, was changing: its practitioners were making use of the new opportunities offered by the abolition of monopolies and guilds and other economic and social changes.

Ongaku zasshi was remarkable in more ways than one. First, from the very first issue (25 September 1890), it included an English title: *The Musical Magazine*. This, together with occasional reports about musical events outside Japan, suggests that Shikama perceived his initiative as having significance beyond Japan. In his launching statement, moreover, Shikama Totsuji compared his initiative with similar ones abroad. Even in the capital of France, 'well-known for its music', publishers of musical

---

21 'Tokyo no onna (34): Biya hōru no gakushu, Inazuna kozō jiken no Shikama Ranko', *Asahi shinbun*, 22 September 1909, Morning.
22 See quote at the beginning of this chapter.
23 True to the customs of the time, the son was adopted into the Shikama family and registered with Tatsu as his mother, while the daughter was registered as an illegitimate daughter: information from copy of the *koseki* (family register) entry for Shikama Totsuji's household, dated 1 April 1929 (Shōwa 14). I thank Totsuji's grandson Shikama Tatsuo for this information; according to him, Totsuji also spent time in Nagano Prefecture.

magazines struggled, he stated with reference to an unnamed weekly musical magazine and the weekly music supplement of *Le Figaro*.[24] Second, regular reports about musical activities from locations across Japan helped create a nationwide network of people (mostly, but not exclusively, teachers) engaged in promoting music. Third, true to the idea of combining the best of all musical worlds, *Ongaku zasshi* included articles and reports on Western and Japanese music, as well as Ming-Qing music.[25] This inclusiveness may well have represented a major contribution to establishing *ongaku* (i.e. 'music') as a concept. The broad coverage was in keeping with Totsuji's advocacy of music reform, for which *Ongaku zasshi* was to provide a forum.

Music had previously been discussed in other journals, such as *Tōyō gakugei zasshi* (The Eastern journal of learning and the arts), established in 1881, and *Dai Nippon Kyōikukai zasshi* (Journal of the Education Society of Japan), established in 1883.[26] But *Ongaku zasshi* provided a specialized forum for all those who embraced the promotion of music as a cause—not least the increasing number of young men and women who, like Totsuji himself, graduated from the Tokyo Academy of Music and, unlike Totsuji but like his brother Jinji, went on to teach in provincial schools. Subscribers to *Ongaku zasshi* received a monthly reminder that they were part of a larger community, linked to other parts of the country and to its capital, and even to the wider world.

Besides regular news about the activities of the Tokyo Academy of Music and other institutions, *Ongaku zasshi* included reports from different regions, probably supplied by teachers at the prefectural teacher training colleges, several of whom would have been Shikama's fellow graduates. Reports from outside Japan informed readers about activities in the Japanese community in Korea and in Taiwan after it became a Japanese colony in 1895, and even North America or Europe. The regional reports often represented the personal impressions of the

---

24 Totsuji Shikama, 'Hakkan no shushi', *Ongaku zasshi* 1 (1890). The magazine is probably *La Revue et Gazette Musicale*; published under different names from 1827 onwards, it ceased publication in 1880.
25 For a list of articles on Ming-Qing music published in *Ongaku zasshi* from 1891–97, see Yasuko Tsukahara, *Jūkyū seiki no Nihon ni okeru Seiyō ongaku no juyō* (Tokyo: Taka Shuppan, 1993), 598–609.
26 Setsuko Mori, 'A Historical Survey of Music Periodicals in Japan: 1881–1920', *Fontis Artis Musicae* 36, no. 1 (1989).

reporter, who may well have been a local actor himself and keen to present his achievements in the best light. This is certainly true of the reports about Sendai, several of which detailed Shikama Totsuji's own activities. They give us valuable information about local institutions and societies, the activities of individuals, and performances; they often included concert programmes.

The magazine's other regular sections were: Music (articles); Songs; Contributions; Miscellaneous Reports; Reference; Miscellaneous Notes; Company Notifications; and Adverts: the first few issues included a serial and some issues had a 'Question and Answer' section.[27] Many of the articles were written by Totsuji himself (under various pen names), at least until issue no. 58, published on 28 May 1896, in which Totsuji announced his return to Sendai. Until then the magazine was published monthly apart from one or two delays. Issue no. 59 was not published until 8 August 1896, by which time *Ongaku zasshi* had been taken over by Kyōeki Shōsha, a major trading company which dealt in educational materials, including sheet music and musical instruments. From no. 61 (25 September 1896), the name was changed to *Omukaku*.[28] The contents changed too. From no. 59 a section with literary contributions (*Bun'en*) was introduced, as were longer, serialized articles by leading experts. Just over a year later, in February 1898, no. 77 became the last issue to be published, although there is nothing to indicate this in the issue itself. Presumably financial difficulties prevented its continued publication.[29] Shikama Totsuji's name appears in *Ongaku zasshi/Omukaku* only a few times after he ceased publishing the journal. In effect, it ceased to be his work after May 1896.

For the roughly five years Shikama Totsuji himself edited and published *Ongaku zasshi*, it provided a wealth of information and food for discussion on subjects such as musical theory, particularly harmony (regarded as the defining characteristic of Western music); Western, Japanese, and Chinese musical instruments and musical genres; as well as Western composers and musicians, starting with Jean-Baptiste Lully in the first issue, perhaps because of his significance as a composer of music played by the French-trained band of the Japanese army.

---

27 *Ongaku; shinkyoku; kisho; zatsuroku; sankō; zassan; mondō; shakoku;* and *kōkoku*.
28 Spelt phonetically, in *hiragana*.
29 Masui, 'Kaidai'.

Presumably, one or both of the returnees from music studies in France acted as Totsuji's informers.[30] Other topics included discussions of the role of music in education, public morality, patriotism, health, and Buddhism.

Songs, in staff or cipher notation and often composed by Totsuji himself, were another regular feature of *Ongaku zasshi*, as were announcements and adverts for his own publishing company, Ongaku Zasshi Sha, and other adverts, mainly for institutions offering music courses and for educational material, sheet music, and musical instruments. Around the time *Ongaku zasshi* was launched, Yamaha Torakusu (1851–1916) and Suzuki Masakichi (1859–1944) embarked on the nationwide distribution of their instruments, and *Ongaku zasshi* regularly carried adverts for Yamaha reed organs and Suzuki violins. Totsuji initially tried to develop the domestic production of violins himself, but gave up when he realized that Suzuki had beaten him to it.[31]

The value of Totsuji's magazine as a primary source regarding musical activities in the 1890s for historians today is obvious. But how was *Ongaku zasshi* received in its time? The magazine itself gives us some clues, as do other contemporary publications.[32] We do not know how many copies of each issue were printed and distributed,[33] but issue no. 2 lists forty-seven places where the magazine was on sale, and no. 5 lists 107. Just over half of the locations were outside Tokyo. In several issues, 'supporters' (the nature of their support is not specified) are listed, totalling about 150 in issues 6 to 18. Many of these were people

---

30   Masui, 'Kaidai', 20, 26.
31   Masui, 'Kaidai', 10. Suzuki Masakichi was not the first Japanese to make violins, but he was the most successful when it came to large-scale production and distribution: see Mehl, *Not by Love Alone*, 72–83.
32   For detailed description and analysis of the supporters, sponsors, and advertisers named in *Ongaku zasshi* as well as feedback from readers and reviews in contemporary publications, see Akio Kusaka, '*Ongaku zasshi* ni miru Shikama Totsuji no keimō katsudō to sono hirogari: juyō no shiten kara (1)', *Aomori Ake no hoshi tanki daigaku kiyō*, no. 24 (1998), http://www.aomori-akenohoshi.ac.jp/images/stories/pdf/college/kiyo/kiyo26.pdf; Akio Kusaka, '*Ongaku zasshi* ni miru Shikama Totsuji no keimō katsudō to sono hirogari: juyō no shiten kara (2)', *Aomori Ake no hoshi tanki daigaku kiyō*, no. 26 (2000), http://www.aomori-akenohoshi.ac.jp/images/stories/pdf/college/kiyo/kiyo26.pdf The following numbers are based on the lists compiled by Kusaka. His lists of supporters overlap, so there are a few duplications.
33   Masui, based on information in *Ongaku zasshi* 36, estimates the total at 600–800 printed copies: Masui, 'Kaidai,' 13.

Totsuji may have met during his studies in Tokyo, including musicians associated with the Tokyo Academy of Music and the imperial court. One of the people named, Nose Sakae, was a graduate of the American Pacific University. Appointed head of Nagano Prefectural Normal School in July 1882, he pioneered the training of music teachers outside Tokyo when he established a training course in that prefecture in January 1886.[34]

In addition, forty-two individuals and organizations who donated money are named: besides Yamaha Torakusu, the largest contributor, these include the Satsuma Biwa Association[35]–an indication that it was not just those involved in Western music who appreciated the magazine. Support also took the form of advertising: the majority of advertisers were based in Tokyo, but a significant number were from other parts of the country.[36] Finally, eleven magazines and twenty-four newspapers from around the country published favourable reviews, having been sent a copy of the second issue and asked for a response.[37] Praise for the magazine typically stressed its rich content and its potential appeal to educators, musicians, music lovers, and even women and children. One enthusiastic supporter even likened Shikama Totsuji to Christopher Columbus.[38]

It seems fair to conclude that even though *Ongaku zasshi* did not make enough money to ensure its continued publication, it was welcomed by contemporaries as a source of information and a forum for discussion. It must have been particularly valuable for music teachers, who were working hard within the localities in which they found themselves to disseminate what they had so recently learnt. The magazine informed (and, possibly, inspired) its readers, not just regarding new music, but also the new musical practices such as music education in schools and public concerts (reports on musical activities included concert programmes). *Ongaku zasshi* would have reminded readers far from the capital with its substantial and growing musical public that they were part of a larger community.

---

34 Yoshihiro Kurata, *Geinō no bunmei kaika: Meiji kokka to geinō kindaika* (Tokyo: Heibonsha, 1999), 208.
35 Kusaka, '*Ongaku zasshi* (1)', 65.
36 Ibid., 68–73. Kusaka lists a total of 139 advertisers, including Shikama Totsuji himself, forty-six of which were based outside Tokyo.
37 Kusaka, '*Ongaku zasshi* (2)', 45.
38 Summarized in Kusaka, '*Ongaku zasshi* (2)', 47.

Ongaku zasshi was Shikama Totsuji's most important and lasting contribution to musical culture in modern Japan, but not his only one. His zeal for music reform drove him to become engaged in a wide range of musical activities, all of which he, of course, advertised and reported on in *Ongaku zasshi*.

Shikama Totsuji's Other Publications

In addition to *Ongaku zasshi*, Shikama Totsuji also published several other works.[39] By 1888 he had authored or co-authored *Kaichū orugan danhō* (A pocket guide to playing the organ) and *Gakki shiyōhō* (How to play musical instruments), as well as two collections of songs: *Katei shōka* (Songs for use in the home, 4 vols, 1887–?) and *Senkyoku shōka shū* (A collection of selected songs, 2 vols, 1888–89). More collections of songs and tutors for self-study followed during the years when he was publishing *Ongaku zassshi*; namely, *Shingaku dokushū no tomo* (A companion to teaching yourself Qing music, 1891); *Tefūkin dokushū no tomo* (A companion to teaching yourself the accordion, 3 vols, 1892); *Satsumabiwa uta* (Collection of songs for *satsumabiwa*, 2 vols, 1892), and *Kanzoku gakki dokushū no tomo* (A companion to teaching yourself wind instruments, 1895). Another collection of *satsumabiwa* song texts as well as of 'miscellaneous' compositions was published with his wife Kotatsu named as the editor: *Kokin zakkyoku shū* (Collection of ancient and modern music, 2 vols, 1894), and *Satsumabiwa uta: Yabu uguisu* (Nightingale in the thicket: *satsumabiwa* songs, composed by Yoshimizu Tsunekazu, 1894).

Like *Ongaku zasshi*, Shikama's other publications reflect his ambition to spread knowledge of suitable music for performance, whether Western, Chinese, or Japanese. Besides, Shikama may well have been motivated by commercial interests at a time when many instrumental tutors for self-study were being published (see the following chapter). Shikama's (and Kotatsu's) interest in the *satsumabiwa* is remarkable,

---

39 The publications listed here are in the catalogue of the National Diet Library, except for Kotatsu's *Yūgi shōka*, which was advertised repeatedly in *Ongaku zasshi* and published by Ongaku Zasshi Sha in 1892; Tokyo University of the Arts has a copy. For *Katei shōka*, the NDL lists only volumes 1–3 (1887–89), while the catalogue at Tokyo University of the Arts includes a fourth volume, but without giving a concluding date.

given that they were from Sendai and the instrument was mainly played in South-Western Japan until the Meiji period, when performers moved to Tokyo and popularized it beyond its region of origin. While Shikama published little apart from *shōka* after giving up *Ongaku zasshi*, he wrote the lyrics for the *biwa* ballad *Ishidōmaru*, based on an old Buddhist morality tale about the young man Ishidōmaru who goes in search of his father, only to find him as a Buddhist monk who does not disclose his true identity to him.[40] The tale had previously inspired other genres, from noh to kabuki and *jōruri* (narrative *shamisen* music). First performed by Yoshimizu, it became known as a masterpiece of his disciple Nagata Kinshin (1885–1927). It is included in the UNESCO Collection: A Musical Anthology of the Orient.[41]

Shikama Kotatsu was also named as the editor of *Yūgi shōka* (Songs for movement games, 1892), published by Shikama's own company, Ongaku Zasshi Sha. Advertisements for this appeared in the issues of *Ongaku zasshi* throughout 1892, starting in number 18 (March 1892). The blurb is the same each time and reads as follows:

> It is in children's nature to be lively (*kappatsu*). Lively children thoroughly enjoy movement games (*yūgi*) and singing (*shōka*). *Yūgi* and *shōka*, moreover, are most important for developing children's intellect and to stimulate their physical education. The editor has paid thorough attention to this and has selected *yūgi shōka* that suit the characteristic nature of the children of our country, and that we believe will help them to gradually progress to refinement (*kōshō*) and nourish their natural virtue (*bitoku*). In particular the movements to each song, with illustrations, will make this book an ideal one for children. The first edition has been highly praised, and a second edition has now been published.[42]

The advertisements each include different pictures of children in Western clothes, suggesting that they were taken from Western books.[43] The preface by the editor is similar in content to the blurb, while a short note

---

40 *Ishidōmaru* was published in 1905, in *Seishin kyōiku teikoku biwa renmashū*, ed. by Yoshimizu Tsunekazu. See Tadashi Shimazu, *Meiji Satsumabiwa uta* (Tokyo: Perikansha, 2001), 56, 208–09.
41 Record 6, side 2.: Noh play, Biwa, and Chanting (1962). See https://discog.piezoelektric.org/musicalanthologyoftheorient.html
42 *Ongaku zasshi* 18 (March 1892), facing p. 1.
43 Further advertisements appeared in *Ongaku zasshi* 22 (July 1892), front inside cover; 27 (December 1892), back cover.

on the following page, by Senka (one of Totsuji's pen names), reiterates the book's purpose, beginning by citing the German pedagogue Carl Kehr (1830–85), part of whose work *Die Praxis der Volksschule* (1877) was published in Japanese by the Ministry of Education in 1880.[44] The collection itself features pictures of children in Japanese dress. The melodies of the nineteen songs are in cipher notation, with brief descriptions of the movements.

Shikama Totsuji, who was clearly influenced by Isawa Shūji, may well have adopted his views on the importance of *yūgi* as well as other aspects of music education. However, the limited coverage of the subject in *Ongaku zasshi* suggests that Totsuji had little more than a passing interest in it. The May 1894 issue carried a short report about influential Japanese in Korea who were planning to establish a private kindergarten and to order musical instruments from Japan.[45] A few issues include *yūgi shōka* by different authors. The August 1896 issue (the first issue published by Kyōeki Shōsha) included a song entitled *Zen'aku mon* (The gates of good and evil) by Kakyōin Shōsen, possibly another pseudonym for Shikama Totsuji or, conceivably, his wife.[46] The tune was known, according to the explanation. As the title suggests, the content was highly moral and it is hard to imagine it appealing to children.

After 1896, Shikama seems to have published little apart from *shōka* and the odd journal article.[47]

Shikama Totsuji as a Performer, Collector and Inventor of Musical Instruments, and Band Instructor

Identifying suitable musical instruments was one of the measures for reforming music that Shikama mentioned in his article on the subject, and articles on a wide range of musical instruments regularly appeared in *Ongaku zasshi*. In July 1892 the magazine even carried a short

---

44 Carl Kehr, *Die Praxis der Volksschule* (8th ed.) (Gotha: E. F. Thienemann, 1877 (1868)). Japanese C. Kehr, *Heimin gakkō ron ryaku* (Tokyo: Monbushō, 1880).
45 'Kaigai no Nihon yōchien', *Ongaku zasshi* 44 (1894) p. 15.
46 'Yūgi shōka Zen'aku mon', *Ongaku zasshi* 59 (1896), p. 23. Kakyōin was the address of the Shikama residence in Sendai.
47 See Chapter 9.

report on Turkish and Middle Eastern musical instruments, based on information from Yamada Torajirō (Sōyū, 1866–1957), a businessman who first travelled to Turkey in 1892 and made a major contribution to relations between the two countries.[48] Shikama's published tutors offered practical help for anyone wishing to learn an instrument without a teacher. He played himself, although how consistently or skilfully is anybody's guess, as our only clues are concert programmes that name him as a performer. He may well have been the type of musician who can pick a tune with relative ease on any instrument they take into their hands. He reportedly played several Japanese and Ming-Qing musical instruments before he enrolled on the training course at the Tokyo Academy of Music, where he would have studied the violin and the piano or reed organ.[49]

He was certainly a collector of instruments. A report in *Ongaku zasshi* in July 1894 listed the following instruments in his collection (classification as in the report):[50]

From Europe:
    Stringed instruments: 1 violin; 1 tenor (viola); 1 cello; 1 mandolin
    Wind instruments: 1 clarinet; 1 *petit flûte* (piccolo flute); 1 *grande flûte* (transverse flute); 1 trumpet
    Instruments with keys: 1 organ; 1 accordion
    Percussion: 1 cymbal; 1 triangle; 1 *chōritsukei* (tuning fork)

From China:
    Wind: 1 *dōshō* (bamboo flute); 9 Shin-*teki* (flutes played in Shingaku); 1 *chanmera* (or *suona*: double reed, oboe-like instrument, originally from Persia); 1 *hitsuriki* (*hichiriki*: double-reed flute)
    Strings: 1 *pipa* (Chinese *biwa*: plucked lute); 5 *gekkin* (round lute with frets); 1 *jahisen* (or *jabisen*: Okinawa *sanshin*, the Okinawan version of the *shamisen*: three-stringed plucked lute); 1 *yōkin* (Chinese, *yangqin*; zither-like instrument); 1 *teikin* (Chinese *tiquin*; two-stringed, bowed instrument); 1 *kokin* (Chinese *huqin*; bowed instrument with two strings); 1 *shichigenkin* (Chinese *guqin*; seven-stringed zither)
    Percussion: 1 *hakuhan* (?*paiban*; clappers) 1 *banko* (Chinese *bangu*; small, high-pitched drum); 1 *dōra* (Chinese *tóngluó*; gong)

---

48   'Konstanchinopuru no gakki', *Ongaku Zasshi* 22 (1892), pp. 14–15.
49   Masui, 'Kaidai', 8, 9. Masui states that Shikama Totsuji played at least the *koto*, *biwa*, and *gekkin*.
50   Totsuji Shikama, 'Kakushu no gakki', *Ongaku zasshi*, no. 46 (1894).

From Japan:
> Wind: 1 *shō*; 1 *hitsuriki* (*hichiriki* double-reed flute used in court music); 1 *yokobue* (transverse flute); 1 *komabue* (type of flute used in *gagaku*); 1 *shinobue* (transverse flute used in kabuki and folk music); 2 *shakuhachi* (end-blown bamboo flute); 8 *hitoyogiri* (a type of *shakuhachi*); 2 *tenfuku/tenpuku* (a type of flute from Kagoshima, similar to the *shakuhachi*); 1 *mokukan* (wooden flute)
> Strings: 4 *senkakin* (Shikama's own invention); 1 thirteen-stringed *koto* (plucked zither); 1 *shamisen* (three-stringed plucked lute); 1 *yakumogoto* (a type of two-stringed *koto*); 1 *nigenkin* (two-stringed *koto*); 1 *chikukin* (three-stringed *koto*, similar to *yakumogoto*, invented in 1886 by Tamura Yosaburō); 1 *satsumabiwa* (plucked lute of the Satsuma-type); 1 Ryūkyū *sanshin* (Okinawan version of the *shamisen*); 1 *chōshisō* (device for tuning a *koto*[51]); 1 Ezo-*koto* (or *tonkori*; plucked instrument of the Ainu)

The lack of Japanese percussion instruments on the list seems surprising. On the other hand, it is remarkable that his collection included a *tonkori*, an instrument of the Ainu, which must have been unfamiliar to most Japanese, as well as two Okinawan *shamisen*: one each listed under Chinese and Japanese instruments, possibly reflecting the ambiguous status of the Ryūkyū kingdom before the Meiji government incorporated it into the Japanese nation. The list of European percussion instruments likewise seems incomplete, given that a previous report listed drums among the instruments for use by Shikama's youth band.

The clarinet was introduced to Japan with the military bands, but is unlikely to have been widely played in other contexts.[52] It was not taught at the Tokyo Academy of Music. Shikama had introduced the clarinet in a previous issue, praising its tone and range and describing it as 'the soul (*konpaku*) of wind instruments' and thus the equivalent of the violin, the 'king (*teiō*) of string instruments'.[53] He played it in concerts on at least two occasions in 1893: a concert in aid of a children's home, organized by Amaha Hideko, who had graduated from the school for the blind;[54]

---

51 See Kosen (Shikama Totsuji), 'Koto no chōshi sōgatten', *Ongaku zasshi* 44 (1894). I thank Prof. Tsukahara Yasuko for drawing my attention to this article.
52 The clarinet is today one of the instruments played by *chindonya*, colourfully dressed street performers who play for advertisers, but this probably represents a later development.
53 Senka [Shikama Totsuji], 'Kurarinetto', *Ongaku zasshi* 30 (1893).
54 'Yūikuin jizen ongaku kai', *Ongaku zasshi* 31 (1893).

and at a *shōka* concert held at a school in his neighbourhood.⁵⁵ What he played is not specified, except that he played solo. At the charity concert, he also played the *hitoyogiri* (three-stringed *koto*) in an ensemble that included the head of the Ōgishi school of *yakumogoto*, as well as his own invention, the *senkakin*, in an ensemble with clarinet, violin (played by Amaha Hideko), and several *koto*.

The mandolin listed among Shikama's stringed instruments was apparently a recent acquisition: according to a short note on the last page (34) of the same issue of *Ongaku zasshi*, it was given to him by an unnamed Englishman. Possibly this was A. Caldwell, who is listed among the supporters of the magazine in the sixth issue and contributed a short article on music published in the following issue both in English and in Japanese translation.⁵⁶ Shikama Totsuji is credited with being the first Japanese to have played the mandolin at a concert. The concert, organized by Shikama himself, took place on 26 August 1894. On 1 August the emperor had formally declared war against China, and the event was billed as a 'Patriotic concert as courageous offering to the state' (*Giyū hōkō hōkoku ongakukai*).⁵⁷ Originally planned for 19 August, it had to be postponed at the last minute because of a death in the imperial family.⁵⁸ The declaration of war was quoted in full in the September issue of *Ongaku zasshi*, followed by Shikama's statement of the rationale for the concert. At a time when everybody had to contribute to the war effort according to their abilities, it fell to musicians to compose and perform music that would encourage the patriotic spirit. The proceeds of the concerts were to go directly to the army.⁵⁹ True to Shikama's broad approach to music, the programme included a mixture of genres: bands playing *gunka* and marches, different styles of *koto* music, reciting, storytelling (*kōdan*), and *nagauta*. Apart from the mandolin, Shikama

---

55 'Seito shōkakai', *Ongaku zasshi* 32 (1893). His eldest daughter Fujiko played the *koto* in both these concerts.
56 A. Caldwell, 'Music', *Ongaku zasshi* 7 (1891).
57 The expression *giyū hōkoku* comes from the Imperial Rescript on Education issued in 1891.
58 Announcements in *Yomiuri shinbun*, 16, 19, and 25. See also *Ongaku zasshi* 47 (1894): 26.
59 Totsuji Shikama, 'Giyū hōkō hōkoku ongakukai kaikai no taii', *Ongaku zasshi* 47 (1894). According to the report of the concert in the same issue, 100 yen were delivered to the army the day following the concert.

also played the *hitoyogiri* in the concert, as previously, together with the head of the Ōgishi school.

The mandolin performance, in a three-part ensemble, was described as Senka *gaku*, Senka being one of several pen names used by Shikama: here, his name (assuming it was his) was given as Koto no ie Shōsen.[60] The other players were Amaha Hideko (violin) and Totsuji's daughter Fujiko (harp/*hāpu*), and they played *Yachiyo jishi* (Lion of eight thousand years). It is not clear what kind of instrument the 'harp' was. If it was a Western harp, it may well have been another first, but no harp is listed among the instruments in Totsuji's collection.[61]

There is no evidence of Totsuji pursuing the mandolin further, and the introduction of the mandolin in Japan in a more lasting way is attributed to Hiruma Genpachi (1867–1936), who graduated from the Tokyo Academy of Music and then studied in Europe, bringing a mandolin home with him in 1901. Totsuji's youngest daughter Kiyoko, however, later played the mandolin professionally.

Shikama's own invention, the *senkakin*, was born from 'my sincere and deep desire to devote myself to reforming the music of our country'.[62] A brief note in the November 1892 issue claimed that the *senkakin* could be used in place of the *koto*, *shamisen*, or *biwa*. The fingerboard (here he seems to be referring to the tonal range) was the same as that of the cello, the viola, and the violin, making it possible to perform music with Western-style harmonies. The note is followed by another, restating the purpose of *Ongaku zasshi* to promote music reform,[63] while an advertisement by the Tanaka Reed Organ Factory included the *senkakin* along with organs and *satsumabiwa*.[64] The merits of the *senkakin* were described in detail in the next issue of *Ongaku zasshi* in a three-page article that included an illustration.[65] After outlining his ideas on music reform (see Chapter 6), Shikama introduced his new instrument, this time spelt with a different

---

60 Masui assumes that this is Shikama Totsuji; the *hitoyogiri* performer appears under the same name in the programme, while in the concert in 1893 Shikama performed as 'Shikama Senka'.
61 Masui, 'Kaidai', 31.
62 *Wagakuni ongaku no kyōsei ni tsukusan to suru no seikishin shukushi*: Totsuji Shikama, 'Senkakin ni tsuite', *Ongaku zasshi*, no. 27 (December 1892), 11.
63 *Ongaku zasshi* 26 (1892), 32.
64 Tanaka Fūgin Seizōsho, 35.
65 Shikama, 'Senkakin ni tsuite'.

character for the 'Sen', the same character as in his home town Sendai.[66] The advantage of the *senkakin*, he asserted, was that its four strings could be tuned in different ways, either G-D-A-E like those of a violin, or A-D-A-D starting an octave below the violin's A string. A capo (*kase*), that is, a device clamped across the strings of the *senkakin*'s long, fretted neck, enabled the player to raise the tuning with ease. This, asserted Shikama, made it easy to play Western or Japanese music or Ming-Qing music. The tonal range of the *senkakin* included lower notes than most Japanese instruments, enabling players to perform pieces with several different parts, including a bass part.

A second article two issues later, by an author who called himself 'Tetteki Bōhyō' (possibly Shikama), again stressed the importance of suitable musical instruments for music reform: the right instrument was as important for a musician as a weapon was to a soldier.[67] After years of research, Shikama had finally developed the *senkakin*, based on the *koto* and the *shamisen*, and enhanced it by adapting characteristics of the violin and the *biwa*. The result was an instrument that sounded exceedingly elegant (*yūbi*) and had a wider range of lower tones than Japanese instruments, making it well-suited for playing harmonies and thus appropriate for the trend towards more complex music. It was not realistic to enforce music reform too quickly, continued the author, as this might lead to an increase in objectionable musical practices (an argument already presented in the first article). The *senkakin*, it was hoped, would provide the essential tool for promoting musical reform.

Subsequent issues of *Ongaku zasshi* included further mentions of the *senkakin* as well as adverts—for a time. Presumably, Tanaka soon gave up production, as the instrument then disappeared from their adverts. From the January 1893 issue (no. 28) the *senkakin* was advertised as being available from Shikama's own company, Ongaku Zasshi Sha. The advertisement praised the instrument as having 'a beautiful form, a superior and clear sound, is easy to play and to carry around. Moreover, the fact that it is suitable for playing Japanese, Chinese, and Western music with a single instrument.' The instrument was claimed to have elicited high praise, and music enthusiasts (*ongaku no shishi*) were urged to try it for themselves. Nevertheless, the *senkakin* failed to gain

---

66 The meaning of both the characters used is the same.
67 Bōhyō Tetteki, 'Senkakin', *Ongaku zasshi*, no. 29 (February 1893).

popularity. Without a published tutor and appropriate sheet music, or a skilled performer to champion the instrument, it did not have much of a chance. The November and December issues of *Ongaku zasshi* included notation for a *senkakin* version of the popular *koto* piece *Yachio jishi* in cipher notation, accompanied by a tablature.[68] Shikama himself played the instrument on at least a couple of occasions. One was at the charity concert on 23 April 1893 already mentioned.[69] That, however, seems to have been the extent of his efforts to promote the *senkakin*, which soon faded into oblivion, as did many musical instruments invented in the nineteenth century, both in Japan and in Europe.

Shikama's concert performances reveal him as an advocate of playing Japanese music on Western instruments, often in ensembles with players of *koto* or *shamisen*. This practice also characterized the youth band founded by Shikama in December 1894, the Tokyo Shōnen Ongakutai. One of the first of its kind, the band's stated aim was 'to avoid vulgar music and practise refined, proper musical compositions in order to promote good public morals and gradually incline (the public) towards the true music of civilization'.[70] According to the regulations published in *Ongaku zasshi*, the band was for boys and girls from the age of ten to the age they entered university. Rehearsals were on three afternoons a week. Participation was to be free, as were the instruments provided, but a maintenance fee had to be paid.[71] The following instruments were listed in the regulations: accordion; *senkakin*; flageolet; small pipe; large drum; small drum; triangle; cymbals; tambourine; flute; clarinet; saxophone; contrabass; bass; and unspecified stringed instruments.[72]

Two months later Shikama could report that the band had featured in the magazine *Fūzoku gahō* (Illustrated magazine of customs): the short article, reprinted in *Ongaku zasshi*, described Shikama as a promoter of reformed music (*kairyō ongaku*) with the aim of supporting education in

---

68 *Yachio jishi* 'Senkakin gakufu', *Ongaku zasshi* 37 (1893): 7–8; 38 (1893): 10; despite the announcement 'to be continued' in no. 38, it does not seem to have been.
69 Item no. 12: 'Yōikuin jizen ongakukai', *Ongaku zasshi* 31 (1893).
70 *yahi naru ongaku o sake yūbi naru seikyoku o renshū shite fūkyō o hiho shi zenji bunmei no shin ongaku ni utsurashimuru*: Regulations for the band in 'Tōkyō Shōnen Ongakutai', *Ongaku zasshi* 50 (1895).
71 An advertisement for members in the following issue stated that a monthly fee of fifty *sen* was payable: *Ongaku zasshi* 51 (1895): 16.
72 'Tōkyō Shōnen Ongakutai', 32. The terminology appears to be derived from French.

the home (*katei kyōiku*) and furthering the reform of society.⁷³ According to the article, the band boasted sixteen kinds of instruments from East and West and performed proper music (*seikyoku*), whether Eastern or Western, old or new, elevated or popular. It played upon invitation at gentlemen's functions. The illustration accompanying the report was drawn from a photograph and showed a group of twelve boys and girls in formal Japanese dress playing a large and a small drum, accordions, side- and end-blown flutes, a triangle, and handheld pagoda bells. Shikama himself, in a Western suit, is standing behind the group, flanked by a background picture of Mount Fuji with a breaking wave at its base, and a large banner bearing the name Tōkyō Shōnen Ongakutai. At the right-hand edge of the picture a Japanese flag and another flag with what may be the name of the band are just discernible. While the band is clearly the main subject of the picture, the flag and Mount Fuji suggest that they are representing the nation and thus Shikama's reform ambitions, which went well beyond training a group of children.

Subsequent reports in *Ongaku zasshi* provide a little more detail about the repertoire, which reportedly included the national anthems of various countries, famous waltzes and polkas, as well as pieces from the *koto* repertoire, *shōka*, and military songs (*gunka*).⁷⁴

Privately established bands were becoming increasingly popular at the time.⁷⁵ A report in *Ongaku zasshi* in September 1895 briefly introduced the ones in Tokyo prefecture, eleven besides Tōkyō Shōnen Ongakutai, one of them another youth band.⁷⁶ In December 1895, a year after founding his own band, Shikama reported that he was finding imitators in other parts of the country as well as Tokyo and offered to assist with instruments and advice.⁷⁷ Indeed, he involved himself in the establishment of a youth band as well as one for adults in Sendai even before he moved there in summer 1896. The fate of the band in Tokyo is not known. Shikama may have travelled to Tokyo while he was based

---

73 'Tōkyō Shōnen Gakutai sōga ni fu shite', *Ongaku zasshi* 52 (1895). See 'Tōkyō Shōnen Ongakutai', *Fūzoku gahō* 97 (1895).
74 'Fuka genzai no ongakutai', *Ongaku zasshi* 53 (1895); 'Tōkyō Shōnen Ongakutai', *Ongaku zasshi* 55 (1895).
75 Yasuko Tsukahara, 'Gungakutai to senzen no taishū ongaku', in *Burasubando no shakaishi: gungakutai kara utaban e*, ed. Kan'ichi Abe et al. (Tokyo: Seikyūsha, 2001), 110.
76 'Fuka genzai no ongakutai'.
77 'Tōkyō Shōnen Ongakutai'.

in Sendai, just as he became active in Sendai while still living in Tokyo; however, it seems unlikely that he would have done so in the long term.

Shikama Totsuji's pedagogical activities included his daughters. The eldest daughter Fujiko (1884–1901) was described by her (hardly unbiased) father in *Ongaku zasshi* as a highly talented musician.[78] She reportedly studied the violin with Rudolf Dittrich from age nine and was said to be even better than Andō Kō.[79] The three who survived into adulthood earned their living as musicians. The eldest, Ranko (1887–1968) reportedly taught music from the age of fifteen, after graduating from Miyagi Prefectural High School for Girls (Miyagi Kenritsu Kōtō Joshi Gakkō) in 1902. When the family moved back to Tokyo in 1906, she taught in the music department of the Matsuzakaya department store in Ueno alongside her father, from whom she eventually took over. She worked there for twenty-seven years. From 1908 to 1909 she studied piano at the Tokyo Academy of Music.[80] In 1909 she received a certain notoriety when the press reported an alleged liaison with an infamous conman. She and her sister Kunie (c. 1891–1969) were described as regular performers on the piano and the violin at Japan's first beer hall (opened in 1899).[81] The conman-scandal pursued Ranko for years: newspaper articles in 1911, 1912, and 1918 referred to it, and so we learn that in 1911 she was still performing at the beer hall, and that in 1918 the sisters were known for their talent and beauty.[82] Not

---

78 'Shikama Fujiko no Kōei', *Ongaku zasshi* 21 (June 1892): 21.
79 'Biya hōru no gakushu'. Dittrich was (1861–1919) was employed as artistic director at the Tokyo Academy of Music from 1888 to 1894. Andō Kō (1878–1963), like her elder sister Kōda Nobu (see Chapter 3), played a pioneering role in the introduction of Western music. Having studied with Dittrich from an early age, she graduated from the preparatory course at the Tokyo Academy of Music, graduating in 1894. After completing her studies at the Academy, she studied in Berlin for three years, before being appointed professor at the Academy in 1903.
80 Yoshihiro Kurata and Shuku Ki Rin, eds., *Shōwa zenki ongakuka sōran: 'Gendai ongakuka taikan' gekan* (Tokyo: Yumani Shobō, 2008), 251. Ishida Tsunetarō, ed., *Meiji fujin roku*, 2 vols. (Tokyo: Tōkyō Insatsu Kabushiki Kaisha, Fujo Tsūshinsha, Hakuunsha, 1908). The year of her birth is given as 1887 by Ishida, which appears to be correct. The inscription on the family grave states that she died in 1968 at eighty-two.
81 'Biya hōru no gakushu'.
82 'Bā to hōru (4): Onna kyūji no Shinbashi hōru', *Asahi shinbun*, 16 September 1911, Morning; 'Jogakusei o mayowasu', *Asahi shinbun*, 22 March 1912; 'Norowaretaru koi no akushu', *Yomiuri shinbun*, 22 March 1912, Morning; 'Inazuma Kozō torawaru Shikama shimai no jōfu nite', *Asahi shinbun*, 26 December 1918, Morning.

much else is known about them. They remained single and presumably made a living by teaching and performing, conceivably benefiting from the post-1945 rise in demand for music lessons.[83] Totsuji's youngest daughter Kiyo (1903–65) played the mandolin professionally, making several recordings during the 1920s and 1930s, some of them together with her sisters. She married Takenaka Kaseiji, a recording engineer.[84] After 1945 Kiyo reportedly ran her own mandolin studio, and, for a time, played in the Orchestra Symphonica Takei, a mandolin orchestra founded by Takei Morishige (1890–1949) in 1915.[85]

The daughters' careers are remarkable, particularly when compared to those of the Kōda sisters, barely a generation earlier: likewise from a samurai family (although from the capital and in the service of the shogun), they only performed in public in concerts under the auspices of the Tokyo Academy of Music and did not make recordings. They would almost certainly have considered playing for money in a beer hall as beyond the pale.[86] Even so, neither could they escape scandal. Kōda Nobu (1870–1946) had to resign from her teaching position at the Academy in 1909 due to allegations of an affair with August Junker, who taught there at the time. Although teaching music presented a viable career for women, the long-standing association of musical performance with the pleasure quarters made performing in public suspect.

Even for men, at least those from samurai families, music as a career was suspect. Shikama Totsuji, being the firstborn, certainly failed to conform to social expectations. Instead of remaining in Sendai and preparing to take over as the head of the family, he followed his younger

---

83   Margaret Mehl, *Not by Love Alone: The Violin in Japan, 1850–2010* (Copenhagen: The Sound Book Press, 2014), 231–47.

84   Information from music yearbooks (1922–41). The one for 1929 lists Kiyo as a Mandolin player: Gakuhōsha, ed., *Ongaku nenkan: Gakudan meishiroku Shōwa 4 nen han* (Tokyo: Takenaka Shoten, 1928), 110. In 1933 she was listed as Shikama Kiyoko but with the addition of Takenaka, her family name: Hitoshi Matsushita, ed., *Kindai Nihon Ongaku Nenkan (Shōwa 8)* (Tokyo: Ōzora Sha, 1997), 41. Subsequent yearbooks in the 1930s list Kiyo and Takenaka Kaseiji at the same address in Kōjimachi. There are several recordings in the National Diet Library and in the sound archives of Osaka College of Music.

85   Renamed Orchestra Symphonica Tokyo in 1987. I have not been able to verify the information about Shikama Kiyo's post-war career.

86   About the Kōda sisters, see Margaret Mehl, 'A Man's Job? The Kōda Sisters, Violin Playing and Gender Stereotypes in the Introduction of Western Music in Japan', *Women's History Review* 21, no. 1 (2012), https://doi.org/10.1080/09612025.2012.645 675

brother to Tokyo, remaining there for several years. He made his living from music; not as part of a respectable teaching career in public schools like his younger brother, but as a freelancer and entrepreneur. He spent a considerable part of the family assets on his ventures, most of which were short-lived. He made his daughters perform in the streets of Sendai as members of his youth bands, hardly an appropriate occupation for samurai daughters.[87] Finally, he abandoned his family for what appears to have been a restless life.

Yet Shikama Totsuji's contributions to the growth and dissemination of music-related activities were important, occurring as they did during the period when Western music was only beginning to reach the wider population outside the capital and the commercialization of music was still in its infancy. Its growing importance and the rising demand for music-related products were reflected in the increasing proportion of adverts in *Ongaku zasshi*. Above all, both Shikama's own activities, and those of the local actors whose achievements were reported in the pages of *Ongaku zasshi*, demonstrate the importance of individual initiative for putting into practice the ideas for music reform advocated by politicians and leading intellectuals, as well as bringing about developments that were not envisaged or endorsed by them. This is further illustrated by the activities of a younger generation of would-be reformers, as well as musical entrepreneurs, who promoted their own version of blending Western and Japanese music.

---

87 According to his grandson Shikama Tatsuo, their cousin, the eldest daughter of Totsuji's brother, was unhappy about this, as she was taunted about it at school: e-mail correspondence 19 and 23 July 2019.

8. Playing Modern: Blending Japanese and Western Music

When we think about it today, it [playing music that mixed Japanese and Western elements (*wayō chōwa gaku*)] was a childish, low-level pastime, but back then it was enjoyed by the populace.¹

Perhaps, rather than listening to and enjoying the music, it was about playing and enjoying the sound; when we consider the traditional music of Japan before the modern era, constrained by status and locality, then being able to simply take up an instrument easily and bring forth a melody on it, must have been an unsurpassable pleasure.²

Shikama Totsuji's enthusiasm for experimenting with musical instruments and styles appears to illustrate Ueno Masaaki's observation perfectly. Living and working as a free agent and entrepreneur, the heir of a former samurai made the most of his newly acquired liberation from the status system. He evidently enjoyed taking up new instruments and playing them. Playing Japanese music on Western instruments was part of his reform agenda; a first step towards the creation of a new national music. At the same time, it was a way of physically acting out civilization in the modern version of *bunmei*, which was based on Western notions of universal progress. The experience of physically acting out *bunmei*, together with the joy of producing a familiar melody

---

1   Hisao Tanabe, 'Meiji makki no hōgakukai', *Kikan hōgaku* 4 (1975): 23.
2   Masaaki Ueno, 'Meiji chūki kara Taishō ni okeru yōgakki de Nihon dentō ongaku o ensō suru kokoromi ni tsuite: Gakufu ni yoru fukyū o kangaeru', *Nihon dentō ongaku kenkyū* 9 (2012): 21, https://rcjtm.kcua.ac.jp/pub/2017web/publications/2012/pdf/09kiyou_ueno.pdf. Parts of the following chapter have previously been published in Margaret Mehl, 'Japan's Early Twentieth-Century Violin Boom', *Nineteenth-Century Music Review* 7, no. 1 (2010), https://doi.org/10.1017/S1479409800001130; Margaret Mehl, *Not by Love Alone: The Violin in Japan, 1850–2010* (Copenhagen: The Sound Book Press, 2014).

on a novel instrument, may well explain the popular appeal of what came to be known as *wayō setchū gaku* (music mixing Japanese and Western elements), *wayō chōwa gaku* (music harmonizing Japanese and Western elements), or *wayō gassō* (Japanese-Western ensemble playing). The practice, which in the following will be referred to as 'blended music' or 'blended performance', could take different forms. Most commonly it involved playing traditional Japanese music of different genres on Western instruments, from sheet music in Western staff or cipher notation. Sheet music was crucial for spreading the practice as well as for enabling traditional pieces to become part of a national repertoire and thus further breaking down one of the divides that characterized the practices of Japanese music.

Its proponents can be roughly categorized as 'reformers' and 'entrepreneurs'. Shikama represented both. The reformers who came after him were recent graduates of the Tokyo Academy of Music. Their arguments for music reform were similar to those of Isawa, Shikama, and others. Unlike their predecessors, however, they had thorough training in Western music, and several were employed in government institutions. Ultimately, these circumstances led them to privilege Western music.

Others, however, embraced blended music as a leisure activity, and enterprising musicians, including performers of indigenous music, promoted the practice by publishing sheet music. This was in itself revolutionary, not just because many of them used Western-style notation, but because it liberated would-be players from the need for a teacher. While the practice came to be looked upon with contempt by the Western-educated elite in Tokyo, it remained popular until at least the time around the First World War, as programmes of concerts in provincial towns, including Sendai, demonstrate.[3] Even when its performance at public concerts declined, it may well have continued to be popular in more private

---

3 Older works on the history of Western music in Japan—their authors perhaps having inherited the snobbism of the Meiji elite—barely mention *wayō gassō* (blended performance). More recently, scholars have tended to regard it as an important stage in the adoption of Western music, although it was relatively short-lived as a result of the increasing tendency to place perceived pure forms of traditional Japanese music and Western art music on their separate pedestals. See, for example, Yasuto Okunaka, *Wayō setchū ongakushi* (Tokyo: Shunjūsha, 2014).

settings: sheet music for the performance of blended music continued to be published and to be available in print well into the twentieth century.[4]

Music Reform in Practice: Graduates of the Tokyo Academy of Music and Blended Music

In 1909, when playing Japanese music on Western instruments was in its heyday, Katō Yōzō published one of the earliest comprehensive histories of Japanese music, which included a brief section on blended music. He defined it as the comparative study of Japanese and Western music, with the aim of making up for the weaknesses of Japanese music with the strengths of Western music in order to create an ideal music (*risōteki no ongaku*). As leading advocates, Katō named Kitamura Sueharu, Takaori Shūichi, and others.[5] Shikama Totsuji he described as a major disseminator of Western music, who pioneered the publication of Japanese music in Western notation in *Ongaku zasshi*.[6] Beyond that he had little to say about the new phenomenon. Interestingly, his short section is followed by one entitled 'The advancement of our countrymen in Europe and America', in which he briefly outlined the achievements of Tanaka Shōhei, as well as Takaori Shūichi and Iwamoto Shōji.[7] The activities of the last two (treated later in this chapter) illustrate another characteristic this new generation of reformers shared with Isawa: they wanted Japan's music to gain international currency.

Kitamura Sueharu: Sheet Music, Kabuki Reform, and Musical Theatre

Even actors who never left Japan appear to have considered a potential audience beyond Japan's borders. Kitamura Sueharu (1872–1931) was among the last students to have studied at the Tokyo Academy of Music under Isawa, when the idea of blending Japanese and Western music

---

4   Ueno, 'Yōgakki de Nihon dentō ongaku'.
5   Yōzō (Chōkō) Katō, *Nihon ongaku enkakushi* (Tokyo: Matsushita Gakki, 1909), 79. The others are Maeda Kyūhachi, Akaboshi Kunikiyo, Ono Asahina, Ōta Kanshichi, and Machida Hisa. Not all of these seem to have been equally prominent, and his list is not exhaustive.
6   Katō, *Nihon ongaku enkakushi*, 80.
7   'Ō-Bei ni okeru hōjin no hatten'; Katō, *Nihon ongaku enkakushi*, 80–81.

had not yet been abandoned. Beginning in 1901, Kitamura published several *nagauta* (a lyrical genre of *shamisen* music) in staff notation with Kyōeki Shōsha, a leading trading company for books and musical instruments as well as a major publisher. The cover page of Kitamura's first publication, *Kanjinchō* (The subscription list), is dominated by the English series title *Japanese Dramatic Music*, followed by the volume number, the title of the piece, and his name in romanized Japanese. Only then follow the Japanese titles. The voice part includes romanized as well as Japanese script. The following two volumes, *Tsurukame* (The crane and the tortoise) and *Echigo jishi* (Lion of Echigo) even include 'Introductory Remarks' in English.

Kitamura had transcribed *Kanjinchō* several years earlier.[8] His interest in publishing Japanese music in staff notation dated back to the early 1890s, when he was still a student at the Tokyo Academy of Music. The son of a prominent scholar in Edo who counted James Hepburn among his acquaintances, Kitamura came into contact with the foreign community at an early age. From 1887 he attended Hepburn's school, Meiji Gakuin. Wishing to study music more thoroughly, he enrolled on Shikama Totsuji's private music course, Tōkyō Shōka Kai. After a year in the Preparatory Department of the Tokyo Academy of Music he continued into the Teacher Training Department in 1891. By then, the initial efforts at combining Western and Japanese music were losing ground, but Kitamura did study the *koto* with Yamase Shōin, and at his graduation in 1893 he performed as a member of a *koto* ensemble, playing Bach.[9] A chance meeting with the wealthy businessman Kashima Seibei (1866–1924) led to the foundation of the Great Japan Music Club (Dai Nihon Ongaku Kurabu) in 1893. Kashima's many interests included brass bands and Japanese theatre. The club's members, who included some of Kitamura's fellow graduates, formed a private ensemble that rehearsed regularly and played Japanese music transcribed by Kitamura.

---

8 The early transcription is lost. Much of the following is based on Yasuto Okunaka, 'Wayō gassō Dōjōji: Kitamura Sueharu ni yoru Nihon ongaku kairyō to zasetsu', *Nagoya Geijutsu Daigaku kenkyūkiyō* 28 (2007); Yasuto Okunaka, 'Gosenfu to iu mediamu no tōjō: Kitamura Sueharu ni totte "saifu" wa nani o imi shita ka', in *Nihon ni okeru ongaku, geinō no saikentō*, ed. Shizuo Gotō (Kyoto: Kyōto Shi Geijutsu Daigaku Nihon Dentō Ongaku Kenkyū Sentā, 2010); Okunaka, *Wayō setchū ongakushi*, 31–68.
9 Okunaka, 'Wayō gassō Dōjōji'.

In his transcriptions Kitamura aimed to be faithful to performance practice. He collaborated with Kineya Rokuzaemon XIII (1870–1940) and his brother Kineya Kangorō V (1875–1917), as well as their father, Rokuzaemon XII (1839–1912). Kitamura would have them play a phrase and write it down; a laborious, slow process (it took two months for the first work, *Kanjinchō*), although with experience they became more efficient.[10]

Kashima and Kitamura also collaborated with kabuki actors. The members were invited to perform at an Inari festival held at the residence of the kabuki actor Ichikawa Danjūrō IX (1838–1903) on 20 and 21 April 1894.[11] The performance of *nagauta* by the club's mixed ensemble of Western instruments and *shamisen* impressed Danjūrō so much that he encored them and they performed *Kanjinchō*. Danjūrō's performance in the kabuki play of that name was one of his signature roles.[12] He was, moreover, a leading representative of the movement for theatre reform. At his suggestion, the club members agreed to collaborate in a performance of *Ninin dōjōji* ('Two people at Dōjō temple') at a charity event at the Kabuki-za in June.[13]

Meanwhile, on 28 April 1894, the club held an inaugural reception, with more performances of *nagauta* on Western instruments and in mixed ensembles, including *Aki no irokusa* (Autumn leaves), *Kanjinchō*, and *Echigo jishi*.[14] *Ninin dōjōji* was duly performed on five days, starting on 15 June; the dancers were Danjūrō's two daughters — another innovation, as performance in the kabuki theatre was prohibited for women before Meiji. Part of the score for the play was subsequently published in the

---

10   Okunaka, 'Gosenfu', 83. The project merited a brief mention in *Ongaku zasshi*: 'Kanjinchō', *Ongaku zasshi* 37 (October 1893).
11   Okunaka, 'Wayō gassō Dōjōji', 348–49.
12   *Kanjinchō*, 'The Subscription List', tells the story of the medieval hero Minamoto Yoshitsune, brother of Yoritomo who, thanks to Yoshitsune's military victories, has established himself as the first shogun. Yoritomo, fearing that Yoshitsune will usurp his power, pursues him. When the fugitives have to pass the barrier of Ataka, his follower Benkei saves him from being discovered by dressing as a priest collecting subscriptions for a temple. Distracting the suspicious guards with offers of sake and his spectacular dance, Benkei sees Yoshitsune's party safely through the barrier.
13   *Ninin dōjōji* is a version of the kabuki play *Musume dōjōji* (published in English as *The Maiden of the Dōjō Temple*), which in turn is based on the noh play *Dōjōji*. The basic theme is a jealous maiden who feels rejected by a priest she fell in love with at the temple, and who returns as a vengeful spirit during the dedication of a new temple bell. *Ninin dōjōji*, first performed in 1835, features two maidens.
14   'Ongaku kurabu', *Ongaku zasshi* 39 (December 1893).

magazine *Kabuki shinpō* (Kabuki news), which had been taken over by the club, backed financially by Kashima. The magazine also published scripts of plays from the private Ichikawa collection, making them publicly available for the first time.[15]

Danjūrō himself performed *Dōjōji* in the role of the female dancer, that is, as the traditional *onnagata*, with the music club's mixed ensemble in January 1896. Danjūrō's performance was praised, but the reception of the music by the critics was largely negative. The heyday of the theatre reform movement had passed anyway, and the ensemble's accompaniment was perceived as intrusive.[16]

The Great Japan Music Club continued its activities for a few more months, but when Kashima ran into financial and personal difficulties it lost his backing and could not survive. Kitamura accepted an appointment at Aomori Normal School, then at Nagano Normal School, returning to Tokyo in 1901, where he worked freelance, performing and publishing music. He continued to believe that transcribing indigenous music was a meaningful contribution to the renewal of Japanese music. Between 1901 and 1909 he published several *nagauta*, with Kyōeki Shōsha: some of these, like *Kanjinchō*, may well have been based on his earlier transcriptions. He continued to publish Japanese music in staff notation in the following decade.[17] Some of the *nagauta* he later recorded with American Columbia, featuring himself, his wife, and Maeda Kyūhachi playing violin and piano.[18] He had previously performed Japanese pieces with his wife (née Amano Hatsuko), another graduate of the Tokyo Academy of Music, in the Mitsukoshi department store, where the couple, joined by Hatsuko's sister, gave regular recitals on the violin and piano between 1906 and 1908.[19]

---

15 Okunaka, 'Wayō gassō Dōjōji', 346.
16 Ibid., 346–47.
17 The National Diet Library (NDL) holds some of his publications. For Kitamura's publications in a 1919 catalogue from Kyōeki Shōsha, see Ueno, 'Yōgakki de Nihon dentō ongaku', 38. The online version of the article includes an appendix with a catalogue from the Osaka-based company Miki Gakki, dated 1923, listing several transcriptions of *nagauta* as music for violin and for piano respectively.
18 The NDL has recordings of *Aki no irokusa*, *Kanjinchō*, and *Tsuki no miyako*.
19 Yūko Tamagawa, 'Mitsukoshi hyakkaten to ongaku: ongaku to shōgyō wa te ni te o totte (Music and Commerce Hand in Hand: Mitsukoshi and Music)', *Tōhō gakuen daigaku kenkyū kiyō* (*Faculty Bulletin, Toho Gakuen School of Music*), no. 23 (1997): 40-41; Yūko Tamagawa, 'Seiyō - Nihon - Ajia: Mitsukoshi hyakkaten no ongaku

Kitamura also composed himself. Three vocal works that he described as *joji shōka* (narrative songs) were premiered in 1903 and 1904: *Suma no kyoku* (Song of Suma), *Roei no yume* (Dream during bivouac), and *Hanare Kojima* (A remote small island).[20] They are forgotten today, although they were successful at the time. *Roei no yume* in particular became quite a hit. Its story was topical: a soldier during a bivouac (scene I) visits his home and his mother in a dream (II), until he is awakened by the sound of the bugle, calling his unit to defend themselves against an enemy attack (III). Composed for male chorus, with female soloist and instrumental interludes, *Roei no yume* was almost certainly premiered at Nagano Normal School, but the first recorded performance took place at a concert by the Wagner Society at Keiō University, held on 28 May 1904, in aid of soldiers fighting in the Russo-Japanese war. The following year, while the war continued, it was performed as a theatrical interlude at the Kabuki-za, with the kabuki actor Ichikawa Komazō (Matsumoto Kōshirō VII, 1870–1949), a disciple of Ichikawa Danjūrō IX, in the role of the soldier. Komazō had been among the actors and musicians associated with the Japan Music Club, where he had also tried his hand at playing Western instruments. Although apparently not the first theatrical performance, it was the first to receive media attention, including detailed reviews that enable a plausible reconstruction.[21] The silent role of the soldier's mother in the second scene (the dream) was acted by Onoe Kikusaburō IV (1860?–1937), accompanied by the female vocal solo, sung off-stage by Kitamura's wife Hatsuko. Komazō acted, spoke lines (based on the text of the work), and sang. The male chorus was positioned as *geza*, on the side of the stage, to the right of the actors. In the third scene, the camp under attack, the soldiers were played by actors and accompanied by the chorus. Most of the staging thus resembled that of traditional kabuki plays, with the exception that Komazō sang some of his lines, and the instrumental sections were played with Western instruments. The performance appears to have been under-rehearsed (attempts to have the kabuki actors sing were abandoned), and the reviewers found much to

---

    katsudō ni okeru ongaku bunka no seiyōka to kokumin ishiki no keisei', *Doitsu bungaku* 132 (2006): 83–84, https://doi.org/10.11282/jgg.132.0_78

20 All three were published by Kyōeki Shōsha in 1904.
21 The following description is based on the detailed analysis in: Yuki Itō, 'Opera to kabuki to "joji shōka" no kyōri: Kitamura Sueharu *Roei no yume*', *Chōiki bunka kagaku kiyō* 19 (2014).

criticize. Nevertheless, the show, which ran from 19 March to 23 April, was a huge success.

Conventional historiography of music in Japan describes this as the first Western-style opera by a Japanese,[22] but this does not do it justice. Kitamura did not compose it with the intention of creating an opera, and the Western-style notation and terminology in the score should be considered in the context of Kitamura's transcriptions of *nagauta*. The opening bars, marked 'Recitativo', bear a striking resemblance to those of Kitamura's *Kanjinchō* transcription, likewise marked 'Recitativo'. It therefore makes more sense to describe the performance as another example of blended music and in the context of efforts to modernize kabuki.[23]

Shōka, as well as children's operettas or 'fairy tale' operas (*otogi kageki*), represent the bulk of Kitamura's own compositions.[24] His opera *Donburako* ('Splash', onomatopoeic), based on the well-known tale of the 'Peach Boy', was published by Kyōeki Shōsha in 1912, with an English title prominently displayed on the front cover: 'Children's operetta Dom-Brako, in Five Scenes, the Plot Founded (sic) on the Japanese Nursery Story, The Momotaro, Word (sic) and Music composed by S. Kitamura'.[25] This was the first work to be staged by the Takarazuka Girl's Opera (Takarazuka Kageki; known today in English as the Takarazuka Revue).

Takaori Shūichi and Iwamoto Shōji: Music Reform and the Global Stage

By the time Takaori Shūichi (?–1919) and Iwamoto Shōji (1881–1954) graduated from the Tokyo Academy of Music, in 1900 and 1901 respectively, music reform was no longer actively pursued there. The two

---

22 For example, Keiji Masui, *Asakusa opera monogatari: rekishi, sutā, jōen kiroku no subete* (Tokyo: Geijutsu Gendai Sha, 1990), 49; Kazushi Ishida, *Modanizumu hensōkyoku: Higashi Ajia no kindai ongakushi* (Tokyo: Sakuhokusha, 2005), 57.

23 See Okunaka, *Wayō setchū ongakushi*, 64, 66–68.

24 The 1923 catalogue by Miki Gakki lists four volumes of music books for lower secondary education with separate volumes of accompaniments, four children's operas, as well as six 'dialogue songs' (*taiwa shōka*), presumably intended for performance by school children. Of the individual songs composed by himself, *Shinano no kuni* (The province of Shinano) is probably the best known and was designated the official song of Nagano prefecture in 1968.

25 Available online through the NDL. (The script and lyrics are in Japanese only.)

were close associates, who, at least in the early years after graduation, pursued the idea of music reform by blending Japanese and Western elements. Following Shikama's example, they founded a music journal in 1901, together with Yamamoto Masao (previously Tsutsumi Masao; 1880–1943), who graduated from the Academy in 1903.[26] This was *Ongaku no tomo* (Friend of music; from April 1905, *Ongaku*), which in 1908 merged with another journal to become *Ongakukai* (Music World). *Ongakukai* appeared monthly from January 1908 to December 1923 and attained the largest readership of all the music magazines of the time.[27] Initially edited by Iwamoto, Takaori, and Yamamoto, the latter took over most of the editorial work when Takaori and Iwamoto left for the United States in spring 1905. While Shikama had demonstrated his awareness of operating in a global context by giving *Ongaku zasshi* an English subtitle, *Ongakukai* went one step further: for several years it boasted an office in New York, and Takaori was the 'Foreign Editorial Manager'.[28] Takaori remained in the United States until 1912.[29] He published regular reports about musical life in America.

Ongakukai, like *Ongaku zasshi*, covered a wide range of music-related subjects. Its contents included new songs, instruction in violin and music theory, discussions about the role of music, information about current trends, and reports about musical activities throughout Japan and abroad. Teaching, particularly of *shōka*, was a major theme, and presumably many of the readers were music teachers in schools.[30] On the whole, *Ongakukai* increasingly privileged Western music, although it included articles on traditional Japanese music (*hōgaku*). Knowing

---

26 For details about the musical magazines, see Setsuko Mori, 'A Historical Survey of Music Periodicals in Japan: 1881–1920', *Fontis Artis Musicae* 36, no. 1 (1989).

27 According to the table of volumes in the reprint edition, the issues were numbered from 1 to 12 each year until Taishō 2 (1913). From January 1914 the numbering is continuous, starting with 147(!), with the final issue being no. 266.

28 For at least part of its period of publication, *Ongakukai* included a colophon page in English that even gave subscription rates in U.S. dollars and described the publication as 'The Ongaku-Kai (Japan's Leading Musical Monthly Journal)'.

29 *Ongakukai* regularly reported on their achievements. Takaori's wife Sumiko was reportedly particularly successful, capitalizing on her exotic appeal. The couple returned to America twice more. See Mehl, *Not by Love Alone*, 97–100.

30 For a brief treatment of the discussions on *shōka* education and *shōka* reform, see Yuji Kawabata, 'Zasshi "Ongakukai" ni miru Meiji-, Taishōki no ongaku kyōiku no jittai ni kansuru kenkyū: shōka kyōiku o chūshin ni', *Ongaku Bunka Kyōikugaku kenkyū kiyō* 29 (2017), https://doi.org/10.15027/42595

as little as we do about the editors—beyond what they wrote for the magazine—we cannot say for sure what changed their attitude, but the years Iwamoto and Takaori spent abroad almost certainly contributed to it.

In 1904, Iwamoto Shōji expressed his views on the need for a new kind of Japanese music in an article published in *Ongaku no tomo* entitled, 'Yūgeiteki ongaku to bijutsuteki ongaku' (Music as an accomplishment and music as an art).[31] He stressed the significance of music as an indispensable part of civilization (*bunmei*), and the need to create a new kind of music modelled on that of the West. According to Iwamoto, it was essential for Japanese to understand the importance of music as an art in order to conduct international relations in a manner befitting civilized (*bunmeiteki*) nations. Music was important for the health of society and for a happy family life: as an example, he cited the role of music in the German empire. The Japanese needed to learn that music was not merely a form of entertainment. Iwamoto did not advocate abolishing Japanese music, but improving it by studying Western music and creating a new form of music that comprised the best of both.[32]

Iwamoto's arguments were similar to those of the earlier advocates of music reform, and like them he saw the publication of sheet music as a way to promote a new kind of music. He and Takaori Shūichi expressed their views in their publication of the sheet music for a *nagauta* piece in staff notation in 1904: *Aki no irokusa*, which they translated as 'Autumn Leaves'. In the preface, Iwamoto extolled the beautiful elements of Japanese music and the way it suited Japanese sensibilities. By publishing the best examples in Western notation, he hoped to promote its study. Takaori, who completed the transcription, even included an English translation of his own preface:

> The musical world of our country, which is in a state of revolution and transition, is busily occupied in producing various kinds of new tunes and airs, all of which unfortunately lack refined taste and gracefulness. If left to its own course, our music will lapse into a lamentable state. My esteemed friend, Mr. Shōji Iwamoto, recognized the necessity of rescuing our music from this prevailing error by the comparative study

---

31 Shōji Iwamoto, 'Yūgeiteki ongaku to bijutsuteki ongaku', *Ongaku no tomo* 6, no. 1 (1904).
32 Iwamoto, 'Yūgeiteki ongaku to bijutsuteki ongaku', 4–7.

8. *Playing Modern: Blending Japanese and Western Music* 213

and harmonious combination of European and Japanese tunes. Through his encouragement, I have been prompted to make a theoretical study of tunes and harmony of our native music. The result is the publication of this little song, entitled 'Akinoirokusa' (Iinge [*sic*: Image] of Autumn Flowers). Although it is far from satisfactory both to the public as well as to the composer himself, as it is his maiden effort, yet the author's work would be more than compensated, if this little volume should become the motive of further inquiry into the proper study of our music, and should prove to be the forerunner of a more enlightened, and eventually a more highly perfected musical work in our country.[33]

Iwamoto and Takaori put their ideas into practice at charity concerts in Shizuoka on 4 and 5 November 1904, during the Russo–Japanese War, in support of soldiers' families.[34] While the mixed programme was not unusual, advertising the Japanese titles as 'music harmonizing Japanese and Western styles' (*wayō chōwa gaku*) was. Five of the eighteen items on the programme were described in this way, two each in the first two parts of the programme (nos. 3 and 9; nos. 3 and 8) and the final performance (Part 3). These were as follows:

Rokudan (Six steps; consisting of *maeuta, kumoi chōshi, hira jōshi*), performed on the piano [?] by Takaori Shūichi, Muraoka Shōtarō, and Takaori Miyaji[35]

Tsurukame (The crane and the tortoise) – violin, piano
    Muraoka Shōtarō, Takaori Shūichi, Iwamoto Shōji

Aki no Irokusa (Autumn leaves) – violin, piano
    Takaori Miyaji, Muraoka Shōtarō, Takaori Shūichi

Yachiyo jishi (Lion of eight thousand years) – violin, piano
    all the Tōkyō Gakuyū Sha members

Kanjinchō (The subscription list)
    Reciting: Takaori Shūichi; piano: Muraoka Shōjirō, Iwamoto Shōji

---

33 Preface dated August 1904: Shūichi Takaori, *Aki no irokusa* (*Nagauta gakufu, Dai 2 shū*) (Tokyo: Gakuyūsha, 1904).
34 'Shizuoka juppei ongakukai', *Ongaku no tomo* 7, no. 2 (1904): 34.
35 This is likely to be a mistake; see the programme of the following concert. *Maeuta* refers to the first song in a piece of the *jiuta* genre, while *kumoi jōshi* and *hira jōshi* describe *koto* tunings.

Of the other items, three songs sung by all the members, as well as Kitamura Sueharu's work, *Roei no yume*, might also qualify as blended music, in that they combined Western-style music with Japanese-themed lyrics. Two of them, *Sanjūyon rentai* (The thirty-fourth regiment) by Muraoka Shōjirō, and *Kogō*[36] by Takaori Shūichi are described as new works. For the third, *Bōyū o natsukashimu* (Remembering a deceased friend), Muraoka is given as the composer, but according to the programme of the concert the group presented in Tokyo three weeks later, Schumann is named. Muraoka Shōtarō (1881–1940) was another student of the Tokyo Academy of Music, although he left without graduating, and from 1907 onwards spent twenty-five years in Dairen, China, composing and performing. The pianist Takaori Miyaji (1893–1963), Shūichi's nephew, graduated from the Tokyo Academy of Music in 1909; he taught at the Academy from 1915 to 1946.

The concert In Tokyo took place on 27 November and again featured a mixed programme.[37] Of the eight items in the first half of the programme, none were explicitly billed as *wayō chōwa*, but two of them were *koto* pieces played on Western instruments: *Rokudan* and *Yachiyo jishi*. The first was performed by Muraoka (voice; *maeuta*): Takaori Shūichi (piano, *kumoi jōshi*), and Sawada Kōichi (*hira jōshi*). The second was performed by the whole group. Sawada also played *Kazoeuta* on the piano; according to the programme, this was the Japanese song, 'Hitotsutoya...', which had been harmonized in America.[38] Murata sang *Bōyū o natsukashimu* (Schumann).

The second part of the concert consisted of two *nagauta*, one by a typical *nagauta* ensemble composed of vocals and *shamisen*. The performers were from the Yoshizumi and Kineya schools, including the *iemoto* Yoshizumi Shōsaburō IV (1876–1972) and Kineya Rokushiro

---

36 According to the programme, this was sung by a chorus; presumably, the song was about the court lady Kogō no tsubone, who features in the *Tale of the Heike* and is a subject of several musical works of different genres. Takaori published a narrative ballad (*jiji shiyoku*) of that title in 1904.

37 'Wayō chōwa juppei ongakukai', *Ongaku no tomo* 7, no. 2 (1904). "Wayō chōwa juppei ongakukai." *Ongaku no tomo* 7, no. 2 (1904): 38–39.

38 *Kazoeuta* (counting song) describes a type of song, and there are several with this title. The volume of kindergarten songs published by the Music Research Committee in 1887 includes a *Kazoeuta*. See Monbushō Ongaku Torishirabe Gakari, ed., *Yōchien shōkashū* (Tokyo: Monbushō Henshūkyoku, 1887).

(1874–1956). They performed *Miikusabune* (The Emperor's warship).[39] The two *iemoto* had joined forces in 1902 and formed an association for the refinement of *nagauta*. They played a decisive role in elevating the status of *nagauta* as a genre in its own right. Both later held appointments at the Tokyo Academy of Music. The participation of musicians from the Kineya and Yoshizumi schools of *nagauta* in the concert, including the final joint performance, demonstrates that efforts at renewal did not only come from those primarily involved with Western music. For the final performance of *Aki no irokusa*, the *nagauta* artists were joined by Sawada Kōichi and Maeda Kyūhachi (piano); Saitō Sauda (organ), and Muraoka Shōjiro and Takaori Shūichi (violin). Maeda, Sawada, and Saitō were Academy graduates.[40] This grand finale featuring blended music proved a great success, according to the (hardly unbiased) report in *Ongaku no tomo*.

Barely two months after the concerts, Takaori Shūichi and Iwamoto Shōji announced that they were leaving for the United States.[41] They left in April 1905, and travelled to Hawaii and North America with virtually no money, planning to live by performing. The timing was auspicious: Japan had just won the war against Russia, so they could expect a heightened interest in their home country. On 21 April they gave a performance in Honolulu at the Mochizuki Club (a restaurant), with a selection of Western and Japanese pieces to 'hearty applause'. According to the short article in *The Pacific Commercial Advertiser*, the two musicians were planning to study in Boston for a year before making their way to Italy.[42]

When they performed in San Francisco in July, their tour was worth half a page in *The San Francisco Call*, with an impressive photograph of

---

39 Not to be confused with a more recent piece from the noh repertoire of that name. In a programme by the Wagner Society on 19 November, *Miikusabune* is described as a piece of the (Yoshizumi?) Shōsaburō School.

40 Maeda Kyūhachi (1874–1943) composed, performed, and taught at the Tokyo Academy of Music from 1901 to 1922, during which time he conducted research into Japanese music; Sawada and Saitō had played Western works in the concert in Shizuoka.

41 Shōji Iwamoto and Shūichi Takaori, 'Kokubetsu no ji', *Ongaku no tomo* 7, no. 4 (1905). See also Katō, *Nihon ongaku enkakushi*, 81; Keiji Masui, *Nihon opera shi – 1952* (Tokyo: Suiyōsha, 2003).

42 'Unique Concert in the Mochizuki Club', *The Pacific Commercial Advertiser*, Honolulu, 22 April 1905, 9.

the two men and an even more impressive description of their alleged status in Japan. The picture had the caption, 'Two Japanese professors of music who discoursed interestingly on oriental melody [...].' In the article, Takaori was described as 'Professor Shuichi Takaori of the Tokio Musical College, "principal of the Japan Musical College," "president of the Takaori Musical Studio,"' while 'Professor Shoji Iwamoto', besides being called 'the black-locked, ivory-skinned Paderewski of Japan', was '"special commissioner of the Musical College of Tokyo, Japan", "president of the Japan Musical College," "proprietor and editor of the Japan Musical Magazine," and "director general of the Tokio Musical College Graduates' Association."'[43] The author of the article (Blanche Partington) had interviewed the duo at their hotel with 'Mr. Mori, the Stanford student' acting as her interpreter. She had not attended their recent concert herself, but she was treated to a short recital by Takaori, who played 'Träumerei', followed by 'an "ancient chorus" arranged by himself, "Akino-Irokusa"', and 'the popular song expressing "The Ecstasy of joy," Scotch and jiggy in character, and with three whole bars of "Bedella" adorning it!' The author liked the last piece best, although she wrote, 'it is dreadful to have to confess' to the fact.

Apparently Takaori did most of the talking, boasting of Japan's achievements in mastering Western music and the high standards at his alma mater, and telling her that his preferred composers were Mozart and Beethoven, who were 'most sympathetic with the Japanese sentiment of all the European composers'. They then discussed Japanese music, and Takaori told her of their hopes for the future of music in Japan. The author found this explained clearly in the preface to *Aki no irokusa* (quoted above), which she quoted in full.[44] She concluded by advertising the forthcoming concert, in which the duo would be playing the *shamisen* and the *koto* as well as the violin and piano.

Presumably, Takaori and Iwamoto gave several performances on their way to Boston.[45] In November 1905 the pair gave a violin and piano recital

---

43 Blanche Partington, 'With the Players and the Music Folk', *The San Francisco Call*, 16 July 1905.
44 Partington, 'With the Players'. Interestingly, the same page carried a short announcement for a Japan-themed play by 'a local man' entitled, 'The Heart of a Geisha'.
45 Iwamoto was stated to be in Boston in an article published in *Ongaku*, 11 no. 6. (April 1907): 15–16.

as well as a performance in Japanese costume with Takaori playing the *shamisen* at a meeting of the National Society of New England Women; the programme included a lecture entitled, 'Why Japan was victorious in the late war'.[46] They may well have continued to perform in order to finance their studies. In December 1912, Takaori and his wife travelled to Europe before returning to Tokyo in May 1913.[47] Iwamoto returned earlier, although when exactly is not clear.[48] With or without Iwamoto, Takaori reportedly played the violin in over sixty hotels in New England over the summer (1911) and earned substantial sums of money.[49]

The real success, however, was Takaori's wife Sumiko; the same report in *Ongakukai* stated that she was more famous than her husband. A former voice student at the Tokyo Academy of Music, she took lessons from the famous singer Geraldine Farrar (1882–1967) in New York.[50] In September 1911, Sumiko became the first Japanese to appear on stage at the Met in a matinee performance of *Madame Butterfly*, although not in a major role.[51] Most of her performances, however, were in vaudeville theatres, with her husband acting as her musical director and as conductor. In an advertisement for a show at Chase's in Washington she was billed as 'Madame Sumiko, the Famous Prima Donna Soprano of the Imperial Opera House, Tokio'. The advertisement also promised 'geisha girls, rickshaw runners etc', suggesting that the event was to be an exotic spectacle rather than a significant musical event.[52] Like the geisha-turned-actress Kawakami Sadayakko, or Miura Tamaki, of *Madame Butterfly* fame, 'Madame Sumiko', ably promoted by her husband, successfully capitalized on Western audiences' fascination with Far Eastern exoticism.[53]

---

46   *New England Magazine*, November 1905, 620.
47   Biō Takaori, 'Gakuyū shishin (26 shin)', *Ongakukai* 6, no. 6 (1913); Biō Takaori, 'Gakuyū shishin (27 shin, 28 shin)', *Ongakukai* 6, no. 7 (1913); Biō Takaori, 'Gakuyū shishin (29 shin)', *Ongakukai* 6, no. 8 (1913); Shūichi Takaori, 'Kikyo raiji', *Ongakukai* 6, no. 6 (1913).
48   Takaori, 'Kikyo raiji'. In February 1913 he was recorded as living in Tokyo in the first part of a register of musicians published in *Ongakukai* (6, no. 2).
49   Masataka Yamamoto, 'Beikoku no gakukai to hōjin no daiseikō', *Ongakukai* 4, no. 7 (1911): 35.
50   This and the following from Masui, *Nihon opera shi – 1952*, 93–94, 129–30.
51   Masui, *Nihon opera shi – 1952*.
52   'Amusements', Display Ad, *The Washington Post*, 10 December 1911.
53   See Mari Yoshihara, 'The Flight of the Japanese Butterfly: Orientalism, Nationalism, and Performances of Japanese Womanhood', *American Quarterly* 56, no. 4 (2004),

Her husband, meanwhile, had taken to conducting. In the same Washington advertisement, he was described as 'the Celebrated Director B.S. Takaori of the Imperial Opera House', who was to conduct 'Alexander's Ragtime Band'. Subsequent engagements in Europe included a performance on 30 December 1912, at the famous Wintergarten Varieté theatre in Berlin.[54] After their return, Takaori directed two operatic works at the Imperial Theatre in Tokyo, the only two works at the time not directed by the Italian Rossi. The Takaoris travelled to America two more times, taking with them other performers and staging exotic shows.[55]

Takaori's transformation from would-be reformer of Japanese music to director of music in variety shows is remarkable, although not entirely surprising. Renewing Japanese music was as much about enhancing Japan's global reputation as it was about educating citizens. Even while expressing the need for Japan to essentially Westernize its performing arts, Takaori appears to have wanted to impress people in Western countries with displays of Japanese achievements. He wrote as much in an article published in *Ongakukai* not long after his return, entitled, 'Hōgaku no kosui kara seiyō no sūhai e' ('From advocating Japanese music to revering Western music').[56] When he enrolled at the Tokyo Academy of Music, he asserted, he preferred Japanese music, having played the *shamisen* from childhood. His Western and Japanese teachers, and even the students, were convinced of the superiority of Western music, while he himself continued to play the *shamisen* even while studying the violin. He came to feel that, although Japanese music had its weaknesses, these were at the same time its strengths. He had resolved to study at the Academy because he felt he needed 'the light of Western science' (*seiyō no kagaku kō*) in order to improve Japanese music.[57] He began to play Japanese tunes on the violin, believing that by doing so he could revive Japanese music, which to him appeared to be doomed. Promoting blended music, he hoped, would preserve the best of Japanese music and convince others, including foreign musicians, that Japanese had a power of expression that Western music lacked.

---

https://doi.org/10.1353/aq.2004.0067
54 Biō Takaori, 'Ōshū man'yū ki (dai 33 shin)', *Ongakukai* 6, no. 4 (1913).
55 Masui, *Nihon opera shi – 1952*, 93–95. See Mehl, *Not by Love Alone*, 96–100.
56 Shūichi (Biō) Takaori, 'Hōgaku no kosui kara seigaku no sūhai e', *Ongakukai* 6, no. 7 (1913).
57 Takaori, 'Hōgaku no kosui kara seigaku no sūhai e', 22.

This, he claimed, was also felt by many Japanese who, although they listened to Western music without aversion, found that ultimately it left them cold. When he travelled to America it was with the double aim of deepening his knowledge of Western music and bringing Japanese music to the West. Citing the example of Arthur Schopenhauer being inspired by Indian thought, he asserted that Japanese music might do something similar for Western musicians. Once in America, however, he not only realized that his aims were contradictory, but also became convinced that Western music had something to offer that he had not yet fathomed, and that Japanese music lacked. This, for him, was the beginning of a monumental spiritual revolution.[58]

Iwamoto's priorities too had shifted. In an article published a few months before Takaori's return he highlighted the responsibility of provincial music teachers for educating not only school children but provincial society in general.[59] He did not discuss the kind of music he had in mind, but school teachers were trained in Western music, and he did not suggest that they promote other kinds, beyond briefly stating that there must be a balance between common music (*zokugaku*) and 'classical music' (*kotengaku*), as both had their characteristics and influenced each other. 'Classical music' does not refer to Western music here; Iwamoto named 'classical' (*kotenteki*) as one of the characteristics of music in the countryside.[60]

Iwamoto's arguments were remarkably similar to those of the earlier propagators of music reform. Like them, he stressed the link between music and civilization (*bunmei*) and the importance of music for improving the customs and morals of the people. He even quoted classical Chinese literature, although not from the Confucian canon, but from a poem by Bai Juyi, who in *Pipa xing* (Song of the lute, 816), laments that he has been banished to a remote district (Xunyang) where there is no music and neither the sound of the lute nor the flute can be heard all year.[61] Iwamoto argued that civilization, including

---

58 Takaori, 'Hōgaku no kosui kara seigaku no sūhai e', 24.
59 Shōji Iwamoto, 'Chihō ongaku kyōshi no sekinin', *Ongakukai* 6, no. 3 (1913).
60 Iwamoto, 'Chihō ongaku kyōshi no sekinin', 8, 11.
61 Translations of this famous T'ang poem include Herbert Giles in *Gems of Chinese Literature* (second edition 1922). See https://en.wikisource.org/wiki/Gems_of_Chinese_Literature/P%C5%8F_Ch%C3%BC-yi-The_Lute-Girl%E2%80%99s_Lament. The poem was well-known in Japan; it famously features in *The Tale of Genji*, in the 'Akashi' chapter.

music, had progressed in the city, but that the countryside, whose people represented the roots of a nation's civilization, lagged behind. Meanwhile, its customs and morals were in decline, and those with responsibility for music in the countryside had to ask themselves how a people who followed the teachings of Confucius and Mencius had come to neglect rites and music. Compared to the city, culture in the countryside had deteriorated and moral decline was the result. The Ministry of Education had been promoting *shōka* nationwide, but its efforts were limited to schools, and had little effect on the people (*kokumin*) in general. The resulting void was filled with vulgar and obscene music (*yahi inwai naru ongaku*).[62] Iwamoto concluded that it was up to music teachers to use their expertise outside as well as inside the schools in order to promote and improve music in the countryside; he suggested three areas of work: 1) Innovations in teaching methods and choice of songs; 2) Promoting and organizing music in the home; 3) Community education, including the organization of movement games associations (Ongaku Yūgi Kai) for children as well as school concerts on public holidays.

Iwamoto's views reflect the Confucian idea of music as an important tool for improving the morals of the people and by extension the whole country. His argument that the individual home (*katei*) is the foundation of the state is another familiar concept from the Chinese classics.[63] But Iwamoto also described the home as a paradise on earth, where the family enjoys peace and happiness, when he recommended music in the home (*katei ongaku*), a new (and Western-inspired) concept, much discussed at the time. His phrase 'our humble little home' (*Waga hanyū no shōsha*) is reminiscent of the Japanese version of 'Home Sweet Home'.[64] Iwamoto frequently referred to Europe and America (Ō-Bei), where, according to him, music outside the big cities, while not the same, was highly developed. He concluded by stating that the quality of music in the countryside should be regarded as closely related to the prosperity

---

62 Iwamoto, 'Chihō ongaku kyōshi no sekinin', 10.
63 The shor-hand (in Japanese) is *shūshin seika chikoku heitenka* (cultivating the person, regulating the family/household, governing the state, ensuring peace in the realm). Versions of this phrase, which links the welfare of the household to that of the state, appear in the 'Record of Music' (Yueji) in the *Book of Rites* (*Reiki*, Chin. *Liji*), as well as in the *Greater Learning* (*Daigaku, Da Xue*).
64 Iwamoto, 'Chihō ongaku kyōshi no sekinin', 9–10.

and decline of the nation's fortunes. The harmony (*chōwa*) between Japanese (or ancient Chinese) and Western civilizations was arguably more successful in the realm of ideas than of practical music-making, and *katei ongaku* remained an unfulfilled dream.[65]

By 1913, *Ongakukai* clearly privileged Western music, particularly the teaching of music in the public education system. Japanese music, while not neglected entirely, was given nowhere near as much space as in *Ongaku zasshi*. Blended music featured hardly at all, except when writers criticized the practice of playing Japanese music on Western instruments. One commentator, writing in 1910, compared Osaka, the city of merchants, unfavourably with Tokyo and described its inhabitants' taste in Western music as superficial and childish: they treated the violin as a variant of the *kokyū* and played popular *koto* pieces on it. All *koto* teachers now had to teach the violin and taught Japanese music, taking payment for each new piece they taught. Others played Japanese pieces on the piano. The businesspeople of Osaka, the author speculated, did not want anything too demanding after a long working day. Thus, he lamented, the violin and the piano, the flowers of Western music, were abused.[66]

Criticism of what he perceived as deviant and backward practice was also expressed in Yamanoi Motokiyo's series 'Baiorin sōhō oyobi gakushū hō' (How to play and study the violin), published in *Ongakukai* in seven instalments in 1912.[67] Yamanoi, a court musician and a graduate of the Tokyo Academy of Music, essentially equated playing Japanese tunes with playing badly.[68] He condemned what he called the *haikara* fashion of playing the violin, supposedly common in Kansai, with the bow held around the middle of the stick rather than close to the nut. The violin, the king of instruments (the Chinese character has the phonetic

---

65 Yūko Tamagawa, 'Kindai Nihon ni okeru katei ongaku ron: "ikka danraku" no mikan no yume', *Tōhō Gakuen Daigaku kenkyū kiyō* 43 (2017).

66 'Ōsaka no yūgei violin' (1909; quoted in Watanabe, Hiroshi, *Nihon bunka modan rapusodi* (Tokyo: Shunjūsha, 2002), 170. 'Gakuhōsei', 'Kansai no ongaku', *Ongakukai* 3.6 (1910): 5–6.

67 Motokiyo Yamanoi, 'Baiorin sōhō oyobi gakushū hō', *Ongakukai* 5, no. 1 (1912). Continued in: 5.2: 39–40, 5.4: 42–47, 5.5: 27–30, 5.10: 41–43, 5.11: 35–36, 5.12: 38–39.

68 Yamanoi studied with Wilhelm Dubravčić, who taught the imperial court musicians, and with Andō Kō and August Junker at the Tokyo Academy of Music. He graduated in 1908. See Tsukahara, See Yasuko Tsukahara, *Meiji kokka to gagaku: dentō no kindaika/kokugaku no sōsei* (Tokyo: Yūshisha, 2009), 21 Appendix.

syllables for the English word 'king' printed above it), deserved better, Yamanoi asserted.[69]

The self-appointed authorities on the nation's music in Tokyo might have abandoned the idea of playing Japanese music on Western interests as immature, but that did not prevent the practice from becoming highly popular in the early twentieth century.

Blended Music as a Commercial Enterprise

While the reformers published traditional Japanese music in staff notation and performed it on Western instruments as part of their agenda for music reform, there was another trend, that, arguably, threatened to thwart their efforts and heightened their sense of urgency.

Playing popular Japanese tunes on Western instruments was not invented by music reformers. The military bands included well-known common music pieces (*zokkyoku*) in their repertoire, and the private bands formed by civilians that began to proliferate in the 1880s naturally selected repertoire that appealed to their audiences with its familiarity. The repertoire of Shikama's youth band likewise included Japanese pieces.

For individuals wanting to try their hand at playing a Western instrument, a substantial number of instrumental tutors and sheet music collections of pieces became available from the end of the century. In the 1890s, the accordion was one of the most widely played Western instruments; from the turn of the century, its popularity was surpassed by the violin. Shikama Totsuji was one of the first to cater to the new trend. He published *Tefūgin dokushū no tomo* (The Accordion: a companion for self-study) in 1890.[70] Shikama employed cipher notation, which would have been familiar to some readers from *shōka* education in elementary schools. Besides *shōka*, the pieces in the collection included marches and Japanese music of various genres. Volume three (1892) includes a brief description of percussion instruments for use in an ensemble (as later

---

69 *Ongakukai*, Vol. 5.5, pp. 2–28. *Haikara* (literally 'high collar') described people superficially aping Western ways, mainly by displaying Western apparel and gadgets, often implying contempt by those using the term.

70 Two more volumes followed: Totsuji Shikama, *Tefūgin dokusho no tomo dai ni shū* (Tokyo: Kyōeki Shōsha, 1891); Totsuji Shikama, *Tefūgin dokusho no tomo dai san shū* (Tokyo: Kyōeki Shōsha, 1892). The first volume is not available through the NDL.

seen in Shikama's youth band), as well as an explanation of accordion fingering and of notation symbols.

In total, at least forty-six music collections for accordion were published in Tokyo and in the Kansai area from 1890 to the end of the Meiji period.[71] Like Shikama's publications, most of them were intended for self-study and aimed at 'beginners', although it is not always evident whether this meant beginners of the instrument or of Western music in general. Nearly all included explanations of basic (Western) musical theory. Several authors described the accordion as particularly suited to self-study.[72] The notation systems used reflected the intended audience: tablature was the most common, used exclusively in more than half of the publications (twenty-six) although not in the same way; another thirteen used it in combination with one or two other systems. Cipher notation followed. Staff notation, exclusively or in combination with other systems, was only used by nine publications in total.[73] Tablature, being instrument-specific, was, of course, not helpful for ensemble playing. Some authors, like Shikama, included hints on playing with others. Machida Ōen (1896), for example, included advice on playing together with *shamisen* and even a tablature for flageolet. He included both tablature and cipher notation.[74]

Even while introducing Western-based musical theory and notation, many collections included only Japanese pieces, variously described as *zokkyoku* (common pieces) or *zakkyoku* (miscellaneous pieces), which also dominated most of the other publications.[75] Machida Ōen divided the fifty-five pieces in his 1896 publication into *shōka* (fourteen); military songs (*gunka*; eight); marches (five); common music (twenty-three), and Qing music (five). Musically, *shōka* and *gunka*, like marches, can

---

71 See Saeko Watanabe, 'Tefūgin no kyokushū ni tsuite: sono kifūhō o chūshin ni', *Ochanomizu ongaku ronshū* 17 (2015), https://teapot.lib.ocha.ac.jp/records/33828 Watanabe examined all the publications available in the NDL and the library of Osaka College of Music. My own observations are based on the twenty-three titles accessible online through the NDL.
72 Watanabe, 'Tefūgin no kyokushū', 15–20. The term *dokushū* is included in thirty-one titles.
73 Watanabe, 'Tefūgin no kyokushū', 20. The accordions imported at the time were diatonic models with ten keys. The system of cipher notation followed the Galin-Paris Chevé method, used in elementary *shōka* education.
74 Ōen Machida, *Tefūgin doku annai* (Tokyo: Tōundō, 1896), 4.
75 Watanabe, 'Tefūgin no kyokushū', 13, 18–19.

be described as 'Western'. The *shōka*, beginning with *Kimigayo*, included several that celebrated national holidays, and in that sense might be described as blended songs. It seems safe to assume that both the *shōka* and military songs would have been familiar to the publication's audience, and the same may well be true of the marches.

The accordion tutors contributed to the dissemination of both knowledge of Western music theory and of repertoire from common music.[76] The latter caused concern for advocates of reform, as is evident from an article in *Ongaku zasshi* whose author, writing from Tokushima, lamented the poisonous influence of obscene and coarse (*inwai yahi*) music being published to satisfy commercial interests.[77] There must have been considerable demand; many of the publications for accordion went through several editions. Buying by mail order was well established, so they could be obtained even in remote parts of the country.

The Violin and Blended Music

In the early twentieth century, the violin began to surpass the accordion in popularity. By January 1907 the magazine *Ongaku sekai* (The world of music) described the violin as the most widely played instrument, and several other newspapers and magazines that year also mentioned its popularity.[78] Two years later, an article in the Ōsaka Asahi newspaper remarked upon the huge popularity of violin lessons.[79] For women, wrote the author, the violin competed with the *koto* as a desirable accomplishment for marriage. The most popular teacher was Kōga Musen, who had come to Osaka in 1888 with the band of the army's fourth division. Kōga Musen (Ryōtarō, 1867–?) who also taught the accordion,[80] believed that people would take pleasure in playing the violin if, rather than struggling with Western pieces, they learnt familiar Japanese tunes. He taught his students to play the violin kneeling on

---

76 Ueno, 'Yōgakki de Nihon dentō ongaku', 23–26.
77 Senoo Shigematsu, 'Ongaku jisshi ni tsuite no chūi', *Ongaku zasshi* 67, no. 32–35 (1897): 33.
78 *Ongaku sekai*, 15 January 1907. This and other examples quoted in Yōko Shiotsu, 'Meijiki Kansai vaiorin jijō', *Ongaku kenkyū* (*Ōsaka Ongaku Daigaku Hakubutsukan nenpō*), no. 20 (2003): 18–19. For the following, see also Mehl, 'Violin Boom'.
79 Quoted in Hiroshi Watanabe, *Nihon bunka modan rapusodi*, (Tokyo: Shunjūsha, 2002), 170.
80 Ueno, 'Yōgakki de Nihon dentō ongaku', 26.

the floor in Japanese style, so that they could comfortably join in an ensemble with *koto* and *shamisen* in the home.

Newspapers and magazines may have actively contributed to the trend as well as catering to it. Articles in the music magazines introduced famous violinists such as Paganini and Sarasate and legendary makers such as Stradivarius, as well as providing practical instructions on how to play the violin. Domestic production had, moreover, resulted in affordable instruments becoming widely available.[81] School teachers, especially those trained at the Tokyo Academy of Music and the prefectural teacher training schools, learnt the violin and used it for teaching *shōka* when no reed organ or piano was available. From around 1890, individual musicians established private music courses or gave individual lessons. Some, like Kōga, were veterans of the military bands, while others had graduated from the Tokyo Academy of Music. In Sendai, Maedako Shinkin, who had trained at the seminary of the Russian Orthodox Church in Tokyo, became one of the most active violin teachers in the city (see Chapter 9). In the 1890s and early 1900s, at least nine teachers offered music courses in Osaka, four in Kobe, and five in Kyoto. From around 1907, advertisements for violin studios in Osaka, Kobe, Kyoto, and Wakayama appear in the newspapers.[82]

It presumably helped that the Japanese were already familiar with stringed instruments, bowed as well as plucked. Takaori wrote that he chose to study violin at the Tokyo Academy of Music because it resembled the *shamisen* most closely.[83] Japan's only native bowed lute, the *kokyū*, was still played as part of a *sankyoku* ensemble with *koto* and *shamisen*, although it was increasingly replaced by the *shakuhachi*. Several types of Chinese fiddles were, moreover, played in Ming-Qing music. It may well be significant that the violin became popular around the time that the popularity of Ming-Qing music suffered a setback during the Sino-Japanese war of 1894–95 (although Ming-Qing music continued to

---

81 According to advertisements appearing in *Ongaku sekai* in 1909 (in the October and November issues) accordion prices started at two yen fifty sen, while Japanese-produced violins started at two yen.
82 Shiotsu, 'Meijiki Kansai vaiorin jijō', 21, 34–35.
83 Takaori, 'Hōgaku no kosui kara seigaku no sūhai e', 22.

be enjoyed well into the twentieth century).[84] The violin could, if played appropriately, blend in well with indigenous stringed instruments.

Indeed, versatility is one of the chief characteristics of the violin. Associated with a wide range of musical genres and styles even within Western music, and played among all classes, it accompanied Europeans wherever they went and, in the late nineteenth century, became an 'instrument of four continents', which often displaced indigenous instruments. Its adoption outside Europe can thus 'be seen as an index to the expansion of European influence over the centuries'.[85] In Meiji Japan, it represented Western civilization.[86]

Given the limited supply of teachers, many attempted to study the violin by themselves, and, as with the publications for the accordion, most of the violin tutors were intended for self-study.[87] Even in the earliest tutors, the repertoire of practice pieces included the odd *sōkyoku*. The first tutor to include common music pieces was *Tsūzoku vaiorin hitorimanabi: shiyōhō no bu; jisshū no bu* (A popular violin self-study book: method section; practical section), first published in 1905. With at least thirty-one print runs by 1926, it was one of the most popular tutors.[88] In the preface the author, Ōtsuka Torazō, stated that he was responding to the rising popularity of the violin, and that the violin blended well with the *koto* and the *shamisen*.[89] In the following years, most tutors included popular common pieces (*zokkyoku*). For example, the practice repertoire in *Vaiorin dokushū no shiori* (A guide to self-study

---

84 For a list of publications of Ming-Qing music (*minshingaku*) sheet music and instrumental tutors published until the end of the Meiji period, see Yasuko Tsukahara, *Jūkyū seiki no Nihon ni okeru Seiyō ongaku no juyō* (Tokyo: Taka Shuppan, 1993), 580–86.

85 Peter Cooke, 'The violin – instrument of four continents', in *The Cambridge Companion to the Violin*, ed. Robin Stowell (Cambridge: Cambridge University Press, 1992), 234.

86 One of the earliest newspaper advertisements for a violin appears on a page with advertisements for factory machines, umbrellas, and top hats 'Violin/Baiorin (advertisement by Jūjiya)', *Tōkyō nichinichi shinbun*, 22 April 1888.

87 Of the thirty-six domestic violin tutors published between 1888 and 1926, twenty-one were explicitly intended for self-study: see Ena Kajino, 'A Lost Opportunity for Tradition: The Violin in Early Twentieth-Century Japanese Traditional Music', *Nineteenth-Century Music Review* 10, no. 2 (2013): 297, https://doi.org/10.1017/S147940981300027X On the publication of violin music, see also Mehl, 'Violin Boom'; Ueno, 'Yōgakki de Nihon dentō ongaku', 27–39.

88 Kajino, 'Lost Opportunity', 297.

89 Torazō Ōtsuka, *Tsūzoku vaiorin hitorimanabi, shiyōhō no bu, jisshū no bu* (Kyoto: Jūjiya Gakkibu, 1909 (7th edn)).

for the violin), published in 1906, included separate sections with *shōka* for Japan's national holidays (eight, including *Kimigayo*), the national anthems of six countries, marches and dances (seven), and *zokkyoku* (ten pieces).[90] Another example, a short treatise published in 1907, consisted of four pages explaining staff notation and musical terms, followed by twenty-four pages of *koto* and *shamisen* pieces (*jiuta*) including lyrics, some of them with parts for ensemble playing.[91]

Some tutors included advice on playing in an ensemble with *koto* and *shamisen*, most remarkably another bestselling tutor, *Violin kōgiroku* (Violin lecture notes), published in Fukuoka in 1913, which by 1933 had been reprinted 151 times.[92] The book, which used both staff and cipher notation, as well as 'do re mi' in Japanese syllables, included a section entitled, 'Posture when playing in a Japanese-style room' with the following advice:

> When playing together with a *koto* or *shamisen* in a Japanese-style room, it is quite inconsiderate (*fuchōhō*) to play the violin standing straight. In other words, because the *koto* and the *shamisen* are played seated, if the violinist alone plays standing up, then the ensemble fails even before it starts playing. Those who insist on standing up saying that is how a violin should be played are unnecessarily inflexible. When people like that happen to play a Japanese piece, they play in a march-like style, turning a gentle and refined *koto* piece into a march and spoiling it completely. A Japanese piece does not require using the bow as roughly as for a Western piece, so it can be played well even sitting down.
>
> To play a Japanese piece, one has to play with the frame of mind (*kimochi*) appropriate to a Japanese piece. One does not hear Japanese songs sung as one sings hymns. It is the same thing. And if you fold a floor cushion twice and put it under your behind while you play, it is more comfortable to bow and your feet will not go numb.[93]

---

90 Teishū Namikoshi, *Vaiorin dokushū no shiori* (Osaka and Tokyo: Yajima Seishindō, 1906). The countries were Britain, the United States, France, Germany, Russia, and Austria.

91 Inosuke Mizohata, *Buwaiorin [vaiorin] no shiori* (Osaka: Kyōwadō Gakki, 1908).

92 Kajino, 'Lost Opportunity,' 297; Nihon Ongaku Tōitsu Kai, (*Tsūshin kyōju*) *Vaiorin kōgiroku* (Fukuoka: Nihon Tōitsu Ongakukai, 1913). There are several pages missing in the version available through the NDL.

93 'Nihon zashiki ni okeru shisei ni tsuite', In Nihon Ongaku Tōitsu Kai, (*Tsūshin kyōju*) *Vaiorin kōgiroku*, 17.

The following page (18) depicts a woman in Japanese dress playing, kneeling on the floor with a low music stand. The caption, besides repeating the advice about the folded cushion, adds that it is acceptable to lower the violin slightly to look at the music.

The above passage not only points out the difference between Western and Japanese musical genres and their performance styles, but also emphasizes the significance both of space and of physical posture and how they relate to the appropriate frame of mind for playing a given piece of music. The mention of people who insisted on playing the violin standing up (although even Western musicians sit down to play in orchestras or chamber ensembles) and who treat *koto* pieces like marches is revealing. Possibly, the staff notation of Japanese pieces encouraged march-like playing because of the visual impact of the two- or four-time rhythms and dotted notes. On the other hand, the observation may have been addressed to the kind of *haikara*-would-be violinists condemned by Yamanoi Motokiyo. It suggests that many people took up the violin because of its significance as a symbol of Western civilization. *Haikara* described people superficially aping Western ways, mainly by displaying Western apparel and gadgets. For the people thus designated, however, adopting *haikara* fashions and in particular an activity such as playing the violin may well have expressed a desire to join in with Japan's modernization project. Playing the violin—or any Western musical instrument—was a way of physically performing Western civilization. Music represented one of the most exalted products of this civilization, and the violin, as readers were regularly reminded, was the king (or, occasionally, the queen) of Western instruments.[94]

One tutor stands out as the only work that actually advertises itself as a violin tutor specifically for Japanese music: (*Hōgaku sokusei*) *Vaiorin tebiki* (A short course of Japanese music for the violin), published in 1913.[95] The author, Machida Ōen (Hisa; ?–1928), was an active promoter of blended music. He had previously published a violin tutor which included a few Japanese pieces,[96] as well as tutors for accordion, *koto*,

---

[94] Several violin tutors praise the violin as the 'king' of Western instruments. Takaori, in his article, cited above, refers to it as 'queen', which is more in line with nineteenth-century Western conceptions of the violin as female.
[95] Ōen Machida, (*Hōgaku sokusei*) *Vaiorin tebiki* (Tokyo: Seirindō, 1913).
[96] Ōen Machida, *Vaiorin dokushū jizai* (Seirindō, 1908).

shamisen, *gekkin*, *minshingaku* flute, harmonica (mouth organ), and *shakuhachi*. In addition, he published collections of *shōka*, *biwa* songs, *hauta*, *zokkyoku*, and *nagauta*.[97]

In his new violin tutor, Machida used staff notation (the earlier tutor used cipher notation), and in the preface he recommended playing Japanese tunes with Western instruments. His explanations of violin playing and musical notation were followed by popular Japanese pieces of different genres, including *Rokudan* and *Echigo jishi*. The book nevertheless concluded with a selection of Western tunes, including 'Boat Song (*Lightly Row*), and 'Rose Song' (*The Last Rose of Summer*), as well as (Western) dances. The final page had a short glossary of Western musical terms. Thus, even while promoting his ideal of playing Japanese music on Western instruments, Machida included the most popular tunes from the school song books; presumably, he could assume that they had become as familiar as the Japanese favourites.[98]

Only four years later, however, in 1917, Machida published a new version of his *Violin tebiki*, this time entitled *Violin sokusei yōgaku tebiki*. This edition included an English title page with the following inscription:

A Short Course for Violin of Western Music

By Owen Machida

Instructor in Uyeno Musical Association of Tokyo

Author of A Short Course for Violin of Japanese Music &&&

The use of English, even in a work that appears to be intended for a Japanese audience, is another indication that playing a Western instrument signalled awareness of and a desire to actively participate in what was perceived to be the modern civilized world. Machida's preface seems to suggest the same: his earlier book, he stated, suited the times and enjoyed a good reception. Now, however, times were progressing, the taste for Western music had spread widely and a national music worthy of an advanced country (*shinkōkoku no kokugaku*) was not far

---

97 See the collections in the NDL. Only some of them are in Western (cipher) notation.
98 *Lightly Row*, known as 'Butterfly' (Chōchō) in Japanese, and *The Last Rose of Summer*, known as 'Chrysanthemum' or 'Flowers in the Garden' (Niwa no chigusa), were among the first Western songs to be used in song collections for kindergartens and schools.

off. The first pages of the book (introducing the violin and the notation system) are almost identical with his previous book, but the practice pieces are *shōka* or famous pieces from the Western repertoire. Evidently, Machida, one of the most prominent propagators of blended music, felt that the fashion was fading.

There is, however, good reason to assume that playing Japanese music on the violin remained popular for longer than Machida's views, or reports (or lack thereof) in *Ongakukai* imply. This is suggested by the considerable amount of sheet music published at the time, and, perhaps even more significantly, by the fact that these publications, including some of Machida's own, remained available for years. Although initially advocated as a measure for music reform, most of the substantial series of individual pieces were published by enterprising individuals, often performers of traditional Japanese music. Twenty-two series have been identified, of which thirteen were issued continuously.[99] The publisher of the earliest one was Nakao Tozan (1876–1956), best known as the founder of the Tozan school of *shakuhachi*. Trained chiefly in the *jiuta* school, he travelled widely in the Kansai area and played with many different local musicians before settling in Osaka and founding his school in 1896. His *shakuhachi* tutor for self-study, published in 1908, although not the first of its kind, is regarded as a major break with the tradition of direct transmission from teacher to student.[100] Tozan also published Western pieces for the *shakuhachi*: one of his *shakuhachi* tutors even includes a picture of a *shakuhachi* player standing (rather than kneeling Japanese style) and using a music stand.[101] Playing Japanese pieces on Western instruments remained more common than the other way round, however.

Nakao had already begun to collaborate with Kōga Musen, with whom he also performed.[102] From 1906 they published a thirty-four-volume

---

99 Kajino, 'Lost Opportunity', 298.
100 Kiku Day, 'The Effect of the Meiji Government's Policy on Traditional Japanese Music During the Nineteenth Century: The Case of the *Shakuhachi*', *Nineteenth-Century Music Review* 10, no. 2 (2013): 275, https://doi.org/doi:10.1017/S1479409813000268
101 Watanabe, *Nihon bunka modan rapusodi*, 173.
102 T. Akutsu and K. Takeishi, 'Meiji jidai ni okeru hōgaku to yōgaku no ongaku shidō no kakawari: Nakao Tozan ni miru shakuhachi to vaiorin gakufu shuppan no keii to sono haikei', *Tōkyō Gakugei Daigaku kiyō - Geijutsu/Supōtsu Kagaku Kakari* 65 (2013), http://hdl.handle.net/2309/134258

series for the violin, including thirty-eight *zokkyoku* pieces.[103] The first volume contained the *koto* piece *Chidori no kyoku* (Song of the Plovers). Besides Nakao, this edition listed Kōga Musen and two other violinists as co-editors. The publications used staff notation throughout. They were intended for playing in mixed ensembles with Japanese instruments.[104] Kōga published his own series from 1910 onwards. The fifty-two volumes included fifty-nine *zokkyoku* pieces. Kōga played the saxophone, but he had also mastered the violin and performed on both.[105] In 1897 he founded a violin ensemble with his students.[106]

Sheet Music and the Nationwide Dissemination of Japanese and Blended Music

Presumably it is because the highly active and prolific Nakao and Kōga were based in the Kansai region, and because musical activities in general are well-documented there, that blended music has been associated with that region.[107] But the sheer amount of sheet music published suggests that it was much more widely practised, and some of the music was published in Tokyo, such as the many and varied volumes published by Machida Ōen for different instruments. One of his first was the *nagauta*, *Dōjoji*, first published in 1907, with a third edition in 1912.[108] His series for violin, published from 1907, consisted of seventeen volumes in staff notation, mostly *nagauta* and *sōkyoku*.[109] Volume 3 of his collection of *hauta* (a genre of short *shamisen* songs) included diagrams of a piano keyboard and a violin fingerboard and presented the songs in cipher notation.[110]

---

103 Kajino, 'Lost Opportunity', 298.
104 Akutsu and Takeishi, 'Nakao Tozan', 6–7.
105 Kajino, 'Lost Opportunity', 298, 306.
106 Ibid., 306.
107 Watanabe, *Nihon bunka modan rapusodi*; Mutsuko Ishihara, 'Meijiki Kansai ni okeru vaiorin juyō no yōsu: wayō setchū genshō ni tsuite', *Ongaku kenkyū* (*Ōsaka Ongaku Daigaku Ongaku Kenkyūsho nenpō*), no. 11 (1993); Shiotsu, 'Meijiki Kansai vaiorin jijō'.
108 Ueno, 'Yōgakki de Nihon dentō ongaku' (p. 19 in the appendix published online).
109 Volume 17, published in 1909, contains a *gidayū* piece; the catalogue at the back announced four more volumes, but it is not clear whether they were published.
110 Ōen Machida, ed., *Hauta shū 3* (Tokyo: Seirindō, 1909). The other volumes do not include Western notation.

Hauta in staff notation were also published by the piano technician Fukushima Takurō (1886–1958), who was likewise based in Tokyo. He also published *koto* pieces (in the version used by the Yamada school) for violin in staff notation.[111] His *Vaiorin dokushū no tomo* (Violin: a companion to self-study, 1910) had a picture on the cover of two people playing the violin: a man in a suit who is standing, and a woman in Japanese dress and sitting in Japanese style (*seiza*), and it included a section on how to tune the violin to a *koto*, *shamisen*, or *shakuhachi*.[112] The practice repertoire included *koto* and *shamisen* pieces. This suggests that even in Tokyo, with its conservatoire and a substantial Western music scene, there was a market for blended music.

Even when the number of new publications declined, existing ones continued to be reprinted.[113] The volumes of Nakao's and Kōga's violin series are listed in a catalogue issued by the Kansai-based music shop Miki Gakki in 1923, which included a substantial number of other publications of Japanese music for violin and various Western instruments, such as a nine-volume series of *nagauta* transcribed by Kitamura Sueharu listed under sheet music for piano.[114] In addition, *Ongakukai* continued to publish advertisements for such sheet music even while its authors rejected the performances of blended music, and even after it had virtually ceased to report on concerts that included such music. Clearly, there was a discrepancy between what the elite propagated and what even readers of *Ongakukai*, who can be assumed to have had an interest in Western music, practised.[115]

Compared to the availability of and demand for sheet music, actual performances are much harder to ascertain: they almost certainly went underreported once the fashion had passed. The declining number of programmes listing performances of blended music that were

---

111 The NDL holds *Hauta zenshū*, vols 1–7, and 9, published 1910, and *Honte rokudan no shirabe, Midare,* and *Chidori no kyoku*, published in 1908, 1911, and 1912; all by Jūjiya in Tokyo.

112 *Vaiorin dokushū no tomo* (Violin: a companion to self-study) Tokyo: Jūjiya Gakkiten, 1910, 26–29.

113 The latest printing of music from Nakao's series appears to have been in 1923, and from Kōga's in 1921: see Kajino, 'Lost Opportunity', 317.

114 Ueno, 'Yōgakki de Nihon dentō ongaku', 41. In the online version, the catalogue is appended to the article. It lists forty-two titles for Nakao's violin series and forty-seven for Kōga's.

115 Ueno, 'Yōgakki de Nihon dentō ongaku', 39.

published in *Ongakukai* does not necessarily reflect reality. In Sendai, where the private music academy Tōhoku Ongakuin regularly gave concerts featuring such music, the programme of a concert in the spring of 1917 featured only two such items, according to *Ongakukai*, and by 1920 blended music did not feature at all.[116] On the other hand, an earlier issue in 1917 contained programmes of a concert in Shuri (Okinawa) and another in Otaru (Hokkaidō).[117] The concert in Shuri was the first organized by a newly formed music association and the programme listed twenty-five items, including solo and ensemble performances of Western music (singing, piano, organ, violin, mandolin), *satsumabiwa*, *chikuzenbiwa*, and *koto*, as well as three items described as 'Ryūkyū ongaku', and one violin and *koto* ensemble playing *Chidori*. The concert in Otaru, described as the third organized by the Katei Ongaku Kai (Association for Music in the Home), likewise featured a mixture of Western and Japanese music; the thirteen items on the programme included one item each with *koto*, *shakuhachi*, *satsumabiwa*; an ensemble of *koto* and *shakuhachi,* and one performance of blended music: the *sōkyoku Chidori,* played by an ensemble of *shakuhachi* and violin. These programmes suggest that far from the major cities, concert programmes featuring a mixture of Western, traditional Japanese, and blended music were not uncommon, and that a popular piece like *Chidori* had become, as it were, national repertoire.

Even if the performance of blended music gradually disappeared from concert programmes, it may well have been played in other more private settings, as was the case with traditional Japanese music. One of them may have been the home. Starting in the last years of the Meiji era, both music magazines and magazines for women published articles discussing music as an important part of family life, and introducing the concept of *katei ongaku*. The term was used in various ways, sometimes, but by no means always, as a direct translation of the German *Hausmusik*. The discourse must be seen in the wider context of social and cultural change at the time, including changing perceptions of the domestic

---

116 *Ongakukai* 188 (June 1917), 60; however, the number of reports on Tōhoku Ongakuin decreased overall.
117 *Ongakukai* 183 (January 1917), 102–03.

space.¹¹⁸ *Ongakukai* published several articles on the subject from the 1910s onwards. Opinions differed markedly on a number of points, including which instruments were the most suitable and whether traditional Japanese music, Western music, or blended music was most appropriate. While most either explicitly or implicitly recommended Western music, others recommended traditional Japanese music, or some kind of blended music; among them were Kitamura Hatsuko (Kitamura Sueharu's wife), and Tōgi Tetteki, a court musician trained in Western music.¹¹⁹ They asserted that Western music was still far removed from people's lives and experiences, and that their preferences could not be changed overnight.

Meanwhile, in 1910, the Dai Nihon Katei Ongaku Kai (Great Japan Home Music Society) was founded in Fukuoka, with the aim of promoting and disseminating appropriate music for music-making in the home, whether Western, Japanese, ancient, or modern.¹²⁰ Besides tutors for self-study, like *Tsūshin kyōju vaiorin kōgiroku* (introduced above), the Society published sheet music for Japanese and Western instruments, including the *koto*, the *shakuhachi*, the violin, and the mandolin. From 1915 until about 1925 it also published a magazine, *Katei ongaku* (Home music), which, although it included educational articles, served mainly as a forum where learners studying by themselves could interact, somewhat like today's social media (some even sent in photos of themselves). Interestingly, the majority of learners interacting through *Katei ongaku* appear to have been male, both students and working men.¹²¹ Music in the home was otherwise regarded as the sphere of women and children, the men being largely absent until they came home from work

---

118 See Jordan Sand, *House and Home in Modern Japan: Architecture, Domestic Space and Bourgeois Culture 1880–1930* (Cambridge, Mass.: Harvard University Press, 2003). For the discourse on music in the home, see Yoshiki Shūtō, 'Narihibiku katei kūkan: 1910–20 nendai Nihon ni okeru katei ongaku no gensetsu', *Nenpō shakaigaku ronshū* (*Kantō Shakai Gakkai* 21 (2008), https://doi.org/10.5690/kantoh.2008.95; Tamagawa, 'Katei ongaku ron'.

119 Kajino, 'Lost Opportunity', 314-16; Tamagawa, 'Katei ongaku ron', 65–67.

120 Ena Kajino, 'Taishōki no tsūshin kyōiku jukōshatachi no ongaku seikatsu: Dai Nihon Katei Ongaku Kai no zasshi "Katei ongaku" kara', *Ongakugaku* 63, no. 1 (2017): 4, https://www.jstage.jst.go.jp/article/ongakugaku/63/1/63_1/_pdf/-char/ja

121 Ibid., 5–71.

and (ideally) found solace in listening to the music rather than joining in.[122]

From 1924, the Society published the 'New Japanese Music' (*shin hōgaku*) of Miyagi Michio (1894–1956). It may well be that it was the fact that they had published Miyagi's piece for *shakuhachi* and *koto*, *Haru no umi* (Sea in springtime) in staff notation in 1931 that enabled the French violinist Renée Chemet (1888–?) to perform the work with Miyagi himself at one of her recitals. The performance, which can be classified as an example of blended music, met a mixed reception.[123] By this time, playing Japanese music on Western instruments had largely been relegated to the private sphere, and we cannot be sure how widespread or popular the practice was.

Blended music has been treated as a stage of transition that helped the Japanese become familiar with Western music. While it may well have been that, it should not be overlooked that it also increased familiarity with different genres of Japanese music, which, thanks to instrumental tutors for self-study and considerable amounts of published texts and notated music, was more widely disseminated than before; this trend only increased with the dissemination of sound media in the 1920s. As well as traditional genres, gramophone recordings around this time included blended music: the Shikama sisters recorded at least two: *Yachiyo jishi* and *Takasago*.[124]

The strict separation of traditional Japanese and Western music was, then, by no means a foregone conclusion. Nevertheless, by the 1920s the trend towards placing both European art music and traditional Japanese music on their separate pedestals, to be kept unsullied by hybridity, had begun. There is a certain irony in the fact that some of the former promoters of blended music, including Kitamura Sueharu and Maeda Kyūhachi, ended up working for the Hōgaku Research Committee at the Tokyo Academy of Music (see Chapter 3), the aim of which was to preserve rather than to renew traditional music.

---

122 Tamagawa, 'Katei ongaku ron', 71–73.
123 For a discussion of the performance, see Kajino, 'Lost Opportunity', 317–18; Mehl, *Not by Love Alone*, 401–02.
124 I thank Hermann Gottschewski for information about recordings by the Shikama sisters.

Another irony is that in the late twentieth century, when efforts were made to re-introduce the Japanese to their musical traditions, this sometimes happened in the form of playing hardy perennials from the European canon or 'Western'-sounding contemporary popular tunes on Japanese instruments. The first track on the accompanying CD to an introduction to Japanese instruments is *Ave Maria* by Bach/Gounod, followed by Bizet's famous minuet from *L'Arlésienne* Suite No. 2, and Saint-Saëns' *The Swan*, played on the *koto* and the *shakuhachi*. The remaining four tracks are instrumental versions of *shōka*; the only one that might be perceived as sounding 'Japanese' is *Jūgoya otsukisan* (Full moon), composed by Motoori Nagayo (1885–1945).[125] Thus a kind of reverse blending of Japanese and Western served to re-introduce young Japanese to the music of their ancestors.

---

125 Norihiro Ishikawa, *Hajimete no wagakki* (Tokyo: Iwanami Shoten (Iwanami junia shinsho), 2003). Fifteen years earlier, the Mutsunowo concert series, organized by two high-profile *hōgaku* musicians Kawamura Taizan (*shakuhachi*) and Kawamura Toshimi (*koto*), made similar efforts to appeal to children by including familiar (Western-style) items. A concert in summer 1989 ended with the theme song of a then-popular computer game named 'Dragon Quest', accompanied by an ensemble of Japanese and Western instruments. (Programme in author's private collection.)

Part Three:
The World, Japan, and Sendai

> Sendai, with its hundred thousand people, is large enough to feel all the currents of modern life. Two hundred miles from Tōkyō, it is sufficiently remote from the beaten path of tourist travel, to escape over-foreignization.[1]

> The people of Tohoku are habitually argumentative, this is often the reason why there is no progress, not in business nor in any other area.[2]

The reasons given by Kate Hansen (1879–1968) for Sendai offering an 'excellent opportunity' for observing what she called 'the average musical consciousness of the Japanese of the present day' are very similar to those that even today make Sendai an interesting case for studying the transformation of musical culture in the late nineteenth and early twentieth century. The notion of an 'average musical consciousness' is, of course, highly questionable, given that how Japanese people experienced the rapid and profound changes that occurred in this period differed vastly depending on which part of Japan they lived in and whether in rural areas or cities. A large number of local studies would be needed in order to identify averages or commonalities throughout Japan with any certainty.[3] But Hansen was right in saying that the major port cities Tokyo, Yokohama, and Kobe were not representative, dominated as they were by foreign influences. Compared to these, the transformation of musical culture progressed more slowly and in different ways in provincial

---

1   Kate Hansen, My Impressions of the Musical Consciousness of the Japanese People, n.d., Personal Papers of Kate I. Hansen, University Archives, PP19, Box 10, Folder 12, Kenneth Spencer Research Library, University of Kansas Libraries, Lawrence, Kansas.
2   TN, 'Sendai Amachū Kurabu kinjō', *Ongakukai* 191 (September 1917).
3   Hiroshi Watanabe, *Nihon bunka modan rapusodi* (Tokyo: Shunjūsha, 2002), 22–24.

towns. In the truly remote areas, on the other hand, developments were so slow that they offer limited scope for study in the period examined here. Sendai, meanwhile, was 'large enough to feel all the currents of modern life'.[4] By the time Kate Hansen arrived in 1907, the northern provincial city had a population of roughly 100,000 and boasted a large number of modern institutions, including a military garrison, schools at all levels, and a university.

Sendai was also the most significant city north of Tokyo, in a region with a reputation for being underdeveloped, an image that lingers to this day. Another aspect of this image is that the Tohoku region is 'traditional', the home of the 'authentic' Japan. The region is known for its flourishing traditional folk performing arts (or what passes for 'traditional' today). European art music, on the other hand, features less prominently: there are few professional ensembles (although Sendai has a professional orchestra, founded in 1973), no conservatoires, and only a small number of music departments at universities, mostly for training teachers. In the nineteenth century, Western music initially took hold slowly, but towards the end of the century the pace quickened, and by the early twentieth century the city could boast a vibrant concert scene with rising standards of music education and increasingly competent performers.

Sendai's status as a provincial centre had historical roots. A castle town (since 1600) and the seat of the Date clan, the rulers of Sendai domain, Sendai became the capital of Miyagi prefecture after the centralization of government in 1871 and thus an important regional centre of the modern state. In 1873 a garrison was stationed in Sendai, and in 1888 it became home to the Second Army Division. The railway line between Tokyo and Sendai was opened in 1887. In 1889, Sendai, with a population of around 90,000, was accorded the administrative status of a city. Although a local trade hub, Sendai was not a major industrial or commercial centre; its importance lay in its role as a centre of local government and of education.

Indeed, Sendai's well-developed school system with a strong foreign presence provided the basis for the rapid advancement of Western music from the end of the nineteenth century onwards. In education, as in other

---

4   Hansen, Musical Consciousness.

areas, there was significant continuity from the Tokugawa era, when the castle town had been the seat of the domain school, Yōkendō.[5] By the nineteenth century, the Date had even established a network of local schools. In addition, there were also numerous private academies (*juku*), several of which morphed into modern schools after the promulgation of the national Education Law in August 1872. Even before that date, several reforms were enacted by the prefectural authorities in Sendai. The domain school suffered disruption during the Restoration wars, but in 1869 it was reorganized to combine the functions of an administrative and an educational institution.[6] In early summer 1872, a government secondary school (the Kanritsu Chūgakkō) was established, with a Department for Western Learning and one for Chinese Learning.

In order to promote Western Learning, Miyagi School of Foreign Languages (Miyagi Gaikokugo Gakkō) was opened in 1874 (renamed Miyagi School of English, Miyagi Eigo Gakkō, at the end of the year), but was closed again in February 1877. In 1873, the second national teacher-training school outside Tokyo was established in Sendai (Miyagi Shihan Gakkō), but this too was short-lived and, in effect, succeeded in 1878 by Sendai Normal School (Sendai Shihan Gakkō), renamed Miyagi Normal School in June 1879.[7]

As elsewhere, the education reforms of Education Minister Mori Arinori in 1886 resulted in more reorganization. Sendai's status as an educational centre was further strengthened with the establishment of the Second Higher Secondary School (Dai Ni Kōtō Chūgakkō) in 1887, which became the Second High School in 1894 (Dai Ni Kōtō Gakkō) following the promulgation of the High School Law. The order for the establishment of the third of the imperial universities, Tohoku Imperial

---

5   For details about education in Miyagi prefecture until 1886, see Kazusuke Uno, *Meiji shōnen no Miyagi kyōiku* (Sendai: Hōbundō, 1973).
6   The Yōkendō was established as the Gakumonjo in 1736 and renamed in 1772. The following summary is based on Uno, *Meiji shōnen no Miyagi kyōiku*. For the Tokugawa period, see also Osamu Ōtō, *Sendai-han no gakumon to kyōiku: Edo jidai ni okeru Sendai no gakuto-ka*, Kokuhō Osaki Hachimangū Sendai Edogaku Sōsho 13, (Sendai: Ōsaki Hachimangū (Sendai Edogaku Jikkō Iinkai), 2009), 38–41.
7   Established as Denshū Gakkō in February 1875, Sendai Normal School was renamed a year later. It included a school for young women (Joshi Shihan Gakkō), opened in 1877. For details about the teacher training schools, see Benjamin Duke, *The History of Modern Japanese Education: Constructing the National School System, 1872–1890* (New Brunswick, NJ: Rutgers University Press, 2009), 147–51.

University (Tōhoku Teikoku Daigaku), was promulgated in June 1907. The first faculty to be established, the College of Agriculture, was actually located in Sapporo, followed in 1911 by the science faculty in Sendai. The medical and engineering departments (later faculties) followed in 1915 and 1919, when the local colleges were transferred to the university. The Faculty of Law and Literature was established in 1922.[8] By the end of the Meiji period, Sendai was thus home to one of only three imperial universities and one of the highly prestigious seven numbered high schools.[9]

The Second High School and, later, Tohoku Imperial University played a major role in the dissemination of Western music. Kate Hansen, discussing the rapid progress between the world wars, observed that the expansion of the university had,

> brought a large number of foreign-trained Japanese to the city, some of whom were ardent concert-goers during their stay abroad. These, with the cooperation of their students, have formed a Music Lovers' Association, for the purpose of promoting professional concerts in Sendai. The first concerts sponsored by this association have been held in the Miyagi College chapel. The members form a very intelligent part of the audience at the public concerts given by our music department.[10]

The private schools included schools established by foreign missionaries of different denominations. They played an important role in the dissemination of Western music, because of the importance given to music instruction (mainly singing hymns) and church music. Missionary activity in northern Japan was significant already from the end of the Tokugawa period, when several young samurai from Sendai, who had left Sendai domain, became converts to the Russian Orthodox Church in Hakodate. They returned to Sendai to form a congregation in 1871, but were imprisoned the following year. After the prohibition of

---

8 The College of Agriculture was transferred to Hokkaido Imperial University in 1918. See Tohoku University website: http://campus.bureau.tohoku.ac.jp/en_tu_ayumi.html
9 The number of imperial universities increased to five within Japan and two in the colonial capitals of Seoul and Taipei in the early twentieth century.
10 Kate Hansen, Thesis: Experiences in Teaching and Developing a Music School in Japan, 1927, updated 1933, Personal Papers of Kate I. Hansen, University Archives, PP19, Box 3, Folder 1, Kenneth Spencer Research Library, University of Kansas Libraries, Lawrence, Kansas.

Christianity ended, the converts from Hakodate founded a provisional church in 1873. The church building was consecrated in 1892.[11] By the end of the Meiji period, Sendai had around fifteen churches.[12] In 1886, Members of the German Reformed Church in America, whose first missionaries came to Japan in 1879,[13] founded two schools in Sendai: Sendai Theological College (Sendai Shingakkō) for boys, which in 1891 became Tohoku College (Tōhoku Gakuin), and Miyagi School for Girls (Miyagi Jogakkō) or Miyagi College.[14] They were followed by Shōkei School for Girls (Shōkei Jogakkō; today Shokei Gakuin University) founded by members of the Woman's American Baptist Foreign Mission Society in 1892, and the Catholic Sendai Schools for Girls (Sendai Jogakkō, now Sendai Shirayuri Women's College), founded in 1893.

In sum, the case of Sendai suggests what kind of conditions were necessary for the musical transformation in the metropolitan centres to reach a provincial city in what was perceived as a backward region. Western music was modern music in that it was performed in modern settings, starting with the military and the education system. Sendai provided both. Schools also served as spaces for the modern institution of the public concert. Another necessary condition was the presence of a sufficient number of individuals with at least rudimentary knowledge of and skill in singing or playing Western music. Here, the foreign missionaries, while not necessarily the movers and shakers, played a vital role as advisors, teachers, and performers. Regular exchanges between local actors and the centre, in this case Tokyo, were another important factor. In the case of Sendai, the centre and the periphery were for several crucial years linked through the person of Shikama Totsuji. Not only did his publication of the music journal *Ongaku zasshi* help create

---

11 According to the website of the Orthodox Church in Sendai, https://www.sendai-orthodox.com/blank
12 Statistical yearbooks for Sendai, Sendai City, *Sendai-shi tōkei ippan* (Sendai: Sendai City, 1901–12). The number for 1907 and 1916 is given as thirteen; for 1906 and 1911 as fifteen.
13 By then Tokyo was already 'well-occupied' in the missionary jargon of the day, so when the chance to found a Christian school in Sendai presented itself, three missionaries from the organization travelled north. See William Mensendiek, *Not without Struggle: The Story of William E. Hoy and the Beginnings of Tohoku Gakuin* (Sendai: Tohoku Gakuin, 1986), 19, 29–46.
14 Today the two are known in English as Tohoku Gakuin University and Miyagi Gakuin Women's University. In the following they will be referred to as Tohoku College and Miyagi College.

a nationwide network of musicians and music teachers, but Shikama also involved himself in activities in his hometown. His brother Shikama Jinji, meanwhile, was a prominent local actor who could provide Totsuji with regular reports for his magazine detailing progress in Sendai.

9. Local Pioneers and the Beginnings of Western Music in Sendai

[…] and becoming the prefecture's first music educator, he was appointed to his alma mater and henceforth he taught at Miyagi Prefecture Normal school, as well as simultaneously holding appointments at Sendai First Lower Secondary School, Sendai Second Lower Secondary School, the Sendai Army Preparatory School, Hōzawa Shōsō School, Miyagi Prefectural Police Training Academy, and others. Not only that: he was constantly on the move as a lecturer, never resting. As a pioneering man of music of his time, our teacher composed the music and lyrics of numerous songs that were sung with pleasure and inspired the people's spirit. Looking back at the progress of music education in our prefecture, it is no exaggeration to call him our unforgettable teacher to whom we owe gratitude (*onshi*).[1]

The above excerpt from a large memorial stone erected honour of Shikama Totsuji's younger brother Shinji's achievements, in front of the main hall of Kōmyōji temple in the northern part of Sendai, testifies to the importance of individual actors in disseminating Western music and the practices associated with it. Although Western music was well established in government institutions by the late 1880s, it took longer for it to become more widely disseminated. Outside the capital and the major port towns with their substantial foreign population, most Japanese had limited opportunities to hear Western music of any kind. In Sendai, the

---

1   From a monument to Shikama Jinji, erected in 1957 at Kōmyōji temple. Hōsawa Shōsō School was established by Hōzawa Miyoji as a private academy (*juku*) for sewing in 1879, and became one of the most respected schools for girls. It still exists today as the (co-educational) high school Meisei Kōtō Gakkō: www.hgm.ed.jp/info/history

first efforts to introduce Western music were made as early as the 1870s, but it was not until the 1880s, when the Tokyo Academy of Music began to train teachers sent by the prefectures, and two missionary schools opened in the city, that the necessary preconditions were created. Even then it took several years until music was taught at all in schools and a concert scene developed. Public concerts, a modern institution even in Western countries, did not take place regularly until well into the 1890s. In in the early ones, performances of traditional Japanese music and arts dominated. The public concert as an institution thus preceded the regular performance of Western music. Over the years, it became a creative space, where the people of Sendai encountered the modern world as it was both represented and shaped through its music.[2]

Most people are likely to have preferred traditional sounds anyway, and as a flourishing commercial city, Sendai naturally offered all kinds of musical entertainment. A list of performing artists and geisha in Miyagi prefecture shows the following figures for performers of traditional musical genres based in Sendai in 1882, totalling 269:

1. Gagaku musicians (*ongaku reijin*) – 11
2. Minshingaku – 24
3. Jōruri – 12
4. Teachers of the above (*dō shosensei mongyō*) – 124
5. Nagauta – 14
6. Shinnai – 12
7. Tokiwazu – 51
8. Kiyomoto – 51
9. *Hayashi* – 12[3]

Apart from court music, Ming-Qing music and *hayashi* (performers in percussion ensembles), the genres mentioned are all types of narrative

---

2   For a discussion of the concert as a creative space, see Chapter 11.
3   *Miyagi shogeijin shōgi ichiran* (Overview of performance artists and geisha in Miyagi), cited in Shin'ya Watanabe, 'Sendai yōgaku no sakigake', *Sendai bunka*, no. 11 (2009): 5. According to Watanabe, he received a copy of the overview from the Shiroishi Doll Warehouse in Miyagi prefecture.

shamisen music.⁴ These art forms remained popular well into the twentieth century, when gramophone recordings and broadcasting provided new platforms for their dissemination.⁵ The introduction of Western music did not in itself lead to their displacement, as the venues and social context of performance differed.

Efforts to introduce Western music into the newly established public school system in Miyagi prefecture began in the 1870s. As we have seen, Ono Shōgorō, one of several young men from Sendai who had been converted to the Russian Orthodox faith in Hakodate, published one of the earliest treatises discussing the role of music in education and arguing in favour of teaching Western music (see Chapter 6).⁶ His call to introduce music into schools was taken up by the school teacher Yano Nariaya (1830–94), who began to teach singing at his elementary school using textbooks published by the Tokyo Normal School for Women. His lessons were not part of the regular curriculum, but hardly any public schools at the time taught singing, so his course would appear to be one of the first of its kind.⁷

This began to change in the 1880s through increased missionary activity and efforts by the local authorities. In September 1882 Imafuku Tatsuo from Miyagi Normal School became the first educator from Sendai to be sent on a short training course at the Music Research Institute in Tokyo. He graduated in July 1883. His certificate detailed his achievements: singing and playing on the organ the first twenty-four songs in the first volume of songs for use in schools (*shōka*).⁸ That

---

4   *Jōruri* is a generic term for narrative *shamisen* music, which, apart from the specific genres named after their founders, including *shinnai*, *tokiwazu*, and *kiyomoto*, also comprised *heikyoku* (narrative vocal genres based on the *Tale of the Heike*), *yōkyoku* (singing in *noh*), and others.

5   Watanabe's explanation. For a brief overview of the vocal narrative genres, which continued to be popular well into the twentieth century, see also Kerim Yasar, *Electrified Voices: How the Telephone, Phonograph, and Radio Shaped Modern Japan, 1868–1945* (New York: Columbia University Press, 2018), 26–29, https://www.degruyter.com/document/doi/10.7312/yasa18712/html

6   Shōgorō Ono, 'Ongyoku no fusei wa jinmin no hinkō o midaru', *Kōshū joshi* 15–17 (1877): Documents relating to the Ono family in the Sendai City Museum; reprinted in: Kanako Kitahara and Sumire Yamashita, 'Kyū Sendai hanshi Ono Shōgorō no ongakuron, Ongyoku no fusei wa jinmin no hinkō o midaru', *Hirosaki Daigaku kokushi kenkyū* 143 (October 2017), https://cir.nii.ac.jp/crid/1010282256804517896

7   Shin'ya Watanabe, 'Sendai yōgaku no sakigake', *Sendai bunka*, no. 11 (2009).

8   Masami Yamazumi, *Shōka kyōiku seiritsu katei no kenkyū* (Tokyo: Tōkyō Daigaku Shuppankai, 1967), 157–58.

same year, Maedako Nobuchika (or Shinkin; 1861 (?)–1929), another convert to the Russian Orthodox Church, returned to his native town. He had studied music at the Russian Orthodox Seminary in Tokyo and subsequently taught church music at several churches. Although his service to the local church appears to have been less than satisfactory,[9] he played an important role as a pioneer of Western music. For decades, his private studio with the impressive-sounding name Tōhoku Ongakuin (Tohoku Academy of Music) trained numerous students in Western music and organized regular concerts featuring both Western music and blended music.[10] He performed himself, as did his daughters Haruko and Nobuko and his son Wataru. Haruko reportedly never married and was active as a violin teacher even after 1945: she died in in her eighties in 1975; she is an example of a pioneer whose professional engagement with Western music extended into the next generation of her family.[11]

The Shikama Brothers in Sendai

It is Shikama Jinji (1863–1941), however, the younger brother of Shikama Totsuji, who is generally described as the first music teacher of note in Sendai.[12] In contrast to Maedako, he was educated in the modern public schools, where he also worked for most of his career. He held appointments at a number of schools in the prefecture for around fifty years, as is evident from the inscription quoted at the beginning of this chapter. The erection of a large memorial stone by grateful students in

---

9   The diary of Bishop Nikolaj has several references to Maedako. In July 1902, after several admonitions and a reduction of his pay, he was dismissed from his post: Kumi Mōri and Takeshi Saitō, Bannai, Tomoko, eds., *Senkyōshi Nikorai no zen'nikki*, 9 vols., vol. 7 (Tokyo: Kyōbunkan, 2007), 82, 159.
10 Reports about this clearly significant institution are conflicting, with both Shikama Totsuji and Madeko named as founders. See the following section on Shikama Totsuji's activities in Sendai.
11 I have found very few sources on Maedako, including a short dictionary entry in Sendai Jinmei Daijisho Kankōkai, ed., *Sendai jinmei daijisho* (2000 (1933)). The dates of his death are from the register at the Russian Orthodox Church in Sendai and from the family grave at Dōrinji temple in Sendai. According to the inscription, Wataru died in Tokyo in 1932 at the age of thirty-seven and Haruko in 1975 (no age recorded).
12 Biographical details in Shin'ya Watanabe, 'Sendai sho no shōka kyōshi Shikama Jinji', *Sendai bunka*, no. 11 (2009); Miyagiken Kyōiku Iinkai, ed., *Miyagiken kyōiku hyakunenshi Vol 4* (Sendai: Gyōsei, 1977), 429; Sakae Ōmura, *Yōkendō kara no shuppatsu: kyōiku hyakunenshi yowa*, vol. 1 (Tokyo: Gyōsei, 1986), 175.

1958, seventeen years after his death, represents an eloquent testimony to the respect his initiatives gained him.

Jinji was already a member of the 'new' generation whose education spanned the period of transition from traditional samurai education to the establishment of the modern school system.[13] Having a traditional education in the Confucian classics, he continued his studies at Miyagi Normal School (Miyagi Shihan Gakkō) from 1878 to 1881. Immediately after graduation at the young age of eighteen, he became principal of Kashima Primary School in the Watari district.

In 1884, Shikama Jinji was sent by his home prefecture to complete a short teacher training course at the institute of the Music Investigation Committee. Candidates had to take an examination, at which Jinji achieved the highest marks. Even Jinji's marks were distinctly lower in the singing test and in arithmetic (where the standard was generally low) than in the other two subjects, reading and essay writing. Although some candidates did miserably, all were admitted to the course, because the number of applicants fell below the institute's quota.[14]

Both of the Shikama brothers graduated in July 1885 (the university's later yearbooks mistakenly give the year as 1886), and Jinji returned to Sendai, where he remained for the rest of his life, and enjoyed a busy and successful career in education.[15] He held concurrent teaching appointments at several schools besides his alma mater, including the ones named in the inscription quoted earlier. He acted as a school inspector and as an invited teacher at schools around Miyagi prefecture. In 1911 he officially retired from Miyagi Normal School, but continued to teach there until 1932. In 1923, he became the fourth principal of Miyagi Prefectural School for the Blind and Dumb (Miyagi Kenritsu Mōa Gakkō), a post he held until September 1933, during which time he significantly contributed to the development of special needs education (*tokushu kyōiku*).

13　Kenneth Pyle, *The New Generation in Meiji Japan: Problems of Cultural Identity, 1885–1895* (Stanford: Stanford University Press, 1969).

14　Yamazumi, *Shōka kyōiku seiritsu katei no kenkyū*, 168–69.

15　A report in *Ongaku zasshi* in April 1896 carried a short note stating that Jinji had been ordered to conduct investigations into music (*ongaku torishirabe*) in Tokyo and stayed there from 2 February to the middle of the month: see *Ongaku zasshi* no. 57 (1896): 30.

Shikama Jinji's activities went well beyond his regular appointments and helped disseminate knowledge of Western music beyond the classroom. In this regard he was typical of local pioneers elsewhere. Reports on musical activities in different parts of Japan regularly appeared in *Ongaku zasshi*, presumably supplied by the local actors themselves. Some highlighted the role of named individuals. Unsurprisingly, Sendai (and sometimes other parts of Miyagi prefecture) featured often in the early issues of *Ongaku zasshi*: almost certainly, Jinji acted as Totsuji's main informant.

The earliest report about musical activities in the prefecture appeared in the second issue of *Ongaku zasshi*. It informed readers that music was being taught at the Second Lower Secondary School, the Normal School, three higher primary schools, and ten standard primary schools, as well as girls' schools, and private sewing schools. The schools had organs, while the violin was used to teach movement games (*yūgi*) at the Normal School and the primary schools. Shikama Jinji had taught summer courses at the Normal School in 1887 and 1889, with sixty-eight participants in total; most of the current teachers had been trained on these courses. He regularly gave summer courses and lectures in different locations in Miyagi prefecture. With children now singing *shōka* when they gathered to play, the vulgar songs of the past would soon be eradicated, the unnamed author of the report remarked optimistically.[16] The participants of the training courses in turn strove to further disseminate music education in the prefecture's schools, and to further their aim, they founded the Miyagi Music Society (Miyagi Ongaku Kai) in 1889.[17] The next report in *Ongaku zasshi* was short, but equally positive about the progress being made; *shōka* could be heard widely, even from errand boys and apprentices (*kozō detchi*); likewise, the sounds of organ, violin, and accordion, as well as Ming-Qing music could often be heard.[18]

The first musical performance in Sendai to be reported in *Ongaku zasshi* took place when the new building of the Second Higher Secondary

---

16   'Miyagi-ken no ongaku', *Ongaku zasshi*, no. 2 (25 October 1890).
17   Regulations in Miyagiken Kyōiku Iinkai, *Miyagiken kyōiku hyakunenshi Vol 4*, 527–29.
18   'Sendai chihō ongaku', *Ongaku zasshi* 13 (1891): 16.

School was inaugurated on 26 October 1891.[19] A military band played ceremonial music (neither the band nor the music are specified),[20] and the event included a sports meeting, accompanied by music. The music teacher, Takagi Tsuguo, conducted an ensemble playing a song he had composed to celebrate the occasion.[21] In the afternoon there was a concert of *koto* music, where *Sansa shigure*,[22] *Rokudan* etc. were performed. After this, a well-known local *shingaku* (Qing music) musician, Mr. Yamashita, intended to perform in honour of the occasion, but the audience had begun to disperse. According to *Ongaku zasshi*, the graceful and cheerful (*yūbi kaikatsu*) sound of the band had absorbed all their attention, and there was no audience for Yamashita's performance, so he went home without having been heard: 'this is how it is with European music and Qing music.'[23]

Subsequent reports suggest that Western music had by no means upstaged the local performing arts. The next report of a concert appeared in the March 1892 issue.[24] It was a charity concert, one of many held in Japan at the time, organized by about ten local people, including musicians and music teachers.[25] Held at the Sendai-za theatre, the concert reportedly drew an audience of two thousand and several hundreds. It lasted all day, and the programme included *gagaku* (performed by the Okabe troupe); two-stringed *koto* (*yakumogoto*, performed by the Haga troupe); *koto* (Yamashita troupe); Qing music (*shingaku*, Yamashita Oikawa troupe); singing (*yōkyoku*, Raishindō Satō troupe); comic noh interlude (*kyōgen*, Suzuki troupe); European music (Maedako troupe); tightrope walking (Wakatayu); *hayashi* (Katata troupe), and kabuki dance (Bandō troupe). The event was reportedly a huge success, raising

---

19   Dai Ni Kōtō Chūgakkō rakusei shiki, *Ongaku zasshi* 14, M24.11, p 13; the event was announced in the preceding issue (13: 16).
20   The announcement in the previous issue of *Ongaku zasshi* included the information that a military band from the army would perform. Presumably, this would have been a band from the local garrison.
21   *Kaikō o shuku suru uta*. The song is published in the same issue of *Ongaku zasshi* (pp. 5–6)
22   *Sansa Shigure* is a local folk song, still well known today.
23   *Nanishiro Ōshūgaku to shingaku korekore no gotoshi*.
24   'Sendai jizen ongaku kai', *Ongaku zasshi* 18 (1892): 19–20.
25   Five of them are named: Kamata Fusan, Yamashita Shōkin, Umehara Eizō, Itō Shōko, and Ichikawa Hiroko.

one hundred yen and eighty-seven sen.[26] The performances were clearly more varied than we would expect at a conventional concert, reminiscent of variety theatre or music hall events.

This report was followed up with a short note in the next issue describing charity concerts in general as a praiseworthy undertaking and commending the recent event in Sendai as an example.[27] As well as raising money for general welfare projects (the money was presented to the local authorities), the purpose of the concert had also been to promote 'our country's traditional music'.[28]

A year later, *Ongaku zasshi* reported another charity concert, described as the third of its kind. Attended by 2,687 people and raising 68 yen 503 sen, it was described as an unprecedented success.[29] The report listed twenty programme items (while implying that there were more), all of them Japanese genres: 1) *imayō* (popular songs of the ancient court); 2) *gagaku* (court music); 3) *kumoi* (*koto* played with a particular tuning); 4) Qing music; 5) *shakuhachi*; 6) two-stringed *koto*; 7) *narimono* (kabuki-theatre style ensemble with drums and flutes); 8) *nagauta* (a sung genre with *shamisen* accompaniment); 9) *nagauta, imayō*; 10) *teodori* (pantomimic dancing similar to that in the kabuki theatre); 11) *gidayu* (a narrative genre with *shamisen*); 12) *nōgaku* (music of the *nō* theatre); 13) *kyōgen* (comic interludes in *nō* theatre); 14) *kiyomoto* (a genre founded in the nineteenth century); (15) *chaban* (a type of short sketch with origins in kabuki theatre); 16) *kiyomoto*; 17) *gentō* (slide show); 18) *satsumabiwa*; 19) *teodori*; 20) *Miyagi no sato jizen no nigiwai* (The prosperity of benevolence in Miyagi village). Given that most of the listed items included several pieces, this concert, like the one previously reported, must have continued for many hours.

A fourth charity concert was announced in the September 1893 issue of *Ongaku zasshi*.[30] The short notice included the information that ten members of the Association for Native Japanese Music (Kokufū Ongaku

---

26 In 1887 the starting salary for a primary school teacher was eight yen a month; ten kilograms of polished rice cost sixty-seven sen in Tokyo in 1892. See Shūkan Asahi, ed., *Nedanshi nempyō: Meiji, Taishō, Shōwa* (Tokyo: Asahi Shinbunsha, 1988), 92, 161.
27 'Jizen ongakukai no bikyo', *Ongaku zasshi* 19 (1892): 21.
28 *Wagakuni jurai no ongaku o hattatsu seshimuru mokuteki.*
29 'Sendai jizen ongaku kai', *Ongaku zasshi* 31 (1893): 19. I could find no report of the second concert.
30 'Sendai jizen ongaku kai', *Ongaku zasshi* 36 (1893): 23. The same page has a note about a Society for researching Qing music (Shingaku Kenkyūkai) established by

Kai) would be coming from Tokyo to perform. This society was founded earlier that year with the aim of preserving, reforming, and promoting the indigenous music of Japan (see Chapter 3). Whether they actually came to perform in Sendai is unclear, as *Ongaku zasshi* published no report after the concert. The November issue carried a report on what appears to be a separate concert, staged at the Sendai-za theatre on 19 November by the Sendai Philanthropy Society (Sendai Jizen Kai; formerly Sendai Jizen Ongaku Kai), again with a programme that included a variety of genres.[31]

Musical associations, established by teachers and others with an interest in promoting music, played an important role in Sendai and elsewhere by organizing regular concerts and lectures. For Shikama Jinji they represented part of his role as a musical pioneer in Sendai. He was a founding member of a music society named Hōmeikai (Phoenix Song Society), established in 1893 with the aim of 'researching the true principles of music and at the same time to promote the essence of reforming customs and habits'.[32] On 14 May 1893 the society organized their first concert in the office buildings of the Tōshōgū shrine, which was attended by over 350 members of the society as well as some 1,500(!) non-members. The programme included *gagaku*, Qing music, *yakumogoto*, *shōka*, *mai*-dance, and *iai* (the art of drawing a sword quickly).[33]

Ongaku zasshi continued to report on the society's activities in the following issues, although not regularly, and the reports vary in detail.[34] The next report described the society's third meeting at the same venue as the first on 10 August 1893.[35] The meeting started at nine o'clock in the morning and was reportedly attended by over fifty members and an audience of several hundred. After the singing of the national anthem and cheers of 'banzai' to the imperial couple and a lecture about music, a varied musical programme followed: the report mentions *gagaku*, Qing music, *yakumogoto*, *Seiyō-gaku* (Western music), and *sōkyoku* (*koto* music).

---

the students of Yamashita Shōkin, who were organizing their tenth regular meeting in Sendai.
31 'Sendai jizenkai no rinjikai', *Ongaku zasshi* 38 (1893): 20–21.
32 'Hōmeikai', *Ongaku zasshi* 33 (1893): 21.
33 Ibid.
34 Other reports about the activities of the Hōmeikai in *Ongaku zasshi* 35 (1893): 15–16; 37 (1893): 19; 38 (1893): 16–17; 41 (1894): 23; 42 (1894): 26; 45 (1894): 31–33.
35 'Hōmeikai', *Ongaku zasshi* 35 (1893): 15–16. I found no report of the second meeting.

The next reported Hōmeikai concert took place on 22 November 1893 in the Gojōkan Hall. Described as a big autumn concert, it included Western music, court music, two-stringed *koto,* and Qing music, as well as lectures (including one by Master of Letters Hiranuma Shukurō, (1864–1938), professor at the Second High School 1888–94).[36] The report does not include all the programme items, but mentions several that were particularly applauded: Shikama Jinji's *Roeikyoku* (song of the encampment); the Qing music piece *Gekkyūden* (Moon Palace) performed by members of the society, and *Rokudan*, performed by an unspecified ensemble consisting Shikama Jinji and two others.

For the following Hōmeikai concert, which took place on 3 June 1894 in the city's Gojōkan Hall, the society had invited the famous *satsumabiwa* artist Yoshimizu Tsunekazu (1844–1910). As a special guest he featured in four of the seventeen items on the programme. According to the report in *Ongaku zasshi*,[37] the audience assembled early in the morning and included staff from the several of the city's schools, prefectural officials, journalists, supporters (*yūshisha*), women, children, and students—about 300 people in all. The concert began at nine o'clock in the morning with the national anthem *Kimigayo* sung by all, standing up, and accompanied by the reed organ and the violin, followed by an address by Shikama Jinji, who was both the current president of the Hōmeikai and the head of the section for Western music. The subsequent performances were as follows: 3) *satsumabiwa* (Yoshimizu Tsunekazu); 4) *wagaku* (*gagaku* composed in Japan) performed on the *koto, shakuhachi,* and *shamisen;* 5) two-stringed *koto;* 6) Qing music; 7) Western music (*seiyōgaku*); 8) *satsumabiwa* (Yoshimizu Tsunekazu); 9) two-stringed *koto;* 10) Qing music; 11) *wagaku;* 12) Western music; 13) *satsumabiwa* (Yoshimizu Tsunekazu); 14) Western music; 15) Qing music; 16) *wagaku* (solo by Yamashita Shōkin);[38] 17) *satsumabiwa* (Yoshimizu Tsunekazu). According to the report in *Ongaku zasshi*, all Yoshimizu's *biwa* performances received especially fervent

---

36 'Hōmeikai', *Ongaku zasshi* 38. (1893): 16–17. The previous issue contained a short note about a lecture organized by the Hōmeikai (p. 19), but there was no mention of a concert.
37 'Hōmeikai daisankai taishūkai gaijō', *Ongaku zasshi*, no. 45 (25 June 1894). The concert was announced in its previous issue. On Tsunekawa, see Chapter 3.
38 Yamashita Shōkin (1848–1918) was a *jiuta* performer and composer.

applause, as did several of the *wagaku* compositions and the Western music performance of *Ukikumo*.[39]

Given that 'music reform' tended to take Western music as its primary model and that Shikama Jinji was regarded as a prime promoter of Western music, the programme is surprising: only three items are billed as Western music (*seiyōgaku*), and at least one of the five titles performed is a traditional piece.[40] In any case, performing a mixture of genres in the same concert and playing Japanese pieces on Western instruments were common practice at the time, although the latter were usually billed as 'blended music' rather than 'Western music'.

The report was followed by the information that the society's regulations had been revised, and cited them in full for the first time.[41] The stated aim was the same as previously reported, that is, 'researching the true principles of music and at the same time to promote the essence of reforming customs and habits' (*ifū ekizoku*; p.32). The genres of music that were to receive particular attention were named: court music, Japanese music (*wagaku*), *yakumogoto*, Western music (*seiyōgaku*), Qing music, and *koto* music. The society had separate sections for these genres (except for *koto* music), and the head for each section was appointed for a year at a time. Four smaller gatherings were held each year, with presentations of research, lectures, and performances, as well as one large gathering in May, where the reports of the society's activities would be given. Eligible members were persons of upright, proper conduct and willing to promote music, and there was a joining fee of thirty sen and a monthly payment of five sen.

The Hōmeikai concert in June 1894 was the last major one to be reported in *Ongaku zasshi*. A shorter report, on the Hōmeikai's fifth general meeting on 8 March 1896, appeared in connection with a longer report on music in Sendai in the fifty-seventh issue.[42] As in previous

---

39 The highlighted *wagaku* pieces are: *Isochidori*, *Yaegoromo*, and *Tsuru no sugomori*.
40 *Rokudan* is the title of a famous *koto* piece attributed to Yatsuhashi Kengyō (1614–84). *Ukigumo* (floating or drifting clouds) is the title of a *shakuhachi* piece (a so-called classical piece or *koten honkyoku*); however, here it is more likely to be a song with the same title composed by the Tokyo Academy graduate Suzuki Yonejirō with lyrics by Ochiai Naobumi and published by Kyōeki Shōsha in 1892. I have not been able to identify the other pieces, *Shizuku no chikara* (strength or power of drops/ dripping), *Shinkōkyoku* (march) and *Roei* (bivouac, camping out).
41 'Hōmeikai daisankai taishūkai gaijō', *Ongaku zasshi* 45 (1894): 31–33.
42 'Sendai tsūshin, Hōmeikai', *Ongaku zasshi* 57 (1895: 22–28 (25).

concerts, the programme included court music, *koto* music, *yakumogoto*, and *satsumabiwa* by the honorary member Yoshimizu Tsunekazu, as well as Western music by the honorary member Shikama Totsuji together with Shikama Jinji. The brothers reportedly performed a military song that roused the brave military men (*yūshō*) in their seats.

Nevertheless, Shikama Jinji seems to have been more active as an organizer than as a performer—hardly surprising, given his limited musical training. He did compose a significant number of *shōka*, an achievement mentioned on the memorial stone. They included school (alma mater) songs (*kōka*) for several schools as well as military songs in connection with the Sino-Japanese and Russo-Japanese Wars, such as *Yuke, yuke, danji, Nihon danji* (Advance, advance, boys, sons of Japan).[43] In 1901 he published *Miyagi-ken kyōdo shōka*, a collection of three songs that described local history and geography.[44] Jinji was, moreover, famed for his skill with words, a result of his early education in the Chinese classics. Apart from the lyrics for some of his songs, he also wrote tributes for teachers who died while carrying out their duties. He was, moreover, a sought-after writer of inscriptions (often under his penname Seidō).[45]

In summer 1896, Shikama Totsuji moved to Sendai, and for a few years he was a significant local actor. The Hōmeikai concert on 8 March 1896 featured him as a guest performer: he had arrived on 6 March and stayed until 30 March. During his stay he rehearsed the newly founded Miyagi Youth Band (Miyagi Shōnen Ongakutai), which performed for the first time at the Sendai Philanthropy Society's eighth spring concert, held at Sendai-za theatre.[46] As with previous concerts, the programme

---

43 He composed songs for at least six primary schools soon after his return from Tokyo: Miyagiken Shōgakkōchō Kai, ed., *Hossoku yonjū shūnen kinen shi: yonjū nen no ayumi* (Sendai: Miyagiken Shōgakkōchō Kai, 1987), 144, 228, 259, 333, 578, 594. The catalogue of Miyagi Prefecture Library records two song collections published locally: Jinji Shikama, *Seishin no uta: dai isshū* (Sendai: Takatō Shoten, 1894); Jinji Shikama and Makino Kōji, *Manshū tetsudō shōka* (Sendai: Fusandō, 1905).

44 Jinji Shikama, ed., *Miyagi-ken kyōdo shōka: dai isshū* (Tokyo: Yoshikawa Hanshichi, 1901).

45 Miyagiken Kyōiku Iinkai, ed., *Miyagiken kyōiku hyakunenshi Vol 2* (Sendai: Gyōsei, 1977), 512. Jinji is mentioned a few times in same work: in vol 2, p. 177, he is listed among those honoured for their contribution to education at the time of the fortieth anniversary of the Imperial Rescript on Education, and also as the composer of the school song for the Normal School.

46 'Sendai tsūshin [April 1896]', *Ongaku zasshi/Omukaku*, no. 57 (28 April 1896): 25 ('Sendai Jizen Kai').

consisted of a mixture of traditional musical and theatrical genres. The performance by the band was a novelty, however. As the first band of its kind in Sendai, it drew applause from the packed hall despite not yet having rehearsed for long.

The founder of the Miyagi Youth Band was Serizawa Fumi, the owner of Sendai's first Western-style laundry business, together with other wealthy local merchants. Shikama Totsuji was listed among the founders and advising teachers of a new youth band in Sendai at a time when he was still based in Tokyo. The founding statement and regulations describe its purpose, as the promotion of proper music (*seisoku naru ongaku no fukyū*).[47] References to the ancient sage kings of China and 'the realm of civilization' (*bunmei no iki*) suggest that, for Shikama at least, the venture was part of the agenda to reform society through music. The businessmen may well have had more mundane objectives in mind. Eligible members were boys from age thirteen to fifteen. Strict discipline was expected, in return for which the boys would be paid twenty sen each time the band was invited to perform. The members reportedly rehearsed with enthusiasm, and the official premiere took place on 25 March in front of an audience of over two hundred, including high-ranking officials and other notables and wealthy merchants.[48] There were speeches (Shikama's own is included in the report), and the boys, resplendent in red trousers and blue caps, played the national anthem and some ten other (unspecified) pieces. Afterwards a photograph was taken, copies of which were to be given to the sponsors. A few days later, the youth band played *Kimigayo* at a daytime reception and concert to celebrate Shikama's mother's sixty-second birthday, where the audience of around two hundred guests included forty-three children and grandchildren from the extended Shikama family. This concert, like the others described here, included a variety of performances in traditional genres, although the violin and mandolin (*mendarin*) are also mentioned.[49]

Shikama Totsuji also actively involved himself in the formation of a band for adults, the Miyagi Ongakutai, although this was not officially

---

47 'Sendai tsūshin [April 1896]', 23.
48 Ibid., 24–25.
49 Ibid., 2–7.

launched until 4 April, when he was back in Tokyo.⁵⁰ The immediate purpose of the band was specific: it was to play on the occasion of the triumphal return of the Second Army Division to its Sendai Garrison after being in action in Japan's new colony, Taiwan. Subsequently, the band would perform by invitation at public and private events, and thus make a practical contribution to the reform of manners and customs (*ifū ekizoku*). The latter once again suggests the agenda of the Confucian-educated music reformer Shikama, as do other phrases in the founding statement:

> Upon earnest reflection, there is nothing like music to bring the human disposition into harmony and to stir the human heart. [...] Japanese music is not useless; it can be sorrowful and move people to shed copious tears; it can also be stirring and excite people so they shout for joy. However, the instruments with which it is performed have a small sound and cannot reach the ears of the audience in a large hall. In this it is inferior to Western music.⁵¹

Although Sendai was the most significant city after Tokyo, Kyoto, and Osaka, the statement continued, its music did not flourish to the same extent, and it lacked a wind band. The recently established youth band was a start, but the founders wanted more, particularly now that the Second Division was about to be welcomed home. The Miyagi Band, consisting of ten members in addition to the band master and his deputy, was to be financed by sponsors. The following instruments were listed: pitch clarinet; grand clarinet (2); piston; alto; baritone; bass; contrabass; cymbals; triangle; grand case; pitch case. A list of supporters followed: four supporting instructors, including the two Shikama brothers; six executives; an officer of the Second Division (in absentia); the prefectural governor, as well as fifty-six other individuals.

By October 1896 Sendai reportedly had four bands: the Miyagi Ongakutai, which was said to be doing well, and three youth bands. For some reason the Tokyo Youth Band was included.⁵² The third one, Shiogama Ongakutai, was founded in the neighbouring port town of Shiogama by two local businessmen. The band had eight to nine

---

50 'Sendai tsūshin [April 1896]', 27–29.
51 Ibid., 28.
52 'Sendai tsūshin [October 1896]', *Ongaku zasshi/Omukaku*, no. 62 (25 October 1896): 39–40.

members and their instruments were the accordion, drums, side-blown flutes, and a triangle. Their repertoire included *shōka* and military songs. The Miyagi Youth Band had nobody to teach them, having broken off their relationship with Shikama Totsuji (no reasons are mentioned). Rather than perform as an accordion ensemble, as Totsuji had intended, its members imitated the adult band, and the thirteen to fourteen members were now playing piston, clarinet, alto, and baritone, which had given rise to concerns about the boys' health. Consequently, the band was not a success. The Tokyo Youth Band included a division for girls, from which five members formed a chamber ensemble that was well regarded and was invited to perform at private functions. The band's repertoire included the national anthems of several countries, famous waltzes and polkas, as well as military songs and *shōka*. By the time the report appeared, Shikama Totsuji had settled in Sendai, but it does not mention the subsequent fate of the Tokyo band.

Totsuji remained in Sendai from May or June 1896 to about 1906, and information about his activities after he relocated is scarce. We can assume that he involved himself in the training of the bands he had helped establish and that he may have supplied reports for *Ongaku zasshi*, while the magazine still existed. Possibly, he eventually took at least the youth band in hand again. He founded a new ensemble for girls. A report in *Ongaku zasshi* published in April 1897 named three bands: the Miyagi Ongakutai for adults; Miyagi Shōnen Ongakutai for young people; and Shikama Senka's (Totsuji's) Joshi Ongakutai for young women.[53] All three were said to be doing well. No further details are given, except a short report about a ceremony in which four musicians from the Miyagi Ongakutai were awarded a certificate for having passed the first stage of training (*zenki gakuka*), and that two or three more awards would soon follow. The band was also preparing for a grand concert to be held soon in celebration of its first anniversary. This would involve all three local bands, as well as including *satsumabiwa*, Oku-*jōruri*, shakuhachi, *koto*, *kokyū* (bowed lute), *shingaku*, *yakumogoto*, piano, one-stringed *koto* (*ichigengoto*), organ, violin, and even sword

---

53 'Miyagi-ken Sendai tsūshin [April 1897]', *Ongaku zasshi/Omukaku*, no. 68 (25 April 1897). It is not clear who wrote the report: the pseudonym is not typical of those Totsuji used. On the bands, see also Hide Henmi, *Sendai hajimete monogatari* (Sendai: Sōdōsha, 1995), 211–15.

dance (*kenmai*), music performed at Shinto shrines (*kagura*), the *laterna magica*/slide show, *hayashi,* and war-like dances. The Shikama brothers were among the organizers. Presumably the concert went ahead, but *Ongaku zasshi* did not report it.

The same report also mentioned that the Miyagi Band had performed at a farewell reception for two former prefectural governors. One of them was Katsumata, himself a supporter of the band, and he praised the band in a speech, describing it as the only private band in North-Eastern Japan that performed the perfect music of a civilized country (*bunmeikoku no kanzennaru ongaku*; p. 36).

During his three weeks' stay in Sendai in March 1896, Shikama Totsuji had not only concerned himself with the performance of Western music. True to his ambitions for reforming Japanese music he and his brother had hosted a meeting at the Shikama residence with three performers of Oku-*jōruri,* a local style of narrative performance to the accompaniment of *biwa, shamisen,* and beating the rhythm with a closed fan. A performance, reportedly attended by at least eighty officials, teachers, and businessmen, made the audience reassess the music: 'what they had generally dismissed as nonsense spouted by itinerant blind performers, had, as they discovered for the first time, a high level of classical elegance (*koga*) compared to other kinds of *jōruri,* and in that respect was similar in to *satsumabiwa*'.[54] In order to raise its value, Shikama Totsuji suggested five areas for reform (*kairyō*): correcting the mistakes in the phonetic spelling of texts; improving the personal appearance of the performers; improving the musical instruments; focusing on the performance of war tales; and providing the audience with printed versions of the texts. Thus elevated, the genre could join *satsumabiwa* as something that could be performed even in front of high-ranking persons. One of the performers, Akaizawa, stayed the night with Shikama Totsuji while he was in Sendai, so they could discus things in more detail, and on that occasion Totsuji wrote a song for him, which he is said to have memorized after hearing it only three times. The report included the lyrics; beginning with proverbs associated with the Confucian canon, they seem unlikely to have had the kind of popular appeal expected from war tales.

---

54 'Sendai tsūshin [April 1896]', 26.

Together, the two reports that appeared in the April and October 1896 issues of *Ongaku zasshi* include details of a broad range of musical activities. Besides the ones already mentioned, they informed readers that *shōka* were now taught in schools across the city and even the more rural districts, with the aid of the organ and the violin (the titles of songs from the standard elementary and higher school textbooks were named). Secondary schools where music was taught by specialized teachers included the private Sendai School for Girls (Sendai Jogakkō, founded in 1893), and the sewing school Shōsō Gakkō, which had established a twice-weekly *shōka* class, taught by Shikama Jinji, in addition to his regular position at the Normal School.[55] Private tuition for aspiring music teachers was provided by the Tōhoku Music Academy (Tōhoku Ongakuin). Established by Shikama Totsuji in the Kakyōin-dōri area of Sendai, it had so many participants from the city as well as the neighbouring prefectures that he even taught on Sundays. Meanwhile Maedako Shinkin was teaching people to play *shōka* on the violin in his home.[56]

Musical instruments and other equipment were sold only by the Takatō bookstore. It had a limited selection, so customers had little choice, and if an item was sold out, they had to wait up to a year until it was re-stocked.

The chief organizers of concerts, the report continued, were the Hōmeikai, dedicated to music reform, and the Philanthropic Society. The latter's concerts, held at the Sendai-za theatre, were more like traditional variety shows, and the audience behaved accordingly, eating their lunch boxes during the performance. Recently, garden parties including performances had become popular, although the spirit of drinking

---

55 'Sendai tsūshin [October 1896]', 38–39.
56 'Sendai tsūshin [October 1896]', 39. The history of Tōhoku Ongakuin is elusive: Shikama Totsuji and Maedako are variously described as its founders. The Kakyōindōri area (today in Miyagino ward, just north-west of Sendai Station) is also where the Shikama residence was located. Possibly the names have been confused: according to a report in April 1897, Shikama Totsuji's establishment was named Tōhoku Ongaku Kai and offered fast-track qualification to teach *shōka* in primary schools. It had forty to fifty members. See 'Miyagi-ken Sendai tsūshin [April 1897]', 36. Meanwhile, a report in 1907 stated that Maedako had recently expanded his school, here referred to has Miyagi Ongaku Kōshūkai, and renamed it Tōhoku Ongakuin. Conceivably, he took over from Shikama Totsuji, who left the city around that time. See 'Miyagi Ongaku Kōshūkai', *Ongaku* 12, no. 2 (1907).

parties prevailed and unless the music performed was of the common popular kind (*zokugaku*) no-one wanted to listen.[57] The report concluded with a series of short notes about different genres of music: *koto* music was very popular among the daughters of better families, and the most popular teachers were Yamashita Shōkin and Itō Matsuko; *yakumogoto* was only taught by one person (Masuda Michie), so only a few had the chance to study it; Ming-Qing music had gone out of fashion in the city but was still enjoyed in the countryside; court music was cultivated by a group of five to six performers who played for ceremonies conducted at temples and shrines, though their performances were not particularly popular. Buddhists had recently begun to include *shōka*, accompanied by the violin and the organ, in their music, and on occasion the Miyagi Youth Band had accompanied *shōmyō* chants at the Honganji Betsuin temple. This had excited the emotions of the believers so much that some had voiced criticism. As for Christians, they mainly sang and played hymns, mixing in the odd *koto* (*sōkyoku*) performance and occasionally organizing charity concerts.

Concerts, according to the report, were still an unfamiliar concept. The impressive programmes often came to nothing because the performers had no notion of time-keeping and much time was wasted waiting for performers arriving late; a bad habit that, according to the report, was not limited to Sendai.[58] This last observation suggests that modern notions of precise clock time had not yet become fully embedded in everyday life.

Thus was the state of musical culture in 1896/7 according to *Ongaku zasshi*. The last few issues contain no reports on Sendai. No magazine devoted to music appeared continuously until the publication of the magazine *Ongakukai* (Music world) from January 1908 onwards, so for about ten years we do not have regular reports from a single source.[59] Clearly, much happened in these years, because by the time *Ongakukai* appeared, the character of the concerts it reported on was different. Although the difference in the focus and scope of the two magazines might to some extent account for the change, it seems likely that it reflects

---

57 'Sendai tsūshin [October 1896]', 40.
58 Ibid., 41.
59 Literary journals reported on music, but not regularly. Local newspapers, including *Kahoku Shinpō*, established in 1897, published information about concerts.

the increasing spread of Western-style music and music-making. While the idea of the public concert, including the charity concert, was adopted already in the 1890s, actual performances consisted largely of established musical genres and the occasional Western-style piece or performance of blended music. Many, if not most, of the concert programmes published in *Ongakukai*, on the other hand, include predominantly, although not exclusively, Western music.

During his time in Sendai, Shikama Totsuji continued to compose songs. In September 1900 he and his brother published their *Railway Song* which detailed the stations on the line from Sendai to Aomori and to Hirosaki, Akita, and Yamagata.[60] Several railway songs were published around this time, celebrating one of the most powerful symbols of modernity and as an aid to learning geography for schoolchildren. The most famous one, about the East Coast (Tōkaidō) line from Tokyo to Kobe, was published in May 1900 and soon reached the status of a popular song: to this day its opening bars signal the approaching trains in stations on that line.

Another joint publication was *Tokkyō shōka* (Moral education songs), published the following year.[61] The collection of twenty-five songs and a short march-like tune without lyrics composed by Fujiko (presumably Totsuji's late daughter) is preceded by the text of the Imperial Rescript on Education in literary Sinitic. Not all the songs were new compositions. They include the national anthem (with an added bass line) and the Sendai folk song *Sansa shigure*. The collection reflects the role accorded by reformers to singing as a means of moral edification.

Totsuji's creation of songs for educational purposes also includes a collection of *Sangyō shōka* (silk industry songs), published in 1901 for the benefit of the workers in the Sano filature, opened in 1886 by Sano Rihachi in the town of Kanayama (now Marumori-Kanayama), south of Sendai.[62] The aim of the collection was to ensure that the overwhelmingly female

---

60 Jinji Shikama and Totsuji Shikama, *Chiiku tetsudō shōka* (Sendai: Yūsenkaku (Yamamoto Otoshirō, 1900)). The Shikamas' song was one of several published about the Tohoku railway lines that year.
61 Totsuji Shikama, *Tokkyō shōka* (Tokyo and Sendai: Gakuyūkan and Yūsenkaku, 1902). Although only Totsuji is named as the author, the introduction was written by Jinji, who is also named as the composer of some of the songs.
62 Ichizō Sano, ed., *Sangyō shōka: Sano Seishijō yō* (Miyagi-ken Igu-gun Kanayama-machi: Sano Ichizō, 1901). Sano Rihachi (?–1915) was an important figure in the history of the silk industry in Meiji Japan. About the silk filature, which exported

workforce sang songs with suitably edifying texts as they worked. Left to their own devices, factory workers often sang songs either deemed vulgar or highly critical of their work conditions.[63] In his preface to the collection, Totsuji expressed the hope that the songs would serve as a replacement for the vulgar and obscene songs (*hika waisetsu*) usually sung by the workers.[64] Concerns about the songs sung by factory girls had previously been the subject of two short reports in *Ongaku zasshi* in 1893. One came from Gunma prefecture and was based on a story from a music teacher named Uchida.[65] The factory girls working in silk production around Maebashi sang while they worked, which helped them work rhythmically and speedily. Unfortunately, the lyrics of the songs were so obscene (*inwai*) that they were dreadful to listen to. For this reason, one factory owner had forbidden the girls to sing, but this had led to a sharp drop in productivity by an average of five to six yen per day, so the prohibition was rescinded. The report concluded that there was an urgent need to include these songs in plans for music reform. The other report came from Hikone, a castle town by Lake Biwa in Shiga prefecture.[66] Here, according to the unnamed informant, efforts were being made to teach appropriate songs in schools, but the vulgar music enjoyed by the townspeople threatened to thwart such efforts. Meanwhile, in the silk filature, a musical box (a *shikōkin*, a Japanese-style box using paper rolls) had been purchased in order to expose the factory girls to appropriate songs (*seikyoku*) instead of the obscene and vulgar songs (*hiwai no zokuuta*) they were singing, so far, however, without effect. Finding a remedy was an urgent task, because the factory girls played a significant role in transmitting obscene songs (*waiyō no denpansha tari*).

Evidently, Shikama Totsuji continued to pursue his ideas about music reform during his time in Sendai. He was, however, only active in his hometown for about ten years. The influence of his brother Jinji on

---

    to the United States, see Rihachi (jun.) Sano, *Sano Silk Filature in North-Eastern Japan* (Tokyo: By the author, 1919).

63 Examples quoted in Patricia Tsurumi, *Factory Girls: Women in the Thread Mills of Meiji Japan* (Princeton: Princeton University Press, 1990).

64 Sano, *Sangyō shōka*.

65 This was presumably Uchida Kumetarō (1861–1941), who had graduated from the Tokyo Academy of Music in 1887 (he taught at the Academy from 1902 to 1909).

66 'Hikone no ongaku', *Ongaku zasshi* 37 (1893).

musical life in Sendai may well have been more lasting. Nevertheless, Totsuji too played a significant role in the development of Sendai's musical culture by bringing his cosmopolitan aspirations to the provincial town and acting as a link with the capital.

Meanwhile, a new local actor, or rather group of actors, had arrived on the scene: the students at the Second High School.

Music in the Second High School

Schools played a major role in the dissemination of Western music, and Sendai, an educational centre, boasted the prestigious Second High School. Music was not formally taught, but from the turn of the turn of the century Western music came to represent a significant extracurricular activity. In 1893, students at the school founded a students' association named Shōshikai. As at the other high schools, members engaged in both educational and recreational activities, cultivated a strong sense of school spirit, and published a magazine, *Shōshikai zasshi*.[67] Meetings of the Shōshikai and its subgroups sometimes included music: at a meeting on 17 October 1902 the musical contributions amounted to a mini-concert. Mrs Dening, whose husband Walter Dening taught at the school,[68] played several piano pieces, while a group of students performed a *kagura* piece on Japanese flutes, and two others performed *Rokudan* on the *shakuhachi* and *koto*.[69]

In 1902 a music club (Ongakubu) was formed within Shōshikai. The driving force behind this was reportedly a new teacher appointed in 1900, Miyoshi Aikichi (1870–1919). A native of present-day Niigata prefecture, Miyoshi graduated from the Imperial University in 1895 with a degree in philosophy. Miyoshi held several teaching appointments before moving to the Second High School, where he taught ethics and became the school's principal in 1911. In addition, he taught at other schools in Sendai, and in his later years tutored two of the imperial princes.

---

[67] Details in Dai Ni Kōtō Gakkō Shi Henshū Iinkai, ed., *Dai Ni Kōtō Gakkō shi* (Tokyo: Dai Ni Kōtō Gakkō Shōshi Dōsōkai, 1979), 107–13. *Shōshi* appears in the work of Mencius, Jin Xin I, and means 'exalted aim' (Legge translation).

[68] Walter Dening, (1846–1913), an English missionary, first came to Japan in 1873. From 1895 he taught English at the Second High School. See Hiroshi Takeuchi, *Rainichi Seiyō jinmei jiten* (Tokyo: Nichigai Associates, 1983), 242–43.

[69] Dai Ni Kōtō Gakkō Shi Henshū Iinkai, *Dai Ni Kōtō Gakkō shi*, 952.

During his brief tenure as principal of the newly founded Nagano Junior High School from 1899 until his move to Sendai, he worked hard to establish extracurricular music classes, inviting a court musician to perform, and having *shōka* taught to *koto* accompaniment. Aspiring to replace the *koto* with a piano, he gathered the school around him and told teachers and pupils that in order to save money for the purchase, the school would not be heated for one winter. The instrument was duly purchased and is reverently preserved in the principal's office, while the anecdote about the 'sacred piano' features in the message from the school's principal to this day.[70] Nevertheless and despite his role in promoting Western music in at least two secondary schools, little is known about Miyoshi's interest in music. In the substantial collection of obituaries, reminiscences, and a selection of Miyoshi's own writings, published in 1931, hardly any of the writers mention music. A few of them name noh singing (*yōkyoku*) as one of his hobbies. In his own draft reminiscences (up to the year 1894), Miyoshi mentions two concerts he attended in Tokyo, one of them a traditional Japanese trio (*sankyoku*) recital in a school classroom, as well as a lecture entitled 'music' by 'Mrs Summers' (presumably Ellen Summers, 1843–1907) at the Tsukiji English Association in 1888, while he attended the First High School. He also recorded submitting an essay entitled 'Gakubu enkaku shi' (history of music and dance) to Professor Konakamura (Kiyonori), the author of the first book-length history of music in Japan, in 1891. Possibly he was also influenced by Raphael von Koeber, one of his professors at the university and a conservatoire-trained pianist, who also taught at the Tokyo Academy of Music.[71]

---

70 Shinano Kyōiku Kai, ed., *Kyōiku kōrōsha retsuden* (Nagano: Shinano Kyōiku Kai, 1935), 392–93; Miyoshi Aikichi Sensei Chōi Kai, ed., *Butsugai Miyoshi Aikichi Sensei* (Tokyo: Miyoshi Aikichi Sensei Chōi Kai, 1931), 47. The latter includes a photo of the piano in the photograph section after p. 246. See also Nagano Prefectural Senior High School, 'Message from the Principal' (Miyamoto Takashi), https://www.nagano-c.ed.jp/naganohs/english/profile/index.html; https://www.nagano-c.ed.jp/naganohs/profile/index.html (accessed 26 July 2021: in July 2020, the English version still carried the 'Message' of the previous principal, who was pictured seated by the 'sacred piano'; the text referring to the piano is the same in both messages).

71 Miyoshi Aikichi Sensei Chōi Kai, *Butsugai Miyoshi Aikichi Sensei*, 16, 21 (second part, after p. 150). This would have been the wife of James Summers (1828–91). The couple, both teachers, came to Japan in 1873.

The only writer who discussed Miyoshi and music in detail stressed the importance Miyoshi attached to musical training in order to cultivate aesthetic sensibilities (*jōsō kyōiku*) as part of a complete education. Miyoshi reportedly described musical and physical training as fundamental to education in ancient Greece. The importance of music education, he asserted, was recognized in East and West: music was the highest of the arts, representing truth, goodness, and beauty. He argued that the emphasis on the material aspects of Western civilization had led to the neglect of the spiritual aspects, and so he supported and promoted the cultural and particularly musical activities of the student association.

Miyoshi's stance seems to have been similar to that of his professor, Inoue Tetsujirō. He was studying in Tokyo at the time of the debate about the continued existence of the Tokyo Academy of Music, in which Inoue participated. Nothing suggests that Miyoshi had a particular liking for Western music. In fact, his well-attested engagement with Buddhism and Confucianism, and his misgivings about the influence of Christianity, particularly among the elite, appear to have been reflected in his attitude to Western music. This is suggested by his notes for a lecture he gave in Sendai on 29 January 1905 at the Chōgyū Kai (presumably a gathering to commemorate the literary critic Takayama Chōgyū, 1871–1902, who had taught at the high school for a short while in 1896–97). In the lecture, entitled 'Nihon ongaku ron' (A discussion of Japanese music) he described the state of music in Japan as divided and aimless, and discussed the decline of Japanese music and its future. Japanese music, he stated, was largely relegated to the realm of entertainment, while the young people in school were exposed only to Western music, which was also embraced by the upper classes and by those returning from study abroad. Japanese music was generally dismissed as coarse, vulgar, and obscene. Music, although international (Miyoshi uses the English word), was a product of the times and of the character of the people embracing it. Unlike the pictorial arts, he asserted, music is abstract and therefore difficult to assimilate without intensive and lasting exposure. Miyoshi was concerned that, while Japanese music would not become extinct, its neglect by the upper classes would cause its decline to continue. He stressed the value of vocal genres in particular, describing Western music as strongest in instrumental genres. He concluded that the adoption of Western music must not result in the neglect of Japanese music.

Miyoshi's attitude to music and to the adoption of Western civilization in general was, like that of Inoue Tetsujirō, Takaori Shūichi and other advocates of music reform, ambivalent. He initiated the music club soon after taking up his appointment in Sendai, with the support of Shikama Jinji, and continued his involvement thereafter, regularly attending the concerts.[72] The activities of the student association did include Japanese music (there was a *biwa* group and a *shakuhachi* group), and we can assume that Miyoshi supported that too. The concerts of the music club, however, featured predominantly Western music.

The first concert took place on 31 January 1903 in the school's hall. Miyoshi was scheduled to give the opening address, which was read by Kurashima because he had fallen ill. The address contained some of the considerations expressed by Miyoshi in the lecture cited above: Japanese music had a tendency to lapse into sadness (*hiai*) and mournfulness (*chintsū*); it was, moreover, often obscene (*hiwai*). Music (and here he appears to refer largely to Western music) should, however, be more than entertainment and technical perfection; he urged the students to contemplate nature and the harmony of the universe when they were not practising, and cited Plato on music's ability to move humans close to the divine.[73]

Unlike the concerts we have examined so far, the published programme featured only Western music:[74]

1. Opening address, read by Mr Kurashima
2. Organ, violin – *Hotaru no Kyoku*[75] – T. Saito, S. Kuzuoka
3. Piano – Galop – N. Rubo[76]

---

72 Heijirō Iwaki, 'Sensei to Ongaku', in *Butsugai Miyoshi Aikichi Sensei*, ed. Miyoshi Aikichi Sensei Chōi Kai (Tokyo: Miyoshi Aikichi Sensei Chōi Kai, 1931).
73 Dai Ni Kōtō Gakkō Shi Henshū Iinkai, *Dai Ni Kōtō Gakkō shi*, 952. There may well have been an unofficial part, such as the 'aftermeeting' described by Kate Hansen in one of her letters: see the following chapter.
74 Cited in *Shōshikai zasshi*, no. 55 (Meiji 36.6.20): 77; the programme is in English: I have kept the original spelling, since it may offer clues for the identification where this is unclear. English translations of Japanese titles are provided by me.
75 Presumably *Hotaru no hikari* (Light of the fireflies, sung to the melody of *Auld Lang Syne*).
76 Probably Kubo, as in the programme for the third concert, where he is listed as performing *Edward Rohlin's Galop*.

4. Violin, violin – *Louisville March*[77] – Mr. Z. Shikama, K. Koriba
5. Piano – *Grand Russian March*[78] – T. Murata
6. Solo – *K. Niina*[79] – S. Koda
7. Chorus – *Dainihon Bochono Uta*[80] – Members
8. Piano – Waltz von F. Eckert – S. Inagaki
9. Chorus – *Mountain Maid's Invitation*[81] – Members
10. Violin, violin – *My Sweet Home (Perinue)*[82] – Mr. Z. Shikama, K. Koriba
11. Piano – *Fröhlicher Landmann*[83] – T. Murata, S. Fukushima
12. Violin – *Ykpauhckar Hozß* (?)[84] – Mr. Y. Okamoto

---

77 Possibly, *Louisville March and Quick Step*, composed for and dedicated to Mrs. A. Bowen by W. C. P. Philada.: Klemm & Brother [between 1831 and 1839].

78 Possibly *The Grand Russian March* by C. P. Francis. Published George Willig, Philadelphia, 1835.

79 Possibly, *Tre giorni son que Nina*, widely ascribed to the composer Giovanni Battista Pergolesi (1710–36). The song was (and is) highly popular, and there are several Japanese-language versions: the earliest, by Yoshimaru Kazumasa, was published in 1912, but that does not preclude the Italian version being known and performed earlier.

80 *Dai Nihon bōchō no uta* / *Song about the Growth of Great Japan*. According to an article in Yomiuri Newspaper in November 1903, the song was being used as a school song by Gumma Prefectural School of Agriculture (Gunma-ken Nōgyō Gakkō). See Yuriko Takashima, 'Kōka o meguru hyōshō bunka kenkyū: kindai kokka seiritsu ni okeru kōka no seitei katei to gendai no sh jōkyō o tekagari ni' (Ph.D. 2013), 25.

81 Lyrics by Thomas Power, various arrangements, c. 1840; published in several collections of songs.

82 *Home Sweet Home*, lyrics by John Howard Payne, music by Henry Bishop.

83 Robert Schumann, Op. 68.10, from his *Album für die Jugend* (Album for the Young)

84 This appears to be Cyrillic, or at least an attempt to print Cyrillic. The most likely transcription is, Украинская ночь (Ukrainskaja notj) meaning 'Ukrainian Night'. Two Russian operas include an aria of that title: (1) Nikolai Andreyevich Rimsky-Korsakov, *May Night* (1879), 'Ukrainian Night and Levko's Song' in Act 3; (2) Tchaikovsky, *Mazepa* (Мазепа), also known as *Mazeppa* (1881–83), based on a poem by Aleksander Pushkin, Mazepa's Monologue in Act 2, Scene 1, Тиха украинская ночь (*Tikha ukraynskaya noch*; 'Quiet is the Ukrainian Night'). Given the frequently imprecise titles in programmes, another possible candidate might be the famous Ukrainian folk song *What a Moonlit Night* (Ніч яка місячна, Nich yaka misiachna), Composed by Mykola Vitaliyovych Lysenko (1842–1912) to lyrics by Mykhailo Petrovych Starytsky (1840–1904). Incidentally Iakov Tichai, who taught music, including violin, first in Hakodate (from 1873) and then in Tokyo at the Russian Orthodox seminary, came from the area of present-day Ukraine, as did Dimitrii Livosvski, who taught violin. See Rihei Nakamura, *Kirisuto-kyō to Nihon no yōgaku* (Tokyo: Ōzorasha, 1996).

13. Chorus – *Tabi no Kure* (Nightfall at journey's end)[85] – Mr. Y. Okuyama, Mr. I. Wakuya, Mr. Y. Okamoto, and four others
14. Violin, violin – Kayser's exercises No. 2[86] – Mr. M. Nakamura, M. T. Sato
15. Solo – *Die Wacht am Rhein*[87] – Mr. Ernst
16. Violin – *Washington March*[88] – Mr. H. Maidako (Maedako)
17. Piano – Schubert's Waltz[89] – Miss Mochidate
18. Solo – *The Holy City* (by Stephens)[90] – Mrs. Gerhald (Gerhard)
19. Solo – *Beyond the Gates of Paradise*[91] – Mrs. Gerhald
20. Piano – Chopin Polonaise[92] – Miss Mochidate
21. Solo – *My Ain Countrie*[93] – Mr. Axling
22. Chorus – *Kimigayo*

---

85 A *shōka*, sung to the melody of *Long, Long Ago*: publications it appears in include a collection edited by Ōwada Tateki and Oku Yoshiisa: *Meiji shōka bassui shōgaku shōka* (Chūōdō 1895). Translation added by myself, the original English-language programme has no translations. See note 74.
86 From Heinrich Ernst Kayser (1815–88), *36 Violin Studies, Op. 20*.
87 Lyrics by Max Schneckenburger (1849), most commonly sung to a melody by Carl Wilhelm (1854), the song functioned as an unofficial national anthem in the German Empire from 1871. The melody was used in college songs for Yale and Dōshisha, the latter in an arrangement by Yamada Kōsaku. An English version was published in Japan in 1903. See Katsuisa Sakai, ed., *Eigo shōka*, 3 vols., vol. 1 (Tokyo: Uedaya, 1903), 10–12.
88 Most likely, *General Washington's March*, also known as 'Washington's march', original score for piano, supposed composer Francis Hopkinson (1737–91). The score in the Library of Congress (Printed and sold by G. Graupner at his musical academy, no. 6 Franklin Street, [1800]) The work includes the melody of the song *Yankee Doodle*.
89 Schubert composed several waltzes.
90 Presumably the highly popular Victorian ballad (1892) by Stephen Adams (pseudonym for Michael Maybrick, 1841–1913), lyrics by Frederic Weatherly (1848–1929).
91 Popular American song (1901); music by Robert A. King (1862–1932), lyrics by Henry V. Neal; possibly Henry Vinton Neal (1848–1931). See http://www.hymntime.com/tch//bio/n/e/a/l/neal_hv.htm
92 Chopin composed several polonaises.
93 *My Ain Countrie*: A sad late Jacobite song of exile; lyrics by Allan Cunningham (1784–1882), who presented several of his own compositions as Jacobite originals. See Scots Language Centre, https://www.scotslanguage.com/articles/node/id/379/type/referance

The members of the chorus, the violinists Kuzuoka and Kōriba, the pianists Murata, Inagaki, and Fukushima, as well as the solo singer Kōda were students.[94] The other performers came from outside the school. 'Mr. Y. Okamoto' is almost certainly Okamoto Fusao; the would-be Cyrillic of the first piece he performed suggests that the 'Y' might stand for the Japanese syllable transcribed as 'fu' according to the Hepburn system, if the types that are specific to Cyrillic were not available.[95] The name Okamoto Fusao appears in later programmes, and in the Japanese versions he is usually described as *kyōshi* or *kōshi*, both of which describe a teacher or professor. He taught the violin at the Second High School, although his name does not appear in the school's staff lists. Learning the violin would have been an extra-curricular activity, so his teaching may well have been an informal arrangement. His background is unknown. In 1909 he was listed (with an address) in *Ongakukai* as the magazine's local representative in Sendai. This would suggest a possible personal connection with the editors through the Tokyo Academy of Music, but his name does not appear in the Academy's student lists,[96] and he might have met them when they came to Sendai as guest performers in concerts. Kate Hansen, who accompanied him on the piano on occasion, believed that he had studied in Tokyo, but that need not have been at the Tokyo Academy of Music. The (pseudo-) Cyrillic letters in connection with his name would suggest that Okamoto, like Maedako, had a connection with members of the Russian Orthodox Church.[97] *Ongakukai* still listed him as their local representative in October 1912, but he is not included in the address list of musicians published in the journal over several volumes in 1913. From 1910 onwards, the name Kumaya Sentarō, with the title *kyōshi*, appears on the school's concert programmes, which suggests that Okamoto had been replaced.

The foreign performers came from the missionary community. Laura Blanche Gerhard (née Ault) was married to Paul Lambert Gerhard

---

94 Dai Ni Kōtō Gakkō Shi Henshū Iinkai, *Dai Ni Kōtō Gakkō shi*, 952–53.
95 The Cyrillic transcription of 'fu' is generally фу (Polivanov system). Note that the initial 'H' before 'Maidako' corresponds to 'N' in English, which would be the first letter of 'Nobuchika', another reading for the characters for 'Shinkin'.
96 I thank Tsukahara Yasuko for confirming this.
97 If he did indeed study in Tokyo, it may have been at the Seminary, or else privately with one of its teachers, such as the violinist Kisu Yoshinoshin, introduced later in this chapter. However, I have found no clear evidence of a Russian connection.

(1873–1949), who had come to Sendai in 1897 to teach at Tohoku College. William Axling (1873–1963) was a Baptist minister who worked in Sendai from 1901 to 1906.[98]

The substantial contributions to the programme by foreign missionaries and teachers remained a feature of the concerts at the Second High School throughout its early years, when few of the school's students had any significant musical training. Not that the foreigners were anything other than amateurs: but at the very least they could be expected to sing hymns and folk songs in tune, and in some cases play musical instruments competently. Most importantly, they had the advantage of being intimately familiar with the music.

For their second concert on 17 May 1903, the organizers of the concert were supported by Kisu Matsusaburō, a local wealthy merchant, the local university graduates' society, and the Miyagi Womens' Association. Together they had invited fifteen members of the Meiji Music Society (Meiji Ongaku Kai), founded in 1898 in Tokyo with the aim of disseminating Western music. But the guests had to cancel at short notice, and instead seven members of the Friends of Music Club (Gakuyū Kurabu) came, all graduates of the Tokyo Academy of Music, most of whom we have already encountered as proponents and performers of blended music (see Chapter 8). They included Kitamura Sueharu, Takaori Shūichi, Maeda Kyūhachi, Muroka Shōtarō, Ishino Gi, and Ōta Kanshichi. Ishino graduated in 1898. He published a volume of practice pieces for the violin in 1907.[99] Ōta, a pianist and a native of Miyagi prefecture, graduated from the Teaching Department of the Tokyo Academy of Music in 1901 and subsequently taught music.[100]

The programme presented by the performers from Tokyo reflected their interest in promoting the performance of blended music, and stood in marked contrast to that of the music club's previous concert as well as most of its subsequent ones. It consisted of three sections, of which the shorter middle section featured performers from the club:[101]

---

98 I have found no information about 'Mr. Ernst'; he may well have been a teacher at the school.
99 Gi Ishino, *Vaiorin renshūkyoku* (Tokyo: Kōseikan, 1907).
100 Ōta plays the piano on a recording of *Aki no irogusa* held in the National Diet Library.
101 *Shōshikai zasshi*, no. 55 (June 1903): 77–78. The programme, like most, is in Japanese.

1. Ensemble: (1) *Huntsmen's Chorus*; (2) *Butterfly Shotten*[102] – (by all performers)
2. Piano solo – *Harō* (Waves)[103] – Maeda Kyūhachi
3. Ensemble – *Rokudan* – Ōta Kanshichi, Muraoka Shōtarō, Takaori Shūichi
4. Violin duo – 'Bēru'[104] – Ishino Gi, Takaori Shūichi
5. Chorus – (1) *Hana* (Flowers/Cherry Blossoms); (2) *Suma no kyoku*[105] (Song of Suma) – all
6. Piano and Violin duo – *Mushi no oto* (The Sound of Insects)[106] – Kitahara Sueharu, Muraoka Shōtarō

—

Chorus – *Yasumasa* (?)[107] – Okamoto Fusao plus seven others
Piano solo – *Midare*[108] (Disarray) – Murata Tsunemichi (member)
Chorus – *Kikori no uta* (woodcutting song)[109] – members

—

1. Ensemble(1) – *William Tell*; (2.) *Swinging Waltz*[110]

---

102 The first is presumably the famous chorus from Carl Maria von Weber's Opera, *Der Freischütz*; the second is presumably *Butterfly Scottish* by James E. Magruder, 1869 (pf. music). See Lester S. Levy Sheet Music Collection, Johns Hopkins University Library: https://levysheetmusic.mse.jhu.edu/collection/040/031
103 Not identified.
104 The transcription is inconclusive. Possibilities include 'veil' and 'vale'; the latter appears more common in titles of popular music.
105 *Hana*: there are several songs of that title; including the well-known *shōka* by Taki Rentarō. *Suma no kyoku* is the title of a *koto* piece, but here it is more likely to refer to Kitamura's opera of that title.
106 There is a *koto* piece of that title, as well as a *kouta*; probably they performed a transcription of the *koto* version.
107 Possibly a spelling error: *Yasumasa* (spelt with a different second character) is the title of a Japanese song based on the melody of 'Das klinget so herrlich' from Mozart's *The Magic Flute*. See Yasuto Okunaka, *Wayō setchū ongakushi* (Tokyo: Shunjūsha, 2014), 11–13.
108 Almost certainly one of several published arrangements of the *koto* piece of that name.
109 More than one possibility: perhaps the song by Ōwada Tateki, to a melody by Lowell Mason.
110 The first is presumably part of Rossini's opera *Wilhelm Tell* (perhaps the overture). The second title, assuming it refers to a specific piece rather than a generic slow waltz, might be the *The Swinging Waltz Song* by Charles A. Davies (Groene, J. C. & Co., Cincinnati, 1885), although it is scored for voice and piano.

2. Piano duo – (1) *Happy New Year March*; (2) *Jolly Sisters Galop*[111] – Muraoka Shōtarō, Maeda Kyūhachi

3. Chorus – National anthems of America and France (in original language) – all

4. Violin solo – *Don Juan* – Ishino Gi

5. Uta (*shamisen* song) – *Kanjinchō*[112] – Kitamura Sueharu

6. Ensemble – *Manzairaku*[113] – all

The concert ended with a closing address by Miyoshi (who is described as the president of the music club) and the national anthem sung twice by all.

The new association must have been eager to make its mark, for it held its third concert less than a week later, on 23 May. As with the second concert, the opening address was given by Kurashima, while Miyoshi's closing address and the national anthem concluded the event. The programme resembled that of the inaugural concert: the formal part, at least, consisted of Western music only, and the efforts of the students were supported by members of the foreign community. Indeed, more foreigners took part, playing a greater variety of instruments. The programme, in English like the first, again contained a mixture of pieces:[114]

1. Piano solo – *Edward Rohlin's Galop*[115] – N. Kubo

2. Chorus – *Robin Redbreast*[116] – Members

---

111 *Happy New Year March* by J. J. Watson. C. A. Fuller (published Shaw, W. F. & Col, 1884); *Jolly Sisters Galop*: Library of Congress has sheet music for two different pieces of that title: (1) By F. L. Blancjour (Philadelphia, Lewis Meyers, 1871); (2) Composed and published by J. N. O. P. Dougherty (Chester, P.A., 1882)
112 See Chapter 8.
113 A well-known celebratory *gagaku* piece.
114 *Shōshikai zasshi* no. 55 (June 1903): 78–79. This programme is in English.
115 I have not been able to identify the piece.
116 Most probably *Robin Redbreast* by Anne Wilhelmina Pelzer (1833-97). She was born into a family of musicians in London and was a successful composer, pianist, concertina player, and teacher there. Her sister, Catherina Pelzer (1821-95), was a celebrated guitar virtuosa. Lyrics by W. Allingham. First published, London 1857. See https://archive.org/details/Robin55298 Another possibility would be the children's song *Little Robin Redbreast* or *Song of the Robin Redbreast*, a popular Victorian Christmas song by Leslie Herbert.

3. Cornet – (1) *Beautiful Isle of Somewhere* (Fearis)[117]; (2) *Of thee, Mother*[118] – Mr Stick

4. Vocal solo – *I love Thee, Dear Country*[119] – Mrs Cleveland

5. 5. Piano – *Potpouri* (Inagaki) – S. Inagaki

6. Vocal solo – *Could I* (Tosti)[120] – Mrs Doering

7. Violin – Galop Allemand[121] – Mr Okamoto, Koriba

8. Vocal solo – *In Old Madrid*[122] – Mrs Gerhard

9. Piano Duet – *Dragon Fighters*[123] – Miss Cleveland, Miss Schneder

10. Vocal solo – *Yume* (Schumann)[124] – S. Koda

11. Solo and Chorus – (1) *Pussy Cats*; (2) *The Duck*; (3) *Fire Song*[125] – Miss Doering

12. Piano – Sonatine de Fr. Kuhlau[126] – T. Murata

13. Mandolin – *Princess Bonnie*[127] – Mr. Stick

14. Chorus (sic) – *In the Starlight*[128] – Miss Mochidate

---

117 *Beautiful Isle of Somewhere* (1897) by John Sylvester Fearis, lyrics by Jessie Brown Pounds (aka 'Somewhere the sun is shining').
118 Possibly, *I Am Dreaming of Thee, Mother* by William R. Scott (1875).
119 Possibly *For Thee, Oh Dear, Dear Country*, popular hymn, sung to several different tunes. Text by Bernard of Cluny (1145), translated by John Mason Neale (1858).
120 Francesco Paolo Tosti (1846–1916): Italian-born composer and music teacher; moved to Britain in 1875.
121 I have only been able to find a piano and harp piece of that name; possibly the item should read 'Galop – Allemande'.
122 *In Old Madrid*; Music by Henry Tortere; lyrics by Clifton Bingham; published 1890.
123 *The Dragon Fighter*: Polonaise by B. Hoffmann, Op. 1.
124 *Yume*: lyrics by Satō Jōjitsu (1839–1908), set to Robert Schumann, *Der Traum*, Op. 146 No. 3.
125 Not identified. Possibly all three come from a single collection of children's songs.
126 Friedrich Kuhlau (1786–1832).
127 Possibly from the musical *The Princess Bonnie*, words and music by William Spenser, premiered in 1894 at the Chestnut Street Theatre, Philadelphia, 1895 Broadway. Extracts were published as *The Princess Bonnie Waltzes*, arranged and composed by Willard Spenser. Published by Wm. H. Keyser & Co., Philadelphia [1894].
128 In the Starlight, by Stephen Glover. Lyrics by J. E. Carpenter. Library of Congress has an edition published by Wyman & Davis, Chicago, 1878. The song features in Laura Ingalls Wilder's 'Little House' books.

15. Violin – *Perdona* (Mozart)[129] – Mr. Okamoto, Miss Nagao, Miss Sato

16. Vocal solo – *Good bye to all, Good bye*[130] – Miss Mochidate

17. Piano Duet – *Witches Frolic*[131] – Miss Cleveland, Miss Schneder

18. Vocal Duet – *Bird Song* (Rubinstein)[132] – Mrs Doering, Mrs Cleveland

19. Vocal Solo – *Abide with Me* (De Koven)[133] – Mrs Stick

20. Piano solo – Polonaise (Chopin); Castignets (Ketten)[134] – Mrs Doering

21. Trio – *Ye Shepherds Tell Me*[135] – Mr. Noss, Mr. Stick, Mr Clayton

22. Chorus – German song (*Immer flott*)[136] – Miss Cleveland, Miss Schneder

23. Trio: piano, organ, cornet – *The Holy City*[137] – Mrs Doering, Mrs Cleveland, Mr Stick

The concert, playing to a packed hall, was deemed a great success. The commentator in the *Shōshikai* magazine gave the unprecedented scope of the event as a reason and speculated that if such concerts were more widely held, this might well contribute towards the reform of society.[138]

---

[129] Presumably a transcription of the duet, *Ah perdona al primo affetto* from Mozart's opera, *La Clemenza di Tito*.

[130] *Good Bye to All, Good Bye* (1901) by the American composer J. Reginald MacEachron.

[131] Franz Behr, *Witches' Frolic*, Caprice, Op. 252 No. 6.

[132] Most likely *Sweetly, Sweetly Sang the Bird* ('Sang das Vöglein', or *The Bird* (Das Vögelein) from a collection of vocal duets by Anton Rubinstein (1829–94), *18 Vocal Duets with Pianoforte Accompaniment*, Op. 48. First German edition listed in Hofmeister 1856; '12 zweistimmige Lieder', Op. 45 and *Zweistimm. Lieder m. Pfte. Neue Ausg 67*, 1881.

[133] Reginald De Koven (1859–1920). *Abide with Me. Sacred Song for Alto*. New York: G. Schirmer (date unknown).

[134] Henry Ketten, b. Baja, Hungary 1848, d. Paris 1883, *La Castagnette*, Op. 94 (1879).

[135] Joseph Mazzinghi (1765–1844), composer, active in London; a pastoral glee scored for three voices and piano.

[136] There seems to be no obvious candidate for this.

[137] Composed by Michael Maybrick (1841–1913), alias Stephen Adams, lyrics by Frederic Edward Weatherly (1848–1929), in 1892, highly popular religious song.

[138] *Shōshikai zasshi* no. 55 (June 1903): 79.

More than half of the twenty-three items (fourteen) were performed by the foreign population, mostly missionaries, and of the nine items performed by Japanese, two were performed by a female singer, while one (no. 15) was played by Okamoto Fusao, together with two young women, possibly students of his from another school. The preponderance of foreigners, most of them from the missionary community, is reflected in the repertoire, which included several hymns (Nos. 3, 4, 19) or songs with Christian content (23). Most of the other pieces, sung or instrumental, might be classified as salon music, understood as a category 'about midway between what is generally known as "popular music" and that called "classic"'.[139]

Reverend J. Monroe Stick (1877–1939), who is named for the first time here, played in many subsequent concerts. A missionary of the Reformed Church in the United States, he came to Japan in 1902 and taught at Tohoku College and, briefly, Miyagi College. During his time at the University of Pennsylvania he had been a leader of the university band. He became a regular performer at concerts, playing several instruments.

More missionaries had arrived on the scene by the time the sixth concert took place, on 15 October 1904: the Methodist missionaries Edwin Taylor Iglehart and Charles Stewart Davison.[140] The number of performers from the Second High School had also increased. They were supported by Japanese performers from outside the school, including the violin teacher Maedako Shinkin, and Shikama Totsuji's eldest daughter Ranko, who played violin both in the ensemble and solo. Having learnt to play Western instruments from an early age, unlike

---

139 See Hoyle Carpenter, 'Salon Music in the Mid-Nineteenth Century', *Civil War History* 4, no. 3 (1958): 291, https://doi.org/10.1353/cwh.1958.0032 The mid-nineteenth century collection of piano music examined by Carpenter includes the kind of repertoire performed in Sendai.
140 Dai Ni Kōtō Gakkō Shi Henshū Iinkai, *Dai Ni Kōtō Gakkō shi*, 953-54. Apparently, there are no reports of the fourth and fifth concerts (I have only been able to check selected issues of *Shōshikai zasshi* myself). Charles Stewart Davison (1877–1920) served as a Presiding Elder in Sendai before moving to Aoyama Gakuin in Tokyo, where Edwin Iglehart (1878–1964) also taught. Edwin Iglehart's brother Charles Wheeler Iglehart (1882–1969) followed him to Japan, and was active in Sendai from 1909 until the First World War). As well as teaching theology at Aoyama Gakuin, Edwin Iglehart presided over the college's first Glee Club and sang himself. He later co-published a short book on music in Japan: Katsumi Sunaga, Edwin Taylor Iglehart, *Japanese Music* (Board of tourist industry, Japanese government railways, 1936).

most Japanese in that period, she was almost certainly more proficient than most of the male high school students at the time. An ensemble played the *Institute March* (1899) and *Brooke's [Chicago] Marine Band March* (1901), both by the American composer, bandmaster, and music publisher Roland Forrest Seitz (1867–1946). Many of his works were dedicated to particular institutions,[141] and his music may well have been introduced to Sendai by Stick, who, as the leader of the university band, had himself requested and received Seitz's *University of Pennsylvania Band March* (1900).[142]

The seventh concert took place on 11 February 1905, a public holiday celebrating the ascension to the throne of the mythical first emperor, Jimmu, in 660 B.C.E. The Russo-Japanese War was still ongoing, but on 2 January the long siege of Port Arthur had ended, and the mood was optimistic. The author of the report on the concert remarked how it boded well for the outcome of the war that Sendai was celebrating the holiday with a concert, while the Russian Neva River Festival that took place every January involved firing cannons. The concert, it was hoped, would encourage the people to keep up their spirits.[143] It began with the singing of the school song, followed by thirteen items and a gramophone record performance to conclude the first part. Most of the performers were students at the school, although Maedako Shinkin played in one ensemble. The only foreigner was Davison, who accompanied two violinists on the organ in two items: an unspecified 'Andante' and *Kriegsmarsch der Priester aus Athalia*, presumably an arrangement of Felix Mendelssohn Bartholdy's work (Op. 74). One of the violinists was Okamoto Fusao. Most of works performed were songs, sung by a small group or played on the violin and the organ.

The second part consisted of a broader range of items, nine in all. It began with *University of Pennsylvania Band March* played by a wind and string ensemble (the Chinese characters are accompanied by the

---

141 The *Institute March* was dedicated to the faculty and pupils of his alma mater, Dana's Musical Institute, Warren, Ohio.

142 Jim McClure, 'Glen Rock's Roland F. Seitz: "By his genius ... he has earned the title of 'Parade Music Prince'"', https://eu.ydr.com/story/news/history/blogs/york-town-square/2013/05/18/glen-rocks-roland-f-seitz-by-his-genius-he-has-earned-the-title-of-parade-music-prince/31589503/

143 Details in Kyūsei Kōtō Gakkō Shiryō Hozon Kai, ed., *Shiryō shūsei kyūsei kōtō gakkō zensho dai 7 kan: seikatsu/kyōyō hen* (2) (Tokyo: Kyūsei Kōtō Gakkō Shiryō Hozon Kai Kankō Bu, 1984), 548–52. Originally published in *Shōshikai zasshi* 65 (1905).

phonetic transcription *ōkesutora*), presumably led by Stick, although his name only appears later in the programme, when he played *The Holy City* on the cornet. The march was followed by a vocal solo by Mrs Kobayashi, the wife of a Japanese scholar, who sang *Satsuma-gata* (Satsuma Bay).[144]

Foreign performers besides Stick and Davison were Mrs Faust and Marie and Margaret Schneder. Shikama Totsuji's daughter Ranko played two solo pieces on the violin, a transcription of a *koto* piece entitled *Hachidan*, and *Overture-Enchantment*.[145] The orchestra concluded with *Palm Branches*, probably the hymn by Jean Baptiste Fauré (1830–1914).[146] This was followed by another gramophone record performance. The gramophone belonged to Doi Bansui (1871–1952), a native of Sendai and professor at the High School since 1900. He had brought it back from Europe the year before, where he had spent over three years studying literature in England, France, and Germany. The audience was treated, among others, to selections from Wagner's *Tannhäuser* and Gounod's *Faust*.

The progress made by members of the school's music club was praised in the society's magazine, and the concert judged to be a success overall, although the chorus number had not gone well, nor had Kobayashi Kōhei's performance on the violin (he played in four duets), apparently because his job as an organizer had left him with too little time to practise.[147]

Only a week after the seventh concert, two more were held on 25 and 26 February 1905.[148] This time the music club had finally managed to secure the participation of leading musicians from Tokyo: seventeen representatives of the Meiji Music Association (Meiji Ongaku Kai)

---

144 Melody by Robert Schumann: see Chapter 6.
145 There are several possible candidates for *Hachidan*. J. Hermann's *Overture; Enchantment* was apparently first published in the collection by J. S. Cox, *J. W. Pepper's Classic Cornet Solos with Piano Accompaniment*. J. W. Pepper, Philadelphia, 1880, https://www.loc.gov/item/sm1880.12569/
146 The programme reads, 'Selection (*Palm Branches*)', which may refer to The Boston Music Company Selection of Popular Salon Music, although I have not been able to verify an edition before 1909.
147 Kyūsei Kōtō Gakkō Shiryō Hozon Kai, *Kyūsei kōtō gakkō zensho 7*, 552.
148 Dai Ni Kōtō Gakkō Shi Henshū Iinkai, *Dai Ni Kōtō Gakkō shi*, 955–56. There is no record of the tenth concert, and after the eleventh concert, on 20 January 1906, the concerts were not numbered in the records.

travelled to Sendai, including its vice-president, Uehara Rokushirō (1848–1913). A music theorist and physicist, Uehara taught at Tokyo Academy of Music and conducted research into acoustics as well as *koto* and *shamisen* music (he himself played the *shakuhachi*). He gave a lecture on Japanese music on 26 February. The leading musician of the group was undoubtedly the violinist Wilhelm (Guglielmo) Dubravčić (1869–1925). Born in Fiume in Italy, Dubravčić had studied at the conservatoire in Vienna. Appointed by the imperial court in 1901 as director of the *gagaku* orchestra and to teach the violin, he remained there until his death.[149] With him were several musicians from established *gagaku* families, namely the Ōno (five members) and the Sono (three members). Another was the violinist and flautist Ōmura Josaburō (1869–1952), a member of the *gagaku* department, as well as the first formally appointed teacher of the flute at the Tokyo Academy of Music, until he moved to Osaka in 1906, where he went on to play a pioneering role in music in the Kansai area. The pianist Maeda Kyūhachi, who had performed in Sendai at the second concert, was also part of the group; he became something of a regular. The group also included the violinist Kisu Yoshinoshin (1868–1951), whose musical career was unusual.[150] Born in Sendai, he enrolled in the seminary of the Russian Orthodox Church in Tokyo in 1881, at a time when the seminary's music department offered more advanced training than almost any other institution in the country. From 1891 to 1894 he studied in St. Petersburg, where his teachers included Nikolai Rimsky-Korsakov, thus becoming one of the first Japanese to study music at a conservatoire abroad.[151] After his return he taught and performed in Tokyo where he opened a private music school. After the earthquake in 1923, he relocated to Sendai where he taught at several schools. He moved back to Tokyo in 1939.

The concert was exceptional in several ways. The audience had to pay to listen, a fact that apparently merited special mention in the report. In

---

149 Irene Suchy, 'Versunken und vergessen: zwei österreichische Musiker in Japan vor 1945', in *Mehr als Maschinen für Musik*, ed. Sepp Linhart and Kurt Schmid (Wien: Literas Universitätsverlag, 1990); Suchy, 'Deutschsprachige Musiker', 187.
150 Former surname, Nakagawa, Christian name Innocenti. See Nakamura, *Kirisuto-kyō to Nihon no yōgaku*, 96–99, 568.8
151 Kisu's return was announced in *Ongaku Zasshi* 50 (January 1895), p. 34. The claim that he had graduated from the conservatoire was probably exaggerated.

return they received the opportunity to hear some of the most advanced performers of Western music active in Japan at the time. Monroe Stick even lent his piano for the occasion, which, in the light of Hansen's later remarks about the high school's own piano, may well have contributed significantly to the quality of the music, as did the absence of student performances. The programme included solo performances, a string quartet (playing a minuet by Boccherini), and a large ensemble that among other things played suitably patriotic compositions, such as two marches composed by Dubravčić and Frantz Eckert celebrating the fall of Port Arthur in the Sino-Japanese and the Russo-Japanese Wars respectively.[152] Even so, holding concerts in wartime apparently gave rise to criticism, and several articles in *Shōshikai zasshi* defended the association's musical activities. In an article about the music club's aims, the author (Watanabe Hideo) stated that it intended to united the fragmented music scene of Sendai. Certainly, the concerts organized by the Second High School brought together different groups of musicians (see Chapter 11).

The eleventh concert on 30 January 1906 again featured students of the school in the first half, while in the second half, performances by outside members dominated. The student performances included a four-part song as well as solo (vocal, organ, and violin) and ensemble items. Okamoto Fusao is described as *kōshi* (instructor) for the first time, although he almost certainly taught members of the club from the beginning. The second part featured mostly foreign musicians before concluding with a march played by a band. Presumably, the next two concerts on 28 April 1906 and 18 January 1907 followed a similar pattern.[153]

The music club's ambitions for disseminating Western music extended beyond Sendai. On 1 April 1907, nine members and their instructor Okamoto left Sendai early in the morning (another member had left for Morioka the previous day) and travelled to Ichinoseki in the south of Iwate prefecture, where they gave a concert in the hall of the lower secondary school (*chūgakkō*) to an audience of around 400.[154] On the following day the group performed in Mizusawa (now part of

---

152 Dai Ni Kōtō Gakkō Shi Henshū Iinkai, *Dai Ni Kōtō Gakkō shi*, 955.
153 Ibid., 56.
154 'Ongakukai hokujō kiji', *Shōshikai zasshi* 76 (1907): 143–44.

Ōshū city), in the town's theatre, with the support of the local youth group. The local people were reportedly particularly keen on the arts, and over 700 attended; more than the theatre could hold, so some had to listen outside. The concert was obviously a social as well as a musical success: at the invitation by teachers of Mizusawa Elementary School, the students returned to Mizusawa on 4 April to celebrate, before returning to Sendai on 5 April.

On 3 April the students gave a concert in the Fujizawa-za theatre in Morioka. The concert was hosted by the city's Christian Youth Association, and the programme is given in the published report. After an opening address and the Second High School's school song, the following items were performed:

Part 1

1. String and wind ensemble *Imperial Gallop*[155]
2. Vocal (three students) – *Heisokutai* (military song about the blockade of Port Arthur in the Russo-Japanese War)
3. Koto – *Tamagawa* (Tama River; Ikutaryū piece) – local performers
4. Vocal solo – *The Maid of the Mill*[156]
5. Instrumental (two students, instruments not specified) – *Rokudan*
6. Vocal solo – *Hana* (Flowers/Cherry Blossoms)
7. Violin solo – Andante – Okamoto *kyōshi*
8. Wind and string ensemble – Quadrille

Part 2

1. Wind and string ensemble – Wedding March[157]
2. Vocal solo – *Zanmu* (Lingering dream)[158]

---

155 Name of a piece by A. Mahler, published J. L. Peters, Cincinnati, 1867.
156 Possibly: The Words by Hamilton Aide. The Music Composed by Stephen Adams. The Anglo-Canadian Music Publishers' Association, Limited, 38 Church Street, Toronto, 1885. See https://levysheetmusic.mse.jhu.edu/collection/137/084
157 Most likely Mendelssohn's.
158 *Shinkyoku* piece, music by Maeda Kyūhachi, published 1906.

3. Organ solo (no work specified)
4. Vocal (four students) – *Chinchin*[159]
5. Koto – *Tsuru no koe* (Voice of cranes) – local supporters (*yūshi*) of Morioka
6. Vocal (two students) – *Roei no yume* (Dream during bivouac)[160]
7. Vocal solo *Kanjinchō*
8. Wind and string ensemble – *Hasenfu* (The shipwreck); operatic song (*kageki*) *Hanare kojima* (Remote island)[161]

The ensemble pieces were played by the whole group. This concert too was reportedly a big success. The report reflects the students' sense of mission, observing that the concert in the Morioka theatre was the first occasion where sales of refreshments in the auditorium were forbidden and people had to remove their hats. The students saw themselves as bringing light into the darkness of the Tohoku wilderness with their refined instrumental music (*kōshō naru kigaku*).[162]

While on tour, the students of the Second High School had to perform the whole programme by themselves or else with local players, rather than enlist the participation of the foreign community. In Sendai, on the other hand, the pattern of the early programmes, with the first part dominated by performances from students and the second with predominantly performances by musicians from outside the school, including the foreign teachers and their families, prevailed for years to come. The foreign performers, although they too were amateurs of varying competence, played a crucial role in the promotion of Western music in Sendai, both as teachers and as performers. It should be emphasized, however, that the staging of regular concerts was initiated by local Japanese actors, such as the Shikama brothers and the students at the Second High School. With the exception of Miyagi College after Kate Hansen's efforts to develop a fully-fledged

---

159 In *katakana* script. I have not been able to identify this.
160 By Kitamura Sueharu: see Chapter 8.
161 No obvious candidate for the first title; *Hanare kojima*, like *Roei no yume*, is one of Kitamura Sueharu's 'narrative songs' (*joji shōka*), published in 1904.
162 'Ongakukai hokujō kiji', *Shōshikai zasshi* 76 (1907): 143–44.

music department, the missionary schools did not play a major role in organizing concerts.

Sendai's Concert Culture around 1907

The concerts organized by the Second High School were the most important ones for the public performance of Western music, at least initially, but other schools also held concerts. In November 1905, Tohoku College celebrated the inauguration of its new school building with a series of events, starting with a charity concert in aid of those suffering from a bad harvest, held at the Sendai-za on 22 November.[163] The concert was supported by the governors of the prefecture and the city and the principals of several schools. Like the high school concerts, this one brought together representatives of different groups, featuring performances by students and teachers from several schools, as well as the Sendai military band. They were joined by an invited musician from Tokyo, the violinist August Junker, a highly trained professional, who performed, taught, and conducted the orchestra at the Tokyo Academy of Music.[164] Foreign performers from Sendai included Florence Seiple, who, like Junker, was conservatoire-trained.[165] Singing, solo and ensemble, dominated the programme, which also included 'whistling' (by a Russian, Paul Witte). Japanese music was represented by two of the ten items in the second part: *Shōchikubai* (Pine, bamboo, and plum blossom), performed on *koto, shamisen, kokyū* (bowed lute), and *shakuhachi*, and *Nihonkai kaisen* (the naval battle in the Sea of Japan), performed on the *biwa*: these were the only two works specified in the programme.

---

163 'Kyōsaku kyūjo jizen ongakukai', *Tōhoku bungaku* 38 (1905).
164 August Junker (1868–1944) studied in Cologne, then in Berlin (with Joseph Joachim), and, after a brief spell with the Berlin Philharmonic Orchestra joined the Chicago Symphony Orchestra, as well as performing as a soloist and with a string quartet. He came to Tokyo in 1898 and was appointed by the Tokyo Academy of Music the following year. Margaret Mehl, *Not by Love Alone: The Violin in Japan, 1850–2010* (Copenhagen: The Sound Book Press, 2014), 54–59.
165 Florence Seiple (1877–1970) came to Japan in 1905 with her husband Reverend William George Seiple (1877–1965), who taught at Tohoku College from 1905 to 1936. She had trained at the Peabody Institute and in Germany. In 1908 she was appointed by Miyagi College, where she taught until 1931. See Chapter 11.

The most prolific organizer of public concerts besides the music club at the Second High School, however, may well have been Maedako Shinkin, who was also one of the most important local teachers, especially when it came to training music teachers for the region's primary schools. Two reports in the short-lived journal *Ongaku* (Music) in April and June 1907 highlighted his achievements.[166] The first stated that he had been training teachers since 1890, and that seventy to eighty percent of music teachers in the primary schools in the prefectures Miyagi, Fukushima, and Iwate were trained by him. The academy's most recent concert had attracted an audience of 1,500. Maedako's importance as a teacher was also highlighted a year later in three reports about music in Sendai published in the newly founded journal *Ongakukai*. According to the first, Tohoku Music Academy (Tōhoku Ongakuin) was founded by Maedako and consisted of three departments: the main department, a regular teacher training department, and an elective department (*honka, futsū shihanka, senka*). Maedako taught violin, organ, *shōka*, and related subjects, and at the time he had around forty students. He had been teaching since about 1887, and by now his numerous graduates included musicians who had made a name for themselves in Kyoto.[167] In subsequent reports, Maedako's Academy was even described as a local leader of Western music (*tōchi seiyō ongaku no jūchin taru Tōhoku Ongakuin nite wa*) and its affiliated society, Kyōseikai, as the only 'society' (the English word in phonetic script is used) dedicated to Western music. It was also praised for its serious, research-based approach: Maedako's efforts stood out from the otherwise frivolous (*keifu naru*) music scene.[168] The Academy was about to send out twelve graduates from its regular course (running for the twelfth time) and was recruiting forty students each for its main, teacher training, and elective departments. In addition, Maedako was listed as a teacher at Tohoku Vocational School for Girls (Tōhoku Joshi Shokugyō Gakkō) and occasional lecturer at the music

---

166 'Miyagi Ongaku Kōshūkai genjō', *Ongaku* 11, no. 6 (1907); 'Miyagi Ongaku Kōshūkai', *Ongaku* 12, no. 2 (1907): 34–35.
167 Hakusuirō [pseud.], 'Sendai-shi no gakukyō (February 1908)', *Ongakukai* 1, no. 2 (1908): 45–46.
168 'Sendai-shi no gakukai', *Ongakukai* 1, no. 4 (1908); Jigensei [pseud.], 'Sendai-shi no gakukyō (June 1908)', *Ongakukai* 1, no. 6 (1908).

club of the Medical School and the Tōka High School for Girls.[169] At the time, members were preparing for a combined public concert and graduating recital. The programme of the concert, which took place on 19 April 1908, was published in the June issue of *Ongakukai*.[170]

Other institutions and associations that promoted music were the music association at the Sendai Medical School (Sendai Igaku Senmon Gakkō) and the Association for Native Japanese Music (Kokufū Ongaku Kai), which promoted the study and performance of indigenous music.[171] The Association, organized by Yamashita Kengyō, devoted itself to the performance of music for *koto* in the style of the Ikuta School, as well as to *kokyū* and *sangen* (*shamisen*), that is, the instruments traditionally played in the three-part *sankyoku* ensemble. If Maedako's academy was the leader of Western music, the Association led the field of Japanese music (*hōgaku*), the report stated.[172]

The Normal School, on the other hand, which ought to be the centre of music for education, was reportedly stuck in its old ways, prioritizing the teaching of notation over instrumental practice, with the result that most of the graduates were not able to teach music. Hope was expressed that a new teacher appointed to the local middle school and coming from Gunma Normal School (Iwaki Hiroshi) would help improve standards.[173]

As a major contribution by a foreign teacher, *Ongakukai* highlighted the Sendai Associated Wind and Strings Band (Sendai Rengō Kangen Gakutai) under the baton of J. Monroe Stick. It had twenty members, including two American pianists, and counted a cornet, piano, violin, and drums among the musical instruments at its disposal. Although *Ongakukai* described Stick as a cornet player, he appears to have been an experienced band leader who mastered several instruments.[174] The band's name hardly appears in programmes, however, so it may have been an ad hoc ensemble, or just a loose association of musicians who

---

169 Tōka Kōtō Jogakkō, a private school founded in 1904.
170 'Tōhoku Ongakuin Ongakukai', *Ongakukai* 1, no. 6 (1908): 49–50.
171 The meanings of *kokufū* include the manners and customs, or, more specifically, the songs and ballads that form part of a country's or a region's traditions.
172 Jigensei [pseud.], 'Sendai-shi no gakukyō (June 1908)'.
173 Ibid.
174 Hakusuirō [pseud.], 'Sendai-shi no gakukyō (February 1908)'.

played together in varying formations. The choirs of Tohoku College and Miyagi College received special mention as the best in the area.[175]

Thus, by around 1907/08, Sendai boasted a lively and varied music scene, with Western music featuring increasingly prominently. The quality of the latter, however, was mixed—hardly surprising, given the limited opportunities for training and listening to outstanding (or even competent) performances. While the Tokyo Academy of Music employed professionally trained foreign teachers and, increasingly, well-trained Japanese staff, teachers in Sendai were generally amateurs when it came to performing. The repertoire would seem to reflect this: much of the music performed consisted of either band music, songs and instrumental pieces found in the pedagogical literature, and popular music, including arrangements of excerpts from operas intended for playing at home.

With the arrival of Kate I. Hansen in autumn 1907 to take up her appointment at Miyagi College, one of the most significant foreign actors appeared on the scene. She was immediately persuaded to participate in the city's musical life, as two concert programmes published in the newly founded journal *Ongakukai* demonstrate. The concerts would have been her first introduction to the local scene. The programmes, reproduced in full here, represent typical examples not only for Sendai but also for other parts of Japan outside Tokyo. The items performed are given here as they appeared in *Ongakukai*. Unlike the Tokyo Academy of Music, where, after the early years, concerts of Western music did not include traditional performances, mixed programmes prevailed in Sendai and elsewhere.[176]

The first concert, organized by the Sendai Association for the Promotion of Music (Sendai Ongaku Shōrei Kai), was held on 26 October 1907, in the Kokubun-chō quarter in the centre of the city. The programme was as follows:[177]

---

175 Ibid.
176 See Chapter 11 for more details about concert programmes.
177 Hakusuirō [pseud.], 'Sendai-shi no gakukyō (February 1908)', 47. The exact venue is not specified.

Daytime Section, Part 1:

1. Choir – *yūshisha* (members of the music association)
2. *Sankyoku* ensemble (traditional Japanese three-part ensemble) – Mr Yamashita *kengyō*[178] et al.
3. Cornett solo – *Tannhäuser: Evening Star* – Mr Stick[179]
4. Piano solo – Miss Hansen
5. Vocal solo – *Boat Song*, Weber – Miss Takeuchi Imako[180]
6. Banjo solo – Mr Zaugg[181]
7. Harmonica solo – *Kārumāchi* – Mr Kawakami Tsutomu[182]
8. Violin solo – Serenade – Mr Okamoto Fusao
9. Vocal solo – Mrs Seiple
10. Piano solo – Allegro and Adagio – Mr Maeda Kyūhachi
11. Mandolin solo – Mr Kawakami Tsutomu

Daytime Section, Part 2:

1. Ensemble performance – members of the association
2. Piano solo – Miss Hansen
3. Harmonica solo – Mr Kawakami Tsutomu
4. Vocal solo – Mrs Seiple
5. Mellophone solo – Mr Stick[183]

---

178 A holder of the highest rank of blind musicians organized in guilds in pre-Meiji Japan.
179 *Song of the Evening Star* from R. Wagner's opera *Tannhäuser*.
180 Takeuchi (or Takenouchi) Imako graduated from the voice department of Tokyo Academy of Music in spring 1907 and had been appointed to teach at the Prefectural Girls' High School. 'Boat Song' may be from Carl Maria von Weber's opera *Oberon*; either Rezia's *Ocean Aria*, or the Mermaid's song *Oh wie wogt es sich schön auf der Flut*, or, possibly the folk song based on a melody from *Oberon*, *Es murmeln die Wellen, es säuselt der Wind* (lyrics by Guido Gössen, 1805–52). See also Item 8, in Part 2.
181 Reverend E. H. Zaugg, a missionary of the Reformed Church in the United States, taught at Tohoku College.
182 Probably *König Karl-Marsch*, composed in 1868 by Carl Ludwig Unrath (1828–1908), which was in the repertoire of the military bands and can be found in a collection of tunes for harmonica first published in 1906.
183 A mellophone is a type of horn, invented in the nineteenth century and played in bands as well as solo; the modern version of the instrument, developed in 1890,

6. *Sankyoku* – Mr Yamashita *kengyō* with others

7. Banjo solo – Mr Zaugg

8. Vocal solo – Weber, *Oberon* – Miss Takeuchi Imako

9. Violin solo – "Māsa" – Mr Okamoto Fusao[184]

10. Piano solo – Mr Maeda Kyūhachi

11. *Biwa* (plucked lute) – Mr Kitajima Hiroshi

Evening Section, Part 1

1. *Sankyoku* – Mr Yamashita *kengyō* with others

2. Harmonica – Mr Kawakami Tsutomu

3. Piano solo – Mr Maeda Kyūhachi

4. Vocal solo – Miss Takeuchi Imako

5. Cornett solo – Mr Stick

6. Piano solo – Miss Hansen

7. Vocal solo – Mrs Seiple

8. Harmonica solo – Mr Kawakami Tsutomu

9. Mandolin solo – Mr Stick

10. Violin solo – *Tenjin no yume* (The angel's/heavenly deity's dream)[185] – Mr Okamoto Fusao

11. Piano solo – Mister Maeda Kyūhachi

---

became popular in the United States. See Alan D. Perkins, Al's Mellophone Page, http://www.alsmiddlebrasspages.com/mellophone/

184 Presumably, the arrangement of a piece from the opera *Martha* by Friedrich von Flotow (1812–83), possibly *Die letzte Rose* (*The Last Rose of Summer*).

185 The title is inconclusive: *tenjin* (heavenly deity) most often refers to the ninth-century scholar and statesman Sugawara no Michizane, who was deified after his death, but there is no obvious candidate for this title, and Okamoto is on record as playing Western pieces, so the title might conceivably refer to a Western piece, such as Anton Rubinstein's *Rêve Angélique* (Op. 10/2), although 'angel' is usually translated as *tenshi*.

Evening section, Part 2

1. Ensemble performance – members of the association
2. Piano solo – Mrs Seiple
3. Harmonica solo – Mr Kawakami Tsutomu
4. Violin solo – Largo – Mr Okamoto Fusao
5. *Sankyoku* – Mr Yamashita *kengyō* with others
6. Vocal solo – Miss Takeuchi Imako
7. Banjo solo – Mr Zaugg
8. Mandolin solo – Mr Kawakami Tsutomu
9. Mellophone solo – Mr Stick
10. Piano solo – Mr Maeda Kyūhachi
11. *Biwa* – Mr Kitajima Hiroshi

The second concert took place only two weeks later, on 9 November, in the auditorium of Sendai Medical School (Sendai Igaku Senmon Gakkō). Described as 'Concert of the Sho Gakkō Rengōkai (Sendai Federation of Schools)', it was organized by volunteers from the school. The performers came from the Normal School, Tohoku Lower Secondary School, the Prefectural High School for Girls, the Second High School, Tohoku College and Miyagi College, and the members of the Sendai Associated Band (Sendai Rengō Ongakutai). Unlike the previous programme, no traditional Japanese music is listed, but that does not necessarily mean that none was performed:[186]

First Part

1. Organ solo – a member of the Association
2. Violin quartet – four members of the men's department of the Normal School
3. Chorus – *Suma no kyoku* (Song of Suma)[187] – students of Tohoku Lower Secondary School

---

186 Hakusuirō [pseud.], 'Sendai-shi no gakukyō (February 1908)', 47–48.
187 By Kitamura Sueharu, published by Kyōeki Shōsha, 1904.

4. Four-part chorus – *Memories of Gallilee*[188] – Komoriya Mitsuo, Yamamoto Tomikazu, Ikeda Kiyoshi, Onikawa Shunzō

5. Violin ensemble – Mazas, Allegro[189] – Saitō Jōzō, Maedako Kiyoshi

6. Chorus – Maran [?] – *Momijigari*[190] – Female students from the Prefectural High School

7. Mellophone solo – Beon [?], *Kanransan* – (Mount of Olives)[191] – J. M. Stick

8. Vocal solo (*shōka*) – *Ryōshū*[192] – Miss Tanaka Ine (Normal School)

9. Violin solo – Madrigal – Saitō Jōzō

10. Chorus – *Aki no yoru*[193] – Mr Ishimori Gōki Mr Ikawa Tadao

11. Piano solo – *American March* – Miss. M. Schwartz[194]

12. Vocal solo – *Ōunahara*[195] – Mr Suzuki Shōkichi (Second High School)

13. Chorus – *March of Victory*[196] – Students of Tohoku College

14. Vocal Solo – *Oberon* by Weber – Miss Takeuchi Imako

---

188 Presumably the hymn of that name: lyrics by Robert Morris (1818–88), music by Horatio R. Palmer (1834–1907).

189 Most likely from the 18 Violin Duos, Op. 38 by Jacques Féréol Mazas (1782–1849).

190 There are several works with this Japanese title, including a part song by Franz Abt; see item 2 in the Second Part. The composer 'Maran' is probably Henri Abraham César Malan (1787–1864), who wrote and composed several hymns.

191 Possibly 'Beon' is a corruption of Beethoven, and the piece is from *Christus am Oelberg* (Christ in the Mount of Olives, Op. 85), such as the 'Hallelujah' chorus.

192 The Japanese version of *Dreaming of Home and Mother*, by John Pond Ordway (1824–80). The Japanese lyrics are by Indō Kyūkei (1879–1943), and were first published in a collection of songs for schools in 1907.

193 Published in 1906 in a compilation of songs for female voices Tateki Ōwada, ed., *Joshi Nisshin shōka* (Tokyo: Dai Nihon Tosho, 1906).

194 Possibly John Philip Sousa, *Stars and Stripes Forever* (1897); Miriam Schwartz was the daughter of Methodist missionaries.

195 Possibly *Ōunahara* (from edition in NDL: Tsubouchi Shōyō, Togi Tetteki): loosely based on Franz Schubert, *Schwanengesang* (Swan Song), D 957, Nr. 12, *Am Meer*, lyrics by Heinrich Heine.

196 Possibly the hymn entitled *March of Victory*, with the first line 'We have lifted our banners' (by E. H. Shannon, published 1883).

Second Part

1. Mixed (*kangen*) ensemble a) *Ze gereeto debuaito*[197] ; b) Waltz – The Sendai Associated Band (Sendai Rengō Ongakutai)
2. Chorus – Aputosu, *Aki no aware* (Sorrows of autumn)[198] – students from the Prefectural Girls' High School
3. Harmonica solo – *Kaaru Maachi*[199] – Komoriya Mitsuo
4. Vocal solo – *Roei no yume*[200] – Mr. Nishiōida Takahira (Normal School)
5. Organ solo – *Sortie* – Miss Kataoka Tamaki
6. Chorus – *Hototogisu* (Cuckoo)[201] – Mr. Nishimaki Hidezō, Mr Koizumi, Mr Kobayashi (Second High School)
7. Chorus – Mendelssohn, *The Maybells and the Flowers* volunteers *yūshi* from Miyagi College
8. Piano solo – Sonata Miss Shionoya Teruko
9. Four-part chorus – Yonsu [?], *Byūtifuru, randoji*[202] – Komoriya Mitsuo, Yamamoto Tomikazu, Ikeda Kiyoshi, Onikawa Shunzō
10. Piano solo – Edward Grieg, *Zug der Zwerge* – Miss K. I. Hansen
11. Voice solo – Mendelssohn *Jerusalem* – Miss Takeuchi Imako[203]
12. Cornett solo – Stick, Polka – J. M. Stick
13. Voice solo – Mrs Seiple

---

197 Probably *The Great Divide: March and Two-Step* composed by Louis Maurice, arranged by Maurice F. Smith, (1872–1925), published by Leo Feist, 1907.
198 Possibly the composer Franz Wilhelm Abt (1819–85), whose works include many part songs, some of which were performed at the Tokyo Academy of Music.
199 See note relating to previous programme, Part 1, item 7.
200 Another song by Kitamura Sueharu (Tokyo: Kyōeki Shōsha, 1904).
201 No obvious candidate; the Japanese children's song, titled *Hototogisu* is of a later date; possibly the English folk song, *The Cuckoo* ('The cuckoo is a pretty bird', or 'Sumer Is Icumen In', also known as 'The Cuckoo Song').
202 Probably *That Beautiful Land*; lyrics by F. A. F. Wood White, music by Mark M. Jones (1834–c. 1905). In 1909 a Japanese version with the title *Nozomi no shima* (Island of hope) was published, with lyrics by Komatsu Gyokugan (Kōsuke, 1884–1966). The performance in this Sendai concert appears to be the first documented one in Japan. See Yoshii Kiyoshi, '"Nozomi no shima" no rūtsu o saguru (Kaiteihan)' (2017), http://www.saeranosushi.sakura.ne.jp/yoshii/nozomi/ThatBeautifulLand_Sum4.pdf
203 Aria from the Oratorio *Paulus*.

14. Piano duet: Wagner, *Tannhäuser* – Mrs Seiple, Miss Hansen
15. *Kimigayo* (national anthem) (sung twice) – all the assembled

Once again, the audience was treated to an eclectic programme that included marches, hymns, selections from operas, salon pieces, and a variety of songs, most, although not all, of them by Western composers, even if they had Japanese lyrics. The performers, students, and teachers came from at least seven different schools. The last item before the national anthem must have been a highlight: both Florence Seiple and Kate Hansen were well-trained musicians, and Richard Wagner, like Beethoven, was better known to Meiji intellectuals through books than through experience of listening to his compositions.[204]

Over the following years Hansen and Seiple (appointed to Miyagi College in 1908) performed regularly in Sendai in addition to teaching music. Miyagi College was the main subject of the last of the four reports on the state of music in Sendai, published in *Ongakukai* in December 1908.[205] The mission school (as readers were reminded) with a newly appointed principal, Henry K. Miller (1866–1936), seemed to be paying particular attention to its music department, which, thanks to the strong American presence, was already more developed than that of other schools. Now the school had strengthened its music education with the appointment of Kate Hansen as pianist. According to one of the school's female teachers, the report went on, students should be expected to be able to play a sonata by the time they graduated; a tall order for a school that did not specialize in music training. Other teachers at the school included J. Monroe Stick (cornet),[206] Florence Seiple (singer), Satō Kazuko (piano), and Uda Masuko (piano), all of whom were enthusiastic promoters of Western music. In addition, Tohoku College had E. H. Zaugg as a music teacher, who, besides playing the banjo, likewise worked hard to proliferate Western music.

---

204 See Toru Takenaka, 'Wagner-Boom in Meiji-Japan', *Archiv für Musikwissenschaft* 62, no. 1 (2005). We cannot know for sure which transcription the two pianists performed, but most piano transcriptions of major orchestral works demand a considerable level of proficiency.
205 'Sendai gakukyō (December 1908)', *Ongakukai* 1, no. 12 (1908).
206 Stick's main appointment was at Tohoku College, but he taught at Miyagi College from 1908 to 1910.

In fact, rather than Miller (who only acted as the school's principal from March 1908 to March 1909), Kate Hansen was the driving force behind the establishment and development of a music department that was one of very few in early twentieth-century Japan offering conservatoire-level training.[207]

---

[207] She acted as deputy principal three times during her pre-war tenure at the college (1916–18; 1924–26, 1934–35), which also suggests that she was perceived as a leader.

10. Foreign Actors: Kate I. Hansen

> The whole system of so-called Occidental music is founded on the Christian religion [...].[1]
>
> If she had been a man, she could have been president of the United States.[2]

While local pioneers were obviously central to the dissemination of Western music, their knowledge and experience of it (and, in some cases, of any kind of music) hardly matched their missionary zeal. In this situation, the presence of a significant foreign community of missionaries and teachers in Sendai played a key role. Not all of them had special expertise, but in the early years even the ability to sing in tune qualified them as models when they performed at local concerts. Several of them could also play an instrument (or even more than one), and a few had trained professionally.

Among these Kate Hansen stands out. Not only was she a trained music teacher, who, moreover, used her furloughs to further qualify herself, but she also had the leadership skills that enabled her to build up a music department whose standards rivalled, and in some respects exceeded, those of the Tokyo Academy of Music. Many of the school's graduates went on to teach music in the northern region and in other parts of Japan. Hansen was unusual, if not unique in other respects. She

---

1   From her last annual report to the Mission Board: quoted in William Mensendiek, *To Japan with Love: The Story of Kate Hansen and Lydia Lindsay of Kansas and Japan* (Sendai: Hagi no Sato Publishing Company, 1991), 107; Dane G. Bales, Polly Roth Bales, and Calvin E. Harbin, *Kate Hansen: The Grandest Mission on Earth from Kansas to Japan, 1907–1951* (The University of Kansas Continuing Education, 2000), 318, https://kuscholarworks.ku.edu/handle/1808/21766

2   Final statement from a panel discussion by Japanese who know Kate Hansen, summarized by William Cundiff as 'A Word Picture of the Missionary'. See Bales, Bales, and Harbin, *Kate Hansen*, 248–54.

taught music in Japan longer than almost any other Western teacher, and certainly longer than those employed by the government. Arriving in September 1907, she worked for Miyagi College until the eve of the Pacific War in 1941. Returning in 1946 to help rebuild the school, she remained for another four years. Her work, and that of her long-time colleague Lydia Almira Lindsey (1880–1971), was recognized by the Japanese government: they were honoured with the Fourth Order of the Sacred Treasure (in absentia) in 1955 and received by the Empress during their visit to Japan in 1961. Nevertheless, like many local, non-state actors, her contribution to music education and musical culture is not widely recognized and she remains largely unknown outside of Miyagi College, which has an auditorium bearing her name.

For the historian, Kate Hansen's significance lies not only in her achievements, but also in her role as an observer of musical life in Sendai, particularly the local people's efforts to master Western music. As well as reports to the mission board and countless personal letters, she wrote two academic theses about music in Sendai: *My Impressions of the Musical Consciousness of the Japanese People*, written during her first furlough in 1912–13 as part of the requirements for the Bachelor of Music, and *Experiences in Founding and Developing a Music School in Japan*, submitted for the Master of Music in 1927 (updated 1933).[3] While her writings show that she took the superiority of Western music for granted and shared the prejudices of her Western contemporaries concerning Japanese music, her description of the occasions and settings in which she heard it and its reception by the Japanese audience highlight the differences between musical worlds. Her reports on local efforts to master Western music are even more illuminating. They might appear excessively derisory and harsh in places, but that is easy to observe with hindsight and in the knowledge of Japan's enormous success in making the foreign music its own within a short time. Hansen reminds us that this success was the result of determined, hard, and sustained effort against considerable odds.

---

3   The letters and thesis manuscripts are kept in the Personal Papers of Kate I. Hansen, University Archives, PP 19, Kenneth Spencer Research Library, University of Kansas Libraries. Hansen wrote regular reports for the mission board, many of which are cited in Mensendieck's biography. However, I was not able to consult these.

A Transnational Life and a Musical Mission

Kate Ingeborg Hansen was born on 5 July 1879 in Logan, in Phillips County, Kansas to Peter Hansen and Alpha Gray Hansen. Her mother's family had British, her father's Danish roots. Peter Hansen emigrated after Denmark's defeat in the war with Prussia (1864) resulted in his native Slesvig being annexed. Like many young men at the time, he had no wish to be conscripted into the Prussian Army. After four years in Wisconsin, he moved to Kansas in 1872. Within a few years, he became a successful businessman and an active member of the local community. He married in 1878. In 1893, the family, which besides Kate included her siblings George Troup (1881), Dane Gray (1883), and Alpha Florence (1886), travelled to Denmark to visit Peter Hansen's Danish relatives.[4] Before leaving America, they visited the Columbian International Exposition in Chicago. The visit may well have sparked Kate Hansen's interest in Japanese culture. The Japanese Phoenix Pavilion was one of the highlights. Among those impressed by it was the twenty-six-year-old Chicago architect Frank Lloyd Wright who later designed several buildings in Japan, most famously the Imperial Hotel in Tokyo (1912–22).[5] Unfortunately, the first volume of Hansen's diary of the trip is lost, so we have no record of her impressions of the American part of the tour.[6]

Arriving at Peter's family home, Ravnskobbel near Sønderborg, Kate and her family spent several months with his Danish relatives. Kate herself was sent to live with her father's sister Marie Thietje, who had married a German. Her father believed that German was a more useful language for his daughter to learn than Danish, and given her later career in music he was proven right. Her early experience of another culture may well have helped prepare her for her work in Sendai. Certainly, it affected her deeply, as her diary shows: her observation of life in the

---

4   Two younger sisters died in infancy. Biographical details based on Mensendiek, *To Japan with Love*; Bales, Bales, and Harbin, *Kate Hansen*.

5   See 'Japan Took Center Stage at Chicago's 1893 World's Fair', Norton Center for the Arts, 2015, http://nortoncenter.com/2015/01/07/japan-took-center-stage-at-chicagos-1893-worlds-fair/ The Kate I. Hansen Collection at the University of Kansas includes (Box 11 Folder 17) *The History of the Empire of Japan*. Printed in English for the Chicago World's Fair 1893. Of course, this in itself is inconclusive, since it is not clear who acquired the book and when.

6   The diary is published in Bales, Bales, and Harbin, *Kate Hansen*, 36–105.

disputed borderlands between Denmark and Germany later found its expression in her musical composition, *Schlesvig* (sic), and she kept in touch with several Danish relatives for the rest of her life.

The family left Denmark in early June 1894, and travelled to New York via Hamburg, Hartlepool, Edinburgh. and Glasgow. On the way, they briefly visited another border region with a history of violent conflict when they made a day trip to Stirling Castle. Kate wrote, 'Everything has seemed like a dream today. The old heroes of Scotland have seemed almost as living beings, while this practical age has seemed far away.'[7] The day appears to have left a lasting impression: years later, a conversation with a Shinto priest at a shrine near Sendai castle about the region's history reminded her of stories about the Highlands and 'their endless clan wars, and you know how I've always liked those.'[8]

Following the family's return to America, Kate attended the public high school in Beloit (about eighty miles from Logan, in Mitchell County), graduating in 1896. During the two previous summers she had attended the Normal School at Phillipsburg, and in August 1896 she passed the Phillips County teacher examination. After a couple of years spent teaching at local schools, giving private music lessons and working in her aunt's millinery shop in Beloit, she enrolled at the University of Kansas at Lawrence in 1899. She earned a music teacher's certificate in 1901 and taught music and German in Denver, Colorado before returning to the University of Kansas in 1903 and graduating with a Bachelor of Arts in 1905.

During both her periods at university, Hansen pursued extracurricular activities and was active in Christian organizations. One of them was the Student Volunteer Movement for Foreign Missions, and in 1901 she pledged to become a student volunteer with the purpose of becoming a missionary.[9] By 1905 she was determined to work as a missionary teacher. On 31 December 1906 she and her friend Lydia Lindsey were appointed by the Reformed Church in the United States to teach at Miyagi Girls' School in Sendai. In a letter to her sister Alpha (b. 1886) Kate wrote, 'Just the school work I have always wanted, in the country

---

7   Bales, Bales, and Harbin, *Kate Hansen*, 102.
8   Kate Hansen (KH) to her mother, 31 January 1926, SRL Box 1, Folder 34.
9   Bales, Bales, and Harbin, *Kate Hansen*, 148.

and even in the very town (or rather city, for Sendai is second only to Tōkyō) where I have always had the greatest interest.'[10]

Kate Hansen and Lydia Lindsay set sail for Japan in August 1907, arriving in Yokohama on 2 September and travelling to Sendai on 5 September. They would both spend most of their subsequent lives in Sendai, teaching at Miyagi College for a total of around forty years. They even took most of their furloughs at the same time.[11] After their arrival at the school in 1907, both mainly taught English and studied the Japanese language. Lindsey continued to teach English language and literature and staged regular school plays. Hansen increasingly devoted herself to teaching music as well as performing in concerts.

At this point a brief examination of Kate Hansen's relationship with music is appropriate. She grew up in a family where music was an integral part of family life: both her own family and her Danish relatives enjoyed playing instruments and singing together as a form of entertainment.[12] Not only Kate herself but also her younger sister Alpha trained as a music teacher. Kate was moreover deeply influenced by her piano professor at the University of Kansas, the German-born Carl Preyer (1863–1947), with whom she worked during all three of her periods of study.[13] Trained in Stuttgart (he subsequently returned to Europe twice to study in Vienna and Berlin respectively), Preyer was one of many German musicians who contributed to the rise of European art music in the United States. He headed the piano department at the University of Kansas for almost forty years. Hansen expressed her passion for music, as well as her awareness of her limitations as a musician, during her long process of soul-searching which resulted in her deciding to devote

---

10   KH to her sister Alpha Florence Hansen (AFH), 27 January 1907, quoted in Bales, Bales, and Harbin, *Kate Hansen*, 156. See also Mensendiek, *To Japan with Love*, 18. The two friends had both applied for the two positions, which were advertised in the *Student Volunteer Magazine*. It is not clear when they first met; Lydia Lindsey entered Kansas University in 1900. Both received their B.A. in 1905. See Mensendiek, *To Japan with Love*, 11, 16, 18.

11   Hansen returned to America for five furloughs between 1907 and October 1941: 1912–13; 1919–20; 1926–28; 1933–34, and 1939–40.

12   There are several references to music-making in her diary of the trip to Denmark.

13   Bales, Bales, and Harbin, *Kate Hansen*, 111–12, 26, 43, 208. Howard F. Gloyne, *Carl Preyer: The Life of a Kansas Musician*. Published by Preyer Memorial Committee, University of Kansas, 1949.

her life to Christian mission.[14] On one occasion she recorded having practised the piano for seven hours that day without feeling tired. A Christmas concert represented 'the seventh heaven': 'Our Professor Preyer outdid even himself. He is wonderful, he is <u>grand</u>.'[15] On another occasion, she wrote what looks like a summary of her feelings:

> My music! I shall never be a great musician, that is certain. I have not the Divine call of genius. Yet I love it. Yet I understand some of it, until it seems a part of my very soul. Yet I can make some people understand good things through it. Yet I can make of it a good and honorable profession.[16]

Ultimately, her love for music was subjected to her work as a missionary and became a way of leading her students to the Christian faith. The role of music in Christian education is a recurring theme in her writings.[17] While this might in part have served to justify her devoting so much of her time not only to teaching music but also to working on her own performance techniques, there is no reason to doubt that it reflected her true belief. She summed up her point of view in 1950, in her last annual report to the Mission Board, in a succinct paragraph:

> The whole system of so-called Occidental music is founded on the Christian religion, and its greatest masters have been saturated with Christianity. They have expressed their Christian thought and feelings in their works, even in supposedly secular ones. A Christian teacher of music, who knows and comprehends these facts, can in the most natural way make music teaching a powerful Christian force, following the august example of Bach himself, a music teacher for most of his life, who said that music must be studied 'to the glory of God,' for if written otherwise it would be nothing but an infernal howling. The teaching of music history is one of the greatest opportunities for Christian influence,

---

14 A 'long diary entry' is quoted in Bales, Bales, and Harbin, *Kate Hansen*, 119-50. It covers the years 1895–1900 and the first entry is dated 5 December 1900. Whether Hansen did not date all her entries or whether the authors of her biography omitted them is not clear.
15 December 1900, Bales, Bales, and Harbin, *Kate Hansen*, 126. Underlined by Hansen. All underlines in the following quotes are by Hansen.
16 Bales, Bales, and Harbin, *Kate Hansen*, 142.
17 For example, Kate Hansen, 'The Japanese Are Learning to Sing', in *Kate Hansen: The Grandest Mission on Earth from Kansas to Japan, 1907–51* (The University of Kansas Continuing Education, 2000 (1914)); Kate Hansen, 'Music Hath Charms', in *Kate Hansen: The Grandest Mission on Earth from Kansas to Japan, 1907–51* (The University of Kansas Continuing Education, 2000).

if done with the right emphasis on religion in general, and our music and the Christian religion in particular. A book should be written on this subject![18]

Hansen's acknowledgement of the close ties between Western music and the Christian religion almost inevitably implied that Western music was superior to any other. Her many dismissive comments regarding Japanese music reflect that assumption. In this she was a typical representative of her times. Her attitude did not change fundamentally, although she later spent a good deal of time and effort on studying Japanese music, created musical arrangements of Japanese songs, and composed works with Japanese themes. Several other foreign teachers did the same, without their expressed views about Japanese music becoming less condescending or coloured by Orientalism.[19]

Hansen's love of music and her ambitions for the school gave her good reasons to continue her musical training during her regular furloughs. For her first furlough she left Japan in July 1912 and returned in March 1914. During this time, she wrote in an article entitled 'Misconceptions and Present Problems' about mission work in general, 'that Japan demands of mission work and workers American standards of efficiency, and is rapidly coming to demand our standard of equipment. "Palm-tree methods" no longer avail here [...].'[20] She followed her own advice to the board by making sure her own qualifications kept up with the rising standards in Sendai. For most of her first furlough she once again enrolled at the University of Kansas to study for a Bachelor of Music, which she was awarded in 1913. During her second furlough from late 1919 (or early 1920) until spring 1921, she studied piano and counterpoint in New York at the Institute of Musical Arts, now the Juilliard School of Music. Most of her third furlough (spring 1926 to summer 1928) Hansen spent at the Chicago Musical College, a private conservatoire founded

---

18 It is quoted by both her biographers. See Mensendiek, *To Japan with Love*, 107; Bales, Bales, and Harbin, *Kate Hansen*, 318.

19 Examples in Irene Suchy, 'Deutschsprachige Musiker in Japan vor 1945. Eine Fallstudie eines Kulturtransfers am Beispiel der Rezeption abendländischer Musik' (Ph.D. doctoral thesis, University of Vienna, 1992). Kate Hansen may well have been advised to make use of Japanese material by her teachers at Chicago.

20 *The Outlook of Missions*, Vol. VI, 2 (February 1914), pp. 81–84. Quoted in Bales, Bales, and Harbin, *Kate Hansen*, 230.

in 1867, studying for a Master's degree in music.[21] She was awarded her Mus.M. with honours in 1927, but continued her studies throughout spring 1928 with the intention of obtaining a doctorate.[22]

Hansen was awarded an honorary doctorate in absentia in January 1930, '[i]n recognition of your broad musicianship, of your general cultural background, of your musical experience, and especially because of the great contribution you are making to the cause of musical education in Japan'.[23] This ended Kate Hansen's formal training, but evidence suggests that she continued to spend substantial amounts of time on piano practice and study.

Kate Hansen and the Music of Others: Sendai's Concert Culture Through Foreign Ears

Hansen's love of music as well as her professional interest made her a keen observer of local musical activities: thanks to her writings, we can almost hear the sounds she describes as well as picture the scenes. The many years she spent in Sendai meant that she was witness to the enormous progress the locals achieved in making Western music their own, as well as the dedication and effort that it cost. At the same time her writings include revealing observations about the practice and performance of traditional music in Sendai during this period of transition. Of course, her descriptions are far from unbiased. Her experience of traditional Japanese music was, moreover, limited: most of it appears to have occurred within the framework of concerts featuring a mixture of Western and Japanese items; that is, in a modern setting rather than in any of the traditional settings for musical performances. For example, only in October 1923 did she attend a Japanese theatre performance for the first time. She did not enjoy it:

---

21 Founded in 1867, Chicago Musical College (now part of Chicago College of Performing Arts) offered Master of Music Degrees from 1917, and became a charter member of the National Association of Schools of Music in 1924. See 'Roosevelt University: The Music Conservatory' (written by Don Draganski, edited by Brian Wis): https://web.archive.org/web/20080417220323/http://ccpa.roosevelt.edu/music/history.htm
22 Mensendiek, *To Japan with Love*, 36, 46, 54–55.
23 Copy of letter in Bales, Bales, and Harbin, *Kate Hansen*, 347.

Last night I was at a Japanese theatre, for the first time in my stay in Sendai, and I hope, for the last time. It began at three in the afternoon, and lasted until midnight. What with the smoking, the bad air, and the terrible racket – for there were gongs and other supposed musical instruments –, and the actors all shouted and yowled at the tops of their voices [...] It was a barbarous performance, with murder and revenge as almost the only theme, and I am glad that it belonged to an art that is dying out, and that we are doing our share to get rid of it. The audience were nearly all older people, and lower-class, old-fashioned looking ones – a great contrast to the audiences we are used to seeing at concerts, for instance.[24]

Hansen's letter obviously reflects her prejudices, including her assumption that Western music was superior and audiences at Western-style concerts were more in tune with modern times. More importantly, it reminds us that there was a whole world of stage performances outside the Western-style concerts, which she hardly experienced at all. One might, moreover, ask how she would have reacted to a comparable class of entertainment in her home country.

First Impressions

Hansen wrote to her family almost every week, and her early letters in particular contain detailed descriptions of performances she witnessed. References to music are most frequent in the letters addressed to her younger sister Alpha Florence Bales, herself a music teacher, until her early death in September 1926 during Hansen's third furlough.[25] In some cases her descriptions of concerts can be compared with the concert programmes published in *Ongakukai*. Her observations contrast starkly with the generally positive reports in that magazine. Hansen's first detailed description of a concert appears in a letter addressed to her sister towards the end of September, which also contains her first descriptions

---

24 KH to her family, 7 October 1923, SRL, Box 1, Folder 31.
25 Personal Papers of Kate I. Hansen, University Archives, PP 19, Kenneth Spencer Research Library, University of Kansas Libraries. Due to limited time, I was only able to consult the letters for the period from her arrival in Japan until the end of 1931, as well as a few around selected dates, but the later letters tended to have fewer reference to music.

of hearing performances on traditional Japanese instruments.[26] According to a brief report in the local newspaper, *Kahoku shinpō*,[27] the concert took place on 23 September and was organized by the music club of the Second High School and held in the school's auditorium. Hansen reported, accurately, that the club had been organizing concerts for the last four or five years, 'and in other ways trying to improve the musical life of the city. As our mission [*sic*] are the musicians they've all been helping and usually give about half the programme.'[28] Hansen too was expected to perform in local concerts, and she played in this one, possibly her first public performance in Sendai. The short newspaper report stated that the concert was a successful affair, attended by several hundred guests. The author of the report also mentioned the items that 'sounded pleasing even to a layperson's ears': an unnamed society member's voice solo, *Ōunabara* (The great sea) and *Coming through the Rye*; J. Monroe Stick's mandolin solo; E. H. Zaugg's vocal solo, *Anvil Song*; Hansen's piano solo; Florence Seiple's solo (voice) recital etc. He particularly praised Takeuchi Imako's voice solo. From the second part he highlighted a society members' recital of *Haisho no tsuki* (The moon in the place of exile); Professor Okamoto's violin solo; Stick's cornet solo and Seiple's and Takeuchi Imako's singing.

Hansen was less impressed, at least by the Japanese musicians:

> They say that the Japanese part of the concert [that is, the Western music performed by Japanese rather than foreign missionaries] has improved immensely in these years – I don't see how it could be worse! They announced an 'orchestra,' and four fellows with violins came out and tried to play a Wagner (think of it, Wagner!) piece; and they all tried to play on the tune, and they were all out of tune and couldn't even keep time together. I thought I should die! But they kept right on – didn't seem to have the least idea they were not giving the finest performance in the world! They were just a sample of the Japanese performance, except one girl who has been through the music school in Tokio, and has a voice and a style of singing we would consider good, even in America [Takeuchi Imako]. And as for the mission we had all kinds of numbers, but they all had accompaniments, and you should have heard the tin pan of a

---

26 Kate Hansen to Alpha Hansen, 22 September 1907; the letter appears to have been continued on 28 September; KH gives a day-by-day description of the previous two weeks, including the concert on 23 September.
27 *Kahoku shinpō*, 25 September 1907.
28 Kate Hansen to Alpha Hansen, 22/28 September 1907.

piano there! As an outlet for my feelings when my turn came (I was especially honoured (!) by being put on twice) I swore [?] that Heller[29] piece at them – just hammered it and banged it out – and it seemed just to suit them; they about went wild over it, and clapped and cheered in the craziest way; and I've been told ever since by Japanese that that was the best thing they had!! [sic] Do I need to say any more about Japanese musical taste? I suppose I'm contributing to the prestige of the school – but my conscience really hurts!

O, but you should have heard the 'aftermeeting' or 'side show', after the foreign music was over; nothing else but the Japanese Satsuma biwa, the great war instrument. One person described it as 'playing violin music without any violin', another as 'singing the full history of the Revolutionary War to the accompaniment of a dish-pan'; but neither is sufficiently vivid. He sang (?) for three-quarters of an hour; first a vocal spasm, then a biwa spasm. And whenever the audience approved his sentiments, they gave out short, sharp yells, like Indian war-whoops. The first time they did it I thought they must be going to massacre the performer; and I really wouldn't have made a move to rescue him; I thought he deserved it![30]

Earlier in the same letter she had described a 'big jollification in our honor' where the entertainment included a *koto* quartet: 'They played a piece a mile long, that certainly was great! The Devil's March can't hold a candle to that! I was really delighted. When I want to swear, I'm going to get a girl to do it for me on a koto!'[31]

The concert she played in, only a week later, apparently appalled her even more:

O, that makes me think of the 'concert.' It was a big charity affair, and I was invited to play an organ solo! I thought nothing could be worse than the Koto Gakko pianos, so I consented. It was in the theatre; a regular big barn, with a gallery; and all the seats were boxes! Literally boxes, the whole lower floor, each about four feet square, and two feet high, and the partitions with about six inch boards nailed to the top for the people to walk on the aisles, of course. The 'concert' began at one o'clock and lasted all day and all night, about. The people came and brought their lunches and camped in those boxes – all on the floor, of course – and

---

29 Stephen Heller (1814–88), pianist and prolific composer of piano works.
30 Kate Hansen to Alpha Hansen, 22/28 September 1907; Box 1, Folder 21.
31 The 'jollification' appears to have taken place on Tuesday, 16 September. *The Devil's March* presumably refers to the *Teufelsmarsch* by the Austrian composer Franz von Suppé (1819–95), from his operetta, *Der Teufel auf Erden* (1878).

tea was served between numbers! I'll not try to describe the Japanese numbers – see the Koto Gakko, only a great deal more of it. But mine! I'd purposely selected a loud march-time piece, to fill the room, and the ancient excuse for an organ with all its stops and loud things out and the pedals going like mad – with all that, it sounded like last dying whisper! But it must have impressed the people; today the minister brought me a Japanese newspaper, with a most wonderful article on me, giving my full history – what they knew – and telling what a wonderful musician I was – 'the greatest musician in Sendai,' as O Masa San translated it![32]

The programme of the concert may well be one of two published in the second issue of *Ongakukai*, dated 26 October 1907 and 9 November 1907 (see Chapter 9). The first programme seems to fit Hansen's description, although the date does not.[33] Even if it is not the one described in Hansen's letter, it provides a good example of the kind of event she experienced soon after her arrival. The programme consisted of two daytime and two evening parts, and Hansen performed in three of them, although what she played is not specified. In the second concert, Hansen played in the second part only: a solo, and a duet with Florence Seiple.[34]

The surviving letters do not include a description of that concert, but playing in at least three concerts in as many months from the day of her arrival must have been a first for her. A letter dated 26 November and addressed to her sister contains a short remark about what seems to have been yet another concert: 'How you would have laughed to hear our "concert"!' Most Japanese, she continued, had no more idea of Western music than monkeys. Because all of it was so unfamiliar, 'they understand the greatest piece of Beethoven's as much and as little – as a rag-time selection. [...] The thing the Japanese appreciate most is length, I played an endlessly long piece out of The Creation for one of my stunts.'[35] Hansen's comment illustrates what she must have realized within a few weeks of her arrival: the people of Sendai, unless they had travelled to Tokyo or spent time abroad, had minimal experience of Western music. While concerts seem to have been fairly frequent, the

---

32   KH to her family, 6 October 1907, SRL, Box 1, Folder 1.
33   'Sendai-shi no gakukyō', *Ongakukai* 1, no. 2 (1908): 45–46. See Chapter 9. I have not been able to verify the date from other sources.
34   Concert of the Sho Gakkō Rengōkai (Federation of Schools) *Ongakukai* 1, no. 2 (1908): 47–48.
35   KH to Alpha, 26 November 1907. Papers, Box 1, Folder 21. I could find no letter for the period between 29 October and 26 November 1907.

scope of music performed was limited. Even 'a rag-time selection' was hardly standard fare, much less 'the greatest piece of Beethoven's'. Far more common were *shōka,* marches, and other short instrumental pieces, or extracts from larger works, presumably taken from instrument tutors and albums.

Some concerts seem to have been spontaneous, disorganized affairs; perhaps particularly the ones staged by students. In January 1908 Hansen wrote to her sister describing 'the funniest mixup' about a concert at the Second High School, where she and other foreign musicians found their names on the programme without having been notified or formally invited. She observed, 'We'd had an experience like that in the fall', after which they told the organizers that they would 'never play again under such circumstances'. In the end only Stick performed at that particular concert.[36] While the students' apparently casual attitude understandably irritated the foreign performers, it demonstrates that it was they who were in charge. Indispensable as foreign participation might have been (at least for the time being), it was not necessarily on their own terms.

Hansen's next detailed description of musical life in Sendai is in a letter to her sister dated 27 May 1908, which starts with a vignette about music in the streets: 'It's really summer today, and except for an awful streetband, which sounds as if all the E flat horns were playing in B flat and all the B flats in something else, it's as quiet and beautiful a Sunday as any one [sic] would want.' The concert held the previous week (23 May) nevertheless showed signs of promise: 'That concert certainly will give Sendai something to talk about for awhile [sic]. It was the first one I've attended out here that didn't have some dreadfully discordant numbers.'[37] Because this concert took place in the school chapel, Hansen was one of the organizers as well as a performer. The chapel offered space for an audience of 700, although chairs had to be borrowed from Tohoku College. Among Hansen's tasks was organizing the checking of *geta* sandals, which had to be left outside the entrance. The audience included school servants but also Count Date with his family, a mix

---

36 KH to Alpha Hansen, 26 January and 2 February 1908. The concert was presumably the one held on 29 January 1908. See 'Sendai shi no gakukai', *Ongakukai* 1, no 4 (1908): 51. Several foreigners, including Hansen, and Stick are named with the piece 'to be determined', although one of Stick's items is billed as *Evening Star*.

37 KH to AFH, 27 May 1908. The concert took place on 23 May: See 'Miyagi Jogakkō ongakukai', *Ongakukai* 1 no. 6 (1908): 49.

of social classes that would surely have been unthinkable a few years previously. Hansen was scarcely in a position to appreciate the novelty and significance of this, however: she was most impressed by the fact that she knew so many people in the audience.

The progamme was eclectic:[38]

Part One

1. Opening Address by president of the Seinenkai (youth association), Tanabe Hisa
2. Gramophone – (five unspecified items) – Prof. Stick
3. *Shōka – Nagare* (Mendelssohn) – Choir of Miyagi Jogakkō
4. Piano – *Spring Song* (Mendelssohn) – Miss Schwartz
5. Banjo and vocal solo – *Asleep in the Deep* (H. W. Petrie[39]) – Prof. Zaugg
6. Cornett solo – *The Lost Chord* (Arthur Sullivan[40]) – Prof. Stick
7. *Shōka – Calm on the Morn* (song celebrating Easter)[41] – Choir of Higashi Rokuban-chō Church
8. Piano Duet – *Rosamunde* (Schubert) – Mrs. Miller, Miss Hansen
9. Koto – *Azuma jishi* (Lion of Azuma; *sōkyoku*) – Tanaka Torako
10. Vocal solo – *Silent Reprehending*[42] (Mozart) – Mrs Seiple

Part Two

11. Piano ensemble – Bolero (Streabbog)[43] – Tonimura Ikiko, Kozasa Aiko, Ujie Tokiko

---

38 'Miyagi Jogakkō ongakukai', 49.
39 1897: lyrics by Arthur J. Lamb.
40 Written 1877: originally for voice and piano. Lyrics by Adelaide A. Proctor (published in 1858).
41 By A. Beirly (see Copyright Catalog, Dec 30–June 27, 1895–96 10, No. 235, Library of Congress. Copyright Office, p. 15).
42 Presumably Mozart's song *Die Verschweigung* (lyrics by Christian Felix Weiße). English translations I have found of titles include 'Discretion' and 'Keeping mum'. Seiple, who studied music in Germany, may well have sung in German, providing her own translation of the title.
43 Louis Streabbog (Jean Louis Gobbaerts, 1835–86), *Bolero pour piano*.

12. Vocal solo – *Violets*[44] – Miss Schwartz
13. Piano solo – Sonata Opus 7 (Beethoven) – Miss Hansen
14. Gramophone – (Five items) – Professor Stick
15. Vocal solo – *Solomon Levi* (University student song)[45] – Prof. Zaugg
16. Poem – *Chikugogawa o kudari*[46] – Professor Naganuma Hakudō
17. Vocal solo – *Heart's Delight* (Gilchrist)[47] – Mrs Seiple
18. Koto ensemble – *Rokudan*[48] – Isawa Nobuko, Iwasaki Kiyoko
19. Piano duet – *Fanfare des dragons*[49] – Uda Masako, Satō Kotoko
20. *Shōka* – *Niji* (Rainbow[50]) – (Rossini) – Miyagi Jogakkō Chorus
21. Closing address – Miller, Principal
22. *Kimi ga yo* (twice) – All

The performances aroused mixed reactions from Hansen:

> How you'd have enjoyed Prof. Naganuma's Chinese poem! It was a wierd [sic] wild chant; every once in awhile it would rise with a regular howl, and then the audience would all howl in chorus; when he'd get extra excited, he'd stamp his foot or shake his fist, and there'd be a chorus of whoops that would make a band of wild Indians look silly. I simply lost all control of myself, and laughed until I was sore – disgraced myself probably. It greatly edified Mr. Degenhart especially, and he threatened next time Mrs. Seiple sang, to join in the chorus the same way. I wonder that the Japanese don't. They had the Satsuma Biwa too – the 'Conquest

---

44 Hardly an unambiguous title. A possible candidate is Roma (words and music), Violets, New York: Leo Feist, 1903.
45 Appears to be associated with college singing: page 27 of *Selected Songs Sung at Harvard College: From 1862 to 1866* (Cambridge: Press of J. Wilson and Sons, 1866).
46 From a poem by Rai Sanyō; composition by Kimura Gakufū; the National Diet Library has a recording of the work dating from 1935. The poem is about the battle of Chikugo River in 1359, during the period of two imperial courts.
47 The American composer and organist William Wallace Gilchrist (1846–1916), *Heart's Delight*, published New York 1886.
48 The famous *koto* (*sōkyoku*) piece.
49 *Fanfare de dragons, esquisse militaire pour piano*. Op. 60 (1867), composed by Frédéric Boscovitz. (Washington, D. C., 1885).
50 Lyrics by Takeshima Matajirō (Hagoromo, 1872–1967), who is better known for the lyrics to Taki Rentarō's famous song, *Hana* (Cherry blossoms). See Tōkyō Geijutsu Daigaku Hyakunenshi Hensan Iinkai, ed., *Tōkyō Geijutsu Daigaku hyakunenshi: Ensōkai hen 1* (Tokyo: Ongaku no Tomosha, 1990), 99.

of Formosa'.⁵¹ But it took only twenty minutes, and during that time I found it convenient to have important business in the hall, so escaped. [...] The audience didn't seem to be as excited about it as they generally get; maybe our training is doing them good.

For the rest we had all sorts of things, from Beethoven to a phonograph. The latter was pretty bad, but it wasn't loud and piercing as they generally are, so I managed to get through it. Mr. Zaugg and Mrs. Seiple each sang twice; Mrs. Miller and I played a duet that lasted fifteen or twenty minutes and nearly tore the insides out of the piano; Ruth Schwartz sang and Miriam played one of Mendelssohn's (Miriam's about fourteen and really has some musical talent); Mr. Stick played; one girl played a koto solo and two a so-called duet (they both play the same thing – there's no idea at all of harmony or different parts); I played the first movement of Beethoven's Op. 7, and mightily astonished the audience with two crashes [?] of chords that about raised the roof; three of our girls played a little piano trio [...].⁵²

Whether the audience really was losing interest in the *biwa* is open to question. They may well have shown more restraint in their reactions because of the foreigners' obvious disapproval. But there were Japanese who agreed with them, such as the reviewer of the Second High School concert in October that year (see the following chapter). The audience reactions to the 'Chinese poem' and the *biwa* performance remind us of the novelty of the Western-style concerts in the form they had taken in the nineteenth century: a quasi-sacred event demanding adherence to a strict etiquette that demanded a passive audience.

The concert indeed became the talk of town it seems: in a letter to her sister dated 7 June, Hansen wrote that it had been 'quite a topic of conversation' and had been reported in 'the Tokyo English paper and by the Tokyo musical magazine'. Tohoku College was planning a concert in imitation of the Miyagi one. Hansen suspected that it would result in an anti-climax as they were asking the same performers to feature at short notice, meaning that they would either have to play the same music or perform under-rehearsed. She herself had claimed a lame wrist

---

51   Presumably *Taiwan iri*, composed by Nishimura Tenshū to commemorate the Japanese invasion in 1895 and the death of Prince Kitashirakawa Yoshihisa (1847–95). See Tadashi Shimazu, *Meiji Satsumabiwa uta* (Tokyo: Perikansha, 2001).
52   KH to AFH, 27 May 1908, Box 1, Folder 22.

and thus avoided having to perform a solo.⁵³ The concert did indeed take place and Hansen wrote about it to her mother:

> [...] and last night we went to the concert at the Tohoku Gakuin, given in imitation of ours. It was not nearly so good, though – the boys are like the Logan Methodists, and get things up on the spur of the moment. We all did our usual stunts – I should think the Japanese would get tired of hearing us at every concert or public affair of any kind. They had some Japanese music that can only be described as similar to the noise old Tom makes when he is put inside the screen, only I believe of the two I'd rather hear Tom! It was enough to make one's hair stand on end. And they had a 'band' – a cornet, two alto horns, and a big bass round [?] horn – all out of tune as I didn't know they <u>could</u> be put out. I'd give two cents to have D.G. hear some of those awful 'bands.'⁵⁴

Even if Hansen did not play solo in this concert, she presumably accompanied other soloists, although the concert programmes in *Ongakukai* only name her in solo items. She mentioned accompanying musicians in several letters. At a concert at the Second High School on 1 May 1909, she accompanied a local violin teacher. This instance of a relatively prominent local musician's effort at performing Western music, together with a *koto* performance at the same concert, represented highlights that provided material for entertaining, if unflattering, descriptions in the next letter to her family:

> Oh, we had a wonderful concert at the Kōtō Gakkō Saturday. I had to play for a man with a fiddle, who never hit the right note, even by accident. The only way I could tell whether we were together was to play in strict time and trust to luck. You never heard anything so appalling in your life – people <u>never</u> play fiddles out of tune at home do they? This one was so bad that even the Japanese – some of them – were amused. Most of the crowd, however, couldn't tell the difference. I never imagined anything could sound as bad. If I don't find some way to get around ever playing for that Fiddler again, I'll know the reason why. And the worst thing is, that he makes his living – giving violin lessons! It would be rather pathetic if it weren't so disgusting – I played the 'Devil's March,' and it pleased the crowd immensely, and they gave me a flowery write-up in the next day's paper!! Guess it sounded so much like their music that it just struck them. – O, that reminds me – they were having an endlessly

---

53   KH to AFH, 7 June 1908, Box 1, Folder 22.
54   KH to her mother 19 June 1908, Box 1, Folder 22. I have not been able to find a programme of the concert. D.G. may be her brother Dane Gray Hansen.

> long piece on the kotos, the women who played them singing a little too, by fits and starts. But they'd had a long interlude, and I was nearly asleep, when they both broke out at the top of their voices – 'Miau' – just like an old tom-cat. I couldn't get my handkerchief stuffed in soon enough and snorted out right before the crowd. It was probably part of a Lament for some dead hero or other, for the Japanese all around had very solemn faces all the time, and I've probably disgraced myself forever, but that was one time too much for me.[55]

According to the programme, most of the concert featured performers from the Tokyo Academy of Music, while locals only played in the third part (six items).[56] Presumably the duet with the violinist she described in the letter was the unspecified violin solo by 'Professor Okamoto' (fifth item on the programme; for Okamoto, see previous chapter). The programme does not mention a *koto* performance. The last item is a *shakuhachi* solo.

Possibly, Hansen did not manage to avoid playing with the 'Fiddler' again, for she includes a description similar to the one above in the thesis she wrote some three years later. The 'orchestra' she refers to may well be the ensemble of the Second High School's music club, which in the early years was led by Okamoto.

> The violin is, next to the organ, the most popular Western instrument in Japan, and the most abused. The 'orchestra' of Sendai consisted of about twelve first violins, a 'cello, and a piano. No two of those violins are ever tuned alike, and they are supposed to be played in unison. Here in America, I marvel how any Westerner can go to one of those concerts. However, to the Japanese audience, the effect is beautiful, and pieces by the orchestra are always encored. One evening, after a peculiarly atrocious performance, one of my piano students said, 'Didn't the orchestra flat a little, Miss Hansen?' I was thankful for small mercies.
>
> The leader of this 'orchestra' is the violin teacher of the city, and is, I believe, a graduate of the Ueno school, but of ten or more years' standing. He, too, finds it quite impossible to tune his violin correctly. When escape was impossible, I have at times played accompaniments for him. He lacks some of the conceit of his countrymen, and is not insulted when told that his instrument is out of tune. But even when the violin is at last in tune, he is unable to hit more than about half of the notes with appropriate correctness. The only [way] in which an accompanist

---

55   KH to AFH, 9 May 1909 Box 1, Folder 22: capitalization is KH's.
56   *Ongakukai* 2, no. 6 (1909): 42. See the following chapter; *Kahoku shinpō*, 26 April 1909.

can keep with him is to play the accompaniment straight through, in metronome time. Usually, in that case, the two end together. And his favorite composer is Bach!⁵⁷

Hansen mentioned the popularity of the violin in letters to her family as well. In 1910 she wrote, 'And when they try to play foreign instruments, they all prefer violins, and they've no idea of playing in tune, but play just as the notation strikes them, generally in good time, but in all sorts of tune. – O yes, and they all insist on playing first – nobody will play second, so they all play at the tune!'⁵⁸ Neither the popularity of the instrument nor the inability to play in tune are surprising. The violin was at the time among the most widely played Western instruments worldwide. One of the most versatile, it appealed to all social classes and could be played in an almost unlimited variety of musical contexts. Playing unfamiliar music on the violin is, however, extremely challenging because it requires the ability to imagine the desired pitch and sound in order to produce them. In the early years of Hansen's time in Japan, most people in Sendai (and elsewhere) simply did not have sufficient opportunity to familiarize themselves with Western music.

Beside her many negative accounts in these early years of her work in Japan, Hansen also reported signs of progress. In a letter to her sister dated 29 March 1908, she wrote: 'But O Kiku San astonished me by playing "the Heavens are Telling" <u>exactly</u> as I had showed her, notes, time, expression and all – it was the best piece of organ playing I've heard from any Japanese! And the class song turned out well too, [...].'⁵⁹ Musical expression was something she usually found lacking in her Japanese pupils. In a letter to her sister dated 15 November 1908 about teaching the piano, she wrote about one of her weekly classes, 'the Japanese are good at technique, and Miriam at expression, and they help and spur each other on.'⁶⁰ The notion that Japanese musicians excel

---

57 Hansen, *Musical Consciousness*, 55–57. By November 1910 Okamoto had been replaced by Kumagai Senta (or Sentarō). The composition of the ensemble is likely to have varied over the years.
58 KH to her family, undated, SRL Box 1, Folder 24 (1910). The sheet seems to be part of a letter, not dated, but '[1]' has been written at bottom. It ends with 'Merry Christmas ...' and refers to a gramophone record of Japanese music Hansen sent to her family.
59 KH to AFH, 29 March 1908, SRL, Box 1, Folder 2.
60 KH to AFH, 15 November 1908, SRL, Box 1, Folder 22. Miriam Schwartz was the daughter of Dr Herbert W. Schwartz (1857–1921), a physician, and his wife Lola B.

at technique but have difficulties with expression has since become a stereotype. During Hansen's early years in Sendai, however, the local people had hardly any opportunity to hear Western art music performed well and thus to learn how expressive playing sounded. Moreover, music teachers, whether in Japan or in Western countries, to this day often fail to convey to their students what exactly is required in order to play expressively.[61]

The last concert described in Hansen's letters before she left Japan for her first furlough took place at Miyagi Jogakkō on 10 May 1912:

> The one thing this week has been our wonderful concert. I'll put in a program. I played all the accompaniments too, so you may imagine how busy it kept me for the last few weeks. People are saying, it was the best thing musically that's ever been given in Sendai, and that's quite a bit, for we've had some very good performers from Tōkyō and Germany. It was certainly the best our school-girls ever did, on the whole, so this five years' music work is ending well.[62]

According to *Ongakukai*, most of the programme was performed by foreigners. Hansen herself played an unspecified sonata by Grieg and Wagner's *Walkürenritt*, together with Mrs Dening. Performances by Japanese (presumably students) included a march for piano (eight hands) by Engelman[63] and a three-part song, *Haru no uta* (Spring song) by Mendelssohn.

Hansen's early descriptions of musical performance suggest that most of the inhabitants of Sendai had not yet gained sufficient understanding of Western music to appreciate or play it. Most of them preferred traditional music, which was performed even at concerts featuring predominantly Western music. Hansen's pupils were eager to learn, however, and by 1912 Hansen's efforts to teach had begun to bear fruit. This no doubt motivated her to pursue further her own understanding and performance of music during her first furlough.

Reynolds Schwartz (1864–1935), Methodist missionaries.

61 See Aaron Williamson, ed., *Musical Excellence: Strategies and Techniques to Enhance Performance* (Oxford: Oxford University Press, 2004), 247–70.
62 KH to her mother, 12 May 1912, Box 1, Folder 26. A version of the programme was published in *Ongakukai* 5.6. The programme in *Ongakukai* does not specify all the performers and pieces.
63 Probably Hans Engelman (1872–1914). See http://ragpiano.com/comps/engelman.shtml

Traditional Japanese Music

Back in America (from autumn 1912), Hansen studied for a Bachelor of Music at the University of Kansas. This temporary return to her homeland represented an opportunity to reflect on what she had observed and learnt in Sendai during her first five years there. Working on her thesis, *My Impressions of the Musical Consciousness of the Japanese People* (henceforth, *Musical Consciousness*), served both purposes. It was almost certainly written for a course she completed in the spring semester of 1913.[64] The work combines a lively narrative detailing her first-hand experiences with more detached descriptions, and efforts at systematic and thoughtful treatment of the indigenous music enjoyed by the people of Sendai, as well as their attempts to master Western music. Hansen expressed her feelings about what she heard more openly than would be considered appropriate by today's academic standards. Her descriptions, moreover, illustrate just how inaccessible Japanese music seemed to her. She realized, however, as her title and introductory remarks show, that her impressions might prove 'misleading' and should 'be taken for what they are, impressions merely, and not scientific facts' (p. 2).

Of her position as an observer she wrote, 'As music teacher in the oldest of these girls' high schools, I was continually in contact with whatever musical life there was in the city, and became quite widely acquainted among its musical people.' (p. 3.) In reality, there is reason to suspect that 'whatever musical life there was' is not entirely accurate: apart from music-making overheard, such as singing in the streets, most of Hansen's encounters with Japanese music took place either at public concerts, themselves a modern innovation, or on other formal occasions.

---

64 College Record, Chicago Musical College; includes award of Doctor of Music, 1 February 1930, and transcripts for her courses at the University of Kansas, SRL PP19 Box 6 folder 1:3 According to the Record, the course was entitled, 'Thesis 2 and 3'. Hansen was awarded the grade I (90–100). Hansen, *Musical Consciousness*. The manuscript is undated, but within it, Hansen refers to her five years in Japan and writes, 'here' in connection with America. Both in the table of contents and in the introduction (bottom of the first of the sixty-three numbered pages) Hansen refers to the work as a 'thesis'. When quoting from this thesis hereafter, I give the page numbers in the text in brackets.

Her experience of performances of Japanese music was largely limited to such occasions.

Hansen described four traditional musical instruments, the *koto*, the *biwa*, the *shamisen*, and the *shakuhachi*, which, she stated, 'are heard everywhere, are commonly studied, and are almost the only native instruments used in concerts'. These, she concluded, were fundamental to the musical consciousness of the Japanese; 'the various gongs, bells, and drums used in the temple worship' (p. 4) apparently did not merit her consideration. Even so, she opined that 'the average Japanese, in my experience, cares more for his Japanese music than the average American cares for anything musical, with the possible exception of the ubiquitous ragtime.' (p. 5.) True to her title, she introduced her treatment of each instrument by describing her impression on the first occasion she heard it. Her subsequent generalizations appear to be based on several performances she had the opportunity to listen to. The *koto* appears to have been the first instrument she heard at length, judging from her letters. In the thesis, she wrote:

> My first impression of the koto was quite pleasant. It was during my first month in Japan that the school gave a tea-party in honor of the new teachers. [...] At last the platform was cleared. Heavy blankets were spread over it, and four cushions were laid carefully on the blankets. Then four of the larger girls appeared, each carrying a wooden instrument, considerably taller than herself, consisting of a box a foot wide, with the top convex; twelve to fifteen strings stretched from one end to the other of the sounding-board; and the same number of triangular bridges, one under each string, at varying intervals up and down the board. The four kotos were placed parallel to each other, at such an angle as to bring the performers' cushions in a straight line, facing the audience. The preparations completed, four of the daintiest little girls, no taller than ten-year old American girls, took their places, sitting flat on the cushions, and began tuning their kotos, moving the bridges up and down the sounding-boards. As they bent over their work, their gay Japanese clothing and their graceful movements made a series of delightful pictures.
>
> Finally, the tuning was over, the four players bowed together until their heads touched their kotos, and the performance began. [...]
>
> There was nothing which I could distinguish as a melody, and the whole piece sounded alike, except that some parts were faster than others. It was all about equally loud. It was all a series of leaps, queer minor intervals mostly, which my Western ears could not classify. It

sounded savage. At last, in the middle of the excitement without any warning, it ended with two slower notes, somewhat like the ones in the beginning. It had not been like anything I had ever heard before, it was rude and weird, but the general effect had been at least more musical than the discords of the English songs sung off the key. Musically, there was something left in Japan to be thankful for. (pp. 5–9.)

Hansen then elaborated on the limitations of the *koto* as she perceived them, concluding that it was not capable of much musical expression (she did, however concede that 'even a musical foreigner' could not appreciate Japanese music). She described the ways it is tuned and the pieces played, which she said were characterized by great leaps from one note to the next. She illustrated her point by giving the intervals of the opening bars 'of a well-known *koto* piece' (*Rokudan*).[65] She continued with a description of how the *koto* was taught:

> While the koto cannot be compared in difficulty with any of our serious musical instruments, the Japanese consider it very hard to master. Most little girls of the present day, in fairly well-to-do families, begin to study the koto when very young, usually before the age of seven. They go every day to the koto teacher's home, and take a lesson of from fifteen to thirty minutes. For several years, they are not supposed to do any practicing, except during their lessons. Everything is taught by rote, there being no printed music. 'Make haste slowly' must be the motto of the koto teacher. The tuning of the koto is supposed to be enough to occupy at least the first three months of the pupil's time. (pp. 11–12.)

To illustrate what she considered the exaggerated claims about the difficulties of mastering the *koto*, Hansen described the experience of her colleague Florence Seiple, who shocked her *koto* teacher by tuning a *koto* within minutes during her first lesson (albeit with the help of a piano), although this process was supposed to take months to learn. She added, however, that Seiple 'did not find all of her study quite so easy as this beginning' (p. 13). The repertoire of the *koto* was limited, according to Hansen, with *Rokudan* being the most popular piece, which was often heard in concerts, 'played on three or four kotos, usually by pretty little girls. It is my opinion that the pleasure the audience derives from this repetition is not one of the ear, but of the eye. The poses of

---

65 The piece is not named. *Rokudan* was one of the pieces available in staff notation in the edition by the Tokyo Academy of Music.

the players, as carefully practiced as their music, would put to shame a teacher of Delsarte.' (p. 13.) She concluded, that while the *koto* was not a superior musical instrument, it was incomparable 'as an instrument for displaying the beauty and grace of a Japanese girl' (p. 13), and speculated that this was a major reason for its popularity.

Whether or not Hansen was right in concluding that even the Japanese audience derived more pleasure from watching the performer than from listening to the music, she had a point when she stated that the visual element in the performance was as significant as the sound. She was also right in identifying *Rokudan* as one of the most popular *koto* pieces. It was also a staple of blended performances (*wayō gassō*), but although these were popular at the time, Hansen described only one experience of hearing one; a concert in the nearby town of Furukawa in 1910: 'O, if you could have heard the koto and violins played together! Nobody would ever believe they were playing the same piece – it was Japanese music too, and they surely ought to be able to do their own music.' Presumably, the problem lay with the violins rather than the *koto*, since they were 'out of tune as only Japanese can make them'.[66] While such performances could occasionally be heard at the kind of concerts Hansen witnessed, in Sendai, they seem to have occurred most frequently at the private music studio Tōhoku Ongaku Gakuin (see the following chapter).

Next, Hansen introduced the *satsumabiwa*, which judging from her description of audience reactions, enjoyed great popularity. She did not share the enthusiasm. Her treatment of the *satsumabiwa* consists of descriptions of two performances, including the first one she heard, at a concert featuring both Western and Japanese music, described in her letter of September 1907 cited earlier. Here is her description of the performance:

> There was a concert, one evening, in the big bare assembly room of the government college. The thousand or more Japanese in the audience had listened patiently and politely, while Japanese and Americans attempted to entertain them with 'foreign' music. They had applauded at the proper times, as far as they knew them, and had done their best to enjoy themselves. The foreigners present, sitting in the front seats, which the courteous Japanese insisted on their occupying, were congratulating

---

66 KH to AFH, 23 October 1910, SRL, Box 1, Folder 24.

themselves that the performance was nearly over. It was time for the last number.

Just then two students appeared with blankets, and spread them on the stage. 'Koto', I thought. They placed a cushion in place. 'Only one koto'. But no pretty little girls and no kotos appeared. Instead, a student brought in an instrument about three feet long, that looked like a cross between a mandolin and a banjo. 'Satsuma biwa', the experienced foreigners whispered, and settled back in their seats. Another student escorted the performer to his seat. He was only an ordinary respectable-looking man, in ordinary dark gray Japanese clothes.

He sat down on his cushion, however, with an air of the gravest importance, and tuned the four strings of his biwa with great care. He looked impressively, first at his audience and then at the ceiling. He closed his eyes, and his face assumed an expression of devout mysticism. Surely, some low, soulful strain would soon delight our weary ears. He opened his mouth – but nothing soft nor sweet came forth. It was a wail, loud enough to be heard half a mile, a high-pitched, strained, discordant yell, that stayed on one note, apparently, nearly as long as the man could hold it with one breath, then wavered in a rude trill that sounded like the last gurgles of a dying man, and ended on a short lower note, thus: [here Hansen included music notes]

While he was getting his breath, after this effort, he played a few notes with a triangular plectrum, about four inches long, that looked like one of the [a proof mark inserted here might indicate a missing word] squares from a drawing class. The tones were about midway between those of a banjo and the noise made by pounding a tin pan, and had no harmonic effect which I could discover. The interlude over, the song, if such it can be called, began again, in about the same style as the first strain, and went on, almost entirely unaccompanied, in a monotonous recitative effect. Whenever the singer paused for breath, the formless interlude was repeated. The performance had gone on for a quarter of an hour, and we were almost exhausted, when the audience began to show signs of excitement. To us, the singing seemed just the same as in the beginning, but it was evidently working up to a climax. All at once, like one man, the whole audience gave a shrill, blood-curdling yell! We nearly jumped out of our seats. Our experienced friends smiled, pulled us down, and whispered something reassuring. After that, for the next half hour, whenever an exciting point was reached, the same short, sharp yell came out. We began to think the performance would last all night, but at last, without any apparent reason, the singer stopped short and made his bow. The house fairly rocked with the applause. Its volume was greater than that called forth by the whole twenty numbers that had preceded this wonderful biwa. This, evidently, was what appealed to the musical consciousness of the people of Sendai. (pp. 14-17.)

Hansen's description of the audience's reaction is as revealing as that of the performance itself. While the foreigners found the performance monotonous and longed for it to end, the Japanese, who had endured rather than enjoyed the preceding Western-style items, clearly knew the piece and eagerly anticipated its climactic moments. Their enthusiastic applause expressed their appreciation and possibly their relief that the entire concert was over.

Hansen's failure to understand Japanese music is dramatically revealed in her description of another performance. By then she had attended local concerts, and on this occasion, she accompanied a recently arrived American teacher (whom she refers to as Miss T.):

> Only once, to me, did the biwa express anything, and then it was the wrong thing! [...] When the interludes came, they were different from any we had ever heard before. The jangling, uncouth instrument gave out such dainty, tinkling notes as we had never believed possible for it. It suggested to me some of Mendelssohn's gay fairy marches, mixed with the clown dances. Between the laughter of Miss T. and the fun of the interludes, even our seasoned gravity was upset. We laughed more than once.
>
> After the concert, we praised the biwa player to some of our Japanese friends, and asked what it had all been about. To our horror, they informed us that it had told the story of a military expedition, only a few years before, in the mountains near Sendai, which had been overtaken by a terrible blizzard, in which hundreds of officers and soldiers had perished. The dainty interludes were supposed to describe the falling of the snow-flakes. As we realized what an unpardonable offence we had committed, for half the audience, probably, had had relations or friends in the luckless expedition, we made a firm resolution never to imagine again that we comprehended any Japanese music. (pp. 17–19.)

The composition that Hansen heard on this occasion was *Fubuki no teki*, and its story is based on a major disaster that occurred in January 1902, in the Hakkōda mountain range in Aomori prefecture (about 350 km from Sendai).[67] During training in preparation for a possible war with

---

67 Known as the Hakkōda Mountains incident (*Hakkōda-san sōnan jiken*). The lyrics of the piece are by Inoue Tokujō (1869–1944), and the work was first published in

Russia, a unit from the Fifth Infantry Regiment of the Imperial Japanese Army's 8th Division was surprised by a blizzard, and 199 out of 210 soldiers died. In more recent times, the tragedy has inspired novels and films; most recently *Hakkōda Mountains* in 2014. The embarrassment Hansen suffered as a result of her blunder may well have increased her dislike of the *biwa*. All in all, she had little to say about the instrument, despite its obvious popularity with the locals:

> The biwa, to the Japanese, is what the minstrel with his harp was to our forefathers. The biwa songs are old legends of battles and heroes, sometimes historical, sometimes mythical, but always exciting. No concert is really complete, in the opinion of the average Japanese, without one of these lengthy recitations. The shortest one I ever heard lasted twenty minutes; the longest, an hour. The biwa is supposed to be a difficult instrument, and many boys and men study it for years. It is not nearly as common, however, as the koto. It has fewer musical possibilities than the koto, its effect depending almost entirely on the words of the song. (p. 17.)

That Hansen had limited opportunity to experience Japanese music in more traditional settings is evident from her discussion of the last two instruments, the *shamisen* (or *samisen*) and the *shakuhachi*. Unlike Hansen's characterization of the *koto* and the *biwa*, her section on the *shamisen* does not begin with the first time she heard it performed at a formal occasion, for reasons which are obvious from her opening paragraph:

> A certain class of tourists place the samisen first among Japanese instruments, because they hear it first, and sometimes hear nothing else. Unfortunately, this ancient instrument, formerly the delight of court ladies and the study of every girl of the middle and upper classes, has fallen into disrepute, probably because it is used so much by geisha and by people even less respectable than geisha. Only a very few good families are still old-fashioned enough to permit their daughters to study the samisen. Accordingly, as it is not considered proper for teachers to witness geisha performances, it was some time before we had an opportunity to hear this instrument at close range. It was associated in our minds with unpleasant encounters with noisy geisha parties, at the tea-houses or hotels, for no such house excludes these parties. It

---

1905 in a collection by Yoshimizu Tsunekazu. See Shimazu, *Meiji Satsumabiwa uta*, 184–86.

is not pleasant to be kept awake half the night by endless thrumming and screaming, like serenades of cats. It is still more unpleasant if one understands the words of the songs, if one may misuse a good word by calling them such. The paper partitions of the rooms did little to deaden the noises, of course. From a few such experiences, I had gotten the opinion that the samisen must be the very worst of Japanese instruments, and must represent the most rudimentary form of the Japanese musical consciousness. (pp. 19–20.)

That, of course, was also the opinion of the music reformers. Hansen did eventually witness a performance after a dinner party when she 'had the opportunity of hearing some of the older songs, with the dances which always accompany them.' (p. 20.) Clearly not impressed with what she heard, she compared the singing style to that of *biwa* performances; the effect, however, of 'the three women wailing in unison' being 'even more doleful than any single biwa singer could produce'. As with a *koto* performance, she felt that the visual impressions, in this case provided by dancers, were far more pleasant than the music:

> However, our attention was soon directed from these unpleasant noises, by the entrance of three or four girls, in beautiful ancient dresses, who began to act out a little play, describing the feelings and the impressions of pilgrims on first beholding Matsushima, the Pine Islands, known and loved by every Japanese as the loveliest spot in all Japan. Whatever might be the defects of the musical setting, the play was very pretty. With few words, but with much of gesture, dances slow and graceful, and tableaux full of picturesque beauty, the players succeeded very well in recalling to us the spell of Matsushima. (pp. 21–22.)

Like the *shamisen*, the *shakuhachi* did not feature prominently in the settings from which Hansen derived most of her experience of Japanese music. This is, perhaps, surprising, for at the time the *shakuhachi* was becoming increasingly popular, with several teach-yourself manuals being published and new schools (*ryūha*) established, most prominently that of Nakae Tozan.[68] Much of the activity, however, appears to have been in the capital and in the Kansai region, and it may well be that the fashion had not reached Sendai.[69] Another reason may be that,

---

68 See Chapter 8.
69 In the concert programmes, the *shakuhachi* appeared in concerts at the Second High School, which had a *shakuhachi* club, as well as at Tōhoku Ongakuin, as part of a

as Hansen noted, it was not played by women at the time. When she did hear it played, she was not displeased with the sounds she heard, judging it 'the most musical of Japanese instruments' (p. 22). Since the *shakuhachi* is the only instrument of those Hansen described that has gained popularity abroad, her verdict comes as no surprise. She also opined that it was the most difficult of the instruments she described: 'To its difficulty, I can bear direct testimony, having had one in the house for some months without being able to make it produce any kind of a sound whatsoever.' (p. 23.) After a brief description of how the instrument is played, she concluded:

> With this very primitive instrument, a good player can produce a great variety of notes, from husky, breathy tones, suggestive of earth-goblins, mists and mysteries, to soft, clear, high notes, like those of the red-birds of Lawrence. He can make trills, almost as beautiful as those on a flute. Certain effects of the wind he can suggest very vividly. In contrast to the barbarian quality of the koto, the harshness of the biwa, the crudeness of the samisen, he can express melancholy tenderness, pleasing fear, even gentle gayety. He uses, in general, the same Japanese scale as the koto player or the biwa or the samisen singer, but the better quality, the power of expression in his tones gives his instrument and entirely new effect. (p. 24.)

Hansen's positive verdict suggests that she had heard at least one performance by a skilled artist. In concerts, on the other hand, it was usually played in ensembles with one or more *koto* and accompanied by singing. The description of such an occasion with which she concluded her discussion of the *shakuhachi* suggests that she did not appreciate the result:

> In Sendai, at one of the concerts, I heard a much-lauded ensemble of three kotos and a shakuhachi, which lasted about half an hour. During the first part, the shakuhachi played alone a great deal, the kotos coming in as interludes, and, as the player was unusually good, the effect was really musical. At about the middle of the piece there was a long passage, lasting about ten minutes, for the kotos alone. It was neither fast nor slow, nor otherwise interesting, and we were growing very sleepy, when, after a short rest, the three women players, with one voice, and that a powerful one, let out a prolonged mi–a–u! From my front seat, I too gave vent to

---

sankyoku ensemble, but there is no evidence of Hansen having attended concerts at the latter.

one short, not-to-be repressed snort of laughter. It was so exactly like the first prolonged yowl of a cat serenade, that even my years of training in Japanese politeness proved powerless. My Japanese neighbors looked at me in mild surprise; to them there was nothing funny in the sound. It was only the beginning of the voice part of the ensemble, a song which lasted ten or fifteen minutes longer, accompanying the koto and the shakuhachi. (pp. 24–25.)

Indigenous singing receives relatively little attention in the thesis, although Hansen mentions the human voice first as expressing 'the purely Japanese musical consciousness' (p. 4) and states that 'unaccompanied singing is heard everywhere in Japan' (p. 26). (I will discuss singing in connection with Hansen's work as a music teacher.)

Hansen summed up her impressions of native music as follows:

It is music well developed above that of barbarous nations, yet retaining many characteristics of barbarism, in its lack of harmony and of design, its harsh tones, its lack of power to express the higher emotions, usually associated with civilization. It gives one the impression that in this art the nation has lagged far behind. [...] When we try to appreciate Japanese music, the best we can say of any piece or instrument is, that it is pretty good, considering that it is Japanese. Japanese music, unlike Japanese art, cannot be measured by a world standard and called good. The Japanese themselves show their comparatively low musical state, in the fact that they also know no names of great musicians which they can place alongside those of their great artists in other lines. The aesthetic nature of one of the most artistic of all races in the history of the world, seems to have spent its force upon arts other than that of sound. In these arts, while learning from the West, they can give as much as they receive. In music, they can give us practically nothing. (pp. 27–29.)

Here, Hansen essentially reiterated the views expressed by Western intellectuals of her day, based on the assumption of a 'world standard' shaped by Western notions of refined music, such as being able to name 'great musicians' (a concept alien to many cultures and of relatively recent date even in the West). Her conclusion that, in contrast to the pictorial arts, no flow of music from Japan to the West could be imagined, has by now proven wrong. Still, it cannot be denied that the exchange has been profoundly asymmetrical, and Hansen regarded this asymmetry as proof 'that the Japanese themselves realize that something is lacking in their music' (p. 29). What she neglected to mention is that even the most avid promoters of Western music regarded it as superior only in certain specific aspects deemed essential to their (and the Japanese government's) modernization project.

Efforts to Master Western Music

Given Hansen's assumption that Western music was superior, she saw no need to discuss the motives for its adoption by the Japanese, and in her treatment of Japanese efforts to master Western music she merely described the process (pp. 29–63). Unsurprisingly, she highlighted the role of Christian missionaries, including the dissemination of hymns and organs; first portable ones, then the larger reed organs. Music education by missionaries preceded government measures, and by the time she arrived in Japan the effects were noticeable:

> Wherever there was a girls' school, the people began to be familiar with the sound of easy Western music. Here and there, a graduate of a girls' school was able to buy a reed organ for herself, and became a musical wonder to her entire neighborhood. In singing, too, the girls' schools took the lead. Their students practiced incessantly, and in addition to their simple hymn tunes they attempted some two- and three-part work. They did, and are still doing good service in teaching Western songs to many thousands of children in Sunday schools. (p. 33.)

Hansen followed her general survey with a brief description of work at her own school in Sendai, before treating the government's measures to disseminate Western music through the education system. She felt ambivalent about the results, particularly in elementary education. Her impression of singing in primary schools was so negative that she felt it might even be counterproductive. Music education in the public schools, she concluded, had so far done little to improve 'the musical consciousness of the mass of the race' (p. 38). Even teachers at secondary level who had trained at the Tokyo Academy of Music were insufficiently qualified for the task:

> Generally speaking, a teacher does his or her best work during the first year or two after graduation. After that, the carefully trained musical sense seems to deteriorate. Also, it is very rare that a Japanese teacher has sufficient musical sense to learn a new piece without help. They are unable to grow. The deterioration shows itself most markedly in the case of those teachers who sing solos, with piano or organ accompaniments.

> At first, they sing reasonably true to the music, but gradually their songs get out of tune, so to speak, and in a few years they are quite unable to sing anything without flatting and sharping most atrociously. Nevertheless, they are doing a great deal to familiarize the people all over the country with Western music, and some of the part-singing of their pupils is quite correct and even pleasing. (p. 27.)

This brought her to the difficulties of teaching singing (pp. 39–52). Although she discussed this subject more thoroughly and systematically in her later thesis, she had already acquired a keen awareness of the specific challenges faced by music teachers, even those who, like herself, were well-trained and had an intimate knowledge of Western music. Teaching the piano was easier, because determination, patience, and persistence went a long way towards mastery of the instrument. Many Japanese, however, underestimated the difficulties of learning music. Hansen gave several examples to illustrate not only the ignorance but also the conceit of some of the Japanese she encountered, particularly of boys and men. A student from the government college (presumably the Second High School), for example, visited Florence Seiple expecting her to teach him to play a Beethoven sonata for a concert the following week (p. 52), although he had never played the piano before. 'The average Japanese boy', Hansen continued,

> indeed, in his attitude toward Western music, is one of the most disagreeably conceited beings imaginable. Profoundly ignorant of it, and with ears which cannot distinguish one tune from another, he yet patronises or criticizes the girls who have studied the piano for years. His respect for the Western teacher prevents his correcting her to her face, but often the playing of certain hymns by pupils of mine has been 'corrected' by boy students who did not know one note from another. Indeed, I learned indirectly that my own hymn-playing in church had been pronounced incorrect by certain boy students, because the hymns were not played as they sang them! However, in a country where students of English have been known to object to imitating an American teacher's pronunciation, on the ground that imitating a foreigner in such a way is derogatory of their 'national pride', almost anything may be expected.
>
> As for the conceit of the young man who has studied a little Western music, it may be imagined. One of my most ridiculous experiences was with the music teacher of a normal school in a provincial city, himself a graduate of the Ueno school [Tokyo Academy of Music]. The friends I was visiting had asked me to give a piano recital, and had invited a number of guests, mostly Japanese ladies. This music teacher was very

patronizing to these ladies, explaining to them what wonderful things they were to hear, with a pompous air which said, 'Of course, I know all about it.' I had chosen descriptive music from Grieg and Schumann mostly, and before each piece, I tried to give them some idea of what it was about, but I did not mention any names of composers. When I had finished, the music teacher made the usual flowery speech of thanks, and then said that in his school, they often had 'classical music'. Could I play anything of that kind, just to let the ladies know how it sounded? [55] 'Why, certainly', I replied politely, 'I will play you a very famous piece by Schumann.' Turning to my pile of music, I slipped out one of the pieces I had played a few minutes before, and repeated it. He explained to the ladies, with great impressiveness, that this was classical music, and much better than any other kind! About that time, my host found it necessary to retire to the hall, whence he did not reappear for several minutes. (pp. 53–55.)[70]

Girls and young women would occasionally display a similar attitude. One of Hansen's former piano students told her that while her husband had bought her an organ so that she could continue to play, she preferred to play the violin, and after two lessons from a local teacher was now continuing by herself (p. 55). The violin was extremely popular, as Hansen noted in her letters more than once. Next to singing and the reed organ or the piano (for those schools who could afford one, including Miyagi College, where Hansen taught), the violin, played solo or in an ensemble, and performances by brass bands, were the most commonly heard. Both appalled Hansen. She summarized what she called the violin situation' by citing the words of a local missionary's daughter who returned to America to study at an Eastern college. In the seven years the daughter lived in Japan she had heard the violin only in the hands of Japanese, but at college she had the chance to hear a recital by the famous violinist Maud Powell (1867–1920). 'The girl wrote home a vivid description of the concert, which had quite carried her away. She ended it thus, "But, Mamma, I never dreamed before, that the violin was really a musical instrument, like the piano!"' (p. 57.)

---

70 Something of this arrogance survived well into the twentieth century. Yoshihara describes the 'hardcore classical fans' as 'a tribe comprised mostly of highly educated men with a penchant for snobbish pride in specialized knowledge'. See Mari Yoshihara, *Dearest Lenny: Letters from Japan and the Making of the World Maestro* (New York: Oxford University Press, 2019), 66.

The wind bands were no better in Hansen's estimation. Wind bands were among the earliest manifestations of Western music in Sendai, and performed frequently. In a letter to her family in 1909 she referred to 'the wonderful Sendai band which was never known to keep the time for two consecutive measures'.[71] As with singing and the violin, however, intonation rather than rhythm was the main problem:

> Even the brass band is out of tune in Sendai. There is a band, with about ten horns of different kinds, which often plays on the street. No two horns are ever tuned to go together. I had grown up in a family of boys who played every instrument in a brass band, but had been quite ignorant before that it was possible to play a horn entirely out of tune. On the occasion of the revision of the American treaty with Japan, the officials of the prefecture, to show their friendly spirit, invited all the American residents to a great tea party in the Court House. We were seated in the place of honor, just below the judges' seats, and behind us were about five hundred of the 'four hundred' of Sendai. After the usual speeches and replies, a band began to play. Nobody at first knew what it was trying to play, but as our hosts all rose, we did likewise. We had been standing some minutes before I realized that it was the 'Star-spangled Banner' in our honor! My neighbor, who was not especially musical, refused to believe my assertion, but it proved correct, and I was quite elated to have been able, once, to identify one piece by a Sendai band. Their favorite piece, by the way, is 'Marching through Georgia', which they assert, is a Japanese tune! (pp. 57–58.)

Hansen nevertheless ended her discussion of Japanese efforts to study and perform Western music on a positive note. Serious students of Western music, Hansen asserted, 'do excellent work' (p. 59). She was particularly impressed with the dedication of her female piano pupils:

> It is possible that in Germany there may be faithful, careful, persistent practice, equal to that of the average Japanese girl student of organ or piano. I have rarely met it in America. Such a girl does exactly as her teacher tells her, down to the smallest detail. They are natural mimics. (p. 59.)

The expression 'natural mimics' appears in Hansen's letters as well.[72] While this sounds like a tired cliché today, for Hansen this clearly

---

71 KH to her family, 7 March 1909, SRL, Box 1, Folder 22.
72 For example, KH to AFH, 22 September 1907, SRL Box 1, Folder 21.

represented her own first-hand experience, as did the now very familiar observations about their ability to master technique but not musical expression. Her students, she asserted, practised for hours, starting at six o'clock in the morning. They were content to practice scales and finger exercises rather than demanding to play 'pieces'. As a result, they generally became more proficient than the average American pupil. But where musical expression was concerned, 'they were absolutely dependent upon their teacher or upon their American classmate. Not more than one pupil in fifty has any feeling for the expression in the music whose notes she knows perfectly. It has not yet penetrated her musical consciousness.' (p. 61.)[73] Still, her best students did well even on that count, and Hansen concluded that the 'musical consciousness' of the Japanese would eventually be transformed successfully, although she expected it to take several generations:

> Such students as these, in the first generation of music study, give one hope that, some day, the Japanese will be a fairly musical race. At present, I should not call them so, even with regard to their native music. This Japanese music, being a lower form, must inevitably give place to the higher form, the Western music. The Japanese are wise in recognizing this fact. They have patience, energy, enthusiasm on their side. They have begun with the best, with Bach and Beethoven. They know nothing of our musical trash. Whether all these things in their favor will be able to make musicians of them, will take several generations to decide. Meanwhile, the lot of the foreign music teachers among them is full of interest. He, or she, is both watching and helping the complete transformation of the musical consciousness of the Japanese race. (p. 63.)

Hansen thus ended *Musical Consciousness* by summarizing a widely held contemporaneous prejudice. But even in Western music, Hansen distinguished between 'the best' on the one hand and 'musical trash' on the other. Not much more than a decade after Hansen wrote her thesis, the increased availability of gramophone recordings and radio broadcasting gave the Japanese ample opportunity to acquaint themselves with both.

That her Japanese students were quicker to learn the mechanics involved in playing the piano than musical expression is hardly

---

73 Interestingly, some of the Japanese music reformers, including Takaori Shūichi and Tanaka Shōhei, expressed the view that Japanese music had an emotional power that Western music lacked.

surprising, given that the latter requires considerable familiarity with the music by hearing it performed. In early twentieth-century Sendai, opportunities to hear European art music played well were extremely limited. Hansen's descriptions, together with the concert programmes, demonstrate as clearly as the written word can do how the people of Sendai inhabited a musical soundscape where indigenous music and poorly performed foreign music, or blended forms, predominated. Only gradually did this change, as Hansen outlined in her Master's thesis, written fifteen years later and based on almost twenty years' experience of teaching in Sendai. She devoted particular attention to the teaching of singing. Compared to the organ or piano, singing posed the greater challenge.

Teaching Japanese Girls to Sing

'The Japanese are born singers. Good voices and good ears are frequent.' Such was the verdict of Eta Harich-Schneider (1894–1986), a pioneer both of modern Cembalo playing and research on the traditional music of Japan. Being 'born singers', they mastered the Gregorian chant taught to them by the first Christian missionaries in the sixteenth century. The Japanese folk song, moreover, 'in its unimpaired condition has always been the best part of Japanese music'.[74]

Nevertheless, learning to sing Western songs well proved a challenge. Western singing differed fundamentally in two ways: first, the use of the voice and the kind of sound aimed for and, second, the tonal system of the music. A singer has to have a precise idea of what sound quality and what notes she is aiming for and then to learn how to produce them. No wonder then, that the first efforts by Japanese at Western-style singing were unlikely to impress foreign observers. Basil Hall Chamberlain, for example, remarked that August Junker, who taught at the Tokyo Academy of Music from 1899 to 1912, had managed to develop 'a pleasing chorus of some eighty singers out of a chaos of disagreeable nasal voices'.[75]

---

74 Eta Harich-Schneider, *A History of Japanese Music* (London: Oxford University Press, 1973), 460, 594.
75 Basil Hall Chamberlain, *Things Japanese: Being Notes on Various Subjects Connected with Japan*, Yohan Classics (Berkeley, CA: Stone Bridge Press, 2007 (1905)), 368.

Kate Hansen would have been the first to acknowledge that this was no mean feat. In her early letters and in *Musical Consciousness* her comments about singing were, if anything, even more scathing than her descriptions of instrumental performances, and she made no attempt to maintain academic detachment in the descriptions of spontaneous singing that followed (p. 26). After two vivid accounts of men breaking into 'gruesome sounds', or a 'howl' on their way home in the evening, she concluded: 'Groups of men on the street, making noises which in this country would result in their making a speedy acquaintance with a police station, are probably neither drunk nor disorderly, but are only giving vent to their feelings in some heroic ballad.' (pp. 26–27.) Hansen must, or course, have been well aware that drunken youths in the street hardly reach *bel canto* standards in the West either. Nevertheless, she felt (or claimed to have felt) the sounds to be so alien that only her experience after some years in Japan enabled her to identify them as singing.

Hansen was more nuanced when describing the singing of Western songs. Even at missionary schools the quality of teaching varied and depended on the initiative of individuals. Many of the first missionaries, Hansen reported, did not even believe that the Japanese could learn to sing.[76] Her own first impressions of singing by the girls at Miyagi College were not entirely negative. In a letter to her sister Alpha, dated 15 September 1907, a week after her arrival in Sendai, she wrote: 'Then they sang an English song, a hymn of some sort. I was surprised at the way they sang. There was no attempt at part singing. But their voices were very clear and they did not screech or strain.'[77] A week later, commenting on another performance at the school, she wrote that the girls 'sang beautifully, in a high, clear voice. The Japanese girls are natural mimics, as I found out.'[78] A few months later, however, she was more critical: 'I sympathize with you about the boys' voices – but they can't hold a candle to the girls, who flat and drag and everything else. However, when I hear Japanese music, and realize that's the kind

---

[76] Hansen, 'The Japanese Are Learning to Sing', 235. (First published in *The Outlook of Missions*, Vol. VI, No. 3 (March 1914), pp. 129–30, 138; The Reformed Church Messenger, February 19, 1914, pp. 2, 20.) See also Hansen, *Musical Consciousness*, 29–30.

[77] Spencer Research Library Box 1, Folder 21.

[78] To Alpha Hansen, 22 September 1907, Box 1, Folder 21.

they've inherited, I wonder they can do as well as they do.'[79] In *Musical Consciousness* she wrote about those early years:

> In the little churches that began to arise, and especially in the Sunday-schools, hymn-singing was carried out with great vigor and enthusiasm, although the tunes were more or less difficult to recognize; neither pitch nor time being much regarded. The tunes, such as they were, became so popular, that many of them were taken over by the Buddhists, supplied with new words, and used in the Sunday-schools started in imitation of the Christian institutions. This practice still persists, and I often heard tunes from the Buddhist boys' school across the street from us, which I could recognize, more or less easily, as familiar American Sunday-school airs. Often the words would be almost unchanged, except by the substitution of the word Buddha for Christ. (pp. 30–31.)

She could, however, report that the situation was improving, thanks to developments like the publication of the union hymnal for all the protestant churches, the increasing number of trained American teachers, and the replacement of portable baby reed organs with larger ones or even with pianos imported from Germany in the 'more advanced' schools (pp. 32–33).[80]

Progress in the government schools, on the other hand, appeared slow to Hansen. By the time she arrived in Japan, graduates from the Tokyo Academy of Music were teaching at high schools (especially those for girls) and teacher training colleges nationwide, but most teachers at elementary schools had minimal training and the results of their efforts reflected this:

> But generally, the singing is done unaccompanied. As few of the teachers are able themselves to sing a major scale, or to tell whether one is sung correctly, the Western singing in public schools is generally unrecognizable as such. Indeed, it is a question in my mind whether this wholesale teaching of Western music by entirely incompetent teachers does not actually hinder Japanese advancement in that art. It is more difficult to teach a Western tune to a graduate of the public schools than to a little child who has never gone to school. So far, as regards Western

---

79 To Alpha Hansen, 20 January 1908, Box 1 folder 22.
80 Hansen was, presumably, referring to *Sambika* (Hymn book). 'Prepared by a Union committee' and published by Kyōbunkan in 1908 (Romaji edition). Data from the National Diet Library. The preface is dated 1903.

music, the musical consciousness of the mass of the race does not appear to have been improved by the public schools. (p. 38.)

The government, in Hansen's estimation, failed to 'recognize the magnitude of the task'. She compared it to teaching a new foreign language in her thesis, *Experiences in Founding and Developing a Music School in Japan* (henceforth *Experiences*), submitted in 1927 as part of the requirements for the Master of Music and updated in 1933.[81] *Experiences* covers some of the same ground as *Musical Consciousness*, but is more concise and tightly structured. The style is sober and more appropriate to an academic thesis. Hansen presents a thorough and systematic account of her efforts to teach her pupils to sing and her work at Miyagi in general. By the time she wrote the thesis, her hopes of a 'fully-fledged conservatory', expressed in a letter to her sister already in 1908,[82] had become a reality. Training at college level, with a three-year higher course and a two-year preparatory course, was added in 1916. 'From next April on, we will have the best music course of any mission school in Japan', Hansen proudly reported to her sister.[83] The course, including the entrance requirements, were based on the one at Kansas University, adapted to local circumstances. Requirements for entry into the postgraduate course were so demanding that in practice, 'nobody but our own very best graduates can get into the higher department, so it will never, or at least not for a long time, have more than five or six in a class [...].'[84]

---

81   Hansen, *Experiences*, 11–12. Mensendiek's biography includes a substantially abridged version of the thesis. See Mensendiek, *To Japan with Love*, 121–31. Mensendiek does not give any information about the manuscript he consulted, which does not seem to be the same as the one in the SRL. For example, in Mensendiek's version (which is also included in Bales' biography), Hansen describes *Musical Consciousness* as an 'essay' rather than a 'thesis'. The most obvious differences are the only musical example with staff notations he cites (although this looks like a mistake by an uninformed copyist). My discussion is based on the manuscript in the SRL.
82   KH to AFH, 21 June 1908, SRL Box 1, Folder 22.
83   KH to AFH, 12 February 1916, SRL, Box 1, Folder 28.
84   KH to AFH, 12 February 1916, SRL, Box 1, Folder 28. Training at college level, with a three-year higher course and a two-year preparatory course, was added in 1916. For the higher course, students had to demonstrate the 'ability to sing at sight, with accurate pitch and rhythm, exercises of the grade of the Ginn Third Music Reader'. On the piano they had to master the first book of Czerny, Op. 299, Heller Op. 47 as well as 'Bach works preparatory to the Inventions, and easy sonatas'. (*Experiences*, pp. 25–26.)

The school now offered a level of training that could compete with the Tokyo Academy of Music and was only matched by one other missionary school, Kobe College, which had established a music department in 1906. By 1924 Hansen could report to the Mission Board: 'We are getting the benefits of all the years of careful work done in our school before the Japanese public had developed an understanding of western music. That pioneer period in music education has passed.'[85] Hansen thus completed *Experiences* fully aware that Western music at Miyagi and in Sendai had come a long way in the twenty years since her arrival.

The path to success, however, was arduous. Missionary boards, like the Japanese government, did not fully realize the difficulties, Hansen asserted, and had failed to send trained teachers. Moreover, music teachers, like teachers of the English language, were apt to lose their own sense of what was correct.[86] To prove her point, she illustrated the difference between the tonality of Western and what she called 'Sino-Japanese' music by describing the popular *koto* piece *Rokudan*, basing her analysis of its tonality on an edition in Western notation.[87] She concluded, 'It is this music, so radically different from Western music, which is even now being heard constantly in the homes, the tea-houses, the theatres and the temples. It formed and still forms the "musical mother-tongue" of the great majority of the Japanese people.' (*Experiences*, p. 11.) Summarizing her early experience in Sendai, Hansen wrote: 'My most vivid musical recollection of those first months and years is of the intense pain I suffered in class, in chapel, wherever Japanese tried to make Western music. The school authorities, Japanese and Americans alike, saw, or rather heard, nothing wrong.' (*Experiences*, p. 16.)

Hansen had already pinpointed specific obstacles ('defects') in *Musical Consciousness*, naming four: 1) the failure of female students to open their mouth; 2) yelling; 3) inability to grasp triple time (although not triplets); 4) pitch. About the first, she stated that Japanese etiquette forbade a woman 'to open her teeth when she talks. This speaking and singing with the teeth firmly closed is so much a habit with all Japanese

---

85   Mensendiek, *To Japan with Love*, 49.
86   On the analogy of learning foreign music and foreign languages, see also Alison M. Tokita, 'Bi-Musicality in Modern Japanese Culture', *International Journal of Bilingualism* 18, no. 2 (2014 (2012)): 159–74, https://doi.org/10.1177/1367006912458394
87   Most likely the one published by the Tokyo Academy of Music: see Chapter 6.

girls, that they are really unconscious of it.' (p. 39.) Still, the habit was relatively easy to deal with, since it could be overcome by having them sing with their finger between their teeth. (*Musical Consciousness*, pp. 39–40; Hansen, *Experiences*, pp. 18–19.)

The second problem she described as 'the idea that Western singing means yelling with all the power of their lungs'. She continued,

> Just why this idea should be so universal, I have never been able to understand fully. [...] In public schools, and in Sunday schools wherever permitted, the accepted method of singing a Western song is to bellow it forth, with all the power of harsh chest tones, until a note is reached so high as to make this impossible. Then there comes a break in the voices, and each singer whatever note he or she can [sic], in strained falsetto. (p. 41.)

In a previous letter to her mother in May 1910, Hansen had expressed her satisfaction with the results of a singing lesson she had given to around one hundred children at a Sunday school in what she described as a 'back-woods' (although it may only have been one of the remoter parts of the city). She succeeded in getting them to 'sing their tune straight, and with a musical tone too – you don't hear that often, for in their common schools they are taught to sing at the top of their lungs and the key doesn't matter at all.'[88] Possibly, the habit derived from the custom of reciting texts aloud together as a means of rote-learning in traditional education, because in a previous letter Hansen had remarked on the noise that she regularly heard from a school she passed in Karuizawa: 'When one goes by, there's a deafening noise of children's voices, for they keep up the, "good old way" in this school of having all the pupils study out loud, and the one with the loudest voice is presumably the best student. The custom seems to have been given up in the Sendai schools.'[89]

At any rate, belting out *shōka* may well have been common, especially among boys. A vivid impression of a first singing class with a new, male teacher in upper elementary school in 1895 is given by the anarchist theorist and labour activist Ōsugi Sakae (1885–1923). Contrasting the

---

88   KH to her mother, 29 May 1910, SRL Box 1, Folder 24.
89   KH to AFH, Karuizawa, 8 August 1909, Box 1, Folder 23.

new arrival with their previous, female teacher, Ōsugi corroborates Hansen's observations,

> Sitting there in front of the organ with his dark face, he held his body erect and his chest stuck out like a soldier's. We waited eagerly to hear what sort of sound was going to come from that organ. It wasn't particularly different from the sound produced by the women teachers with their gentle faces. Yet despite the dark face and dishevelled hair, his large fingers raced across the keys with a liveliness and skill that were not at all clumsy, and his playing gave us a feeling of exhilaration. Then he began to sing. His wide mouth filled his whole dark face and from it came a deep bass that reverberated throughout the classroom. Up to then we had heard only women teachers sing, their lips pursed and voices barely audible. Now under his influence we became exuberant, opened our mouths as wide as possible and sang as loudly as we could.[90]

The difficulties with rhythm observed by Hansen, particularly triple time rhythms (pp. 42–43), are attested in other sources. Foreigner participants in the balls held at the Rokumeikan back in the 1880s remarked on the Japanese dancers' problems with the waltz.[91] But Hansen observed problems even with hymns (not known for their rhythmic complexity), and, during the rehearsal of Mendelssohn's *Wedding March* for a pupil's wedding, the bridegroom 'went along with his head down. anxiously watching his feet and counting time until Okayama San, who seems to be O Masa San's best friend at present, got alarmed lest he do the same at the ceremony.'[92] Of course, in this case, apprehension rather than a lacking sense of rhythm may have been the cause. The same o-Masa-san, now Masa Sato, wrote about another wedding, where she herself played Mendelssohn's march and neither bride nor groom could keep time and arrived at the altar far too early: 'Probably they lost their minds and their feet were going fast.' She explained, 'As Miss Hansen knows well, Japanese are very stupid to keep time to the 6/8 time. Miss Hansen has a hard time to let the school girls keep time straight when she plays

---

90 Sakae Ōsugi and Byron K. Marshall, *The Autobiography of Ōsugi Sakae translated with annotations by Byron K. Marshall*, Voices from Asia; 6, (Berkeley, Calif.: University of California Press, 1992), 42.
91 Examples in Margaret Mehl, 'Dancing at the Rokumeikan — A New Role for Women?', in *Japanese Women: Emerging from Subservience, 1886–1945*, ed. Gordon Daniels and Hiroko Tomida (Folkestone, Kent: Global Oriental, 2005).
92 KH to AFH, 23 April 1910, Box 1, Folder 24.

march.' Chieko (presumably her daughter), on the other hand, was good at keeping time, 'even to the 6/8 time march.'⁹³

Nevertheless, rhythm was relatively easy to correct, as Hansen reported in an early letter to her sister:

> [...] and to their other great fault, not keeping time, I've been able to apply a remedy since we've had the chapel piano, for I make so much noise they simply have to keep time. We've put them through a regular siege of the songs they were the worst on; I've played the bass so heavy that it sounds like a bass drum and they can't help keeping time; and at last I've got them 'broken in' so that when I begin a prelude, they listen as attentively as if their lives depended on it, and come in in exactly the same time, for they've learned I won't either wait or hurry for them. But such times as I've had bringing it about! I'm afraid some mornings the foreigners present haven't gotten much out of chapel, for sometimes I've gone through a whole song, perhaps with the whole school a half measure or so behind me, or afterward, when the more musical ones began to 'catch on,' there have been whole songs when part of the school sang all the way through in one kind of time and part in another! Two or three songs I would never let them sing – 'Lead, Kindly Light' is one, but they persisted in choosing it at prayers, so I've just succeeded in getting them so they can sing it and actually keep together! They sing low, though, in fear and trembling, and listen to the piano at every note. They'll get it, though; and there's one comfort, so long as the piano and I stay, we'll never have this kind of a siege again, for the majority will always know how to sing, and the rest will learn from them.⁹⁴

Pitch, on the other hand, presented the greatest difficulty and the one on which most of the efforts described in *Experiences* were concentrated. Hansen mentioned inability to sing or play at correct pitch in several early letters. Of a Sunday school she attended soon after her arrival, taught by o-Masa-san, she wrote to her family, 'the Japanese don't seem to have any idea of feeling or the key. O Masa San led and the other girl played, and they did their best, but those youngsters just opened their mouths and yelled, [...].'⁹⁵

---

93   Miyagi Jogakkō, 6 April 1916, Masa Sato to 'My dear friend' (AFH?), SRL, Box 1, Folder 28.
94   KH to AFH, 21 June 1908, SLR Box 1, Folder 22.
95   KH to her family, 6 October 1907, SRL, Box 1, Folder 21. There seems to be a bit more on the subject, but next part of the letter is illegible.

Despite the daunting obstacles, Hansen could report a measure of improvement even in her earliest letters. She was greatly helped by the appointment of Florence L. Seiple in 1908. Trained as a singer at the Peabody Institute and in Berlin, she taught music alongside Hansen until at least 1931.[96] As early as June 1908 Hansen wrote to her sister about a 'really wonderful change in the chapel singing this term; and the other piano. [sic]'. 'Mrs Seiple', she continued, 'has certainly done wonders in improving the quality of the voices this term – they imitate her and they don't flat any more, to speak of – [...].'[97]

Getting their pupils to sing in tune consistently remained a challenge, however. Hansen devoted systematic efforts to investigating the cause even in her earliest years in Sendai when she could not concentrate all her time on teaching music. *Experiences* contains a concise account of her conclusions. (*Experiences*, pp. 17–22.)

She soon ruled out 'lack of interest or effort' in the face of her pupils' obvious determination and enthusiasm. Likewise, 'lack of knowledge of musical theory'; the students had learnt some rudiments of musical theory in primary school, on which they could build by studying the available books. Lack of rhythmic sense, being comparatively easy to resolve, she also ruled out.

Eventually Hansen identified two 'fundamental defects'. The second of these, not mentioned in her earlier thesis, was 'the lack of power of paying concentrated attention. Japanese girls were not expected to think very deeply' (*Experiences*, pp. 17–22). Even this was relatively easy to resolve, by strict drills, making them sing alone during lessons, and generally bringing home to them the realization that studying music was as serious and difficult as studying English or maths. In a postcard addressed to her sister and dated 13 December 1914 she describes how she went about this task:

> They've gotten to the point where they beg me to just let them have plenty of chances to sing alone in class – when it used to take all my diplomacy to induce them to try it alone on very special occasions. You see, I flunked about a fourth of the school last spring! I enjoyed doing it too, for they'd

---

96 She was married to William George Seiple, who taught at Tohoku College from 1905 to 1936 and acted as director at Miyagi from March 1908 to 1911.
97 KH to AFH, 21 June 1908, SLR, Box 1, Folder 22.

gotten the idea while I was gone that they didn't have to work in music. I believe they are convinced now that they were mistaken.[98]

The first and greatest 'fundamental defect', however, was pitch, and this could only be remedied by intensive, constant practice that targeted its root. Hansen's thorough investigation revealed that difficulties with pitch were specific rather than general. She tested her incoming students and discovered a number of what she called 'deaf spots' (*Experiences*, p. 19). Most of them centred on the ascending major scale. Within this the most difficult succession was from the sixth to the seventh to the eighth degree. The next most difficult point was the (major) third step; most students had difficulties distinguishing a major third from a minor third.

A key experience that gave Hansen valuable insights into the problem of pitch occurred when she practised Schubert's *Erlking* with her best chorus in 1910 (in a three-part arrangement).[99] In October 1910, she wrote to her sister:

> I've attempted a most ambitious thing in the chorus arrangement – three-part – of Schubert's Erlking. It really isn't much harder for them, though, than a single major tune that any American youngster could sing. Their ideas of difficulty aren't ours, anyway, and easy intervals for us are next to impossible for them, and vice versa. But the Erlking appeals to them mightily, and they get into a white heat of enthusiasm at every practice – as do I![100]

She again mentioned rehearsing 'Erlking' in a subsequent letter, and after the successful performance of the work, she wrote at some length about what she called an 'experiment'.[101] She had made them learn it all by ear, 'just to see if that would get the Japanese flatting out of their voices – and it did; there was only one false note in it and that an inconspicuous one. But it took from a half hour to an hour's practice every day for two months!' The tutor who helped her drill the students 'developed such an ear that on the night of the performance she said she couldn't hear a thing but the one false note!' She described the tutor,

---

98 KH to AFH, 13 December 1914, SRL, Folder 27.
99 Hansen, *Experiences*, 19. Hansen wrote, 'in about my fifth year', but according to her letters home, she rehearsed the work in her fourth year, autumn 1910.
100 KH to AFH, 9 October 1910, SRL Box 1, Folder 24.
101 KH to AFH, 3 December 1910, Box 1, Folder 24.

whom she could trust to conduct individual practice, as a 'great help in getting the kinks out of the altos, who <u>would</u> flat on sol – do every time it came in'. The tutor did equally well in drilling the altos in a Brahms song, 'when I'd despaired'. Summarizing the students' strengths and weaknesses Hansen told her sister,

> you should have heard the way they'd all sing augmented seconds and all such outlandish intervals perfectly true on the first trial, and flat and get away miles from the tune whenever it struck a major scale! Beside sol-do, the thing that floored them most was la-ti-do. They were <u>weeks</u> getting that! But those chromatic passages were play to them, and the queer intervals at the end they sang unaccompanied, with almost no trouble at all. It was an interesting experiment; but I'm glad it's over. [102]

When she discussed the experience in *Musical Consciousness*, she expressed her surprise at the ease with which the fifty girls memorized the three-part arrangement and mastered its at times intricate rhythms: 'The passages with the eight notes in the song against the three in the accompaniment were no more difficult than any other passage.' (pp. 33–34.) But what intrigued her even more was the immense difficulty they had with short ascending scale passages, in contrast to the diminished fifth in the last phrase of the melody, which they sang correctly 'from the very first time they heard it, while an American singer, who was learning at the same time, had considerable trouble with this interval.' (p. 46.) In *Experiences* (pp. 19–20) she described her observations in more detail, again contrasting the difficulty the girls had with the ascending notes in the passage, 'Willst, feiner Knabe du mit mir gehn?' with the ease with which they mastered, 'In seinen Armen das Kind war todt', singing the final phrase 'with absolutely true pitch after I had played it for them once on the piano'. Even after extended and intensive practice, however, the problem had not been overcome for good: two weeks later 'when the concert was repeated unexpectedly with only two or three days for practice, they sang it almost as badly as at the beginning.'

It has to be said, though, that the difficulties with the scale passage described by Hansen here may well be experienced by European or North American choirs, depending on the age and experience of the

---

102 KH to AFH, 3 December 1910, Box 1, Folder 24.

singers and the musical context.[103] Possibly, after years in Japan, Hansen overestimated the abilities of the average American church or school choir.

Having identified the specific problems with pitch, Hansen set about developing a remedy. After returning from her first furlough with a Mus. B., she put together a series of books with ear-drill exercises, similar to those of the Ginn series for teaching music reading that the school had adopted as text books in music theory,[104] but based on the specific difficulties her students wrestled with. She was helped in her drill work by competent assistants, as her letters about rehearsing *Erlkönig* show. In *Experiences* (p. 24) she described how she recruited tutors from the most promising graduate students whom she had singled out for informal classes, covering 'all the mechanical parts of teaching the subject'. When she compared the students' achievements in the written ear-drills with those in their other subjects, she discovered that 'musical intelligence and general intelligence', and particularly English reading, corresponded closely.

Relentless ear-drilling, combined with written exercises and regular graded tests produced results,

> even beyond my hopes. The singing classes learned very quickly what concentration meant. Remarkable accuracy in pitch was developed in a year or so. Chapel and entertainments ceased to be painful. Real singing became possible, and independent singing of parts. I was able to organize a choir of schoolgirls to sing every Sunday in the largest church in Sendai, learning a hymn or a simple anthem in two or three parts for each service. (*Experiences*, p. 23.)

Letters to her family described other early successes. At a show in November 1914, a few months after her return from her first furlough, the students performed a pantomime based on Longfellow's *Hiawatha*. The accompanying 'incidental music' included a song by Charles Wakefield Cadman, 'slightly altered in the title to fit the proprieties in Japan'. The song (sung as Hiawatha stands by Minnehaha's grave) is

---

[103] This was confirmed to me by Mark Baumann, organist of the German church St Petri in Copenhagen, who has experience with both adults' and children's choirs (conversation, August 2016).

[104] Ginn's *The New Educational Music Course* (1906) by James Mc Laughlin and W. W. Gilchrist.

billed in the programme as 'Along the Spirit Way', which is the last line of the verse. The actual title is, 'Far Off I Hear a Lover's Flute', one of Cadman's *Four American Indian Songs* (Op. 45). Hansen gave a glowing evaluation of the singer's performance:

> The girl has a really good voice, and can get good tones up to high a; and Mrs. Seiple drilled her. You should have heard her do that last octave jump, landing absolutely true on high g, with a very soft tone, then swelling into a long full tone and letting it die away very gradually. It was the best thing of the kind we ever had here.[105]

From Hansen's description we can conclude that her student, in mastering the challenges posed by the deceptively simple melody in terms of intonation and breath control, succeeded in conveying the kind of expression Hansen otherwise found performances by Japanese tended to lack.

The best instrumental performance in the same show, wrote Hansen, was a sonata played on two pianos (four hands), the allegro from the Mozart's Piano Sonata No. 5 in G major, K. 283 with an added accompaniment of a second piano by Edvard Grieg. Compared to singing, Hansen discussed her experiences with teaching the piano and organ only briefly in *Experiences*, presumably because they presented less of a challenge.

> During all this time, I had been teaching piano and organ. Mechanically, the results had been good. Japanese girls as a rule have good hands, are excellent mimics, and are far more zealous in practicing than American girls. Memorizing had, however, been almost impossible, and of course spontaneous expression was almost unknown. After the introduction of ear-drill, memorizing became very easy. Japanese girls have naturally good memories, for their former education, especially in Japanese music, consisted almost wholly of memorizing. All that was necessary was for them to learn really to <u>hear</u> the Western music they were studying. (*Experiences*, pp. 24–25.)

Thanks to effective training of the musical memory, a student from the first graduating class of the newly established college department astonished her audience by playing Beethoven's entire 'Moonlight'

---

[105] KH to AFH, 30 November 1914. Details of the pieces performed according to the programme: 'Twenty-third Anniversary of the Miyagi Jo Gakko Literary Society', 27 November 1914. SRL, Box 5, folder 13.

Sonata, 'the one Western piece known by reputation to every educated Japanese' (*Experiences,* p. 27) from memory. Two years later, another student gave the first graduating recital at which she both sang and played the piano, performing 'a Bach Fugue, a Beethoven sonata, several modern pieces, and the last movement of the Mendelssohn G minor concerto' from memory (*Experiences,* p. 28).

Singing, meanwhile, progressed to the point that the school could boast a chorus of eighty to one hundred voices, with all members having passed an examination in sight-singing equivalent to the entry requirements for the music course. In 1926 they performed Mendelssohn's *St Paul Oratorio*. According to Hansen, 'it marked a step in the musical history of Japan, for it was the first time that a Japanese chorus had sung the whole of a standard oratorio.' (*Experiences,* p. 32.) Even the contralto solos were sung by a Japanese graduate from the college course. Voice graduates, like the piano graduates, had to prepare graduating recitals (Hansen attached programmes of the 1933 recitals in the appendix of the thesis).[106]

Some of the school's graduates stayed on as teachers in the music department. At the time Hansen wrote *Experiences*, the department usually employed six Japanese teachers in addition to three conservatoire-trained Americans. To prevent the problem of deteriorating skills soon after graduation that Hansen had observed earlier, the teachers were carefully supervised and given sufficient opportunity for study and practice in the school's studios. In addition, they each received a weekly lesson with their head of department. According to Hansen, these measures were effective: 'Although Japanese music teachers as a rule do their best work during the first year or so after graduation, this policy has made our Japanese faculty increasingly efficient the longer they teach.' (*Experiences,* p. 34.) Retaining the Japanese teachers, however, was a problem, as they usually gave up their job when they married, 'and music teachers seem to be especially desirable in the marriage market' (*Experiences,* p. 34).

Besides training school teachers, the music department obviously laid stress on training church musicians who could play the organ and instruct children at Sunday schools to sing hymns. Hansen reported that

---

106 Hansen also began to refer to the music department as a 'Conservatory' from around 1926: see Mensendiek, *To Japan with Love*, 54.

Miyagi was currently providing organists and pianists for about twenty-five Sunday schools, and that she herself made an effort to visit one of these schools each Sunday to give advice to her students. In this work too, Hansen reported remarkable achievements, citing the National Secretary of the Christian Literature Society, who, during a visit to the Sendai churches remarked, 'Such church music is impossible in Japan anywhere outside of Sendai.' (*Experiences*, p. 35.) Hansen, however, did not let herself become complacent: 'Ear-drill, largely written, continues to be the foundation of all instruction. "Eternal vigilance" is certainly the price of true pitch in Japan.' (*Experiences*, p. 32.)

Hansen's detailed description of the challenges she faced as a teacher of Western music to the Japanese, the measures she developed to overcome them, and the successes she achieved, provide us with a clear idea of what a tortuous process the adoption of Western music was for the Japanese and how slow it was in the early years—something that we rarely hear about in the predominant narrative of the success story. Ultimately, however, Kate Hansen, like her fellow missionaries, regarded mastery of Western music as a means rather than an end in itself. In this they resembled the Confucian-educated Meiji leaders who advocated music as a tool for reforming the people's manners and customs. In her reports to the mission board, Hansen identified teacher training as one of the department's most important tasks, both in order to secure the future of the school and to extend the influence of Christian teachers.[107] Even in her academic thesis, Hansen made no bones about this: 'From the beginning, the historical relation of Western music to Christianity has been made clear to all music students. The majority of those entering the Conservatory are already identified with some church, and all of the others have become Christians before graduation.' (*Experiences*, p. 34.)

But while both the Japanese leaders and the foreign missionaries promoted music as a tool for their respective non-musical ends, Hansen's personal passion for music extended well beyond her work as a missionary and educator. This fact would not have been lost on the Japanese. They would also have observed that making music was an important leisure activity for foreigners; one that was, moreover,

---

[107] Reports for 1934–36; 1942, quoted in Mensendiek, *To Japan with Love*, 61–62, 75–76.

perceived as entirely respectable—at least when it was enjoyed in genteel homes, in church, and at public concerts.

Hansen's characterizations of the different kinds of native music serve as a useful reminder of how different traditional Japanese and modern Western music were. It is difficult to gauge whether the fact that most of her hearing experience took place in concerts rather than traditional settings diminished or increased the sense of alienness. Either way, Hansen's experience of alienness reminds us that most Japanese must have experienced similar feelings when confronted with Western music. The difference, however, was that Hansen had no qualms about dismissing Japanese music as backwards, while for the Japanese the alien music represented modern times. Hansen's attitude towards Japanese music was, moreover, to a significant extent shared by the Japanese elite.

Given the alienness of Western music, it is hardly surprising that initial efforts by the Japanese to perform it produced mixed results. But the examination of concert programmes in the following chapter demonstrates the zeal with which local actors in Sendai organized concerts and performed in them. Arguably, the quality of the resulting performances was less important than the act of performing.

11. The World in Sendai

> Nevertheless, it is really thanks to her [Kate Hansen] that we can savour such complex harmonies even here in the back and beyond of Tohoku. If it were not for her, this gathering would probably have amounted to nothing.[1]

> Sendai is an extraordinary place; a place where really serious concerts are held.[2]

Before recorded music became widely available, music could only be heard through live performances, and concerts represented an important vehicle for disseminating Western music, as well as certain indigenous genres. But the public concert, a modern institution imported from the West, did more than that. We might look upon it as a 'creative space' where the people of Sendai encountered the wider world.[3] While the literal space of the concert is a confined venue, the 'creative space' has no fixed boundaries. Within it, at a particular historical moment, people and their ideas interact, and all sides of the encounter are affected, with unpredictable outcomes. The character of the interactions is not necessarily defined by a particular power structure, or by notions of original and copy; the foreign and the indigenous mix and overlap in complex ways.[4] Concerts thus represented a space in which music was

---

1 Masao [pseud.], 'Ongakukai hihyō: jūgatsu sanjūichi nichi yūshi ongakukai zakkan', *Shōshikai zasshi* 83 (1908): 149.
2 'Kakuchi no ongaku', *Ongakukai* 225 (July 1920).
3 For the concept of 'creative space', see Denise Gimpel, 'Introduction', in *Creative Spaces: Seeking the Dynamics of Change in China*, ed. Denise Gimpel, Bent Nielsen, and Paul Bailey (Copenhagen: NIAS Press, 2012); Denise Gimpel, *Chen Hengzhe: A Life between Orthodoxies* (Lanham, Maryland: Lexington Books, 2015), 5–7. The title and some of the content of this chapter were inspired by Jeanice Brooks' paper, 'The World in My Parlour: Imperial Encounters in Sentimental Songs' (20th Congress, International Musicological Society, Tokyo, 2017).
4 Gimpel, 'Introduction', 2, 5, 6–7.

performed and listened to. Music, however is always 'music with', and the effects of staging or attending concerts do not result exclusively from the music itself.[5]

Most of the concerts examined in this chapter were staged in schools by students and teachers and with the aim of presenting achievements in the mastery of (chiefly Western) music and of educating the local public. Arguably, concerts did more than that: they linked the local people to the wider world, and they did so in three ways. First, the concerts were an occasion for direct encounters between the Japanese organizers, performers, and listeners with members of the foreign population, particularly the teachers at the missionary schools. Second, a significant part of the repertoire performed and listened to consisted of works played and enjoyed worldwide. Third, many of the pieces performed evoked foreign places or past times; other worlds, in short, and thus had the potential to widen the horizons of the imagination of the listeners. Much has been said about the nation as an imagined community. The world of nations and the global community too are imaginary constructs, as is the notion of modernity. Although the commonalities of modernity include major political, social, and economic changes,[6] another defining characteristic is the idea of progress and the consciousness of a major rupture with the past and traditional ways of life.[7] In the face of the experience of loss that results from this rupture, 'music becomes a site of both nostalgia and anticipation'.[8] The concerts enabled participants, whether performers or audience, to experience themselves as part of the global community and to participate in 'a globally shared culture of modernity'.[9]

---

5   See Tia DeNora and Gary Ansdell, 'What Can't Music Do?', *Psychology of Well-Being: Theory, Research and Practice* 4, no. 23 (2014): 6, https://doi.org/10.1186/s13612-014-0023-6

6   See Chapter 1.

7   Hugh De Ferranti and Alison Tokita, eds., *Music, Modernity and Locality in Prewar Japan: Osaka and Beyond* (Farnham, Surrey: Ashgate, 2013), 10, https://doi.org/10.4324/9781315596907 The experience of a rupture with the past is also a major theme in Julian Johnson's analysis of musical modernity. See Julian Johnson, *Out of Time: Music and the Making of Modernity* (Oxford: Oxford University Press, 2015), 13–46, https://doi.org/10.1093/acprof:oso/9780190233273.001.0001 .

8   Daniel Chua, quoted in Johnson, *Out of Time*, 16.

9   De Ferranti and Tokita, *Music, Modernity and Locality*, 10.

By the early twentieth century, concerts featuring exclusively or predominantly Western music were becoming a fixture of cultural life in Sendai. Significantly, the early concerts featured predominantly Japanese or blended (*wayō setchū*) music. The concert as an institution thus predated the public performance of Western music. In the course of the 1920s, visiting artists from overseas began to perform in Sendai, while the impact of gramophone recordings and radio broadcasts made itself felt. Recordings separated the performer from the listener. They could and did profoundly change the experience of listening to a live performance; increasingly, the works performed at the concerts were already familiar to the audience from listening to recordings. Thus the period examined in this chapter, while largely determined by the availability of concert programmes in *Ongakukai*, represents a particular, transitional, historical moment: a time when a measure of familiarity with certain kinds of Western music, namely *shōka* and music played by bands, had been acquired, but the range of music performed was limited and the standard of performance modest.

Admittedly, we are on uncertain ground for several reasons. *Ongakukai* was published between January 1908 and November 1923 and reported on concerts held in Sendai between 26 October 1907 and 19 February 1921: forty-five in all, between two and six for each year.[10] The published programmes (most reports included a programme) represent but a fraction of the concerts held in Sendai. The number of unreported concerts is impossible to tell, although information from local newspapers and other sources might fill some of the gaps.[11] Some reports included a general characterization of the music scene. For example, in the April 1908 issue, it was reported that there were fewer concerts than in the previous year: while four to five concerts were held between January and March in 1907, in the current year the only event that could be called a concert was the seventeenth concert of the Second High School.[12] Whether or not a report was published presumably depended on the initiative of individuals and, perhaps, the number of items submitted to *Ongakukai* for publication from sources throughout

---

10 For a chronological list of the concerts reported in *Ongakukai*, see the appendix.
11 I have not been able to examine in detail reporting in local papers. From what I did see, coverage in *Kahoku shinpō*, for example, was at best patchy.
12 'Sendai-shi no gakukai', *Ongakukai* 1, no. 4 (1908): 50.

the country. Programmes were published after the event, but may well have been prepared in haste and without confirming details with the performers, which would account for the lack of detail or the remark 'to be determined'. Individual items, moreover, may well have been swapped around or changed on the day. As an exact record of any given concert, programmes may therefore not always be reliable, but they do give us an idea of overall trends.

Identifying individual items on the programmes represents another challenge. Even the idea of an exact specification of the pieces to be performed at a given event may well have seemed outlandish at the time, and the programmes examined here rarely provide the details we expect from concert programmes today. Typically, they describe the items as instrumental (naming the instrument or instruments) or vocal; as solos, ensembles (duet, trio etc.), 'orchestra', or chorus. It is not always clear whether the groups sang or played in unison or in different parts; in some programmes, performances of part songs are explicitly described as such. The title of the piece performed follows, and sometimes the name of a composer. Titles were generally given in transliteration or in Japanese translation. Transliteration was not standardized and the Japanese script does not allow accurate representation of foreign names. With some titles, it can be anybody's guess what language was transliterated.

Japanese titles are no less ambiguous. In some cases we cannot even be sure whether the title represents a work from the Western repertoire or a Japanese piece, traditional or contemporary. 'Tsuki' (moon), for example, can be the title of a *koto* piece or of any number of *shōka*. The tunes of Western songs, both folk songs and art songs, were often given lyrics that had nothing to do with the original ones, such as Schumann's *Zigeunerleben*, which morphed into *Satsuma-gata*, before the German lyrics were translated.[13] There are (at least) three songs with the title *Ōtōnomiya* (an alternative name for the Kamakura Shrine), two of them sung to the tune of Friedrich Silcher's song, *Der alte Barbarossa*; the third one a *shōka* published by the Ministry of Education. For some songs, the foreign lyrics were translated more than once. The same song could appear under different titles, which may reflect the source of the notated

---

13   See Chapter 6.

music.[14] For instrumental pieces, nondescript titles like 'Andante' may well designate practice pieces from instrumental tutors.

Given all these uncertainties, some of the identifications of programme items cited here are merely educated guesses.[15] Because of this and the limited number of sample programmes, no attempt at statistical analysis is made here. As an indication of general trends, however, the forty-odd programmes of varying detail and accuracy, covering the period from autumn 1907 until February 1921, do provide valuable evidence of musical activities at the grassroots level.

Even if we assume that the programmes are representative and give a fair indication of what was performed, they do not tell us how the performances were received. The audiences are difficult to identify, but it seems safe to conclude that many of them would have been associated with the performers, such as family, friends, or fellow students. We have limited information about entrance fees. Sometimes fees are mentioned in a way that suggests that they were the exception rather than the rule. Many if not most of the concerts held in schools may have been free. We rarely receive an indication of what Japanese listeners actually experienced when they listened to what was performed. Published reviews are not always telling. One detailed review of a concert by the Second High School (cited in this chapter) appears to be penned by the kind of arrogant man characterized by Kate Hansen in *Musical Consciousness*. If he is to be believed, the audience at the concert had little if any appreciation for art music.

Concerts were organized by different actors, most of them Japanese and associated with one of Sendai's many schools, which also provided the venue for the majority of concerts. Other organizers included local associations, and venues included churches and the Sendai-za theatre. Some of the concerts were joint efforts involving several groups. Foreign actors were prominent in the concerts organized at the Second High School, as well as at the mission schools. Most of the local performers were teachers and students. Most of the invited performers were associated

---

14 A useful source for researching song titles is the database at Kunitachi College of Music Library: Dōyō/shōka sakuin, https://www.lib.kunitachi.ac.jp/shiryo/shoka/

15 In making such guesses, I have assumed that by the twentieth century, sheet music that was available in Europe and North America may well have found its way to Sendai, whether through trade or through informal channels.

with the Tokyo Academy of Music. Among the public schools, the Second High School is represented with the highest number of concerts (nine), followed by Miyagi Prefecture Normal School (eight).[16] Of the private institutions, Tōhoku Ongakuin led with nine concerts, followed by Miyagi College (five). Other schools were represented with one to three concerts, while eight concerts were staged by various associations.

The concert programmes examined reveal significant differences, but also broad similarities. Most of them featured predominantly Western music; whether because of the magazine's decreasing coverage of Japanese music in general, or because performers of Japanese music favoured other settings is hard to tell. 'Western music', however, is a blanket term, and the programmes published in *Ongakukai* illustrate the wide variety of musical performances it covered.

An exception is a programme of a concert organized by the Association for Native Japanese Music (Kokufū Ongaku Kai) that took place on 8 April 1908.[17] The concert consisted of a daytime and an evening section, with fourteen and twelve items respectively.[18] The programme of the evening section ran as follows:

1. *Tsuyugoromo* (A Cloak of Dewdrops) (2 *koto*, 1 *sangen*)

2. *Nihon nishiki* (Japan Brocade)[19] (3 *koto*, 2 *sangen*)

3. *Sue no chigiri* (Pledge of Eternal Fidelity) (2 *koto*, 1 *sangen*)

4. *Ume no ukihashi* (The Bridge of Dreams) (3 *koto*, 1 *sangen*)

5. *Chidori (no) kyoku* (Song of the Plovers) (3 *koto*)

6. *Hagi no tsuyu* (Dew on the Bush Clover) (*koto, sangen, shakuhachi*)

7. *Dewa no kyoku* (Song from Dewa Province) (3 *koto*)

8. *Sato no akatsuki* (Daybreak in the Village) (*sangen, shakuhachi*)

9. *Miyagi (no) kyoku* (Song from Miyagi) (2 *koto, sangen*)

---

16 Including the normal schools for men and women after their separation in 1913.
17 'Sendai Kokufūkai ongakukai', *Ongakukai* 1, no. 6 (1908): 48–49.
18 Unlike in most cases, the evening section precedes the daytime one in the report. Four items were the same in both sections.
19 Possibly a misprint for *Yamato nishiki*, a composition by the *jiuta* performer and composer Yamashita Shōkin.

10. *Shin aoyagi* (New Song of the Green Willow) (*koto, sangen, shakuhachi*)

11. *Sanzan/Mitsuyama*[20] (*koto, sangen*)

12. *Shōchikubai* (Pine, Bamboo, and Plum) (*koto, sangen, shakuhachi*)

Most if not all the pieces appear to be in the *jiuta* genre, originally a *shamisen* genre and adopted by Ikuta Kengyō (1656–1715), founder of the Ikuta-school of *koto* music.[21] He developed *jiuta* into a chiefly instrumental genre (*tegotomono*), often played by ensembles, including *koto* and *shamisen* (usually called *sangen* in this context). Later, the *sankyoku* ensemble, consisting of *koto*, *shamisen*, and *kokyū* (bowed lute) or *shakuhachi* became common.[22] Ikuta *jiuta* is an example of a regional style (originating from the Kansai region) that attained nationwide currency from the late nineteenth century. *Miyagi no kyoku* was composed by Yamashita Shōkin (1848–1918). Another concert of predominantly *koto* and *shamisen* music took place on 30 August 1915 at the Sakuragaoka Public Hall and featured well-known performers from Tokyo.[23]

Judging from the programmes in *Ongakukai*, Japanese and blended music were most often performed in concerts at the private Tōhoku Ongakuin (Tohoku Music Academy).

Tōhoku Ongakuin

Headed by Maedako Shinkin (1861?–1929), Tōhoku Ongakuin (Tohoku Academy of Music) was exceptional: a large private music studio that regularly organized concerts. As a major player in the dissemination of Western music it predated the Second High School, the other major organizer of concerts (see Chapter 9). Its main importance may well have been as an institution that trained teachers rather than as an

---

20 Possibly a misprint for Mitsuyama (written with an additional character), which is the title of a *jiuta* piece by Mitsuzaki Kengyō.

21 Number 5, *Chidori no kyoku*, here played on *koto* only, is a *koto* piece in the Meiji shinkyoku style. For a brief explanation for most of the pieces named here, see the website of the International Shakuhachi Society: https://www.komuso.com/pieces/index.pl?genre=-1

22 William P. Malm, *Traditional Japanese Music and Musical Instruments* (Tokyo: Kodansha International, 2000), 170, 99, 208–09.

23 'Sendai Sōkyoku Sangen Gassōkai', *Ongakukai* 168 (1915): 87.

organizer of concerts, but its outreach organization, Kyōseikai, as well as the descriptions, 'Spring concert' and 'Autumn concert', suggests that public concerts were an integral part of the Academy's activities and that the nine concerts reported in *Ongakukai* represent a mere fraction of the concerts actually held. Unlike the concerts at the Second High School, which depended on the initiative (or lack thereof) of the students at any given time, the Tōhoku Ongakuin remained in the hands of Maedako Shinkin, who was, moreover, ably supported by family members, particularly his daughter Haruko, who would have been at least in her teens by 1908 and whose name features in every concert.[24] Her sister Nobuko graduated from the Music College of the East (Tōyō Ongaku Gakkō) in March 1917.[25] Shinkin's son Wataru, who died in Tokyo in 1932 at age thirty-five, may well have studied music in Tokyo, like his sister: some of the violin pieces he reportedly performed are fairly advanced.[26] Otherwise not much is known about the family.

In contrast to the Second High School, Maedako Shinkin's academy did not rely on foreign support: the performers, besides Shinkin himself and members of his family, were (presumably) his students and, on occasion, guest performers. Another marked difference from most of the concerts organized by schools was the high number of blended (*wayō setchū*) performances including guest performers who played Japanese instruments.

Blended performances, together with a few pieces played exclusively on Japanese instruments, featured prominently in the two concert programmes in 1912. The 'Twenty-first commemorative concert'[27] on 20 October 1912, in which a total of twenty-four items were performed, included seven ensemble pieces played on the violin, *koto*, *shamisen*, and

---

24 She died in 1975, reportedly in her eighties.
25 Midori Takeishi, 'Meiji/Taishō no Tōyō Ongaku Gakkō: Ensō ni kansuru kiroku, shiryō', *Tōkyō Ongaku Daigaku kenkyū kiyō* 29 (2005): 29, https://core.ac.uk/download/pdf/230043973.pdf Nobuko is also recorded as a member of the school's alumni organization. Maedako Nobu (variously spelt) features in concerts in April 1912 (no names in 1913 programme), 1914; April 1917; November 1920, as well as the Tohoku University concert that year.
26 His death is recorded on the stone of the family grave at Dōrinji in the Shintera area of Sendai.
27 There appears to be a mistake in the counting; see previous year. *Ongakukai* 5, no. 12 (1912): 64–65.

shakuhachi in various combinations, and a Japanese piece performed as an organ solo:

3. One *koto*, two *shamisen*, three violins (title not specified)
6. Organ solo – *Echigo jishi* (Echigo lion dance)
7. *Shakuhachi*, violin, *shamisen*: Nagauta *Echigo jishi*[28]
9. *Shamisen*, violin – *Harusame* (Spring rain)[29]
13. *Shakuhachi*, two violins (or violin and *koto*) – *Shōjō tsuru* (The crane on the pine tree)[30]
17. *Shakuhachi, shamisen,* violin – *Chidori* (Plovers)[31]
20. Violin and *shamisen* – *Kokaji* (The swordsmith)[32]
23. *Koto, shakuhachi,* violin – *Hagi no tsuyu* (Dew on the bush clover)[33]

In addition, item 12, *Haru no kyoku* (Spring song)[34] performed with four violins may also have been a *koto* piece, although the title could conceivably describe a Western one. The Western music on the programme consisted of *shōka*, popular vocal or instrumental excerpts from operas, marches, salon pieces, and pieces with unspecific titles like 'Andante' or 'Serenade' and no composer named. The concert was special in that it featured a visiting *shamisen* player from the Kineya school (Kineya Rokukei), described as famous, who, as well as playing in the mixed ensemble items, performed two items in a duo with *shakuhachi* (15. *Tamagawa*, 22. *Yachiyo jishi*) and one with *shamisen* (19. *Kanjinchō*), as well as concluding the concert with an unspecified solo.

---

28 *Echigo jishi* is the title of both a *jiuta* and a *nagauta* piece (with the former considered one of the main sources for the latter). In this case, the *jiuta* would seem the more likely version, but the programme explicitly says, *nagauta*. The organ performance may well have been based on a different version.
29 *Jiuta*.
30 *Sōkyoku* from the Yamada school.
31 *Sōkyoku* from the Ikuta School, see programme of the Kokufū Kai.
32 *Nagauta* piece, composed for *shamisen* in 1832 by Kineya Katsugoro (I or II).
33 There is a piece of that title in both the Ikuta and the Yamada schools, the former being of the *jiuta* genre.
34 Or 'Ode to spring': *sōkyoku* in the style of Meiji shinkyoku from the Ikuta School, composed by Yoshizawa Kengyo II.

More typical, perhaps, was the programme of a concert on 3 November 1916. Although the Academy regularly held an autumn concert, the report in *Ongakukai* states that this particular one was held in celebration of the special holiday (investiture of the crown prince) and was attended by several hundred people.[35] The programme was as follows:

1. Organ solo – *Golden Dream*[36]
2. Two-part singing (unspecified) – Six members of youth group
3. Organ solo – *Tsuki* (Moon)[37]
4. Organ and violin – *Yūhō* (Friend)
5. Organ solo – *Tsuru kame* (Crane and tortoise)[38]
6. *Shakuhachi*, violin, *sangen* – *Chidori* (Plovers)
7. *Shōka* chorus – *Tanoshiki wagaya* (Our happy home)[39]
8. Violin duo – *Shukuten māchi* (Celebratory march)
9. Violin and *sangen* – *Haru no kyoku* (Spring song)[40]
10. Violin, organ – March
11. *Shakuhachi, violin, sangen* – *Yūgao* (Evening face)
12. Organ solo – *Hail Columbia*
13. Violin, *koto, shakuhachi* – *Shin Takasago* (New *Takasago*)
14. Mandolin solo (no piece named)
15. Violin, *koto, shakuhachi* – *Aki no kyoku* (Autumn song)
16. Violin solo – Largo
17. *Koto, sangen* – *Ataka* (probably *Ataka no matsu*/The Pines at Ataka, a *nagauta*)

---

35 *Ongakukai* 182 (1916), 48.
36 Presumed transliteration. The Library of Congress has sheet music for a piano piece with that title by Joe A. Stipp (Church & Co., John, Cincinnati, 1871). See https://www.loc.gov/item/sm1871.03480/
37 Possibly a *sōkyoku* (Ikuta School) of this title, but it could also be one of several *shōka* with the same title.
38 *Tsuru kame no kyoku* is the title of a *sōkyoku* from the Ikuta School and of a *nagauta*.
39 There are several possible *shōka* with this title, including *Home, Sweet Home*.
40 This and the following items 11, 13, 15, are *sōkyoku* from the Ikuta School.

18. Violin solo – Romance
19. Violin, *koto, shakuhachi* – *Shōjō no tsuru* (A crane in the pines, Yamada school)
20. Violin (solo)[41]
21. Violin duo – Romance
22. Violin, *sangen, shakuhachi* – *Tamagawa*
23. Violin solo – 'Kosucherutora ni bu'[42]

In later years, the proportion of blended items in the programmes seems to have declined, and the programme of the last concert reported in *Ongakukai*, which took place on 13 November 1920 in Sanbanchō Kumiai Church, contains none at all. The number of programmes is too small to conclude with certainty that this reflects a trend, but if so, this would parallel the general trend of the time (see Chapter 8). As in the previous example, most of the Western pieces named in the programmes are *shōka*, marches, and instrumental pieces, but, unusually, specific titles and the composer's name are given for nearly all the items.[43] The programme was as follows (the performers, presumably all affiliated with the Academy, are only named for some items):

Part 1

1. Violin duet – *Tsubame wa kaeru* (The swallows fly home) – by Abt[44]
2. Male voices, 4-part – A. *Good Night* – by 'Watkings'[45]; B. *Tayutau kobune* (The drifting small boat) – by Knight[46]

---

41 'Vaiorinkinbo(po?)iseru'; possibly, a misprint for Tannhäuser.
42 This looks like a misprint. The performer is Maedako Shinkin, and it seems likely that he played a movement from a concerto, possibly in A (if the 'ra' stands for 'la' on the do re mi scale, and 'ni bu' might conceivably refer to the second movement).
43 'Tōhoku Ongakuin Shūki ensōkai', *Ongakukai* 230 (1920): 34.
44 *Wenn die Schwalben heimwärts ziehn/ When the Swallows Homeward Fly*, by Franz Wilhelm Abt (1819–85).
45 The most likely transcription.
46 *Rocked in the Cradle of the Deep*, lyrics by Emma Hart Willard, music by Joseph Philip Knight, first published in 1840. The Japanese lyrics are by Kondō Sakufū, who wrote lyrics for numerous foreign songs. See Mamiko Sakamoto, 'Kondō Sakufū to sono yakushikyoku saikō', *Toyama Daigaku Kyōiku Gakubu kiyō A* (*bunkakei*) 50 (1997).

3. Violin trio – *Sayogaku* (serenade) – by Haydn

4. Violin quartet *Mune yori mune e* (From breast to breast/Heart to heart) – by Mozart

5. Baritone (tenor?) solo – *Sayogaku* – by Schubert[47]

6. Violin duet – *Lovely Rose*[48]

7. Soprano solo – *Subete o shireru kimi yori* (From you who knows everything) – Mozart[49]

8. Piano duet – *Sasayaki* (Whisper) – by Gillet[50]

9. Violin solo *Tanoshiki waga ya* (Our happy home) variations – by Sousa[51]

Part 2

1. Mixed choir – *Butō* (Dance) – by 'Shuyotto'[52]

2. Violin trio – From Opera, *The Barber of Sevilla* (sic; unspecified) – by Rossini

3. Organ solo – *Happy Moments* – by 'Uaresu'[53]

4. Violin quartet – Chor aus *Euryanthe* – by Weber[54]

5. Female vocal duo – *Tsukiyo* – (Moonlit night) – by 'Dēmusu'[55]

6. Violin solo – *Malaguena* – by Sarasate

---

47 Possibly Schubert, *Ständchen*, although this is generally sung by a tenor.
48 No composer specified; possibly *Go Lovely Rose* by Henry Lawes (1596–1662); or Roger Quilter, *Go Lovely Rose*, op. 24/3.
49 *Voi che Sapete*, aria from *The Marriage of Figaro*.
50 Probably Ernest Gillet (1856–1940), whose compositions include *Doux murmure* for piano.
51 Presumably, John Philip Sousa, *Home, Sweet Home*, variations for violin and piano.
52 Conceivably Eduard Schütt (1856–1933), whose songs include *Elfentanz*.
53 Possibly 'In Happy Moments' from the opera *Maritana* by William Vincent Wallace (1812–65); music from *Maritana* was on the programme of concerts at the Second High School in 1913 and 1915, as well as one at Sendai Higher Secondary School for Girls in 1917.
54 Most likely the 'Hunter's Chorus' in Act III of *Euryanthe* by Carl Maria von Weber.
55 There are several songs of that name by both Japanese and foreign composers. Maedako Nobuko and Wataru sang a duet with the title *Tsukiyo* at a concert given by Tohoku University and supported by members of Tōhoku Ongakuin on 1 May 1920, where Mendelssohn is named as the composer.

7. Violin duet – *La paloma* (Spanish serenade) – by Yradier[56]
8. Soprano solo – *Ware wa samayou* (I wander about) – by Gounod[57]
9. Mixed chorus – *Yū no kyoku* (Evening song)[58]

The consistent inclusion of composers' names might suggest a new awareness of the distinctiveness of the individual works, even if they were part of edited collections. There are fewer *shōka* than the previous concerts, and although most of the pieces can be described as fairly elementary, others, like *Voi che sapete* are more demanding, and Sarasate's *Malaguena* (played by Maedako Shinkin's son Wataru) is certainly well above beginners' level.

That the Tohoku Academy of Music was still perceived as a major player in the Western music scene around 1920 is suggested by the fact that members of the Academy took part in the concert organized by students of Tohoku Imperial University on 1 May 1920.[59]

The Second High School

The music club at the Second High School was the most important organizer of concerts featuring predominantly Western music in the first years of the twentieth century. The number of concerts is, however, difficult to determine, and might have been lower than that of the concerts given by Tōhoku Ongakuin. The Shōshikai association's magazine reported a total of eleven concerts before 1908, but reporting appears to have been irregular, particularly after 1908.[60] *Ongakukai* reported nine concerts with programmes between 1908 and 1920. The irregularity both of concerts held and of reporting is presumably explained by the fact that the students' level of initiative and activity varied from year to

---

56 Sebastián Yradier (1809–65); one of the most recorded pieces ever.
57 Charles Gounod wrote numerous songs, a few of which were given Japanese lyrics. Possibly, *Ave Maria*, which Maedako Nobuko sang in the concert given by Tohoku University that same year.
58 No composer specified. Possibly, Josef Rheinberger (1839–1901), *Abendlied* Op. 69, Nr. 3.
59 'Tōhoku Teikoku Daigakusei yūshi ongaku ensōkai', *Ongakukai* 225 (1920): 29.
60 For the period 1908 onwards *Shōshikai zasshi* recorded only one concert that was not reported in *Ongakukai*.

year; the spring concert in 1915, moreover, took place after an extended period of national mourning following the death of the Meiji emperor.[61]

While the members of the music club relied heavily on the participation of the foreign community, the extent of their involvement appears to have varied, and lessened over time. Relations with members of the foreign community may have been less close after the conclusion of the pioneering phase. With the gradual increase of music teaching in schools, new students entering the high school may well have felt more confident in their own abilities. Either way, just under six years after its first concert, the musical offerings and levels of competence in performance continued to be mixed. The concert on 31 October 1908, for example, included *shōka*, short instrumental solos, and two marches played by an 'orchestra'. Besides foreigners, several Japanese women performed: Mrs Kobayashi was the wife of a professor at the school and may have trained at the Tokyo Academy of Music; the others were, presumably, students from other schools. A review of the concert, which according to *Ongakukai* attracted a large audience, was published in *Shōshikai zasshi*. The author, who called himself 'Masao', may have been an older student; at any rate a young man who prided himself on his superior knowledge and powers of appreciation.[62] The programme was as follows:

Part 1

1. Orchestra – *Gallop* – Members
2. Piano – 'to be determined' – Miss Hansen[63]
3. Two-part singing – 'Orubōrudo, uotchi'[64] – Miss Izumi Kyōko (with one more)
4. Harmonica – *College March* – A member
5. *Shakuhachi* solo – *Kaze-ki no kyoku*[65] – Mr Adachi Kochō

---

61 *Ongakukai* 164 (1915), 71.
62 'Sendai Kōtō Gakkō ongakukai', *Ongakukai* 2, no. 1 (1909): 51; 'Ongakukai hihyō: jūgatsu sanjūichi nichi yūshi ongakukai zakkan', *Shōshikai zasshi* 83 (1908): 149–51. *Shōshikai zasshi* did not include the programme, but the review suggests that at least the first part was largely as reported in *Ongakukai*.
63 Kate Hansen does not seem to have written about this concert in her letters.
64 I have not been able to identify this piece.
65 Possibly, *Kaze to ki to mizu to,* from the Tozan School.

6. Violin duet – Andante (Gluck)[66] – Mr Okamoto Fusao, Mr Isawa Yoshiaki

7. Vocal solo – *Satsuma-gata* (Satsuma Bay)[67] – Mrs Kobayashi

8. Cornet solo – *Natsukashi no hahaue* (Longing for Mother) (Stick)[68] – Mr Stick

Part 2

1. 'Orchestra' (*kangengaku*) – *Kriegsmarsch*[69] – Members

2. Four-part chorus – *Aki no urami* (Regrets of autumn) – Miss Izumi Kyōko (with three others)

3. Harmonica solo – *Polka* – A member

4. *Shakuhachi* solo – *Zangetsu* – Mr Adachi Kochō

5. Vocal ensemble – *Yasumasa*; *Hanabi*[70] – Miss Nagao Seiko, Miss Nagao Tomoko (with two others)

6. Violin solo – *Rekorēto*[71] – Mr Okamoto Fusao

7. Vocal solo – *Apyū*[72] – Mrs Kobayashi

8. Piano solo – (to be determined) – Miss Hansen

9. Mellophone solo – *Oh Master Take me through the Gate*[73]

Part 3

---

66 Most likely 'Dance of the Blessed Spirits' from Gluck's opera *Orfeo ed Euridice* (Act II Scene 2).
67 See Chapter 6.
68 Possibly the same piece as Stick performed on 23 May 1903, entitled 'Of Thee Mother' (*I Am Dreaming of Thee, Mother*?); another possible candidate would be *Dreaming of Home and Mother* by John Pond Ordway (1824–80; composed 1851). Stick may have arranged an existing composition for cornet rather than composed a new one.
69 Presumably Mendelssohn's *Kriegsmarsch der Priester aus Athalia*, which was also performed in the Second High School's seventh concert on 11 February 1905: see Kyūsei Kōtō Gakkō Shiryō Hozon Kai, ed., *Shiryō shūsei kyūsei kōtō gakkō zensho dai 7 kan: seikatsu/kyōyō hen* (2) (Tokyo: Kyūsei Kōtō Gakkō Shiryō Hozon Kai Kankō Bu, 1984), 550.
70 For *Yasumasa*, see Chapter 7. *Hanabi* (Fireworks) is presumably another *shōka*; there are several possible candidates.
71 I have not been able to identify the piece.
72 Or 'Abyū' (piece not identified).
73 Presumably a hymn (not identified).

Opera – *Kaichōon* (Sound of the Tide)[74] – Members

Masao, the (presumably) self-appointed critic, was not impressed with the concert, concluding that 'artistically, there was no performance of overpowering force'.[75] His criticism began with the school song by the association's members, which apparently preceded the programme: 'one would expect people born as men to sing out', he observed and suggested that if they could not do better, it would be better to have the audience join in. Nor was he impressed by the 'orchestra', which in his opinion did not deserve that name. His criticism of the harmonica performance (item 4) was particularly harsh:

> Properly speaking, to even think of the harmonica as a musical instrument seems misguided. If it must be played at all, a march or similar might be acceptable. But when some hybrid version of 'Echigo jishi' or 'Rokudan' is played, blaring out so-called compound notes – oh my goodness, I involuntarily blushed with shame. It is like a beggar gate-crashing an evening reception on the Emperor's birthday. [...] If you want to play that kind of thing, do it for a gathering of maid servants on the upper floor of your lodgings.[76]

Clearly, the reviewer had no time for blended performances. When it came to more traditional Japanese performances like the *shakuhachi* solo that followed, he had to admit his ignorance and make up for it by quoting from a Chinese classic: apparently not uncommon among reviewers commenting on Western music they were unfamiliar with.[77] Significantly, this reviewer resorted to the same ploy when commenting on music he felt he ought to be familiar with, but which, as he admitted, he had not listened to with great attention.

---

74 The most likely candidate for the title is the modern kabuki play by Hasegawa Shigure (1879–1941) submitted from a competition held by *Yomiuri shinbun* in 1905 and premiered to acclaim in 1908 at the Kabuki-za in Tokyo in 1908. Another possibility is some kind of performance based on the collection of mostly French and Belgian poems translated by Ueda Bin in 1905. Some of these were set to music by Torii Tsuna (1886–1966), a violinist and composer who graduated from the Tokyo Academy of Music in 1906 and taught there for many years. However, the manuscripts of her compositions at Tokyo University of the Arts date from the 1930s, so this seems unlikely.
75 Masao [pseud.], 'Hihyō', 149.
76 Ibid. According to the programme in *Ongakukai*, the piece played was a march. According to Masao, he played *Karl March* in the second part of the programme.
77 Compare Kume's reference to 'Hakusetsu'; see Chapter 2.

He was more confident in his evaluation of the piano and violin performances (items 2 and 6). Kate Hansen's performance did not pass muster: before concluding that her performance was an asset (see the quote at the beginning of this chapter), he asserted:

> Miss Hansen's piano playing is certainly more than the fingerings of a novice's unskilled hand. However, precisely because her technique [he uses the foreign word] is flawless, one might, with the greatest respect, put it negatively, and say that it is like a music box. It still lacks the power to impress deeply and cannot be acknowledged to represent the life and soul of true art.[78]

Ironically, his criticism mirrors Hansen's remarks about Japanese performers, although, if her own description of her performance (in another concert) of *The Devil's March*, a popular salon piece and hardly the last thing in high art, is anything to go by, Masao may well have had some justification for his remarks.

His comment on the violin duet's performance was even more scathing: 'I will merely point out that on the violin you should not make a sound like the whining of a mosquito suffering from a lung disease.'[79] Mrs Kobayashi's solo performance of *Satsuma-gata*, too, had him in the role of the discerning authority. Having heard it performed by a chorus at the Tokyo Academy of Music five or six years previously, he felt he could appreciate it more than the other members of the audience. He did, however, express his preference for the choral version and for the more recent Japanese lyrics by Ishikuro Kosaburō, who had translated the German text rather than compose an entirely different one.[80] Even if Mrs Kobayashi (who may conceivably have trained and learnt *Satsuma-gata*, at the Tokyo Academy) did not wish to sing the new lyrics, he remarked, she should at least have announced Schumann's song with the new translated title, 'Rurō no tami' (The vagrant people/gypsies), although the audience probably would not understand the words of either.

---

78 Masao [pseud.], 'Hihyō', 149.
79 Ibid.
80 First performed at the Tokyo Academy of Music with this title on 9 October 1908, although Ishikuro Kosaburō is only named at a concert on 8 and 9 June 1912. See Tōkyō Geijutsu Daigaku Hyakunenshi Hensan Iinkai, *Ensōkai hen 1*, 279, 343.

The lyrics of two other songs likewise gave him cause for criticism. *Aki no urami* he had heard sung as *Haha naki wagaya* (Our home without a mother),[81] the words of which fit the tune better in his opinion. The song *Yasumasa*, on the other hand, he pronounced ill-chosen: the 'la la la(tsu) la la la la la' was 'a bit too unartistic', although the song was still better than the likes of *Roei no yume*.[82] Recalling Hansen's remarks about ignorant self-appointed experts in Western music, one wonders whether he realized that the composer of the music of *Yasumasa* was Mozart. On the other hand, Mozart's composition and the Japanese lyrics cannot be described as a good fit.[83] The critic's low opinion of Kitamura's *Roei no yume*, together with his remarks about song lyrics and about playing Japanese tunes on a harmonica, suggests that he favoured Western art music. Indeed, he even appealed to the organizers to ban unmusical instruments like the accordion and the *biwa* from future concerts.[84] Kate Hansen would surely have approved.

If Masao was critical of several performers, he had equally harsh words for the behaviour of the audience. Having praised J. Monroe Stick's cornet solo, he remarked, 'this man's serious approach to his art never fails to fill me with respect.'[85] He contrasted this with the attitude of the audience, who 'hoot and heckle and confuse a concert with a playground' and who 'shout ridiculous nonsense as they enter'.[86] He expressed his contempt for the audience again after praising the bass singer in the vocal quartet: 'Of course one cannot expect the hooting crowd (*yajiren*) to appreciate the appeal of the bass singer. The soprano will attract attention on the strength of her beauty alone, but the manly (*otoko rashii*), truly deep voice that comes from the innermost heart (*haifu*) is too sober (*shibui*) for them and does not hold their interest.' The mob, he continued, might be satisfied by a female playing the *koto*, but knew no greater pleasure than listening to the *biwa* or a band accompanying Asakusa street artists. He suggested that such people should be discouraged from attending or at least urged to keep quiet.

---

81 Possibly *What is home without a mother.* By Alice Hawthorne (Septimus Winner, 1827–1902). New York: H. De Marsan (Data from the Library of Congress).
82 See Chapter 8.
83 Okunaka, *Wayō setchū ongakushi*, pp. 11–16.
84 *Ongaku no kankei no nai biwa toka tefūgin to ka* Masao [pseud.], 'Hihyō', 151.
85 Masao [pseud.], 'Hihyō', 150.
86 Ibid.

The assertion that the (predominantly male?) audience appreciated the female performers for their appearance rather than their musical performance resembles Kate Hansen's remarks in her discussion of the *koto* in *Musical Consciousness*; another indication that Western observers' disdain for popular Japanese music was matched by the local elites' contempt for music they deemed 'common'.

The 'so-called opera' performed in the third and final part of the concert presented Masao with another opportunity to express his contempt for the undiscerning masses, who seemed to enjoy the spectacle, although he himself thought that the only redeeming feature was Mrs Kobayashi's beautiful singing.[87]

While the participation of foreigners in the concerts of the Second High School may have decreased over the years (the sample of programmes examined is too small to be sure), musicians from the Tokyo Academy of Music continued to perform at the invitation of the Second High School as they had done at the second concert in 1903. They performed at the school again at least in 1909 and 1913, as well as at other Sendai concerts.[88] For the concert on 1 May 1909, forty students arrived on 30 April, an event that merited advance announcements in the local newspaper *Kahoku shinpō*.[89] The guests performed a total of ten pieces, for piano, strings, and voice. Not all the works are specified (or identifiable), but they included a Romance for Cello solo by Georg Goltermann;[90] an unspecified work for piano trio, and the vocal solo, *Ninin no heishi* (*Die beiden Grenadiere*),[91] described by *Kahoku shinpō* as 'a masterpiece (*kessaku*) by (Heinrich) Heine set to music by the great German composer Schumann', as well as a choral rendition of the song *Ōtōnomiya*, based on a song by the German composer Friedrich Silcher.[92]

---

87 Masao [pseud.], 'Hihyō', 151.
88 'Sendai Nikō ensōkai', *Ongakukai* 2.6 (June 1909): 42. The *Ongakukai* report on their performance in the concert on 5 October 1913 stated that this was the third or fourth occasion. See 'Sendai ni okeru Dai Ni Kōtō Gakkō Gakuyūkai ensōkai', *Ongakukai* 6.1. (November 1913): 66–67.
89 'Sendai Nikō ensōkai', *Ongakukai* 2.6 (June 1909): 42; *Kahoku shinpō*, 26 April 1909, p. 2, and again on 1 May.
90 Georg Eduard Goltermann (1824–98); presumably one of the *3 Romances sans paroles* for solo cello, Op. 90.
91 Today more generally translated as *Futari no tekidanhei*.
92 Silcher's four-part arrangement of *Der alte Barbarossa*, a poem by Friedrich Rückert (1788–1866). Although this is not the only song with the title *Ōtōnomiya*, this is the most likely version, because of its association with the Tokyo Academy of Music.

The song is another example of the type of blended performance practised in the early years of the Tokyo Academy of Music: a Western composition—in this case a four-part chorus—sung with Japan-themed lyrics.

We can assume that the singing by the students of the Tokyo Academy of Music was of a higher standard than that of their hosts, who also sang on this occasion. The audiences of Sendai, moreover, would have had little chance to hear a cello played competently: much less in a chamber ensemble.

The third part of the concert, consisting of six items with local performers, began with a four-part string ensemble of members of the Music Association playing 'Tannhäuser'; possibly a performance similar to the one described by Kate Hansen after her first experience of a concert at the Second High School. Okamoto, who played an unspecified violin solo (presumably accompanied by Kate Hansen), was still described as *kōshi* in the programme, but by the concert on 22 November 1910 he appears to have been replaced by Kumagai *kōshi*.[93]

A clear indication of the school's ambition to present Western music at its most impressive were the efforts to perform as an orchestra, or at least a larger ensemble. The programme of the sixth concert on 15 October 1904 already included a band of sorts, although the majority of players may have come from outside the school.[94] In fact, it is hard to determine what exactly was behind the term *kangengaku* (generally translated as 'orchestra') in each case. In the concert on 23 September 1907, 'orchestra' described 'four fellows with violins', according to Kate Hansen. The *kangengaku* in the concert on 31 October 1908 did not merit the name either, according to the reviewer; nor did the *kangen gassō* in 1910: ten players led by the new teacher. In June 1915 a report in *Ongakukai* stated that the school finally had an orchestra (*kangengaku*) and that a full orchestra was planned for the near future. Even so, the description of the items on the programme of the recent concert makes this a dubious assertion. Although four out of a total of eleven items

---

Ōtonomiya (or Daitōnomiya) refers to the Kamakura shrine (Kamakura-gū) or to the fourteenth-century imperial prince who is enshrined there.

93 See *Ongakukai*, 4.1 (January 1911), 73. Kumagai Senta graduated from Tōyō Ongaku Gakkō in 1910: see Takeishi, 'Meiji/Taishō no Tōyō Ongaku Gakkō', 29.

94 Dai Ni Kōtō Gakkō Shi Henshū Iinkai, *Dai Ni Kōtō Gakkō shi*, 953–54.

are described as a 'string ensemble' (*gengaku gassō*) and one as a 'string and wind ensemble' (*kangen gassō*), the titles of the pieces suggest the usual fare of works arranged for a variety of instrument combinations. A possible exception is the 'first string ensemble' item, an adagio from an unspecified symphony.[95] Symphony orchestras were still a rarity in Japan in 1915.

The people of Sendai nevertheless had a chance to hear a major ensemble performing to a high standard at a concert on 23 October 1920, the last one at the Second High School reported in *Ongakukai*: a string orchestra and chorus consisting of students and staff from the Academy performed the *Grand March* from *Tannhäuser* under the baton of Gustav Kron.[96]

In 1915 *Ongakukai* described the concerts organized by the music aficionados (*yūshi*) of the Second High School as 'the centre of the musical world in Sendai'.[97] This may, of course, have been the (hardly unbiased) view of a local observer: the ambitions of the music club clearly exceeded the skills and resources of the students. In the early twentieth century, it would have been rare to have learnt the violin or the piano from an early age, particularly for young men. Nor would they have had the opportunity to hear a symphony concert, much less a Western-style opera, so it is hardly surprising that the 'opera' *Kaichōon* or what the programmes describe as an 'orchestra' did not merit the name. But the students who organized the concerts succeeded in bringing together local musicians with different backgrounds who performed a wide range of works. Even allowing for the small number of programmes sampled and the appearance of the same piece under different names, there seems to be relatively little repetition. By hosting

---

95 'Nikō yūshi ongakukai', *Ongakukai* No. 164 (T. 4.6), p. 71: 1915 (no date given). The other pieces had the titles *Bara no hanaen* (Rose Garden); *Shōri no hata no shita* (probably 'Unter dem Siegesbanner' by Franz von Blon, 1861–1945), and *Kinkonshiki* (probably Jean Gabriel-Marie, 1852–1928, *La Cinquantaine*). The 'wind and string' ensemble performed *Hana yamome*, which may well have been the same selection of excerpts from Lehar's *The Merry Widow* performed by a 'string ensemble' at a concert on 5 October 1913 (*Ongakukai* 6.11 (1913): 66–67).

96 'Dai Ni Kōtō Gakkō ongaku ensōkai', *Ongakukai* 230 (December 1920), 34. See also the report in Gakuyūkai, *Ongaku 11.12* (*December 1920, 51*) in Tōkyō Geijutsu Daigaku Hyakunenshi Hensan Iinkai, ed., *Tōkyō Geijutsu Daigaku hyakunenshi: Ensōkai hen 1* (Tokyo: Ongaku no Tomosha, 1990), 515–16. Gustav Kron (1874–?) succeeded August Junker at the Academy in 1913 and taught there until 1925.

97 '[...] Sendai gakukai no chūshin', *Ongakukai* 164 (1915): 71.

concerts with musicians from Tokyo, the school made it possible for their local audience to hear works that could not otherwise be performed in Sendai.

Miyagi Normal School

Miyagi Normal School (Miyagi Shihan Gakkō) trained both male and female students until the founding of Miyagi Normal School for Women in 1913. Although the required subjects for future teachers included music, musical training was basic, and the criticism of music education at the school expressed in *Ongakukai* in one its earliest reports is likely to have been well-founded, judging from the available concert programmes.[98] We can assume that concerts were held regularly, perhaps twice yearly. They consisted mainly of *shōka*, as often as not sung in unison, with a few pieces for violin, piano, or organ. The instrumental pieces are not always specified in the published programmes, and are likely to have come from the teaching literature.

The relatively low level of performance and the limited range of genres performed do not, however, mean that the concerts did not contribute significantly to the musical education of Sendai audiences. The concert on 4 March 1911, for example, reportedly drew an audience of around 1,500; presumably it included a large number of parents, since the first part consisted of performances by pupils of the affiliated elementary school. Of the thirty musical items, nearly all were songs, sung solo or in groups of varying sizes. Two were violin solos, one of them performed by a man from the main school (he also performed in the second part); the third instrumental piece was an unspecified ensemble performance by volunteers from the main school.[99]

The second part consisted of thirty-five items (including an opening address by Shikama Jinji and a closing address by the head of the school), again mostly singing. Six items were instrumental performances: an organ solo and a violin ensemble (pieces not specified); violin and organ, *Hail Columbia March*; violin ensemble, *Donauwellen*; violin, Adagio

---

[98] 'Sendai shi no gakujō', *Ongakukai* 1, no. 6 (1908): 46. See Chapter 9.
[99] *Ongakukai* 4, no. 4. (1911), 61.

(unspecified); violin, *Jūdan no kyoku* (Ten steps).[100] The songs are all given with Japanese titles, except for two that are spelt in *katakana* and were presumably sung in English, as they both appear in a three-volume collection of *shōka* in English published in 1910: *Massa's in de Cold, Cold Ground* and *Home Sweet Home*.[101] The former, composed in 1852, is one of Stephen Foster's plantation songs, some of which gained worldwide popularity.[102] Three items were billed as *tokuhon shōka* (reading textbook songs) without a specific title. These were songs based on the texts in the national readers used in elementary schools. The Ministry of Education published its first collection in 1910, but by then several had been published by individuals.

Subsequent concerts followed a similar pattern. The concert on 2 March 1912, the sixth, according to *Ongakukai*, included twenty-five musical items, six of them instrumental (violin and organ). In addition, a guest violinist, Hongō Kōshirō, performed two pieces: *Siciliano* and *Berceuse de Jocelyn*.[103]

In March 1914, *Ongakukai* reported progress at the Normal School following the appointment of a new professor, who arranged concerts with good musicians in order to cultivate the students' taste in music. The concerts of the previous October, with students from the Tokyo Academy of Music, had fuelled the enthusiasm of teachers and students alike.[104] The concert on 7 February was deemed a great success, with 300 students performing, as well as children from the affiliated school, afficionados from the Second High School, and guest performers, including the violinists Hongō Kōshirō and Kumagai Senta. The

---

100 Items 5, 9, 13, 18, 21, and 26. *Donauwellen* is written phonetically; 'Koroshibia shikōkyoku' looks like a misprint, while *Hail Columbia (March)*, played on the organ or organ and violin appears on programmes of concerts at the Second High School (1905) and Tōhoku Ongakuin (1914, 1916); *Jūdan no kyoku* or *Midare* is a *sōkyoku* piece.

101 Items 19 and 24. See Katsuisa Sakai ed., *Eigo shōka shū* (Tokyo: Uedaya Shoten, 1903): vol. 1: 6–9; vol 2: 16–19.

102 See Chapter 2.

103 From the opera *Jocelyn* by Benjamin Godard (1849–95). I have not been able to find information about Hongō: he is listed as a composer in a catalogue of sheet music for songs in the Taishō era: Junko Konishi, 'Taishōki "uta" shiryō mokuroku', *Ōsaka Ongaku Daigaku Hakubutsukan Nenpō* 25 (2010), https://dl.ndl.go.jp/info:ndljp/pid/10313756

104 'Miyagi-ken Shihan Gakkō', *Ongakukai*, 149 (1914): 56. The concert was hosted by the Second High School.

reporter nevertheless regretted the small number of violin players, due to the fact that violin was not part of the standard curriculum. In fact, the published programme only included one solo violin performance by Hongō, while Kumagai is listed as a singer in a two-part song, *Tabi no yoru*.[105] The other instrumental items were the organ (six items), the piano (two), as well as two string ensembles of the students from the high school.

Hongō and Kumagai may have been regulars; perhaps they taught at the school on a casual basis. They also performed at the concert at the Normal School for Men on 26 February 1916: Hongō played a violin solo in the first part of the programme, accompanied by Kumagai. Kumagai also sang tenor in a choral number. In the second part (in which Hongō's name did not appear), Kumagai played a violin solo. The concert concluded with a string ensemble whose members were described as volunteers (possibly students from the Second High School) and presumably played violins, while Kumagai played the cello; they were accompanied by a female teacher.[106] Except for one more violin item in the first half (the performer is not named), the other instrumental performances were on the organ or piano (three each). All in all, ten of the thirty-two items on the programme were instrumental; the others were songs, mostly *shōka*. Among them, *Tipperary Song*, sung solo, may well have been a first in Sendai. *It's a Long Way to Tipperary*, first published in 1912 and recorded in 1914, is very much associated with the First World War. Japan had entered the war as an ally of Britain, and the Japanese navy saw battle both in Asia and in the Mediterranean. Compared to the Russo-Japanese War ten years earlier, however, the war was remote. The other items on the programme were not particularly warlike (if one discounts the usual military marches); indeed, the same singer's other offering was *Hanyū no yado* (Our humble dwelling), the Japanese version of *Home, Sweet Home*.

---

105 *Wanderers Nachtlied* (The wanderer's night song), music by Anton Rubinstein (Op. 48). There are at least three Japanese versions; the duet version listed in the Kunitachi database has lyrics by Hatano Juichirō (1851–1908). The duet was also performed at a concert at Tohoku University in 1920.

106 No piece is specified for Hongō's performance or the string ensemble. Kumagai played *Madrigal* by Achille Simonetti (1857–1928) and *Gavotte* by François-Joseph Gossec (1734–1829). Both are popular pieces to this day, and can be found in the Suzuki violin tutors, among others. The female teacher was Hoshizawa Toshiko, teacher at Prefectural Girls' High School.

The predominance of *shōka* over instrumental numbers was even more evident in the concert of the Normal School for Women on 24 February 1917: twenty-four out of the twenty-seven musical items were vocal (the programme specified the number of parts). They included Schumann's *Zigeunerleben*, now with the translated title *Rurō no tami* and (presumably) sung with the translated lyrics by Ishikuro Kosaburō.

A year later, *Ongakukai* reported the appointment of a new teacher, Inose, who performed for the first time at the concert on 16 February 1918, playing *Ave Maria* on the violin.[107] Another innovation was a new music club, the Orfeo Club, formed by afficionados at the school. The last item before the concert ended with the school song was *Gunkan māchi* (Warship march), performed by a chorus and string ensemble consisting of students and afficionados. Composed and arranged by Japanese, it is still one of the most-performed Japanese marches.[108] The programme included one performance by a foreigner, Mrs 'Genzā', who sang *The Mission of a Rose*.[109]

Singing, much of it in unison, also predominated in the concert in 1918, interspersed with performances on the violin, piano, or organ, usually solos or duets. The overall pattern of the concerts thus seems to have remained fairly similar during the period examined here. Standards are likely to have risen, as recorded in *Ongakukai*, but this is hard to tell from concert programmes alone. Unlike the Second High School, the curriculum of the Normal Schools included music, so the concerts served as an opportunity for the students to show what they had learnt. Nevertheless, performers from outside the school were invited as well, so the concerts were in part a joint effort involving the cooperation of different local groups. The last concert reported in *Ongakukai*, held on 19 February 1921, represented a major initiative, including as it did performances by pupils and teachers of several schools. The programme,

---

107 No composer is named; presumably, Gounod.
108 Lyrics by Toriyama Hiraku (1837–1914). The music arranged in 1900 by Setoguchi Tōkichi (1868–1941), based on a song of his own (*Umi yukaba*, 1897) with the addition of a trio based on compositions by Tōgi Sueyoshi (1838–1904) and Ōtomo Kotodatsu (Yakamochi, ?–?). For details, see Masajirō Tanimura, *Umi no gunka to reishiki kyoku: Teikoku Kaigun no ongaku isan to Kaijō Jieitai* (Shuppan Kyōdō Sha, 2015).
109 Spelt in *katakana* phonetic script: lyrics by Clifton Bingham (1859–1913); music by Frederic H. Cowen (1852–1935).

which consisted of thirty-two musical items, nineteen vocal and thirteen instrumental ones, was as follows:

1. Ensemble – A. *Gaisen seru shōgun o miyo* (See the Conquering Hero Comes) (Handel)[110]; B. *Kanashiki enbukyoku* (Sad waltz) (Ivanovich)[111] – string ensemble
2. Unison singing – A. *Kyōshū* (Longing for home); B. *Sakura* ('Cherry blossoms')[112] – Main department, first year
3. Piano solo – *Battle of Waterloo*[113] – second year
4. Vocal solo – *Tsubame* (Swallows) – pupils from affiliated school[114]
5. Violin solo – *Madrigal*[115] – fourth year
6. Unison singing – A. *Yoru* (Evening); B. *Chishima* (Kurile Islands?)[116] – Kita Gobanchō Higher Elementary School
7. Piano and violin – *Csikós Post* (Necke)[117] – two third-year students
8. Chorus, two-part – *Shun'ya no yume* (Dream on a spring night)[118] – Higashi Nibanchō Higher Elementary School
9. *Shōka* – A. *Mittsu no fune* (Three ships) (round); B. *Yoru no o-yashiro* (Shrine in the evening)[119] (two-part) – First High School for Women (Daiichi Kōtō Jogakkō)

---

110 From *Judas Maccabäus*.
111 Presumably Ion Ivanovici (or Josef Ivanovich; 1845–1902), the composer of *Donauwellen* (Waves of the Danube), features under various titles and in different forms in several programmes examined; possibly *Seufzer-Walzer* (Sigh Waltz). Of course, it might be just another version of *Donauwellen*.
112 There are several possible candidates for both titles.
113 Probably *The Battle of Waterloo*, by G. Anderson.
114 There are several songs of this title, including one in the first collection of songs for elementary schools published by the Music Research Committee, based on *Come, Come Pretty Bird* (lyrics and music by John H. Hewitt, 1801–90; 1938).
115 Possibly the same 'Madrigal' by Simonetti that appears in the programme of the school's concert in February 1916.
116 Both titles defy precise identification, but are most likely to come from the *shōka* textbooks for elementary schools. 'Chishima' appears in the first line of the song *Dōhō subete rokusenman* (Our sixty million brethren) from the sixth volume of *Jinjō shōgaku shōka*, published by the Ministry of Education in 1914.
117 *Csikós Post Galop* by Hermann Necke (1850–1912).
118 I have not been able to identify this.
119 *Yoru no yashiro*: lyrics by Yoshimaru Kazumasa, based on melody by Kreutzer; possibly Conradin Kreutzer (1780–1849). *Mittsu no fune* may be a translated Western

10. Piano solo – *Wiener Marsch*[120]

11. Male voices, three-part – A. *Yū no inori* (Evening prayer); B. *Yamato Takeru*[121]

12. *Shōka* – (no title given) – Higashi Nibanchō Jikka Kōtō Jogakkō

13. Vocal solo – *Komori uta* (Lullaby) – students from Tōka High School for Girls (Tōka Kōtō Jogakkō)

14. Piano solo – Allegro (Beethoven) – third-year student

15. Mixed chorus – A. *Koishiki haha* (Beloved mother); B. *Taihei no homare* (In praise of peace)[122] – Kenkyūkai members from the schoo)

16. Piano solo – *Ito tsumugu onna* (Raff)[123] – performed by Prof. Yoshii, Dai Ichi Joshi Kōtō Gakkō

Part 2

17. Unison – *Tanoshiki misono* (Pleasant garden)[124] – six girls from the affiliated elementary school

18. Unison – A. *Kono kimi kono kuni* (This ruler, this land); B. *Enyūkai* (Banquet)[125] – second-year students

---

song, but there is also a *sōkyoku* (with song) piece of that name, which appears in a collection published by the Tokyo Academy of Music (*Sōkyokushū*, 1914).

120 By Carl Czerny.
121 Yamato Takeru is a mythical imperial prince whose story is told in the *Record of Ancient Matters* (*Kojiki*). There are several songs with this title. The Kunitachi database has an entry for a three-part setting by Albert Methfessel (1785–1869), a German composer whose works include part-songs for male voices. (Lyrics by Fujimura Tsukuru).
122 *Koishiki haha* not identified; *Taihei no homare* can be found in Naruse Jinzō, ed., *Shinpen jogaku shōka*, vol. 4 (Osaka: Miki Sasuke, 1927 (1926)); the volume includes a title, *Kokyō no haha*. Gabriel Marie is given as the composer. No lyricist is named; the preface states that the lyrics have been added with consideration for a good fit with the music, so presumably the editor is the composer.
123 Joachim Raff (1822–82) ; *La Fileuse*, étude de concert opus 157 n°2.
124 Not identified.
125 *Enyūkai* (Garden party—written with a different character), lyrics by Takeshi Morisako, music by August Söderman (1832–76); *Kono kimi*, lyrics by Yoshimaru Kazumasa, music by François-Adrien Boieldieu (1775–1835), from his opera *Jean de Paris*. The collections cited in the Kunitachi database are of a later date, but presumably the songs were published in earlier collections.

19. Violin duet – Allegro (Bōmu)[126] – students from the extracurricular course at the Dai Ichi Kōtō Jogakkō
20. Mixed voices – *Sansaijo* (Three females)[127] – female students
21. Vocal solo – *Ongaku ni yosu* (To music)[128] – fourth-year student
22. Piano solo – *Hochzeitsmarsch* (Wedding march)[129] – fourth-year student
23. Female voices, three-part – *Shungyō* (Spring dawn)[130] – Tōka High School for Girls, fourth-year students
24. Organ solo – Fantasia and Fugue (Bach) – Ichikawa, teacher at the school
25. Mixed voices – *Haru no uta* ('Spring song')[131] (a cappella) – female teachers from city schools and Kenkyūkai members from this school
26. Piano solo – Fantasy (Mendelssohn) – Professor Imai from the Tōka High School for Girls
27. Violin solo – Romance (Wieniawski?)[132] – Tejima, teacher at the Sendai High School for Girls
28. Male four-part Chorus – *Rurō no tami* (*Zigeunerleben*) – from school
29. Piano duet – *Kalif of Bagdad*[133] (Boieldieu) – Miyagi Jogakkō teachers Ono, Satō

---

126 Most probably the Austrian violinist, violin teacher, and composer Joseph Michael Böhm (1795–1876).
127 *Sansaijo* from the Monbushō *shōka* collection for elementary schools for the fifth year, 1913.
128 Possibly Schubert, *An die Musik*.
129 Presumably Mendelssohn.
130 Lyrics by Nakamura Akika, music by Johann Friedrich Reichardt (1752–1814).
131 Possibly, Mendelssohn, *Vier Lieder*, Op. 100: III. Frühlingslied or *Sechs Lieder im Freien zu singen*, Op. 59: II. *Frühzeitiger Frühling*.
132 Possibly, Henryk Wieniawski's Romance from Concerto No. 2 d minor, Op. 22, II. Romance: Andante non troppo, which is not quite as virtuosic as some of Wieniawski's other works.
133 *Le calife de Bagdad* (The caliph of Baghdad), opéra comique in one act by the French composer François-Adrien Boieldieu; the overture is still popular today.

30. Chorus, three-part – A. *Lascia ch'io pianga* (Handel);
    B. *Lindenbaum* (Schubert)[134] – Chorus of the Engineering Department of Tohoku University (Tōhoku Daigaku Kōgaku Senmonbu)

31. Wind and string ensemble (clarinet; violins 1, 2, and 3; cello) – A. Moment Musical (Schubert); B. Minuet (Beethoven) – afficionados from music club at Tohoku Imperial University

32. Mixed chorus – a cappella *Kōen no uta* (Festive merriment song)[135] – female teachers from city schools and Kenkyūkai members from this school

The concert brought together teachers and students from several schools in Sendai: besides the Normal School and its affiliated schools, performers came from at least six other institutions, ranging from elementary schools to the Imperial University. The Second High School is not named, but some of its music enthusiasts may have joined the larger ensembles. No foreign performers are named; unlike twenty or even ten years earlier, there were enough experienced Japanese teachers and performers. The overall programme did not differ significantly from previous ones: more than half of the thirty-two items were songs; only thirteen were instrumental performances, with most of the titles suggesting a fairly elementary level, except, perhaps, those played by teachers (assuming they were played with a reasonable level of competence). The works do, however, represent a wide range of musical styles in a single concert, something that by this time may well have been appreciated by the more experienced concert-goers in the audience. Some of the pieces may have been familiar to them from previous performances.[136]

Compared to most other programmes, particularly the early ones, this one included a fair number of works from the canon of the composers generally perceived as the greatest representatives of European art music: Händel (items 1; 30); Bach (24); Beethoven (14; 31); Schubert (21; 30; 31); Mendelssohn (22; 26; possibly, 25); and Schumann (28). Clearly,

---

134 There are several choral arrangements of both.
135 Lyrics by Yoshimaru Kazumasa; music by August Söderman (1832–76): *Eine Bauernhochzeit*.
136 This is difficult to gauge, because of the small sample of programmes, but works like *Csikós Post* and *Zigeunerleben* appear on multiple programmes.

local actors on the Sendai music scene had made both the institution of the concert and the music performed at it their own.

Miyagi College

The highest standards of performance by local players may well have been achieved in the concerts organized by Miyagi College. Certainly, levels of ambition were high, as Kate Hansen's activities demonstrate. The college regularly held concerts and recitals (significantly more than the five reported in *Ongakukai*), as well as other events that included musical performance: the annual graduation ceremonies, for example, would have included musical recitals, as did the programme of the 'Twenty-third Anniversary of the Miyagi Jo Gakko Literary Society' on 27 November 1914.[137] In addition, the recital by Florence Seiple reported in *Ongakukai* in 1915 would not have been the only one. Kate Hansen's 'little private recital' mentioned in a letter to her sister in February 1908 may well have been the first of several.[138] But while all these events would have exposed locals to Western music, they were not always open to the general public. Most of the performers in the concerts reported in *Ongakukai* were foreigners, predominately missionary teachers and their families. Whether *Ongakukai* found these concerts more newsworthy, or whether concerts with performances by the female students tended to be for a restricted audience is hard to tell. Although Kate Hansen did not mention it, the more conservative families in Sendai may well have had reservations about letting their daughters perform in public concerts.

The programme of the concert described by Kate Hansen in May 1908 (see previous chapter) is the most varied of those published in *Ongakukai*: none of the others include Japanese music, although that does not mean that none was performed. Still, as Miyagi College's musical ambitions rose, they may well have felt they could dispense with such concessions to their audience. These were concerts where the local audience had the opportunity to hear works from the what today is perceived as the standard repertoire, such as a Beethoven sonata, performed by Kate

---

[137] This was presumably the event referred to as a 'Christmas show' in Kate Hansen's letter. See previous chapter: programme in Hansen Papers, SRL.

[138] KH to AFH, 2 February 1908, Box 1 Folder 22; the collection at the SRL includes several programmes of recitals by KH.

Hansen or Mrs Denning—or at least a single movement. We cannot be sure that the entire work was performed in each case: Hansen and Denning may not have played the entire sonatas by Grieg and Beethoven respectively at the concert on 10 May 1912, of which Hansen wrote to her mother that it was regarded as 'the best thing musically that's ever been given in Sendai'.[139] The other twelve items on the programme were songs or short instrumental pieces. The concert ended with Wagner's *Walkürenritt* for piano for four hands played by Hansen and Dening, a performance that must have represented an impressive finale. The other offerings do not appear very different from those at other concerts, but the experience of regularly performing in public may well have resulted in a rise in standards of performance among the foreigners as well as the Japanese. Hansen performed the *Walkürenritt* again in a school concert on 11 March 1916, with Mrs Kriete.[140]

By 1912 Miyagi College was already known for the quality of its music: two years earlier, *Ongakukai* had described it as an 'authority in the musical world of Sendai' and praised the concert held on 16 June 1910.[141] The concert featured performances by three sisters, the daughters of Henry Mohr and Emma Marie Landis, Presbyterian missionaries and teachers at Meiji Gakuin College in Tokyo. Possibly the programme in *Ongakukai* is incomplete, as it only lists nine items, all played by the sisters: for piano duet, *Spanish Dance* and *Polish Dance* by Moszkowski[142] and an unspecified piece from Gounod's opera *Faust*; for piano solo, *La fileuse* by Raff; 'Nocturne' for left hand by the Russian composer Scriabin (the programme mentions his nationality); a work by Chopin, and *La Polka de la Reine* by Raff;[143] for violin, a fantasy by Vieuxtemps; *Bohemian song* by Antonín Dvořák and *Barcarole* by Hauser, and *Romance* by Beethoven.[144]

---

139 See Chapter 10.
140 *Ongakukai* 174, 54.
141 'Sendai Miyagi Jogakkō ongakukai', *Ongakukai* 3, no. 7 (1910): 53.
142 Moritz Moszkowski (French: Maurice Moszkowski; 1854–1925), a German composer, pianist, and teacher of Polish-Jewish descent, composed numerous small-scale pieces for piano, including Spanish and Polish dances (Op. 12 and Op. 55).
143 *La fileuse* (The spinning maid) by Joachim Raff (1822–82), Op. 157 no. 2; Prelude and Nocturne for left hand, Op. 9, D-flat major, composed in 1894 by the Russian composer Scriabin; if 'uorufu' in the programme is not a misprint for 'waltz', it might conceivably be the prelude dedicated to Wolff, although supposedly not published until 1918; Raff's *Polka de la Reine* (Op. 95, composed 1861).
144 Henri Vieuxtemps (1820–81) wrote more than one violin work with 'Fantasia' in the title; the best known is the *Fantasia appassionata* for violin and orchestra, Op. 35

According to *Ongakukai* the three young ladies had chosen pieces that suited the people of Tohoku. The (unnamed) commentator particularly praised the Fantasy by Vieuxtemps and the *Faust* duet, and concluded that the three performers had truly contributed to the local music scene.[145]

The Landis sisters performed again the following year: in a letter to her sister dated 21 May 1911 and describing the twenty-fifth anniversary concert at Tohoku College on 16 May (of which she enclosed the programme), Kate Hansen wrote, 'The Landis girls are the same ones who helped with a concert here last spring, when they were just back from Germany. They really play well.'[146] Indeed, the programme of the concert in 1910 suggests that the three sisters, although still in their teens, were highly proficient on their instruments.[147]

Recitals by the teachers at Miyagi College represented a new format for the local audience. Hansen describes one she gave on 9 June 1914 as 'the first of its kind ever held in Sendai'. The school had invited the local foreigners and 'all the Japanese we knew of who had studied any music, the parents of all the schoolgirls, a lot of the common-school teachers and principals, all our own alumnae and students, and a crowd of other people of the kind we want to get interested in our school.' Hansen played the programme from memory, a first for her and 'terrifying in some ways'.[148] She was supported by Carl D. Kriete and his wife Beth

---

(c.1860), which is also performed with piano; Dvořák wrote several short pieces for violin, but seemingly none by that title; the Japanese 'Bōto no uta' by 'Hūsaa' Miska most probably refers to the Austro-Hungarian violinist and composer Miska Hauser (1822–87), whose numerous salon pieces include 'Op. 16. No. 1, Barcarole', published in 6 *Pièces p. Violon av. Acc. de Pfte.* Wien, Müller (Hofmeister); the programme does not specify which of the two violin romances by Beethoven was performed.

145 *Ongakukai* 3, no. 7 (1910), 53. Sadie Lea Weidner was the school's principal from 1909 to 1913; Hayasaka was the registrar.
146 KH to AFH, 21 May 1911, SRL Box 1 Folder 25. In the same letter she describes Mrs Denning as their best player, albeit subject to performance nerves.
147 Their parents, Henry Mohr Landis (1857–1921) and Emma Marie Landis (1859–1935), who was German-born, married in 1888 and came to Japan the same year, where they taught at Meiji Gakuin, where they spent their entire working life. Their (presumably) firstborn, Fritz (b. 1889) died in infancy; they were survived by three daughters and two sons. See Meiji Gakuin Rekishi Shiryōkan, ed. Meiji Gakuin Rekishi Shiryōkan shiryōshū dai 13 shū: 'Meiji Gakuin no gaikokujin senkyōshi' Segawa Kazuo ikōshū. Tokyo: Meiji Gakuin Rekishi Shiryōkan, 2018, 49–50. Obituaries in Samuel John Umbreit, ed. *The Christian Movement in Japan, Korea and Formosa: A Yearbook of Christian Work, Twentieth Annual Issue* (Federation of Christian Missions Japan, 1922), 299–300; *Japan Christian Yearbook* (Nippon Dempo News Agency, Tokyo: 1936), 321–22.
148 KH to her family, 14 June 1914, SRL Box 1, Folder 27.

(the couple was based in Yamagata), whom she described in a letter to her sister as 'thorough musicians'.[149] Carl Kriete had sung baritone in the choir as a student, while Beth, a pianist, was conservatoire-trained.

A year later, on 16 April 1915, Florence Seiple gave a recital accompanied by Hansen, who also played solo. The reporter for *Ongakukai* speculated that Seiple may have hoped to become an opera singer, because her impressive rendering of an aria from *Samson and Delilah*, 'where Delilah seduces Samson', suggested that it was a forte of Sendai's 'primadonna'.[150] Presumably, this was *Mon cœur s'ouvre à ta voix* from Act 2 of Camille Saint-Saëns' opera; indeed a daring choice for a missionary wife. Seiple's other offerings, songs by Johannes Brahms and the American Romantic composer Edward Alexander MacDowell (1860–1908), were more conventional.

The school's first graduation recital, on 22 March 1919, was another landmark. Of course, graduation concerts were common by then, but they involved groups of graduates and other members of the school, rather than a single individual. 'I think we have set a new standard for this part of Japan', Hansen wrote the following day and continued:

> It's a long way back from this to the concerts they used to have here, when audiences of a couple thousand people would listen gravely for half an hour at a time to boy students' playing exercises and scales with one finger and imagine they were hearing Western music! They were still having them in my first year or two in Sendai. Now there is a considerable public which is beginning to know quite a bit about what music really is, and that helps our school, of course.[151]

The concerts at Miyagi College probably reached a smaller and less diverse audience than those held at the Normal School. For those who did attend, however, they represented an opportunity to hear major works of European art music as well as what we today might regard as salon pieces, played to a relatively high, sometimes professional

---

149 KH to AFH, 10 June 1914, SRL Box 1, Folder 27 (a programme is included at the back of the same folder), Carl D. Kriete (1883–1962), who from 1930 to 1940 served as seventh president of Miyagi College, and his wife had come to Japan in 1911. Beth (née Martin) Kriete (1883–1962), who taught at Miyagi from 1935 to 1941, had studied music at Arnold School of Music, Cincinnati College of Music. See 'Miyagi Gakuin no yakuin mata wa kyōin de atta senkyōshi', *Miyagi Gakuin Shiryō Shitsu nenpō/Miyagi Gakuin Archives of History Review* 18/19 (2011/2012).
150 'Sendai tsūshin', *Ongakukai* 164 (1915): 70–71.
151 KH to her family, 23 March 1919, SRL, Box 1 Folder 29.

standard. Performances would have included the oratorios Kate Hansen mentioned in *Impressions*, although, possibly, performed in a church service rather than a concert.[152]

Japanese students and audiences, however, were not the only ones whose experience of Western art music increased and deepened. While Hansen only hints at it in her letters, she —and presumably her Western colleagues —also developed and progressed. In Sendai they had opportunities to perform that they might not have had to the same extent if they had stayed in their home countries. They may well have been more confident, knowing as they did that their audience (at least initially) were undiscerning, and have chosen works they might not otherwise have dared to play in public. Of Hansen we know that she took every opportunity to further her skills and knowledge. She revised her initially low opinion of the audience, and her choice of repertoire pieces like *Devil's March* were replaced with sonatas by Beethoven and Grieg. We might also ask ourselves whether Florence Seiple would have performed Delilah's aria of seduction for an audience in an American provincial town. Miyagi College provides a striking illustration of how the musical encounter affected all the parties involved, not just those generally perceived to be at the receiving end.

Other Institutions

Concerts were also organized at other schools, but they may well have been smaller, less public affairs. At any rate, only a few were reported in *Ongakukai*, and not all reports included a programme. One that did was a concert held on 23 March 1917 at Sendai High School for Girls.[153] The programme listed an opening and a closing address and nine musical items: vocal, piano, and violin solos and a violin duet. The duet was played by Hongō and Kumagai (the latter described as an external teacher). That same year, on 21 November 1917 a concert held at Shōkei School for Girls was reported, with a programme of eight items: chorus, vocal solo, piano, and organ.[154] Neither of these two was significantly

---

152 *Ongakukai* has no report of an oratorio performance.
153 'Sendai Kōtō Jogakkō sōbetsu ongakukai', *Ongakukai* 187 (1917): 73–74.
154 'Sendai Shōkei Jogakkō ongakukai', *Ongakukai* 195 (1918): 72–73.

different from the other programmes described. Performers at Shōkei included Mrs Iglehart, the wife of a Methodist missionary.

Local societies also organized concerts. In December 1916, *Ongakukai* reported the establishment of the Sendai Musical Amateur Club (Sendai Ongaku Dōkō Kurabu).[155] The club had been formed in November with the intention to refine the local people's musical sensibilities and to study and cultivate Western music, perceived as being underdeveloped in the city, which did not even have a dedicated concert hall.[156] The inaugural concert on 18 November, in the auditorium of the Second High School, featured three performers from Tokyo: Tōgi Tetsusaburō (violinist), Ōwada Aira (singer and cellist), and Hirota Ryūtarō (composer and pianist).[157] All three were graduates of and teachers at the Tokyo Academy of Music. While the programme was not unlike others in Sendai at the time, it included two string quartet items, in which the local violinists Hongō and Kumagai joined the guests (each playing second violin in one), as well as two piano trio performances.[158] The concert was deemed a success, attracting an audience of 1,400.

The club organized another concert in May 1917, again with musicians from Tokyo. This time Tōgi and Ōwada were joined by the pianist Sakakibara Naoshi and the soprano singer Takeoka Tsuruyo.[159] Besides Mendelssohn's piano trio in G minor (performed by Tōgi and Owada, with Sakakibara at the piano), a string quartet by Haydn in G major,[160] and Mozart's *Eine kleine Nachtmusik*, the audience were

---

155 'Ongaku ensō taikai', *Ongakukai* 182 (1916): 48; for the programme see Sendai Chōmarusei [pseud.], 'Sendai gakukyō (February 1917)', *Ongakukai* 184 (1917): 61.
156 Sendai Chōmarusei [pseud.], 'Sendai gakukyō (February 1917)'.
157 'Ongaku ensō taikai', *Ongakukai* 182 (1916): 48. Tōgi (1884–1952), who came from a *gagaku* family, graduated from the Tokyo Academy of Music in 1905, where he taught from May 1906 until January 1908. Ōwada (1886–1962) taught *shōka* at the Academy from 1907 to 1913. Hirota (1892–1952) taught at the Academy from 1914 to 1939 and was also a member of the Hōgaku Research Committee. See Tōkyō Geijutsu Daigaku Hyakunenshi Hensan Iinkai, ed. *Tōkyō Geijutsu Daigaku hyakunenshi: Tōkyō Ongaku Gakkō hen 2.* (Tokyo: Ongaku no Tomosha, 2003), 1566; 1551; 1572 (Hirota).
158 Only the titles of the movements are named, not the actual works. In the quartet items, Hirota played the viola part, according to the programme.
159 'Sendai Amachua Kurabu shunki ensōkai', *Ongakukai* 189 (1917): 46. Takeoka is not named in the programme, but her identity is evident from another report published in a later issue. See 'Sendai Amachua Kurabu kinkyō', *Ongakukai* 191 (1917): 54–55. The city hall was completed in May 1916.
160 The programme describes it as '*to chōchō* (7 ban)', but this may be an error: Haydn wrote several quartets in G major, none of which is identified as 'no. 7'.

treated to Beethoven's 'Moonlight' Sonata (or at least a movement from it) and the final movement of Mendelssohn's violin concerto in E minor.[161] Again, the local violinists Hongō and Kumagai took part.[162] This concert too was described as a success, with 1,300 people attending in the newly built city hall. According to *Ongakukai*, this was all the more noteworthy because of the difficulties of organizing concerts in provincial towns. Another report in *Ongakukai* two months later even claimed that the audience had numbered 2,500 and praised Takeoka's singing, adding that her songs had become popular among the local girls. Nevertheless, Takeoka was not actually named together with the other guest performers from Tokyo, and her name did not appear in the programme: since no other singer is named, she presumably sang *Hiru no yume* (Midday dream), composed by Fukada Sada, and the soprano part in an unspecified duet from Mozart's opera *Don Giovanni*, with Ōwada Aira singing the other part.[163] Possibly, the omission was due to a notion that the name of a young woman who had only graduated the previous month did not merit a mention together with the famous stars, or else she had been roped in at the last minute. Takeno continued into the graduate department and went on to an impressive career as a performer and pedagogue, as well as a co-founder in 1926 of what today is Kunitachi College of Music.

The author of the report concluded by praising the work of the society, but then ended on a critical note. The habit of people in Tohoku to argue about everything hampered progress: 'Those who devote themselves to music and while teaching at one school go to the extreme of interfering with the staging of other concerts, are behaving outrageously. Those who aim to further the growth of music must eliminate these members as quickly as possible.'[164] The cooperation of different parties evinced by several of the concert programmes was clearly far from self-evident.

---

161 'Sendai Amachua Kurabu shunki ensōkai', *Ongakukai* 189 (1917): 46l.
162 Kumagai is listed as taking the viola part in the string quartet performances.
163 Presumably *La ci darem la mano*, the most famous duet from the opera, although 'jichūon' in the programme usually means 'tenor', and the part of Don Giovanni is scored for bass or baritone.
164 TN, 'Sendai Amachū Kurabu kinjō', *Ongakukai* 191 (1917): 55.

Representing the Nation and the World in Sendai

By the early 1920s, then, participation in concerts whether as listener, performer, or organizer, had widened and diversified, with new actors, such as the Amateur Club and members of Tohoku Imperial University, appearing on the scene. The people of Sendai had the opportunity to hear a wide range of Western music, sometimes performed to a high standard. As for Japanese music, the reporters for *Ongakukai* were chiefly concerned with Western music, so other sources would have to be consulted in order to reach definite conclusions, but the absence of references to Japanese music in the later reports, together with its disappearance from published concert programmes, suggests that the distance between the two musical worlds had increased.

Judging from the sample of concert programmes published in *Ongakukai*, performances varied between the different organizing institutions and over time. Nevertheless, some general characteristics are discernible. Performances included solos and vocal and instrumental ensembles ranging from duets to small orchestras. The predominant musical instruments were the piano or (reed) organ and the violin, and, in Japanese music, the *koto* and the *shamisen* as well as the *satsumabiwa*. The local musicians consisted mainly of students and their teachers, among them the foreign teachers and other members of the foreign community. Visiting musicians most commonly came from the Tokyo Academy of Music.

The repertoire consisted largely of *shōka*, hymns, and fairly elementary instrumental pieces. The number and variety of *shōka* published in Japan by this time means that close examination would require a study of its own. The later collections increasingly included compositions by Japanese. Indeed, for *tokuhon shōka* (reading textbook songs) this could not be otherwise, since the text was a given. Even *shōka* not specifically described as such were often based on the contents of school textbooks. Setting existing lyrics to a tune represented a marked departure from the adoption of *shōka* in the early days of the Tokyo Academy of Music, when Western tunes had to be fitted with suitable Japanese lyrics.

Chronologically, the repertoire ranged from the European Baroque era to contemporary music. Among the instrumental pieces, marches were particularly frequent, reflecting the strong presence of military-style music in the repertoire of nineteenth-century Western music. Many items might be classified as salon pieces, with the term used in a broad sense to include both music composed chiefly for playing at home and arrangements of popular excerpts from larger works such as operas and oratorios, including works largely forgotten today, such as unspecified items from Flotow's opera *Martha* (conceivably, *The Last Rose of Summer*, the melody of which would have been familiar to most Japanese from one of the earliest *shōka*); or from Wallace's *Maritana*.[165] Other operatic favourites included Carl Maria von Weber and Richard Wagner.[166]

The most iconic 'great masters', on the other hand, are strikingly underrepresented. Beethoven, for example, for all the reverence the Japanese expressed for his name, (as attested by Kate Hansen) and for all his status as the icon of European art music, is conspicuous by his absence in most of the programmes examined. He is named (or can be definitely identified) as a composer in seven of the programmes examined, four of them performed by foreigners at Miyagi College or musicians from the Tokyo Academy of Music.[167] Mozart, that other iconic composer, is named in eight concert programmes (twice in two of them), with two of them featuring local Japanese performers.[168]

The breadth of the repertoire reinforces the understanding of these concerts as a creative space in which the imagination, stimulated by the sonic experience and the different titles that described its elements, could roam beyond the borders of the city and the prefecture to encompass the whole Japanese nation, and the world beyond its

---

165 *Martha:* ('Māsa') Sendai Association, October 1907; Second High School, January 1908; Miyagi Shihan, February 1918; possibly Tohoku University, May 1920 ('Maruta'); William Vincent Wallace (1812–65), *Maritana*: Second High, October 1913 (probably); Second High, November 1915; Sendai Girls' High, 1917); Tohoku Academy of Music, 1920.
166 Works by Weber were included in at least eight of the programmes examined; pieces from *Tannhäuser* in at least five.
167 Performances by Japanese include an organ solo by a fourth-year student at Miyagi Normal School for Men, 26 February 1916, playing an unspecified funeral march (from Op. 26?), and a piano solo as well as an ensemble performance at a concert by the Miyagi Normal School, 26 February 1916; an unspecified funeral march (from Op. 26?), 19 February 1921; an unspecified allegro and a minuet respectively; the ensemble members came from Tohoku University.
168 Second High School, 1903 and 1920; Miyagi College, May 1908, 1916; Normal School, 1914; Amateur Club 1917; Imperial University, 1920 (2); Tohoku Academy, 1920 (2).

borders. The extent of the familiarity of the pieces would have varied, from Japanese and blended music, and *shōka* that by the 1900s had been sung for many years, to the marches and dances that were staples of military and civilian band performances, and, finally, Western popular songs and instrumental works that evoked faraway and mythical places, and, less often, chamber music and solos that might be described as art music proper.

The programme of the concert at the Normal School in 1921, introduced above, includes examples of all of the (Western-style) genres mentioned. The opening work, *See the Conquering Hero Comes* from Händel's *Judas Maccabäus*, is an example of a work based on a story from Biblical times. The popular chorus has been adapted and arranged in many forms, and had probably been performed at previous concerts.[169] Another example is the *War March of the Priests* from Mendelssohn's *Athalia* (Op. 74), which in the nineteenth century was as popular as his *Wedding March*, performed in the same concert (item 22), and appeared on at least three programmes in Sendai.[170] Other exotic settings are the (Middle Eastern) Orient, represented by *The Caliph of Baghdad* (29), and the gypsy camp portrayed in Schumann's *Zigeunerleben* (28), now sung with translated lyrics.[171] Gypsies are also evoked in Sarasate's *Zigeunerweisen*, still one of the most popular violin pieces in Japan (and elsewhere); the performance by Tōgi Tetteki at the Sendai Amateur Club's spring concert in 1917 (billed as *Rurōshi no uta*) may well have been a Sendai first, given its level of difficulty.

The audience would not have known this, but François-Adrien Boieldieu, the composer of *The Caliph*, also composed the tune of *Kono kimi kono kuni* (This ruler, this land; item 18), a patriotic song that begins with 'The height of Mount Fuji, the depth of Lake Biwa...'. The famous landmarks would have been almost as distant as a foreign country to

---

169 For example, Pt 2, item 3 in the Second High School concert in November 1910 lists a string ensemble of *gaika* (victory song), which may well be Händel's chorus, which appears in the repertoire of violin tutors.

170 Second High School, February 1905; and October 1908 (ensemble); Miyagi Jogakkō, May 1912 (organ). About the popularity of *Athalia*, see Marian Wilson Kimber, 'Performing "Athalia": Mendelssohn's Op. 74 in the Nineteenth-Century Choral World', *The Choral Journal* 49, no. 10 (2009).

171 *The Caliph of Baghdad* was also performed at a concert held at Miyagi College in June 1916. *Zigeunerleben* (with the translated title *Rurō no tami*) was also programmed at the Normal School for Girls in February 1917.

most of the population of Sendai before the political unification of the country and construction of the railway network. If *Chishima* (Kurile Islands; item 6B) is, as seems likely, the song *Dōho subete rokusenman* (Our sixty million brethren), then the opening lines, 'From Karafuto and Chishima in the North to Taiwan, Penghu, and the eight provinces of Korea in the South', describe the extent of the Japanese empire at the end of the Meiji era. The (mythical) beginnings of the Japanese nation are the subject of *Yamato Takeru* (11). The song of the *Gunkan māchi* (Warship march), on the other hand, performed at the Normal School concert in February 1918, bore the message that Japan had to protect itself against a potentially hostile world.

Many compositions in other concerts evoked foreign nations or regions in their titles. The concert programme with the Landis sisters (16 June 1910) alone included a 'Spanish' and a 'Polish' dance as well as a 'Bohemian song', while two composers were described as French and Russian respectively. The names of several marches included place names; for example, the Second High School concert on 31 March 1903 included the *Louisville March, Grand Russian March* and *Washington March*.[172] The American patriotic song *Hail Columbia* featured in several concerts.[173]

Perhaps as a counterweight to a world that had become larger and, even while fascinating, more threatening, *shōka* expressing a nostalgic longing or a sense of loss were popular items. In the 1921 programme examined here, *Kyōshū* (Longing for home; item 2) and *Koishiki haha* (Beloved mother; 15) almost certainly fall into this category. The all-time favourite, however, was *Home, Sweet Home,* which was sung or played in several concerts either in English, or in Japanese, as *Hanyū no yado* (Our humble dwelling) or *Tanoshiki wagaya* (Our happy home).[174] Even in the sentimental evocation of the home—another modern construct—the Japanese in Sendai and elsewhere were in tune with their contemporaries in the English-speaking world. *Home Sweet Home*, composed by Henry R. Bishop and premiered as part of Payne's 1823 operetta *Clari, or the Maid of Milan*, became one of the most popular sentimental songs of the

---

172 See Chapter 9.
173 Second High School, 11 February 1905; Normal School, 4 March 1911; Tōhoku Ongakuin, 25 October 1914 and 3 October 1916.
174 *Tanoshiki wagaya* might also be one of several other songs with that title.

nineteenth century (and beyond), widely circulated as sheet music and sung by amateurs at home and by professional singers on the stage.[175] The song has since featured in American films, and plays a central part in Ichikawa Kon's 1956 film *The Burmese Harp*. Early in the film, a company of Japanese soldiers find themselves surrounded by British in a remote Burmese village. They sing *Home, Sweet Home* with Japanese lyrics in order to trick the British soldiers into believing that their presence has not been noticed by the Japanese. But as they prepare for a surprise attack, the British soldiers respond by singing the same song with its English lyrics. The Japanese soldiers surrender and learn that the war ended three days previously. In this scene, singing together, albeit in different languages, is represented as 'a unifying act', through which the soldiers on opposing sides recognize their common humanity.[176]

War, of course, represents a major break with the past, both for the nations and the individuals involved. But modernity itself is defined by the notion of progress and rapid movement away from the past. Nostalgia, a melancholic sense of irretrievable loss, depends on this notion and is a quintessentially modern phenomenon.[177] Music gave expression to that loss. Julian Johnson describes the nineteenth-century Lied as 'a vehicle of nostalgia' and as 'one of the most explicit genres of musical re-membering, defined by a peculiarly modern quality of temporal dissonance to which it gives exemplary form.'[178] The examples he analyses are art songs from the classical canon, but the characterization would seem to apply to the songs by composers like Stephen Foster and Henry Rowley Bishop. For Japan and other non-Western countries, the break with the past was particularly extreme because it involved being confronted with cultural traditions radically different from their own.[179]

---

175 Bridget Bennet, 'Home Songs and the Melodramatic Imagination: From "Home, Sweet Home" to *The Birth of a Nation*', *Journal of American Studies* 46, no. 1 (2012): 178, https://doi.org/10.1017/S0021875811001356

176 For a detailed discussion of the episode and its effect on Japanese and Anglophone viewers respectively, see Stephen Parmelee, '"Such Inexplicable Pain": Kon Ichikawa's The Burmese Harp', *Christian Scholar's Review* 40, no. 4 (2011), https://christianscholars.com/such-inexplicable-pain-kon-ichikawas-the-burmese-harp/

177 Peter Fritzsche, 'Specters of History: On Nostalgia, Exile, and Modernity', *The American Historical Review* 106, no. 5 (2001): 1589, 95, https://doi.org/OI: 10.2307/2692740; Johnson, *Out of Time*, 26, 85.

178 Johnson, *Out of Time*, 37.

179 De Ferranti and Tokita, *Music, Modernity and Locality*, 10.

Nostalgia is strongly present in Japan's culture today, musically and otherwise, something generally ascribed to the abruptness and rapidity of Japan's course of modernization, Westernization, and urbanization.[180]

The modern space of the concert brought inhabitants of Sendai from diverse backgrounds together for the purpose of performing and listening to music. This in itself was new. Through the foreign music they encountered the world outside Japan. Whether as listeners or performers, they could, simultaneously with their contemporaries in other parts of the world, imagine and experience themselves as part of a much wider world than the provincial city they lived in, or even the nation it belonged to. By performing the music, they were simultaneously performing an imagined worldwide community: symbolically 'keeping together in time' and (increasingly) in tune with the modern world of nations.

---

180 Jennifer Milioto Matsue, *Music in Contemporary Japan*, Focus on World Music Series, (New York: Routledge, 2016), 55–58.

Conclusion

The international environment Japan found itself in in the late nineteenth century meant that in order to survive without being colonized it had no choice but to somehow unite the people in solidarity and strive to enrich and strengthen the country, and become a civilized nation. The Meiji government intended public education to foster a new type of citizen that, while submitting to the demands of the nation, would act as an independent individual, and for this purpose music (singing *shōka* with one voice) was deemed indispensable. One aspect of songs is that they move people with the literary quality and content of the lyrics. Equally important, however, is the act of matching them with sound [...] We should note that, however hackneyed the lyrics may be, it is song which, just as the drum call creates discipline, synchronizes the pitch and tempo of the all the voices of people present in a given place.[1]

When we reflect on some of the conclusions reached in this exploration of musical universality, irony may seem to abound. We share perceptual mechanisms and processes, but the result is that we develop mental schemata that make some foreign music sound strange. We share some universal preferences, but most are not on the surface, and their compatibility with many structural possibilities results in musical diversity, not similarity. Music's impact on our sense of security and its power to create group cohesion makes it serviceable for sectarian purposes.[2]

By the early 1920s, musical culture in Sendai had been transformed: 'We are having real professional concerts in Japan now, even in Sendai, and the way the Japanese are getting to appreciate them is wonderful. [...] The

---

1 Yasuto Okunaka, *Kokka to ongaku: Isawa Shūji ga mezashita Nihon kindaika* (Tokyo: Shunjūsha, 2008), 237. See also Benedict Anderson, *Imagined Communities* (London: Verso, 1991), 145.
2 Kathleen Marie Higgins, *The Music between Us: Is Music a Universal Language?* (Chicago: University of Chicago Press, 2012), 181–82, https://doi.org/10.7208/chicago/9780226333274.001.0001

Japanese are going to be ahead of us in music in a couple of generations, if our folks don't improve',[3] wrote Kate Hansen in 1923. In her thesis in 1927, she gave three main reasons for the transformation. First, Japan's increasing wealth as a result of the war boom allowed more people to buy instruments, even pianos, and practise playing them at home. None of her early pupils had a piano at home, despite coming from wealthy families. Second, phonographs became popular (no doubt also a result of increased wealth), as did recordings of Western music, with the effect of 'training their ears in a remarkable way'. Third, 'real artists' (Hansen's expression) began to visit, including European refugees, particularly destitute White Russians after the revolution. Hansen added a fourth reason that was applicable in Sendai: the efforts by professors of Tohoku Imperial University, who had often studied abroad and heard concerts in Europe, and worked hard to promote concerts by top-class artists in Sendai.[4]

Hansen's letters in the 1920s contain several references to rising musical standards. On 10 February 1924, she wrote to her family that a local primary school had acquired a piano, 'the first one for that purpose in the city'.[5] She herself was invited to play at its inauguration, and some of the teachers at the school had taken lessons at Miyagi College in preparation for the event.[6] A few months later she mentioned an example of increased familiarity with Western music: 'Curiously enough, as I was walking home the day before the concert, I heard a man, a very ordinary-looking one, whistle the airs of both the Mendelssohn and the Lohengrin marches, somewhat out of tune, to be sure, but quite recognizably.'[7]

Foreign artists touring Japan began to include Sendai in their itinerary, and found an appreciative audience. About Efrem Zimbalist's

---

3   KH to 'Aunt Kate' (Troup Cookingham), Karuizawa, 1 August 1923, SRL Box 1, Folder 31.
4   Hansen, Kate. Thesis: Experiences in Teaching and Developing a Music School in Japan. (1927, updated 1933. Personal Papers of Kate I. Hansen, University Archives, PP19, Box 3, Folder 1, Kenneth Spencer Research Library, University of Kansas Libraries, Lawrence, Kansas), 27–30. Research tends to back up her observations. See Margaret Mehl, *Not by Love Alone: The Violin in Japan, 1850–2010* (Copenhagen: The Sound Book Press, 2014), 121–31.
5   KH to her family, SHL Box 1, Folder 32.
6   KH to her family, 17 February 1924, Box 1, Folder 32.
7   KH to her family, 8 June 1924.

visit in 1930, Hansen wrote, 'The great event of this week was the concert by Zimbalist, the first one in Sendai by any artist of his reputation. [...] I think Mr. Zimbalist had expected a very backwoods kind of audience, and was extremely surprised to find a lot of conservatory students and people who know about music.'[8] In subsequent letters, Hansen wrote about concerts in Sendai given by Leonid Kreutzer, the French pianist Gil-Marchex, Jascha Heifetz, Zimbalist again, Konrad Liebrecht, and Mischa Elman.[9] Kreutzer and Liebrecht had fled from the Nazis and settled in Japan. Other refugees from Germany included the German philosopher Karl Löwith (1897–1973), who taught at Tohoku Imperial University from 1936 to 1941. His wife was 'an excellent amateur violinist', and playing together with her gave Hansen 'a chance to know things I've never played in before'.[10] That same year, 1937, Hansen had her first experience of hearing music broadcast by radio from Germany at the house of an acquaintance: 'the very first time we've done this in Sendai, and now, for the first time, I'm really wishing for a radio.'[11]

By the 1930s, then, the provincial town's links to the wider world had noticeably increased. Europe, meanwhile, was becoming 'provincial' in the sense that its cultural dominance was eroding. Emigrants from Europe in the early twentieth century mostly settled in America rather than Asia. By the end of the century, however, European art music was just as much at home in Asia as in Europe or the USA, if not more so.[12]

Until well into the twentieth century, narratives that assumed the superiority of European art music in order to explain its dominance were common. Since then, it has become fashionable to link the spread of Western music with 'the crimes of colonialism'.[13] While such a link

---

8   KH to her family, 18 October 1930, SRL Box 1, Folder 36. Zimbalist toured Japan six times between 1922 and 1935: see Mehl, *Not by Love Alone*, 138–39. KH's papers include a programme of a recital in Sendai on 5 June 1935 (Box 5, Folder 13).
9   Leonid Kreutzer: KH to her family 10 May 1931; Henri Gil-Marchex (1894–1970) and Heifetz: 25 Oct 1931, Folder 37; Konrad Liebrecht: 3 June 1935; Elman 14 February 1937.
10 KH to her family, 28 February 1937, Folder 42.
11 KH to her family, 11 January 1937, Folder 42.
12 Nicholas Cook, 'Western Music as World Music', in *The Cambridge History of World Music*, ed. Philip Vilas Bohlman (Cambridge: Cambridge University Press, 2013), https://doi.org/10.1017/CHO9781139029476 Spitzer makes the same point: see Michael Spitzer, *The Musical Human: A History of Life on Earth* (London: Bloomsbury, 2021), 272.
13 For a recent example, see Spitzer, *Musical Human*, 258–67 and passim.

cannot be denied, the reality is more complex. As Liebersohn rightly observes: 'To capture the complexity of musical encounters is to go against the cliché of an imposition tout court of Western culture on the rest of the world, countered by the revolt of indigenous cultures.'[14] Japan is a case in point. It is worth repeating here that not only did Japan escape being colonized: Japan itself became a colonizing power and contributed to the global dissemination of Western music in its colonies. Comparing Japan with the United States, which in the period examined here became the most powerful of Western nations, demonstrates that political and cultural dominance did not necessarily go hand in hand; a sense of inferiority and a reverence for Europe as the musical heartland persisted in both Japan and the USA.[15]

In what follows, the five assertions presented in the introduction and elaborated upon in the preceding chapters will be revisited in order to shed further light on the complex processes involved in Japan's musical modernization and to attempt to answer the question posed in the introduction about what music might contribute to our understanding of Japan's modern history.

First, Western music attracted the attention of government officials and individuals not because of its intrinsic merits, but because of its functions within the modern state. For the general public it came to be associated with modernity, because it was performed in and by modern institutions. Second, while government efforts centred on strengthening the nation and moulding its citizens, all the actors we have examined, both official and non-official, were acutely conscious of being part of a global community of nations in which they wanted to be accepted as equals by the leading powers. Third, and closely to related to the first two, the ultimate relegation of traditional music to a niche existence did not mean that it became insignificant. Indeed, it assumed a vital role in the re-imagining of Japanese culture. Fourth, 'Western music' is a blanket term, and European art music proper was arguably the least important genre to be introduced, at

---

14 Harry Liebersohn, *Music and the New Global Culture: From the Great Exhibitions to the Jazz Age* (Chicago: University of Chicago Press, 2019), 9, https://doi.org/10.7208/9780226649306

15 The same point has been made regarding China. See Richard Curt Kraus, *Pianos and Politics in China: Middle-Class Ambitions and the Struggle over Western Music* (New York and Oxford: Oxford University Press, 1989), 202.

least initially. Our examination of concert life in Sendai reveals that concert programmes were dominated by *shōka*, marches, pieces from the pedagogical literature, and items that might be subsumed under the term 'salon music'. And fifth, there is good reason to accept that many of the effects of hearing and making music described in the research literature on the subject are real and support the argument that engaging with Western music (as well as approaching traditional music in a new way) was a means of engaging with global modernity itself and playing an active part in shaping it.

Beside the army and navy, the school system was the most significant modern institution through which Western music was first introduced. Isawa Shūji, the most important actor behind the introduction of music into the public education system, had limited musical expertise or interest in music *per se*. Emphasizing these deficiencies, however, obscures the breadth of his educational vision. This becomes clear when his role as a promoter of Western music is related to his other activities.[16] Isawa understood the power of music when combined with movement, and with language, to promote all aspects of education: physical, intellectual, linguistic, and moral. This is evident from his pioneering efforts in Aichi to introduce movement games as part of elementary education. Both schools and the military employed synchronized movements to music to support the Meiji government's agenda of educating citizens. If the Japanese really are more group-orientated than most—and the cliché persists, although scholars have long been critical of it[17]—then the systematic promotion of singing together and of synchronized movement to music since the Meiji period may well represent a more plausible explanation than the demands of rice cultivation.

Indeed, performing synchronized movements to music is not limited to schools or the army. In 1928, the national broadcasting cooperation (NHK) introduced an institution that has endured almost continuously to this day: radio callisthenics (*rajio taisō*). The concept originated in the United States in 1925, the year radio broadcasting was introduced

---

16 This is the major contribution of Okunaka's book: see Okunaka, *Kokka to ongaku*.
17 See, for example, Hans Dieter Ölschleger et al., eds., *Individualität und Egalität im gegenwärtigen Japan: Untersuchungen zu Wertemustern im Bezug auf Familie und Arbeitswelt* (Munich: Iudicium, 1994), 31–47.

into Japan, and aroused Japanese interest almost immediately.[18] It took the form of a three-minute series of simple exercises to piano accompaniment broadcast every morning at the same time. As with the drum and fife bands, one might question the description of the simple piano accompaniment as 'music', but the sounds are certainly what we would call 'Western'. Moreover, over the years, *rajio taisō* (together with the merits of rising early) became the subject of several *shōka*, including *Rajio* in the Ministry of Education textbook for primary schools (second year) issued in 1932.[19]

More recently, song and movement in the form of dance were mobilized in support of the upcoming 2020 Tokyo Olympics by the organizing committee, who in 2017 released a video with an updated version of the 1964 classic song *Gorin ondo*, complete with a new choreography that included a version for the wheelchair-bound.[20]

Isawa is often described as having given little consideration to aesthetic education, but that is not entirely true. For the early collection of *shōka* compiled under Isawa's auspices, poets and prominent stylists were engaged to compose suitable lyrics. Many of the songs in the first song book are about nature and the seasons and exemplify basic Japanese poetic conventions. Others express longing for home and family. The lyrics of *Hotaru* (Fireflies), sung to the tune of *Auld Lang Syne*, one of the most culturally significant songs from the early *shōka* repertoire, combined nostalgia with love for the nation and the need to protect it. Today, the strongly patriotic verses are forgotten, and the main reason for its significance and enduring popularity may well be

---

18 Kerim Yasar, *Electrified Voices: How the Telephone, Phonograph, and Radio Shaped Modern Japan, 1868–1945* (New York: Columbia University Press, 2018), 118–26, https://www.degruyter.com/document/doi/10.7312/yasa18712/html; Mark Jewel, 'The First Primary School Songbook of 1881: A Study and Translation (1)', *Journal of Liberal Arts (Waseda University)* 143 (2017). See also Ryan Moran, 'Securing the Health of the Nation: Life Insurance, Labor and Health Improvement in Interwar Japan', *Japan Forum* 31, no. 2 (2019), https://doi.org/10.1080/09555803.2018.1461677 For a recent description of current practice in present-day Japan, see 'The Lifelong Exercise that Keeps Japan Moving', WorkLife (Japan 2020), BBC, updated 19 June 2020, https://www.bbc.com/worklife/article/20200609-the-life-long-exercise-that-keeps-japan-moving

19 See liner notes to the compilation, *Rajio taisō no subete: Rajio taisō 75nen no ayumi*. CD, King Records, 2003, KICG 3079.

20 See, for example, 'Tokyo 2020 Olympics get song and dance treatment', BBC News, Asia, 25 July 2017, https://www.bbc.com/news/av/world-asia-40712985

the tradition, transmitted from America, of singing it at graduation.[21] Whether or not lyrics of *shōka* were overtly nationalist, their melodies and rhythms helped shape the words and phrases and made them more memorable, while the act of singing together reinforced the sense of belonging to a community, whether local, national, or even global.

Research on singing in schools and on sports has often focused on their use, or abuse, in the service of the nation. The abuses of music by dictatorial regimes and for fuelling aggression have, of course, been identified and analysed. Unsurprisingly, musical culture in Nazi Germany, where the myth of a special German link with music persisted, has received particular attention.[22] In Japan in the period from the 1930s to the end of the Second World War, the already patriotic content of *shōka* in the textbooks issued by the Ministry of Education became increasingly militaristic and thus provides a stark reminder of music's potential to divide as well as to unite. Combining the unfixed emotional power of music with specific meanings expressed through the power of words can produce a formidable tool for the manipulation of minds and emotions. During the Second World War, *shōka* sung in schools played a significant role in mobilizing pupils for the war effort and did so far more effectively than more obvious propaganda forced on the people by an authoritarian government.[23] Discourse analysis of a large number of letters written by kamikaze pilots, for example, has revealed that their

---

21 For a translation of all the songs in the first songbook, see Jewel, 'The First Primary School Songbook of 1881: A Study and Translation (1)'. For the significance of fixed occasions for singing *Auld Lang Syne*, see Morag J. Grant, *Auld Lang Syne: A Song and its Culture* (Cambridge: Open Book Publishers, 2021) https://doi.org/10.11647/OBP.0231

22 For a summary of Germany's ambivalent relationship with music, see Celia Applegate, *The Necessity of Music: Variations on a German Theme* (Toronto: University of Toronto Press, 2017), 296–313, https://doi.org/10.3138/9781487511593 Synchronized, rhythmical movements have been similarly discredited: see William McNeill, *Keeping Together in Time: Dance and Drill in Human History* (Cambridge, MA: Harvard University Press, 1997), 151.

23 For a detailed linguistic and discursive analysis of *shōka* in the government textbooks and the psychological mechanisms behind them, see Luli van der Does-Ishikawa, 'A Sociolinguistic Analysis of Japanese Children's Official Songbooks, 1881–1945: Nurturing an Imperial Ideology through the Manipulation of Language' (Doctor of Philosophy, University of Sheffield, 2013), https://core.ac.uk/download/pdf/19775967.pdf

self-representations in their writings reflect the contents of *shōka* they grew up singing in school.²⁴

But while nationalism causes division and conflict between nations, it also constitutes a set of shared assumptions about the world: internationalism and globalism represent the other side of the same coin, and music can serve both. Kume Kunitake may have had difficulty making sense of the musical performances he heard at the Boston Jubilee, but he had no trouble in understanding music's usefulness for promoting patriotism when he observed military bands of different nations performing their brand of patriotic music. Music, as well as being a tool of patriotism, can and does serve as a force of global integration. While the bands of different countries had their own repertoire, the musical idiom was shared, as were musical practices and innovations, which circulated across national borders.²⁵

Japanese reformers realized that, in order to join the concert of nations, they needed a distinctive national music that—literally— harmonized with that of the other nations. Westerners solved the paradox by cultivating the myth of music as a universal language. The national musics of Western countries could be regarded as dialects, that is, in essence, compatible. Japanese music, however, differed fundamentally from Western music, and when Chamberlain applied the notion of dialect to Japanese music, he must have been aware that it was far-fetched. Isawa, in his writings, tried to prove that Japanese and Western music have shared roots, an even more far-fetched idea.

Ultimately, the dilemma was resolved by allocating Western and Japanese music to separate spheres and by placing European art music and the various genres of traditional music (in some cases in sanitized forms) on their separate pedestals. Western music was the music of global modernity, performed in modern spaces, including occasions when the nation—as a member of the world of nations—was affirmed and celebrated. Meanwhile, indigenous musics—re-imagined as *hōgaku*, a term that brought together previously separate musical worlds— represented national distinctiveness. Horiuchi Keizō (1897–1983), music

---

24 Luli van der Does-Ishikawa, 'Contested Memories of the Kamikaze and the self-representations of Tokkō-tai youth in their missives home', *Japan Forum* 27, no. 3 (2015), https://doi.org/10.1080/09555803.2015.1045540 See in particular 370–73.

25 Applegate, *Necessity*, 228, 30.

critic and author of a history of (mostly Western) music in modern Japan (1968), presents the case in a nutshell, characterizing *yōgaku* and *hōgaku* as follows:

> *Yōgaku* is based on the folksongs and folk dances of all the peoples of Europe and America, and so the artistic progress in each country has influenced the others, and thus the distinctiveness of each people has gradually weakened and their musical compositions have taken on a mode of expression that gives rise to a shared emotion that transcends ethnic feelings. This characteristic of transcending ethnicity must be a major reason why *yōgaku* has so many devotees in Japan.
>
> *Hōgaku*, on the other hand, relies on modes of expression that are completely rooted in the nature, language, and customs of Japan. Because of this, rather than compositions that might arouse emotions shared by the whole human race, it tends to be limited to specific characteristics that only appeal to people within a narrow sphere.[26]

By the time Horiuchi was writing (the 1960s), this process of role allocation was complete. *Hōgaku* (in the meaning of traditional music) was marginalized, but treated as an essential national asset. By this time, the solution also satisfied more recent Western expectations, that non-Western countries remain faithful to their own culture and preserve its supposed authenticity, rather than adulterate it in the name of modernization.[27] The exaggerated respect for *honba*, the heartland of European art music as the only place where allegedly authentic classical music can be heard,[28] has its correlation in the cultivation of (supposedly) pure Japanese musical tradition.[29]

The close association of Western music with modernity is illustrated in an episode described by the writer Nagai Kafū (1879–1959), who had far more first-hand experience of Western music than the early reformers, having spent five years in the United States and France and attended numerous opera and concert performances. During his voyage

---

26 Keizō Horiuchi, *Ongaku Meiji hyakunen shi* (Tokyo: Ongaku no tomo Sha, 1968), 2.
27 Hiroshi Watanabe, *Nihon bunka modan rapusodi*, (Tokyo: Shunjūsha, 2002), 17–21. Yasar seems to adopt the same attitude when he alleges that the Japanese committed 'cultural suicide' by adopting Western music: Yasar, *Electrified Voices*, 82.
28 The attitude is alive and well, even while scholars such as Cook are stating that East Asia has in effect become the new centre of European art music. See Beata M. Kowalczyk, *Transnational Musicians: Precariousness, Ethnicity and Gender in the Creative Industry* (Routledge, 2020), 47.
29 Watanabe, *Nihon bunka modan rapusodi*, 8.

from France back to Japan in 1908 he felt the urge to express his feelings in a 'beautiful [Western-style] song in the most beautiful voice I can muster.' He found the various Japanese musical genres inadequate for the purpose, even while lamenting his inability to express his sentiments in music. That his dismissal of Japanese genres as unsuitable for his intention was almost certainly related to his specific situation rather than a blanket rejection of Japanese music, is suggested by his observation that noh chanting was 'completely out of place on a state-of-the-art steamship in the twentieth century.'[30]

The opera fan Kafū can be assumed to have had in mind an aria rather than a *shōka*. For most Japanese at the time, however, Western music would have meant the mixture of musical genres played by military and civilian bands: the songs taught in schools, as well as popular songs and transcriptions of popular classics for performance in the home. The works from European art music included in this mixture would have been either chamber music with piano and violin or arrangements of extracts from the symphonic and operatic repertoire. Most Japanese never had the opportunity to even hear the latter in the way the composer intended them: defining genres of European art music could not be directly experienced in Japan until well into the twentieth century. Even small-scale works could rarely be heard performed competently.

This also means that before the advent of recorded music, the possibilities for faithfully imitating Western examples were limited. This is a fact that needs spelling out in order to counter another conventional narrative, which claims that the Japanese (and by extension other Asians) have not fully mastered European art music, but that they merely imitate. They are, so the stereotype goes (and as we have heard) technically proficient but lack the ability to express the music. Those who continue to repeat this narrative are clearly not aware of the extent to which Western music has dominated the Japanese soundscape since the late nineteenth century. To be sure, Japanese students (like the ones taught by Kate Hansen) proved to be accomplished mimics, but learning by imitation is not limited to certain cultures. Even Mozart, that icon of the European notion of 'genius', was a mimic.[31] It is the

---

30 Quoted in Yasar, *Electrified Voices*, 74.
31 Spitzer, *Musical Human*, 45.

'corrosive and misunderstood conception'[32] of 'genius' that underpins the assumption that, while technical accomplishment can be acquired, musical expression requires some undefined special quality that cannot easily be learned. Until recently (and perhaps even today), expressive skills were rarely explicitly taught.[33] Hansen's early observation that most—not all! —of her pupils were unable to play expressively cannot be dismissed, but is easily explained by the fact that the girls had hardly any opportunity to hear and familiarize themselves with the sound of the music they were studying. Expressive skills can be learned, but the musician has to know what quality of sound they are aiming for and that knowledge is acquired through the experience of listening to performances.

Gramophone records were therefore a major game-changer. By the time they became widely available and affordable, in the 1920s, the early channels for the reception of Western music were well-established, which meant that there was a firm basis for the reception of art music—as well as other kinds of music—through recordings. The timing was an important factor in the thoroughness with which the Japanese made Western music their own, because in the early phase of its introduction the only way to experience music was by live performance. Gramophone recordings did enable and even encourage imitation, not only in Japan.

This did not apply solely to art music or even Western music in general. Recordings also made indigenous musical genres more widely accessible. Even before that, and before the introduction of Western music could make itself felt, the traditional musical praxis transformed as a result of political, social, and economic changes. These included the regulation and standardization of court music, the abolition of guilds and monopolies, the gradual disappearance of barriers between social classes and geographical locality, as well as changing gender roles. The commercialization of artistic and leisure pursuits, which had already begun in the Tokugawa period, offered new opportunities, and musicians, such as Nakao Tozan, made good use of them. Publishing and selling self-study manuals, song texts, and sheet music, whether

---

32 Ibid., 44.
33 Patrik N. Juslin et al., 'Feedback Learning of Musical Expressivity', in *Musical Excellence: Strategies and Techniques to Enhance Performance*, ed. Aaron Williamson (Oxford: Oxford University Press, 2004), 247.

of Western, Japanese, or blended music, could be both part of a reform agenda and a way to generate income by catering for new markets. Either way, these were largely grassroots activities, but the result was that, even without direct government intervention, traditional genres were transformed by a certain amount of standardization and by the nationwide dissemination of repertoire. Self-study manuals, moreover, made it possible to learn a traditional instrument without binding oneself to the traditional system of transmission.[34] Recordings made and issued by indigenous companies reinforced this trend.

While arguing that Western music, when it was introduced in the nineteenth century, represented universal civilization, progress, and modernity, we have not discussed how far the music itself was inherently 'modern'. Cook suggests that music of the Western classical tradition may well have even more power than music in general to transcend time and place. He names the omnipresence of European art music in (contemporary) Seoul as an example, but he could just as well have named Tokyo. According to Cook, 'classical instrumental music signifies autonomy, the availability of values not tied to time and place', or, in other words, universal values. To what extent this is an 'ideological deception' is of limited significance, as long as it is widely believed. Western classical music serves as a 'musical utopia',[35] which can become a powerful force when it is combined with collaboration.

To people unfamiliar with Western music (classical or otherwise), it would have been first and foremost modern (a universal value, one might say) by association. Essentially, it constituted the soundtrack to the nation's modernization project.[36] Advocates of music reform did occasionally mention musical elements: they would describe Japanese music as doleful, implying that Western music was experienced as more upbeat and suggested progress. Certainly, the musical character of marches and the majority of *shōka* would seem to justify that perception. Nevertheless, in this book, I have treated the nature of the music itself as secondary even while insisting that that music was more than just another element in the reform package.

---

34 The *shakuhachi* in particular appears to have been well served with published manuals, if the NDL holdings are anything to go by.
35 Cook, "Western Music as World Music', 93–94.
36 My use of the word 'soundtrack' here is inspired by Spitzer, *Musical Human*, 67–99.

What, then, makes music special? What do we learn from our examination of music and music-related activities in Japan in the period under investigation? In order to attempt an answer, we must first and foremost remind ourselves that music results from human activity, and that this activity always takes place in a particular historical, geographical, social, and cultural context, with which it is inextricably bound up and upon which its effects and efficacy depend.

The 'power of music' (or *ongaku no chikara* in Japanese) is a long-standing cliché and the subject of myths, whether Orpheus' lyre or Yasumasa's flute. Perhaps it was never invoked more fervently than in the wake of the triple disaster in Northern Japan in 2011. Among the many musical initiatives, the concerts given by members of the Sendai Philharmonic Orchestra were among the earliest, and, with the founding of the Center for Recovery Through the Power of Music in Tohoku, the orchestra placed their efforts on a firm organizational footing. These and other musical activities received much media attention. On closer examination, however, the effects were mixed, and depended very much on extra-musical factors. Nakamura Mia, who examined media reports and conducted ethnographic fieldwork, concluded that 'music as social mediation is distinctly capable of amplifying empathy', but that the power of music depends on 'what music is played and how it is contextualized'.[37] She also concluded that, while in the immediate aftermath of the disaster, those affected could derive comfort from listening, as time went on, the role of active participation increased.[38]

From a different angle, but with similar emphasis on active participation, Tia DeNora and Gary Ansdell argue that music certainly has the potential to enhance health and well-being, or what they call 'a capacity to flourish', but they ascribe this not to the music per se, 'but rather what is done with, done to and done alongside musical engagement'.[39] Citing a longitudinal study involving music therapy, they

---

37 Mia Nakamura, 'Reconsidering the Power of Music: Recovery Concerts and Songs after the 2011 Japan Earthquake', *Senri Ethnological Studies* 105 (2021), https://minpaku.repo.nii.ac.jp/record/8708/files/SES105_06.pdf

38 Mia Nakamura, 'Music Sociology Meets Neuroscience', in *The Oxford Handbook of Music and the Body*, ed. Youn Kim and Sander L. Gilman (Oxford University Press, 2019 (online)), 136.

39 Tia DeNora and Gary Ansdell, 'What Can't Music Do?', *Psychology of Well-Being: Theory, Research and Practice* 4, no. 23 (2014): 9, https://doi.org/10.1186/s13612-014-0023-6

present a list of seventeen positive effects observed over time. Several of these would seem applicable to the case of Sendai examined here, in particular the following: musical activity provided,

1. 'a pretext for social relating'
2. 'a set of events that can be recalled and thus contribute to a sense of accumulating identity'
3. 'opportunities for interaction with others (and thus opportunities to forge relationships)'
4. 'opportunities for musicianship'
5. 'a medium for reframing identities'
6. 'a means for sharing information that might be harder to share through talk alone'[40]

As we have seen, music brought together individual actors, local and foreign, in order to promote music according to their respective goals. The modern institution of the concert became an important creative space for musical encounters. While Kate Hansen and other observers with knowledge of Western music derided or bemoaned the low standards of performance or the audience's lack of understanding, these were not the most significant aspects of the encounters. Arguably, the experience generated by performing (or listening) is what mattered. European art music represented the apex of Western civilization and what Cook calls 'musical utopia', in the sense that it was imagined as much as (or more than) it was performed. The fact that the Western music played in Sendai came, as it were, from the lower ranks of the art music repertoire is of limited significance compared to the player's consciousness of being part of a larger edifice: great music and, ultimately, modern civilization. The 'four fellows with violins' attempting to play an extract of a Wagner opera were perhaps not so different from the British amateur string quartet at the other end of the twentieth century attempting one of Beethoven's notoriously challenging late works, whose violinist told their coach: 'I know that to you we're all making a horrible bloody noise,

---

40 DeNora and Ansdell, 'What Can't Music Do?,' 7–8. The numbering is mine. The study, referred to as 'BRIGHT' is not the main focus of the article and not described in detail.

but we're not hearing that! We're hearing Beethoven.'[41] Of course, we cannot know for sure what exactly the four students were hearing, but we can be sure that it was not mere noise.

Participating in a concert of Western music or even blended music, whether as a performer or a listener— often the audience would be expected to join in the national anthem— meant sharing a space with people one would not usually associate with. *Shōka* with patriotic Japanese lyrics, whether of foreign origin or composed by Japanese in what we might call an international idiom, reinforced their awareness of being citizens of the modern nation of Japan. The increasingly global repertoire, meanwhile, linked the people in Sendai with those in other parts of the world. They could imagine themselves as actively participating in the modern world of nations. As Cristina Magaldi has argued for Rio de Janeiro in the early twentieth century, cultural connections among the urban centres worldwide were strengthened through the international circulation of music. The music popular at the time thus created a 'community of transnational feeling' and fuelled curiosity about foreign places.[42]

In sum, if we refrain from regarding the performance of a musical work as a faithful representation of a piece whose meaning is perceived as unchanging, and instead focus on the performance 'as an opportunity in which music allows people to do something with it while it itself does something', we can appreciate even a musically excruciating performance as a positive act in which new meanings are produced and a new future is imagined.[43] The students of the Second High School, and performers and listeners throughout the country and across social divides, were thus involved in imbuing the music they played with new meanings and imagining themselves as citizens of a democratic nation and of the modern world.

---

41   Quoted in Peter Mountain, *Scraping a Living: A Life of a Violinist* (Bloomington IN and Milton Keynes, UK: Authorhouse, 2007), 246.
42   Cristina Magaldi, 'Cosmopolitanism and World Music in Rio de Janeiro at the Turn of the Twentieth Century', *The Musical Quarterly* 92, no. 3–4 (2009): 335, https://doi.org/10.1093/musqtl/gdp021
43   Nakamura, 'Music Sociology Meets Neuroscience', 136. Nakamura's main focus is 'retelling' and memory work after experiencing trauma, but the 'retelling' is part of an effort to imagine a better future.

The role of music not only in social bonding within a society but as a bridge for cross-cultural communication and solidarity is discussed by the philosopher Kathleen Higgins. The author's evident love for music might cause a reader to suspect that she is excessively optimistic about what music can accomplish, but her treatment is nuanced, and she draws upon work from several disciplines. Higgins's central argument is that 'people from around the globe can be brought together by one another's music.'[44] She ends by making a case for familiarizing oneself with music from other cultures. Music, according to Higgins, 'intimates [...] a sense of a broader world beyond music'.[45] It 'communicates vitality and engages our sense of connection with the larger environment and those within it.'[46] Higgins further argues that the 'powerful awareness of sharing life with others in the world' impressed on us by music represents 'a source of basic security'.[47] This sense of security is a condition for music's potential to 'shake people up and encourage change'.[48]

Higgins admits that the claims she makes for music providing a sense of security 'presupposes that the music is in a style that is familiar (or becoming so)'.[49] In the absence of familiarity, the awareness of sharing in something larger might still be there, but the emotions aroused may well be negative. We saw an example of a *shōka* with lyrics that presented the wider world as a threat,[50] and the history of modern Japan certainly shows an ambiguous relationship with the outside world. On the other hand, by combining the foreign music with familiar language, poetic conventions, or historical events, *shōka* also served as a way to render the music familiar and indigenize it. In concerts, familiarization was further promoted by including traditional Japanese as well as foreign music and by blended performances. By the time concerts of predominantly Western music were staged in Sendai, marches and *shōka* at the very least had become an integral part of the musical soundscape and may

---

44 Higgins, *Music between Us*, 1.
45 Ibid., 105.
46 Ibid., 168. More broadly, on the significance of shared sonic experience, see Ruth Finnegan, *Communicating: The Multiple Modes of Human Communication* (2nd edition) (London: Routledge, Taylor & Francis Group, 2014 (2002)).
47 Higgins, *Music between Us*, 144.
48 Ibid., 147.
49 Ibid., 148.
50 See Chapter 11.

well have contributed to feelings of security and of being at home in the modern world.

Western music in Japan, then, was linked to modernity right from the arrival of Perry's ships. Japan's modernization owed much to the fact that the Japanese, both at the state and at the individual levels, successfully harnessed the power of music, or more precisely, of 'doing things with music'.[51] Engaging with Western music not only became an important way to create a powerful national community, but also, through musical experience shared across time and space,[52] to actively participate in the emerging global community of nations.

---

51 DeNora and Ansdell, 'What Can't Music Do?', 7–8.
52 As Ruth Finnegan points out, 'sonic symbols' can transcend time and space. See Finnegan, *Communicating: The Multiple Modes of Human Communication* (2nd edition), 90.

Appendix: Chronological List of Concerts in Sendai Reported in *Ongakukai*

Date – Title, Location or Venue (if specified[1]); Volume/Issue/Page

26 October 1907 – Sendai Association for the Promotion of Music (Ongaku Shōrei Kai), Kokubun Quarter, city of Sendai (venue not specified); Vol. 1.1. (February 1908), 47.

9 November 1907 – Concert of the Sendai Association of Schools (Sho Gakkō Rengōkai), Sendai Medical College auditorium; Vol. 1.1. (January 1908), 47–48.

29 January 1908 – Sendai Second High School Concert (Seventeenth concert); Vol. 1.4. (April 1908), 51.

12 April 1908 – (Eighth) Concert of the Sendai Association for Native Japanese customs (Sendai Kokufūkai); Vol. 1.6. (June 1908), 48–49.

19 April 1908 – Tōhoku Ongakuin Concert (Twelfth Graduation Concert), Vol. 1.6 (June 1908), 49–50.

23 May 1908 – Miyagi College (Miyagi Jogakkō) Concert; Vol. 1.6 (June 1908), 49.

31 October 1908 – Sendai [Second] High School Concert ('Eighteenth');[2] Vol. 2.1. (January 1909), 51.

---

1 For the Second High School, the venue is always the school auditorium, so this has been omitted. Unless otherwise stated, the reports in *Ongakukai* included concert programmes. I have included concerts that were not reported in *Ongakukai*, information about which I found in other sources these are given in square brackets.

2 The number 'eighteenth' seems doubtful: according to the Shōshikai magazine, the eleventh concert was held on 20 January 1906, with the next concerts on 28 April and on 28 January 1907; the concerts were no longer numbered in the magazine after the eleventh. See Dai Ni Kōtō Gakkō Shi Henshū Iinkai, *Dai Ni Kōtō Gakkō shi*, 956–57.

27 February 1909 – Third Concert of Miyagi Normal School; Vol. 2.4. (April 1909), 38–39.

1 May 1909 – Second High School Concert (with students from the Tokyo Academy of Music); Vol. 2.6. (June 1909), 42.

[22 April 1910 – Second High School Concert][3]

10 June 1910 – Charity Concert: Disaster Relief for the Great Aomori Fire, Sendai-za Theatre; Vol. 3.7. (July 1910), 53. (No concert programme included.)

16 June 1910 – Miyagi College Concert, school auditorium; Vol. 3.7. (July 1910), 53.

22 November 1910 – Second High School Yūshikai[4] Concert, school auditorium; Vol. 4.1. (January 1911), 73.

4 March 1911 – Miyagi Prefecture Normal School Practice Concert, school auditorium; Vol 4.4. (April 1911), 61.

16 May 1911 – Tohoku College Concert (25th anniversary), school auditorium; Vol. 4.6. (June 1911), 40. (programme in Vol. 4.7, 45.)

2 March 1912 – Miyagi Prefecture Normal School (Sixth concert); Vol. 5.4. (April 1912), 68.

28 April 1912 – Tōhoku Ongakuin Concert (Tenth concert of the Ongakuin Kyōseikai), in the academy, Sendai Higashi Nibanchō; Vol. 5.6. (June 1912), 68.[5]

[4 May 1912 – Second High School concert][6]

10 May 1912 – Miyagi College, school auditorium; Vol. 5.6., 68.

20 October 1912 – Tōhoku Ongakuin (Twenty-first commemorative concert); Vol. 5.11. (December 1912), 64.

5 October 1913 – Sendai Concert of the Tokyo Academy of Music Alumni Association, auditorium, Second High School; Vol. 6.11. (November 1913), 66–67.

26 October 1913 – Tōhoku Ongakuin, Academy's auditorium, Sendai Higashi Nibanchō; Vol. 6.12. (December 1913), 56.

7 February 1914 – Miyagi Prefecture Normal School (with *yūshi* from Second High School), school auditorium; No. 149 (March 1914), 56–57.

---

3 Not reported in *Ongakukai*; date according to the published history of the Shōshikai.
4 'Yūshikai' might be translated as 'association of 'afficionados'; it is not clear whether this represents a formal society or just the members of the music club within the Shōshikai.
5 Also brief note in *Kahoku shinpō*, 28 April 1912, 5.
6 According to announcement with programme excerpt in *Kahoku shinpō* (29 April 1912), 2.

25 October 1914 – Tōhoku Ongakuin Autumn Concert; No. 158. (December 1914), 39.

[27 November 1914 – Miyagi College twenty-third anniversary concert. (Programme in Kate I. Hansen Papers, SRL.)]

16 April 1915 – Miyagi College auditorium, recital by Mrs Seiple; No. 164 (June 1915), 70–71.

Undated, 1915 – Second High School Yūshi Concert; No. 164 (June 1915), 71.

30 August 1915 – Sendai Sōkyoku Sangen Gassōkai: concert with famous *koto* and *shamisen* performers from Tokyo), Sakuragaoka Public Hall; No. 168 (October 1915), 87.

13 November 1915 – Second High School: Concert to mark the Enthronization of the Taishō Emperor; No. 170 (December 1915), 87.

26 February 1916 – Miyagi Normal School for Men (Miyagi Danshi Shihan Gakkō); No. 174 (April 1916), 53–54.

11 March 1916 – Miyagi College; No. 174 (April 1916), 54.

3 June 1916 – Sendai Christian Church Sunday School Concert, at Miyagi College; No. 178 (August 1916), 75.

3 November 1916 – Tōhoku Ongakuin, at the Academy; No. 182 (December 1916), 48.

18 November 1916 – Recital with leading musicians from Tokyo, organized by the local music lovers' club (Ongaku Dōkō Kurabu),[7] supported by volunteers from the Second High School; auditorium of the Second High School; No. 182 (December 1916), 48. (Programme in No. 184, February 1917, 60–61.)

24 February 1917 – Miyagi Normal School for Women (Miyagi Joshi Shihan Gakkō, second concert); No. 187 (May 1917), 73.

23 March 1917 – Sendai High School for Girls, Farewell Concert; No. 187 (May 1917), 73–74.

29 April 1917 – Tōhoku Ongakuin Spring Concert, at the Academy; No. 188, (June 1917), 60.

26 May 1917 – Sendai Amateur Club's Spring Concert; No. 189 (July 1917), 46.

17 November 1917 – Second High School, school auditorium; No. 195 (January 1918), 72.

21 November 1917 – Shōkei School for Girls, Concert; No. 195 (January 1918), 72–73.

16 Feb 1918 – Miyagi Normal School, including afficionado (*yūshi*) club 'Orfeo'; No. 197 (March 1918), 69–70.

---

7 This seems to be the same as the Sendai Amachua Kurabu.

[Undated] – Eleventh Graduation Concert (private), Sendai High School for Girls; No. 199 (May 1918), 41. (No programme.)

30 May 1919 – Tohoku College (Tōhoku Gakuin; fundraising concert for new school building), Sendai-za theatre; No. 213 (July 1919), 50.

9 November 1919 – Tōhoku Ongakuin Autumn Concert, in Higashi Sanbanchō 5 Jōkan; No. 219 (January 1920), 44–45.

1 May 1920 – Concert by Afficionados of Tohoku Imperial University, auditorium of the Faculty of Engineering; No. 225 (July 1920), 29.

23 October 1920 – Second High School Concert; No. 230 (December 1920), 34.

13 November 1920 – Tōhoku Ongakuin Autumn Concert, Higashi Sanbanchō Kumiai Church; No. 230 (December 1920), 34.

19 February (Sat) 1921 – Miyagi Prefecture Normal School (organized by societies within the school), school auditorium; No. 234 (April 1921), 48–49.

Bibliography

Abe, Hiroshi. *Chūgoku no kindai kyōiku to Meiji Nihon*. Tokyo: Fukumura Shuppan, 1990.

Aikawa, Yumi. *'Enka' no susume*. Tokyo: Bungei Shunjū, 2002.

Akita, George. *Evaluating Evidence: A Positivist Approach to Reading Sources on Modern Japan*. Honolulu: University of Hawai'i Press, 2008.

Akutsu, T., and K. Takeishi. 'Meiji jidai ni okeru hōgaku to yōgaku no ongaku shidō no kakawari: Nakao Tozan ni miru shakuhachi to vaiorin gakufu shuppan no keii to sono haikei'. *Tōkyō Gakugei Daigaku kiyō - Geijutsu/Spōtsu kagaku kakari* 65 (2013): 1–14. http://hdl.handle.net/2309/134258

'Amusements'. Display Ad, *The Washington Post*, 10 December 1911, TA3.

Anderson, Benedict. *Imagined Communities*. London: Verso, 1991.

Applegate, Celia. 'Introduction: Music Among the Historians'. *German History* 30, no. 3 (2012): 329–49. https://doi.org/10.1093/gerhis/ghs039

— *The Necessity of Music: Variations on a German Theme*. Toronto: University of Toronto Press, 2017.

Atkins, Taylor E. *Blue Nippon: Authenticating Jazz in Japan*. Durham, N.C.: Duke University Press, 2001.

Atkins, Tayor E. 'The Dual Career of "Arirang": The Korean Resistance Anthem that Became a Japanese Pop Hit'. *The Journal of Asian Studies* 66, no. 3 (2007): 645–87. https://doi.org/http://www.jstor.org/stable/20203201

Avila, Eric. *American Cultural History: A Very Short Introduction*. Oxford: Oxford University Press, 2018.

'Bā to hōru (4): Onna kyūji no Shinbashi hōru'. *Asahi shinbun*, 16 September 1911, Morning, 5.

Bales, Dane G., Polly Roth Bales, and Calvin E. Harbin. *Kate Hansen: The Grandest Mission on Earth from Kansas to Japan, 1907–1951*. The University of Kansas Continuing Education, 2000. https://kuscholarworks.ku.edu/handle/1808/21766

Bauer, Wolfgang. *China und die Hoffnung auf Glück: Paradiese, Utopien, Idealvorstellungen in der Geistesgeschichte Chinas*. Munich: dtv, 1974.

Bayly, Christopher Alan. *The Birth of the Modern World 1780–1914: Global Connections and Comparisons*. Malden, MA: Blackwell, 2004.

Beckerman, Michael. 'Henry Krehbiel, Antonín Dvorák, and the Symphony 'From the New World'. *Notes* 49, no. 2 (1992): 447–73. https://doi.org/10.2307/897884

Beckingham, Carolyn. *Moribund Music: Can Classical Music be Saved?* Brighton: Sussex Academic Press, 2009.

Bell, Alexander Melville. *Visible Speech: The Science of Universal Alphabetics on Self-Interpreting Physiological Letters for the Writing of All Languages in One Alphabet, Illustrated by Tables, Diagrams and Examples*. Inaugural Edition ed. London/London and New York: Simpkin, Marshall & Co./N. Trübner & Co., 1867.

Bennet, Bridget. 'Home Songs and the Melodramatic Imagination: From "Home, Sweet Home" to *The Birth of a Nation*'. *Journal of American Studies* 46, no. 1 (2012): 171–87. https://doi.org/10.1017/S0021875811001356

Beyer, Friedrich-Heinz. 'Deutsche Musik in Japan: Völkisch-nationale Musikpflege im Fernen Osten'. *Zeitschrift für Musik*, no. 6 (June) (1941): 393–96.

Bieber, Hans-Joachim. *SS und Samurai: Deutsch-Japanische Kulturbeziehungen 1933–1945*. Munich: iudicium, 2014.

Blacking, John. *How Musical is Man?* Seattle: University of Washington Press, 1973.

Blanning, Tim. *The Triumph of Music: Composers, Musicians and Their Audiences, 1700 to the Present*. London: Allan Lane (Penguin), 2008.

Bod, Rens. *A New History of the Humanities: The Search for Principles and Patterns from Antiquity to the Present*. Oxford: Oxford University Press, 2015 (2013). (De Vergeten Wetenschappen, 2010).

Bohlman, Philip V. *World Music: A Very Short Introduction*. Oxford: Oxford University Press, 2002.

Boyle, Edward. 'Imperial Practice and the making of Modern Japan's Territory: Towards a Reconsideration of Empire's Boundaries'. *Geographical Review of Japan Series B* 88, no. 2 (2016): 66–79. https://doi.org/10.4157/geogrevjapanb.88.66

Braun, Christoph, and Ludwig Finscher, eds. *Max Weber: Zur Musiksoziologie (Nachlaß 1921)*. Edited by M. Rainer Lepsius Horst Baier, Wolfgang J. Mommsen, Wolfgang Schluchter, Johannes Winckelmann, Max Weber Gesamtausgabe. Tübingen: J. C. B. Mohr (Paul Siebeck), 2004 (1921).

Brenner, Helmut. 'Absorption und Adaption als Faktoren traditioneller Music in Lateinamerika'. *Archiv für Musikwissenschaft* 62, no. 1 (2005): 1–12. https://doi.org/https://www.jstor.org/stable/25162318

Bruce, Robert V. *Bell: Alexander Graham Bell and the Conquest of Solitude*. Boston: Little, Brown and Company, 1973.

Bull, Michael, and Les Back, eds. *The Auditory Culture Reader*. Oxford: Berg, 2003, [2020 edn:] https://doi.org/10.4324/9781003086895

Bull, Michael, and Les Back. 'Introduction: Into Sound'. In *The Auditory Culture Reader*, edited by Michael Bull and Les Back, 1–20. Oxford: Berg, 2003.

Bunkachō (Agency of Cultural Affairs). 'Nihon no uta hyakusen'. *Bunkachō geppō* 2007, no. 2 (2007): 38–39. https://www.bunka.go.jp/tokei_hakusho_shuppan/hakusho_nenjihokokusho/archive/pdf/93732401_03.pdf

Caldwell, A. 'Music'. *Ongaku zasshi* 7 (1891): 9–10.

Carpenter, Hoyle. 'Salon Music in the Mid-Nineteenth Century'. *Civil War History* 4, no. 3 (1958): 291–99. https://doi.org/10.1353/cwh.1958.0032

Chai, Ch'u, and Winberg Chai, eds. *Li Chi (Book of Rites): An Encyclopedia of Ancient Ceremonial Usages, Religious Creeds, and Social Institutions, translated by James Legge*. 2 vols. Vol. 2. New Hyde Park, New York: University Books, 1967.

Chamberlain, Basil Hall. *Things Japanese: Being Notes on Various Subjects Connected with Japan*. Yohan Classics. Berkeley, CA: Stone Bridge Press, 2007 (1905).

Chiba, Yūko. *Doremi o eranda Nihonjin*. Ongaku no Tomosha, 2007.

Conrad, Sebastian. *What is Global History?* Princeton: Princeton University Press, 2016.

Conrad, Sebastian, Hans Martin Krämer, and Tino Schölz, eds. *Geschichtswissenschaft in Japan: Themen, Ansätze und Theorien*. Göttingen: Vandenhoeck & Ruprecht, 2006.

Cook, Nicholas. *Music: A Very Short Introduction*. Oxford: Oxford University Press, 2000.

— 'Western Music as World Music'. In *The Cambridge History of World Music*, edited by Philip Vilas Bohlman, 75–100. Cambridge: Cambridge University Press, 2013.

Cooke, Peter. 'The violin – instrument of four continents'. In *The Cambridge Companion to the Violin*, edited by Robin Stowell, 234–48. Cambridge: Cambridge University Press, 1992.

Cottrell, Stephen. *Professional Music-Making in London: Ethnography and Experience*. SOAS Musicology Series. Aldershot: Ashgate, 2004.

D'Ausilio, Alessandro, Giacomo Novembre, Luciano Fadiga, Peter E. Keller. 'What can music tell us about social interaction?' *Trends in Cognitive Sciences* 19, no. 3 (2015): 111–14. https://doi.org/10.1016/j.tics.2015.01.005

Dai Ni Kōtō Gakkō Shi Henshū Iinkai, ed. *Dai Ni Kōtō Gakkō shi*. Tokyo: Dai Ni Kōtō Gakkō Shōshi Dōsōkai, 1979.

Darwin, John. *After Tamerlane: The Rise & Fall of Global Empires, 1400–2000*. London: Penguin Books, 2007.

Day, Kiku. 'The Effect of the Meiji Government's Policy on Traditional Japanese Music During the Nineteenth Century: The Case of the *Shakuhachi*'. *Nineteenth-Century Music Review* 10, no. 2 (2013): 265–92. https://doi.org/doi:10.1017/S1479409813000268

De Ferranti, Hugh, and Alison Tokita, eds. *Music, Modernity and Locality in Prewar Japan: Osaka and Beyond*. Farnham, Surrey: Ashgate, 2013.

Deloria, Philip J. *Indians in Unexpected Places*. Lawrence, KS: University Press of Kansas, 2004.

DeNora, Tia, and Gary Ansdell. 'What Can't Music Do?'. *Psychology of Well-Being: Theory, Research and Practice* 4, no. 23 (2014): 1–10. https://doi.org/10.1186/s13612-014-0023-6

Dittrich, Rudolf. 'Beiträge zur Kenntnis der japanischen Musik.' *MOAG* 6, no. 85 (1897): 376–91.

— *Nippon Gakufu 2: Zehn japanische Volkslieder gesammelt und für das Klavier bearbeitet*. Leipzig: Breitkopf und Härtel, 1894.

— *Nippon Gakufu. Sechs japanische Volkslieder gesammelt und für das Klavier bearbeitet*. Leipzig: Breitkopf und Härtel, 1894.

— *Rakubai: Fallende Pflaumenblüten: Japanische Lieder mit Koto für Klavier bearbeitet*. Leipzig: Breitkopf und Härtel, 1894.

Douai, Adolf. *The Kindergarten: A Manual for the Introduction of Froebel's System of Primary Education into Public Schools, and for the Use of Mothers and Private Teachers*. New York: E. Steiger, 1872 (4th ed.).

Duke, Benjamin. *The History of Modern Japanese Education: Constructing the National School System, 1872–1890*. New Brunswick, NJ: Rutgers University Press, 2009.

Dyck, Noel, and Eduardo P. Archetti. *Sport, Dance and Embodied Identities*. Oxford: Berg, 2003.

Ehrlich, Cyril. *The Music Profession in Britain Since the Eighteenth Century: a Social History*. Oxford: Clarendon Press, 1985.

— *The Piano: A History*. Revised edition. Oxford: Oxford University Press, 1990 (1976).

Ellis, Alexander J. 'Appendix to Mr. Alexander J. Ellis's Paper on "The Musical Scales of Various Nations" Read 25th March 1885'. *Journal of the Society of the Arts* 33, no. 1719 (30 October 1885): 1102–11. http://www.jstor.org/stable/41335239

— 'On the Musical Scales of Various Nations'. *Journal of the Society of the Arts* 33, no. 1688 (27 March 1885): 485–527. http://www.jstor.org/stable/41327637

Enomoto, Yasuko. *Shanhai ōkesutora monogatari: Seiyōjin ongakukatachi no yume*. Tokyo: Shunjūsha, 2006.

Eppstein, Ury. *The Beginnings of Western Music in Meiji Era Japan*. New York: Edwin Mellen, 1994.

Etō, Toshiya. *Vaiorin to tomo ni: Nani o uttatte iru ka shiritai*. Tokyo: Ongaku no Tomosha, 1999.

Fend, Michael. 'Witnessing a "Process of Rationalisation"? A Review-Essay of Max Weber's Study on Music'. *Max Weber Studies* 10, no. 1 (2010): 101–20. https://doi.org/10.15543/MWS/2010/1/9

Ferranti, Hugh de. 'Taming the Reciting Voice: *Satsumabiwa* Text-scores and their Roles in Transmission and Performance'. *Context: Journal of Music Research* 31 (2006): 137–49.

Fineberg, Joshua. *Classical Music, Why Bother? Hearing the World of Contemporary Culture through a Composer's Ears*. New York: Routledge, 2006.

Finnegan, Ruth. *Communicating: the Multiple Modes of Human Communication (2nd edition)*. London: Routledge, Taylor & Francis Group, 2014 (2002).

— *The Hidden Musicians: Music-Making in an English Town*. Cambridge: Cambridge University Press, 1989.

Flavin, Philip. 'Meiji shinkyoku: The Beginnings of Modern Music for the Koto'. *Japan Review: Journal of the International Research Center for Japanese Studies*, no. 22 (2010): 103–23. https://nichibun.repo.nii.ac.jp/record/211/files/JN2204.pdf

Fogel, Joshua A. *Articulating the Sinosphere: Sino-Japanese Relations in Space and Time*. Cambridge MA: Harvard University Press, 2009.

Fritzsche, Peter. 'Specters of History: On Nostalgia, Exile, and Modernity'. *The American Historical Review* 106, no. 5 (2001): 1587–618. https://doi.org/OI: 10.2307/2692740

Fujimoto, Hiroko. 'Meiji 20 nendai no Tōkyō Ongaku Gakkō to Nihon Ongakukai'. *Ochamomizu ongaku ronshū*, no. 8 (2006): 11–23.

Fujita, Rinko. 'Music Education in Modern Japanese Society'. In *Studies on a Global History of Music*, edited by Reinhard Strohm, 140–56. London: Routledge, 2018.

'Fuka genzai no ongakutai'. *Ongaku zasshi* 53 (1895): 1–5.

Fukuhara, Masae. 'Yōchien sōsetsuki ni okeru "yūgi" no dōnyū ni kansauru kenkyū: Tanaka Fujimaro no hōkoku monjo o tegakari ni'. *Taiikugaku kenkyū* 51 (2006): 635–47.

Fukuzawa, Yukichi. 'On De-Asianization by Fukuzawa Yukichi, March 16, 1885'. In *Meiji Japan through Contemporary Sources*, edited by Tokyo The Centre for East Asian Cultural Studies, 3 vols. Vol. 3, 129–33. Tokyo: The Centre for East Asian Cultural Studies, 1972.

Fulcher, Jane F., ed. *The Oxford Handbook of the New Cultural History of Music*. Oxford: Oxford University Press, 2011.

Furukawa, Takahisa. *Kōki, Banpaku, Orinpikku: Kōshitsu burando to keizai hatten*. Tokyo: Chūō Kōronsha, 1998.

Gakuhōsha, ed. *Ongaku nenkan: Gakudan meishiroku Shōwa 4 nen han*. Tokyo: Takenaka Shoten, 1928.

Galliano, Luciana. *Yōgaku: Japanese Music in the Twentieth Century*. Lanham, Maryland, and London: The Scarecrow Press, 2002.

Gant, Andrew. *Music*. Ideas in Profile: Small Introductions to Big Topics. London: Profile Books, 2017.

Garon, Sheldon. 'Rethinking Modernization and Modernity in Japanese History: A Focus on State-Society Relations'. *Journal of Asian Studies* 53, no. 2 (1994): 346–66. https://doi.org/10.2307/2059838

Geiger, Heinrich. *Erblühende Zweige: Westliche klassische Musik in China*. Mainz: Schott, 2009.

Gienow-Hecht, Jessica C. E. 'Introduction'. In *Music and International History in the Twentieth Century*, edited by Jessica C. E. Gienow-Hecht, 1–30. New York/Oxford: Berghahn, 2015.

— *Sound Diplomacy: Music and Emotions in Transatlantic Relations, 1850–1920*. Chicago: University of Chicago Press, 2009.

Gimpel, Denise. *Chen Hengzhe: A Life between Orthodoxies*. Lanham, Maryland: Lexington Books, 2015.

— 'Introduction'. In *Creative Spaces: Seeking the Dynamics of Change in China*, edited by Denise Gimpel, Bent Nielsen and Paul Bailey, 1–23. Copenhagen: NIAS Press, 2012.

Gluck, Carol. 'The End of Elsewhere: Writing Modernity Now (AHR Roundtable).' *American Historical Review* 116, no. 3 (2011): 676-87. https://doi.org/10.1086/ahr.116.3.676

Godart, G. Clinton. 'Spencerism in Japan: Boom and Bust of a Theory '. In *Global Spencerism: The Communication and Appropriation of a British Evolutionist* edited by Bernard Lightman, 56–77 Leiden: Brill, 2016.

Gordon, Andrew. *A Modern History of Japan: From Tokugawa Times to the Present* (4th International Edition). Oxford: Oxford University Press, 2020.

Goto-Jones, Christopher. *Modern Japan: A Very Short Introduction*. Oxford: Oxford University Press, 2009.

Gottschewski, Hermann. 'Nineteenth-Century *Gagaku* Songs as a Subject of Musical Analysis: An Early Example of Musical Creativity in Modern Japan.''. *Nineteenth-Century Music Review* 10, no. 2 (2013): 239–64. https://doi.org/10.1017/S1479409813000256

Gottschewski, Hermann, and Kyungboon Lee. 'Franz Eckert und „seine" Nationalhymnen. Eine Einführung'. *OAG Notizen*, no. 12 (2013): 27–30. http://www.oag.jp/images/publications/oag_notizen/Feature_II_-_Kimigayo.pdf

Grant, Morag J. *Auld Lang Syne: A Song and its Culture*. Cambridge: Open Book Publishers, 2021. doi:https://doi.org/10.11647/OBP.0231

Groemer, Gerald. 'The Rise of "Japanese Music"'. *The World of Music* 46, no. 2 (2004): 9–34. https://www.jstor.org/stable/41699564

Gruhn, Wilfried. *Geschichte der Musikerziehung: Eine Kultur- und Sozialgeschichte vom Gesangsunterricht der Aufklärungspädagogik zu ästhetisch-kultureller Bildung*. Second ed. Hofheim: Wolke, 2003.

Hahn, Tomie. *Sensational Knowledge: Embodying Culture through Japanese Dance*. Middletown, Connecticut: Wesleyan University Press, 2007.

Hakusuirō [pseud.]. 'Sendai-shi no gakukyō (February 1908)'. *Ongakukai* 1, no. 2 (1908): 45–48.

Hall, Bonlyn G. 'The American Education of Luther Whiting Mason'. *American Music* 6, no. 1 (1988): 65–73. https://doi.org/10.2307/3448346

— 'Luther Whiting Mason's European Song Books'. *Notex, Second series* 41, no. 3 (1985): 482–91. https://doi.org/10.2307/941157

Hammerstein, Reinhold. *Die Musik der Engel: Untersuchungen zur Musikanschauung des Mittelalters*. Bern: Francke, 1962.

Hanna, Judith Lynne. *To Dance Is Human*. Austin: University of Texas Press, 1980.

Hansen, Kate. 'The Japanese Are Learning to Sing'. In *Kate Hansen: The Grandest Mission on Earth from Kansas to Japan, 1907–1951*, 235–38: The University of Kansas Continuing Education, 2000 (1914).

— 'Music Hath Charms'. In *Kate Hansen: The Grandest Mission on Earth from Kansas to Japan, 1907–1951*, 245–47: The University of Kansas Continuing Education, 2000.

— My Impressions of the Musical Consciousness of the Japanese People. n.d. Personal Papers of Kate I. Hansen, University Archives, PP19, Box 10, Folder 12, Kenneth Spencer Research Library, University of Kansas Libraries, Lawrence, Kansas.

— Thesis: Experiences in Teaching and Developing a Music School in Japan. 1927, updated 1933. Personal Papers of Kate I. Hansen, University Archives, PP19, Box 3, Folder 1, Kenneth Spencer Research Library, University of Kansas Libraries, Lawrence, Kansas.

Harich-Schneider, Eta. 'European Musician in Japan'. *XXth Century (Shanghai)* 3, no. 6 (1942): 418–21.

— *A History of Japanese Music*. London: Oxford University Press, 1973.

Havens, Thomas R. H. *Artist and Patron in Postwar Japan: Dance, Music, Theater and the Visual Arts, 1955–1980*. Princeton, NJ: Princeton University Press, 1982.

Henmi, Hide. *Sendai hajimete monogatari*. Seindai: Sōdōsha, 1995.

Herd, Judith Ann. 'Western-influenced "classical" Music in Japan'. In *The Ashgate Research Companion to Japanese Music*, edited by David W. Hughes and Alison McQueen Tokita. Aldershot, UK: Ashgate, 2008.

Hernández, Javier C. 'Violinist Apologizes for "Culturally Insensitive" Remarks About Asians'. *The New York Times*, 28 June, updated 11 November 2021. https://www.nytimes.com/2021/06/28/arts/music/pinchas-zukerman-violinist-asians.html

Hewett, Ian. *Music: Healing the Rift*. New York: Continuum, 2003.

Higgins, Kathleen Marie. *The Music between Us: Is Music a Universal Language?* Chicago: University of Chicago Press, 2012.

'Hikone no ongaku.' *Ongaku zasshi* 37 (1893): 17–18.

Hiramoto, Mie. 'Slaves Speak Pseudo-Toohoku-ben: The Representation of Minorities in the Japanese Translation of Gone with the Wind'. *Journal of Sociolinguistics* 13, no. 2 (2009): 249–63. https://doi.org/ https://doi.org/10.1111/j.1467-9841.2009.00406.x

Hirata, Kimiko. 'Meiji 20 nendai no Nihon ongaku kan: Tōkyō Ongaku Gakkō zonhai ronsō o tōshite'. *Ningen hattatsu bunka gakurui ronshū*, no. 8 (2008): 45–54. https://www.lib.fukushima-u.ac.jp/repo/repository/fukuro/R000002158/16-51.pdf

'Hōmeikai daisankai taishūkai gaijō'. *Ongaku zasshi*, no. 45 (25 June 1894): 31–33.

Horiuchi, Keizō. *Ongaku Meiji hyakunen shi*. Tokyo: Ongaku no tomo Sha, 1968.

Horowitz, Joseph. *Classical Music in America: A History of Its Rise and Fall*. New York: Norton, 2005.

Hosokawa, Shuhei. 'In Search of the Sound of Empire: Tanabe Hisao and the Foundation of Japanese Ethnomusicology'. *Japanese Studies* 18, no. 1 (1998): 5–19. https://doi.org/10.1080/10371399808727638

— 'Ongaku, Onkyō/Music, Sound'. In *Working Words: New Approaches to Japanese Studies*, 1–22. 20 April. Center for Japanese Studies, UC Berkeley, 2012. http://escholarship.org/uc/item/9451p047

Howe, Sondra Wieland. *Luther Whiting Mason: International Music Educator*. Warren, MI: Harmonie Park Press, 1997.

Howe, Sondra Wieland, and Mei-Ling Lai. 'Isawa Shūji, Nineteenth-Century Administrator and Music Educator in Japan and Taiwan'. *Australian Journal of Music Education* 2 (2014 (2011)): 93–105. https://files.eric.ed.gov/fulltext/EJ1061986.pdf

Howell, David L. *Geographies of Identity in Nineteenth-Century Japan*. Berkeley and Los Angeles: University of California Press, 2005.

Howland, Douglas R. *Translating the West*. Honolulu: University of Hawai'i Press, 2002.

Hughes, David W., and Alison McQueen Tokita, eds. *The Ashgate Research Companion to Japanese Music*. Aldershot, Hampshire: Ashgate, 2008.

Iguchi, Junko. 'Osaka and Shanghai: Revisiting the Reception of Western Music in Metropolitan Japan'. In *Music, Modernity and Locality in Prewar Japan: Osaka and Beyond*, edited by Hugh De Ferranti and Alison Tokita, 283–99. Farnham, Surrey: Ashgate, 2013.

'Inazuma Kozō torawaru Shikama shimai no jōfu nite'. *Asahi shinbun*, 26 December 1918, Morning, 5.

Inoue, Satsuki. 'Tsunekawa Ryōnosuke to Meijiki Nihon no Ongaku'. *Aichi Kenritsu Geijutsu Daigaku kiyō*, no. 41 (2011): 19–31. https://doi.org/10.34476/00000014

Isawa, Shūji. 'Aichi Shihan Gakkō nenpō'. *Monbushō nenpō* 2 (1875): 361–68.

— 'Ongaku kairyō no koto'. In *Isawa Shūji: Yōgaku kotohajime - Ongaku torishirabe seiseki shinpōsho*, edited by Masami Yamazumi, 288–95. Tokyo: Heibonsha, 1971 (1884).

Ishida, Kazushi. *Modanizumu hensōkyoku: Higashi Ajia no kindai ongakushi*. Tokyo: Sakuhokusha, 2005.

Ishida Tsunetarō, ed. *Meiji fujin roku*. 2 vols. Tokyo: Tōkyō Insatsu Kabushiki Kaisha, Fujo Tsūshinsha, Hakuunsha, 1908.

Ishihara, Mutsuko. 'Meijiki Kansai ni okeru vaiorin juyō no yōsu: wayō setchū genshō ni tsuite'. *Ongaku kenkyū* (Ōsaka Ongaku Daigaku Ongaku Kenkyūsho nenpō), no. 11 (1993): 101–10.

Ishikawa, Norihiro. *Hajimete no wagakki*. Tokyo: Iwanami Shoten (Iwanami junia shinsho), 2003.

Itō, Yuki. 'Opera to kabuki to "joji shōka" no kyōri: Kitamura Sueharu *Roei no yume*'. *Chōiki bunka kagaku kiyō* 19 (2014): 136–19 ([sic]; *migi* 41–58).

Iwaki, Heijirō. 'Sensei to Ongaku'. In *Butsugai Miyoshi Aikichi Sensei*, edited by Miyoshi Aikichi Sensei Chōi Kai, 228–32. Tokyo: Miyoshi Aikichi Sensei Chōi Kai, 1931.

Iwamoto, Shōji. 'Chihō ongaku kyōshi no sekinin'. *Ongakukai* 6, no. 3 (1913): 7–12.

— 'Yūgeiteki ongaku to bijutsuteki ongaku'. *Ongaku no tomo* 6, no. 1 (1904): 4–7.

Iwamoto, Shōji, and Shūichi Takaori. 'Kokubetsu no ji'. *Ongaku no tomo* 7, no. 4 (1905).

Iwano, Yūichi. *Ōdō rakudo no kōkyōgaku: Manshū – shirazaru ongakushi.* Tokyo: Ongaku no Tomosha, 1999.

Jackson, Myles W. 'From Scientific Instruments to Musical Instruments: Tuning Fork, Metronome, and Siren'. In *The Oxford Handbook of Sound Studies*, edited by Trevor Pinch and Karin Bijsterveld, 201–23: Oxford University Press, 2012.

Jacobowitz, Seth. *Writing Technologies in Meiji Japan: A Media History of Modern Japanese Literature and Visual Culture.* Cambridge, MA: Harvard University Press, 2015.

Jameson, Frederic. 'Foreword'. In *Noise: The Political Economy of Music*, edited by Brian Massumi, vii–xiv. Minneapolis: University of Minnesota Press, 1985.

Janz, Tobias, and Chien-Chang Yang. 'Introduction'. In *Decentering Musical Modernity: Perspectives on East Asian and European Music History*, edited by Tobias Janz and Chien-Chang Yang, 9–39. Bielefeld: Transcript, 2019.

Jewel, Mark. 'The First Primary School Songbook of 1881: A Study and Translation (1)'. *Journal of Liberal Arts (Waseda University)* 143 (2017): 73–94.

Jigensei [pseud.]. 'Sendai-shi no gakukyō (June 1908)'. *Ongakukai* 1, no. 6 (1908): 46.

'Jinbutsu dōsei.' *Ongakukai*, no. 160 (1915): 60–61.

'Jogakusei o mayowasu.' *Asahi shinbun*, 22 March 1912.

Johnson, Henry. 'A Modernist Traditionalist: Miyagi Michio, Transculturalism, and the Making of a Music Tradition'. In *Rethinking Japanese Modernism*, edited by Roy Starrs, 246–69. Leiden: Brill, 2012.

Johnson, Julian. *Out of Time: Music and the Making of Modernity.* Oxford: Oxford University Press, 2015.

— *Who Needs Classical Music? Cultural Choice and Musical Value.* New York: Oxford University Press, 2002.

Juslin, Patrik N., Anders Friberg, Erwin Schoonderwaldt, and Jessika Karlsson. 'Feedback Learning of Musical Expressivity'. In *Musical Excellence: Strategies and techniques to enhance performance*, edited by Aaron Williamson, 247–70. Oxford: Oxford University Press, 2004.

Kajino, Ena. 'A Lost Opportunity for Tradition: The Violin in Early Twentieth-Century Japanese Traditional Music'. *Nineteenth-Century Music Review* 10, no. 2 (2013): 293–321. https://doi.org/10.1017/S147940981300027X

— 'Taishōki no tsūshin kyōiku jukōshatachi no ongaku seikatsu: Dai Nippon Katei Ongaku Kai no zasshi "Katei ongaku" kara'. *Ongakugaku* 63, no. 1 (2017). https://www.jstage.jst.go.jp/article/ongakugaku/63/1/63_1/_pdf/-char/ja

'Kakuchi no ongaku'. *Ongakukai* 225 (July 1920): 9.

Kaminuma, Hachirō. *Isawa Shūji.* Jinbutsu sōsho. Tokyo: Yoshikawa Kōbunkan, 1962.

Kanda, Kōhei. 'Kokugaku o shinkō subeki no setsu'. *Meiroku zasshi* 18 (1874): n.p.

— 'On Promoting Our National Music'. In *Meiroku Zasshi: Journal of the Japanese Enlightenment*, Edited and Translated by William R. Braisted, 235–37. Cambridge, Massachusetts: Harvard University Press, 1976.

'Kanjinchō'. *Ongaku zasshi* 37 (October 1893): 20.

Kartomi, Margaret J. 'The Processes and Results of Musical Culture Contact: A Discussion of Terminology and Concepts'. *Ethnomusicology* 25, no. 2 (1981): 227–49. https://doi.org/10.2307/851273

Kasahara, Kiyoshi. *Kurobune raikō to ongaku*. Tokyo: Yoshikawa Kōbunkan, 2001.

Katō, Yōzō (Chōkō). *Nihon ongaku enkakushi*. Tokyo: Matsushita Gakki, 1909.

Katsuyama, Yoshiaki. 'Furēberu no undō yūgi ron ni kansuru ikkōstsu: shūdan yūgi ni yoru ningen keisei ron o chūshin ni'. *Nagoya Daigaku Kyōiku Gakubu kiyō* 33 (1986): 79–89.

Kaufmann, Walter. *Musical References in the Chinese Classics*. Detroit Monographs in Musicology. Detroit: Information Coordinators Inc., 1976.

Kaviraj, Sudipta. 'An Outline of a Revisionist Theory of Modernity'. *European Journal of Sociology* 46, no. 3 (2005): 497–526. https://doi.org/10.1017/S0003975605000196

Kawabata, Maiko. 'Virtuoso Codes of Violin Performance: Power, Military Heroism and Gender (1789–1830)'. *19th-Century Music* 28 (2004): 89–107. https://doi.org/10.1525/ncm.2004.28.2.089

Kawabata, Yuji. 'Zasshi "Ongakukai" ni miru Meiji-, Taishōki no ongaku kyōiku no jittai ni kansuru kenkyū: shōka kyōiku o chūshin ni'. *Ongaku Bunka Kyōikugaku kenkyū kiyō* 29 (2017): 71–76. https://doi.org/10.15027/42595

Kealiinohomoku, Joann. 'Dance Culture as a Microcosm of Holistic Culture'. In *New Dimensions in Dance Research: Anthropology and Dance - The American Indian. Proceedings of the Third Conference on Research in Dance*, edited by Tamara Comstock, 99–106. New York: Committee on Research in Dance, 1972.

Kehr, C. *Heimin gakkō ron ryaku*. Tokyo: Monbushō, 1880.

Kehr, Carl. *Die Praxis der Volksschule (8th ed.)*. Gotha: E. F. Thienemann, 1877 (1868).

Ketelaar, James Edward. *Of Heretics and Martyrs in Meiji Japan: Buddhism and Its Persecution* Princeton: Princeton University Press, 1990.

Kim, Hio-Jin. *Koreanische und westliche Musikerausbildung: Historische Rekonstruktion - Vergleich - Perspektiven -*. Marburg: Tectum, 2000.

Kim, Jin-Ah. 'Transfer und Aneignung. Europäische Kunstmusik in Korea'. *Asien* 143 (April 2017): 47–63. https://asien.asienforschung.de/wp-content/uploads/sites/6/2018/01/143_abs_Kim.pdf

Kimber, Marian Wilson. 'Performing "Athalia": Mendelssohn's Op. 74 in the Nineteenth-Century Choral World'. *The Choral Journal* 49, no. 10 (2009): 8–23.

Kitagawa, Kakushō. *Biwa Seisuiki: Shirazaru biwa no konjaku monogatari*. Osaka: Fūeisha, 2016.

Kitahara, Kanako, and Kenji Namikawa, eds. *Kindai ikōki ni okeru chiiki keisei to ongaku: tsukurareta dentō to ibunka sesshoku*. Kyoto: Mineruba Shobō, 2020.

Kitahara, Kanako, and Sumire Yamashita. 'Kyū Sendai hanshi Ono Shōgorō no ongakuron, "Ongyoku no fusei wa jinmin no hinkō o midaru"'. *Hirosaki Daigaku kokushi kenkyū* 143 (October 2017): 33–45.

Kleeman, Faye Yuan. *In Transit: The Formation of the Colonial East Asian Cultural Sphere*. Honolulu: University of Hawai'i Press, 2014.

Koga Masao Ongaku Bunka Shinkō Zaidan (The Masao Koga Music and Culture Promotor Foundation). *Yume jinsei o kanadete*. Tokyo: Koga Masao Ongaku Bunka Shinkō Zaidan, 2004.

'Kokufū ongaku reikai'. *Ongaku zasshi* 45 (25 June 1894): 30–31.

Kojima, Yasunori. 'Ogyū Sorai ichimon no ongaku shikō to sono reigaku kan'. In *Reigaku bunka: Higashi Ajia no kyōyō*, edited by Yasunori Kojima, 312–41. Tokyo: Perikansha, 2013.

Konakamura, Kiyonori. *Kabu ongaku ryakushi*. Tokyo: Konakamura Kiyonori, 1888.

Konishi, Junko. 'Taishōki "uta" shiryō mokuroku'. Ōsaka *Ongaku Daigaku Hakubutsukan Nenpō* 25 (2010). https://dl.ndl.go.jp/info:ndljp/pid/10313756

Kosen (Shikama Totsuji). 'Koto no chōshi sōgatten'. *Ongaku zasshi* 44 (1894): 6–7.

Koshikakezawa, Mai. 'Senoo gakufu kara miru Taishō jidai no yōgaku juyō'. *Tōkyō Geijutsu Daigaku Ongaku Gakubu kiyō* 41 (2015): 29–43.

Koshiyama, Shōzō. *Satsuma biwa*. Tokyo: Perikansha, 1983.

Kowalczyk, Beata M. *Transnational Musicians: Precariousness, Ethnicity and Gender in the Creative Industry*. Routledge, 2020.

Kōzu, Senzaburō. 'Mondai tōgi'. In *Tōkyō Geijutsu Daigaku hyakunenshi: Tōkyō Ongaku Gakkō hen 1*, edited by Tōkyō Geijutsu Daigaku Hyakunenshi Hensan Iinkai, 363–64. Tokyo: Ongaku no Tomosha, 1987 (1891).

Kramer, Lawrence. *Why Classical Music Still Matters*. Berkeley and Los Angeles: University of California Press, 2007.

Kraus, Richard Curt. *Pianos and Politics in China: Middle-Class Ambitions and the Struggle over Western Music*. New York and Oxford: Oxford University Press, 1989.

Krebs, Gerhard, and Bernd Martin, eds. *Formierung und Fall der Achse Berlin-Tōkyō.* Munich: iudicium, 1994.

Kriege, Matilda H. *The Child, Its Nature and Relations: An Elucidation of Froebel's Principles of Education. A Free Rendering of the German of the Baroness Marenholtz-Bülow.* New York: E. Steiger & Co., 1872.

Kume, Kunitake. *The Iwakura Embassy 1871–73: A True Account of the Ambassador Extraordinary and Plenipotentiary's Journey of Observation through the United States of America and Europe.* Edited by Graham Healey and Chushichi Tsuzuki. 5 vols. Vol. 1: The United States of America, Kamiyakiri, Matsudo, Chiba: The Japan Documents, 2002.

— *The Iwakura Embassy 1871–73: A True Account of the Ambassador Extraordinary and Plenipotentiary's Journey of Observation through the United States of America and Europe* Edited by Graham Healey and Chushichi Tsuzuki. 5 vols. Kamiyakiri, Matsudo, Chiba: The Japan Documents, 2002.

Kurata, Yoshihiro. *Geinō no bunmei kaika: Meiji kokka to geinō kindaika.* Tokyo: Heibonsha, 1999.

Kurata, Yoshihiro, and Shuku Ki Rin, eds. *Shōwa zenki ongakuka sōran: 'Gendai ongakuka taikan' gekan.* Tokyo: Yumani Shobō, 2008.

Kusaka, Akio. '*Ongaku zasshi* ni miru Shikama Totsuji no keimō katsudō to sono hirogari: juyō no shiten kara (1)'. *Aomori Ake no hoshi tanki daigaku kiyō,* no. 24 (1998): 55–73. http://www.aomori-akenohoshi.ac.jp/images/stories/pdf/college/kiyo/kiyo26.pdf

— '*Ongaku zasshi* ni miru Shikama Totsuji no keimō katsudō to sono hirogari: juyō no shiten kara (2)'. *Aomori Ake no hoshi tanki daigaku kiyō,* no. 26 (2000): 41–60. http://www.aomori-akenohoshi.ac.jp/images/stories/pdf/college/kiyo/kiyo26.pdf

'Kyōsaku kyūjo jizen ongakukai'. *Tōhoku bungaku* 38 (1905): 104.

Kyūsei Kōtō Gakkō Shiryō Hozon Kai, ed. *Shiryō shūsei kyūsei kōtō gakkō zenho dai 7 kan: seikatsu/kyōyō hen (2).* Tokyo: Kyūsei Kōtō Gakkō Shiryō Hozon Kai Kankō Bu, 1984.

Lebrecht, Norman. *The Maestro Myth: Great Conductors in Pursuit of Power.* New York: Citadel Press, 1993.

Lee, Angela Hao-Chun. 'The Influence of Governmental Control and early Christian Missionaries on Music Education of Aborigines in Taiwan'. *British Journal of Music Education* 23, no. 2 (2006): 205–16.

Lehtonen, Lasse. '"March from the Age of Imitation to the Age of Creation": Musical Representations of Japan in the Work and Thought of Shinkō Sakkyokuka Renmei, 1930–1940'. Doctoral Dissertation, University of Helsinki, 2018. https://helda.helsinki.fi/handle/10138/233760

Lehtonen, Lasse. 'Western Art Music Taken to Heart by the Japanese'. *Finnish Music Quarterly* [online], 2 April 2020. https://fmq.fi/articles/western-art-music-japan

Levitin, Daniel. *This Is Your Brain On Music: Understanding a Human Obsession.* London: Atlantic, 2008 (2006).

Liebersohn, Harry. *Music and the New Global Culture: From the Great Exhibitions to the Jazz Age.* Chicago: University of Chicago Press, 2019.

Lincicome, Mark. *Imperial Subjects as Global Citizens: Nationalism, Internationalism, and Education in Japan.* Lanham, MD: Lexington Books, 2009.

Lincicome, Mark E. *Principle, Praxis, and the Politics of Educational Reform in Meiji Japan.* Honolulu: University of Hawai'i Press, 1995.

Lippman, Edward A. *Musical Thought in Ancient Greece.* New York and London: Columbia University Press, 1964.

Lubinski, Christiana, and Andreas Steen. 'Travelling Entrepreneurs, Travelling Sounds: The Early Gramophone Business in India and China'. *Itinerario* 41, no. 2 (2017): 275–303. https://doi.org/10.1017/S0165115317000377

Machida, Ōen, ed. *Hauta shū 3.* Tokyo: Seirindō, 1909.

— (*Hōgaku sokusei*) *Vaiorin tebiki* Tokyo: Seirindō, 1913.

— *Tefūgin doku annai.* Tokyo: Tōundō, 1896.

— *Vaiorin dokushū jizai.* Seirindō, 1908.

MacKenzie, John M. *Orientalism: History, Theory and the Arts.* Manchester: Manchester University Press, 1995.

Magaldi, Cristina. 'Cosmopolitanism and World Music in Rio de Janeiro at the Turn of the Twentieth Century'. *The Musical Quarterly* 92, no. 3–4 (2009): 329–64. https://doi.org/10.1093/musqtl/gdp021

Malm, William P. 'Chinese Music in the Edo and Meiji Periods in Japan'. *Asian Music* 6 no. 1/2 (1975): 147–72. https://doi.org/10.2307/833846

— *Traditional Japanese Music and Musical Instruments.* Tokyo: Kodansha International, 2000 (1959).

Mark, Michael L. *A Concise History of American Music Education.* Lanham, MD: Rowman & Littlefield Education, 2008.

Masao [pseud.]. 'Ongakukai hihyō: jūgatsu sanjūichi nichi yūshi ongakukai zakkan'. *Shōshikai zasshi* 83 (1908): 149–51.

Masui, Keiji. *Asakusa opera monogatari: rekishi, sutā, jōen kiroku no subete.* Tokyo: Geijutsu Gendai Sha, 1990.

— *Nihon opera shi - 1952.* Tokyo: Suiyōsha, 2003.

— 'Ongaku zasshi (Omukaku) kaidai.' In *Ongaku zasshi (hōkan),* 5–33. Tokyo: Shuppan Kagaku Sōgō Kenkyūsho, 1984.

Matsue, Jennifer Milioto. *Music in Contemporary Japan*. Focus on World Music Series. New York: Routledge, 2016.

Matsumoto, Zenzō. *Teikin yūjō: Nihon no vaiorin ongaku shi*. Tokyo: Ressun no Tomosha, 1995.

Matsushita, Hitoshi, ed. *Kindai Nihon Ongaku Nenkan (Shōwa 8)*. Tokyo: Ōzora Sha, 1997.

McClary, Susan. 'Afterword: The Politics of Silence and Sound'. In *Noise: The Political Economy of Music*, edited by Brian Massumi, 149–58. Minneapolis: University of Minnesota Press, 1985.

McNeill, William. *Keeping Together in Time: Dance and Drill in Human History*. Cambridge, MA: Harvard University Press, 1997.

Mehl, Margaret. 'Between the Global, the National and the Local in Japan: Two Musical Pioneers from Sendai'. *Itinerario* 41, no. 2 (2017): 305–25. https://doi.org/10.1017/S0165115317000389

— 'Chinese Learning (*kangaku*) in Meiji Japan'. *History* 85 (2000): 48–66. https://doi.org/10.1111/1468-229X.00137

— 'Dancing at the Rokumeikan - A New Role for Women?'. In *Japanese Women: Emerging from Subservience, 1886-1945*, edited by Gordon Daniels and Hiroko Tomida, 157–77. Folkestone, Kent: Global Oriental, 2005.

— 'From Classical to National Scholarship: Konakamura Kiyonori's History of Music in Japan (1888) and Its Foreign-Language Prefaces'. *History of Humanities* 8, no. 1 (2023): 99–120. https://doi.org/10.1086/723948

— *History and the State in Nineteenth-Century Japan: The World, the Nation and the Search for a Modern Past (Second edition with new preface)*. Copenhagen: The Sound Book Press, 2017 (1998).

— 'Introduction: Western Music in Japan: A Success Story?'. *Nineteenth-Century Music Review* 10, no. 2 (2013): 211–22. https://doi.org/10.1017/S1479409813000232

— 'Japan's Early Twentieth-Century Violin Boom'. *Nineteenth-Century Music Review* 7, no. 1 (2010): 23–43. https://doi.org/10.1017/S1479409800001130

— 'A Man's Job? The Kōda Sisters, Violin Playing and Gender Stereotypes in the Introduction of Western Music in Japan'. *Women's History Review* 21, no. 1 (2012): 101–20. https://doi.org/10.1080/09612025.2012.645675

— *Not by Love Alone: The Violin in Japan, 1850–2010*. Copenhagen: The Sound Book Press, 2014.

— *Private Academies of Chinese Learning in Meijji Japan: The Decline and Transformation of the Kangaku Juku*. Copenhagen: NIAS Press, 2003. https://doi.org/10.4324/9780203507162

— 'Transmutations of the Confucian Academy in Japan: Private Academies of Chinese Learning (kangaku juku 漢学塾) in Late Tokugawa and Meiji Japan as a Reflection and Motor of Epistemic Change'. In *Confucian Academies in East Asia*, edited by Vladimír Glomb, Eun-Jeung Lee and Martin Gehlmann, 126–56. Leiden: Brill, 2020.

— 'Verbote der Bon-Tänze in den Präfekturen Kashiwazaki und Niigata (1872/73)'. In *Wege zur Japanischen Geschichte: Quellen aus dem 10. bis 21. Jahrhundert in deutscher Übersetzung*, edited by Anke Scherer and Katja Schmidtpott, 97–103. Hamburg: Gesellschaft für Natur- und Völkerkunde Ostasiens, 2020.

Meissner, Kurt. *Deutsche in Japan*. Tokyo: OAG, 1961.

Melvin, Sheila, and Jindong Cai. *Rhapsody in Red: How Western Classical Music Became Chinese*. New York: Algora, 2004.

Mendenhall, Thomas C. 'Japan Revisited after Thirty Years'. *The Journal of Race Development* 2, no. 3 (January 1912): 224–35.

Mensendiek, William. *Not without Struggle: The Story of William E. Hoy and the Beginnings of Tohoku Gakuin*. Sendai: Tohoku Gakuin, 1986.

— *To Japan with Love: The Story of Kate Hansen and Lydia Lindsay of Kansas and Japan*. Sendai: Hagi no Sato Publishing Company, 1991.

Mervart, David. 'Meiji Japan's China Solution to Tokugawa Japan's China Problem'. *Japan Forum* 27, no. 4 (2015): 544–58. https://doi.org/10.1080/09555803.2015.1077881

Mitsui, Toru. 'Interaction of Imported and Indigenous Music in Japan: A Historical Overview of the Music Industry'. In *Whose Master's Voice: The Development of Popular Music in Thirteen Cultures*, edited by Alison J. Ewbank and Fouli T. Papageorgiu, 152–74. Westport, Connecticut: Greenwood Press, 1997.

— *Popular Music in Japan: Transformation Inspired by the West*. New York: Bloomsbury Academic & Professional, 2020.

'Miyagi-ken no ongaku'. *Ongaku zasshi*, no. 2 (25 October 1890): 16–17.

'Miyagi-ken Sendai tsūshin [April 1897]'. *Ongaku zasshi/Omukaku*, no. 68 (25 April 1897): 36–37.

'Miyagi Gakuin no yakuin mata wa kyōin de atta senkyōshi'. *Miyagi Gakuin Shiryō Shitsu nenpō/Miyagi Gakuin Archives of History Review* 18/19 (2011/2012): 19–60.

'Miyagi Ongaku Kōshūka'. *Ongaku* 12, no. 2 (1907): 34–35.

'Miyagi Ongaku Kōshūkai genjō'. *Ongaku* 11, no. 6 (1907): 28–29.

Miyagiken Kyōiku Iinkai, ed. *Miyagiken kyōiku hyakunenshi Vol 2*. Sendai: Gyōsei, 1977.

— ed. *Miyagiken kyōiku hyakunenshi Vol 4*. Sendai: Gyōsei, 1977.

Miyagiken Shōgakkōchō Kai, ed. *Hossoku yonjū shūnen kinen shi: yonjū nen no ayumi*. Sendai: Miyagiken Shōgakkōchō Kai, 1987.

Miyashita, Kazuko. 'Foster's Songs in Japan'. *American Music* 30, no. 3 (2012): 208–325. https://doi.org/10.5406/americanmusic.30.3.0308

Miyoshi Aikichi Sensei Chōi Kai, ed. *Butsugai Miyoshi Aikichi Sensei*. Tokyo: Miyoshi Aikichi Sensei Chōi Kai, 1931.

Mizohata, Inosuke. *Buwaiorin [vaiorin] no shiori*. Osaka: Kyōwadō gakki, 1908.

Monbushō Ongaku Torishirabe Gakari, ed. *Sōkyokushū*. Tokyo: Monbushō Henshūkyoku, 1888.

— ed. *Yōchien shōkashū*. Tokyo: Monbushō Henshūkyoku, 1887.

Moran, Ryan. 'Securing the Health of the Nation: Life Insurance, Labor and Health Improvement in Interwar Japan'. *Japan Forum* 31, no. 2 (2019): 211–34. https://doi.org/10.1080/09555803.2018.1461677

Mōri, Kumi, and Takeshi Saitō, Tomoko Bannai, eds. *Senkyōshi Nikorai no zen'nikki*. 9 vols. Vol. 7. Tokyo: Kyōbunkan, 2007.

Mori, Setsuko. 'A Historical Survey of Music Periodicals in Japan: 1881–1920'. *Fontis Artis Musicae* 36, no. 1 (1989): 44–50.

Morris, Ivan. *The Nobility of Failure: Tragic Heroes in the History of Japan*. Tokyo: Tuttle, 1982 (1975).

Mountain, Peter. *Scraping a Living: A Life of a Violinist*. Bloomington IN and Milton Keynes, UK: Authorhouse, 2007.

Mueller (Müller, Leopold Benjamin Karl). 'Einige Notizen ueber die Japanische Musik'. *Mitteilungen der Gesellschaft für Natur- und Völkerkunde Ostasiens* 1, no. 6 (1874): 13–22, Plates I-IX. https://oag.jp/books/band-i-1873-1876-heft-6/

Müller, Leopold Benjamin Karl. 'Einige Notizen ueber die Japanische Musik'. *Mitteilungen der Gesellschaft für Natur- und Völkerkunde Ostasiens (MOAG)* 1, no. 6, 8, 9 (1873–76): (06) 13–19, 21–31 (08) 41–48 (09) 19–35.

Murayama, Shigeo. *Meijiki dansu no shiteki kenkyū*. Tokyo: Fumaidō, 2000.

Nagahara, Hiromu. *Tokyo Boogie-Woogie: Japan's Pop Era and its Discontents*. Cambridge, MA 2017.

Nagai, Yoshikazu. *Shakō dansu to Nihonjin*. Tokyo: Shōbunsha, 1991.

Nakai, Kitarō. 'Ongaku Gakkō haisezaru bekarazu'. In *Tōkyō Geijutsu Daigaku hyakunenshi: Tōkyō Ongaku Gakkō hen 1*, edited by Tōkyō Geijutsu Daigaku Hyakunenshi Hensan Iinkai, 358–59. Tokyo: Ongaku no Tomosha, 1987 (1891).

Nakamura, Kōsuke. *Kindai Nihon yōgaku josetsu*. Tokyo: Tōkyō Shoseki, 2003.

Nakamura, Mia. 'Music Sociology Meets Neuroscience'. In *The Oxford Handbook of Music and the Body*, edited by Youn Kim and Sander L. Gilman, 127–42: Oxford University Press, 2019 (online).

— 'Reconsidering the Power of Music: Recovery Concerts and Songs after the 2011 Japan Earthquake'. *Senri Ethnological Studies* 105 (2021): 63–77. https://minpaku.repo.nii.ac.jp/record/8708/files/SES105_06.pdf

Nakamura, Rihei. *Kirisuto-kyō to Nihon no yōgaku*. Tokyo: Ōzorasha, 1996.

— *Yōgaku dōnyūsha no kiseki: Nihon kindai Yōgakushi josetsu*. Tokyo: Tōsui Shobō, 1993.

Namikoshi, Teishū. *Vaiorin dokushū no shiori*. Osaka and Tokyo: Yajima Seishindō, 1906.

Nettl, Bruno. *Encounters in Ethnomusicology: A Memoir*. Warren, MI: Harmonie Park Press, 2002.

Nihon Fūzokushi Gakkai, ed. *Shiryō de kataru Meiji no Tōkyō hyakuwa*. Tokyo: Tsukubanesha, 1996.

Nihon Ongaku Tōitsu Kai. *(Tsūshin kyōju) Vaiorin kōgiroku*. Fukuoka: Nihon Tōitsu Ongakukai, 1913.

Niigata-ken, ed. *Shin Niigata-kenshi: Shiryō hen 14 (Kindai 2: Meiji ishin hen II)*. Niigata: Niigata-ken, 1983.

Nishihara, Minoru. *'Gakusei' Bētōven no tanjō*. Tokyo: Heibonsha, 2000.

Nitaku Ichiin Koji. 'Aete yo no shokusha ni shissu'. In *Tōkyō Geijutsu Daigaku hyakunenshi: Tōkyō Ongaku Gakkō hen 1*, edited by Tōkyō Geijutsu Daigaku Hyakunenshi Hensan Iinkai, 361–62. Tokyo: Ongaku no Tomosha, 1987 (1891).

Nolte, Eckhard, and Reinhold Weyer, eds. *Musikalische Unterweisung im Altertum: Mesopotamien - China - Griechenland*. Edited by Eckhard Nolte, Beiträge zur Geschichte der Musikpädagogik. Frankfurt a. M. et al.: Peter Lang, 2011.

Nomura, Kōichi, Kenzō Nakajima, and Kiyomichi Miyoshi. *Nihon yōgaku gaishi: Nihon gakudan chōrō ni yoru taikenteki yōgaku no rekishi*. Tokyo: Rajio Gijutsusha, 1978.

'Norowaretaru koi no akushu'. *Yomiuri shinbun*, 22 March 1912, Morning, 3.

Nose, Shūichi. 'Kei taisō no kindai Nihon taiikuka Kyōiku katei e no dōnyū ni kansuru shiteki kōsatsu (A historical review on the curricular adoption of light gymnastics into modern Japanese physical education)'. *Taiiku kenkyū: Japan journal of physical education, health and sport sciences* 28, no. 3 (1983): 177–83.

Okada, Akeo. 'Europäische Klassik in Japan - eine düstere Diagnose'. In *Musik in Japan*, edited by Guignard Silvain, 179–97. Munich: iudicium, 1994.

Okano, Ben. *Metteru Sensei: Asahina Takashi, Hattori Ryōichi no Gakufu, Bōmeisha Ukurainejin shikisha no shōgai*. Tokyo: Rittōmyūjikku, 1995.

Ōkubo, Toshiaki. *Nihon kindai shigaku no seiritsu*. Ōkubo Toshiaki rekishi chosakushū 7. Tokyo: Yoshikawa Kōbunkan, 1988.

Okunaka, Yasuto. 'Gosenfu to iu mediamu no tōjō: Kitamura Sueharu ni totte "saifu" wa nani o imi shita ka'. In *Nihon ni okeru ongaku, geinō no saikentō*, edited by Shizuo Gotō, 81–90. Kyoto: Kyōto Shi Geijutsu Daigaku Nihon Dentō Ongaku Kenkyū Sentā, 2010.

— *Kokka to ongaku: Isawa Shūji ga mezashita Nihon kindaika*. Tokyo: Shunjūsha, 2008.

— 'Shōka ni yoru shintai no kokuminka: Isawa Shūji no kyōiku shisō no ichi sokumen'. *Kaitoku* 68 (2000): 27–43.

— 'Wayō gassō Dōjōji: Kitamura Sueharu ni yoru Nihon ongaku kairyō to zasetsu'. *Nagoya Geijutsu Daigaku kenkyūkiyō* 28 (2007): 337–52.

— *Wayō setchū ongakushi*. Tokyo: Shunjūsha, 2014.

Ölschleger, Hans Dieter, Helmut Demes, Heinrich Menkhaus, Ulrich Möhwald, Annelie Ortmanns, and Bettina Post-Kobayashi, eds. *Individualität und Egalität im gegenwärtigen Japan: Unterschungen zu Wertemustern im Bezug auf Familie und Arbeitswelt*. Munich: Iudicium, 1994.

Ōmori, Seitarō. *Nihon no yōgaku*. 2 vols. Vol. 1, Tokyo: Shinmon Shuppansha, 1986.

Ōmura, Sakae. *Yōkendō kara no shuppatsu: kyōiku hyakunenshi yowa*. Vol. 1, Tokyo: Gyōsei, 1986.

'Ongaku kurabu'. *Ongaku zasshi* 39 (December 1893): 19.

Ono, Shōgorō. 'Ongaku okosu beshi.' *Kōshū joshi* 14 (1877).

— 'Ongyoku no fusei wa jinmin no hinkō o midaru'. *Kōshū joshi* 15–17 (1877).

Ōnuma, Yoshiki, ed. *Konakamura Kiyonori nikki*. Tokyo: Kyūko Shoin, 2010.

Osterhammel, Jürgen. *Die Verwandlung der Welt: Eine Geschichte des 19. Jahrhunderts*. Munich: C. H. Beck, 2009.

— 'Globale Horizonte europäischer Kunstmusik, 1860–1930'. *Geschichte und Gesellschaft* 38, no. 1 (2012): 86–132. https://doi.org/10.13109/gege.2012.38.1.86

— *The Transformation of the World: A Global History of the Nineteenth Century*. Princeton: Princeton University Press, 2014.

Ōsugi, Sakae, and Byron K. Marshall. *The Autobiography of Ōsugi Sakae translated with annotations by Byron K. Marshall*. Voices from Asia; 6. Berkeley, Calif.: University of California Press, 1992.

Ōtō, Osamu. *Sendai-han no gakumon to kyōiku: Edo jidai ni okeru Sendai no gakuto-ka*. Kokuhō Osaki Hachimangū Sendai edogaku sōsho 13. Sendai: Ōsaki Hachimangū (Sendai Edogaku Jikkō Iinkai), 2009.

Ōtsuka, Torazō. *Tsūzoku vaiorin hitorimanabi, shiyōhō no bu, jisshū no bu*. Kyoto: Jūjiya Gakkibu, 1909 (7th edn).

Ōwada, Tateki, ed. *Joshi Nisshin shōka*. Tokyo: Dai Nihon Tosho, 1906.

Parakilas, James, and E. Douglas Bomberger. *Piano Roles: Three Hundred Years of Life with the Piano*. New Haven: Yale University Press, 1999.

Park, William. 'The Lifelong Exercise that Keeps Japan Moving'. WorkLife (Japan 2020), BBC, Updated 19 June, 2020. https://www.bbc.com/worklife/article/20200609-the-life-long-exercise-that-keeps-japan-moving

Parmelee, Stephen. '"Such Inexplicable Pain": Kon Ichikawa's The Burmese Harp'. [In English]. *Christian Scholar's Review* 40, no. 4 (2011): 393–405. https://christianscholars.com/such-inexplicable-pain-kon-ichikawas-the-burmese-harp/

Partington, Blanche. 'With the Players and the Music Folk'. *The San Francisco Call*, 16 July 1905, 19.

Piao, Chunli. 'Nagasaki no minshingaku to Chūgoku no minshin jichō shōkyoku kenkyū'. *Chūkyō Daigaku Bunka Kagaku Kenkyūsho/Fukuoka Daigaku Jinbun Gakubu (Cultural Science)* 17, no. 2 (2006): 48–22. [sic]

Pinch, Trevor, and Karin Bijsterveld. 'New Keys to the World of Sound'. In *The Oxford Handbook of Sound Studies*, edited by Trevor Pinch and Karin Bijsterveld, 1–36: Oxford University Press, 2011. https://doi.org/10.1093/oxfordhb/9780195388947.001.0001

Pyle, Kenneth. *The New Generation in Meiji Japan: Problems of Cultural Identity, 1885–1895*. Stanford: Stanford University Press, 1969.

— 'Profound Forces in the Making of Modern Japan'. *Journal of Japanese Studies* 32, no. 2 (2006): 393–418.

Rathert, Wolfgang, and Bernd Ostendorf. *Musik der USA: Kultur- und Musikgeschichtliche Streifzüge*. Hofheim: Wolke, 2018.

Ravina, Mark. *To Stand with the Nations of the World: Japan's Meiji Restoration in World History*. New York: Oxford University Press, 2017.

Reich, Nancy. 'Women as Musicians: A Question of Class'. In *Musicology and Difference: Gender and Sexuality in Musical Scholarship*, edited by Ruth A. Solie, 125–46. Berkeley: University of California Press, 1995.

Rempe, Martin. 'Cultural Brokers in Uniform: The Global Rise of Military Musicians and Their Music'. *Itinerario* 41, no. 2 (2017): 327–52. https://doi.org/10.1017/S0165115317000390

— *Kunst, Spiel, Arbeit: Musikerleben in Deutschland, 1850 bis 1960*. Göttingen: Vandenhoeck & Ruprecht, 2020.

Rempe, Martin, and Claudius Torp. 'Cultural Brokers and the Making of Glocal Soundscapes, 1880s to 1930s'. *Itinerario* 41, no. 2 (2017): 223–33. https://doi.org/doi:10.1017/S0165115317000420

'Japan Took Center Stage at Chicago's 1893 World's Fair'. Norton Center for the Arts, 2015, 1, http://nortoncenter.com/2015/01/07/japan-took-center-stage-at-chicagos-1893-worlds-fair/

Rieu, Alain-Marc. 'The syndrome of "overcoming modernity": Learning from Japan about ultra-nationalism'. *Transtext(e)s Transcultures. Journal of Global Cultural Studies* 9 (2014): 1–23. https://doi.org/DOI: 10.4000/transtexts.552. https://journals.openedition.org/transtexts/552

Roberts, Luke S. *Performing the Great Peace: Political Space and Open Secrets in Tokugawa Japan*. Honolulu: University of Hawaii Press, 2012.

'Rōhō no amachua ōkesutora Suwa kōkyōgakudan sōritsu 80 shūnen'. *Sarasate*, no. 11 (2006): 101.

Ronge, Bertha, and Johann Ronge. *A practical guide to the English kinder-garten (children's garden): for the use of mothers, nursery governesses, and infant teachers : being an exposition of Froebel's system of infant training: accompanied by a great variety of instructive and amusing games, and industrial and gymnastic exercises, also numerous songs, set to music and arranged to the exercises*. London: J. S. Hodson, 1855.

Ross, Alex. *The Rest is Noise: Listening to the Twentieth Century*. New York: Picador, 2007.

Ruoff, Kenneth J. *Imperial Japan at its Zenith: The Wartime Celebrations of the Empire's 2,600th Anniversary*. Ithaca, NY: Cornell University Press, 2010.

Saegusa, Shigeaki. *Kyōten dōchi kurashikku*. Tokyo: Kino Bukkusu, 2014.

Saitō, Kei. *<Ura> Nihon ongakushi: ikei no kindai*. Tokyo: Shunjūsha, 2015.

Sakai, Katsuisa, ed. *Eigo shōka shū.*. 3 vols. Vol. 1. Tokyo: Uedaya, 1903.

Sakamoto, Mamiko. 'Kondō Sakufū to sono yakushikyoku saikō'. *Toyama Daigaku Kyōiku Gakubu kiyō A (bunkakei)* 50 (1997): 11–22.

— *Meiji chūtō ongaku kyōin no kenkyū: "Inaka kyōshi" to sono jidai*. Tokyo: Kazama Shobō, 2006.

Sakurai, Masato, Heruman Gochefuski, and Hiroshi Yasuda. *Aogeba tootoshi: maboroshi no genkyoku hakken to 'Shōgaku shōkashū' zenchikuseki*. Tokyo: Tōkyōdō Shuppan, 2015.

Sand, Jordan. *House and Home in Modern Japan: Architecture, Domestic Space and Bourgeois Culture 1880–1930* Cambridge, Mass.: Harvard University Press, 2003.

Sano, Ichizō, ed. *Sangyō shōka: Sano Seishijō yō*. Miyagi-ken Igu-gun Kanayama-machi: Sano Ichizō, 1901.

Sano, Rihachi (jun.). *Sano Silk Filature in North-Eastern Japan*. Tokyo: By the author, 1919.

Sauerbrey, Ulf. 'Froebelian Pedagogy: Historical Perspectives on an Approach of Early Childhood Education in Germany'. In *Guójì jiàoyù réncái péiyù zhī cèlüè yánjiū (Talent Development for International Education)*, edited by Sophia Ming-Lee Wen, 168–96. Taiwan: Tian Ming Sheu/National Academy for Educational Research, 2016.

Savigliano, Marta E. *Tango and the Political Economy of Passion*. Boulder: Westview Press, 1995.

Schmidt, Volker H. 'How Unique is East Asian Modernity?'. *Asian Journal of Social Science*, no. 39 (2011): 304–31. https://doi.org/10.1163/156853111X577596

Schoenbaum, David. 'Countries and Western: The Geopolitics of Music'. *The Wilson Quarterly* Winter (2015). http://wilsonquarterly.com/quarterly/fall-2014-the-great-wars/what-spread-classical-music-tells-us-about-globalization/

Schweikert, Norman. *Interview with Iwakura Tomokazu*. 1995. Cassette tape, Rosenthal Archives of the Chicago Symphony Orchestra.

'Seito shōkakai'. *Ongaku zasshi* 32 (1893): 19–20.

'Sendai-shi no gakukai'. *Ongakukai* 1, no. 4 (1908): 50–51.

Sendai Chōmarusei [pseud.]. 'Sendai gakukyō (February 1917)'. *Ongakukai* 184 (1917): 60–61.

Sendai City. *Sendai-shi tōkei ippan*. Sendai: Sendai City, 1901–1912.

'Sendai gakukyō (December 1908)'. *Ongakukai* 1, no. 12 (1908): 35.

Sendai Jinmei Daijisho Kankōkai, ed. *Sendai jinmei daijisho*, 2000 (1933).

'Sendai tsūshin [April 1896]'. *Ongaku zasshi/Omukaku*, no. 57 (28 April 1896): 23–28.

'Sendai tsūshin [October 1896]'. *Ongaku zasshi/Omukaku*, no. 62 (25 October 1896): 38–41.

Service, Jonathan. 'Harmony outside the Iron Cage: Tanaka Shōhei's Strategic Deconstruction of the Music-Theoretical Edifice'. *History of Humanities* 2, no. 2 (2017): 375–87. https://doi.org/10.1086/693320

Shaw, George Bernard. 'A ladylike tremolando in Richmond'. In *Music for Love*, edited by Christopher Driver, 286–90. London: Weidenfeld & Nicolson, 1994 (1890–94).

Shigematsu, Senoo. 'Ongaku jisshi ni tsuite no chūi'. *Ongaku zasshi* 67, no. 32–35 (1897).

Shigeno, Yasutsugu. 'Fūzoku kabu genryū kō'. In *Zōtei Shigeno hakushi shigaku ronbunshū*, edited by Toshiaki Ōkubo, 4 vols. Vol. 1, 435–62. Tokyo: Meicho Fukyūkai, 1989.

Shikama, (Totsuji) Senka 'Ongaku kairyō ippan'. *Ongaku zasshi*, no. 38 (November 1893): 1–2.

— 'Ongaku kairyō ippan (ctd.)'. *Ongaku zasshi*, no. 39 (1893): 1–2.

Shikama, Jinji, ed. *Miyagi-ken kyōdo shōka: dai isshū*. Tokyo: Yoshikawa Hanshichi, 1901.

— *Seishin no uta: dai isshū*. Sendai: Takatō Shoten, 1894.

Shikama, Jinji, and Makino Kōji. *Manshū tetsudō shōka*. Sendai: Fusandō, 1905.

Shikama, Jinji, and Totsuji Shikama. *Chiiku tetsudō shōka*. Sendai: Yūsenkaku Yamamoto Otoshirō, 1900.

Shikama, Totsuji. 'Giyū hōkō hōkoku ongakukai kaikai no taii'. *Ongaku zasshi* 47 (1894): 5–6.

— 'Hakkan no shushi'. *Ongaku zasshi* 1 (1890): 1–3.

— 'Kakushu no gakki'. *Ongaku zasshi*, no. 46 (1894): 25–26.

— 'Senkakin ni tsuite'. *Ongaku zasshi*, no. 27 (December 1892): 10–13.

— *Tefūgin dokusho no tomo dai ni shū*. Tokyo: Kyōeki Shōsha, 1891.

— *Tefūgin dokusho no tomo dai san shū*. Tokyo: Kyōeki Shōsha, 1892.

— *Tokkyō shōka*. Tokyo and Sendai: Gakuyūkan and Yūsenkaku, 1902.

— 'Yamato miyage no jo'. *Ongaku zasshi* 46 (1894): 18–19.

Shikama, Totsuji (Shōsen Itsudo). 'Nihon ongaku'. *Ongaku zasshi* 21 (1892): 9–11.

[Shikama, Totsuji] Senka. 'Kurarinetto'. *Ongaku zasshi* 30 (1893): 8.

Shimazu, Tadashi. *Meiji Satsuma-biwa uta*. Tokyo: Perikansha, 2001.

Shinano Kyōiku Kai, ed. *Kyōiku kōrōsha retsuden*. Nagano: Shinano Kyōiku Kai, 1935.

Shiotsu, Yōko. 'Meijiki Kansai vaiorin jijō'. *Ongaku kenkyū* (Ōsaka *Ongaku Daigaku Hakubutsukan nenpō*), no. 20 (2003): 11–38.

'Shizuoka juppei ongakukai'. *Ongaku no tomo* 7, no. 2 (1904): 34.

Shōken Koji. 'Ongaku Gakkō no hitsuyō ni tsuite'. In *Tōkyō Geijutsu Daigaku hyakunenshi: Tōkyō Ongaku Gakkō hen 1*, edited by Tōkyō Geijutsu Daigaku Hyakunenshi Hensan Iinkai, 358. Tokyo: Ongaku no Tomosha, 1987 (1891).

Shūkan Asahi, ed. *Nedanshi nempyō: Meiji, Taishō, Shōwa*. Tokyo: Asahi Shinbunsha, 1988.

Shūtō, Yoshiki. 'Narihibiku katei kūkan: 1910–20 nendai Nihon ni okeru katei ongaku no gensetsu'. *Nenpō shakaigaku ronshū* (*Kantō Shakai Gakukai* 21 (2008): 95–106. https://doi.org/10.5690/kantoh.2008.95

Signell, Karl. 'The Modernization Process in Two Oriental Music Cultures: Turkish and Japanese'. *Asian Music* 7, no. 2 (Symposium on the Ethnomusicology of Culture Change in Asia (1976): 72–102. https://doi.org/10.2307/833790

Small, Christopher. *Musicking: The Meanings of Performing and Listening*. Middletown, CT: Wesleyan University Press, 1998.

Spencer, Paul. *Society and the Dance*. Cambridge: Cambridge University Press, 1985.

Spitzer, Michael. *The Musical Human: A History of Life on Earth*. London: Bloomsbury, 2021.

Suchy, Irene. 'Deutschsprachige Musiker in Japan vor 1945. Eine Fallstudie eines Kulturtransfers am Beispiel der Rezeption abendländischer Musik'. Doctoral thesis, University of Vienna, 1992.

— 'A Nation of Mozart-Lovers: Das Phänomen abendländischer Kunstmusik in Japan'. *Minikomi* (*Informationen des akademischen Arbeitskreises Japan*) 1994, no. 1 (1994): 1–8.

— 'Versunken und vergessen: zwei österreichische Musiker in Japan vor 1945'. In *Mehr als Maschinen für Musik*, edited by Sepp Linhart and Kurt Schmid, 89–121. Wien: Literas Universitätsverlag, 1990.

Sugano, Fuyuki. *Konoe Hidemaro: Bōmei ōkesutora no shinjitsu*. Tokyo: Tōkyōdō Shuppan, 2017.

Suzuki, Seiko. '"Kagaku" to shite no Nihon ongaku kenkyū: Tanabe Hisao no gagaku kenkyū to Nihon ongakushi no kōchiku'. Doctoral thesis, University of Tokyo, 2014.

Suzuki, Shin'ichi. *Nurtured by Love: The Classic Approach to Talent Education*. Miami: Suzuki Method International, Summy-Birchard Inc., 1983.

Suzuki, Yonejirō. 'Ongaku Gakkō zonhai ni tsuite'. In *Tōkyō Geijutsu Daigaku hyakunenshi: Tōkyō Ongaku Gakkō hen 1*, edited by Tōkyō Geijutsu Daigaku Hyakunenshi Hensan Iinkai, 359–61. Tokyo: Ongaku no Tomosha, 1987 (1891).

Takahashi, Haruko, Sachiko Kishimoto, and Kichiji Kimura. 'Isawa Shūji no "yūki" ni kansuru ikkōsatsu'. *Chūkyō taiikugaku kenyū* (*Chūkyō Daigaku Gakujutsu Kenkyūkai*) 16, no. 1 (1975): 67–80.

Takaori, Biō. 'Gakuyū shishin (26 shin)'. *Ongakukai* 6, no. 6 (1913): 53–57.

— 'Gakuyū shishin (27 shin, 28 shin)'. *Ongakukai* 6, no. 7 (1913): 56–58.

— 'Gakuyū shishin (29 shin)'. *Ongakukai* 6, no. 8 (1913): 54–56.

— 'Ōshū man'yū ki (dai 33 shin)'. *Ongakukai* 6, no. 4 (1913): 45–47.

Takaori, Shūichi. *Aki no irokusa* (*Nagauta gakufu, Dai 2 shū*). Tokyo: Gakuyūsha, 1904.

— 'Kikyo raiji'. *Ongakukai* 6, no. 6 (1913): 10–11.

Takaori, Shūichi (Biō). 'Hōgaku no kosui kara seigaku no sūhai e'. *Ongakukai* 6, no. 7 (1913): 21–24.

Takashima, Yuriko. 'Kōka o meguru hyōshō bunka kenkyū: kindai kokka seiritsu ni okeru kōka no seitei katei to gendai no sh jōkyō o tegakari ni'. Ph.D., 2013. https://doi.org//10.15006/32665A4729

Takeishi, Midori. 'Meiji/Taishō no Tōyō Ongaku Gakkō: Ensō ni kansuru kiroku, shiryō'. *Tōkyō Ongaku Daigaku kenkyū kiyō* 29 (2005): 27–48. https://core.ac.uk/download/pdf/230043973.pdf

— ed. *Ongaku kyōiku no ishizue: Suzuki Yonejirō to Tōyō Ongaku Gakkō*. Tokyo: Shunjusha, 2007.

Takenaka, Toru. 'Isawa Shūji's "National Music": National Sentiment and Cultural Westernization in Meiji Japan'. *Itinerario* 34, no. 3 (2010): 97–118. https://doi.org/10.1017/S0165115310000719

— 'Wagner-Boom in Meiji-Japan'. *Archiv für Musikwissenschaft* 62, no. 1 (2005): 13–31.

Takeuchi, Hiroshi. *Rainichi Seiyō jinmei jiten*. Tokyo: Nichigai Associates, 1983.

Tamagawa, Yūko. 'Kindai Nihon ni okeru katei ongaku ron: "ikka danraku" no mikan no yume'. *Tōhō Gakuen Daigaku kenkyū kiyō* 43 (2017): 57–76.

— 'Mitsukoshi hyakkaten to ongaku: ongaku to shōgyō wa te ni te o totte (Music and Commerce Hand in Hand: Mitsukoshi and Music)'. *Tōhō gakuen daigaku kenkyū kiyō (Faculty Bulletin, Toho Gakuen School of Music)*, no. 23 (1997): 27–59.

— 'Seiyō - Nihon - Ajia: Mitsukoshi hyakkaten no ongaku katsudō ni okeru ongaku bunka no seiyōka to kokumin ishiki no keisei'. *Doitsu bungaku* 132 (2006): 78. https://doi.org/10.11282/jgg.132.0_78

Tanabe, Hisao. 'Meiji makki no hōgakukai'. *Kikan hōgaku* 4 (1975): 20–23.

— *Meiji ongaku monogatari*. Tokyo: Seiabō, 1965.

Tanaka, Takako, Akiko Odaka, and Hideharu Umeda. 'Taishōgoto no denpan to henyō: Taiwan, Indoneshia oyobi Indo no jirei'. *Kyōto Kyōiku Daigaku kiyō* 120 (2012): 121–37.

Tanimura, Masajirō. *Umi no gunka to reishiki kyoku: Teikoku Kaigun no ongaku isan to Kaijō Jieitai*. Shuppan Kyōdō Sha, 2015.

Tao, Demin. 'Tominaga Nakamoto no Ongakukan: "Gakuritsukō" no kenkyū'. In *Nihon kangaku shisōshi ronkō: Sorai, Nakamoto oyobi kindai*, 103–23. Suita: Kansai Daigaku Shuppanbu, 1999.

Tetteki, Bōhyō. 'Senkakin.' *Ongaku zasshi*, no. 29 (February 1893): 9.

Tindall, Blair. *Mozart in the Jungle: Sex, Drugs and Classical Music*. London: Atlantic Books, 2005.

TN. 'Sendai Amachū Kurabu kinjō'. *Ongakukai* 191 (September 1917): 54–55.

Togi, Masataro. *Gagaku: Court Music and Dance*. New York: Weatherhill, 1971.

Tokita, Alison M. 'Bi-Musicality in Modern Japanese Culture'. *International Journal of Bilingualism*, no. online (2012): 0(0) 1–16. https://doi.org/10.1177/1367006912458394

Tokyo Academy of Music, ed. *Collection of Japanese Koto Music*. Tokyo: Department of Education, 1888.

Tōkyō Geijutsu Daigaku Hyakunenshi Hensan Iinkai, ed. *Tōkyō Geijutsu Daigaku hyakunenshi: Ensōkai hen 1*. Tokyo: Ongaku no Tomosha, 1990.

— ed. *Tōkyō Geijutsu Daigaku hyakunenshi: Tōkyō Ongaku Gakkō hen 1*. Tokyo: Ongaku no Tomosha, 1987.

— ed. *Tōkyō Geijutsu Daigaku hyakunenshi: Tōkyō Ongaku Gakkō hen 2*. Tokyo: Ongaku no Tomosha, 2003.

'Tokyo no onna (34): Biya hōru no gakushu, Inazuna kozō jiken no Shikama Ranko'. *Asahi shinbun*, 22 September 1909, Morning, 5.

'Tōkyō Shōnen Gakutai sōga ni fu shite'. *Ongaku zasshi* 52 (1895): 10–11.

'Tōkyō Shōnen Ongakutai'. *Ongaku zasshi* 55 (1895): 18–19.

'Tōkyō Shōnen Ongakutai'. *Fūzoku gahō* 97 (1895): 22 (illustration p. 4).

'Tōkyō Shōnen Ongakutai'. *Ongaku zasshi* 50 (1895): 31–32.

Tsukahara, Yasuko. 'Gungakutai to senzen no taishū ongaku'. In *Burasubando no shakaishi: gungakutai kara utaban e*, edited by Kan'ichi Abe, Shūhei Hosokawa, Tomomasa Takazawa, Mamoru Tōya and Yasuko Tsukahara, 83–124. Tokyo: Seikyūsha, 2001.

— *Jūkyū seiki no Nihon ni okeru Seiyō ongaku no juyō*. Tokyo: Taka Shuppan, 1993.

— 'Meiji 30 nen no kunaishō shikibushoku gagakubu'. *Tōkyō Geijutsu Daigaku Ongakubu kiyō*, no. 31 (2006): 89–112. https://geidai.repo.nii.ac.jp/records/505

— *Meiji kokka to gagaku: dentō no kindaika/kokugaku no sōsei*. Tokyo: Yūshisha, 2009.

— 'Nihon ongaku no kindai kara gendai'. In *Nihon no dentō geinō kōza: ongaku*, edited by Nihon Geinō Bunka Shinkōkai and Kokuritsu Gekijō, 459–80. Kyoto: Tankōsha, 2008.

Tsurumi, Patricia. *Factory Girls: Women in the Thread Mills of Meiji Japan*. Princeton: Princeton University Press, 1990.

Tsurumi, Patricia E. *Japanese Colonial Education in Taiwan, 1895–1945*. Cambridge, Mass.: Harvard University Press, 1977.

Turino, Thomas. *Music as Social Life: The Politics of Participation*. Chicago and London: The University of Chicago Press, 2008.

Ueno, Masaaki 'Meiji chūki kara Taishō ni okeru yōgakki de Nihon dentō ongaku o ensō suru kokoromi ni tsuite: Gakufu ni yoru fukyū o kangaeru'. *Nihon dentō ongaku kenkyū* 9 (2012): 21–42. https://rcjtm.kcua.ac.jp/pub/2017web/publications/2012/pdf/09kiyou_ueno.pdf

Umeda, Hideharu. 'Bari shima nishi bu Pupuan mura ni denshō sareru taishōgoto o kigen to suru gakki mandorin'. *Shizuoka Bunka Geijutsu Daigaku kenkyū kiyō* 19 (2018): 165–70. https://suac.repo.nii.ac.jp/records/1551

Umihara, Tōru. *Nihonshi shōhyakka: Gakkō*. Tokyo: Kondō Shuppansha, 1979.

Uno, Kazusuke. *Meiji shōnen no Miyagi kyōiku*. Sendai: Hōbundō, 1973.

van der Does-Ishikawa, Luli. 'Contested Memories of the Kamikaze and the self-representations of Tokkō-tai youth in their missives home'. *Japan Forum* 27, no. 3 (2015): 345–79. https://doi.org/10.1080/09555803.2015.1045540

— 'A Sociolinguistic Analysis of Japanese Children's Official Songbooks, 1881–1945: Nurturing an Imperial Ideology through the Manipulation of Language'. Doctor of Philosophy, University of Sheffield, 2013. https://core.ac.uk/download/pdf/19775967.pdf

van der Linden, Bob. 'Non-Western National Music and Empire in Global History: Interactions, Uniformities, and Comparisons'. *Journal of Global History* 10 (2015): 431–56. https://doi.org/10.1017/S1740022815000212

Vianna, Hermano. *The Mystery of Samba: Popular Music and National Identity in Brazil*. Chapel Hill and London: The University of North Carolina Press, 1999.

'A Violin Virtuoso.' *The Japan Times*, 21 February 1898.

'Violin/Baiorin (advertisement by Jūjiya)'. *Tōkyō nichinichi shinbun*, 22 April 1888, 8.

Wade, Bonnie C. *Composing Japanese Musical Modernity*. Chicago: University of Chicago Press, 2014.

— *Music in Japan*. Oxford: Oxford University Press, 2005.

'Waga Ongaku zasshi'. *Ongaku zasshi*, no. 17 (February 1892): 16.

Watanabe, Hiroshi. *Nihon bunka modan rapusodi*. Tokyo: Shunjūsha, 2002.

— *Saundo to media no bunka shigengaku: kyōkai senjō no ongaku*. Tokyo: Shunjūsha, 2013.

Watanabe, Saeko. 'Tefūgin no kyokushū ni tsuite: sono kifūhō o chūshin ni'. *Ochanomizu ongaku ronshū* 17 (2015): 13–30. https://teapot.lib.ocha.ac.jp/records/33828

Watanabe, Shin'ya. 'Sendai sho no shōka kyōshi Shikama Jinji'. *Sendai bunka*, no. 11 (2009): 6–7.

— 'Sendai yōgaku no sakigake'. *Sendai bunka*, no. 11 (2009): 4–5.

'Wayō chōwa juppei ongakukai'. *Ongaku no tomo* 7, no. 2 (1904): 38–39.

Weber, Max. '[Zur Musiksoziologie]'. In *Max Weber: Zur Musiksoziologie (Nachlaß 1921)*, edited by Christoph Braun and Ludwig Finscher. Max Weber Gesamtausgabe, 145–280. Tübingen: J. C. B. Mohr (Paul Siebeck), 2004 (1921).

Wehler, Hans-Ulrich. *Modernisierungstheorie und Geschichte*. Göttingen: Vandenhoeck & Ruprecht, 1975.

Whitney, Clara. *Clara's Diary: An American Girl in Meiji Japan*. Tokyo: Kodansha International, 1981 (1979).

Williamson, Aaron, ed. *Musical Excellence: Strategies and techniques to enhance performance*. Oxford: Oxford University Press, 2004.

Yamamoto, Masataka. 'Beikoku no gakukai to hōjin no daiseiko'. *Ongakukai* 4, no. 7 (1911): 34–36.

Yamanashi, Makiko. *A History of the Takarazuka Revue Since 1914: Modernity, Girls' Culture, Japan Pop*. Leiden: Global Oriental, 2012.

Yamanoi, Motokiyo. 'Baiorin sōhō oyobi gakushū hō'. *Ongakukai* 5, no. 1 (1912): 32–35.

Yamashita, Sumire. 'Tōhō seikyō no ongakaku to shizoku'. In *Kindai ikōki ni okeru chiiki keisei to ongaku: tsukurareta dentō to ibunka sesshoku*, edited by Kanako Kitahara and Kenji Namikawa, 171–203. Kyoto: Mineruba Shobō, 2020.

Yamazumi, Masami, ed. *Isawa Shūji: Yōgaku kotohajime - Ongaku torishirabe seiseki shinpōsho*. Tokyo: Heibonsha, 1971.

— *Shōka kyōiku seiritsu katei no kenkyū*. Tokyo: Tōkyō Daigaku Shuppankai, 1967.

Yang, Kuei-Hsiang. 'Minshingaku: Nagasaki ni tsutaerareta Chūgoku ongaku'. *Ochanomizu Joshi Daigaku Daigakuin Ningen Bunka Kenkyūka (Journal of the Musicological Society of Ochanomizu University)* 2 (2000): 70–80. https://teapot.lib.ocha.ac.jp/record/33890/files/KJ00004857924.pdf

Yasar, Kerim. *Electrified Voices: How the Telephone, Phonograph, and Radio Shaped Modern Japan, 1868–1945*. New York: Columbia University Press, 2018.

Yatabe, Ryōkichi. 'Ongaku Gakkō ron'. In *Tōkyō Geijutsu Daigaku hyakunenshi: Tōkyō Ongaku Gakkō hen 1*, edited by Tōkyō Geijutsu Daigaku Hyakunenshi Hensan Iinkai, 354–56. Tokyo: Ongaku no Tomosha, 1987 (1891).

'Yōikuin jizen ongakukai'. *Ongaku zasshi* 31 (1893): 17–18.

Yoshihara, Mari. *Dearest Lenny: Letters from Japan and the Making of the World Maestro*. New York: Oxford University Press, 2019.

— 'The Flight of the Japanese Butterfly: Orientalism, Nationalism, and Performances of Japanese Womanhood'. *American Quarterly* 56, no. 4 (2004): 975–1001. https://doi.org/10.1353/aq.2004.0067

— *Musicians from a Different Shore: Asians and Asian Americans in Classical Music.* Philadelphia: Temple University Press, 2007.

Yuasa, Yasuo. *The Body: Toward an Eastern Mind-Body Theory.* Albany: State University of New York Press, 1987.

'Yūikuin jizen ongaku kai'. *Ongaku zasshi* 31 (1893): 17–18.

Yumoto, Kōichi. *Bakumatsu Meiji ryūkō jiten.* Tokyo: Kashiwa Shobō, 1998.

Yung, Bell. 'The Nature of Chinese Ritual Sound'. In *Harmony and Counterpoint: Ritual Music in Chinese Context*, edited by Bell Yung, Evelyn S. Rawski and Rubie S. Watson, 13–31. Stanford, CA: Stanford University Press, 1996.

Zon, Bennett. 'Science and Religion'. In *The Oxford Handbook of Music and Intellectual Culture in the Nineteenth Century*, edited by Paul Watt, Sarah Collins and Michael Allis, 387–408: Oxford University Press, 2020.

Zuck, Barbara A. *A History of Musical Americanism.* Ann Arbor, MI: UMI, 1980 (1978).

Zweig, Stefan. 'Lafcadio Hearn'. In *Das Japanbuch: Eine Auswahl aus den Werken von Lafcadio Hearn*, 1. Frankfurt a. M.: Rütten & Loening, 1923 (1911).

Index

accordion 109, 190, 193, 198, 222–226, 228, 248, 257, 362
African American music 82–84
Aichi Normal School (Aichi Shihan Gakkō) 145–146
Aikawa, Yumi 41
Ainu people 19, 94, 194
amateur 43, 45, 48, 61, 74, 91, 94, 96, 99, 105, 107, 115, 270, 281, 285, 385, 389, 400
American Civil War 30, 64, 66–70, 73, 82
ancient Greece 12, 131, 139, 265
Andō, Kō (née Kōda) 200, 221
Applegate, Celia 7, 10, 16
Arirang (song) 58–60
Asahina, Takashi 57
Asakusa Opera 112
Association for Musical Games (Ongaku Yūgi Kai) 220
Association for Music in the Home (Katei Ongaku Kai) 233
Association for Native Japanese Music (Kokufū Ongaku Kai) 99, 250, 284, 350

Bell, Alexander Graham 147–151
Bell, Alexander Melville 148–149
Bewegungsspiele (movement games) 141–142
Bion Kai (Association for Beautiful Sound) 112
biwa (plucked lute) 35, 91, 94, 98–99, 120, 164, 191, 193, 196–197, 229, 252, 258, 266, 282, 303, 308, 314, 317–321, 362. See also *chikuzenbiwa*; See *heikebiwa*, *satsumabiwa*, *teikoku biwa* ('imperial' *biwa*)

Blackstone, Tsianina Redfeather 81–82
Blanning, Tim 16, 42, 44, 47–48
Bod, Rens 16
body (and music) 14, 130, 145, 178
Book of Rites 129, 169, 220
Boston 67–71, 73–74, 149, 215–216, 394
Bridgewater Normal School 147, 151–153
Buddhism 12, 94, 96, 160, 188, 191, 260, 265, 330
bunmei (civilization) 128–129, 131, 159, 203, 212, 219
bunmei kaika (civilization and enlightenment) 36, 128, 170

Cadman, Charles Wakefield 81–82, 339–340
  Four American Indian Songs 81, 340
  Shanewis 81–82
Cai, Yuanpei 53
Chamberlain, Basil Hall 135, 137, 152, 328, 394
chamber music 97, 105, 117, 228, 257, 364, 383, 396
charity concert 45, 166, 195, 198, 207, 213, 249–250, 260–261, 282, 303
Chemet, Renée 235
Chiba, Yūko 41
Chicago 64, 73, 282, 295, 299
chikuzenbiwa 98, 233
children's song. See *dōyō*
Chinese learning. See *kangaku*
Christianity 33, 51, 81, 101, 107, 131, 241, 265, 275, 293, 296, 298–299, 323, 328, 330, 342

cinema 115–116
cipher notation 126, 188, 192, 198, 204, 222–223, 227, 229, 231
civilization. *See bunmei*
civilization and enlightenment. *See bunmei kaika*
clarinet 100, 193–195, 198, 256–257, 373
classical music 2–3, 26, 31–32, 41–42, 46, 50, 61, 63, 70, 75, 93, 96, 120–123, 219, 325, 395, 398. *See also kurashikku* (Western classical music); *See also Nihon koten ongaku* (Japanese classical music)
colonialism 29, 39, 47, 49, 51, 54–55, 58–59, 66, 149, 151, 389
Committee for Research into Traditional Japanese Music (Hōgaku Kenkyū Kakari) 111
common music (*zokugaku*) 104
concert. *See* charity concert; *See* public concert
Confucianism 18, 24, 53, 90, 125, 129–131, 136, 140, 170, 182, 219–220, 247, 256, 258, 342
conservatoire 23, 44, 82, 88, 104, 121, 123, 155, 179, 232, 238, 264, 278, 282, 292, 299, 341, 377
creative space 244, 345, 382, 400
cultivated music 77, 84, 158
  compositional 77
  conceptual 77
cultural resources studies (*bunka shigen gaku*) 9

Dagron, Gustave Charles 101
Dai Ni Kōtō Chūgakkō. *See* Second Higher Secondary School, Sendai
Dai Ni Kōtō Gakkō. *See* Second High School, Sendai
Dai Nihon Katei Ongaku Kai. *See* Great Japan Home Music Society
Dai Nihon Ongaku Kurabu. *See* Great Japan Music Club
dance hall 44, 57, 115–116

Darwinism 132, 151–152
Dazai, Shundai 130
DeNora, Tia 399
Department of Court Ceremonies 96, 102
Dittrich, Rudolf 104–106, 155, 200
dōyō (children's song) 272, 290
dual structure. *See nijū kōzō*
Dubravčić, Wilhlem (Guglielmo) 221, 278–279
Dvořák, Antonín 77–80, 375–376
Dwight, John Sullivan 70, 72, 85

Eckert, Franz 54–55, 101–102, 104–105, 107, 267, 279
education 21, 23, 41, 49, 52–54, 66–69, 103, 108, 110, 122, 131, 139, 147, 150, 152–156, 162, 170, 182, 185, 189, 192, 220–221, 238, 243, 248, 265, 284, 291, 294, 300, 323, 332, 366
Ehrlich, Cyril 15
Ellis, Alexander J. 29, 163–164
emotion 12–14, 31, 59, 75, 93, 133, 155, 176, 260, 322, 327, 393, 395, 402
enka (sentimental popular ballad) 2, 31, 41, 78
Eurocentrism 33, 37–38, 73

Farrar, Geraldine 217
Fenton, John William 101–102
Ferris Seminary 103
First World War 16, 24, 55, 58, 75, 110, 122, 182, 204, 275, 368
Fletcher, Alice 80–81
folk music 47, 55, 58–59, 79–80, 160, 194, 249, 261, 267, 286, 290, 328
folk performing arts. *See minzoku geinō*
Foster, Stephen 83–85, 367, 385
France 120, 159, 185, 188, 227, 272, 277, 395–396
Froebel, Friedrich 141–146
Fujiwara, Yoshie 112, 114
Fukuzawa, Yukichi 31, 36

Fulcher, Jane 10

gagaku song 144
Gaisberg, Frederick 57
Gakusei (1872) Education Law 103, 239
Geidai. *See* Tokyo University of Fine Arts and Music (Tōkyō Geijutsu Daigaku, Tōkyō Geidai)
Gekkan gakufu (Monthly scores) 109
gekkin (lute with round, flattish body) 91, 183, 193, 229
gidayū (popular narrative *shamisen* genre) 117, 120, 158, 160, 231
Gienow-Hecht, Jessica 10, 13
global history 7, 11, 19, 32
globalization 5–6, 10–11, 17, 19, 22, 24, 29–30, 42, 46, 48–55, 125
gramophone recording 46, 54, 57–58, 113, 116–117, 235, 245, 276–277, 311, 327, 347
Great Japan Home Music Society (Dai Nihon Katei Ongaku Kai) 234
Great Japan Music Club (Dai Nihon Ongaku Kurabu) 206, 208
Great National Peace Jubilee (Boston) 70
Greece (ancient). *See* ancient Greece
gunka (military songs) 110, 195, 199, 223
gymnastics. *See taisō*

Hansen, Alpha Florence 295–297, 301, 305, 308, 329
Hansen, Kate Ingeborg 25, 237–238, 269, 279, 306, 312, 339, 345, 374, 376, 378
  appointment at Miyagi College 285, 291
  correspondence with family 301
  development of music study at Miyagi College 281, 292–293, 332–333, 336, 374
  dislike of the *biwa* 319
  early life 295

  emigration to Japan 297
  interest in Japanese culture 295
  musical training 300, 313
  observations of musical life in Sendai 106, 240, 294, 300, 302, 308–309, 311, 314–318, 320–330, 341–343, 349, 362–364, 374, 382, 388–389, 400
  public performances 286–287, 290–291, 302, 304–305, 307, 309–310, 358–359, 361, 364, 374, 377
  relationship with music 297
  teaching experiences 331, 334–335, 337–338, 340, 396–397
Harbin 55–56
Harich-Schneider, Eta 26, 89, 328
Hasegawa, Ichirō (Ch'ae Kyuhwa) 58
Hasegawa, Shigure 360
Hatano, Juichirō 368
Hattori, Ryōichi 57
hauta (short *shamisen* song) 168, 229, 231
hayashi (flute and drum ensemble in traditional theatre) 244, 249, 258
heikebiwa 98, 111
Helmholtz, Helmut 111
Hepburn, James 103, 206, 269
hichiriki (double-reed pipe) 160, 193–194
Higgins, Kathleen 402
Hiruma, Genpachi 196
history. *See* global history; *See* local history
Hohmann, Christian Heinrich 68–69
Hokkaido 19, 65–66, 240
Hōmeikai (Phoenix Song Society) 251–254, 259
hybridization 89, 235
hymn 53–55, 81, 84, 96, 103, 227, 240, 260, 270, 273, 275, 277, 289, 291, 323–324, 329–330, 334, 339, 341, 359, 381
  Buddhist hymn 96
  Protestant hymn 53, 96, 103

Ichikawa, Danjūrō IX 207–209
iemoto system 93, 214–215
Ikuta school (Ikuta-*ryū*) 98–99, 284, 351, 353–354
Imperial Hotel 295
Imperial Theatre 112–113, 218
Imperial University. *See* Tokyo Imperial University (Tōkyō Teikoku Daigaku)
India 31, 49, 57–58, 110, 178
Indianism (movement) 79–83
Inoue, Tetsujirō 169–170, 265–266
intonation 61, 111, 326, 340
Ishikuro, Kosaburō 166, 361, 369
Ishino, Gi (Iwao, Takashi) 270–272
Italy 47, 112, 120, 215, 278
Iwakura Embassy 36, 63–64, 66, 71, 143
Iwamoto, Shōji 205, 210–213, 215–217, 219–220
Iwate prefecture 279

Japanese music. *See Nihon koten ongaku* (Japanese classical music); *See Nihon ongaku* (Japanese music)
jazz 2, 31, 42, 57, 60, 74, 83, 85, 115–116
Jews 56, 114
jiuta (sung genre of traditional music with instrumental interludes) 98, 213, 227, 230, 252, 350–351, 353
Johnson, Julian 39–40, 46, 346, 385
joji shōka (narrative songs) 209, 281
jōruri (generic term for narrative *shamisen* music) 97, 160, 191, 257–258. *See also* Oku-*jōruri*
Jūjiya (musical store) 109, 232
Junker, August 40, 73–74, 201, 221, 282, 328, 365

kagura (generic term for Shintō music) 94, 160, 258, 263
kamikaze 393
kanbun. See Sinitic
Kanda, Kōhei 157–158, 179

kangaku (Chinese learning) 21, 129–130, 133, 135–136, 140, 183
kangengaku ('orchestral' ensemble) 359, 364
Kanjinchō (The subscription list) 206–208, 210, 213, 272, 281, 353
Kansai area 19, 41, 56–57, 98, 107, 113, 117, 221, 223, 230–232, 278, 320, 351
katei (household, home) 199, 220–221, 233
Katei ongaku (*Hausmusik*, music played in the home) 220–221, 233–234
Katei ongaku (magazine) 234–235
Katei Ongaku Kai. *See* Association for Music in the Home
Katō, Yōzō 205
Kawakami, Sadayakko 217
kayōkyoku (popular songs) 31, 60, 78, 118
kazoeuta (counting song) 214
Kimi ga yo (Japanese national anthem) 102, 307
kindergarten 102, 141–145, 154, 192, 214
Kineya (family and school of *shamisen* artists) 207, 214–215, 353
Kishi, Kōichi 114, 119
Kisu, Yoshinoshin 269, 278
Kitamura, Hatsuko (née Amano) 234
Kitamura, Sueharu 126, 205–210, 214, 232, 234–235, 270–272, 281, 288, 290, 362
kiyomotobushi (style of narrative performance with *shamisen*) 97
Kobayashi, Ichizō 113
Kobe 22, 56, 107, 116, 225, 237, 261, 332
Kōda, Kō. *See* Andō, Kō (née Kōda)
Kōda, Nobu 74, 105, 200–201
Koeber, Raphael von 264
Koga, Masao 58, 119
Kōga, Musen (Ryōtarō) 126, 224–225, 230–232

kōka (school/alma mater songs) 27, 254
Kokufū Ongaku Kai. *See* Association for Native Japanese Music
kokugaku (National learning) 133–135
kokugaku (National music) 100, 104, 164, 229
kokyū (bowed lute) 94, 98, 184, 221, 225, 257, 282, 284, 351
komusō (mendicant monks) 94
Konakamura, Kiyonori 133–137, 264
Konoe, Hidemaro 114–115
Korea 25, 31, 51, 54–55, 57–60, 102, 119, 136, 151, 186, 192, 384
kouta (short *samisen* song) 117, 271
Kōzu, Senzaburō 165–166, 170
Krehbiel, Henry 78–79
Kron, Gustav 40, 365
Kumaya, Sentarō 269
Kume, Kunitake 63–64, 71–72, 133, 394
Kunitachi College of Music (Kunitachi Ongaku Daigaku) 166, 349, 380
kurashikku (Western classical music) 26, 75
Kyōeki Shōsha 187, 192, 206, 208–210, 253, 288
Kyoto Imperial University 115
Kyoto University Orchestra 56

Laska, Josef 115
Leroux, Charles 101
Levitin, Daniel 6
Liebersohn, Harry 29, 390
local history 254
Lombardi, Luca 9
Lully, Jean-Baptiste 187

Machida, Ōen 223, 228–231
Madame Butterfly (opera) 82, 114, 165, 217
Maedako, Haruko 246, 352
Maedako, Nobuchika (Shinkin) 225, 246, 259, 269, 275–276, 283–284, 351–352, 355, 357

Maedako, Wataru 246, 352, 356–357
Maeda, Kyūhachi 205, 208, 215, 235, 270–272, 278, 280, 286–288
mandolin 193, 195–196, 201, 233–234, 255, 273, 286–288, 302, 317, 354
Mason, Lowell 67–68, 271
Mason, Luther Whiting 68–70, 74, 85, 104, 147–148, 151, 153–155, 157, 162–163
Matsuno, Clara (née Zitelmann) 102, 144
Matsuzakaya department store 108, 200
McClary, Susan 6
McNeill, William H. 14
Megata, Tanetarō 139, 147–148, 153
Meiji Music Society (Meiji Ongaku Kai) 107, 270, 277
Meiji Restoration 5, 30, 35, 37, 88, 94, 99, 128, 166
Meiji Six Society (Meirokusha) 157, 183
Mendelssohn, Felix 276, 280, 290, 306, 308, 312, 318, 334, 341, 356, 359, 372–373, 379–380, 383, 388
Mendenhall, Thomas 89
Metter, Emmanuel 56
Mikado, The (opera) 97
military band 1, 14, 43, 54, 71, 95, 101, 110, 172, 194, 222, 225, 249, 282, 286, 394
minshingaku (Ming and Qing dynasty music) 27, 90, 173, 226, 229, 244
minstrel show 83–84
min'yō (folk song) 2, 94
minzoku geinō (folk performing arts) 94, 238
Mitsukoshi department store 108, 208
Miura, Tamaki 82, 114, 217
Miyagi Band (Miyagi Ongakutai) 255–258
Miyagi College (Miyagi Jogakkō, Miyagi Gakuin) 5, 23, 240–241, 275, 281–282, 285, 288, 290–291, 294, 297, 306–307, 312, 325, 329,

331–332, 336, 342, 350, 372, 374–378, 382–383, 388
Miyagi Gakuin. *See* Miyagi College
Miyagi Jogakkō (Miyagi School for Girls). *See* Miyagi College
Miyagi, Michio 54, 119, 235
Miyagi Music Society (Miyagi Ongaku Kai) 248
Miyagi Normal School (Miyagi Shihan Gakkō) 239, 243, 245, 247, 366, 382
Miyagi Ongakutai. *See* Miyagi Band
Miyagi Prefectural Police Training Academy (Miyagi-ken Junsa Kyōshūsho) 243
Miyagi Prefectural School for the Blind and Dumb (Miyagi Kenritsu Mōa Gakkō) 247
Miyagi School for Girls (Miyagi Gakuin Women's University). *See* Miyagi College
Miyagi Shōnen Ongakutai. *See* Miyagi Youth Band
Miyagi Youth Band (Miyagi Shōnen Ongakutai) 254–255, 257, 260
Miyoshi, Aikichi 263–266, 272
Morioka 279–281
movement games (*yūgi*). *See yūgi*
Mozart, Amadeus 31, 165, 216, 271, 274, 306, 340, 356, 362, 379–380, 382, 396
  The Magic Flute 165, 271
musical modernity 19, 37–41, 43, 45, 59–60, 132, 346
Music College of the East (Tōyō Ongaku Gakkō) 52, 108, 171, 352, 364
Music Investigation Committee (Ongaku Torishirabe Gakari) 101, 103–104, 153–154, 163, 167, 172, 183, 247
musicking 9–12, 16
musicology 7–8, 16, 29, 38, 49, 132, 163
  ethnomusicology 3, 7–8, 38, 47, 112

music-related activities (*ongaku katsudō*). *See ongaku katsudō*
Music Research Institute (Ongaku Torishirabe Sho). *See* Music Investigation Committee (Ongaku Torishirabe Gakari)

Nabeshima, Naohiro 107
Nagai, Kafū 395
Nagano Prefectural Normal School 189, 208–209
Nagata, Kinshin 191
nagauta (genre of *shamisen* music) 97, 106, 195, 206–208, 210, 212, 214–215, 229, 231–232, 250, 353–354
Nagoya 108, 110
Nakamura, Mia 399
Nakao, Tozan 97, 126, 230–232, 397
naniwabushi (ballads sung to *shamisen*) 98, 120
national anthem 16, 55, 71, 102, 151, 199, 227, 251–252, 255, 257, 261, 268, 272, 291, 401
National Institute of Gymnastics (Taisō Denshū Sho) 152–153
nationalism 29, 47–48, 76, 88, 393–394
National learning. *See kokugaku*
National Music Course 68–69, 147
nation-building 17, 19–20, 24, 30, 65, 85, 133
Native American music. *See* Indianism (movement)
Nettl, Bruno 3, 6, 11
new *hōgaku* (*shin hōgaku*) 235
New Symphony Orchestra (Shin Kōkyō Gakudan) 115
NHK (Japan Broadcasting Association) 56, 115, 391
Nihon Gakki. *See* Yamaha (company)
Nihon koten ongaku (Japanese classical music) 93
Nihon ongaku (Japanese music) 4, 174, 265
nijū kōzō (dual structure) 41, 121
Nomura, Kōichi 120

Nose, Sakae 189
nostalgia 35, 84, 346, 384–385, 392

Ogyū, Sorai 130, 158
Okamoto, Fusao 267–269, 271, 273–276, 279–280, 286–288, 302, 310–311, 359, 364
Okinawa 57, 65, 193–194, 233
Oku-*jōruri* 257–258
Ōmura, Josaburō 278
ongaku (music) 9, 26, 131, 133–135, 137, 159–160, 186
Ongaku (Music; edited by Tsutsumi Masao) 211, 216
Ongaku (Music; magazine by Tokyo Academy of Music alumni) 109
ongaku kairyō (music reform) 21, 174–175
ongaku katsudō (music-related activities) 9–10, 21, 42, 202, 399
ongaku no chikara ('power of music') 399
Ongaku no tomo (Friend of music) 211–212, 215
Ongaku sekai (The world of music) 109, 224–225
Ongaku Torishirabe Gakari. *See* Music Investigation Committee
Ongaku Torishirabe Sho (Institute of Music Investigation). *See* Music Investigation Committee (Ongaku Torishirabe Gakari)
Ongaku Yūgi Kai. *See* Association for Musical Games
Ongakukai (Music world) 109, 211, 221
ongyoku (musical performance) 99, 133–134
Ono, Shōgorō 134, 158, 245
Orientalism 8, 49, 119, 299
Osaka 22, 56–57, 91, 108, 116–118, 201, 208, 221, 223–225, 227, 230, 256, 278
Osaka Mitsukoshi Band 108
Osaka Philharmonic Orchestra 56–57
Osterhammel, Jürgen 5, 10, 65

Ottoman Empire 50
Ozawa, Seiji 121

Paci, Mario 56
Paganini, Nicolo 5, 225
Partington, Blanche 216
pentatonic scale 78, 154
Perry, Commodore Matthew 1, 33, 64, 84, 101, 403
Pestalozzi, Johann Heinrich 67, 152
pitch 93, 119, 132, 139, 164, 256, 311, 330–332, 335, 337–339, 342, 387
plantation song 1, 79, 84, 367
Preyer, Carl 297–298
provincialization 6, 37
public concert 23, 43–44, 107, 110, 112, 189, 204, 240–241, 244, 261, 283–284, 313, 343, 345, 352, 374

Qing music 27, 90–92, 173, 176, 183, 185–186, 190, 197, 223, 225–226, 244, 248–253, 260

radio 54, 98, 115–116, 118, 327, 347, 389, 391
radio callisthenics. *See rajio taisō*
railway songs. *See tetsudō shōka*
rajio taisō (radio callisthenics) 391–392
Rakusekisha 150
Ramsegger, Hans 107
recording company 47, 117
recording technology 46–47, 57
reed organ 46, 109–110, 160, 184, 188, 193, 225, 252, 323, 325, 330
reigaku (rites and music) 18, 90, 125, 134, 137, 160–161, 182, 220
rhythm 31, 93, 131–133, 141–142, 258, 326, 331, 334–335
Rimsky-Korsakov, Nikolai 267, 278
rites and music. *See reigaku*
riyō (rustic popular song) 117
Robbio, Augusto 5
Roei no yume (song) 209, 214, 281, 290, 362

Rokudan (*koto* piece) 100, 164, 213–214, 229, 249, 252–253, 263, 271, 280, 307, 315–316, 332, 360
Rokumeikan (Deer Cry Pavilion) 102–103, 334
Rolland, Romain 60, 117
Ross, Alex 13, 17
Rurō no tami (*Zigeunerleben*) 166, 361, 369, 372, 383
Russian Orthodox Church 158, 161, 225, 240, 245–246, 267, 269, 278
Russians 56, 161, 388
Russo-Japanese War 182, 209, 254, 276, 279–280, 368
ryūkōka (popular songs) 58–59, 118
Ryukyu Islands 19, 65, 84

Saegusa, Shigeaki 31–33, 60–61
Saigō, Takamori 166
Sangyō shōka (silk industry songs) 261
sankyoku ensemble 97, 225, 264, 284, 321, 351
Sarasate, Pablo 225, 356–357, 383
  Zigeunerweisen 383
sarugaku (form of popular theatre, preceding noh) 158
satsumabiwa 35, 98–99, 190, 194, 196, 233, 250, 252, 254, 257–258, 316, 381
Satsuma-gata (song) 166, 277, 348, 359, 361
Sauvlet, Guillaume 104, 107
Schumann, Robert 166, 214, 273, 277, 325, 348, 361, 363, 369, 373, 383
  Zigeunerleben 166, 348, 369, 372–373, 383
science 8, 12, 37, 60, 66–67, 87, 132, 139, 152, 156, 158, 167, 218, 240
Second Higher Secondary School, Sendai (Dai Ni Kōtō Chūgakkō) 239, 248
Second High School, Sendai (Dai Ni Kōtō Gakkō) 239
Second World War 114, 119, 393

Seiple, Florence 282, 286–288, 290–291, 302, 304, 306–308, 315, 324, 336, 340, 374, 377–378
Sendai Dai Ni Kōtō Chūgakkō.
  See Second Higher Secondary School, Sendai
Sendai Dai Ni Kōtō Gakkō.
  See Second High School, Sendai
Sendai Jogakkō (Sendai School for Girls) 241, 259
Sendai Medical School (Sendai Igaku Senmon Gakkō) 284, 288
Sendai Musical Amateur Club (Sendai Ongaku Dōkō Kurabu, Sendai Amachua Kurabu) 379
Sendai Philharmonic Orchestra 399
Sendai Shingakkō (Sendai Theological College) 241.
  See Tohoku College (Tōhoku Gakuin)
senkakin (musical instrument) 178, 194–198
Senow Gakufu (sheet music series) 109
Seoul 54, 58, 240, 398
Shanghai 53, 55–57, 113, 116
sheet music 22, 91, 109, 164, 169, 176–177, 183, 187–188, 198, 204–205, 212, 222, 226, 230–232, 234, 272, 349, 354, 367, 385, 397
Shibusawa, Eiichi 107
Shigeno, Yasutsugu 133–137
Shikama, Fujiko 195–196, 200, 261
Shikama, Jinji 23, 182–184, 186, 242–243, 246–248, 251–254, 256, 258–259, 262, 266, 281, 366
Shikama, Kiyoko 183, 196, 201
Shikama, Nobunao 181–182, 184
Shikama, Ranko 183, 200, 275, 277
Shikama, Tatsu (Kotatsu) 185, 191
Shikama, Totsuji 21–23, 37, 100, 108, 126, 129, 172–187, 189–206, 211, 222–223, 241, 243, 246–248, 254–259, 261–262, 275, 277, 281
shingaku (Qing music) 27, 176, 190, 193, 249–250, 257

shinkyoku (new *koto* music) 98, 353
Shōkei Jogakkō (Shōkei School for Girls) 241, 378–379
shōmyō (Buddhist chant) 94, 260
Shōnen Ongakutai (youth band) 198–199, 254, 257
Shōshikai (student association of the Second High School) 263, 274–276, 279, 357–358, 405
singing
  by factory workers 262
  in schools 52, 54, 66–67, 71, 84–85, 103–104, 110, 133, 150–151, 153–154, 156, 245, 247–248, 323–325, 328–330, 332–333, 336, 339, 341, 366, 369, 393–394
    learning 66, 101, 103, 110, 145–146, 150–151, 154, 156, 159, 245, 261, 328, 339
Sinitic 72, 130–131, 135–137, 181, 261
Sino-Japanese War (1894–95) 56, 91, 97, 225, 254, 279, 332
Sinosphere (East Asian cultural sphere) 20, 63, 127–128, 135
Small, Christopher 9
Society for Western Music (Yōgaku Kyōkai) 102
Sōgakudō 172
sōkyoku (*koto* music) 98, 177, 226, 231, 233, 251, 260, 306–307, 353–354, 367, 371
sound studies 8
staff notation 22, 32, 49, 60, 85, 111–112, 141, 164, 176, 206, 208, 212, 222, 227–229, 231–232, 235, 315
Steinberg, Michael P. 6
Stick, J. Monroe 273–277, 279, 284, 286–291, 302, 305–308, 359, 362
Strok, Avray 113
Suzuki, Masakichi 110, 188
Suzuki, Shin'ichi 117, 121
Suzuki, Yonejirō 52, 108–109, 171, 253
symphony orchestra 2, 40, 45, 55–56, 73–74, 88, 108, 114–115, 120
  in Japan 40, 56, 74, 108, 114–115

  in United States 73, 120
synchronicity 20, 65
synchronized movement 24, 391

taishōgoto (modern type of *koto*) 110
taisō (gymnastics) 143, 145, 391–392
Taiwan 51, 53–54, 58, 139, 149–151, 186, 256, 384
Takahashi, Fumiyo 150
Takano, Shigeru 99
Takaori, Shūichi (Biō) 126, 205, 210, 212–215, 266, 270–271, 327
Takaori, Sumiko 211, 217
Takarazuka Girls' Opera (*Shōjo Kageki*) 210
Takarazuka Revue 113, 210
Takarazuka Symphony Orchestra 113, 115
Tanabe, Hisao 47, 112
Tanaka, Fujimaro 139, 143, 145, 148, 153
Tanaka, Shōhei 29, 111–112, 163, 197, 205, 327
tango 31, 57, 60
Tateyama, Zennōshin 111
technology 16, 42, 45–47, 57, 90, 116
teikoku biwa ('imperial' *biwa*) 99
tetsudō shōka (railway songs) 40, 110, 261
theatre reform (*engeki kairyō*) 97, 155, 158, 207–208
Tichai, Iakov 267
tōa ongaku (East Asian music) 47
Tōgi (family of court musicians) 234, 369, 379, 383
Tohoku Academy of Music (Tōhoku Ongakuin) 233, 246, 259, 283, 320, 350–352, 356–357, 367, 382, 384
Tohoku College (Tōhoku Gakuin) 241, 270, 275, 282, 285–286, 288–289, 291, 305, 308, 336, 376
Tōhoku Gakuin. *See* Tohoku College
Tohoku Imperial University (Tōhoku Teikoku Daigaku) 239–240, 357, 373, 381, 388–389
Tohoku region 184, 238

tokiwabushi 97
Tokkyō shōka (collection of moral education songs) 261
Tokugawa shogunate 33, 36, 64, 91
tokuhon shōka (reading textbook songs) 367, 381
tokuiku shōka (moral education songs) 169
Tōkyō Geidai (Tōkyō Geijutsu Daigaku). *See* Tokyo University of Fine Arts and Music
Tokyo Higher Normal School (Tōkyō Kōtō Shihan Gakkō) 102, 143, 150, 152–154, 167, 184, 245
Tokyo Imperial University (Tōkyō Teikoku Daigaku) 52, 115, 166
Tokyo Municipal Music Society (Tokyo Municipal Music Society (Tōkyō Shichū Ongaku Kai) 107
Tokyo Normal School for Women (Tōkyō Joshi Shihan Gakkō) 102, 143, 153–154, 245
  Kindergarten Department (Fuzoku Yōchien) 102
Tokyo Olympics (2020) 392
Tōkyō Ongaku Gakkō zonhai ronsō (controversy over the continued existence of the Tokyo Academy of Music) 167
Tōkyō Shichū Ongaku Kai. *See* Tokyo Municipal Music Society
Tōkyō Shōkakai (private music school) 184
Tōkyō Shōnen Ongakutai. *See* Tokyo Youth Band
Tokyo University of Fine Arts and Music (Tōkyō Geijutsu Daigaku, Tōkyō Geidai) 122–123, 190, 360
Tokyo Youth Band (Tōkyō Shōnen Ongakutai) 198–199, 256–257
tonkori (zither with vertically stretched strings played by the Ainu) 194
Torii, Makoto 166
tōyō ongaku (Oriental music) 47

Tōyō Ongaku Gakkō. *See* Music College of the East
tsugarujamisen (modern *shamisen* style from Northern Japan) 2
Tsukahara, Yasuko 9, 194, 269
Tsunekawa, Ryōnosuke 184
tuning fork 132, 164, 193

Uehara, Rokushirō 278

variety theatre. *See yose*
Verbeck, Guido 141
violin tutor 226, 228–229, 368, 383
visible speech 148–150

Wagener, Gottfried 107
Wagner, Richard 40, 117, 215, 277, 286, 291, 302, 312, 375, 382, 400
Wagner Society 209, 215
Waseda University 52
Watanabe, Hideo 279
Watanabe, Hiroshi 3–4, 9, 41
wayō chōwa gaku (music harmonizing Japanese and Western elements) 22, 27, 203–204, 213
wayō gassō (Japanese-Western ensemble playing) 22, 27, 204, 316
wayō setchū (mixing Japanese and Western elements). *See* blended music
Weber, Max 38–39, 48
Western music. *See yōgaku*
'Western music complex' 41
Whitney, Clara 107
women 44, 97, 104–105, 113, 161, 186, 189, 201, 207, 224, 233–234, 239, 252, 257, 275, 310, 320–321, 325, 334, 350, 358
World Peace Jubilee (Boston) 71
World War I. *See* First World War
World War II. *See* Second World War

Xiao, Youmei 52

yakumogoto (two-stringed plucked zither) 194–195, 249, 251, 253–254, 257, 260

Yamada, Kōsaku 114–115, 119, 268
Yamada, Torajirō (Sōyū) 193
Yamaha (company) 110, 121, 188–189
Yamaha, Torakusu 110, 188, 189
Yamamoto, Kyūzaburō (agent) 113
Yamamoto (Tsutsumi), Masao 211
Yamanoi, Motokiyo 221, 222, 228
Yamashita, Shōkin 251, 252, 260, 350, 351
Yasuda, Yuitsu (MP) 169
Yasumasa (song) 165, 271, 359, 362, 399
Yatabe, Ryōkichi 155, 167
yōgaku (Western music) 18, 26, 121, 123, 229, 395
Yōgaku Kyōkai. *See* Society for Western Music
Yōkendō (Sendai domain school) 158, 182, 183, 239
yōkyoku (noh singing) 96, 182, 245, 249, 264
yonanuki scale 78, 118
yose (variety theatre) 98, 250
Yoshimizu, Tsunekazu 99, 190, 191, 252, 254, 319
youth band 108, 194, 198, 199, 202, 222, 223, 255, 256, 257
yūgi (movement games) 143, 144, 145, 146, 152, 191, 192, 248
yūgi shōka 144, 191, 192
Yung, Bell 7
yūshisha (supporters, afficianados) 252, 286

Zaugg, E. H. 286, 287, 288, 291, 302, 306, 307, 308
zokugaku (common music) 26, 90, 136, 158, 163, 174, 176, 178, 219, 222, 223, 224, 226, 260
Zukerman, Pinchas 25

About the Author

Margaret Mehl is a historian of modern Japan with a special interest in musical culture. She is currently an Associate Professor at the University of Copenhagen, having previously held appointments at the universities of Cambridge, Edinburgh, Stirling, and Berlin. As well as a doctorate from the University of Bonn, Margaret Mehl holds a Dr. Phil. (Habilitation) from the University of Copenhagen. She has lived and worked in Japan as a researcher on several occasions, where she has had affiliations with the University of Tokyo, and with Waseda University. Margaret Mehl has published widely on the history of historiography, education, and music in modern Japan. Her previous books include *History and the State in Nineteenth-Century Japan* (which has been translated into Japanese), *Private Academies of Chinese Learning in Meiji Japan: The Decline and Transformation of the* Kangaku Juku, and *Not by Love Alone: The Violin in Japan, 1850–2010*.

When she is not reading, writing or teaching, Margaret Mehl enjoys playing her violin and has performed in amateur orchestras and chamber ensembles in several countries.

Author website: www.MargaretMehl.com

About the Team

Alessandra Tosi was the managing editor for this book.

Lucy Barnes proofread this book. Adèle Kreager created the index.

Jeevanjot Kaur Nagpal designed the cover. The cover was produced in InDesign using the Fontin font.

Cameron Craig typeset the book in InDesign and produced the paperback and hardback editions. The text font is Tex Gyre Pagella and the heading font is Californian FB.

Cameron also produced the PDF, and HTML editions. The conversion was performed with open-source software and other tools freely available on our GitHub page at https://github.com/OpenBookPublishers.

Jeremy Bowman produced the EPUB edition.

This book has been anonymously peer-reviewed by experts in their field. We thank them for their invaluable help.

This book need not end here...

Share

All our books — including the one you have just read — are free to access online so that students, researchers and members of the public who can't afford a printed edition will have access to the same ideas. This title will be accessed online by hundreds of readers each month across the globe: why not share the link so that someone you know is one of them?

This book and additional content is available at:
https://doi.org/10.11647/OBP.0374

Donate

Open Book Publishers is an award-winning, scholar-led, not-for-profit press making knowledge freely available one book at a time. We don't charge authors to publish with us: instead, our work is supported by our library members and by donations from people who believe that research shouldn't be locked behind paywalls.

Why not join them in freeing knowledge by supporting us:
https://www.openbookpublishers.com/support-us

Follow @OpenBookPublish

Read more at the Open Book Publishers BLOG

You may also be interested in:

Classical Music
Contemporary Perspectives and Challenges
Michael Beckerman and Paul Boghossian (eds)

https://doi.org/10.11647/obp.0242

Tellings and Texts
Music, Literature and Performance in North India
Francesca Orsini and Katherine Butler Schofield (eds)

https://doi.org/10.11647/obp.0062

Auld Lang Syne
A Song and its Culture
Morag Josephine Grant

https://doi.org/10.11647/obp.0231

www.ingramcontent.com/pod-product-compliance
Lightning Source LLC
Chambersburg PA
CBHW060348250426
43667CB00051B/2467